ARABIC DOCUMENTS FROM MEDIEVAL NUBIA

Arabic Documents from Medieval Nubia

Geoffrey Khan

In consultation with Grzegorz Ochała, Pamela Rose, Robin Seignobos and Naïm Vanthieghem

UNIVERSITY OF CAMBRIDGE
Faculty of Asian and Middle Eastern Studies

OpenBook Publishers

https://www.openbookpublishers.com

Any digital material and resources associated with this volume will be available at https://doi.org/10.11647/OBP.0391#resources

Semitic Languages and Cultures 24

ISSN (print): 2632-6906
ISSN (digital): 2632-6914

ISBN Paperback: 978-1-80511-230-3
ISBN Hardback: 978-1-80511-231-0
ISBN Digital (PDF): 978-1-80511-232-7

DOI: 10.11647/OBP.0391

Cover image: Fortress of Qasr Ibrim - on a cliff above the Nile in Nubia. Print from David Roberts' *Egypt & Nubia* (London: F.G. Moon, 1846-49), v. 2, pt 5. Library of Congress, Reproduction number LC-USZC4-3998, https://commons.wikimedia.org/wiki/File:Fortress_of_Ibrim--Nubia-David_Roberts.jpg.
Cover design: Jeevanjot Kaur Nagpal

The main fonts used in this volume are Charis SIL, Scheherazade New, SBL Greek, and Segoe UI Historic.

CONTENTS

Preface xi

1. Introduction 1
2. The Arabic Documents from Qaṣr Ibrīm 15
3. The Correspondence with Eparchs 49
4. Other Correspondence and Accounts 129
5. Legal Documents 145
6. Coinage 185
7. Taxes 193
8. Lists of Commodities 195
9. Titles of Officials 205
10. Slaves and Servants 235
11. The Socio-Economic Situation Reflected by the Documents 253
12. Script and Layout 263
13. Language 277
14. Maps 285

Documents and Translations 287

Method of Editing 289

1 Letter to the Eparch Uruwī 291

2 Letter to the Eparch Uruwī 295

3 Letter to the Eparch Uruwī 303

4 Letter to the Eparch Uruwī 309

5 Letter to the Eparch Uruwī 315

6 Letter to the Eparch Uruwī 321

7 Letter to the Eparch Uruwī 325

8 Letter to the Eparch Uruwī 329

9 Letter to the Eparch Uruwī 335

10 Letter to the Eparch Uruwī 347

11 Letter to the Eparch Uruwī 351

12 Letter to the Eparch Uruwī 357

13 Letter to the Eparch Uruwī 361

14 Letter to the Eparch Uruwī 369

15 Letter to the Eparch Uruwī 373

16 Letter to the Eparch Uruwī 379

17 Letter from the Eparch Uruwī 387

18 Letter from the Eparch Uruwī 393

19 Letter to the Eparch Īsū 397

20 Letter to the Eparch Īsū 403
21 Letter to an Eparch 409
22 Letter to an Eparch 417
23 Letter to an Eparch 423
24 Letter to an Eparch 431
25 Letter to an Eparch 437
26 Letter to al-Bazīl, the Deputy of the Eparch Darmā 445
27 Letter to the Secretary of the Eparch Uruwī 449
28 Letter to a Commander 455
29 Letter to a Commander 459
30 Letter to a Dignitary 465
31 Letter to a Dignitary 477
32 Letter to a Dignitary 483
33 Letter to a Dignitary 487
34 Letter to a Dignitary 493
35 Letter 499
36 Letter 503
37 Letter 509
38 Letter 515

39 Letter 521

40 Letter 527

41 Poem of a Traveller 529

42 Account 533

43 Account 541

44 Lease of Land (Rajab 518 AH/August 1124 AD) 547

45 Lease of a Boat (566 AH/1170 AD) 551

46 Document of Testimony and Document of Sale 559

47 An Acknowledgement of a Debt and Testimonies 575

48 Marriage Contract and Acknowledgement 583

49 Documents relating to Divorce 597

50 Acknowledgement relating to Divorce (15th Jumādā II 430 AH/14th March 1039 AD) 603

51 Marriage Contract and Testimony 605

52 Court Record relating to Marriage 613

53 Letter relating to a Marital Dispute 617

PREFACE

This book has been long in the making. The journey started in the early 1990s when Elizabeth Sartain came to visit me in Cambridge and asked whether I would be willing to take on the task of editing the medieval Arabic documents from Qaṣr Ibrīm. These documents had been discovered by the Egypt Exploration Society in excavations at the site (now largely submerged in lake Nasser in the south of Egypt). I accepted the invitation with enthusiasm, since I saw that these documents would constitute an important complement to the medieval documents in Arabic script from the Genizah, which I was working on at that time. Elizabeth had produced a handlist of the documents and preliminary English translations of a some of them, and these formed a very helpful foundation for the task of producing a full edition.

Soon after starting work on the documents, however, it became clear to me that the work on the project was fraught with many challenges. The decipherment of the documents was very slow due to the highly cursive nature of the script. In the early stages of the project, it became clear to me that I would not be able to have direct access to the original documents but had to work on photographs. Furthermore, I had difficulty finding photographs of all the documents in Elizabeth Sartain's handlist. Derek Welsby, who was a curator at the British Museum in the 1990s, kindly helped me identify a certain proportion of the photographs. Further help was offered to me more recently by the curators Julie Anderson and Loretta Kilroe. I finally managed to find images of all the documents with the help of Pamela Rose, a former director of excavations at Qaṣr Ibrīm. Pamela also generously devoted much time to explaining to me all the complicated numbering systems of the documents used by the Egypt Exploration Society and wrote sections on the archaeological context of the discovery of the documents for the introduction of the edition.

As work on the edition progressed, I appreciated more and more how important the documents are for the history of Nubia in the medieval period. I am grateful to Robin Seignobos, one of the leading historians of medieval Nubia, who has given me encouragement over the last few years to complete the task and helped me in many ways. He clarified for me numerous details of the historical context of the documents and supplied to me many references to historical sources.

The book was immensely improved by the detailed comments that I received from the two peer-reviewers, Grzegorz Ochała and Naïm Vanthieghem. Grzegorz supplied to me numerous pertinent references to Nubian sources and generally helped me contextualise the book within the current state of Nubian studies. Naïm generously devoted an immense amount of time to the checking of my readings of the documents and suggested numerous improvements.

On account of the generous help offered to me by Pamela, Robin, Grzegorz and Naïm, I have included their names in the credits on the main title page.

Many other people also kindly offered me help and advice over the long years in which this book gradually took shape.

I greatly benefited from reading some of the texts with students and post-doctoral researchers, many of whom suggested readings that were better than my own. These young scholars include Ursula Bsees, Mohamed Ahmed, Mohammad Shomali, Lorenzo Bondioli and Tobias Scheunchen.

Marina Rustow offered much encouragement at various stages of the project. In 2015 I read some of the documents with her and her students when I was a fellow at the Institute of Advanced Studies in Princeton. She also offered helpful comments on the final draft of the book.

The superb work on medieval Nubian history by Giovanni Ruffini was an important foundation for many parts of the historical introduction of the book. Giovanni kindly read the final draft of the book and offered many helpful commments.

The economists Phil Armstrong and Ioana Negru kindly advised me on certain aspects of my historical analysis of the documents.

Krisztina Szilagyi and Anne Burberry carefully proofread the book and recommended several improvements. Anne prepared the final camera-ready copy of the book.

Other scholars who offered comments on various details of the draft of the book and drew my attention to various sources include Adam Łajtar, Sebastian Richter, Stefanie Schmidt, Andrew Marsham, Gabriel Gerhards, David Bramoullé, Joost Haagen, Vincent van Gerven Oei, Craig Perry, Ahmed Kamal, Artur Obłuski, Gertrud van Loon, Magdalena Wozniak and Alexandros Tsakos.

My post-doctoral researchers Shuan Karim and Masoud Mohammadirad kindly helped me create the maps for the book.

To all these people I am deeply grateful. I should also like to acknowledge the support of the Institute of Advanced Studies in Princeton, where I worked on the project when I was a fellow there in 2015. I am also immensely grateful to the Egypt Exploration Society for entrusting to me the edition of these precious documents and patiently waiting nearly thirty years for the appearance of the edition.

Geoffrey Khan

Cambridge, December 2023

1. INTRODUCTION

The geographical term Nubia is typically used to refer to a region that extends from the first cataract of the Nile, just south of Aswan, to the confluence of the Blue and White Niles, near Khartoum below the sixth cataract. The western boundary is in the Libyan desert and the eastern boundary is the Ethiopian plateau northwards, but these delimitations are somewhat vague. The core of Nubia is the Middle Nile from Aswan to Khartoum (Williams and Emberling 2020, 2).

The rocky cataracts and associated stretches of shallow water make the river more difficult to navigate than the Upper Nile above the first cataract. Since travel north and south historically relied primarily on river travel, the first cataract was a natural border that typically coincided with a political boundary between Egypt and Nubia in antiquity and the Middle Ages. There have been some periods of history, however, in which Egypt and Nubia have been politically united.

Lower Nubia, which formed the geographical background of most of the documents published in this volume, is the portion of the Nile valley, approximately 350 kilometres in length, between the first and second cataracts. This region now spans the south of Egypt and the north of the Republic of Sudan. Upper Nubia is the region of Nubia that lies south of the second cataract.

The Nubians are a group of people who speak some form of the Nubian language, which belongs to the Nilo-Saharan family of languages. The term 'Nubian' first appears in written sources in the Kushite period (seventh century BC–fourth century

 https://doi.org/10.11647/OBP.0391.01

AD; Rilly 2008). They are mentioned by Strabo (*Geography* VII), quoting Eratosthenes (276–196 BC), who refers to them by the term *Noubai.* They originally inhabited the region of Kordofan and Darfur and subsequently moved into the Central Nile valley and migrated to the north after the end of the Meroitic dynasty in the fourth century AD. Modern archaeologists and historians, however, are cautious of regarding the migrating Nubians as an ethnically uniform people (Vantini 1981, 25; Welsby 2002, 7; Williams and Emberling 2020, 3). In the fifth century AD, the Nubians gradually pressed down the Nile from territories north of the second cataract and became established in northern Nubia (Obłuski 2014, 35). Subsequently, through partial conquest and settlement of the Nubians, the spoken language of the region shifted to Nubian.

Greek sources also refer to a group of people called the *Nobates,* who were a nomadic people originating in the Libyan desert and settled south of Aswan in late antiquity. According to Halm (1998, 66), they were distinct in origin from the *Noubai.* The Byzantine emperor Diocletian (284–305 AD) settled the *Nobates* south of the first cataract and contracted them with an annual payment to prevent raids into the territory of the empire from the south. By the Islamic period, descendants of the *Noubai* and the *Nobates* were referred to in Arabic sources by the single term *al-Nūba.*

Christianity was introduced into Nubia in the sixth century AD under the auspices of the church organisation of Byzantine Egypt, and subsequently the churches of the region came under the jurisdiction of the Coptic patriarchate of Alexandria

(Gadallah 1959; Vantini 1981, 33–50; Welsby 2002, 31–67; Swanson 2007; Tsakos 2021). There is archaeological evidence for the establishment of Christianity at Qaṣr Ibrīm near the beginning of the sixth century (Adams 1996, 5). At that period, Nubia consisted of three kingdoms (Tsakos 2021, 2):

(i) Nobadia, with its capital in Pachōras (Faras), north of Wādī Ḥalfa, apparently extending from Aswan to the third cataract;
(ii) Makuria, with its capital in Dongola.[1] This controlled the territory up to some point between the region of Abu Hamed/Mograt Island and the junction of the Nile with the River Atbara;
(iii) Alodia, with its capital in Soba near Khartoum, extending to an unknown area in Gezira between the Blue and White Niles.

These kingdoms emerged from competing chiefdoms that developed after the collapse of the Kushite kingdom based in Meroe in the fourth century AD (Welsby 2002, 15–16; Tsakos 2021, 4). The names of the kingdoms given above are based on those that are found in Greek Byzantine sources. The Arabic and indigenous Nubian names are as follows:

[1] The archaeological site known as Old Dongola (in Arabic *Dunqulā al-ʿAjūz*) lies about 80 kilometres south of the modern town of Dongola.

Table 1: Arabic and indigenous Nubian names of Nubian kingdoms

Byzantine	**Arabic**	**Nubian**
Nobadia	al-Marīs	Migi
Makuria	al-Muqurra	Dotawo
Alodia	ʿAlwa	Aroua

The nomadic Beja tribes (known in early sources as the Blemmyes) of the eastern desert remained mainly pagan at this period.

In 19 AH/640 AD, the Muslim general ʿAmr ibn al-ʿĀṣ began his invasion of Egypt. ʿAmr sent small parties of raiders into Nubia on several occasions, but these were forced to retire discomfited. ʿAbd Allāh ibn Saʿd ibn ʾAbī Sarḥ, who subsequently succeeded ʿAmr as commander of Egypt in 25 AH (646–7 AD), discontinued these raids and made terms with the Nubians. In 31 AH/651–2 AD, ʿAbd Allāh led a well-equipped expedition into Makuria and laid siege to Dongola, under the rule of the Nubian king Qalidurut. According to al-Maqrīzī, the king in Dongola sued for an armistice, which was accepted by ʿAbd Allāh. In the version of events recorded by the earlier historian Ibn ʿAbd al-Ḥakam (d. 257 AH/871 AD; *Futūḥ Miṣr*, 169–89), however, the Nubians were the victors in the battle (Spaulding 1995, 584). According to al-Maqrīzī's account, ʿAbd Allāh concluded peace with the king on the basis of a treaty known in Arabic as *baqṭ*, from Greek *πάκτον*. Al-Maqrīzī (*Ḵiṭaṭ*, I:369–70) reproduces the text of this, citing a book, now lost, by ʿAbd Allāh ibn Sulaym al-ʾAswānī (tenth century AD).[2] This imposed on the Nubians the duty of paying an annual tribute of 360 slaves.

This was an unusual treaty. The normal treaty made by the Muslims, referred to as a *ṣulḥ*, was issued when they occupied and gained mastery of a country, absorbing it into *dār al-ʾIslām*. These conditions did not hold in the case of their campaign against Nubia. The *baqṭ*, therefore, is best characterised as a 'truce' (*hudna*) or 'neutralisation' (*muwādaʿa*), terms that are used in some sources (Forand 1971, 113). Nubia, therefore, was neither *dār al-ʾIslām* ('place of Islam') nor *dār al-ḥarb* ('place [that is the target] of religious war').

Bar Hebraeus (*Chronography*, 134) cites the following statement of a Nubian king regarding the *baqṭ*: "Inasmuch as they (i.e., the Arabs) have cut off (their shipments), we also have cut off (ours)." This reflects an interpretation of the *baqṭ* as an agreement of mutual exchange, not a punitive imposition.

The wording of the *baqṭ*, according to al-Maqrīzī, was as follows:

> This is the treaty issued by the *ʾamīr* ʿAbd Allāh ibn Saʿd ibn ʾAbī Sarḥ to the chief of the Nūba and to all the people of his kingdom, a treaty binding upon all the Nubians, great and small, from the boundary of Aswan to the boundary of ʿAlwa. ʿAbd Allāh ibn Saʿd ibn ʾAbī Sarḥ gave them security and a truce, valid between them and the

---

[2] Al-Maqrīzī's material is quoted from a book entitled كتاب اخبار النوبة والمقرة وعلوة والبجة والنيل 'The Book of Nubia, Muqurra, ʿAlwa, the Beja and the Nile' by ʿAbd Allāh ibn Sulaym al-ʾAswānī, which has not survived (Kheir 1989).

neighbouring Muslims of Upper Egypt, as well as the other Muslims and the *ḏimmī*. You, Nubian people, will be safe with the guarantee of God and His Prophet Muḥammad, that we shall not fight you and shall not wage war upon you, nor shall we carry out raids, as long as you keep the condition laid down between us and yourselves: that you enter our country in transit only, not for the purpose of settling there; we also shall enter your country in transit without settling there. You must protect any Muslim or anyone who is under our protection, if he settles in your country or travels through it, until he leaves it. You must return any fugitive slave belonging to the Muslims who seeks asylum in your country; you must deliver him to the country of Islam. You must likewise return any Muslim who fights against the Muslims; you must drive him out of your country to the country of Islam, without befriending him or without hindering him in any way.... You must give 360 slaves every year, whom you will hand over to the *ʾimām* of the Muslims. They must be chosen from slaves (*raqīq*) of your country, adults, without bodily defects, both male and female, excluding old men, old women and sucklings. You will hand them to the governor (*wālī*) of Aswan.[3] The Muslims do not undertake to drive away enemies who may attack you, or prevent them from attacking you, from the frontier of ʿAlwa to the territory of Aswan. If you give shelter to any slave of the Muslims, or you kill a Muslim, or an ally, or if you allow any damage to be done to the mosque which the Muslims have built within your town, or you retain any part of the 360 men, the treaty and truce will be cancelled, and we and you shall return (to hostility) until God judges between us, for He is the best

---

[3] It is generally thought that the delivery would have been made at al-Qaṣr, a fortress on the border of Nubia (Gascoigne and Rose 2012).

> Judge. Upon these conditions we are bound by the covenant of God and His Promise and that of His Prophet Muḥammad; you, on your side, stand pledged to us by those you hold most holy in your religion, the protection of Christ, the protection of the Apostles and the protection of those persons whom you hold in the highest respect in your religion and your community. May God be witness between us and you on this.
>
> Written by ʿUmar ibn Šarḥabīl in Ramaḍān 31 AH (652 AD)

The term *baqṭ* is used in the *History of the Patriarchs of Alexandria,* in the biography of the Patriarch Benjamin (622–661 AD), to refer to the tribute that the Emperor Heraclius (610–641 AD) paid to the Muslims after the battle of the Yarmūk (636 AD; Seignobos 2016, 55). The term in the Nubian treaty, therefore, appears to have referred specifically to the unilateral obligation to deliver a tribute of slaves rather than to the agreement as a whole. As remarked, this was not the spirit of the original agreement, which was rather a truce (*hudna*) ratified by the mutual exchange of gifts.

Other aspects of al-Maqrīzī's account of the *baqṭ* indicate that it is unlikely to be an accurate record of the original agreement.[4] The text of the treaty recorded by him contains several anachronisms. The most conspicuous of these is the condition

---

[4] According to Ibn ʿAbd al-Ḥakam, the *baqṭ* treaty was preserved in an archive in the Egyptian capital until the building was destroyed by fire (Hinds and Sakkout 1981, 214–15). The likelihood, however, that the original document would have survived in archives until later centuries has been called into question by Forand (1971).

relating to the upkeep by the Nubians of a mosque in Dongola. Another possible anachronism is that the *baqṭ* treaty is said to have been negotiated with the Makurian king of Dongola and be binding on the people of his kingdom from the frontier of the land of Aswan to the border of the land of ʿAlwa (the Arabic term for Alodia). The Makurian king was, therefore, presumed to be sovereign over all of the northern Nubians, indicating that Nobadia by this time had been annexed by Makuria and ceased to exist as an independent political entity. The unification of Nobadia and Makuria under the king of Dongola is reflected by Greek and Coptic inscriptions from Lower Nubia dating to the first decade of the 700s (Ruffini 2020, 761). According to Halm (1998, 64), however, the two kingdoms were unified only during the reign of king Merkurios of Dongola (696–c. 710 AD), so the original *baqṭ*, which was drawn up in 31 AH/652 AD, must have been negotiated with the king of Nobadia.

According to Seignobos (2016, I:70–75), al-Maqrīzī is likely to have taken the text of the *baqṭ* treaty from the work of al-ʾAswānī (tenth century AD), upon whom he is dependent for most of his information on Nubia. The presence of a mosque in Dongola is referred to by Ibn Ḥazm (384–456 AH/994–1064 AD; *Jumal Futūḥ al-ʾIslām* II:129). This suggests that there was a Muslim community there in the Fatimid period. Further evidence for this is a Muslim funerary stele datable to the Fatimid period that was discovered in Dongola.[5]

[5] This is being prepared for publication by Robin Seignobos.

Ibn ʿAbd al-Ḥakam (d. 257 AH/871 AD; *Futūḥ Miṣr*, 188–89), records two versions of the *baqṭ*. One was similar to the terms recorded by al-Maqrīzī, but the other, referred to as a *hudna* 'truce', imposed far fewer demands on the Nubians and required them only to return Muslim captives in the immediate aftermath of the battle and not deliver an annual quota of slaves. Spaulding (1995, 584) argues that the latter was the original understanding by the Nubian authorities of the agreement, whereas the first version was the prevailing interpretation of the Islamic theorists of the early Abbasid period. It is relevant to note that some sources refer to the *baqṭ* as a mutual presentation of a gift (*hadiyya*) rather than a tax or tribute (*jizya*), e.g., Ibn Ḵurradāḏbih (Forand 1971, 116).[6] The very use of the term *baqṭ*, which is an Arabicisation of the Greek term *πάκτον*, suggests that it was essentially a continuation of the settlement made by Diocletian with the *Nobates*, based on mutual benefit, to secure the southern border of the Byzantine empire at the first cataract. The *baqṭ* was made with the descendants of the *Nobates* of the Byzantine period, i.e., with the kingdom of Nobadia. Al-Masʿūdī, indeed, states that the *baqṭ* was made with the king of *Marīs*, a term used to refer to the territory of Nobadia (Halm 1998, 68–70).

By the ninth century, according to Spaulding, the Muslims had begun to believe that the *baqṭ* had been a fixed written

[6] Several Coptic letters were discovered at Qaṣr Ibrīm that are addressed to the eparch and datable to the eighth century AD. These relate to Egyptian–Nubian treaty obligations. They mention the Nubians' obligation to return runaway slaves, but do not mention the obligation to deliver a quota of slaves (Joost Hagen, personal communication).

document that legally bound the Nubians in perpetuity to a status of subordination to the Islamic caliphate with a substantial annual tribute in the form of slaves.[7] There are frequent accounts in the sources of the failure of the Nubians to deliver the quota of slaves and this may have been due to the fact that the Nubians did not accept the Abbasid Muslim interpretation of the *baqṭ*, rather than due to an intentional infringement of a written treaty. According to al-Maqrīzī (citing al-ʾAswānī), the defeated Nubians dutifully paid their annual tribute under the *baqṭ* for about two centuries after the Islamic conquest of Egypt, up to the reign of the Abbasid caliph al-Muʿtaṣim (218–27 AH/833–42 AD). We know, however, that this version of events is not accurate, since a surviving original letter on papyrus (see §2.2 below) written by the first Abbasid governor of Egypt in 141 AH/758 AD claims that the slave quota had not been delivered for several years. A Nubian delegation visited al-Muʿtaṣim in 221 AH/836 AD to negotiate the terms of the *baqṭ* and secured an agreement to have the number of slaves reduced by two thirds (Vantini 1970; Forand 1971, 116; Kheir 1989, 69–70). The available data in historiographical sources concerning *baqṭ* shipments indicate that

[7] The delivery of a set number of slaves (commonly 360) appears as a standard component of a number of reported incidents during the early Arab conquests in Africa (Savage 1992, 359). As remarked, al-Maqrīzī gives the number 360 as the quota in his version of the *baqṭ*. There are a few small variations of this number in versions of the *baqṭ* appearing in other sources, e.g., those of al-Masʿūdī, Ibn ʿAbd al-Ḥakam, ʾAbū al-Buḥturī and Ibn al-Furāt (Seignobos 2016, 78).

they fell far short of the quota mentioned in al-Maqrīzī's version of the *baqṭ* treaty (Spaulding 1995, 591–93).[8]

There was an advantage to the Arabs in maintaining independent Nubia as a supplier of slaves, since Muslims and Christians under their patronage could not be enslaved. The Nubians, in exchange for the slaves, received various Egyptian goods.

The weakness of the central government of Egypt during the Ṭūlūnid (254–92 AH/868–905 AD) and Ikšīdid (323–58 AH/935–69 AD) dynasties gave the Nubians and local Beja tribes an opportunity to resume the sporadic raiding of Upper Egypt. When the Fatimids assumed power in 358 AH/969 AD, the *baqṭ* is reported to have been in arrears. According to Ibn Sulaym al-ʾAswānī, he was sent by the Fatimid general Jawhar in an embassy to the king of Dongola to discuss payment of the *baqṭ*.[9] The specific outcome of these negotiations is not recorded. Forand (1971, 121) hypothesises that the *baqṭ* fell into disuse and was only restored in 674 AH/1276 AD by the Mamluk ruler Baybars al-Bunduqdārī. The reality emerging from the documents published in this volume seems to be that the *baqṭ* was not discontinued but rather manifested itself in a way that conflicts with the view presented by the historiographical sources.

---

[8] For other discussions of the *baqṭ*, see Brett (1969); Brunschvig (1975); Renault (1989).

[9] This is quoted by al-Maqrīzī in his *al-Muqaffā* (Troupeau 1954; Kheir 1989, 36).

In the Fatimid period there were generally good relations between Egypt and Nubia without military interventions.[10] One factor conditioning these good relations may have been that the Shiʿite Fatimid dynasty needed new alliances to counterbalance the traditionally Sunni régimes of the Middle East. This is reflected by the fact that many Nubians were appointed to important positions in the Fatimid court and army (Vantini 1981, 129–30; Lev 1987; Tsakos 2021, 18). Also, by the twelfth century, the threat of the Seljuk Turks and the Crusaders made the Fatimid régime increasingly dependent on the development of international trade to supply and fund their military defences (Bramoullé 2012).

At some point around this time, Alodia (Arabic ʿAlwa) became united with Nobadia and Makuria (Arabic al-Muqurra)[11] under a single king (§3.3).

After the Ayyubids took control of Egypt in 567 AH/1171 AD, there were renewed hostilities in the south. Saladin sent his brother Šams al-Dawla with a force that seized and captured the citadel of Qaṣr Ibrīm in 568 AH/1173 AD, an episode that may be reflected in destruction levels encountered during excavations

---

[10] There were some exceptions. Al-Maqrīzī (*ʾIttiʿāẓ al-Ḥunafāʾ bi-ʾAḵbār al-ʾAʾimma al-Fāṭimiyyīn al-Ḵulafāʾ*; Beshir 1975, 21), for example, states that in 556 AH/1161 AD "the King of the Nubians marched against Aswan with twelve thousand horsemen and massacred a great multitude of Muslims."

[11] The original vocalism of this Arabicised word seems to have been al-Muqurra rather than al-Maqurra. The vocalism al-Muqurra is found in Yāqūt's *Kitāb Muʿjam al-Buldān* (Ruffini and Seignobos 2020).

within its cathedral. Subsequently, however, the occupying force was withdrawn. The Mamluks undertook sustained military action against the south after a Nubian attack on ʿAyḏāb and Aswan in 673 AH/1275 AD (Seignobos 2015). This allowed the Islamic element in the local population to gain power. According to the historiographical sources, the payment of the *baqṭ* was disrupted during the tumultuous relations between the Ayyubids and the Nubians, but its terms remained in force and a payment was made in the Mamluk period by Nubia even in 667 AH/1269 AD after the Mamluks had taken effective control of Dongola in 658 AH/1260 AD and installed a Nubian puppet king.

ʾAbū al-Makārim (d. 1208 AD; *Taʾrīḵ al-Kanāʾis wa-l-ʾAdyira*, 272) reports that there were thirteen kings in Nubia, who ruled the land under the supremacy of the Great King.[12] According to Hendrickx (2011), these were eparchs who held sway locally over various parts of the Nile Valley. There is no clear evidence, however, for this number of eparchs at this period. The existence of one such eparch based at Qaṣr Ibrīm is referred to in the medieval documents published in this volume. He governed Lower Nubia where kings of Nobadia once ruled.[13]

The accounts of Ibn Sulaym al-ʾAswānī indicate that the import trade in Lower Nubia was mainly in the hands of Muslim entrepreneurs, who, after the ninth century, were allowed to

---

[12] This work was mistakenly attributed to ʾAbū Ṣāliḥ by the editor of the text, B. T. A. Evetts, in 1895; cf. den Heijer (1996).

[13] Unpublished Coptic letters to the eparch of Qaṣr Ibrīm datable to the eighth century address the eparch as ‘king’ (Joost Hagen, personal communication).

travel and to settle freely in the northern part of the country. Lower Nubia was given special status as a free-trade zone between Christian Nubia and Muslim Egypt. Under the aegis of these Muslim entrepreneurs, Lower Nubia developed a monetary, or at least semi-monetary, economy. On the other hand, trade beyond the second cataract by Muslims remained restricted. The principal commodity that Nubia exchanged for Egyptian commodities was slaves.[14]

---

[14] For further details of the historical background, see Adams (1977, 459–507; 1996, 6–7).

2. THE ARABIC DOCUMENTS FROM QAṢR IBRĪM

2.1. The Site of Qaṣr Ibrīm

Qaṣr Ibrīm (Old Nubian *Silimi*, Greek and Coptic *Phrim*, Latin *Primis*) is an archaeological site situated between the first and second cataracts of the Nile, now in Egypt about 240 km south of the first cataract. In the Middle Ages this was Lower Nubia (Nobadia). The long history of occupation of Qaṣr Ibrīm ranges from the end of the New Kingdom of Pharaonic Egypt in the eleventh century BC to 1812 AD in the Ottoman period. It was a major citadel city built on a bluff that originally rose nearly perpendicularly 70 m above the Nile floodplain or 90 m above the low Nile (Adams 1996, 1; Lane 2000, 490). Its location reflected its strategic and defensive role in Nubia.

Qaṣr Ibrīm is first mentioned in the works of Pliny (*Natural History*, VI:35, 181–82) and Strabo (*Geography*, XVII:1, 54) in relation to the events of 23 BC, in which an invading force of Nubians drove out a Roman garrison and took possession of the citadel. They refer to the place by the name *Primis*. This is likely to be a Latinisation of the indigenous toponym *Pedeme*, which starts to appear in Meroitic funerary stelae around the same period (Adams 1996, 4). This subsequently developed into *Phrim* in Greek/Coptic and *ʾIbrīm* in Arabic. In medieval and Ottoman Arabic documents, the place is referred to as *qalʿat ʾIbrīm* 'the citadel of Ibrīm'. The term *qaṣr*, therefore, is likely to have been late, possibly added after the site was abandoned.

 https://doi.org/10.11647/OBP.0391.02

After the construction of the Aswan High Dam in the 1960s, however, Qaṣr Ibrīm became flooded by the waters of Lake Nasser and is now reduced to a small island.

Figure 1: Qaṣr Ibrīm in 1826 (Lane 2000, figure 152)

Figure 2: Qaṣr Ibrīm as the waters of Lake Nasser were rising in 1966 (Rose 2011, 2)

Figure 3: Qaṣr Ibrīm in 2008

A licence to excavate Qaṣr Ibrīm was granted to the Egypt Exploration Society as part of the International Campaign to Save the Monuments of Nubia (Säve-Söderbergh 1987). The first season of excavations was in 1961. The city had been abandoned in 1812, during the Ottoman period, more or less intact (Rose 2011). Its fortification walls, the agglomeration of Ottoman houses and the cathedral building (converted to a mosque) at the centre of the city were all well preserved.[1] The Ottoman garrison was made up initially of Bosnian mercenaries and its descendants remained there until they were finally evicted in the year 1811.

In the first season in 1961, it was decided to focus on riverside cemeteries, which were in immediate danger of the rising flood waters (Mills 1982). Excavations of the citadel began in

[1] See the description by Lane (2000, 490–91), who visited the site in 1826.

1963, directed by J. Martin Plumley of the University of Cambridge. There were further seasons of excavations in 1964, 1966, 1969, 1972 and thereafter every two years down to 2006, which was the twenty-sixth and final season. In 1972 the University of Kentucky and American Research Center in Egypt joined the Egypt Exploration Society as sponsors of the excavations in Qaṣr Ibrīm. Between 1976 and 1988 the excavations were directed by William Y. Adams of the University of Kentucky. In 1988 the direction of the excavations was taken over by Mark Horton of the University of Bristol and subsequently in 1996 by Pamela Rose (Adams 1996, 12; Rose 2011).

During the various excavations, a very large number of artefacts and texts were discovered at the site of Qaṣr Ibrīm from the various historical layers of its occupation. The texts include material written in Egyptian hieroglyphs, Demotic, Meroitic, Latin, Greek, Old Nubian, Coptic, Arabic and Turkish (Adams 1979). In the Middle Ages, Old Nubian was the spoken language of Nubia, but written material preserved in Qaṣr Ibrīm from this period is written in four languages, viz. Old Nubian, Arabic, Coptic and Greek. Old Nubian was used for a wide range of documentary and literary writings. Coptic and Greek were mainly restricted to Christian religious texts.

The Arabic texts are mainly documentary and relate to diplomacy and commerce. They are datable to throughout the Islamic period. They include an Arabic papyrus from the middle of the second century AH/eighth century AD, documents from the medieval period and documents from the Ottoman period.

2.2. The Arabic Papyrus

The Arabic papyrus discovered at Qaṣr Ibrīm, which was published by Hinds and Sakkout (1981), is the longest extant papyrus written in Arabic. It is 53.5 cm wide and 264.5 cm long, and consists of 69 lines. It is a letter written in 141 AH/758 AD by the newly installed Abbasid governor of Egypt to the king of Dongola, complaining of the Nubians' failure to fulfill some of their obligations under the *baqṭ* treaty. The letter had evidently been forwarded by the king of Dongola to the eparch at Qaṣr Ibrīm, as the official most directly concerned. This was put in a storage crypt.

2.3. Medieval Scrolls

Plumley (1975b) published two scrolls discovered at Qaṣr Ibrīm containing the same text (with slight differences of wording) in Bohairic Coptic and Arabic respectively. The Arabic document contains 58 lines. Each scroll contains a Letter Testimonial (known in Arabic as *taqlīd*) from the Patriarch Gabriel IV (1370–78 AD) to the people of Nubia, informing them that he had consecrated a new bishop, Timotheos, in the place of their deceased bishop, Athanasios, and instructing them to receive and enthrone Timotheos in his see.

2.4. Documents from the Ottoman Period

In a series of two volumes, Hinds, in collaboration with Sakkout and Ménage, published a corpus of documents from Qaṣr Ibrīm that are datable to the Ottoman period, written in Arabic and Turkish (Hinds and Sakkout 1986; Hinds and Ménage 1991). The

Ottomans took control of Upper Egypt and Lower Nubia in the 1570s. The documents are datable to the seventeenth and eighteenth centuries. They consist mainly of legal documents relating to land and administrative documents relating to military affairs, mostly connected with the pay of the Turkish garrison.

2.5. The Medieval Documents Published in this Volume

2.5.1. Preliminary Remarks

In addition to the published Arabic documents that have been described above, a number of medieval Arabic documents discovered at Qaṣr Ibrīm have so far remained unpublished. These throw new light on relations between Egypt and Nubia in the High Middle Ages, especially in the Fatimid period. They are of particular importance since previous historical studies from the perspective of Arabic sources have been almost entirely based on historiographical sources, often written a long time after the events described and distorted by tendentious points of view. The medieval documents from Qaṣr Ibrīm are firsthand witnesses to the interaction of Egyptians and Nubians and the reality of how the *baqṭ* operated.

Preliminary work on many of these medieval documents was carried out by Elizabeth Sartain. She produced a handlist of the documents and translations of some of them, which were published by Adams (2010, 249–55). In the mid 1990s she passed the documents on to me to prepare them for publication.[2] The present volume presents the edition of the majority of this corpus of unpublished medieval documents. The edited documents, as far as can be established, are datable to the eleventh and twelfth centuries in the second half of the Fatimid period.

Several of the medieval documents from Qaṣr Ibrīm are not included in the edited corpus, mainly due to their fragmentary state. Also, it should be noted that the Arabic texts discovered in the excavations also included some fragments of literary texts. These also are not included in the edited corpus, with the exception of a poem that appears to have been written by a travelling merchant. In addition, some Old Nubian manuscripts containing also Arabic text were discovered in Qaṣr Ibrīm (see the plates in Ruffini 2014) and at least one Coptic manuscript containing Arabic (Adams 1996, 220–24). The Arabic portions of these bilingual texts are also not included in this volume.

The task of preparing the edition brought numerous challenges. Although I had Elizabeth Sartain's handlist, I was not able to get access to the original documents. Most of them are understood to be in the collection of the Museum of Islamic Art in Cairo, though some were subsequently transferred to the Nubian Museum in Aswan. Moreover, I initially did not have a full collection of the photographs of the corpus. With the help of Julie

---

[2] In addition to photographs of the documents, Elizabeth Sartain passed on to me a series of notes on the documents and the unpublished manuscript of a lecture entitled 'Nubian-Egyptian Relations in the Late Fatimid Period: The Sudan Trade', which she delivered at the Middle Eastern Studies Association conference, North Carolina, 1993.

Anderson and Loretta Kilroe at the British Museum, where the Qaṣr Ibrīm archive is now kept, I was able to acquire a few of the missing photographs as well as photographs of some documents that were not in Sartain's handlist. This was greatly facilitated by a spreadsheet prepared by Robin Seignobos that collated my collection of photographs with Sartain's handlist. I was eventually able to acquire the remaining missing photographs with the help of Pamela Rose, a former director of excavations, who allowed me to have access to the full digital photographic copy of the artefacts and texts discovered at Qaṣr Ibrīm.

2.5.2. Numbering Systems[3]

It was standard practice for objects, including the Arabic documents discussed here, to be assigned **object numbers**, either as individual items or in groups. This was done by the archaeologists working at the site. In early seasons, the number was usually in the form of the year followed by a sequence number; this was later superseded by a number giving the date followed by a sequence number (e.g., 74.1.23/5 is the fifth object catalogued from those found on 23rd January 1974). In later seasons, where several pieces were found together in a single context, a subsidiary letter or number could be added to the final number to designate the individual pieces (e.g., 78.2.13/45A; 74.1.29/11.7). It is clear, however, that in early seasons (at least up to and including 1974) not all finds were allocated individual object numbers,

[3] This section was written by Pamela Rose. All archival sources cited here are now housed in the Department of Egypt and Sudan, British Museum.

and in the case of texts, the pieces without object numbers were grouped together by language without, as far as it is possible to establish, separating them by provenance. These groups are known only by their registration number.

The **registration number** refers to the number given to individual finds or groups of similar finds in the official Egyptian Antiquities Service register book. This documented which finds were transferred from the site to the Cairo Museum (or, later, to magazines in Aswan), where the objects were then stored prior to dispersal via the division process or for retention in the museum. The registration number took the form of the year and a sequence number, thus 74/12, or simply a sequence number without a year. Individual objects thus often have both an object number (the site record) and a registration number (its entry in the official register book).

Most of the objects were photographed on site, and have one or more **excavation photograph numbers** associated with them. They have a format giving the year, film number and frame number, e.g., 1966A_P06_21A-22. Frequently, the excavation photograph numbers have more than one frame number, as in the example just given. This indicates that two separate photographs, typically of the recto and of the verso, were taken. Sometimes the film number was elaborated to reflect the photographer, or type of film used, so that in the example above, 'P' indicates that the photographer was J. Martin Plumley. The excavation numbers and photograph numbers were related by means of a log book.

All the Arabic documents discussed below were transferred to the Cairo Museum, and thence, at least in the case of the 1966 documents, to the Museum of Islamic Art in Cairo, where they were assigned **Museum of Islamic Art inventory numbers** in the series 23973, i.e., 23973.1, 23973.2, etc. This number was written on the documents in Arabic numerals. The museum inventory numbers for documents from the 1974 and 1978 excavations are not known. Three of the documents from the 1966A excavations have been assigned the inventory numbers Add. 01, Add. 02 and Add. 03 in Sartain's handlist. The origin of these numbers is unclear.

Finally, following a project conducted by Dr J. Hall of Würzburg University to scan all black and white photographs from Qaṣr Ibrīm, the digital images of the documents have also been assigned an **image number** in the digital collection of images.

Due to the complexity of all these various systems of numbers, it was decided to assign each edited document in this corpus an edition number and to refer to this edition number in any discussion about the document. The edition numbers run from **1** to **53** and are in bold font throughout the book (except in the indexes). The excavation photograph numbers, the digital image numbers and the museum numbers of each document are listed at the beginning of the edition of each document. The object numbers and registration numbers are also indicated, where these can be recovered. Unfortunately, not all of these can be identified and matched with the edition numbers.

2.5.3. Provenance of the Documents[4]

2.5.3.1. 1966

The majority of texts discussed here come from the excavation season conducted in early 1966 (season 1966A). None of them was studied on site and no object numbers were assigned to them, as outlined in Plumley's introduction to Hinds and Sakkout (1986). They were photographed in 1966 only after transport to the Cairo Museum at the end of the season: the photographic log notes for each image only "Arabic mss, Cairo museum" and does not give any further details. Plumley, however, notes that it was the "earlier Arabic" from the excavation that was photographed in 1966 (Hinds and Sakkout 1986, vii–viii).

One of the most important finds of the 1966A season, a sealed pot found in an Ottoman house seen to contain multiple containers and bundles of Arabic documents, was not further investigated that year. By 1968, when Plumley returned to Egypt to continue documentation of the 1966 finds (excavation seasons were not possible in 1967 or 1968), the pot and its contents had been transferred to the Museum of Islamic Art, and the documents themselves opened, catalogued and registered without regard for details of their origin, along with some or all of the "earlier Arabic." This is clear because a number of the documents were photographed in both 1966 and 1968. Some documents were only photographed in 1968, raising the possibility that at least some of these came from the previously unopened

[4] This section was written by Pamela Rose.

documents within the pot. Indeed, Plumley comments that the pot's contents included earlier Arabic material of "the twelfth and thirteenth centuries" as well as Ottoman-period documents (Hinds and Sakkout 1986, viii). The photographic log books for 1968 list all photographs as "Arabic mss Jan to March 1966 in Islamic Museum photographed in Jan 1968" and note the museum accession number.

The official registration book from the 1966A season lists the contexts of all the Arabic documents transferred to Cairo after the excavation. These are:

Table 2: Contexts of all Arabic documents transferred to Cairo after the excavation

Registration Number	**Comment**
66A/10–18	The pot and its contents, dated as "Bosnian" (i.e., Ottoman).
66A/20	"Collection of manuscript fragments (mainly Arabic. Possibly some Turkish)" from houses 295–310,[5] "Bosnian."
66A/27	Page of Arabic manuscript, 30 × 15 cm in size, from room 196, "Bosnian."
66A/111	Collection of Arabic mss, from Tomb T2, Christian and Islamic.

The dating assigned to the fragments relied on context rather than the properties of the documents themselves, and it is possible that earlier documents were present in later contexts.

[5] For the architectural plan and the numbering of the houses, see Adams (1996).

These are the only Arabic materials sent to Cairo from the 1966A season. If we accept Plumley's statement that it was only the "earlier Arabic" that was photographed that same year, then the documents with 1966 photograph numbers must come from 66A/111, Tomb T2. This was one of four chambers cut into a rock face to the south of the cathedral. All were robbed when found, but T2 contained memorial stelae of bishops of Ibrīm, below which, on the floor, were manuscripts in Coptic, Old Nubian and Greek, as well as the Arabic noted above. Plumley thought that together these "may well be the remains of one period of the library and archives of Ibrīm" (Plumley 1966, 11; see also Adams 2010, 54–56). It should be added, however, that a few Arabic fragments were found in the 1966B season, in December of that year. They were given registration number 66B/22, and, as registered pieces, must have been taken to Cairo Museum at the end of the excavation season. There are no photographs and no further information, apart from provenances including the North Temple Plaza and the 'Bosnian' plaza south of house B63. Thus it is unknown whether they might be amongst the pieces photographed by Plumley in the Museum of Islamic Art in 1968.

2.5.3.2. 1974

Some of these documents were recorded in Plumley's photographic log for 1974 with object number 74.1.29/11.x. Another site photographer, Violet MacDermot (VM in the table below), also photographed documents with the same object number (74.1.29/11) without suffixes, but these were Old Nubian texts. Thus the object number covered a context containing documents in multiple languages. Object number 74.1.29/7 also included both Arabic and Old Nubian fragments. The remaining Arabic texts were either unmarked, or have a number in a circle: numbers 10, 25 and 27 can be identified. These appear to relate to numberings allocated by MacDermot whilst photographing the assemblage with register number 72/12. No other locational data is given in the photographic log books. One might suppose that Plumley photographed the 'important' documents (which perhaps also merited separate find numbers) and left the smaller, unnumbered fragments to the second photographer.

Table 3: Numbers associated with documents photographed in 1974

Edition no.	Object no.	VM number	Registration no.
19		27 in circle	74/12
20		25 in circle	74/12
27	74.1.29/11.7		
28	74.1.29/11.2		
29	74.1.29/11.1		
30	74.1.29/11.3		
32	74.1.29/11.6		
33	74.1.29/11.6		
38	74.1.29/11.4		
39	74.1.29/11.5		
42	74.1.29/7		
43		10 in circle	74/12
44	74.1.29/11.4		

Since objects received their numbers based on the day of their discovery, their provenance can be identified by reference to site records. On 29th January 1974, workmen were removing floors of house LC1–6, rooms 1 and 2. According to Plumley's daybook:

> During the clearing of the floor of room 1 a small quantity of mss in Arabic and Old Nubian were recovered. However, in the adjoining room 2 a much greater quantity of mss was found. Mostly written in Arabic with a few documents in Old Nubian, these mss appear to be, in the main, letters. First examination shows that a number are complete and are possibly to be dated to the twelfth or thirteenth century.

These are presumably papers underlying the *mastaba* noted in the preliminary report (Plumley 1975a, 6–7). The pottery record for the room 2 location formalises it as "sherds associated with archive cache." In the same room, found the next day, was a sealed vessel containing Old Nubian leather scrolls (including dates 1155 or 1156), a Coptic scroll and an Arabic page.

Adams (1996, 47–50, 214–16) describes LC1–6 (redesignated as House 177) as an "eparchal house" and notes several more documents from it:

> In the loose fill beneath the floor of Room 1 were found several small folded papers which appear to be letters to the eparch ([object numbers] 69.2.8/3, 7, 8; [registration number] 69/26; [registration number] 74/12). In the fill beneath the stone-flagged entrance step to Room 2 were more papers, bearing texts both in Arabic and Old Nubian ([object number] 74.1.29/11).

Thus, following Adams, the materials in the present volume would come from both rooms in the house. It should be noted that some scholars subsequently questioned Adam's interpretation of the house (Wojciechowski 2011; Ruffini 2012b, 19). Several of the documents that Adams states were discovered in the house, however, can now be confirmed to be letters to the eparch and are included in the current corpus.

2.5.3.3. 1978

The photographic log for 1978 records the discovery of Arabic documents as object number 78.2.13/45A-E (registration number 276). The provenance was LC1–22, room 1, upper fill. LC1–22 (redesignated as structure 199) is a small, somewhat nondescript, single room (Adams 2010, 37) without any other distinguishing features. The fact that the texts were found in the upper fill means that they were not necessarily originally associated with the room.

The description of the find is as follows:

> [Five] Arabic texts in cloth.
>
> Cloth dyed blue-green in which are mss on strong brown paper. Cloth is z-spun cotton tabby, indigo dyed, almost a square. Mss are folded carefully. All in black ink. D is folded from one end, all others from both ends then doubled to half width.
>
> A. Side 1: ends of 16 lines. Side 2: Beginnings of 13 lines (including signature?). Top & bottom cut, other side torn. 26.9 × 9.6 cm [edition no. **49**].
>
> B. Side 1: 16 complete lines & 3 short ones lower left. Side 2: Blank. Bottom and left side cut. 16.6 × 27 cm [edition no. **52**].
>
> C. Side 1: complete length of 12 lines, 1 short one interlineated & 3 short lines upside down crammed in. Side 2: 5 lines, inverted, including signature?, complete, and 2 divided lines. 17.7 × 13.8 cm [edition no. **53**].

D. Side 1: 14 lines, probably complete, but bottom surviving line is cut through horizontally. Other side blank. 6 × 17.6 cm [edition no. **50**].

E. Side 1: Complete, 21 lines, some split (near bottom) into two parts. Side 2: 6 lines complete. 18.1 × 27.1cm [edition no. **51**].

The photographs of these documents are the following:

1978_A102_12–12A, 1978_A102_14–14A–1978_A102_19–19A. These include edition nos **51–53**.

1978_B09_06A-07–1978_B09_13A-14, 1978_B09_16A-17–1978_B09_18A-19. These include edition nos **49–50**.

1978_B11_23–23A, 1978_B19_05A-06.

These are a dossier of legal documents, discovered bound together in a cloth, that relate to the turbulent marital affairs of a certain Maryam ibnat Yuḥannis (**49**, **50**, **51**, **52**, **53**). They may have been gathered together by Maryam. It is significant that the documents were written in Upper Egypt. It would appear that Maryam moved to Qaṣr Ibrīm later in life.

2.5.4. Overview of the Content of the Documents

The medieval Arabic documents in the corpus that is edited in this volume include letters, accounts, legal documents and one poem written by a traveller.

Many of the letters constitute correspondence between Muslim merchants, who were based in Aswan, and the Nubian eparch in Qaṣr Ibrīm. The corpus also includes correspondence between merchants and Muslim dignitaries, such as *ʾamīrs*, and correspondence between merchants.

The accounts were written by the Muslim merchants and mention many of the commodities that are found also in the letters.

In the Middle Ages, the region of Lower Nubia was governed by a royal deputy of the king of Dongola based at Qaṣr Ibrīm, whom I refer to as an eparch, his Greek title, following the custom of historians of Nubia. He appears to have been mainly concerned with the conduct of relations with Muslim Egypt.

A large proportion of the medieval letters discovered at Qaṣr Ibrīm are from merchants who were members of the Arab tribal group known as the Banū al-Kanz. The Banū al-Kanz can be traced in origin to a migration of a part of the Arab tribe of Rabīʿa from Arabia to Upper Egypt in the third century AH/ninth century AD, attracted to the gold and emerald mines in the region (Holt 2012). They amalgamated through intermarriage with the local Beja tribe, which controlled the region between the Red Sea coastline and the eastern banks of the Nile River. They eventually gained control of Aswan, the mines of Wādī al-ʿAllāqī and the frontier zone. In Fatimid times, the ruler of this Arab-Beja tribe was the *de facto* governor of Aswan. Their power derived in a large measure from their control of trade with Nubia and the caravan route to the Red Sea port of ʿAyḏāb. They had considerable wealth and were patrons of literature and scholarship. The documents of the corpus edited in this volume cast important new light on the activities of the Banū al-Kanz.

In 396 AH/1006 AD, the ruling sheikh of the Banū al-Kanz, ʾAbū al-Makārim Hibat Allāh, assisted the Fatimid caliph al-Ḥākim in the capture of a political rival, ʾAbū Rakwa, who nearly overthrew al-Ḥākim's régime. For this service, ʾAbū al-Makārim was given the title Kanz al-Dawla 'Treasure of the Dynasty'.[6] The title became hereditary and was assumed by subsequent leaders of the tribe throughout the Fatimid period. It was due to this that the tribe as a whole came to be known as the Banū al-Kanz. The present-day Kenuz Nubians are thought to be their descendants.

Since the *baqṭ* agreement was a non-aggression treaty, the Arab tribesmen had little scope for raiding for booty, so they began to participate in commerce. Aswan was a commercial network linking overland trade routes from the Red Sea and the Upper and Lower Nile.

The Banū al-Kanz were not independent from the Fatimid state and the Kanz al-Dawla reported to the Fatimid governor of Qūṣ. The Fatimid government granted the Kanz al-Dawla responsibility for regulating Fatimid diplomatic relations and commerce with Nubia, tax collection in the frontier villages, protecting the mines of Wādī al-ʿAllāqī and travellers and caravans passing through their sphere of control.

The Banū al-Kanz came into periodic conflict with the Ayyubids and subsequently also with the Mamluks. Eventually, in the fourteenth and fifteenth centuries, they were forced to migrate southward into northern Nubia, where they helped accelerate the expansion of Islam (Garcin and Tuchscherer 2012; Seignobos 2016, I:380–85). They assimilated into the Nubian culture and adopted the Nubian language, although they remained

---

[6] For the sources for this, see Beshir (1975, 16 n. 2).

Muslims. They assumed control of the Kingdom of Makuria in the early fourteenth century and intermarried with the Nubian royal family, creating a new branch of Nubian people who today are speakers of the Dongolawi (Andaandi) and Kenzi (Mattokki) languages (Ruffini 2019, 114; 2020, 766). The royal throne hall in Dongola was subsequently converted into a mosque (Godlewski and Medeksza 1987).

The letters of the edited corpus provide new insights into relations between Egypt and Nubia. In particular, they demonstrate the important role played by the Banū al-Kanz and by the Nubian eparch in the region.

A detailed analysis of the letters will be given in the ensuing pages, but we may summarise the contribution of the letters to our understanding of relations between Egypt and Nubia in the Fatimid period as follows.

According to historiographical sources, the *baqṭ* remained in force until the full islamicisation of Nubia in the fourteenth century (Cuoq 1986, 75). There is a reference to a Fatimid vizier doubling the *baqṭ* payment owed by the Nubians as a punitive measure and a report (Beshir 1975, 19–20) that the Fatimid ruler al-ʾAfḍal

> wrote to the governor of Upper Egypt to send an army to the borders of the country of the Nubians and to send an emissary to them in order to renew upon them the stipulated quota that had been established by tradition, which is three hundred and sixty heads of slaves every year. Before doing this he should collect from them the arrears of what was due from them in the past.

The letters of the edited corpus, however, do not allude to the purported requirement of the *baqṭ* agreement for the Nubian king to make a delivery of a specific quota of slaves to the Egyptian governor in Upper Egypt in exchange for commodities. Rather, the letters reflect a situation in which the eparch administered the exchange of slaves for goods with individual Muslim merchants who were the agents of the Kanz al-Dawla, the Fatimid government representative in Aswan. The eparch required the Muslims to enter Nubia peacefully and the Kanz al-Dawla required the eparch to reciprocate by guaranteeing the merchants' protection. This was an equipollent diplomatic reciprocity that appears to have been the original spirit of the *baqṭ* agreement, as has been discussed above. It was not a predatory practice that aimed at humiliating Nubia and stripping its wealth. It cannot be excluded, of course, that the formal delivery of a quota of slaves was running in parallel with these interactions with individual merchants, but there is no evidence for this in the corpus. If such deliveries of quotas were taking place at this period, one would have, indeed, expected to find references to them in the correspondence with the eparch.

One of the letters (**24**) refers to a slave (*raqīq*) that the eparch bestowed (*ʾanʿamathu*) upon the writers. This indicates that the process involved was conceived of as the exchange of diplomatic gifts rather than barter of commodities for slaves. This would be in line with the way diplomatic relations between agrarian Northeast African states were conducted (Kapteijns and

Spaulding 1988; 1990; Spaulding and Kapteijns 1994; Spaulding 1995, 584–86).[7]

Reciprocal gift exchange in pre-industrial societies fostered cohesion and peaceful relations between the groups in the absence of protection from a supra-regional dominant political power. According to the model of diplomatic gift exchange in pre-industrial societies proposed by Sindzingre (2017, 12), this is likely to have involved the process of making a gift to create a debt for the receiving group, i.e., exchanging a gift for a debt of reciprocity. A gift is, in principle, voluntary, though this is a polite fiction and reciprocity is expected (Mauss 2002, 3–4). A gift, therefore, is a bid by the giver to gain trust from the recipient (Caillé 2007, 49). Negru (2009) describes a gift that is made with such an expectation of reciprocation as an 'impure gift', which contrasts with a 'pure gift' without any such expectation. It is the 'impure' characteristic of diplomatic gifts that builds social cohesion. There is evidence in the letters for such debts in gift exchanges between the Muslim merchants and the eparch. This would impose an obligation on the receiving group to make a similar exchange in return, thus maintaining a circulation of gifts and debts that would bind the groups. The altruism of gift-giving motivated by the expectation of reciprocation created social cohesion more powerfully than market exchanges. This was because it had evolved as a trait of small hunter-gatherer societies centuries before the development of monetary markets and so was deeply embedded in human psychology (Trivers 1971).

---

[7] For diplomatic gift exchanges in the Islamic world, see Cutler (2001) and al-Qaddūmī (1996).

Such gift-giving, with its social motivations, lies outside market activity but, as Sindzingre (2017) emphasises, even in the pre-industrial age there were never purely non-market societies. This holds true for the activities of the Muslim merchants reflected in the letters in our corpus. The merchants subsequently sold the slaves as commercial commodities. These were market exchanges and not gift exchanges. Yāqūt (d. 626 AH/1229 AD; *Muʿjam al-Buldān*, IV:515), indicates that in his day (early thirteenth century AD) there were vibrant slave markets on the Egyptian–Nubian border.[8] There is no evidence from the letters of a situation such as that described by al-Masʿūdī (d. 345 AH/956 AD; *Murūj al-Ḏahab* I:132–33), in which there was a regular delivery of quotas of slaves at the border town of Nubia, al-Qaṣr, which were distributed to a variety of officials. It cannot be excluded that such descriptions of the delivery of quotas were fictional constructs of tendentious historiography relating to the *baqṭ* rather than reflections of reality.

Beshir (1975, 21) hypothesises that one of the motivations for the slave trade may have been the increasing demand for slave soldiers in the army. There was a vast expansion of the black infantry corps of the Fatimid army during the reign of

[8] For an examination of the evidence for the external trade of Nubian slaves in the Middle Ages, including their acquisition for service in the army, see Edwards (2011). For slave markets, see Rāġib (1993). Nubian domestic slaves were being sold in Cairo at this period, as shown by the Genizah document published by Perry (2019). For other medieval documents attesting to the acquisition of Nubian slaves, see Bruning (2020, 685).

al-Ḥākim (386–411 AH/996–1021 AD; Lev 2013, 61). It is significant, however, that the letters in our corpus frequently refer to slaves by the terms *waṣīf* and *waṣīfa* (§10.2), which designated slaves who were destined for domestic service (Goitein 1967, 131; Rāġīb 2006, II:23–25). The import of slaves for military service may have taken place by different routes. There is evidence for the import of slaves, for example, through the Red Sea port of Quṣayr (Guo 2004, 43). This appears, however, to be on a small scale. Travellers to Egypt during the eleventh and twelfth centuries mention kidnapping and organised slave raids to the south and southeast of Aswan. It is possible that these raids provided a large proportion of the slaves appearing on the Egyptian markets (Perry 2017, 134).

The diplomatic gift exchange was formally between the eparch, who represented the Nubian king, and his Muslim counterpart, the Kanz al-Dawla, who represented the Fatimid government. Within this system, however, the merchants, who were the agents of the Kanz al-Dawla, appear to have made individual monetary gain through the sale of slaves in Egypt. Thus, the Muslim merchants became entrepreneurs by interfacing with this administered gift exchange. In this respect, the situation was a mixed economy, not private enterprise nor a wholly statist economy.[9]

---

[9] According to Hudson (2010, 12), this is how Ancient Mesopotamian economies worked. Cf. the remarks of Welsby (2002, 202–3) regarding trade in medieval Nubia. Frenkel (2017, 147), in her study of slavery in the Genizah documents, points out that Jewish merchants did not in

The term 'entrepreneur' is a seventeenth-century French term denoting "a person who entered into a contractual relationship with the government for the performance of a service or the supply of goods. The price at which the contract was valued was fixed and the entrepreneurs bore the risks of profit and loss from the bargain" (Kirzner 1979, 39; see also Renger 2000, 155). According to Hudson (2010, 12), "an entrepreneur seeks economic gain either with his own money or, more often, operating with borrowed funds or managing the assets of others (including public institutions) to make something over for himself by cutting expenses or creating a business innovation." It is likely that this is not far from how the Muslim merchant entrepreneurs in our corpus were operating viz-à-viz the Kanz al-Dawla and the eparch. There was a symbiotic and complementary relationship between the administering institutions and the mercantile enterprise. They did not act by themselves for their own individual interest, but as part of a system. Indeed, the letters in our corpus refer to mercantile partnerships (§9.22).

There are also many references in the Arabic documents to monetary transactions, some of them with the eparch, though it appears that these never involved the purchase of slaves. In some cases, the merchants apologise for not having ready cash for transactions that do not involve slaves (e.g., **21**r, margin, 1), which suggests that monetary purchase was expected in such transactions. Ruffini (2012b, 171–206; 2019) has shown that medieval Nubia was integrated into the currency system of Egypt

---

principle deal in slaves, since the import of slaves to Egypt was in the hands of high-ranking Muslim officials.

and coins travelled at face value and were not treated simply as bullion. It is easiest to interpret these monetary transactions with the eparch as market exchanges. These would have been extensions of the Egyptian market economy into Nubia, which were carried out on the back of the diplomatic gift exchanges.

This is, therefore, a further reflection of an entrepreneurial mixed economy of market and non-market exchanges (Hudson 2010, 12). It is important to note that, since the slaves acquired by gift exchange were subsequently sold in Egyptian markets, the reciprocal gift exchanges must have been based on the comparison of abstract values of a monetary standard established by a market economy. Despite being expressed as a gift exchange, the delivery of slaves effectively took the form of a substitute for money. Indeed, the merchants sometimes complained if the slaves were defective in some way, since their market value would have been reduced. The exchange did not have the characteristics of barter, in which the parties compared their immediate needs of particular commodities (Grierson 1978, 11). An exchange of substitutes for money that were subsequently sold, indeed, was tantamount to a market exchange of commodities. Gifts are typically not sold. It would appear, therefore, that even the exchange of slaves for commodities had this distinctive property of a market exchange. Although this exchange was, arguably, in its substance a market exchange, its form was presented and conceptualised as a gift exchange, reflected, for example, by the reference to the 'bestowing' of a slave upon the merchants. It was this external form of the exchange as a gift exchange that served the purpose of creating social cohesion and peaceful relations, which was the spirit of the truce (*hudna*) between Egypt and Nubia. The fact that it was a market exchange in its substance is likely to have facilitated the exchange, since the Muslim merchants and indeed the eparch were working within the Egyptian monetary market economy.

There is evidence from the letters that merchants made individual commitments of loyalty to the eparch and the king in order to conduct trade in Nubia and be afforded protection (see **9**). This is another manifestation of the individualisation of diplomatic trade and gift exchange. They were representatives of groups, but the exchanges with the eparch and the king were on an individual level and these were controlled by individual controls of loyalty.

The merchants mention only small numbers of slaves in their letters, which were received by individual merchants, and no overall quota. It should be noted that this conflicts with the historiographical sources listed by Beshir (1975), mainly al-Maqrīzī, which report up to five deliveries of *baqṭ* payments during the Fatimid period, consisting of substantial numbers of slaves and luxury goods.

Since, at earlier periods, the Muslim interpretation of the *baqṭ* tended to be a unilateral obligation to pay tribute, it is likely that one common reason why Nubians failed to cooperate was their perception that the Muslims violated a principle of reciprocity, which was a key feature of diplomatic relations between agrarian Northeast African states (Spaulding 1995, 584–86). This reciprocity would have been present in the individual-level gift exchange of slaves for commodities as described above. One may say that the situation reflected in the letters of individual-level gift exchanges, which were implicitly market exchanges, combined with explicit market exchanges reflects the mutually accepted way in which the *baqṭ* was able to operate.

The letters confirm to some extent the description given by al-ʾAswānī of an open trade zone for Muslim merchants in Lower Nubia between the first and second cataracts. This was an arrangement designed to allow safe trade between potentially hostile political domains, which did not allow Muslim merchants close to the king and his centre of power in Dongola. Parallels to such arrangements can be identified elsewhere in pre-industrial societies. Polanyi (1963), who has extensively studied many such "ports of trade," as he calls them, stresses that they are administered rather than free markets.[10] The trade zone in Lower Nubia was administered by the king through his eparch. As far as can be seen, the merchants traded exclusively with the eparch and his staff, and so foreign trade was a royal monopoly. The political authority of the eparch was associated with his economic power. Nubian documents relating to land sale from Qaṣr Ibrīm indicate that eparchs were big land owners (Ruffini 2016a, 17, 197).

Scholars have compared medieval Nubia to the kingdom of early modern Dahomey in West Africa, which is described by Polanyi (1966) as consisting of a port of trade separated from the remainder of the kingdom. Ruffini (2012b, 61–68) cautions against applying Polanyi's portrayal of Dahomey to medieval Nubia without qualification. According to Polanyi, royal monopolies

---

[10] I am grateful to the economist Phil Armstrong for discussing with me Polanyi's economic model.

function by the redistribution of wealth in society. Following this model, the royal monopoly on the trade with the Arab merchants would be assumed to have resulted in redistribution of goods by the eparch and the king. According to Ruffini (2012b, 67, 102–3), however, the Nubian documents that he has studied indicate that gift giving in the Christian period was in the private sphere, as acts by private citizens rather than the eparch and the king. Moreover, we see from the Nubian documents that the king did not claim ownership over all land and the Nubian people were not considered to be his slaves. Some historians of Nubia, such as Jay Spaulding (e.g., Spaulding 1995), David Edwards (e.g., Edwards 2004), Ali Osman (e.g., Osman 1982) and Giovanni Ruffini himself, have argued that a more accurate insight into some aspects of medieval Nubia can be gained by the study of modern societies of Northeast Africa. As we have seen, Spaulding in particular retrojects modern customs of diplomatic reciprocity in royal monopolies in Northeast African societies to the functioning of the *baqṭ* in medieval Lower Nubia.

We learn from the documents of our corpus that Muslims had settled within the trade zone. This is confirmed by the discovery of Muslim gravestones, mainly dating to the ninth–eleventh centuries AD, between the first and second cataracts (Edwards 2019, 968–69; Seignobos 2021). Arabic ostraca datable to this period have, moreover, been discovered in sites within the trade zone other than Qaṣr Ibrīm, for example Debeira West (Shinnie and Shinnie 1978, Plate LII). The letters indicate, furthermore, that some Arabic-speaking Muslims appear to have worked in the service of the Nubian eparch, such as his secretary (*kātib*), who took care of the eparch's Arabic correspondence.

The letters show us also that in reality the Muslim merchants were not totally restricted to this trade zone. Several letters refer to Muslim merchants visiting the capital Dongola and also Soba, the capital of ʿAlwa, which at that period was united with Makuria and Nobadia, in order to conduct trade with the king. This was another component of the royal monopoly that operated separately from the trade zone. This direct trade with the king appears not to have been totally demonetised, as there is a reference to a monetary payment by the king (**9**r:26). The exchanges with the king, therefore, appear to have included market exchanges.

Ruffini (2019) argues that the economy of the Nubian state was monetised with Islamic currency in both Lower Nubia and Upper Nubia and was integrated with the Egyptian economy in a single currency zone. Nubia was economically dependent on Egypt, but exerted its agency to adapt Egyptian economic standards to local ideological needs and local expressions of power.

It is significant that Aswan is referred to in the Arabic letters of the corpus as a *ṯaġr* 'boundary' (e.g., **19**r:3) and Aswan is described in this way also in the works of the medieval geographers, e.g., al-ʾIṣṭaḵrī (d. 346 AH/957 AD; *Masālik al-Mamālik*, 51). This term was typically used to designate a port or inland boundary at the edge of Muslim territory that faced a non-Muslim enemy (Brauer 1995, 12–16; Seignobos 2010). According to al-Maqrīzī (*Ḵiṭaṭ*, I:367), up to the end of the Fatimid period, there was a permanent garrison of armed soldiers in Aswan ready to protect the border (*ḥifẓ al-ṯaġr*) from incursions of Nubians and blacks (*al-Nūba w-al-Sūdān*). The economic integration of Nubia with Egypt did not correspond to the political boundary between them and commercial interactions, therefore, required the peace-making element of diplomatic gift exchanges.

Furthermore, the letters indicate that the king was dependent on Egypt for military supplies and so Egyptian merchants played a role in guaranteeing the security of the king and his régime. It is likely for this reason that they were given permission to conduct trade directly with the king in Dongola and Soba—letter **39** indicates that a Muslim merchant had travelled to Soba to sell supplies for the king's army. The Muslims were, moreover, given diplomatic gifts of land within Lower Nubia by the king, apparently as an exchange for military and political aid in periods of tension with Egypt or during dynastic struggles (see document **21**). So, there was a mixture of market and non-market exchanges.

Just as there were private commitments of loyalty made between the merchants and the eparch, there were private commitments of loyalty made between the Muslims and the king. While operating in Nubia, Muslims had the status of loyal Nubian subjects, who made formal commitments of allegiance, rather than visiting Egyptians with safe conduct. This would have created a higher level of security for the Nubians when dealing with the Muslim merchants. Another possibility is that these commitments of loyalty reflect that the Muslims concerned were, in fact, residents of Nubia and regular subjects of the king. This is not, however, a necessary conclusion.

Diplomatic gift exchange in the restricted trade zone in Lower Nubia, on the one hand, and the military and political aid supplied to the king in exchange for diplomatic gifts of land and royal trading concessions, on the other hand, both supplemented by market exchanges, were strategies to increase the economic power of the king and his eparch, and to maintain the political security of the régime. As we have seen, the nature of the activities in the trade zone of Lower Nubia was further determined by the original spirit of the truce (*hudna*), which required equipollent reciprocity and mutual protection.

The legal documents of the corpus include a lease of land (**44**), a lease of a boat (**45**), documents of sale of land (**46**), an acknowledgement of a debt (**47**) and marriage contracts and other documents relating to marriage (**48–53**). These documents were drawn up within the jurisdiction of a Muslim *qāḍī* in Egypt, in most cases, it seems, in Aswan.

The parties concerned included both Muslims and Nubians. The fact that they were discovered in Qaṣr Ibrīm indicates that some of the parties must have been resident in Nubia at some point. They reflect the settlement of Nubians in Upper Egypt and the settlement of Muslims in Nubia. Indeed the documents of sale **46** recto and **46** verso seem to be relating to plots of land south of Aswan in Nubia. Document **44** refers to a Nubian resident in Lower Nubia who served as a Fatimid military officer with an estate (*ʾiqṭāʿ*) in Upper Egypt. Presumably, he owed allegiance to both the Fatimid and Nubian authorities. Likewise, the Muslim merchants operating in Nubia appear to have owed allegiance to both the Kanz al-Dawla, the representative of the Fatimid government, on the one hand, and also the Nubian eparch and king, on the other. This system of dual loyalty maintained peaceful Egyptian–Nubian relations.

In this context, it should be noted that the majority of the people serving the Muslim merchants operating in Nubia, such as their slave boys (*ġilmān*, sing. *ġulām*), appear from their names to have been Nubians. Some of those who served the merchants, moreover, were resident in Nubia (see §10).

All this reflects the integration and symbiosis of Egyptians and Nubians in the society of the region across the political border between Upper Egypt and Lower Nubia.

In what follows, I shall divide the description and analysis of the documents into three main groups: the correspondence with eparchs (§3), other correspondence and accounts (§4) and legal documents (§5). This has the advantage of drawing attention to distinctive features of each of the groups of documents. Some features relating to the life and work of the Muslim community, however, inevitably cut across groups of documents. Following the treatment of these three categories of documents, I present a series of inventories and studies that relate to the entire corpus.

3. THE CORRESPONDENCE WITH EPARCHS

3.1. Preliminary Remarks

Twenty-five of the documents of the corpus constitute correspondence with the eparchs who were based in Qaṣr Ibrīm. A large proportion of these are letters sent to the eparch Uruwī (**1–16**). There are two letters sent by the eparch Uruwī (**17–18**), two letters sent to the eparch Īsū (**19–20**) and five letters sent to an unnamed eparch (**21–25**). One letter (**26**) is written to the deputy of the eparch Darmā and one to the secretary of the eparch Uruwī (**27**).

3.2. The Eparchs

3.2.1. Uruwī

The eparch Uruwī figures more prominently than any other eparch in the corpus. The name of Uruwī is represented in the Arabic documents in most cases with the orthography اروى, in one case اوى (**9**v, address, right column, 2) and in another case روى (**27**r:3). The name of this eparch appears in Old Nubian documents with the orthography ⲟⲩⲣⲟⲩⳝⲓ 'Ourouwi', e.g., P. QI IV 109, verso, line 20, where he is mentioned as the one who regulates work and payment, and P. QI IV 95, where he is mentioned as the recipient of the document. According to Grzegorz Ochała (personal communication), however, the latter document is likely to have been written before Ourouwi became eparch.

 https://doi.org/10.11647/OBP.0391.03

In Nubian orthography, the digraph ⲟⲩ can represent either short [u] or long [u:] (Van Gerven Oei 2021, 36). The Arabic orthography اروى would appear to reflect the pronunciation [uruwi:], with short [u] vowels and the Arabic *wāw* corresponding to the glide ⳝ [w] in the Nubian orthography ⲟⲩⲣⲟⲩⳝⲓ 'Ourouwi'. The Arabic orthography روى (**27**r:3) would reflect the elision of the first vowel [ruwi:], which would be a phonetic process that would be more expected for a short vowel than a long vowel. It also indicates that the stress did not fall on the initial syllable of [uruwi:].

A few of the Arabic letters of the corpus that are addressed to Uruwī contain evidence that they were written during the reign of the Fatimid caliph al-ʿĀḍid li-Dīn Allāḥ, who was in office from 555 AH/1160 AD to 567 AH/1171 AD. Some of the names of the writers of the letters that appear in the address have the epithet العاضدى *al-ʿĀḍidī*, which indicates that they were affiliated to al-ʿĀḍid (**1**v, address, left column, 5; **8**v, address, left column, 5). One letter reports the news of the killing of the vizier Šāwar by Šīrkūh (**6**r:7), which we know took place in the year 564 AH/1169 AD. So Uruwī's term of office must have extended to at least 564 AH/1169 AD.

The sender of the Nubian letter P. QI IV 94 is ⲟⲩⲣⲟⲩⲏⲗ (Ourouēl) "the eparch of Nobadia." It is likely that this was a variant form of the name ⲟⲩⲣⲟⲩⳝⲓ 'Ourouwi'. The vowel represented by ⲏ in Old Nubian was, in fact, pronounced [i] or [i:] (Van Gerven Oei 2021, 35), although historians normally transcribe it as ē. So ⲟⲩⲣⲟⲩⲏⲗ would have been pronounced [urui:l].

The successor of the eparch Uruwī is likely to have been the eparch Masē, who is referred to in a dossier of Nubian documents compatible with a date before 1172 (Ruffini 2012b, 214).

3.2.2. Darmā

Letter **26** is addressed to al-Bazīl, the deputy (*al-nā'ib*) of the eparch Darmā, i.e., vice-eparch. Vice-eparchs are mentioned in various Nubian documents, e.g., P. QI III 38, P. QI III 40, P. QI III 49, P. QI III 50, P. QI IV 67, P. QI IV 69, P. QI IV 84, P. QI IV 94, P. QI IV 102. The name al-Bazīl appears to be the name Basil with intervocalic voicing.[1]

The eparch Darmā referred to in **26** can be identified with the eparch Darme (ⲇⲁⲣⲙⲉ). He is mentioned in a protocol of a Nubian proclamation dated 22nd August 1155 issued by King Moses George (P. QI III 30) and also in the Nubian document P. QI IV 109. In letter **26**, his name is represented by the Arabic orthography درما, indicating that the final vowel was pronounced long. The Nubian character ⲉ, which is written at the end of the

[1] Intervocalic voicing is attested in Old Nubian for the velar consonant ⲕ /*k*/, which is sometimes represented between vowels as ⲅ /*g*/. This voicing of intervocalic velars occurs also in modern Nubian languages (Van Gerven Oei 2021, 36, 408). The Old Nubian character ⲥ /*s*/ occasionally interchanges with the Nubian character ⲍ /*z*/ in Nubian names. This is found in intervocalic position, e.g., ⲉⲗⲉⲓⲍⲁⲃⲉⲧ for ⲉⲗⲉⲓⲥⲁⲃⲉⲧ (Mina 1942, no. 107), and also in word-initial position, e.g., ⲍⲁⲏⲗ for ⲥⲁⲏⲗ (Hellström 1970, I:235; II, Corpus Y, no. 232:1 and pl. 157:5), ⲍⲓⲙⲉⲱⲛⲓ for ⲥⲓⲙⲉⲱⲛⲓ (Zyhlarz 1932, 187–90). It is significant that the distinction between [s] and [z] is not phonemic in modern Nubian languages, e.g., Nobíin (Bell 1971, 118).

name ⲇⲁⲣⲙⲉ, represents either a short or long vowel. The fact that the Arabic transcription of the name has final *mater lectionis ʾalif* rather than *mater lectionis yāʾ* suggests that the final Nubian vowel was heard as a mid-low vowel [ɛː] rather the a mid-high vowel [eː].

The name of the writer of letter **26**, which appears in the address, has the epithet العاضدى *al-ʿĀḍidī*, as do the writers of the letters to Uruwī **1** and **8**. This indicates that he was affiliated to al-ʿĀḍid (555 AH/1160 AD–567 AH/1171 AD). Indeed, most of the other titles of the writter of **26** are identical to those of the writers of **1** and **8** and it is likely that **1**, **8** and **26** were sent by the same person.

Letter **23**, which is written to an unnamed eparch, mentions the name Darmā in a somewhat obscure passage:

> He entered Aswan and gathered the slaves [i.e., servants] of Darmā and brought me to them and said to me that "the Master of the Horses has ordered me to take over the administrative office." (**23**r:9–10)

This Darmā appears to have been an official of some kind but was not the eparch ('Master of the Horses'). Several Nubian documents dating from 1155 to 1187, which is likely to coincide with the date of **23**, refer to men called Darme with various official titles including *ŋeshsh* of the *domestikos* and *meizoteros* (Ruffini 2012b, 268–69). The functions of these officials are not completely clear. The term *domestikos* was used in the Byzantine empire as a title for both officials with military duties and those with civil administrative duties. In Nubian sources, the eparch of Nobadia is sometimes referred to as the *domestikos* of Pak̲ōras. The *ŋeshsh* and the *meizoteros* were lower ranking officials.

3.2.3. Īsū

Letters **19** and **20** are addressed to the eparch Īsū. In **19** his name is spelt يسوا and in **20** ايسوا. An eparch with the name ⲓⲏⲥⲟⲩ is mentioned in the Nubian document P. QI IV 101. This name is normally transcribed Iēsou by historians, but one should take into account that the Nubian vowel represented by the letter ⲏ was pronounced [i] or [iː] (Van Gerven Oei 2021, 35). The spelling ⲓⲏⲥⲟⲩ, therefore, would have been pronounced [iiːsū] or simply [iːsuː] without an initial glide. The Arabic orthographies يسوا and ايسوا are likely to have both been intended to represent the pronunciation [iːsuː].[2]

The Nubian document P. QI IV 101, which mentions Iēsou [Īsū], is likely to be datable to around 1155, since a certain Papasa *k̠artoularios*[3] mentioned in this document could be identified with a man of the same name and title in P. QI III 30, which is dated 22nd August 1155. As we indicated already, P. QI III 30 is a Nubian proclamation issued by King Moses George, which mentions the eparch Darme. The eparch Iēsou [Īsū], therefore, must have been in office shortly before or shortly after 1155. The date of the document, 1155, was roughly the period in which Moses George is thought to have succeeded his uncle King David, and he reigned until around 1190 (Ruffini 2012b, 247–48). The document P. QI IV 101, which mentions the eparch Īsū, refers to King

[2] Cf., furthermore, the variant spellings of the name in Nubian sources: DBMNT / TM Nam 3410 (ⲓⲏⲥⲟⲩⲋ): DBMNT NamVar 300288 (ⲓⲏⲥⲟⲩ), 300218 (ⲓⲥⲟⲩ), 301143 (ⲓ̅ⲥ̅ⲟⲩ), 300907 (ⲉⲓⲥⲟⲩ), 300984 (ⲉ̅ⲥ̅ⲟⲩ).

[3] This literally means 'archivist', though the precise duties of this official are not clear.

David (ⲇⲁⲩⲧⲓ Dauti) and not King Moses George. So Īsū's office of eparch must have begun in the reign of King David before 1155.

We could infer from the fact that Darme was eparch in 1155 and that his office extended into the reign of al-ʿĀḍid (555 AH/1160 AD–567 AH/1171 AD) that the eparch Īsū preceded the eparch Darme.

There is evidence, however, that Īsū was still eparch during the reign of Moses George. The Arabic document 1974_V08_24–24A,[4] which is not included in the present corpus, is apparently a pen exercise containing various addresses. This includes the following:

ابى الخير يسو وزير الملك مويس احياه الله وارشده

'ʾAbū al-Ḵayr Īsū, vizier of the King Mūyis, may God cause him to live and guide him.'

ابى الخير يسو... وزير الملك مويس ادام الله مملكته

'ʾAbū al-Ḵayr Īsū... the vizier of King Mūyis, may God cause his kingdom to endure.'

This indicates that the eparch Īsū (represented here as يسو without the final ʾ*alif*) was the vizier of king Mūyis, who can be identified as Moses George. So Īsū's term of office extended into the reign of Moses George.

One possibility is that the periods in which Darme and Īsū were eparchs overlapped. This may have been because the two eparchs were in conflict. The Nubian document P. QI IV 101, which mentions the eparch Īsū, was, in fact, written by another

[4] This is part of registration number 74/12 and part of object number 74.1.29/7.

eparch called Asouwil, who appears to be in conflict with the eparch Īsū. Such rivalries between competing eparchs could, therefore, occur.

The Arabic letter **27**, which is addressed to the secretary of the eparch Uruwī, indicates that Uruwī was the son of the preceding eparch.[5] Unfortunately there is a lacuna in the document where his father's name would have appeared. Given the preceding discussion, it is not clear whether his father was Darme or Īsū. In the edition of **27**, however, I have tentatively offered the reading يسو Īsū in the lacuna, since there is no trace of the rising *hasta* of the final *ʾalif* of درما above the lacuna and the lacuna is sufficiently small for us to expect to see the top of an *ʾalif*. As we have seen, the orthography يسو, without an *ʾalif*, is attested in the document 1974_V08_24–24A, which is discussed above.

Ruffini (2012b, 247–48) presents evidence that an eparch called Joasse in Nubian sources coincided chronologically with the reign of King Moses George and also with that of his predecessor King David, who was his uncle. The names Īsū and Joasse are too different to be the alternative names of the same person. Perhaps Joasse was yet another eparch overlapping with Īsū and/or Darme.

---

[5] For a discussion of the possible hereditary nature of the office of eparch, see Hendrickx (2011). Robin Seignobos presented a paper on this subject at the 15th International Conference for Nubian Studies, Warsaw, 2022, which he is currently preparing for publication.

3.3. Titles of the Eparchs

In the openings of the letters to the eparchs and in the addresses on the verso, the eparch is given various titles. These include the following:

الاكشيل *al-ʾikšīl* (passim)
اروى خياخ *ʾUruwī ḵiyāḵ* (**4**v, address, right, 2; **6**v, address, right, 2)
اروى بن خياخ *ʾUruwī ibn ḵiyāḵ* (**1**v, address, right, 2; **3**v, address, right, 2; **5**v, address, right, 2; **8**v, address, right, 2; **11**v, address, right, 2; **12**v, address, right, 2)
اوى بن خياخ *ʾU(r)uwī ibn ḵiyāḵ* (**9**v, address, right, 2)
وزير الملك 'vizier of the king' (passim)
النائب عن الملك 'the deputy of the king' (**1**v, address, right, 2; **3**v, address, right, 2; **5**v, address, right, 2; **6**v, address, right, 2; **11**v, address, right, 2)
النائب عن الملك بقلعة ابريم 'the deputy of the king in the fortress of Ibrīm' (**1**v, address, right, 2; **3**v, address, right, 2)
النائب عنه بقلعة ابريم 'his (i.e., the king's) deputy in the fortress of Ibrīm' (**8**v, address, right, 2)
النائب بقلعة ابريم 'the deputy in the fortress of Ibrīm' (**9**v, address, right, 2)

The Arabic form الاكشيل (*ʾal-ʾikšīl*) represents the Nubian official title *ikšīl*. In Nubian script this is represented as ⲉⲕ̄ϣⲓⲗ with a stroke over the ⲕ, which indicates that it was preceded by ⲓ, i.e., it is equivalent to ⲉⲓⲕϣⲓⲗ *eikšil*. The vowel digraph ⲉⲓ was pronounced as short [i] or long [iː] and ⲓ, likewise, represented short [i] or long [iː] (Van Gerven Oei 2021, 34–38). The *mater lectionis yāʾ* after the *šīn* in the Arabic orthography الاكشيل and the lack of a *mater lectionis* before the *kāf* suggest that the Nubian word ⲉⲓⲕϣⲓⲗ was heard with a short vowel in the first syllable and a long vowel in the second syllable, i.e., *ikšīl*.

The term ⲉⲓⲕϣⲓⲗ *ikšīl* is attested in various medieval Nubian sources. It usually occurs in the Nubian sources in combination with the word *k̲oiak* (ⲭⲟⲓⲁⲕ), originally an Egyptian month name, in the phrase *k̲oiak-ikšil*. The character *k̲* only occurs in loanwords in Nubian (Van Gerven Oei 2021, 37). The title *k̲oiak-eikšil* was often, but not exclusively, borne by the Nubian eparchs. Ruffini (2012b, 45–56), in his detailed study of the title, argues that it may have been used as an inherited honorific as well as an official title. According to Ruffini (2012, 52), the term *k̲oiak-eikšil* literally denoted an official who held authority over the month of K̲oiak. This Egyptian month was originally the time of a festival celebrating Osiris's victory over death, but the festival came to be associated in medieval Christian Nubia with the celebration of Christmas, the key festival of the year, socially, politically and economically. Ruffini suggests that the obligation to host feasts can be seen as a form of enforced wealth redistribution. Van Gerven Oei (2021, 18) is of the opinion that the term *k̲oiak-eikšil* has its origin in a "pre-Nubian" substrate language.

In the Arabic letters, the title اكشيل *ʾikšīl* does not appear in combination with a word corresponding to *k̲oiak*. The term *k̲oiak*, however, can be identified in the form written حياح without diacritics, which appears in the addresses of some of the letters. I propose to read this خياخ. In some medieval Nubian and Greek sources, the first vowel of the term *k̲oiak* in the phrase *k̲oiak-eikšil* is represented by a front vowel, which is transcribed by the editors as *ei* or *i*, e.g., *k̲eiakišši*, *keiakshshi*, *kiak(i)šš(i)l*, *k̲eiakiššika* (ⲭⲉⲓⲁ̄ⲕϣϣ̄ⲓⲕⲁ *k̲eiakiššika* < *k̲eiak-ikšil* + accusative *ka*).[6] As remarked, the Nubian digraph ⲉⲓ represented a vowel that was pronounced as [i] or [iː]. So, it is possible that خياخ was intended to represent the pronunciation *k̲iyāk̲*. The occurrence of velar fricative *k̲* sounds in خياخ indicates that it was a loanword in Nubian. Modern dialects of Nubian do not have this sound in their sound inventory (cf., e.g., Bell 1971) and it is generally thought that it did not occur in Old Nubian. The form of the word with velar fricatives may be a reflection of its pronunciation in Coptic. The month name *k̲oiak* is attested in numerous variant forms in Coptic. Some variants in the Sahidic dialect have fricatives in both initial and final position, as in the form خياخ, e.g., ⲭⲟⲓⲁⲭ, ⲭⲓⲁⲭ, ⲭⲓⲁϩⲉⲭ (Crum 1939, 133; Ochała 2011, 228; Richter 2022). The final *k̲āʾ* rather than *kāf* in the form خياخ appears to reflect a lenition of the final stop /*k*/ of *k̲oiak* to a fricative after a vowel, resulting in the pronunciation *k̲iyāk̲*. Although the fricative sound *k̲* is generally thought not to occur in Old Nubian, lenition of postvocalic *k* to *k̲* in a Nubian name appears to be reflected also by the personal name ماريخرة (**4**v:1, 5; **6**r:4; **9**v:19). This can be interpreted as a variant of the attested Nubian name Marikouda,[7]

---

6 http://www.medievalnubia.info/dev/index.php/Offices_and_Titles, accessed 28 March 2024; Van Gerven Oei (2021, 166, 317, 407). I have normalised the transcriptions of the editors to some extent in conformity to my system of transcription.

7 DBMNT / TM Nam 33354: DBMNT NamVar 300149 (ⲙⲁⲣⲓⲕⲟⲩ̀ⲇ́), 301474 (ⲙⲁⲣⲓ̀ⲕ́).

in which the *k* and the *d* of the name would have undergone lenition, resulting in the fricative *k̠* and the sonorant *r* respectively, i.e., Mārīk̠ura. There is a diacritical dot over the *k̠ā*ʾ of ماريخرة in **4**v:1 and **6**r:4. The interchange of *d* with *r* is attested in other Nubian names, e.g., Menakourra < Menakouda, Maššoura < Maššouda. So, the final fricative in خياخ may also have developed by a process internal to Nubian.

In the Arabic documents, the term *k̠iyāk̠* is not used in combination with the title *ʾikšīl*, in a phrase corresponding to the Nubian term *k̠oiak-eikšīl.* Rather, it is used in combination with the proper name Uruwī, e.g., اروى خياخ *ʾUruwī k̠iyāk̠* (**4**v, **6**v). The proper name takes the place of the title *eikšil* in the Nubian phrase. The word *k̠iyāk̠* appears to be used as a nominal attribute of *ʾUruwī*. In Arabic such attributes would be expressed either by apposition (*badal*) or by a genitive annexation construction (*ʾiḍāfa*), in which the dependent attribute follows the head, i.e., either 'Uruwī, *k̠iyāk̠*', or 'Uruwī of *k̠iyāk̠*' respectively. The Nubian phrase *k̠oiak-eikšil* can be interpreted as a nominal compound expressing a genitive type of attributive relationship, i.e., *eikšil* of *k̠oiak*. In such constructions, which are productive in Nubian, the attibutive nominal is placed before the head noun (Van Gerven Oei 2021, 396), e.g., *ŋon-kouda* lord-servant, i.e., 'servant of the lord'. Such Nubian compounds often express kinship relations, e.g., *soŋoj-as* 'soŋoj-daughter = the daughter of a soŋoj (official)', *eŋ-ŋal* 'mother-son = brother'. In several of the Arabic documents, the relationship between Uruwī and *k̠iyāk̠* is presented as one of kinship by the linking term *ibn* 'son of':اروى بن خياخ *ʾUruwī ibn k̠iyāk̠* 'Uruwī son of *k̠iyāk̠*' (**1**v, **3**v, **5**v, **8**v, **11**v, **12**v). We learn from document **27**, a letter to the secretary of Uruwī, that Uruwī was the son of an eparch. The *ḵiyāḵ* in the phrase 'Uruwī son of *ḵiyāḵ*', therefore, is likely to be referring to Uruwī's father, who is designated by the title *ḵiyāḵ*. The phrase اروى خياخ in **4**v and **6**v is likely, therefore, to mean 'Uruwī of *ḵiyāḵ*' (*ʾiḍāfa*), which would correspond to Nubian genitive compounds expressing kinship relationships.

In some cases, the name of the eparch in the Arabic documents is combined with the Arabic patronymic (*kunyā*) ʾAbū al-Ḵayr 'father of goodness'. This is found in combination with the names of Uruwī, Īsū and Darmā:

ابو الخير اروى (**15**v, address, right, 3)
ابى الخير اروى (**7**v, address, right, 2)
ابى الخير يسوا (**19**v, address, right, 1)
[ا]ب[ى] الخير ايسوا (**20**v, address, right, 2)
ابى الخير درما (**26**v, address, right, 2)

The patronymic ʾAbū al-Ḵayr 'father of goodness' is widely attested in medieval Arabic sources. It is metaphorical and alludes to a praiseworthy quality, like the patronymic ʾAbū al-Faḍl 'father of merit' (Wensinck 2012). According to al-Qalqašandī (*Ṣubḥ al-ʾAʿšā*, V:410), in correspondence emanating from the chancery, a patronymic was used in the address of the addressee when the sender wished to honour him. The fact that it is used with all three eparchs, Uruwī, Īsū and Darmā, suggests that it had an honorific descriptive function.

It is noteworthy that, in the letters to the eparchs, the addresses that contain the phrase ʾAbū al-Ḵayr do not contain the term *ḵiyāḵ*. It is possible that the patronymic ʾAbū al-Ḵayr was intended as an Arabicised form of the term *k̲iyāk̲*, which took its place in the addresses of these documents. There is a certain phonetic resemblance in its first syllable.

A standard title of the eparchs that appears in the letters is صاحب الخيل *ṣāḥib al-k̲ayl* 'Master of the Horses'.

In printed editions of some medieval Arabic historiographical sources, the Nubian eparch is referred to as صاحب الجبل *ṣāḥib al-jabal* 'Master of the Mountain', e.g.,

> ولهذه الناحية وال من قبل عظيم النوبة يعرف بصاحب الجبل
>
> 'This region has a governor from among the Nubian élite who is known as Master of the Mountain.' (Al-Maqrīzī [d. 845 AH/1441 AD], *K̲iṭaṭ*, I:352 [citing al-ʾAswānī])
>
> وَيعرف صَاحب هَذِه الْوِلَايَة عِنْد النّوبَة بِصَاحِب الْجَبَل
>
> 'The one in charge of this region is known among the Nubians as Lord of the Moutain.' (Al-Maqrīzī [d. 845 AH/1441 AD], *al-Sulūk*, II:199)
>
> ويسمى من يتولى هذه الولاية، عند النوبة، صاحب الجبل
>
> 'The one who governs this region is called by the Nubians Master of the Mountain.' (Al-Nuwayrī [d. 733 AH/1333 AD], *Nihāyat al-ʾArab*, XXXI:40)
>
> وكتب إلى صاحب الجبل وهو نائب صاحب دنقلة
>
> 'and he wrote to the Master of the Mountain, who is the deputy of the ruler of Dongola.' (Al-Nuwayrī [d. 733 AH/1333 AD], *Nihāyat al-ʾArab*, XXVIII:183)

Compare also ʾAbū al-Makārim (d. 1208; *Taʾrīk̲ al-Kanāʾis wa-l-ʾAdyira*, 324), where "the Master of the Mountain" is also mentioned.

Apparently taking his lead from this, Browne (1989, 218; 1996, 160) proposed that the Nubian title of eparchs *soŋoj* had this meaning, deriving it from *sa* 'lord' and *ŋoj* 'mountain'. According to Van Gerven Oei (2021, 16), however, *soŋoj* originated in the "pre-Nubian" substrate of the language. As remarked above, moreover, in Old Nubian compound nominals, the attributive nominal is placed before the head noun (Van Gerven Oei 2021, 396), so the expected order would be 'mountain-lord'.

In some of the Arabic documents in the corpus, the second term in this Arabic title is written with diacritics that indicate that the reading of the term should be صاحب الخيل *ṣāḥib al-ḵayl* 'Master of the Horses' rather than صاحب الجبل *ṣāḥib al-jabal* 'Master of the Mountain', e.g.,

Figure 4: Examples of diacritics indicating the reading 'Master of the Horses': **13**r (top left), **22**r (top right), **2**v (middle left), **3**v (middle right), **11**v (bottom left)

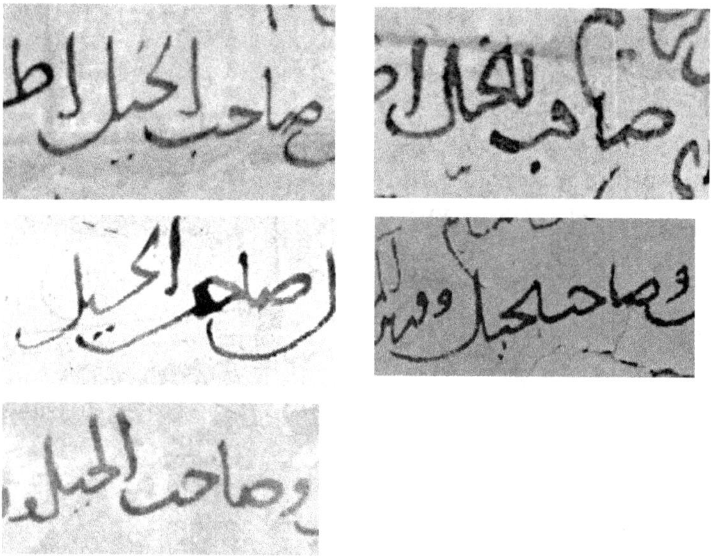

The term *ṣāḥib al-ḵayl* 'Master of the Horses' is attested in various published medieval Arabic sources as a title of an official, often in a military context, e.g., al-Zubayr ibn Bakkār (d. 256 AH/ 870 AD), *al-ʾAḵbār al-Muwaffaqiyyāt*, 211; al-Ṭabarī (d. 310 AH/ 922 AD), *Taʾrīḵ al-Rusul wa-l-Mulūk*, III:384; al-Qāḍī ʿIyāḍ (d. 544 AH/1149 AD), *Tartīb al-Madārik*, III:332; Ibn al-ʾAṯīr (d. 630 AH/ 1233 AD), *al-Kāmil fī al-Taʾrīḵ*, IV:202; Ibn Manẓūr (d. 711 AH/ 1311 AD), *Muḵtaṣar Taʾrīḵ Dimašq*, XX:332; al-Maqrīzī (d. 845 AH/1441 AD), *Ḵiṭaṭ*, I:372. In some published sources, the *ṣāḥib al-ḵayl* is explicitly stated to be responsible for horses, e.g.,

صاحب الخيل يبث خيلًا لتأخذ له أخبار العدو

> 'The Master of the Horses sends horses in order get for him news of the enemy.' (Al-Maʿarrī [d. 449 AH/1057 AD], *al-Lāmiʿ al-ʿAzīzī*, 459)

وخرج إلى عامر فوجه معه خيلا. وأمر صاحب الخيل أن يأخذ به على طريق قرنة

> 'He went out to ʿĀmir and sent horses with him and ordered the Master of the Horses to take him on the Qarna road.' (Al-Nuwayrī [d. 733 AH/1333 AD], *Nihāyat al-ʾArab*, XXIV:113)

فإن أردت نزولا أمرت صاحب الخيل... فوقفت خيله متنحّية من معسكرك

> 'If you want to alight, command the Master of the Horses and stop his horses as they leave your camp.' (Al-Qalqašandī [d. 821 AH/1418 AD], *Ṣubḥ al-ʾAʿšā*, X:234)

I have, indeed, identified one published medieval source that uses the term *ṣāḥib al-ḵayl* apparently to refer to the Nubian eparch:

فسار الهذيل في طلبه إلى أعمال صاحب الخيل، وهو المقيم في أوّل عمل النّوبة

> '(The ʾ*amīr*) Huḏayl went in pursuit of him to the districts of the Master of the Horses, who dwelt in the first district of the Nubians.' (Al-ʾAnṭākī [d. 458 AH/1066 AD], *Kitāb al-Ḏayl*, 478–79)

It does not necessarily follow, however, that the title *ṣāḥib al-jabal* 'Master of the Mountain' in the other published sources mentioned above is a corruption based on a misreading of the Arabic word الحىل without diacritical dots. Some sources refer to the division of Lower Nubia into a northern and southern district known as *al-ʿAlī* and *al-Jabal* respectively. Qaṣr Ibrīm would have been in *al-Jabal* district and so the designation of the eparch as *ṣāḥib al-jabal* would have related to this district (Seignobos 2015, 564). Various medieval sources refer to a geographical feature of Lower Nubia called *jabal al-janādil* 'mountain of the cataracts', e.g., Ibn al-Wardī (d. 852 AH/1448 AD; *Ḵarīdat al-ʿAjāʾib*, 139), who states that the "ships of the Egyptians and Sudanese reach this mountain." Trimingham (1965, 64) suggested that *ṣāḥib al-jabal* was an abbreviation of *ṣāḥib jabal al-janādil* (cf. also Hendrickx 2011, 320–21).

The question arises as to why the eparch should have the title of *ṣāḥib al-ḵayl* 'Master of the Horses'. It is significant that several of the letters in the corpus refer to the transport of horses (*ḵayl*) to the eparch. The most significant letter is **22**, which mentions a complaint by the eparch that the supply of horses (*ḵayl*) for the Nubian army by the Fatimid authorities has stopped. This indicates that the Fatimid ruler was supporting the Nubian army.

An essential component of the army was the cavalry. The letter indicates that the eparch was responsible for mustering the horses for military purposes. Some historical sources state that the Arabs supplied horses to the Nubians in exchange for slaves as part of the terms of the *baqṭ*, e.g., Ibn ʿAbd al-Ḥakam (d. 257 AH/871 AD), *Futūḥ Miṣr*, 59.

The supply of horses to the eparch is mentioned also in other letters, e.g., "When he (the bearer of this letter) is present (with you), ask him about your horses (*ḵaylika*)" (**23**r:19); "Let me and the Nubians know about the transport of the horses (*al-ḵuyūl*)" (**33**:16).

Some letters, furthermore, refer to the delivery to the eparch of military equipment, such "the helmet (*al-ḵūḏa*),... the three scabbards (*qurub*) and the spear (*al-rumḥ*)" (**31**v:1).[8] Letter **23**r:4, 5 refers to the delivery of muzzles (*al-kimāmāt*), which may relate to accoutrements of horses for military purposes. The

[8] For references to helmets in medieval Nubia in other sources see Zarroug (1991, 89) and Spaulding (1998, 49). Many spearheads have been found in Nubian archaeological sites (Shinnie 1961, fig. 29: 5 and 6; Daniels and Welsby 1991, fig. 64: 103 and 104; Adams 2010, pl. 21: e and f; Adams and Adams 1999, pl. 6.5D: b). The medieval Arab historians indicate that the Nubians were excellent archers and were given the nickname *rumāt al-ḥadaq* 'pupil-smiters' (Trimingham 1965, 61; Halm 1998, 68). The Nubians had a unique style of archery and manufactured bows and arrows themselves (Zieliński 2015). This explains why they are not referred to as merchandise carried by the Muslim merchants. I am grateful to Gabriel Gerhards for drawing my attention to several of these references.

account **43**v:4 refers to 'army wool' (*ṣūf ʿaskarī*), which was presumably a military supply.

The eparch's title *ṣāḥib al-ḵayl*, therefore, is likely to designate a core military duty of the holder of the office. This, however, was clearly not his exclusive activity. He was responsible for facilitating all types of trade on behalf of the Nubian king, as well as having other fiscal and administrative functions (Adams 1977, 464–66; 1996, 225; Hendrickx 2011).

There is a parallel with the Roman title *magister equitum* 'Master of the Horses', 'Master of the Cavalry', who served as the deputy of a Roman dictator (head of state). In Roman administration, the *magister equitum* could operate independently of the cavalry in various political roles subordinate to the dictator (Sherwin-White and Lintott 2015; Gizewski 2006). The term was used in the Byzantine empire under Constantine (fourth century AD; Lee 2018). The latest attestation is in 411 AD (Martindale 1980, 1181), but it appears not to be attested in the later Byzantine period.[9] According to Henrickx (2011, 304–7), the office of Nubian eparch in Lower Nubia would have been created on the model of the Roman and Byzantine office of governor after the unification of Nobadia and Makuria. Since by this period the Byzantine governor was no longer called *magister equitum*, it is problematic to regard the parallel with the eparch's Arabic title to be

[9] It is not found in *Prosopographie der mittelbyzantinischen Zeit* (Lilie et al. 2013). I am grateful to Andrew Marsham and Giovanni Ruffini for drawing my attention to this reference and the previous references in this paragraph.

the result of a direct calque. The parallel, however, seems too striking to be a coincidence.

There is some evidence from other sources that the Nubian eparch had a military role. In parallel Nubian and Greek versions of a work known as *The Book of the Investiture of the Archangel Michael*, St Michael is referred to in Greek as ἀρχιστράτηγος 'commander-in-chief' and as *soŋoj* in Nubian (Tsakos 2023, 147–49). The title *soŋoj* is the usual Nubian term for eparch. Moreover, St Michael in this text is said to be wearing red and this can be compared to the red attire of military saints in Nubian iconography (Magdalena Wozniak, personal communication).

The Nubian title 'Lord of the Horses' *mourtin ŋod* is attested in the Nubian land sale document P. QI III 37, published by Browne (cf. Ruffini 2012b, 83). In this document, the title is associated with a man called Ḵael, whom Browne (P. QI III, p. 85) identifies with a Ḵael mentioned in the Nubian document P. QI III 34 of his corpus, who bears the title *soŋoj*, and so would be an eparch.[10] In the protocol of P. QI III 37, however, it is stated that Adama was eparch (*soŋoj*) at that time. The title *mourtin ŋod* in this document, therefore, would appear to be a military title of somebody who was not eparch.

Various titles of the eparch found in the Arabic letters relate to the geographical scope of his authority. These include the following:

---

[10] See the discussion in Ruffini (2012b, 83), who cautions against identifying all these titles with the eparch.

متولى بلاد مريس واعمالها *mutawallī bilād Marīs wa-ʾaʿmālihā* 'the governor of the Land of Marīs and its districts' (**2**v, address, right, 3; **10**v, address, right, 2; **14**v, address, right, 2; **16**v, address, right, 2; **24**v, address, right, 1–2)

متولى بلاد المريس واعمالها *mutawallī bilād al-Marīs wa-ʾaʿmālihā* 'the governor of the Land of al-Marīs and its districts' (**21**v, address, right, 2)

متولي اعمال بلاد المريس *mutawallī ʾaʿmāl bilād al-Marīs* 'the governor of the districts of the land of al-Marīs' (**21**r:2)

متولى القلعة الابريمية وبلاد مريس *mutawallī al-qalʿa al-ʾibrīmiyya wa-bilād Marīs* 'the governor of the fortress of Ibrīm and the land of Marīs' (**7**v, address, right, 2)

متولى بلاد مريس *mutawallī bilād Marīs* 'the governor of the land of Marīs' (**17**v, address, right, 2–3)

متولى بلاد المقرة والمريس *mutawallī bilād al-Muqurra wa-l-Marīs* 'the governor of the land of al-Muqurra and al-Marīs' (**15**v address, right, 2–3)

متولى ابريم وبلاد مكن *mutawallī ʾIbrīm wa-bilād Migin* 'the governor of Ibrīm and the land of Nobadia' (**22**v, address, right, 2)

متولى بلاد مريس مكن واعمالها *mutawallī bilād Marīs Migin* 'the governor of Marīs Nobadia' (**19**v, address, right, 2)

The topographical name مريس *Marīs* or المريس *al-Marīs* in the addresses of many of the Arabic letters is an Arabicised form of the Coptic term ⲙⲁⲣⲓⲥ *Maris* 'southern country'. In Coptic, it is used to designate both Upper Egypt and also Lower Nubia, the latter being the territory designated by the Arabicised form مريس

Marīs (Crum 1939, 300).[11] The capital of *Marīs* was Faras (Greek/ Coptic Pak̲ōras). Some of the eparchs had the title of '*domestikos* of Faras' in Nubian documents (Ruffini 2012b, 34, 38, 50, 208). The Arabicised form *Marīs* designates the region of northern Nubia that corresponded geographically to the earlier kingdom of Nobadia. According to al-ʾAswānī, the southern boundary of *Marīs* was the village of Bīstū just south of the third cataract (al-Maqrīzī, *K̲iṭaṭ*, I:353). South of this was the region of the earlier kingdom of Makuria (Arabic *al-Muqurra*). South of Makuria was the earlier kingdom of Alodia (Arabic *ʿAlwa*). The Arabic term *al-bilād al-qibliyya* 'the southern land' is found in **16**r:7, which appears to be an Arabic calque of the Coptic *Maris*. The term *al-bilād al-baḥriyya* 'the northern land' occurs in **24**v:3, which is presumably referring to the region of Aswan north of Nobadia. Letter **24**v:1–3 refers to 'the news from the north' (*al-ʾak̲bār al-baḥriyya*) and letter **38**r:5 mentions 'a town in the north' (*bilād baḥrī*). Some letters use the term *bilād al-Nūba* 'land of the Nubians' (**14**r:3; **16**r:10; **32**:6; **45**:7) to refer to the zone of Lower Nubia where the Muslim merchants operated. It is relevant to note here that in the papyrus document dated 758 AD that was published by Hinds and Sakkout (1981, 218), the addresee is given the title *ṣāḥib Muqurra wa-Nūba* 'the master of Muqurra and Nūba', where *Nūba* is used as an Arabic equivalent of Nobadia (i.e., *al-Marīs*) and this is likely to be the sense of *bilād al-Nūba* in the documents cited above.

---

[11] I am grateful to Joost Hagen for pointing this out to me.

At the period when the Arabic letters were written, the former kingdoms of Nobadia and Makuria were united under a single king based in Dongola. The text of the *baqṭ* treaty (al-Maqrīzī, *Ḵiṭaṭ*, I:323–24) states that this was a "covenant binding upon the Nūba… from the frontier of Aswan to that of ʿAlwa," indicating this unity. This is also confirmed by al-Yaʿqūbī (*Taʾrīḵ*, I:217), who wrote in 278 AH/891 AD:

> The Nūba have become two kingdoms. The first is the kingdom that they call Muqurra…. The capital of their kingdom is Dongola. It is they who made peace with the Muslims and pay them *baqṭ*…. The other Nubian kingdom, which they call ʿAlwa, is much more dangerous than Muqurra. Its capital is called Soba.

There is evidence that by the Fatimid period also Alodia (ʿAlwa) had lost its independent status and was under the king of Dongola (see below).

Letter **15** contains the title *mutawallī bilād al-Muqurra wa-l-Marīs* 'the governor of the land of al-Muqurra and al-Marīs', indicating that the eparch's authority extended across the united kingdom of Nobadia and Makuria. A number of decrees of Nubian kings have been discovered in Qaṣr Ibrīm, which reflect the centralisation of the administration in Dongola, indicating that the kings of Dongola were involved in the affairs of Lower Nubia at local levels (Ruffini 2016a; 2020, 763).

The form مكن in the address of **19** and **22** would seem to be an Arabic transcription of the Nubian topographic element *migin* in the title *migin soŋoj* 'the eparch of Nobadia', which is attested in Nubian sources (Ruffini 2012b, 34). The form *migin* is a genitive form of *migi-*. The *kāf* of Arabic was perceived to be the closest approximation to the Nubian sound /g/.

The Arabic term *mutawallī* in the titles is used in Fatimid administrative and legal documents as a title of the head of government offices and institutions (Khan 1993a, 106, 107, 175, 342, 358, 416, 434).

3.4. The Correspondents with the Eparch

We learn from the addresses of the letters about the identity of the correspondents with the eparch. In most cases, these are the senders of the letters. Letters **17** and **18** are sent by the eparch Uruwī, so the correspondents are the recipients.

Many of the correspondents are members of the Banū al-Kanz. Some are high-ranking *ʾamīr*s. These include the leaders of the Banū al-Kanz, known as Kanz al-Dawla (**1**, **8**, **26**). The family tree and succession of the leaders of the Banū al-Kanz in the eleventh and twelfth centuries, the period of the Qaṣr Ibrīm corpus, are represented below in Figure 5 following Seignobos (2020, 141). Those who are recorded as having the title of Kanz al-Dawla are marked with an asterisk. The exact dates of the periods of their leadership are not known.

Figure 5: Leaders of the Banū al-Kanz in the eleventh and twelfth centuries

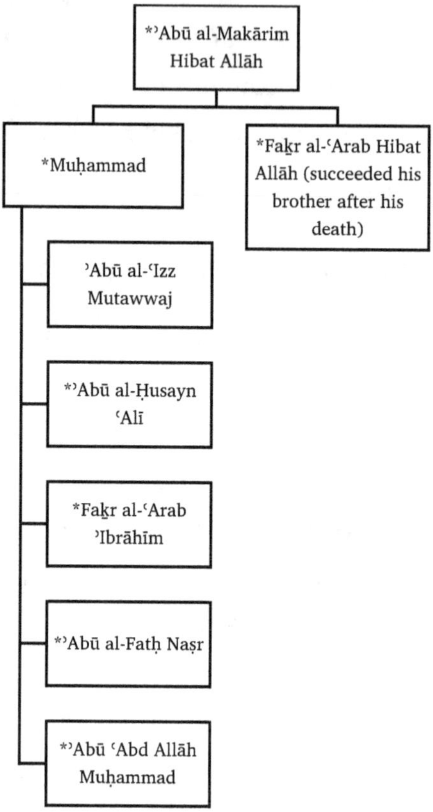

In the addresses of the letters sent by Kanzī leaders, the senders have elaborate honorific titles. The addresses of **1** and **8** contain the name Kanz al-Dawla ʾAbū Manṣūr Mutawwaj. This appears to be the same as the Kanz al-Dawla called ʾAbū al-ʿIzz Mutawwaj in the genealogy of Seignobos reproduced in Figure 5. Letters **2** and **7** are from *ʾamīrs* who are sons of the Kanz al-Dawla. According to the addresses, these have the names Tanwīr (**2**, reading not certain) and Naṣr (**7**). In **2**, it is indicated that Tanwīr is son of the Kanz al-Dawla ʾIbrāhīm ibn ʿAlī ibn Mutawwaj ibn ʾAbī Yazīd al-Ḥanafī. The genealogy of the Kanz al-Dawla ʾIbrāhīm ibn ʿAlī ibn Mutawwaj corresponds to the succession in the family tree in Figure 5. Tanwīr, the son of ʾIbrāhīm, evidently did not serve as the Kanz al-Dawla. It was rather ʾIbrāhīm's son Naṣr who succeeded him to this office, as shown in the genealogy in Figure 5. The sender of letter **7** is described in the address as "the commander Naṣr, the son of the commander Kanz al-Dawla," which was presumably this Kanz al-Dawla Naṣr ibn ʾIbrāhīm. The address of **26** indicates that the sender was Faḵr al-ʿArab Kanz al-Dawla. This is likely to be the Kanz al-Dawla Faḵr al-ʿArab ʾIbrāhīm who appears in the genealogy above.

The address in **2** attaches the *nisba* al-Ḥanafī to the Kanz al-Dawla ʾIbrāhīm ibn ʿAlī ibn Mutawwaj ibn ʾAbī Yazīd. The Banū al-Kanz claimed descent from the tribe of the Banū Ḥanīfa. The *nisba* al-Ḥanafī is attested in inscriptions from Aswan relating to Kanzī *ʾamīrs*, e.g., RCEA III, nos 2391, 2392; Wiet (1971, no. 54 [p. 37]).

The senders of several letters have a Kanzī *nisba* but no title indicating their rank. These include Lāmiʿ ibn Ḥasan al-Kanzī (**3**, **4**, **5**, **6**, **9**, **12**), Ḥusayn ibn Ḥasan al-Kanzī (**14**, **16**—he is explicitly stated to be the brother of Lāmiʿ in **16**r:5), Ḥāmid al-Kanzī (**10**), ʾAbū al-Ṯanāʾ Ḥāmid al-Kanzī (**11**—presumably the same person as the sender of **10**). Lāmiʿ ibn Ḥasan was the sender of letter **36** and his son Manṣūr was the sender of **30**, which were not sent to eparchs.

The other correspondents with the eparchs do not have Kanzī *nisbas*. They include an *ʾamīr* ʾAbū Manṣūr ʿAjīl (**22**). He is given elaborate honorific titles: "the prosperous, auspicious and most gracious commander, the commander, victor of the religion, sword of the Commander of the Faithful, ʾAbū Manṣūr ʿAjīl, son of the sincere commander Hilāl al-Dawla, our elder Kanz al-Dīn."

One of the correspondents is Ḥiṣn al-Dawla ibn al-ʿAsqalānī (**13**), the title indicating that he had some connection to the Fatimid government. A man with the name Ibn al-ʿAsqalānī appears also in the text of letter **9**, where he is said to be in the entourage of the Nubian king, and an *ʾamīr* with the title Ḥiṣn al-Dawla is the addressee of letter **28**. The Kanzī sender of letter **9**, Lāmiʿ ibn Ḥasan, complains bitterly that Ibn al-ʿAsqalānī has impeded his activities in the court of the Nubian king.

The sender of letter **21** is the son of a judge: ʿAbd Allāh ibn al-Qāḍī al-Rašīd ʿAlī ibn al-Zubayr. The sender of **23** is an official with the title *Ṣāḥib al-Sawārī* 'the Master of the Shipmasts'. The other correspondents have no official title in the address: Muḥammad ibn Ramaḍān al-Ḥājj (**15**), ʾAbū al-Ṭāhir (**17**), al-Ḥusayn ibn Muḥammad (**20**). A man with the name ʾAbū al-Ṭāhir appears in the body of letter **9**r:4 (ʾAbū al-Ṭāhir ibn Tarīk) and in the account **42**r (left, 14). According to the address of letter **34**, the recipient was ʾAbū al-Ḥasan ʿAlī, son of the elder, the preacher (*al-dāʿī*) ʾAbū al-Ṭāhir ʿUbayd Allāh ibn ʾAbī Turʿa.

The sender of **21**, ʿAbd Allāh ibn al-Qāḍī al-Rašīd ʿAlī ibn al-Zubayr, belonged to a family who had influential positions in the Fatimid administration. His brother al-Qāḍī al-Rašīd ʾAḥmad appears particularly prominently in the medieval sources. Al-Maqrīzī (*al-Muqaffā al-Kabīr*, I:325) gives the full genealogy of ʾAḥmad as follows:

> ʾAḥmad ibn ʿAlī ibn ʾIbrāhīm ibn Muḥammad ibn al-Ḥusayn ibn Muḥammad ibn Falīta ibn Saʿīd ibn ʾIbrāhīm ibn al-Ḥasan, al-Qāḍī al-Rašīd (the Rightly-Guided Judge) ʾAbū ʿAlī al-Ḥusayn ibn al-Qāḍī al-Rašīd Sadīd al-Dawla (the Rightly-Guided Judge, Just One of the Dynasty) ʾAbū al-Ḥasan ʾIbrāhīm ibn al-Qāḍī al-Rašīd al-Mufawwaq Ṯiqat al-Mulk (the Rightly-Guided Judge, the Prosperous, Trust of the Kingdom) ʾAbū ʾIsḥāq, known as Ibn Zubayr al-Qurašī al-ʾAsadī al-ʾAswānī

This indicates that ʿAbd Allāh and ʾAḥmad came from a large family of judges. According to al-Maqrīzī (*al-Muqaffā al-Kabīr*, I:181), the grandfather of ʿAbd Allāh and ʾAḥmad, ʾIbrāhīm ibn Muḥammad ibn al-Ḥusayn ibn Muḥammad ibn al-Zubayr, was the judge of Qūṣ, who "was alive in the year 471 AH/1078–79 AD." The grandfather is mentioned in the legal document **47**r:3–4, which is dated 515 AH/1121 AD, during the reign of the Fatimid caliph al-ʾĀmir. Letter **21** mentions ʿAbd Allāh's sons—Qāsim, ʾAbū ʿAbd Allāh and Hibat Allāh—and his paternal cousin, the judge ʾAbū al-Faḍl Muḥammad ibn Ḥusayn, as well as ʿAbd Allāh's grandfather. ʾAbū al-Faḍl Muḥammad ibn Ḥusayn was judge of Aswan in 518 AH/1124 AD (Garcin 1976, 117).

ʿAbd Allāh's brother ʾAḥmad was an envoy of the caliph al-Ḥāfiẓ to Yemen but was executed by the vizier Šāwar on suspicion of attempted rebellion in 562 AH/1167 AD; cf. al-ʾIdfūwī (d. 748 AH/1347 AD), *al-Ṭāliʿ al-Saʿīd*, 98–102, 364; al-Maqrīzī, *al-Muqaffā al-Kabīr*, I:325. ʾAḥmad had another brother called Ḥasan al-Qāḍī al-Muhaḏḏab, who was imprisoned and died one year earlier (Lev 1998, 62–79; Smoor 2006). ʾAḥmad's brother ʿAbd Allāh, who was the sender of **21**, was, therefore, likely to be out of favour with the Fatimid government (Sartain 1993, 25–26). By contrast, the *ʾamīrs* of the Banū al-Kanz have elaborate titles in the addresses explicitly declaring their loyalty and affiliation to the Fatimid caliph.

The family tree of the members of the family of ʿAbd Allāh ibn al-Qāḍī al-Rašīd ʿAlī ibn al-Zubayr who are mentioned above can be reconstructed as follows:[12]

Figure 6: The Banū Zubayr

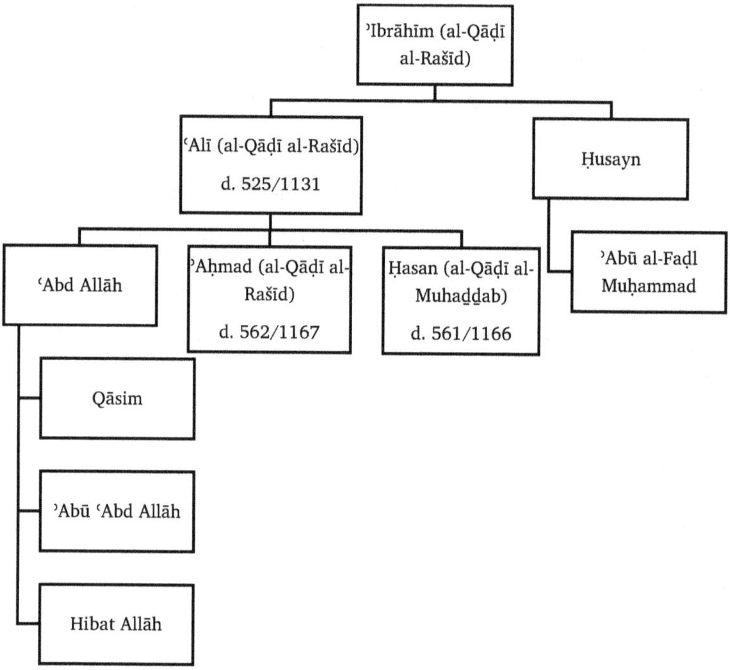

All this indicates that the correspondents with the eparch did not form a uniform group and in some cases had conflicting interests.

[12] A detailed study of the wider family of the Banū Zubayr is in preparation by Robin Seignobos. Some details of the tree presented here are dependent on his research.

The senders and recipients of the correspondence with eparchs are summarised in the table below:

Table 4: Senders and recipients of the correspondence with eparchs

	Sender	Recipient
1	Kanz al-Dawla ʾAbū Manṣūr Mutawwaj	The Ikšīl, Master of the Horses, Uruwī ibn Ḵiyāḵ
2	ʾAbū al-Futūḥ Tanwīr ibn Kanz al-Dawla ʾAbū ʾIsḥāq ʾIbrāhīm ibn ʿAlī ibn Mutawwaj ibn ʾAbī Yazīd	The Ikšīl, Master of the Horses, ʾAbū al-Ḵayr Uruwī
3	Lāmiʿ ibn Ḥasan al-Kanzī	The Ikšīl, Master of the Horses, Uruwī ibn Ḵiyāḵ
4	Lāmiʿ ibn Ḥasan al-Kanzī	The Master of the Horses, Uruwī Ḵiyāḵ
5	Lāmiʿ ibn Ḥasan al-Kanzī	The Ikšīl, Master of the Horses, Uruwī ibn Ḵiyāḵ
6	Lāmiʿ ibn Ḥasan al-Kanzī	The Ikšīl, Master of the Horses, Uruwī Ḵiyāḵ
7	The commander Naṣr, son of the commander Kanz al-Dawla	The Ikšīl, Master of his (the king's) Horses, ʾAbū al-Ḵayr Uruwī
8	Kanz al-Dawla ʾAbū Manṣūr [Mutawwaj]	The Ikšīl, Master of the Horses, Uruwī ibn Ḵiyāḵ
9	Lāmiʿ ibn Ḥasan al-Kanzī	The Ikšīl, Master of the Horses, Uruwī ibn Ḵiyāḵ
10	Ḥāmid al-Kanzī	The Ikšīl, Master of the Horses, Uruwī
11	ʾAbū al-Ṯanāʾ Ḥāmid al-Kanzī	The Ikšīl, Master of the Horses, Uruwī ibn Ḵiyāḵ
12	Lāmiʿ ibn al-Ḥasan al-Kanzī	The Ikšīl, Master of the Horses, Uruwī ibn Ḵiyāḵ
13	Ḥiṣn al-Dawla ibn al-ʿAsqalānī	The Ikšīl, Master of the Horses, Uruwī

14	Ḥusayn ibn Ḥasan al-Kanzī	The Ikšīl, Master of the Horses, Uruwī
15	Muḥammad ibn Ramaḍān	The Ikšīl, Master of the Horses of the King, ʾAbū al-Ḵayr Uruwī
16	Ḥusayn ibn Ḥasan al-Kanzī	The Ikšīl, Master of the Horses, Uruwī
17	Master of the Horses, Uruwī	ʾAbū al-Ṭāhir
18	Uruwī (?)	—
19	The judge ʾAbū al-Faḍl Muḥammad ibn al-Fātiḥ ibn ʿAbd Allāh al-Ḥusaynī	The Ikšīl, Master of the Horses, ʾAbū al-Ḵayr Īsū
20	Al-Ḥusayn ibn Muḥammad [ ] Naṣr [ ]	Master of the Horses, ʾAbū al-Ḵayr Īsū
21	ʿAbd Allāh ibn ʿAlī ibn al-Zubayr	The Ikšīl, Master of the Horses
22	ʾAbū Manṣūr ʿAjīl ibn Hilāl al-Dawla, Kanz al-Dīn	Master of the Horses
23	The Master of the Shipmasts (*ṣāḥib al-sawārī*)	The Ikšīl
24	—	[ʾAbū] al-Ḵayr
25	—	—
26	The commander Kanz al-Dawla	Al-Bazīl, the deputy of the Master of the Horses, the Ikšīl, ʾAbū al-Ḵayr Darmā
27	ʾIbrāhīm ibn ʿAbd al-Raḥmān	ʿUbayd Allāh ʿAlī, the secretary (*kātib*) of the Master of the Horses

3.5. The Content of the Correspondence with the Eparch

3.5.1. Courtesy and Equality

Many passages in the correspondence express mutual respect, courtesy, gratitude and an acknowledgement that the power relationship between the Muslims and the eparch was one of equality, e.g.,

Letters sent by Muslims to the eparch:

> Whatever kindness and good he (the Ikšīl) does in his (the bearer of the letter's) regard, I shall appreciate and be thankful for. (**8**r:12–13)
>
> There is no greater generosity performed by the Ikšīl than what the Ikšīl will have done with regard to the duty of showing respect, kindness and polite hospitality for the leader Saʿāda. (**10**r:7–10)
>
> As for the merchants, the Master of the Horses does not require instruction from me regarding their situation. Your reputation is good among the people. (**2**v:3–4)
>
> As for the statement of the Ikšīl—may God cause his support to endure—that I have shown neglect for his status and have not inquired about him, the situation is not like that. I recognise his eminence, and am steadfast in my love for him and my gratitude to him in all circumstances. (**15**r:6–8)
>
> Moreover, I know how I am loved by you. (**2**v:6)

Letters sent by the eparch to Muslims:

> The Master of the Horses kisses your honourable hand and makes a request to your honour. What is requested from

> my lord is that you do goodness and kindness to your slave (the Master of the Horses). His (i.e., of the Master of the Horses) two wives send their best wishes. You are always so kind. (**17**r:11–13)

> Your slave (i.e., the writer) kisses your hand and legs, and warmly welcomes a letter from your honour. (**18**r:12–13)

> Whatever it may be (that you need), I shall hasten to ensure that people take it and come to you, and I shall send it—they will do it. I shall write to keep you informed. I am your slave in the land. (**18**v:1–2)

This spirit of courtesy and equality is expressed also in the addresses of many of the letters, e.g.,

> (Sent) to the brother, the Master of the Horses (**22**v)

> (Sent by) one who is grateful for his munificence, Muḥammad ibn Ramaḍān, the pilgrim (**15**v)

> (Sent by) one who is grateful to him and his friend Lāmiʿ ibn al-Ḥasan al-Kanzī (**12**v)

> (Sent by) one who is grateful for his kindness, the Master of the Horses and vizier of the king, Uruwī, governor of the land of Marīs (**17**v)

3.5.2. Request for Protection

The main purpose of many letters in the corpus is to request the eparch to offer protection and correct treatment to the bearer of the letter, and to ensure that they are able to carry out their business without impediment, e.g.,

> I [request] that… you ensure that he (the bearer of the letter) proceeds safely to his colleagues, and that you then take care of this colleague of mine and protect him, and also his colleagues in the armed garrison post. (**19**v:5–6)

In several cases, the letter requests the eparch to protect a servant of the sender and carry out business with him, e.g.,

> The bearer of this (letter) is my loyal and respectful companion, Oua, who is my servant (*ḵādim*).... Please treat him well and correctly and provide him with his requirements. (**6**r:3–5)

> I have sent my slave boy (*ġulām*), who is called Šarīf, with a brown camel to his honourable presence. I want you to receive it from me. I have not written you a letter or sent to your presence anything before today, and I praise God for that. So take the camel and do not let him (Šarīf, the servant) be detained by a single day. Then send him to Papa, my servant (*ḵādim*), who carries out my business, for I shall be cut off from him, if there is a delay. (**7**r:3–9)

The statement below in letter **3** apparently refers to the fact that the operation of the merchants' boats in Nubia required authorisation from the eparch:

> and the lofty, most glorious and munificent presence, may God establish his happiness, has graciously released (*ʾaṭlaqat*) the boats. (**3**r:5–6).

In several cases, the writer makes it clear that the protection of the Muslim bearer of the letter was a duty of the eparch, i.e., under the terms of the non-aggression pact between the Muslim government and the Nubian king. The Muslims had no executive authority, but rather the executive authority was with the Ikšīl. The Ikšīl was expected to exercise his executive authority to protect and care for Arab merchants, e.g.,

> The Ikšīl cannot show them opposition in anything small or big, but should show honour to the aforementioned

> leader and care for him and for his companions who are travelling with him. (**1**r:6–7)

> The Ikšīl, therefore, needs to protect them and care for them in accordance with their rights, and all the more so since they belong to those whose right (to protection) is obligatory and the service of whom is a compulsory requirement. (**3**r:9–10)

> The Ikšīl knows what is required with regard to the restraint of his companions and the imposition upon them of obligations and the prevention of those who oppose him with harm and damage. (**3**, margin, 3–5)

> (I report) the arrival of the carrier of (this letter) to the land of the Nubians.... He is somebody who should be treated correctly, protected and cared for. He has a right to your customary protection, so that he is able to have access to the administrators and others of your slaves and servants, because it is incumbent upon your honour to protect and care for him in your customary way until he returns... since he has a good reputation. (**14**r:3–7)

> The Ikšīl does not need my recommendation with regard to him or my reassurances to show him respect and treat him well. (**8**r:8–10)

> (I inform) that the bearer of these lines is the Head (*al-raʾīs*), may God decree his safety, and he must be shown favour and respect. (**26**r:3–5)

The writer of **3** requests the eparch to grant him the executive authority to provide protection to the bearer of the letter:

> Please arrange for his letter to be sent to me with authorisation for me to offer the leader Saʿāda respectful treatment until it (his work) is finished. (**3**v:3–4)

In letter **16**, there is a reference to a man with the title of *ḵalīfa* 'agent' claiming his salary from the deputy of the eparch. This official belonged to the community of Muslim merchants and so the payment of his salary was entailed within the protection and support for Muslims that the eparch was expected to offer:

> I would like a letter to be sent to all the administrators requesting them to protect the places of Lāmiʿ and his slaves and likewise my places and my slaves. You know that they all perform good services to the king and to you. The agent (*al-ḵalīfa*) mentioned that he has instructions and he adhered to all of these. He wrote to Ibn ʿImrān, the deputy (*nāʾib*) of your honour, asking him about his salary and he gave him his usual salary. (**16**r:13–16)

In letter **11**, the request for the eparch's protection relates to financial support of the bearer, who is a son-in-law of the writer:

> My son-in-law, who is called ʾAbū ʿAbd Allāh Muḥammad ibn ʿAbd al-Raḥmān, the merchant, has come (to you). He has suffered the loss of a debt owed to him by some spendthrift people known as the sons of Kajja.... You have an obligation to him, for my money is with your majesty. (**11**r:3–4, **11**r, margin, 5)

In the absence of the eparch from Ibrīm, the writer of letter **27** asks his secretary to draft a letter for him that will put an end to malicious gossip against him. He reinforces his request by paying a respected elder to intercede for him with the secretary. The writer also appeals to the precedent of the eparch's father's favourable treatment of him:

> The slave will ask my master the elder ʿUbayd Allāh to encourage him (the secretary) to draft a letter for me and send it to me with the Master of the Shipmasts. This is what I need the most from my master (the eparch). In the days of his father, my master the Master of the Horses, nobody opposed me in anything.... I have sent (this letter) to him with the Master of the Shipmasts and we shall request him to pay one dīnār as cash commission to my master the elder ʿUbayd Allāh. (**27**r:17–v:8)

3.5.3. Permission to Leave Nubia Safely

If the bearer of the letter is a servant, the writer sometimes requests that the eparch does not detain him, indicating that the servant required permission to leave Nubia, e.g.,

> When the bearer of this letter reaches you, release him and send him away quickly, so he can reach me, if God wills, because I want to send him to the north to carry out some errands for me. (**2**r:6–8)

A passage in letter **3** suggests that the permission of the eparch is required for the boats of the Muslims to leave Nubia:

> The lofty, most glorious and munificent presence, may God establish his happiness, has graciously released (*ʾaṭlaqat*) the boats. (**3**r:5–6)

The writer of letter **4** requests the eparch to ensure that his colleagues return from Nubia downriver safely:

> Let the people go down (the river) without fear. We have released (*ʾaṭlaqnā*) the people (apparently meaning: we have authorised them to travel). (**4**v:7)

3.5.4. Protection of Property

Several of the Muslim writers of the letters had landed property within Nubia. The writer of **16**, Lāmiʿ ibn Ḥasan al-Kanzī, requests the eparch to protect his properties (*mawāḍiʿ* 'places') and 'his slaves' (*ʿabīdihi*), i.e., Lāmiʿ's administrative staff:

> I would like a letter to be sent to all the administrators requesting them to protect the places of Lāmīʿ and his slaves and likewise my places and my slaves (*ʿabīdī*). (**16**r:13–14)

Al-ʾAswānī refers to Muslim residents (*qāṭinūn*) in Lower Nubia (al-Maqrīzī, *Ḵiṭaṭ*, I:352). According to al-Masʿūdī (*Murūj al-Ḏahab*, III:40–43), during the reign of the Abbasid caliph al-Maʾmūn (r. 198–218 AH/813–33 AD), some Muslims living in Aswan owned estates located inside Nubia. These estates had been bought from Nubians during Umayyad and earlier Abbasid times. Muslim gravestones, mainly dating to the ninth–eleventh centuries AD, have been discovered between the first and second cataracts (Edwards 2019, 968–69). Ruffini (2012b) demonstrates from a study of Nubian documents that private land tenure existed in medieval Nubia. He adduces parallels with modern Nubian society, in which the acquisition of land is associated with Nubian identity. If this is retrojected back into the Middle Ages, then the acquisition of land by Muslim Arabs could reflect an assimilation into Nubian society, or at least a recognition of the equipollent relationship of Nubians and Egyptians in the spirit of the *baqṭ*.

3.5.5. Communications with the Nubian King

Al-ʾAswānī indicates that the northern region of Nubia (Marīs) between the first and second cataracts of the Nile was open to Muslims (al-Maqrīzī, *Ḵiṭaṭ*, I:307):

> It is a district open to Muslims who have property in the nearer part and trade in the districts beyond where some of them are domiciled.

In the legal document of the corpus **45**r:7, this region that is open to Muslims is referred to as *al-islāmiyya*.

The region south of the second cataract was closed to Muslims (al-Maqrīzī, *Ḵiṭaṭ*, I:307):

> At the beginning of the cataracts of the country of Nubia lies a village called Taqwā (modern Wādī Ḥalfa) on level ground where the Nubians' boats ascending from al-Qaṣr on the borders of their country stop. No boats are allowed to pass this place, nor is any Muslim or any other allowed to ascend the river further except by permission of the Master of the Mountain.

In the letters of the corpus, the town of Aswan is called a *ṯāgr* 'border' (**19**r:3; **45**:19), since it was the urban administrative centre that lay closest to the border of Nubia. According to al-ʾAswānī, the border of Nubia in the north was at the village of al-Qaṣr, on the east bank of the Nile just south of Bilāq (Philae). In this place there was an armed garrison (*maslaḥa* or *musallaḥa*) post (al-Maqrīzī, *Ḵiṭaṭ*, I:307). It was situated one mile south of Bilāq and six miles south of old Aswan (al-Masʿūdī [d. 345 AH/ 956 AD], *Murūj al-Ḏahab*, I:133; Lane 2000, 462).

In letter **19**v:6, the writer requests the eparch to protect the people 'in the garrison post' (*al-maslaḥa/al-musallaḥa*) and this is likely to be referring to the garrison of al-Qaṣr. The letter shows that the garrison was within Nubian territory and so under the authority of the eparch. According to al-ʾAswānī, the Nubian king George requested the Abbasid caliph al-Muʿtaṣim (r. 218–27 AH/ 833–42 AD) to remove the garrison post from al-Qaṣr, since the garrison was on Nubian soil (al-Maqrīzī, *Ḵiṭaṭ*, I:372). Two mosques were built around the middle of the eleventh century just south of the fortress (Bloom 1984; Gascoigne 2008). These were under Muslim control, though a church upon which one of the mosques was built seems to have been under Nubian control, judging by the following description by ʾAbū al-Makārim (d. 1208 AD; *Taʾrīḵ al-Kanāʾis wa-l-ʾAdyira*, 100b; translation by Evetts, 274):

> There is a church of the glorious angel Michael (*Miḵāʾīl*) which overlooks the river, and is situated between the land of Nubia and the land of the Muslims; but it belongs to Nubia. Near it there is a mosque which has been restored; and also a castle which was built as a fortress (*ḥiṣn*) on the frontier between the Muslims and Nubians, and is at the extremity of the Nubian territory.

References to al-Qaṣr disappear after the Fatimid period and the fortress may have ceased to be used. Remains of the fortress have survived to modern times in the site known as Ḥiṣn al-Bāb ‘fortress of the gate (to Nubia)’, which has been excavated by archaeologists (Gascoigne and Rose 2012).

The documents in our corpus demonstrate that the southern boundary of the open region between the first and second cataracts was in principle observed by the Muslims in the Fatimid period. This is shown clearly by the legal document **45** (566 AH/

1170 AD), which records the lease of a boat by two Muslims from a Christian to travel upstream from Bilāq (Philae) to Nubia for the sake of trade. The document specifies that the stopping place in the south must be the Island of Michael (*jazīrat Mikā'īl*).[13] This was the island known in Nubian as Meinarti, which lay just north of the second cataract, a short distance upstream of the modern town of Wādī Ḥalfa. Excavations of levels of Meinarti datable to the Fatimid period have revealed spacious houses, reflecting prosperity. One house was presumably the residence of an important official and had four store rooms (Adams 2003; Welsby 2002, 124–27). The site is believed to have been the occasional residence of the Nubian eparch of Nobadia and to have played an important role in the control of trade to points further up the Nile. Two Greek funerary inscriptions that were discovered there include the title *k̠oiak-eikšil,* one of which refers to an eparch. (Ruffini 2012a, 49–50)

Many of the letters of the corpus show that the eparch acted as an intermediary between the Muslims and the Nubian king in Dongola, which was necessary due to the restriction on travel beyond the second cataract.

The second cataract, however, was not a hard border for Muslims. According to al-ʾAswānī, no boats, of Muslims or others, could cross the second cataract without the permission of the eparch. A further border was situated at Maqs al-ʾAʿlā, "six stages" (*marāḥil*) south of the second cataract, beyond Baṭn al-Ḥajar,

[13] In the document the name is spelt with *kāf* (*Mikā'īl*), whereas in ʾAbū al-Makārim's text it is spelt with a *k̠ā'* (*Mik̠ā'īl*). These are two variant forms of the name in Arabic.

possibly to be identified with the modern town of ʿAkaša (Seignobos 2010, 20). To cross this border, permission was needed from the king (al-Maqrīzī, *Ḵiṭaṭ*, I:353). So, travel south of the second cataract was in principle possible for Muslim merchants so long as they had the necessary permission.

Several of the letters indicate that the Muslim merchants travelled to the court of the king in Dongola with authorisation from the eparch.

The writer of letter **13** requests the eparch to send him a letter to facilitate the conduct of trade with the king:

> If God wills, I shall travel to the king after the festival. I ask for your kindness to write a letter to the slave of the king requesting him to deliver to me the consignment that he promised me. Please could this be done through your agency.... Send your letter to me, so that a group of merchants can enter (to see the king) with me, for you would thereby help them in their livelihood. (**13**v)

It appears from the following passage in **13** that the eparch was not always comfortable about Muslims travelling to the king:

> As for what he has (i.e., you have) mentioned about the situation of the journey to the king and his (i.e., your) saying that he is (i.e., you are) afraid, well, praise be to God the Exalted, I am not a soldier of the king's army that I should be feared. I am a man who is a merchant, I am his slave and his servant. (**13**r:4–9)

On several occasions, the letters mention the dispatch of messengers (generally referred to as *ġulām* 'slave boy') to the king to carry out the business of their Muslim masters. It is likely that the journey to Dongola was difficult. The third cataract and Baṭn al-Ḥajar were not navigable by boats during the low water season of the Nile and this may have been why merchants preferred not to make the journey themselves:

> The slave boy of the ruler has set off together with my slave boy to the king. (**22**r:9–10)

> I was intending to send a messenger to the king with the merchandise that I have bought for him for ten dīnārs and the horse that I have prepared for him, and equipment that he requested from me. (**9**v:7–9)

The writer of letter **9**, Lāmiʿ ibn Ḥasan al-Kanzī, reports that his slave boy was impeded at the court of the king by an apparently rival Muslim merchant called Ibn al-ʿAsqalānī, who is probably the same as the writer of letter **13**, Ḥiṣn al-Dawla ibn al-ʿAsqalānī:

> My slave boy arrived humiliated and wronged by Ibn al-ʿAsqalānī.... For is Ibn al-ʿAsqalānī the king and we his slaves and his grovellers? (**9**v:9–17)

On some occasions, the writers of letters request the eparch to convey letters to the king on their behalf. The writer of letter **22**, a Muslim *ʾamīr*, refers to the provision of military aid in the form of the delivery of horses by the Fatimid ruler to the Nubian king. The *ʾamīr* requests the eparch to convey a letter to the king with regard to this shipment rather than sending a letter directly to the king:

> As for your saying that the ships conveying the horses have stopped, I was intending to (send them) until the order of the ruler, may God make his reign eternal, reached me by the hand of his brother, the governor of our land, together with a letter to the king informing him (the king) that if he (the king) needed an army (*ʿaskar*), he (the ruler) would

> send it to him, but he (the ruler) has prohibited me from sending to you the first instalment of the horses until these messengers (i.e., my slave boy and the slave boy of the ruler) arrive (at the king). For the slave boy of the ruler has set off together with my slave boy to the king. Please, please allow them passage, after showing them due honour and respect, to the king, and request him in your letter not to delay them for a single hour. (**22**r:5–9)

Letter **21** casts important light on another dimension of relations between Muslims and the Nubian king. The writer, ʿAbd Allāh ibn al-Qāḍī al-Rašīd ʿAlī ibn al-Zubayr, informs the eparch that he has sent two of his sons to Nubia:

> I sent two of my sons, called Qāsim and ʾAbū ʿAbd Allāh to Erkinun in order for them to dwell there, as your guests and the guests of the king, may God preserve his life. I did not send them for trade nor for benefit through selling and buying. Rather, I sent them to be at the disposition of the king and (stay) in his land until God permits. I shall convey to them cloth for them to send to the king, may God preserve his life, so that they can see his crown (i.e., have an audience with him) and become one of his subjects (literally: slaves). (**21**r:3–8)

The town of Erkinun may be possibly identified with the modern village of Argíin (also spelt Argîn and Arqin) in Lower Nubia on the west bank of the Nile just north of Wādī Ḥalfa (Ṣabbār and Bell 2017, 27; Salvoldi and Geus 2017, 82). So the sons were not sent directly to the king in Dongola, but rather used this as a base in Nubia. The writer goes on to say that various members of his family, including his father "the rightly-guided judge," his grandfather and his cousin, the judge ʾAbū al-Faḍl, had a similar relationship of service to the Nubian king.

His father and cousin are said to have been envoys of the Fatimid ruler. It was his father who strove to make a peace treaty between the Fatimid ruler and the Nubian king David at a time of political instability. The writer, ʿAbd Allāh, says that, when he was young, he himself travelled to visit the Nubian king with his cousin. Moreover, another son of his, Hibat Allāh, also visited the court of the Nubian king on a previous occasion.

As remarked above (§3.4), ʿAbd Allāh ibn al-Qāḍī al-Rašīd ʿAlī ibn al-Zubayr was a member of an influential family, many of whom held high offices in the Fatimid administration. It would have been expected, therefore, that the Fatimid ruler sent them on diplomatic missions to Nubia. According to **21**r:18, the family owned property in Nubia "from which we have a livelihood."

There is, however, another factor in the relations of the Banū al-Zubayr with the Nubian king. ʿAbd Allāh's brother, al-Qāḍī al-Rašīd ʾAḥmad ibn ʿAlī, was executed by the vizier Šāwar on suspicion of attempted rebellion; cf. al-ʾIdfūwī (d. 748 AH/1347 AD), *al-Ṭālīʿ al-Saʿīd,* 98–102, 364. It is possible, therefore, that ʿAbd Allāh was seeking asylum for himself and his children in Nubia with a view to shifting his allegiance to the Nubian king (Sartain 1993, 25–26). ʿAbd Allāh requests the eparch to act as intermediary with the king in order to make the necessary arrangements for this, including the provision of dwelling places in Lower Nubia:

> If you would do the kindness of sending a letter to the king, may God preserve his life, informing him of everything I have mentioned and my wish to come to his country, then please do so. Also obtain for me from him a letter from the king to the Master of the Horses /to you/ instructing that

> he treats me and my sons well and treats me in the same way as my forefathers, and instruct you in the letter to provide me with a house in Ibrīm, a house in Adminna and a house in Erkinun, so that I can build them and I can live in whichever of these houses I wish together with my sons. (**21**r:21–26)

One should, however, be cautious about drawing conclusions about shifts of allegiance to the king from statements about service. In several letters, sent by men who seem otherwise to be loyal to the Fatimid ruler, the writers make statements such as the following:

> As for what you have said with regard to the service of the king, we are all his servants and slaves of the crown (i.e., his subjects). (**22**r:4–5)

> I am the servant of the king and his deputy. (**9**r:27–margin, 1)

The following passage in letter **9** indicates that the writer's service to the king, provision of supplies and commitment to the protection of the eparch's subjects has formed a close relationship between him and the eparch. Moreover, this closeness has come about "in the presence of the bishop:"[14]

> Does not the Master of the Horses think that what brings me and you together close in the presence of (*bi-ḥuḍūr*) the bishop is that I provide him with provisions and I remain in the service of the king and the protection of your companions? (**9**r, margin, 11–v:1)

[14] There were four bishoprics in Lower Nubia, including Qaṣr Ibrīm, Kourte, Faras and Sai (Łajtar and Derda 2019; Tsakos 2021, 10).

The phrase “in the presence of the bishop” gives the act of ‘coming close’ a legal sanction, just as a legal act is frequently stated in medieval Arabic legal documents to have been conducted in the presence of witnesses or of a judge. This procedure evidently formed the legal basis of the relationship between Muslim merchants and the Nubian authorities. The passage suggests that, as with legal contracts, the obligations were contracted between individual parties, rather than being based exclusively on a government-level pact, as is generally thought to have been the case with the government-level *baqṭ* of the earlier Islamic period.

One possibility is that the reference to the writer’s loyalty and service to the eparch and the king like a loyal Nubian subject reflects that the writer’s primary residence was in Nubia. This, however, is not necessarily the case. It could rather reflect a security measure imposed on the merchants. A further reflection of the loyal allegiance of the merchants to the Nubian authorities while operating in Nubia is seen in the following wording in letter **20**:

> May he (the Master of the Horses) not cease to allow me to act as his agent (*ʾināba ʿanhu*) in trade, to carry out his needs and for any service. (**20**r:12–margin, 1)

The implication of this is that the merchant is acting on behalf of the eparch. Again, this does not necessarily reflect that the merchant owed overall exclusive loyalty to the Nubian eparch, but rather that while operating in Nubia he had the status of being in service to the eparch.

Regarding ʿAbd Allāh ibn Zubayr’s request in **21** for houses in Nubia, this also does not necessarily reflect a shift in allegiance. ʿAbd Allāh alludes to the fact that his family already had property in Nubia, from which they derived an income:

> Our property (*ʾamlākunā*), from which we have a livelihood, is in their country. (**21**r:18)

We know from other sources that Muslims had acquired land in Nubia (see, for example, §3.5.4). Moreover, there is evidence that there was a mosque in Dongola in the Fatimid period and a Muslim funerary stela datable to the Fatimid period has been discovered there. This indicates that there was a Muslim community in the town already at this period (Seignobos 2016, I:70–75). The request of ʿAbd Allāh ibn Zubayr in **21** for houses in Nubia, therefore, should be seen in the light of this incipient Muslim settlement in Nubia. It is probably significant that the location of all the houses that ʿAbd Allāh specifies is in Lower Nubia, north of the second cataract, where other Muslim settlements were concentrated. The Nubian king made the boundary of the second cataract a constraint not only on mercantile travel but also on Muslim settlement.

A passage in letter **23** appears to be referring to the quashing of a rebellion by Nubians in Aswan against the Nubian king, which reflects loyalty to the king:

> When they heard that the Nubians had rebelled against the king, he (the servant of the writer) killed them. (**23**r:7–8)

These passages evidently express loyalty and respect for the authority of the king rather than a shift of allegiance. Note also the title *al-ḥaḍra al-makḏūma* (literally 'the served presence') in **16**r:5, which seems to be referring to the king.

The following passage from letter **2** appears to be alluding to a Muslim commander's commitment to protect the land of the Nubian king:

> The commander has written that he will arrive and he will give instructions for your sake and for the sake of the carrying out of your requests. He also mentions (the need) to safeguard the subjects and protect the merchants who are travelling to you from among the merchant community (and mentions) the country of the king and its guarding and protection. (**2**r:13–16)

In letter 21, ʿAbd Allāh mentions three Nubian kings, viz. داوود, مويس and باسيل. The first two may be identified with the kings David and Moses George, whom scholars have identified from other Nubian sources as having their reigns in the twelfth century.[15] In some Nubian documents, Moses George is referred to by the single name Moses, as in, e.g., the Nubian letter P. QI III 31. The name Mūyis appears to be a variant form of the name Moses, corresponding perhaps to the attested forms of the name Mōēs and Mōēsēs.[16] In the Arabic document 1974_V08_24–24A, which is not included in the present corpus and is apparently a pen exercise, various addresses are written describing the eparch Īsū as the 'vizier of King Mūyis' (*wazīr al-malik Mūyis*).

---

[15] http://www.medievalnubia.info/dev/index.php/Kings, accessed 1 March 2024. The reading of موس as مويس and its identification with King Moses George was proposed by Robin Seignobos.

[16] http://www.medievalnubia.info/dev/index.php/Names, accessed 1 March 2024.

According to the extant Nubian sources, the chronological sequence of kings was David followed by his nephew Moses George. David's reign predated 1155, which is the date of the proclamation of King Moses George (P. QI III 30). The reference to a peace treaty (*ṣulḥ*) between the Fatimid ruler and the Nubian king David at a time of political turbulence and instability (**21**r:11–12) may be referring to a raid that is reported by al-Maqrīzī (*ʾItti‘āẓ al-Ḥunafāʾ bi-ʾAḵbār al-ʾAʾimma al-Fāṭimiyyīn al-Ḵulafāʾ*; Beshir 1975, 20) to have been made by the Nubian king in 501 AH/1107 AD and its aftermath. The ruler of Egypt at the period was the vizier al-ʾAfḍal Šāhanšāh:

> And in it (this year) came the news that the King of the Nubians mobilised by land and water and decided to march against Upper Egypt. Al-ʾAfḍal sent an army to Qūṣ and ordered the governor of Qūṣ to march himself to the borders of the country of the Nubians. But there came the news of the rising of the King's brother against him and his murder. The strife among them intensified until the members of the royal household were exterminated and a boy was installed in the monarchy. His mother sent begging al-ʾAfḍal's forgiveness and asking him not to send against them someone to raid them. He wrote to the governor of Upper Egypt to send an army to the borders of the country of the Nubians and to send an emissary to them in order to renew upon them the stipulated quota that had been established by tradition, which is three hundred and sixty heads of slaves every year.

Letter **21** suggests that the king Basil mentioned there preceded Moses George and David, since the king whom the grandfather of the writer visited was Basil, whereas the father of the writer and the writer himself visited Mūyis (Moses George). This earlier Basil may have been a king of Alodia at Soba,[17] since the letter (**21**r:10–11) could be interpreted as referring to the visit to Basil by the writer's grandfather in Soba. At that period Alodia had not been united with Makuria (see below). There was, however, a king Basil on the throne of Makuria in 1089, which may have been the king that the writer's grandfather saw (Vantini 1981, 128; Welsby 2002, 89, 260). This Basil was succeeded by a king George in 1132, who in turn was succeeded by King David.[18]

The Nubian proclamation dated 22nd August 1155 issued by King Moses George (P. QI III 30) confirms that this king was on the throne at that time. The text states that it was written in the third month since he became king, succeeding his uncle King David, and he seems to have ruled until around 1190 (Ruffini 2012b, 247–48). The name of the eparch to whom **21** was sent is not specified in the address. Since the writer refers to his visits to King Moses George, it is likely that this was the king that was ruling at the time the letter was written. As we have seen (§3.2), the reign of Moses George appears to have overlapped with the term of office of the three eparchs mentioned elsewhere in the

---

[17] This was the interpretation of Adams (2010, 252).

[18] http://www.medievalnubia.info/dev/index.php/Kings, accessed 1 March 2024. According to Michałowski and Gerster (1967, 37), Basil was the grandfather of Moses George. It is not clear, however, what their source is for this. They mention it in connection to an inscription on a wall painting in the cathedral at Faras, but according to the latest interpretations of this, it does not contain a reference to Basil (Łajtar 2009, no. XIII; Jakobielski et al. 2017, 432).

corpus, Uruwī, Darmā and Īsū, so it is not possible to be certain about the identity of the eparch addressed in the letter.

In the description of the visits by the writer of **21** and his family to King Moses George (Mūyis), it is stated that in some cases the king was in Soba and in some cases he was in Dongola:

> My cousin, the judge ʾAbū al-Faḍl travelled to visit the king Mūyis as a messenger of the ruler to Soba. I myself travelled with my cousin when I was young to Soba to visit king Mūyis. I was received by him very well. My son, Hibat Allāh, travelled to the just king Mūyis, while he was in Dongola, and was received very well by him and he bestowed gifts of honour upon him. (**21**r:13–16)

Soba was the capital of the kingdom of Alodia (ʿAlwa), situated on the north bank of the Blue Nile, a few miles above its confluence with the White Nile. This passage suggests that at this period Makuria, Nobadia and Alodia were all united under King Moses George. The court of the king seems to have been itinerant between Dongola and Soba. This itinerant court of a Nubian king is alluded to also in letter **39** of the corpus, which was written by a merchant who had travelled to Soba:

> If the king had come to us in Soba, we would not have stayed in the country more than a month or two months, but… we are with the merchandise that we have for the king and his army, but we have found that there is only little (business) in the land. (**39**r:8–11)

The implication is that the writer was expecting the king to come to Soba, but his travel had been delayed. So this also would be evidence of an itinerant court. Moreover, the Nubian eparch must have had the power to grant permission to Muslims to travel to Alodia as well as to Makuria. It is possible that the king left Soba for Dongola in the rainy season between June and September, and so would have been expected to be back in Soba by the time the merchant wrote letter **39** on 10th Šawwāl 485 AH/13th November 1092 AD (the exact date is mentioned in the letter). The king may have followed the old 'king's road' in the Bayuda, which in the Kushite period used to connect the towns of Meroe and Napata (Lohwasser 2013, 425–28).

This unification of the kingdoms is confirmed by some Nubian and Greek inscriptions that describe King Moses George as the ruler of Makuria and Alodia (Łajtar 2009; Van Gerven Oei 2011, 253–55; Jakobielski et al. 2017, 434). He is given this title also in an unpublished Coptic letter that was discovered at Qaṣr Ibrīm.[19] King George (d. 1157), the precedessor of King David, is described in a Nubian memorial inscription discovered in Wādī al-Naṭrūn as ascending to "the throne of the two dominions" on 28th June 1132 AD, the two dominions apparently being Makuria and Alodia (Van Gerven Oei 2011, 235–36). Adam Łajtar has informed me that he is aware of an unpublished Nubian document (74.1.30.6), which refers in its protocol to a ruler of Makuria and Alodia. Włodzimierz Godlewski discussed the unification of the kingdoms in several of his papers (e.g., Godlewski 2008; 2010). He speculates that this may have arisen through marriage alliances between the royal families of Makuria and Alodia.[20] This was the culmination of an increasing rapprochement

[19] The English translation of this appears in Adams (1996, 227–29).

[20] I am grateful to Adam Łajtar for drawing my attention to these references.

between the two kingdoms since the Arab invasion of Nubia in the seventh century. By the eighth century, Makuria had shifted from the Chalcedonian creed to the Coptic creed, in conformity with Alodia's church (Welsby 2002, 34–35). In the eighth and ninth centuries, there is evidence of Makurian influence on the architecture and pottery of Soba (Danys and Zielińska 2017, 182–83). Intermarriage between the royal families of Makuria and Alodia had begun already in the tenth century (Welsby 2002, 89). By the middle of the twelfth century, Nubian sources refer to the Nubian state by the native term Dotawo, the earliest being the proclamation of Moses George (P. QI III 30) dated 22nd August 1155, where it refers to the united kingdoms of Makuria and Alodia (Łajtar 2009, 94; Ruffini 2016b, 550). In the early thirteenth century, the region of Alodia was overrun by raiders from the south called Damādim and Soba was destroyed (Gerhards forthcoming).

3.5.6. Trade

A passage in letter **24** indicates that the Muslim writers are dependent on the goodwill of the eparch's director of administration (*mutawallī*) without the latter putting capital into business transactions in a partnership (*qarīḍa*). The allusion seems to be to the dependence of the Muslim merchants on the authorisation of the eparch and his administrators to carry out trade:

> His slaves [kiss the ground] before him and report to him that it has not been concealed from him that his slaves (i.e., the writers) were dependent on the administrative director in his presence without being in financial partnership. (**24**r:4–6)

Many letters mention commodities of trade. In most cases, these are items of trade between the Muslim writers and the eparch. As has been shown in §3.5.5 above, some letters refer to trading by Muslim merchants with the Nubian king, either directly or through the intermediary of a messenger.

Commodities that were delivered to the eparch by the Muslim merchants include herbs and spices, vinegar, clothes and textiles, furniture, containers, bitumen, military equipment and horses (see §8 for details). Archaeological finds in the region provide evidence of imports of pottery, including glazed wares, glass, textiles and paper (Adams 1996, 95–99; 2010, 69–72; Welsby 2002, 183–201; Edwards 2019, 969–70). The delivery of horses was in some cases clearly intended for military purposes. This applies, for example, to letter **22**, which refers to a complaint by the eparch that the supply of horses (*ḵayl*) for the Nubian army by the Fatimid authorities has stopped. In some cases, however, a horse was sent as a diplomatic gift to the eparch, e.g.,

> I have sent you a mare of excellent quality (*farasan jayyidatan*) from my horses (*ḵaylī*) for your personal benefit by the hand of my slave boy Yaḥyā. (**22**r:17–18)

In letter **7**, the writer tells the eparch that he has sent him a camel, apparently as a diplomatic gift rather than as an item of trade:

> I have sent my slave boy (*ġulām*), who is called Šarīf, with a brown camel to his honourable presence. I want you to receive it from me. (**7**r:3–5)

The most frequently mentioned items that were received by the Muslim merchants from the eparch are slaves. In the medieval period, the Nubians retained control of the sourcing of dark-skinned slaves, most likely in the Upper Nile valley, Kordofan and Darfur, although they no longer controlled the sources of luxury items such as ivory and ebony, since access to these had retreated too far to the south (Ruffini 2019, 106).

The generic term for slaves that appears in the letters is *riqq* or *raqīq*. When a specific number of slaves is intended, these terms are often combined with the numerical classifier *raʾs* 'head', e.g., *al-raʾsayn al-raqīq* 'the two (heads of) slaves' (**4**r, margin, 3; **9**r, margin, 8–9), *al-raʾs al-raqīq* 'the (head of) slave' (**24**r:7). In **25**v:11, 'two slaves' are denoted by the phrase *al-raʾsayn* alone. Alternatively, the writers refer to specific slaves by the terms *waṣīf* (male) and *waṣīfa* (female), which designate slaves that were destined for domestic service (Goitein 1967, 131; Rāġīb 2006, II:23–25). The letters also mention slave girls as items of trade, which are referred to by the term *jāriya*.

Letter **18**, sent by the eparch Uruwī, refers to the delivery of wheat (*ḥabāʾib al-qamḥ*) to the merchants by the eparch. In letter **17**, also sent by Uruwī, the eparch says that he has sent a lantern (*sirāj*) to the merchant for the merchant's mother.

Letter **9**, referring to trade with the king, indicates that the Muslim merchant received, or expected to receive, horses and servant women and cash from the king:

> I am owed by the king two horses. He has sent me two good-for-nothing, aged slave women (*jāriyatayn ʿajāyiz*) and six dīnārs. (**9**r:25–26)

This passage indicates that the term *jāriya* did not necessarily always refer to young girls.

The range of goods received by the Muslims from the Nubians is considerably more restricted than the lists of commodities that are recorded by the historiographical sources. In addition to slaves, these latter sources refer to ivory, leopard skins, dates, ebony for furniture manufacture, spears, emery, alum, exotic live animals such as monkeys, lions, leopards, elephants and giraffes and especially cattle and camels (Beshir 1975; Spaulding 1995, 588).

It is significant that only small numbers of slaves and slave girls are mentioned in the correspondence. As discussed already (§2.5.4), these are best interpreted as diplomatic gifts. There is no evidence of the merchants being the agents of a mass delivery of slaves by the Nubians to the Fatimid authorities, such as the "three hundred and sixty head of slaves" that was required of the Nubians in the earlier *baqṭ* treaty. Furthermore, there is no mention of the *baqṭ* in the documents of the corpus.

The letters reflect a semi-monetary economy in Lower Nubia. The units of money mentioned include dīnārs and dirhams. Gold dīnārs constituted the standard money and silver dirhams were of lower value. A cash payment is referred to as *ḥaqq ʿayn* (literally: 'what is owed of cash'). For more details about coinage, see §6.

Terms of capacity and weight used in correspondence with the eparch include *raṭl* 'litre' (vinegar **15**v:3), *ʾirdabb* (wheat **18**r:5) and *ʾūqiya* 'ounce' (**15**v:3, 5).

Some letters indicate that the merchants sold the slaves that they received from the eparch for cash. The following passage from letter **9** indicates that the merchant sold a slave for cash in order to purchase scented goods for the eparch. There was, therefore, an intermediate monetary transaction in the exchange of merchandise between the merchants and the eparch:

> As for the purchase of the goods that you mentioned (in your letter), allocate the expenditure to the elder ʾAbū al-Ṭāhir.... When your slave boy informed me that you needed the goods, I delivered him (the slave) to the broker and he auctioned him and acquired (the offer of) five dīnārs. I then went to your slave boy and consulted him concerning his sale and sold him for five dīnārs, on the grounds that there is nobody in the land and none of the people have anything. We have dealt with the orders for scented goods. (**9**r:5–12)

Letter **25** refers to the sale of a slave girl and two slaves:

> The slave girl was inspected and the price paid for her was ten dīnārs, but they found that she was crippled and they returned her. I had offered her for sale to a woman for twelve dīnārs and seven dirhams in a private transaction. (**25**v:7–8)

> As for the two slaves (*al-raʾsayn*) who are with them, they paid to me for them thirty-two dīnārs, for an equivalent exchange of thirty-six, each dīnār (having this exchange value). They have also paid more, at a rate of a dīnār, two and three. (**25**v:11–12)

The following terse statement by a Muslim merchant in letter **37** suggests that the merchant writers of the letters were also buyers of slaves in the markets in Aswan:

> As for slaves (*al-raqīq*), there is nothing in Aswan. (**37**v:4–5)

The following passage from letter **4** suggests that the Muslims sometimes used slaves received from the eparch to pay debts in lieu of monetary payment:

> Then I wrote to you concerning the condition of the two slaves who are to be sent to my creditor ʾAbū al-Ḍubāʿ, but you have not sent them to me and I do not know whether your servant has given us a share. (**4**r, margin–v:1)

There is evidence in the letters also of direct monetary transactions with the eparch. Letter **20**, for example, refers to the receipt of cash from the eparch for the purchase of commodities:

> His slave boy, Bišr, arrived on Wednesday as I was leaving for the land of Nubia. I found in it (the letter) that the Master of the Horses sent three dīnārs. (**20**r:4–5)

These were presumably Egyptian dīnār coins that were in circulation in Nubia rather than gold bullion.

In the following passage from letter **9**, the writer instructs the eparch to assign the payment to another merchant:

> As for the purchase of the goods that you mentioned (in your letter), allocate the expenditure (*al-nafaq*) to the elder ʾAbū al-Ṭāhir. (**9**r:5–6)

The letters sometimes refer to the sending by the merchants of cash to the eparch, e.g.,

> I have sent to you dirhams, two pieces in cash (*ḥaqq ʿayn qiṭʿatayn*), two boxes, a leather bag and bitumen. (**9**v:19–20)

There is no reference, however, to the Muslims purchasing slaves from Nubia with money. Letter **24** refers to a slave (*raqīq*) that the eparch bestowed (*ʾanʿamathu*) upon the writers. The choice of the verb *ʾanʿama* 'to bestow' indicates that the Muslims did not purchase the slave for money, but rather the slaves were transferred to the Muslims as a diplomatic gift. As argued in §2.5.4, however, the gifts were based on the comparison of abstract values of a monetary standard established by a market economy. The fact that the writers complain that the slave was sick in the passage below indicates that the Muslim merchants treated the receipt of slaves as part of a reciprocal exchange of diplomatic gifts. Reciprocity would be impaired if the gift was defective in some way and of reduced monetary value:

> They inform him that the slave (*al-raʾs al-raqīq*) whom he bestowed (*ʾanʿamathu*) upon his slaves (*mamālīkihā*, i.e., the writers of this letter) through the agency of Bazilī was sick (*marīḍa* sg.f), and that his slaves (*mamālīkihā*, i.e., the writers) wanted to return her. (**24**r:6–8)

In letter **17**, the eparch Uruwī says explicitly that he is sending a slave girl as payment for what is owed:

> I have sent a slave girl (*jāriya*) with ʾIbrāhīm (as payment) for what is owed together with her two children. (**17**r:5–6)

The passage below, from letter **4**, is further evidence for the practice of exchanging slaves from the eparch for goods supplied to the eparch by the Muslims:

> I have taken note of it and the fact that he stated that he (the eparch) has sent to me a female slave, and has sent to me a slave girl with Jawhar (the name of a slave boy), and that I have only been able to send to him two turbans with difficulty and a seat. As for the first (i.e., the aforementioned) female slave, she has not reached me in his consignment so that I may take possession of her, my honour, Master of the Horses, and I shall not correspond with you

> nor give you consignments of cloth as gifts until what you send is at my disposal. (**4**r:3–8)

The writer of letter **9** says that he bought aromatic herbs, spices, sugar and butter for the eparch from a market, since he was not able to find these commodities "in the land" at market prices. The term 'the land' without qualification seems to be used by the merchants to refer to Aswan and its environs. The 'market' referred to, therefore, is likely to have lain further afield:

> We have dealt with the orders for scented goods. We did not find in the land anything of these that the merchants reckoned to be at market prices. Moreover we did not find the (sufficient) outlay for the goods. So, I sent your slave boy together with my messenger to the market (*al-sūq*) and he bought... (**9**r:11–14)

The writer of **15** states that he had to send to Qūṣ to buy commodities since they were not available locally (presumably in Aswan):

> As for the situation of the trade consignment, since your honour requested it, when I reached the land, I asked about it, but did not find any of it. I did not want to neglect this and so I sent somebody to Qūṣ to buy it. (**15**r:9–12)

It is relevant to note that, from the late eleventh century, there was a decline in the importance of Aswan and a concomitant growth of Qūṣ as a garrison and centre of administration and trade (Garcin 1976, 79–84).

Letter **16** mentions the market of the cloth-merchants:

> He has just written a letter saying that he cannot make it to the market of the cloth-merchants (*sūq al-bazzāzīn*). (**16**v:3–4)

The merchants often used middlemen for the purchase of commodities for the eparch, as seen, for example, in the following passage from letter **20**, which refers to the payment of commission to the middleman:

> I asked on your behalf for bitumen (*zift*) to be bought for you before I left the land. I collected three dirhams commission (*ḥaqqan*) in order for him to buy for him (i.e., the Master of the Horses) the bitumen. (**20**r:4–6)

Letter **9** refers to the use of the services of a broker (*simsār*) by a merchant:

> I delivered him (the slave) to the broker (*al-simsār*) and he auctioned him and acquired (the offer of) five dīnārs. (**9**r:8–9)

Prices of commodities were subject to inflation, as seen in this passage from letter **9**:

> If the goods become more expensive, we will not sell them to those taking refuge in the houses with the women due to the inflation. No goods remain in the market. The price of all the spices in the market that I have mentioned has doubled. (**9**r:19–22)

The writers of letters to the eparch refer in some cases to the trade in coins, involving varying exchange rates, e.g.,

> Let them send to me in this final hour of mine these nineteen dīnārs and eight dirhams, at the rate of five for every dīnār. I have made inquiries about the exchange rate on my side and I found it to be seven, but I traded them at the better rate of six and a half. If I do not go ahead with this transaction, the exchange will be more, and you will lose due to a higher exchange rate. I have acquired gold dīnārs. I have sent at the time (of the transaction) a mail relating

> to it with Yūsū as payment of the amount in coin. But there is nothing that would suit you. If there were anything at all, here or elsewhere, I would have sent it to you. However, cash is something that we cannot control (i.e., we have no control over its value) and we have not found an executive officer. (**25**r, margin–v:5)

In some cases, the writers apologise for not having ready cash (*ḥaqq ʿayn*) to pay to the eparch and so they exchange other commodities, e.g.,

> I ask forgiveness, since I have written this letter from Dendur. If I were in Aswan, I would have sent him cash, so that trusting friendship may accompany what this (letter) says, if God wills. (**20**v:1–2)

> I have sent a piece of an Iraqi striped garment (*šuqqat burd ʿirāqī*) in lieu of a cash payment (*bi-rasm ḥaqq ʿayn*). Please forgive me. (**21**r, margin, 1)

This indicates that a monetary transaction was expected in these circumstances, but coins were in short supply.

Although only very few coins datable to this period have been excavated by archaeologists in Nubia, there are ample references to coins and monetary payments in extant Nubian documents and accounts (Ruffini 2012b, 171–80; 2016a; 2019; see also Vorderstrasse 2012).

Letter **9**, referring to trade with the king, indicates that the Muslim merchant received, or expected to receive, dīnārs from him:

> I am owed by the king two horses. He has sent me two good-for-nothing, aged slave women (*jāriyatayn ʿajāyiz*) and six dīnārs. (**9**r:25–26)

This appears to conflict with the following statement of al-ʾAswānī, who claims that Upper Nubia was demonetised (al-Maqrīzī, *Ḵiṭaṭ*, I:353; translation by Vantini 1975, 604):

> Here (south of the second cataract) neither the dīnār, nor the dirham are of any use because they do not use money in their transactions, except with the Muslims beyond the cataract. They do not buy or sell with money, but carry out their transactions by the exchange of slaves (*raqīq*), cattle, camels, iron tools and grains.

The passage in letter **9** is at the very least evidence that dīnārs were in the possession of the king in Dongola. It is not clear whether they had the function of money for market exchanges or for diplomatic gifts of gold.

The standard means of transportation of goods by the merchants that is mentioned in the letters to the eparch is the river boat, referred to generically as *markab* (pl. *marākib*). The following passage from **25** shows that navigation of the river was impeded in the cold season due to the wind:

> Cold will be upon me (soon) and I shall not be able (to carry out my business) and the Marīsī wind will not allow me to arrive. So, tell them to hurry up to carry out my requests and deliver the slave to me. (**25**r:14–15)

In general, sailing upstream to Nubia was difficult, as stated in letter **25**:

> You know that going downriver (to Aswan) is easy and going upriver (to Nubia) is difficult. (**25**v:6)

The Muslim merchants prefer to avoid travelling during the fast of Ramaḍān:

> I have desisted from journeying to the king only in consideration of the fact that Ramaḍān is a difficult month and I am anxious about travelling on the road before breaking the fast. If God wills, I shall travel to the king after the festival. (**13**r, margin, 2–v:1)

3.5.7. Complaints

A number of letters express complaints to the eparch. Some of these relate to issues concerning trade. The writer of letter **4** complains about the lack of delivery of slaves:

> As for the aforementioned female slave, she has not reached me in his consignment so that I may take possession of her, my honour, Master of the Horses, and I shall not correspond with you nor give you consignments of cloth as gifts until what you send is at my disposal. (**4**r:5–8)

> Then I wrote to you concerning the condition of the two slaves (*al-raʾsayn al-raqīq*) who are to be sent to my creditor ʾAbū al-Ḍubāʿ, but you have not sent them to me and I do not know whether your servant has given us a share. (**4**r, margin, 3–v:1)

The writer of letter **25** complains to the eparch that a Muslim *ʾamīr* has not fulfilled his requests relating to a slave, since he requires authorisation from the eparch. The writer requests the eparch to send the necessary authorising letter:

> As for the commander (*al-ʾamīr*), I visited him one day and he said to me "We shall carry out your requests," but I have not seen him again since and they do not allow me to visit him.... He said to me "When the letter comes from the Master of the Horses, I shall carry out your requests."... Write your letter to the commander that this slave belongs

> to the king and that he should bring it down (the river) so that the requests of the king be fulfilled out of respect. (**25**r:6–13)

In some cases the writer complains about the condition of the slaves that have been delivered, e.g.,

> They inform him that the slave (*al-ra'ʾs al-raqīq*) whom he bestowed upon his slaves (*mamālīkihā*, i.e., the writers of this letter) through the agency of Bazilī was sick, and that his slaves (i.e., the writers) wanted to return her, but the messenger (*al-rasūl*) whom she accompanied became ill, and that the slave girl (*al-jāriya*) and her son, Rāhim, your slave boy (*ġulāmaka*), were examined before purchase three times, and that she and her son have died. (**24**r:6–10)

The writer of letter **24** reports that the eparch's carrier has absconded and asks him to recover the goods that have been lost:

> Your carrier has absconded. Please arrange for your command to be issued to some of your slaves to extract forcibly from him what is appropriate, God willing. (**24**v:5–7)

Some letters complain about the treatment of the writer's colleagues or servants in Nubia, e.g.,

> Every year a large number of boats travel to your land and your colleagues badly mistreat them. This year the people from the port (of Aswan) were hindered in two ways. One of these is the injustice done to them by the people of the land and the other is the lack of produce.... I have sent two boats and everything in them is mine. I would like the Ikšīl to ensure that nobody obstructs them. (**5**r:4–8, margin, 1–3).

> I wrote to you concerning the condition of my servants (*ʿabīd*) but you did not reply. (**4**r, margin, 2)

The writer of letter **9** complains to the eparch about the treatment of his servant at the court of the king and defective merchandise delivered by the king, it not being possible to complain to the king directly:

> What I wish to inform the Ikšīl of is that my slave boy Kablām has arrived at the court of the king, but he (the king) has shown little gratitude for what I have undertaken for him. I am owed by the king two horses. He has sent me two good-for-nothing, aged slave women and six dīnārs.... my relationship with you has been spoiled since the king treats my slave boy in such a bad way. (**9**r:23–26, margin, 6–8)

3.5.8. Political Events

Some of the letters to eparchs mention political events. The clearest example of this is letter **6**, which reports the news of the killing of the vizier Šāwar by Šīrkūh. This took place in the year 564 AH/1169 AD, so the letter must have been written shortly after this:

> As for the news, God has protected us from the evil of Šāwar and he has been killed by the hand of Šīrkūh, the military commander, may God protect him, and has taken on the viziership to bear the burden of evil that is to come. (**6**r:6–8)

The writers of letter **24** tell the eparch that the news they have heard about disturbances in the north (i.e., north of Nubia) has prevented them from coming to Nubia:

> If it was not for the news we have heard from the north (*al-ʾaḵbār al-baḥriyya*) and the strife of the land, your slaves (i.e., the writers) would have made sure to present

> ourselves before you to kiss the ground and to perform their obligations. (**24**v:1–3)

Letter **4** contains an obscure reference to the outcome of a battle:

> The commander Treasure of the Dynasty (*Kanz al-Dawla*) arrived after victory, slaughter and God's victory. (**4**v:2–3)

3.6. The Structure of the Letters

3.6.1. Opening

Many of the letters to eparchs open, after the *basmala*, with the verb اعلم *ʾuʿlimu* 'I inform'. This takes as its object the eparch, who is referred to by his titles, and, after various blessings, is followed by the content of the report, e.g.,

اعلم الاكشيل وصاحب الخيل ووزير الملك... توجه القائد سعادة

> 'I inform the Ikšīl, Master of the Horses, vizier of the king... that the leader Saʿāda has set off.' (**1**r:2–3)

اعلم الاكشيل وصاحب الخيل ووزير الملك... انه يعلم ما وصل كتابه الى به في حال المسافرين من المراكب وغيرهم

> 'I inform the Ikšīl, Master of the Horses, vizier of the king... that his letter to me has referred to the condition of the travellers from the boats and of others.' (**3**r:2–4)

اعلم الاكشيل وصاحب الخيل ووزير الملك... ان متحملها صاحبى ومحسن تكرمتى اوه وهو خادمى

> 'I inform the Ikšīl, Master of the Horses, vizier of the king... that the bearer of this letter is my loyal and respectful companion, Oua, who is my servant.' (**6**r:2–4)

اعلم الاكشيل صاحب الخيل ووزير الملك متولى اعمال بلاد المريس...
اننى سيرت ولدين من أولاد

'I inform the Ikšīl, Master of the Horses, vizier of the king, the governor of the districts of the land of al-Marīs,... that I sent two of my sons...' (**21**r:2–3)

اعلم الاكشيل ووزير الملك وصاحب الخيل... توجه موصل هذا الكتاب

'I inform the Ikšīl, vizier of the king, Master of the Horses... that the bearer of this letter has set off.' (**2**r:2–5)

[ا]علم الاكشيل وصاحب الخيل... انه يعلم ان فى كل سنة...

'I inform the Ikšīl, Master of the Horses... that he knows that every year...' (**5**r:2–4)

اعلم صاحب الخيل [ووزير الملك]... وصولى الى ثغر اسوان حماه الله

'I inform the Master of the Horses [and vizier of the king]... of my arrival at the border of Aswan, may God protect it.' (**19**r:2–3)

In some letters, the titles of the eparch are preceded by an honorific term of address consisting of the word *ḥaḍra* 'presence'. After such openings, the eparch is generally referred to in the body of the letter by a 3sg.f pronoun, which agrees with *ḥaḍra*:

اعلم الحضرة السامية الاجلية الاكشيل وصاحب الخيل... توجه صهرى

'I inform the exalted and glorious presence, the Ikšīl and Master of the Horses... that my son-in-law has set off (to you).' (**11**r:2–3)

اعلم حضرة مولاى صاحب الخيل... وصول كتاب على يده غلامها ابس

'I inform the presence of my lord, the Master of the Horses... of the arrival of a letter by the hand of your slave boy Ipisi.' (**16**r:2)

In letter **14**, the initial اعلم *ʾuʿlimu* has been omitted by mistake:

>اعلم< حضرة مولاى الاجل صاحب الخ{لد}يل ووزير الملك... وصول متحملها الى بلاد النوبة

'(I inform) the presence of my majestic lord, the Master of the Horses and vizier of the king... of the arrival of the bearer of this letter to the land of the Nubians.' (**14**r:2–3)

The opening with اعلم is used also in **26**, which is addressed to a deputy eparch:

اعلم البزيل النائب عن صاحب الخيل بقلعة ابريم... ان متحمل هذه السطور الرئيس

'I inform al-Bazīl, the deputy of the Master of the Horses in the fortress of Ibrīm... that the bearer of these lines is the Head.' (**26**r:2–4)

Letter **7** opens with the formula كتبت... معلما له 'I have written... informing him':

كتبت... معلما له... انى قد وجهت غلامى يسمى شريف

'I have written... informing him... that I have sent my slave boy, who is called Šarīf...' (**7**r:2–4)

Several letters contain the obeisance formula 'the slave kisses the ground' in the opening:

عبد حضرة مولاى الاكشيل ووزير الملك... المملوك يقبل الارض والذى يريد علمه ان

'The slave of my honourable lord, the Ikšīl and vizier of the king... the slave kisses the ground and what he wishes him to know is that...' (**23**r:2–4)

مملوك الحضرة السامية الـ[ـا]جلية الكريمة... يقبل الارض بين يديها وينهى اليها... الذى يريد علمه ان وصلنى كتابك وقراته وفهمت ما فيه

'The slave of the lofty, most glorious and munificent presence... kisses the ground before him and reports to him... that what he wishes him to know is that your letter has arrived and I have read it and I have understood what is in it.' (**25**r:2–5)

سبب اصدار هذه المناجاة... حضرة مولاى الاكشيل صاحب الخيل وزير الملك... مماليكها [يقبلون الارض بيـ]ـن يديها وينهون اليها انها

'The reason for sending this message,... my honourable lord, the Ikšīl, Master of the Horses, vizier of the king,... his slaves [kiss the ground] before him and report to him that...' (**24**r:2–5)

Within the body of letter **24**, the writers refer to the act of obeisance to the eparch by kissing the ground in a potential audience with the eparch:

If it was not for the news we have heard from the north (*al-ʾak̲bār al-baḥriyya*) and the strife of the land, your slaves (i.e., the writers) would have made sure to present ourselves before you to kiss the ground (معولين علي المثول بين يديها لتقبيل الارض) and to perform their obligations. (**24**v:1–3)

Letter **27**, which is written to the secretary of Uruwī, requests the secretary vicariously to kiss the hand of the eparch:

العبد يسل حضرة مولاى الشيخ الاجل الكاتب... قبول يدى مولاى الاجل صاحب الخيل روى بن مولاى الاجل [ ]

'The slave asks my honourable master, the sublime elder, the secretary,... to kiss the hands of my sublime master, the Master of the Horses, (U)ruwī the son of my sublime master.' (**27**r:2–3)

Letter **8** opens directly with the report of the departure of a colleague with the verb *tawajjaha*:

توجه... متحملها القائد حسن بن القائد شجاع الدولة اسحق متولى الباب

'The bearer of this letter, the leader Ḥasan, the son of the leader Šujāʿ al-Dawla ('the Courage of the State') ʾIsḥāq, the administrator of the gate, has set off (to you).' (**8**r:1–4)

Some letters to eparchs open with the verb *waṣala* 'to arrive' in a phrase that reports the arrival of a letter from the addressee. This is also the opening of the letter sent by the eparch to the Muslim merchant ʾAbū al-Ṭāhir (**17**). The letters with these openings, therefore, are responses to letters:

وصل كتاب الاكشيل وصاحب الخيل... ووقفت عليه

'The letter has arrived from the Ikšīl and the Master of the Horses... and I have taken note of it.' (**4**r:2–3)

وصل كتاب صاحب الخيل ووزير الملك... وكتاب اخر الى الشيخ ابو الطاهر بن تريك

'The letter of the Master of the Horses and vizier of the king... has arrived and another letter for the elder ʾAbū al-Ṭāhir ibn Tarīk.' (**9**r:2–4)

وَصل كتاب مولاي الاكشيل صاحب الخيل... ووقفت عليه وقوف مسرور بوروده مبتهج بوفوده

'The letter of my master the Ikšīl, Master of the Horses,... has arrived and I have read it, happy at its arrival and delighted at its delivery.' (**13**r:2–4)

وصل كتاب صاحب الخيل ووزير الملك... ووقفت عليه وسررت بوصوله

'The letter of the Master of the Horses and vizier of the king... has arrived, and I have taken note of it and am pleased with its arrival.' (**20**r:2–3)

وصل كتاب حضرة مولاى صاحب الخيل... اما ما ذكرته عن

'The letter of your honour, my lord, the Master of the Horses... has arrived. As for what you have said with regard to...' (**22**r:2–4)

وصلتنى كتب حضرة مولاى الاكشيل وزير الملك... ووقفت عليها واحطت علما بما لديها

'The letters of my honourable lord the Ikšīl, vizier of the king... have reached me and I have read them and taken note of their contents.' (**15**r:2–4)

This opening formula is found also in **17**, which was sent by the eparch Uruwī to the Muslim merchant ʾAbū al-Ṭāhir. The addressee is not given any honorifics:

وصل كتاب ولدى... وقراته وفهمت مضمونه

'The letter of my son... has arrived and I have read it and noted its contents.' (**17**r:2–3)

The title of the eparch is followed by a blessing that opens with the formula اطال الله بقاه 'may God prolong his life'. A variant of this is found in **10**, in which the object of the verb is the title of the eparch:

اطال الله بقا صاحب الخيل

'May God prolong the life of the Master of the Horses.' (**10**r:2)

In openings in which the eparch is addressed by the honorific term *ḥadra* ‘presence’, the blessing contains a 3sg.f pronoun:

حضرة مولاى صاحب الخيل اطال الله بقاها

‘the presence of my lord the Master of the Horses, may God prolong his life’ (**22**r:2)

حضرة مولاى الاكشيل ووزير الملك اطال الله بقاها

‘the presence of my lord, the Ikšīl, vizier of the king, may God prolong his life’ (**23**r:2)

Letter **7** is exceptional in having a 2nd person pronoun in the formula:

كتبت اطال الله بقاك

‘I have written, may God prolong your life’ (**7**r:2)

The wish for the prolongation of life is followed by other blessings, which are more variable in form but typically open with the verb وادام ‘and may He (God) cause to endure’, e.g.,

وادام حراسته ونعمته

‘and cause his protection and wellbeing to endure’ (**1**r:3)

وادام عزه وهلك عدوه وضده

‘and cause to endure his strength, and cause his enemy and opponent to perish’ (**2**r:3–4)

وادام حراسته ونعمته

‘and cause to endure his protection and well-being’ (**3**r:3)

وادام عزه وكبت عدوه

‘and cause his power to endure and crush his enemy’ (**4**r:2–3)

وادام حراسته وسلامته ونعمته

'and cause his protection, safety and wellbeing to endure' (**5**r:3)

وادام تاييده وحراسته وسلامته ونعمته

'and cause his support, protection, safety and wellbeing to endure' (**6**r:3)

وادام عزك ونعماك وتمكينك وكبت اعداك

'and cause your strength, your wellbeing and your power to endure, and suppress your enemies' (**7**r:2–3)

وادام تاييده وسعادته وسلامته ونعمته

'and cause his support, happiness, safety and wellbeing to endure' (**8**r:3)

Letter **7** has 2nd person pronouns:

وادام عزك ونعماك وتمكينك وكبت اعداك

'and cause your strength, your wellbeing and your power to endure, and suppress your enemies' (**7**r:2–3)

The formula opening with اعلم 'I inform' in the present tense and the obeisance formula المملوك يقبل الارض 'the slave kisses the ground', or variants thereof, are strategies of the writer to express that he is in the virtual presence of the addressee. Such formulas, which present the writer as having a virtual audience before the addressee, are a feature of petitions and other documents addressed to the Fatimid rulers (Khan 2008, 893–95). The obeisance formula was introduced into petitions during the reign of al-ʾĀmir (495–524 AH/1101–1130 AD). It is not found in petitions to earlier Fatimid caliphs (Khan 1990, 24–26). The introduction of the formula at the time of al-ʾĀmir appears to reflect a development in Fatimid court ceremonial protocol in his reign, whereby the custom of kissing the ground in the presence of the caliph was reintroduced after having been discontinued for some time. This is alluded to in the chronicle of the vizier Ibn al-Maʾmūn al-Baṭāʾiḥī (Fuʾād Sayyid 1983, 21):

> اجتمع امرا الدولة لتقبيل الارض بين يدى الخليفة الامر على العادة التى قررها مستجدة
>
> 'The ʾ*amīrs* of the state gathered to kiss the ground before the caliph al-ʾĀmir according to the custom that he had re-established.'

There are, however, some differences from documents addressed to Fatimid rulers. Petitions and documents addressed to Fatimid rulers do not use the verb اعلم in their openings. Furthermore, blessings opening with the formula اطال الله بقاه are not used in documents addressed to Fatimid rulers. It is, however, used in letters addressed to Fatimid dignitaries below the rank of ruler (Khan 1993a, 310), e.g., T–S 28.8 (ALAD 98, two petitions to Fatimid judges) and T–S Ar.4.10 (ALAD 97, a petition to a Fatimid dignitary). Absent from the blessings is the verb خَلَّدَ 'may He make eternal', which is a distinctive feature of the blessings on Fatimid viziers, who became the de facto rulers in the late Fatimid period (Khan 1993a, 308–9), e.g., خلد الله تعالى ملك المجلس العالى 'may God, the exalted, make eternal the rule of the lofty seat' (T–S Ar.39.391, ALAD 82, petition to the vizier Ibn al-Sallār)

The openings of letters to the eparch, therefore, exhibit some characteristics of letters to Fatimid dignitaries and rulers.

It is worth noting that contemporary Nubian letters often open with the expression of obeisance 'I pay homage to you' as if the writer were in a virtual audience (Ruffini 2016a), indicating that the Arabic formulas of obeisance would be what was expected in Nubian society.

Some of the letters do not present the address to the recipient as a virtual audience in the spatio-temporal situation of the addressee, but rather open the letter with a verb in the *qatala* form, which is idiomatically translated by an English present perfect, e.g., وصل 'has arrived', توجه 'has set off'. The deixis of such verbs is not to a virtual audience before the addressee, but rather to the spatio-temporal situation of the writer. They thus express physical separation from the addressee. This is a characteristic of most letters that are not addressed to the eparch in the corpus (§4.6.1).

3.6.2. Closure

The letters to and from the eparch typically close with formulaic expressions of politeness, including the following.

3.6.2.1. Offer of Service in Return for a Request

> So may his (the Ikšīl's) letter be dispatched to me with (instructions) for me to execute (a service) for his sake, for I am ready to execute that for him. I am grateful to him for this, if God wills, the Mighty and Magnificent. (**1**r:8–1, margin, 1)

> If you have any need, write to me concerning it, if God, the Mighty and Glorious, wills. (**5**v:2)

If you have any need, write to me and let me know about it, if God, the Exalted and Majestic, wills it. (**6**r, margin, 1–2)

So, may the Ikšīl (send) a letter and do not omit to ask me in it to carry out his needs. (**8**r:14)

Is the Ikšīl not in need of something? Let him give instruction for it to be carried out and I would be grateful (for the opportunity to do the service), if God, the Mighty and Magnificent, wills. Praise be to God alone. (**10**r, margin, 1–5)

Whatever needs your illustrious honour has, I am committed to carrying out your needs and obeying your instruction. (**16**v:1–2)

Whatever request you have, write to me, and I shall carry it out and perform my duty, whether it be small or large. (**20**r:11–12)

Whatever need you have, you would please me by allowing me to carry it out. (**22**r:18–margin, 1)

3.6.2.2. Request for the Sending of News

Send me your news. (**9**v:21)

Do not delay sending letters to me about your news. (**16**r:16)

Your slave (i.e., the writer) kisses your hand and legs, and warmly welcomes a letter from your honour. (**18**r:12–13, letter from Uruwī)

I request that he writes—for which I would be most grateful—concerning his news and his situation. I would be glad of that and delighted, if God wills. (**19**r:7–8)

3.6.2.3. Sending of Greetings

I send to you warmest greetings and also to those within your care greetings.' (**7**r:9–10)

I send the honourable Master of the Horses the warmest greetings, the purest love and respect, wishes for future good, if God wills. (**15**v:5–7)

3.6.2.4. Closure Formulas

Such expressions of politeness are then generally followed by various formulaic elements. These include:

(i) The *ḥamdala* (الحمد لله وحده 'praise be to God alone')

(ii) Blessings on the Prophet Muḥammad (with slight variations), e.g.,

وصلواته على سيدنا محمد نبيه واله وسلام

'and His (God's) blessings be upon our Lord Muḥammad, His prophet, and his family, and peace' (**2**r, margin, 1)

وصلواته على سيدنا محمد نبينا وسلامه

'and His blessings on our Lord Muḥammad, our prophet, and His peace' (**4**v:6)

وصلواته على سيدنا محمد نبيه وسلامه

'and His blessings on our Lord Muḥammad, his prophet, and His peace' (**5**v:3–4)

وصلواته على محمد ومن خلفه وصحبه وسلم تسليما وسلامه

'and His blessings be upon Muḥammad, those who succeeded him and companions, and may He save (them), and His peace' (**19**r:9)

(iii) The *ḥasbala* (حسبنا الله ونعم الوكيل 'Our sufficiency is God. What a fine keeper is He!'). This is omitted in **26** (letter to al-Bazīl, the deputy of the eparch Darmā).

3.6.3. Postscripts

Several letters contain postscript notes after the formulaic closure, e.g., **2**v:1–8; **4**v:7–8 (separated from text above by a check mark); **16**v:3–4; **17**v:1–4; **24**v, margin, 1–2.

4. OTHER CORRESPONDENCE AND ACCOUNTS

4.1. Correspondents

Letters **28–40** are not sent to the eparch or his office, but rather constitute miscellaneous pieces of correspondence. Most of these are within the Muslim community. Letter **36** appears to be addressed to some kind of Nubian official. Document **41** is a poetic description by the writer of his journey on a boat, presumably on the route between Aswan and Nubia. Documents **42** and **43** are business accounts. We learn from letter **9** that such accounts were enclosed with letters:

> A record of the goods and their purchase is enclosed in this letter of mine. It has been inserted with a note of all expenditure. (**9**r:22–23)

Letters **28–34** are addressed by merchants to high-ranking dignitaries. The addressee of **28** and **29** is identified as an *ʾamīr* 'commander'. Letter **28** was addressed to the *ʾamīr* Ḥiṣn al-Dawla. This is likely to be Ḥiṣn al-Dawla ibn al-ʿAsqalānī, who was the writer of letter **13** and the man called Ibn al-ʿAsqalānī who is reported in letter **9** to be at the court of the Nubian king. Letter **29** is addressed to *al-ʾamīr ʾIbrīm*, which presumably means 'the commander at Ibrīm'. The address of this letter is الى ابريم ان شا الله 'to Ibrīm, God willing'.

The addressees of letters **30–34** are not explicitly identified as *ʾamīr*s, but are shown to be dignitaries of some kind by the lofty terms of address in the opening or by their contents, e.g.,

https://doi.org/10.11647/OBP.0391.04

حضرة مولاى حضرة مولاى الشيخ الاجل اطال الله بقاه وادام عزه وعلاءه
وضعف سناه وتمكينه وكبت بالذل حسدته واعداه

> 'My honourable lord, the most illustrious elder, may God prolong his life and cause his strength and his ascendance to endure, and double his splendour and his power, and crush in humility his enviers and his enemies.' (**30**r:2–3)

حضرة مولاي الشيخ الاجل اطال الله بقاها وادام تاييدها وعلاها ورفعتها
وسناها وسموها وارتقاها وكبت بالذل المهين حسدتها واعداها

> 'My honourable master, the most illustrious elder, may God prolong his life and cause his strength, his exaltedness, his ascendance, his splendour, his loftiness and his elevation to endure, and crush in vile humility his enviers and enemies.' (**31**r:2–4)

حضرة مولاى وولى واخى على اطال الله بقاها وادام سموها وسناها وتمكينها
وكبت حسدتها وعداها

> 'My honourable master, my friend and brother, ʿAlī, may God prolong his life and cause his exaltedness, his splendour and his power to endure, and crush his enviers and enemies.' (**34**r:3–4)

In the address of **30**, it is stated that the sender was "Manṣūr ibn Lāmiʿ ibn Ḥasan, by the order of Ḵalīfa ibn Ḥasan." This was, presumably, the son of Lāmiʿ ibn Ḥasan al-Kanzī, who was the sender of several of the letters to eparchs (**3**, **4**, **5**, **6**, **9**, **12**). The address also contains the phrase ليصل ابريم 'May it reach Ibrīm'.

Letters **35–40**, as far as can be seen from their surviving addresses and opening formulas, were addressed to people of lower rank or no clear official rank. The recipient of letter **36** appears to have been some kind of Nubian official. The sender of this letter was Lāmiʿ ibn Ḥasan al-Kanzī, who, as remarked, was the sender of several of the letters to eparchs. The other letters of this group appear to be correspondence between friends or family members.

As can be seen, therefore, some of the senders of the letters of the group **28–40** were members of the Banū al-Kanz. The Kanz al-Dawla and Kanzī officials are mentioned in the body of a number of the letters of this group, e.g.,

> I inform you, my son, that I had sent you the advance consignment immediately after asking the commander, Kanz al-Dawla, may He cause his power to endure, (to dispatch it). (**29**r:4–5)

> So, talk to him and inform him that the author of the letter brought by Ṭāʾī is an elder sent by the judge. He is the deputising son of the Kanzī judge. (**30**r, margin, 15–17)

> If the ruler, may God strengthen his victory, has validly received their poll-tax, through the services of the Pride of the Arabs, Kanz al-Dawla, may God cause his elevation to endure, he knows what the ruler, may God strengthen his victory, has undertaken to support the livelihood of the two from the one who sold them and the ruler's son, the exalted, glorious, noble, rightly-guided and powerful presence, who safeguarded their return, gathered (funds) for supporting their families that could be lived off. (**32**:2–4)

> I, God willing, shall go to ʿUbayd, Kanz al-Dawla, the Greatest of the Progeny, the Noble One. May God, the Mighty and Glorious, preserve the brotherhood that is between us. (**33**:4)

The correspondents of letters **28–40** are summarised in the table below:

Table 5: Correspondents of letters **28–40**

	Sender	Recipient
28	—	—
29	ʿAbd al-Karīm ibn al-Ḥasan	ʾAbū al-Qāsim Hibat Allāh ibn Muḥammad ibn al-ʾAʿmā
30	Manṣūr ibn Lāmiʿ ibn Ḥasan	ʾAbū Muḥammad ʿĪsā ibn Muḥammad ibn Ḥasan
31	—	—
32	—	—
33	—	—
34	Muḥammad ibn ʿUbayd Allāh ibn al-Ḥasan ibn ʿAlī	ʾAbū al-Ḥasan ʿAlī ibn ʾAbū al-Ṭāhir ʿUbayd Allāh ibn ʾAbī Turʿa
35	ʿAlī ibn Muṣʿab	ʾAbū Finjān ibn Fakka
36	Lāmiʿ ibn Ḥasan al-Kanzī	al-Qarṭamaq Mašal al-Farīk
37	Jāmiʿ	Ḵalīl, ʿUmar and ʿUṯmān
38	Muḥammad ibn ʾAbū Ḥayy	Danī ibn Kannān
39	—	Bū Ḥasan
40	—	—

4.2. Overview of Subject Matter

The letters belonging to the group of correspondence **28–40** relate to various topics. As expected, the dominant focus in many of the letters is trade, typically with copious references to specific commodities and monetary payments. Some letters allude to relations with the eparch and the Nubian king. Letter **38** describes problems with agricultural cultivation in an *ʾiqṭāʿ* situated on an island and requests the help of the addressee to find more cultivators. The writer says

> They... moved the plough from the island and took it to the town of Edfu. (**38**:8–9)

On the other side of the letter, there is a document of lease (**44**) that records the lease of a share of the property of Danī ibn Kannān on "the island known as ʾAbū Fāris to the west of the border of Nubia." This suggests that the island mentioned in **38** was in Egypt close to the border of Nubia.

Several letters are of a personal nature and include expressions of emotion to the writer's family and friends. The writer of letter **30** describes how he has been in pursuit of two runaway servants, who fled to Nubia.

4.3. Relations with the Nubian King

There are references to relations with the Nubian king in letters **33** and **39**. Various passages in letter **33** indicate that the addressee, whose identity is not clear, acted as an intermediary between the writer and the Nubian king, e.g.,

> This is so that you be aware of it so that I can have an audience with the king. Please bring us to my lord the king, God willing.... for you are the conveyor of my letter to my father and to my honourable lord the king. (**33**:5–6)

The addressee is evidently a high-ranking Muslim dignitary, presumably an *ʾamīr*, and not the eparch, who would normally be expected to convey letters to the king. This is shown by passages such as the following in the letter, which indicates that the addressee's father was an *ʾamīr*:

> my father commanded me that when I needed any instructions, we should write to your father, the commander (*ʾamīr*) on the desert river. (**33**:2–3)

The letter refers to the renewal of the governorship of his father by the Nubian king. Presumably what is intended is the authority for his father to command the operations of the Muslims within Nubia:

> I inform you, may God give you life, that the king, may God give him life, has renewed the governorship (*al-wilāya*) of my father. The king said (this) to him when he admitted the man arriving with him. (**33**, margin, 1)

If this interpretation of **33** is correct, then it suggests that high-ranking Muslim dignitaries had privileged access to the king.

Letter **39** was written by a Muslim merchant who had travelled to Soba to deliver merchandise to the Nubian king and his army, but at the time of writing the king had not yet made an appearance:

> If the king had come to us in Soba, we would not have stayed in the country more than a month or two months, but… (We are) with the merchandise that we have for the king and his army, but we have found that there is only little (business) in the land. (**39**r:8–10)

The precise content of the merchandise for the king's army is not specified. Some letters of the corpus refer to the delivery to the eparch of military equipment including "the helmet (*al-ḵūḏa*),… the three scabbards (*qurub*) and the spear (*al-rumḥ*)" (**31**v:1). Gabriel Gerhards (personal communication) has suggested that the goods that the merchant supplied to the king may have included mail armour. Fragments of this, greatly corroded, have been discovered in excavations in Soba (Daniels and Welsby 1991, figures 65, 109).

The writer of **39** says he misses his family, but does not seem to be the only Muslim visitor to the region, as suggested by the following passage:

> Please make an effort to send us your news with whomsoever may happen to travel to the land of Nubia. We would be happy about that and be able to be informed about what he knows about your situation. We are only meeting one another by chance. (**39**r:7–8)

According to al-ʾAswānī, who visited Nubia in the second half of the tenth century, there was a Muslim quarter in Soba (Kheir 1989, 53). Already al-Yaʿqūbī (d. 292 AH/897–8 AD) states that Muslims visited Soba (*Kitāb al-Buldān*, 174).

Letter **39** is unusual in that it provides the exact date on which it was written:

> We arrived in Soba in the last ten days of the month of Ramaḍān in the year four-hundred and eighty-five (1092 AD). I am writing this letter on the tenth day of Shawwāl (18th November 1092 AD). (**39**r:11–12)

Letter **30** describes how he pursued two runaway servants (*ḵādimayn*) but turned back at the Nubian border, indicating that Muslims, in principle, required permission to enter Nubia:

> When I was notified that they had arrived in his (the eparch's) land, I turned back (from my pursuit of) them. (**30**r:8)

4.4. Grain for Nubians

Letter **36**, which appears to be addressed to some kind of Nubian official, refers to shipment of grain to Nubia:

> The lack of produce this year has not been concealed from you and the condition of the people. No ship would have been sent this year, had I not opened the store and sold to the people of your land. (**36**r:6–8)

This appears to be referring to a shortage of grain in Nubia. The delivery of grain to Nubia by the Muslims was one of the terms of the *baqṭ* treaty (cf. al-Maqrīzī, *Ḵiṭaṭ*, I:370). There are several extant Nubian documents containing disbursement orders of grain issued by the eparch (e.g., P. QI II 23, P. QI III 49, P. QI IV 94). These disbursements, which show that the eparch was responsible for the supply of grain, were apparently from public stores or the eparch's personal store (Adams 1996, 226–27).

It is significant that the passage in letter **36** indicates that the grain was sold to the Nubians. As was discussed above (§2.5.4), in the period in which the letters were written, the mutual obligations of Muslims and the Nubians were contracted between individuals, as suggested by a passage in letter **9**:

> Does not the Master of the Horses think that what has brought me and you together close in the presence of the bishop is that I provide him with provisions and I remain in the service of the king and the protection of your companions? (**9**r, margin, 11–v:1)

4.5. Trade

The letters of this group of correspondence refer to numerous commodities of trade. These include herbs and spices, clothes and textiles, jewellery, furniture, fuel and military equipment (see §8 for a full list), which, it seems, were intended for shipment to

Nubia. This range of commodities also appears in the accounts **42** and **43**.

There are also references in the letters to slaves and slave girls, which would have been received from Nubia. Letter **37** refers to the lack of slaves in Aswan:

> As for slaves (*al-raqīq*), there is nothing in Aswan, or only a few. By God, bring your slave girl with you. (**37**v:4–6)

Letter **31**v:4 mentions the acquisition of a 'freedman' (*mawlā*).

Letter **30** refers to what appears to be a business partnership (*šarika*), which includes the writer's slave boy (*ġulām*):

> Inform the Master of the Horses about the person who is with you and tell him that he (the person with you) is the son of the sister of the judge, Nūr al-Dīn, and he is a member of the partnership (*al-šarika*) of which Nūr al-Dīn is a member. (**30**r:15–16)

> I have brought into partnership (*ʾašraktu*) with him my wife and my slave boy, Ramaḍān and Rāšid, the mariner (*al-baḥḥār*), who is with him and those of the Nubians [ ] (**30**r, margin, 6–9)

This letter also mentions a 'partner' (*šarīk*), presumably a 'business partner':

> Moreover, I would not have desisted from travelling to Ibrīm in the current situation, but I did not know whether I had a friend or acquaintance in it (Ibrīm) after you departed from it upriver and Ṭāʿī was absent. So I desisted from coming to the partner (*al-šarīk*), because I did not dare, and, moreover, he could not have helped me (anyhow). (**30**r:10–11)

Letter **29** refers to the advance consignment of goods (*al-ʿīna*). This appears to have been a delivery of goods that the recipient of the letter had paid for in advance:

> I inform you, my son, that I had sent you the advance consignment immediately after asking the commander, Kanz al-Dawla, may He cause his power to endure (to dispatch it), and he sent it with a reliable person indicating that he would meet ʿAbd al-Bāqī and deliver it to him. He went on part of the way, but then returned, and it (the advance consignment) has remained with us until this day. I have (now) sent it to you with ʿAbd al-Bāqī. It contains nine *raṭls*.... I paid to ʿAbd al-Bāqī a sixth of a dīnār apart from the fee for the credit (*ʾujrat al-ʿīna*) that would remain with you of an eighth of a dīnār. (**29**r:4–9, 17–18)

The letters and accounts use the units of measure *raṭl* (blue wool **34**r:8; herbs and spices, bitumen **43**) and *wayba* (cartham seed **43**v:1).

In the Fatimid period, several *raṭls* were used. The one used for weighing bread and meat was 144 dirhams, i.e., 444.9 g. The one used for spices (called *raṭl fulfulī*, pepper *raṭl*) and also for cotton was 150 dirhams, i.e., 463 g. The one used for flax, which was called *raṭl layṯī*, was 200 dirhams, i.e., 617.96 g. The one used for honey, sugar, cheese and metals, which was called *raṭl jarwī*, was 312 *dirhams*; i.e., 964 g (Ashtor and Burton-Page 2012). A *wayba* was 15 litres (1/6 of an *ʾirdabb*) or 11.6 kg of wheat (Hinz 1955, 52).

As in the letters to eparchs, in the correspondence **28–40** there is frequent mention of the buying and selling of commodities by monetary transactions.

There are references to the sending of cash payments, which are typically referred to by the term *ḥaqq ʿayn*, i.e., cash to pay what is due, e.g.,

> What I have sent is a cash payment (*ḥaqq ʿayn*). This is because, when ʿUbayd Allāh decided to travel to you, I sent this enclosed with it for you quickly in haste. (**33**:16–17)

In some cases, a commodity is substituted for cash payment, as seen in the following passage. The writer feels obliged to apologise, which indicates that cash was the preferred means of payment:

> I have sent with the bearer of the letter a dyed garment (*musaqqaʿ*) in place of the payment in cash (*ḥaqq ʿayn*). Please forgive me. (**36**v:2–3)

Letter **30** refers to the wages (*nafaqa*) that are due to the writer from the addressee, indicating that there was an employment relationship:

> I have been informed that I shall not have my wages from him (the addressee) (*nafaqatuhu*) until when he returns. (**30**r:8)

The standard means of transportation of goods by the merchants that is mentioned in this group of letters is the river boat, referred generically as *markab* (pl. *marākib*).

The merchants were typically passengers and the boats were navigated by a crew. This is clear from the poetic description of a voyage on a boat in **41**. In letter **30**, there is a reference to "Rāšid, the mariner (*al-baḥḥār*)" (**30**r, margin, 7). Merchants had to pay for transport by boat, as seen in **31**:

> I asked (them to allow me) to come with them and all that has prevented me is the cost of the transport. It is not appropriate for me to go up (the river) and leave the cost of the transport behind me (i.e., without paying it). (**31**r:6–8)

The legal document **45** records the lease by two Muslim merchants of a light boat known as a *zallāj* 'gliding boat', which appears to have been navigated by them alone.

Passages in letters **31** and **37** indicate that merchants sometimes travelled on land by horse (*ḥiṣān*). Various overland routes were available, the main one from Ibrīm to Aswan being via the oasis of Kurkur in the western desert (Paprocki 2019; Ducène 2007; Davies and Welsby 2020). The journey, however, was evidently very gruelling:

> As for other matters, I journeyed beyond al-Marīs and arrived at Aswan. My horse (*ḥiṣānī*) was covered in dust (and exhausted). (**31**r:4–5)

> For God's sake, encourage one of your group to come to me, for my horse is weak and I cannot come to you. (**31**v:2–3)

> What I wish to inform you of is that I have arrived in Aswan and both I and the horse (*al-ḥiṣān*) are exhausted. (**37**r:4–5)

Horses were sometimes transported by boat, as seen in the following passage from **37**:

> Come only in a boat (*markab*). Do not bring a horse (*faras*). When you come down (the river), take my horse and go back up (the river). (**37**v:7–9)

The writer of letter **30** indicates that he hired the services of a muleteer:

> I hired a muleteer (*mukārī*) and travelled to the person who is his (the commander's?) lieutenant (*k̲alīfatuhu*). (**30**v:6)

For rapid travel, camels were used, as seen in letter **30**, in which the writer describes his hot pursuit of runaway servants:

> After the flight of the servant, I rode a Nubian camel throughout the day and night and I did not rely on any of the servants to undertake the search for them. (**30**v:2–3)

The Muslim merchants preferred to avoid travelling during the fast of Ramaḍān:

> The only reason I did not come to you after you arrived was that I wanted to spend the fast of Ramaḍān with my family. (**30**v:1)

Letter **34** refers to a caravanserai (*k̲ān*), which appears to have been used by visiting merchants on their travels:

> On another matter, I have sent to you by the conveyer of this letter (*mūṣil hād̲ā al-kitāb*) a *raṭl* of blue wool (*ṣūf ʾaz-raq*) to the caravanserai (*k̲ān*) of Fatḥ the dyer (*al-ṣabbāġ*), (**34**r:7–8)

4.6. The Structure of the Letters

4.6.1. Opening

Letter **35** opens with the abbreviation بسملة *basmala* rather than the full formula.

Letter **31**, which is addressed to a dignitary, opens with the present tense verb اعلم 'I inform', which is a feature of the letters to eparchs:

اعلم حضرة مولاي الشيخ الاجل

'I inform my honourable master, the most illustrious elder…' (**31**r:2)

Most letters of this group, however, open with the formula كتابى '(This is) my letter', e.g.,

كتابى الى حضرة مولاى وولى واخى على

'(This is) my letter to my honourable master, my friend and brother, ʿAlī.' (**34**r:3)

كتابى الى اخى وسيدى واعز الخلق على وعندى

'(This is) my letter to my brother and my lord, the dearest person to me.' (**35**r:2)

كتابى الى الأخ خليل وللاخ عثمان وعمر

'(This is) my letter to my brother Ḵalīl and my brother ʿUṯmān and ʿUmar.' (**37**r:2–3)

كتابى اليك يا والدى والعزيز على وعندى

'(This is) my letter to you, my father, who is dear to me.' (**38**r:2)

كتابى اليك يا والدى والعزيز على

'(This is) my letter to you, my father, who is dear to me.' (**39**r:2)

Letter **29** opens with the formula كتبت اليك 'I have written to you', which has a similar sense to كتابى اليك:

كتبت اليك يا ولدى العزيز على الامير ابريم

'I have written to you, my son, who is dear to me, the commander (at) Ibrīm.' (**29**r:2)

Letter **36** opens with the report of the arrival of a letter:

كان كتاب الخليفة مشل انكرة سلمه الله وصلنى على يد عبيده

'The letter of the lieutenant Mašal Ankara, may God keep him safe, has reached me by the hand of his servants.' (**36**r:2–3)

Letter **40** opens with a request for news:

اسال عن اخباركم فيسرنى سماعى لما اختار منها

'I (write to) ask about your news, for it would make me happy to hear something of this that I would treasure.' (**40**:2)

The addressee is addressed by various titles expressing respect and affection, as seen in the examples above. The titles of the addressees of letters **31** and **34**, who are dignitaries, include the term *ḥaḍra* 'presence'. The kinship terms والدى 'my father' and الاخ/اخى 'my brother/brother' are likely metaphorical expressions of endearment. The term ولدى 'my son' in the opening formula of **29** may be a genuine kinship relationship. Alternatively, it could be a term of endearment to a person who is younger than the sender. The phrase ولدى occurs twice in a list of greetings at the end of **34** (v:1, 2), where it seems indeed to be a kinship relationship. It is relevant to note, however, that in **17**, which is a letter from the eparch Uruwī, the eparch addresses the Muslim merchant in the opening formula as ولدى. Here it is difficult to interpret the word as a genuine kinship relation. There is always the possibility, however, that the orthography is defective and والدى 'my father' was intended.

The blessings after the addressee's title are similar to those in the letters of the correspondence with the eparch. The first formula is 'may God prolong his/your/their life' (اطال الله بقاه, اطال الله بقاك, اطال الله بقاهم, اطال الله بقاها). This is followed by an assortment of further blessings, which vary according to the status of the addressee. Letters to dignitaries typically have blessings expressing wishes for the preservation of the addressee's high office, e.g.,

اطال الله بقاها وادام سموها وسناها وتمكينها وكبت حسدتها وعداها

> 'May God prolong his life and cause his exaltedness, his splendour and his power to endure, and crush his enviers and enemies.' (**34**r:3–4)

اطال الله بقاه وادام تاييده وعلاه ورفعته سناه

> 'May God prolong his life and cause to endure his strength, his elevation, his ascendance and his splendour.' (**35**r:2–3)

4.6.2. Closure

The letters of this group close with the three formulaic elements that are found in the correspondence with the eparch, namely (i) the *ḥamdala,* (ii) blessings on the prophet Muḥammad and (iii) the *ḥasbala.* In **29**, only the *ḥasbala* occurs. In **30**, the blessings on the prophet are omitted.

5. LEGAL DOCUMENTS

5.1. Document 44: Lease of Land (Rajab 518 AH/ August 1124 AD)[1]

This document records a lease by a certain Raḥma ibn Saʿīd, from a man called Danī ibn Kannān, of shares of land in Danī's estate (*ʾiqṭāʿ*), which was assigned to him by 'the office of the (Fatimid) ruler' (*dīwān al-sulṭān*). The sheet of paper on which the document was written also contains letter **38**, which was addressed to Danī ibn Kannān. Letter **38** is likely to have been written first, with the address on the verso, and the legal document **44** was subsequently written in the space under the address. In the legal document, Danī has the gentilic al-Šaḵriyābī. This relates to Wādī al-Šaḵriyābī, which is mentioned in an Arabic document from the Ottoman period found at Qaṣr Ibrīm (Hinds and Sakkout 1986, document no. 27). In this Ottoman document, Wādī al-Šaḵriyābī is said to be *min ʿamal ʾIbrīm* 'in the administrative district of Ibrīm'. In letter **38**, Danī has the title *al-ʿaqīd*, which appears to have denoted a 'military officer'. In Fatimid Egypt, an *ʾiqṭāʿ* typically consisted of agricultural land leased to a military grantee (*muqṭaʿ*) for a sum of money payable to the treasury (see §9.16).

It is indicated in document **44** that the estate was located on the island of ʾAbū Fāris lying 'to the west of the border of

---

[1] I published a preliminary edition of this document in Khan (2013). Several of the readings in the present edition differ from those of the preliminary edition.

 https://doi.org/10.11647/OBP.0391.05

Nubia' (بالغرب من حد النوبة). This seems to indicate that the estate was on one of the islands in the area of the first cataract of the Nile lying to the west of the border of Nubia, which was situated at the village of al-Qaṣr on the east bank of the Nile just south of Bilāq (Philae; §2.5.4). The *ʾiqṭāʿ* estate, which was bestowed by the Fatimid government, must have been outside of Nubian territory.

The 'office of the ruler' (*dīwān al-sulṭān*) was presumably the *dīwān al-ʾiqṭāʿāt*, which is mentioned by al-Maḵzūmī (*Kitāb al-Minhāj*, 70).

The lessee leased "three shares from twenty-four shares in total, held in common." This division into twenty-four shares is connected with the laws of inheritance, in which the shares of the heirs are calculated in twenty-fourths (Grohmann, APEL I, 172). This lease of land from an *ʾiqṭāʿ* was a form of subletting, whereby the lessee had right to three parts out of twenty-four of the income on the land.

The lessor, Danī ibn Kannān, was evidently not resident on the land. The fragmentary address of letter **38** reads "[The land] of Marīs... to the leader Danī ibn Kannān," which suggests that Danī was resident in Marīs. This would explain why the document containing **38** and **44** was found in Qaṣr Ibrīm. Furthermore, Wādī al-Šaḵriyābī, to which Danī's *nisba* relates, was situated within the administrative district of Ibrīm. A *muqṭaʿ* frequently lived away from his *ʾiqṭāʿ* (Rabie 1972, 63). We have here, therefore, the case of a Fatimid military officer resident in Nubia. The writer of letter **38** to Danī calls himself in the address "his (i.e., Danī's) son (*waladihi*), Muḥammad ibn ʾAbū Ḥayy." The fact that the writer was called Muḥammad indicates that he was a Muslim. This may imply that Danī was a Muslim. The term *walad,* however, is often used in the letters as a polite metaphorical term to designate somebody of subordinate status, so Danī may have been a Nubian Christian, which is what his name suggests. If so, then we would have here a case of a Nubian resident in Nubia who served as a Fatimid military officer.

The letter **38**, which mentions agriculture, is presumably referring to the cultivation of the *ʾiqṭāʿ* in question.

The lease is for a period of one year "beginning in (the Coptic month of) Kīhak (December–January)." The name Kīhak is a variant name of the Coptic month name Koiak, which is also spelt كياك in Arabic. The use of a Coptic month to specify the start date was due to the fact that the collection of land tax (*k̲arāj*) was calculated according to the *k̲arājī* year, which corresponded to the Coptic solar year consisting of 365 days. The Muslim lunar (*hilālī*) year was shorter than the *k̲arājī* year by approximately eleven days. Thirty-three lunar years corresponded to thirty-two solar years (Ibn Mammātī [d. 606 AH/1209 AD], *Kitāb Qawānīn al-Dawāwīn,* 358). Land tax (*k̲arāj*) related to agricultural produce and was collected seasonally at the time of the harvest, i.e., according to the solar year. The administration of the *k̲arāj*, however, worked with lunar years. In order to prevent complications, the solar year was periodically brought into line with the lunar year. This was achieved by disregarding one solar year every thirty-three lunar years. The operation was termed تحويل السنة الخراجية الى السنة الهلالية (al-Qalqašandī [d. 821 AH/1418 AD], *Ṣubḥ al-ʾAʿšā,* XIII:54–55). The last *taḥwīl* of the Fatimid period was undertaken by al-ʾAfḍal ibn Badr al-Jamālī in 501 AH/1107–8 AD. Before this, it had been neglected for about 132 years, with the result that the lunar year had overtaken the solar year by four years. The Fatimids failed to issue an order for a *taḥwīl* when it fell due in 534 AH/1139–40 AD, which resulted in a two-year gap between the lunar year and the *ḵarājī* year in 567 AH/1171–72 AD after the fall of the Fatimid régime (Rabie 1972, 133–34). Letter **38**, which is addressed to Danī ibn Kannān and is written on the back of the sheet, relates to cultivation and mentions that the harvest will be in the month of Baramhāt, i.e., the Coptic month corresponding to March–April.

In line 7, it is stated that the lessor received the rent from the lessee in full (تاما وافيا). In line 8, however, it is indicated that the lessor allowed the lessee to pay in instalments. The phraseology referring to receipt in full must be a slavish use of a fixed formula that was not appropriate in this particular case. A similar contradiction of a formula expressing full receipt with the reality of only a partial receipt is found in the acknowledgement document **47**v.

The structure of document **44** corresponds broadly to that of extant documents of lease from Fatimid Egypt (Khan 1993a, 143–47). The components consist of:

1. *Basmala*
2. Opening formula
   The document opens with the formula استاجر فلان من فلان 'so-and-so leased from so-and-so'. Muslim legal documents were declarative instruments. The transactions were described in an objective style with the parties referred to

in the third person. In documents of lease, the transaction is written from the point of view of the lessee (*al-mustaʾjir*).

Most extant documents of lease from the Fatimid period open with a demonstrative pronoun: هذا ما استاجر فلان من فلان 'this is what so-and-so leased from so-and-so'. This is the case also in contemporary documents of sale, which typically open هذا ما اشترى فلان من فلان 'this is what so-and-so bought from so-and-so'. The formula with the demonstrative pronoun is likely to be the original one. The demonstrative pronoun and the objective style arose from the fact that the legal formularies had their roots in monumental types of legal text, which were originally intended for public display. The demonstrative pronoun originally referred to the object on which the text was inscribed. The exophoric reference of the demonstrative of the original monumental formula to a surrounding physical structure on which an inscription was written was subsequently transferred to the textual object of a document (Khan 2019). Documents of lease that open directly with the verb استاجر are attested in other sources (Khan 1993a, 143).

3. Identification of the parties
4. Identification of the property that is leased
5. Specification of the period of lease
6. Amount of rent and terms of payment
7. Constituent acts of the transaction
8. Warranty

The documents lack the following components that are characteristic of documents of lease:

Validity formula (اجارة صحيحة 'with a valid lease')
Specification of the rights of the lessee
Indication that the parties separated physically after the transaction
Confirmation that the transaction was witnessed
Witness clauses

The lack of witness clauses is surprising. The validity of a legal transaction was dependent on it being witnessed by accredited witnesses (*ʿudūl*). Documents of lease typically include autograph testimonies of witnesses consisting of a declaration that the witness has testified to the acknowledgement by the lessor and the lessee of the contents of the document, e.g., شهد فلان على اقرار الآجر والمستاجر بما فيه 'so-and-so testified to the acknowledgement of the lessor and the lessee of what is in it' (Khan 1993a, 147). The lack of witness clauses may reflect that the doucument was a copy of an original that was made as private record.

The structure of the warranty clause in the document requires some comment, since it contains an archaism for the period.

The structure of Arabic legal formulas developed over time. Major changes were made in the Abbasid period. The changes originated for the most part in the Abbasid heartlands in Iraq in formularies that were developed by Islamic legal scholars. The new Arabic formulaic structures were disseminated across the Islamic world (Khan 1994). They were first introduced in the Abbasid heartlands in Iraq and the eastern Islamic provinces, then spread westwards to Egypt. As a consequence of this process of development, the formulae of documents in peripheral geographical areas were liable to preserve at a particular historical period archaic features that had been replaced in more central areas. This is reflected not only in the aforementioned movement of formulae from the Islamic heartlands in the east to Egypt in the west, but also within Egypt itself.

Previous research on medieval Arabic legal documents from Egypt has shown that innovations that appear in legal documents in the political centre in Fusṭāṭ and Cairo are not found at the same period in documents from Upper Egypt, which preserve more archaic structures (Khan 1993a, 7–55).

The first cataract of the Nile was on the periphery of the Islamic world. According to the trends in the development of formulae described above, the Arabic legal documents written there would be expected to preserve features that had been replaced in the political centre in Fusṭāṭ and Cairo. This is indeed reflected by the warranty clause in document **44**, which has preserved an early feature that is no longer found in legal documents further north in Egypt.

Document **44** contains (in lines 9–11) the following warranty formula against a claim from a third party:

فما ادرك المستاجر المذكور من درك من ديوان السلطان اعز الله نصره او من احد من الناس كلهم كان على هذا دنو بن كنان خلاصه والخروج اليه ما يلزمه حكم شروط المسلمين وضمانهم

'Whatever claim comes upon the aforementioned lessee from the Office of the Ruler, may God strengthen his victory, or from anybody, it is the duty of Danī ibn Kannān to

> clear it and pay him what is required by the law of the legal instruments of the Muslims and their warranty.'

It is significant that the government 'Office of the Ruler' is presented in the warranty as a potential source of a claim. This would, therefore, be a guarantee against an objection by the government to the subletting of land of the *ʾiqṭāʿ*.

The earliest documentary attestation of such a warranty clause is found in a document datable to the middle of the second century AH/eighth century AD from Khurasan (145 AH/762 AD; Khan 2007, 141–43, document 25):

فما ادراكك من سبل ابرهيم او غيره فعلى خلاصه بما عسر وهان

> 'Whatever claim comes upon you from ʾIbrāhīm or anybody else, it is my duty to clear it with whatever (is necessary), be it difficult (for me to pay) or easy.'

Such warranties are characteristic of transactions of sale or leases of landed property. The formula of this document from Khurasan is close to the formula of the warranty clause of documents of sale that is recommended by the second-century Iraqi jurists. ʾAbū Ḥanīfa (d. 150 AH/767 AD) and ʾAbū Yūsuf Yaʿqūb (d. 182 AH/798 AD) proposed the following formula:

فما ادرك فلان بن فلان فى ذلك من درك فعلى فلان بن فلان خلاص ذلك او رد الثمن

> 'Whatever claim is made against so-and-so son of so-and-so, it is the duty of so-and-so son of so-and-so to clear that or return the price.'[2]

---

[2] This has been preserved in al-Ṭaḥāwī's *Kitāb al-Šurūṭ al-Kabīr* (ed. Wakin 1972, Text 21).

The formula of Yūsuf ibn Ḵālid (d. 189 AH/805 AD) and his pupil Hilāl ibn Yaḥyā was (Wakin 1972, Text 21):

فما ادرك فى هذه الدار... من درك... فعلى فلان بن فلان خلاص ذلك كله

'Whatever claim is made against this house, it is the duty of so-and-so son of so-and-so to clear all that.'

The elements of the warranty clause that were developed by the jurists in Iraq can be traced to pre-Islamic sources. The use of the term *ḵalāṣ* in sense of 'clearing' or 'cleansing' a transaction of third-party claims has numerous semantic parallels in legal documents of the pre-Islamic Near East. These include documents written in Greek, Aramaic and Akkadian, the earliest being Middle Babylonian and Middle Assyrian Akkadian texts.[3] It is particularly remarkable that the Arabic term *ḵalāṣ* itself is attested in Nabatean legal documents datable to the first century AD (Yadin et al. 2002, documents nos. 1, 2 and 3; also p. 227).

The Egyptian jurist al-Ṭaḥāwī (d. 321 AH/933 AD) modified the formula slightly, notably by replacing the term *ḵalāṣ* 'clearing' with different phraseology (Wakin 1972, § I 2.0):

فما ادرك فلان بن فلان فى ما وقع عليه هذا البيع... فعلى فلان بن فلان
تسليم ما يجب عليه فى ذلك من حق

'Whatever claim is made against so-and-so son of so-and-so with regard to that which this sale concerns... it is the duty of so-and-so son of so-and-so to deliver whatever debt he owes with regard to that.'

---

[3] See Frantz-Murphy (1988); Greenfield (1992b; 1992a); Yaron (1958). For further details, see Khan (1994, 212–14).

The term *ḵalāṣ* was still retained, however, by the jurist al-Saraḵsī (d. 448 AH/1056 AD; *Kitāb al-Mabsūṭ*, XXX:173), who was active in Central Asia in the fifth century AH/eleventh century AD:

فما ادرك فلان بن فلان من درك فى هذه الدار فعلى فلان بن فلان خلاصه حتى يسلمه له

'Whatever claim is made against so-and-so son of so-and-so with regard to this house, it is the duty of so-and-so son of so-and-so to clear it by delivering it to him.'

The term *ḵalāṣ* is not used in the warranty formulas of later jurists, including that of al-Marġīnānī (sixth century AH/twelfth century AD) in his work *al-Fatāwā al-Ẓahīriyya*. Al-Marġīnānī, like al-Saraḵsī, was active in Central Asia (Khan 1993a, 49–51).

Warranty clauses in documents of sale of buildings or landed property opening with the phrase *mā ʾadraka fulān ibn fulān* and using the term *ḵalāṣ* to refer to the duty of the seller to clear claims of a third party are not attested in Egyptian documents before the third century AH/ninth century AD. The earliest case I am aware of is BAU 11 (276 AH/889 AD, Fayyūm):

فما ادرك فلان بن فلان فى الشرا من درك علقة او تباعة لاحد من الناس...
فخلاص ذلك ونفاذه لازم لفلان بن فلان بالغ ما بلغ

'Should any claim be made against so-and-so the son of so-and-so with respect to this purchase by way of attachment or right due to any person… the clearing and execution of that is the obligation of so-and-so the son of so-and-so, whatever it may amount to.'

The term *ḵalāṣ* in the second half of the formula is, however, attested in a document of sale of animals that is datable to the 150s AH/760s–770s AD (Rāġīb 2006, no. XV):

فان ادعا احدا من الناس البقرتين فعلى عبد العزيز بن سليمن خلاصهما

'If any person claims these two cows, then it is the duty of 'Abd al-ʿAzīz ibn Sulaymān to clear them (of claims).'

The use of the term *ḵalāṣ* is attested in documents from Upper Egypt down to the fifth century AH/tenth century AD, e.g., APEL 72 (460 AH/1068 AD, ʾAsyūṭ):

كان على هذا البايع خلاصه كاين ما كان وبالغ ما بلغ

'It is the duty of this seller to clear it, whatever it is and whatever it may amount to.'

Documents from al-Fusṭāṭ at this period, however, do not use the term but rather exhibit a warranty formula that is based on the one recommended by al-Ṭaḥāwī. This reflects the fact that the documents from the Upper Egyptian countryside were more conservative of earlier traditions than those of the Egyptian capital (Khan 1993a, 26–28, 51–55).

Now, returning to the lease in document **44** from Qaṣr Ibrīm, we have noted that the warranty clause contains the term *ḵalāṣ* to express the clearing of claims. Against the background of the development of the formula of the warranty clause that has just been described, we see that the Ibrīm document, written in 518 AH/1124 AD, is the latest document attested so far that preserves this term. This formulaic archaism can be interpreted as reflecting the peripheral position in the Islamic world of the provenance of the document.

Another attestation of the term *k̲alāṣ* in the warranty of a legal document from Qaṣr Ibrīm has been preserved in the fragmentary document 1978_B10_08A-09[4] (not included in this edited corpus): [...] نفاده وضمانه وخلاصه [...] 'its execution, its warranty and its cleansing'.

5.2. Document 45: Lease of a Boat (566 AH/1170 AD)

This document records the lease of a boat by two Muslim dignitaries from a Christian. The two Muslim lessees have elaborate titles and are identified as accredited witnesses:

> The two elders, the notable (*al-makīn*) Guardian of the Dynasty (*walī al-dawla*) ʾAbū al-ʿUmar Hibat Allāh ibn al-Ḥasan ibn ʾIbrāhīm ibn Ṭalʿa and the dignitary (*al-wajīh*) Glory of the Dynasty (*jalāl al-dawla*) ʾAbū al-Ḥusayn ʿAlī ibn ʾIbrāhīm ibn ʿAlī ibn Nahray, the two certified witnesses of the border town of Aswan (**45**:2–3)

The titles containing the element *al-dawla* indicate that they had some kind of affiliation to a government office. For the origin of such titles, see Rosenthal (2012).

The lessor and owner of the boat is identified as Sirāj ibn Mario, the Christian from al-Muqurra (al-Muqurrī).

The boat is identified as a *zallāj*, which literally means 'gliding (boat)'. The two Muslims hired the boat in order to conduct trade in the region that was open to the Muslims between the first and second cataracts, referred to in the document as

[4] Object number 78.2.20/7, registration number 79/276; provenance LC1-17 Room 2, below floor 1; size 7 × 6 cm.

al-islāmiyya (written السلامية). It is stated that the *zallāj* had the capacity of a load of one hundred and fifty irdabbs. Al-ʾIdfūwī (d. 748 AH/1347 AD; *al-Ṭāliʿ al-Saʿīd*, 26) refers to a 'large *zallāj* that had a capacity of two thousand irdabbs of sugar' (زلاجا كبيرا يسع الفى اردب سكرا). The *zallāj* in document **45**, with a capacity of one hundred and fifty irdabbs, was clearly smaller. It was also smaller than boats referred to in many of the letters of the corpus by the term *markab* (pl. *marākib*). These were larger boats that carried a greater number of passengers.

After a detailed description of the components of the *zallāj*, the document states that the purpose of the lease is to transport goods "to the border of the region where Muslims have the right to travel (*al-islāmiyya*)," from Bilāq (Philae) to the Island of Michael (*jazīrat Mikāʾīl*) in the Land of the Nubians. Bilāq was identified by the medieval geographers as the last town before the Nubian border and the first navigable point south of the first cataract (Seignobos 2010, 14–15). The Island of Michael, which was known in Nubian as Meinarti, lay just north of the second cataract.

The period of the lease is three months "beginning in Kīhak (10th December–8th January) and ending on the last day of ʾAmšīr (9th March), the Coptic months, within the year 566 AH (1170 AD) with the stipulation that they sail downstream from the Island of Michael on the first day of Baramhāt (10th March), the Coptic month" (**45**:8–9). The rent for this period is specified as fifteen dīnārs (**45**:10).

After a description of the constituent acts of the transaction, a condition is added that if they stayed in the Island of

Michael later than the beginning of Baramhāt, they would have to pay a proportion of their cargo to the lessor as a penalty.

Then follows an indication of taxation duty (*maks*): "Duty was not liable on it going upstream, but was liable on it going downstream, in accordance with customary practice" (**45**:15–16).

The transaction is stated to have been made and witnessed "in the border town of Aswan on the 20th day of the month of Rabīʿ I of the year 566 (1st December 1170 AD)" (**45**:19).

There follow then two autograph witness clauses.

The following components can be identified in the structure of the documents:

1. *Basmala*
2. Opening formula
   This opens with a demonstrative pronoun: هذا ما استاجر فلان من فلان 'this is what so-and-so leased from so-and-so', which is the usual opening of leases in the Fatimid period.
3. Identification of the parties
4. Identification of the item leased and the purpose of the lease
5. Specification of the period of lease
6. Amount of rent and terms of payment
7. Constituent acts of the transaction
8. Validity formula: وعقد الاجر منهما عقدا صحيحا 'the lessor made a valid contract with them' (**45**r:16)
9. Confirmation that the transaction was witnessed, specifying the place and date
10. Autograph witness clauses.

Under each of the witness clauses, there is a cipher which can be tentatively read as فى تاريخه 'on its date'. In each case it appears to have been written by a different hand from that of the witness. This is evidently an example of secondary verification of the testimony of the witnesses, known as *šahāda ʿalā šahāda* 'testifying to a testimony'. One of the functions of this was to supplement the primary witnesses whenever there was some element within a contract, or added to it, that might weaken the contract or expose it to a claim. The secondary witnesses strengthened the validity of the contract (Wakin 1972, 68–69). Another example of secondary witnessing is seen in the Fatimid contract of sale published in Khan (to appear 2024), where the clause شهد عندى ذلك والثقة بالله 'This was witnessed in my presence, and my trust is in God' is written under each of the witness clauses.

The document lacks a component that indicates the physical separation of the parties and a warranty, which are found in some leases of the Fatimid period.

5.3. Document 46 Recto: Document of Testimony

Item **46** of the corpus is a sheet containing two legal documents. The document on the recto is a testimony opening شهد الشهود المسمون في هذا الكتاب 'The witnesses named in this document bore testimony'. The document on the verso is a document of sale opening هذا ما اشترى 'This is what X bought'.

The text on the left side of the document of testimony has been lost, whereas no text has been lost from the document of sale. This may suggest that the testimony was written first and later, after the document became damaged, the sheet was re-used to write the text of the document of sale on the verso on the surviving writing material. For this reason, the testimony is considered to be the recto and the document of sale the verso.

The testimony and the documents of sale relate to different transactions.

Since the text of the testimony on the recto is fragmentary, the details of the transaction that it records are obscure in places. The surviving text of the document includes the phrase شركة صحيحة ماضية نافذة 'a valid, effective, operative partnership (*šarika*)' (**46**r:31). The witness clauses at the end of the document refer to "the acknowledgement by the seller and the buyer." This indicates that the transaction was a sale of property as a partnership. There appear to have been two sellers. The name of one of these is given as Muḥammad, son of the commander, Kanz al-Dawla ʾAbū al-Makārim Hibat Allāh at the beginning of the document (**46**r:3). This was the Kanz al-Dawla Muḥammad, who appears in the family tree of holders of the office of Kanz al-Dawla in §3.4. The name of the second person is lost in the lacuna at the end of line 3, but it must have been Ġalyūn ibn Sulaymān ibn Ġalyūn, who is mentioned later in the document (**46**r:7), where it is stated that he has been "named in this document." He is said to be from the village of Dendur, which was situated in Lower Nubia on the west bank of the Nile between Aswan and Qaṣr Ibrīm. This person is the buyer in the document of sale on the verso, where his name is given as Ġalyūn ibn Sulaymān al-Kanzī (**46**v:2).

Both sellers, therefore, were Kanzīs and at least one had settled within Lower Nubia. The property that is sold is said to be "in the possession of them both, not in the possession of one of the two of them" (**46**r:6), which indicates that the sellers themselves were in partnership. The purpose of the transaction was evidently to bring a further person into the partnership. This appears to have been "Pāpāy, the daughter of Ampātā, the Christian woman" (**46**r:9), to whom shares of the property were sold.

As far as can be inferred from the fragmentary text, several plots of land were involved in this transaction of sale, though they are treated as a single lot in the sale. These plots appear to have been situated in the region of the town of Aswan, which is mentioned in **46**r:18. The first of these is said to 'border on (literally: bend towards) the land of Nubia on the west' (وانحرف الى بلد النوبة في الغرب) and border on the Nile in the east (**46**r:11–12). A village is mentioned with a name that could be read as هنداو and identified with the village of Hindāwī south of Aswan (Salvoldi and Geus 2017, 70). If this is correct, then the plot would be situated in Nubia.

Its length is "nine cubits, according to (the length of) cubit that is in current use (*ḏirāʿ al-ʿamal*)" (**46**r:10). This type of cubit is referred to in many Egyptian sources. According to al-Maqrīzī (*Ḵiṭaṭ*, I:380), it was equivalent to the so-called *Hāšimī* cubit, which was introduced by the Abbasids during the reign of al-Manṣūr (136–58 AH/754–75 AD). Hinz (1955, 55) calculates its length as approximately 66.5 cm. For references to *ḏirāʿ al-ʿamal* in the medieval sources, see Grohmann (1954, 173–74).

Included in the sale are watering places (*wird* **46**r:21) and a building with an upper and lower floor. The rights of the property include the right to drink from its water well (شرب من بئر مائه,

46r:24) and the right of access to all its amenities. The transaction includes also "four cows and two bulls and... forty head of riding animals" (**46**r:26–27).

Al-Ṭaḥāwī gives models of documents that were used in order to admit another person into a partnership (*šarika*) in the ownership of a property (ed. Wakin 1972, IV 8.0). These do not correspond to the formulary of **46** recto, which is a document of testimony (*šahāda*).

When a person bought a property, two documents were drawn up. One of these is what is referred to as the *ʾaṣl* 'origin, base, foundation', i.e., a foundational certificate of his ownership. This is a document of sale written from the perspective of the buyer, opening هذا ما اشترى فلان 'this is what so-and-so bought'. The second of these was a document of *šahāda* 'a document testifying in his support to the validity of his ownership'.

Many such documents of *šahāda* from the Middle Ages are extant. They typically open with the formula شهد الشهود المسمون اخر هذا الكتاب .. على اقرار فلان 'The witnesses at the end of this document have borne testimony... to the acknowledgement of so-and-so' or slight variants of this. Examples of *šahāda* documents relating to the transfer of property include Vienna: National Library 10254 (ed. Thung 2006, 66–67). Such documents can be considered to record acts of secondary witnessing (*šahāda ʿalā šahāda*) in order to strengthen the protection of the contract against claims (Wakin 1972, 68–70). Al-Ṭaḥāwī (III, *al-Buyūʿ*, 12.0–12.2) recommends that such *šahāda* documents contain a copy of the full text of the *ʾaṣl* document and the names of its witnesses.

Our document **46** recto is, therefore, a document of secondary witnessing strengthening the validity of a primary *ʾaṣl* document of partnership, which is not extant.

5.4. Document 46 Verso: Document of Sale

This document records the purchase of a plot of land by Ġalyūn ibn Sulaymān al-Kanzī from Fak̲r ibn Furayj ibn Mīnā al-ʾIsamnāwī. As we have seen, Ġalyūn ibn Sulaymān was a partner in the partnership recorded on the recto.

Ġalyūn bought "seven cubits, (measured) in the cubit of the elbow (*d̲irāʿ al-mirfaq*), held in common (*mušāʿ*), of all the land known as Šabb Šalūl in the east opposite the village known as Murwā" (**46**v:5–7). The latter could perhaps be identified with the village of Murwaw (Salvoldi and Geus 2017, 70), situated between Aswan and Qaṣr Ibrīm on the west bank of the Nile. If this is correct, then the plot would be situated in Nubia.

The term *mušāʿ* 'held in common', which is generally used in reference to shares of property, was inserted as an addition above the line. This term indicates that the seven cubits constituted a share of the whole plot and that this share was not a discrete portion but rather a share in joint ownership. The same is likely to apply to the nine cubits of the plot mentioned in the document of testimony on the recto.

The southern boundary "extends to a piece of land known (by the name) of the aforementioned purchaser recently" (**46**v:7–8). This suggests that the transaction recorded in this document extended Ġalyūn's ownership of land. "The eastern boundary extends to the desert and the western boundary extends to the Nile"

(**46**v:10–11). This indicates that the plot was located on the east bank of the Nile.

The rights of the property acquired by the purchaser include the right to drink from its water well (**46**v:11–12).

The formula of the document conforms broadly to that of documents of sale of the period. It does not contain an explicit warranty clause, but the warranty is covered by the generic statement "according to the requirements of the condition of sale of the Muslims, and their warranties and stipulations (ضمانهم وشروطهم)" (**46**v:20–21).

5.5. Document 47: An Acknowledgement of a Debt and Testimonies

The recto of **47** contains an acknowledgement document (*ʾiqrār*). A document of acknowledgement records a formal recognition of rights on the part of a declarant (*al-muqirr*) to a beneficiary (*al-muqarr lahu*) regarding an object of recognition (*al-muqarr bihi*). This gained legal validity due to its being made in the presence of accredited witnesses. This type of document appears to have been based on pre-Islamic models (Khan 1994, 204–12).

In the *ʾiqrār* on **47** recto (dated Ramaḍān 515 AH/November 1121 AD), ʿUbayd Allāh ibn Ḥasan, the trader (*al-jallāb*), acknowledged that he owed Merki ibn Abrām one and a half dīnārs. Merki, who, judging by his name, was a Nubian, is stated to have been a freedman of the judge ʾAbū al-Ḵayr ʾIbrāhīm ibn Muḥammad ibn al-Ḥusayn ibn Muḥammad ibn al-Zubayr. This judge belongs to the Banū Zubayr, a prominent family of judges in the Fatimid period, some of whose members are mentioned in other documents of the corpus (see §3.4). The sender of **21**, ʿAbd Allāh ibn al-Qāḍī al-Rašīd ʿAlī ibn al-Zubayr, was the grandson of the judge ʾAbū al-Ḵayr ʾIbrāhīm.

The verso of **47** contains two testimonies instigated by the creditor Merki ibn Abrām in connection with the complicated recovery of the debt owed to him. The testimonies open with the formula اشهدنى مركى بن ابرام 'Merki ibn Abrām called me to witness' and are written by an accredited witness.

The first testimony declares that Merki 'has received in full' (قبض واستوفا **47**v:2) a debt that is owed by ʿUbayd Allāh ibn Ḥasan, and released him fully from this debt. This is qualified, however, by the statement that the debtor only "paid a quarter of a dīnār and an eighth of gold," i.e., not the full debt of one and a half dīnārs. The statements of full receipt were presumably taken slavishly from the fixed formula of receipts and then this was qualified.

The second testimony declares that Merki "has received in full from ʿAbd Allāh, a freedman, substituting for his father, a quarter, a sixth and an eighth of a dīnār... on behalf of his debtor ʿUbayd Allāh ibn Ḥasan." ʿAbd Allāh was the son of ʿUbayd Allāh ibn Ḥasan, who paid on the latter's behalf. Again Merki released his debtor "with a release of full receipt." This is then qualified by the statement that his debtor still owed him the remaining quarter and two sixths of a dīnār. The remainder of the document indicates that this release was made "after he (the creditor) had received a legal injunction (*ḥukm*) against him (the debtor) for the remainder," which was ratified by an oath sworn by God.

Another witness finally adds a note in a different hand at the end of the document that he had witnessed everything that the other witness witnessed. This was, therefore, a *šahāda ʿalā šahāda*, i.e., a secondary act of witnessing. This second witness states that he was present at the receipt of the injunction against him (i.e., against the debtor) and "the injunction was written above" (كتب الحكم اعلاه). This presumably refers to the fact that in the document that contained the injunction, the injunction was written above and the witnesses added their signatures below.

5.6. Document 48 Recto: Marriage Contract (23rd Rabīʿ I 484 AH/15th May 1091)[5]

The recto of document **48** contains a marriage contract, which is written in a wide landscape type of format. The formula opens, after the *basmala*, as follows:

هذا ما اصدق فلان فلانة وتزوجها به

'This is what so-and-so (the bridegroom) granted to so-and-so (the bride) and married her with it' (**48**r:2–3)

This is referring to the bridal gift, known as *ṣadāq* or *mahr*, which the bridegroom is obliged to give to the bride in consideration of the rights that a husband acquires over the wife. This is based on the Qurʾān 4:4: وَءَاتُوا۟ ٱلنِّسَآءَ صَدُقَٰتِهِنَّ نِحْلَةً 'Give women their bridal gifts as a free offering'.

According to Islamic law, a marriage contract is made between the bridegroom and the bride's *walī*, i.e., her 'representative'

[5] An edition of document **48** was made by ʿĪsā (2000). My reading differs in a number of places.

or 'guardian'. The *walī* is mentioned later in the document, where it is stated:

> The groom named in this document accepted from the representative (of the bride) named with him in it the contract of marriage mentioned in this document on the condition of the aforementioned endowment. (**48**r:9–10)

This indicates that the groom undertook the constituent acts of the contract with the *walī* rather than the bride. It was the custom, however, for the bridal gift to be given to the bride and not to the *walī* (Schacht et al. 2012).

The names of the bridegroom and the bride are given with a long genealogy, which indicates that the two were related:

> *Bridegroom*: Muḥammad, known as ʾAbū ʿAbd Allāh ibn ʾIsmaʿīl ibn Ḥusayn ibn ʾIbrāhīm ibn Ḥusayn {ibn ʾIbrāhīm} ibn ʾAṣfar ibn Maymūn ibn Baydūs ibn Basūn (**48**r:2)
>
> *Bride*: ʾUmm al-Ḥasan ibnat ʿAlī ibn ʾAḥmad ibn Ḥusayn ibn ʾIbrāhīm ibn Ḥusayn ibn ʾAṣfar ibn Maymūn ibn Baydūs ibn Basūn (**48**r:2–3)

The second phrase 'ibn ʾIbrāhīm' in the geneaology of the bridegroom, which is enclosed in curly brackets, appears to be a dittography. It does not appear in the geneaology of the bride or in the genealogy of the son of the bridegroom on the verso (**48**v:3).

The bridal gift was twenty-three dīnārs, but, as was the custom, only a portion of this, viz. eight dīnārs, was paid at the time of the drawing up of the contract. The remainder would be paid after the passage of five years. The amount of the bridal gift and the terms of the postponed portion of the payment differ considerably across the surviving medieval marriage contracts (Grohmann 1934, I:71–72; Mouton et al. 2013, 43–45). The sum of twenty-three dīnārs is in the lower half of the attested amounts of the bridal price in the documents, which can exceed 100 dīnārs. The bride price in contract no. 5 of the corpus of marriage contracts from Damascus (ed. Mouton et al. 2013, 89–90), for example, is 110 dīnārs.

The *walī*, i.e., the guardian of the bride who represented her, was "the noble preacher (*al-šarīf al-ḵaṭīb*) ʾAbū ʿAlī Muḥammad ibn Ḥaydara ibn al-Ḥusayn ibn al-Ḥasan al-Ḥusaynī." This man is mentioned by al-ʾIdfūwī (d. 748 AH/1347 AD) in his *al-Ṭāliʿ al-Saʿīd* (414). Al-ʾIdfūwī saw in Aswan a document written by him dated 527 AH/1132–33 AD. At that time he was apparently *qāḍī* of Qūṣ. According to Islamic law, the *walī* of the bride should be preferably her father. If the father is not alive or available, then the *walī* should be her paternal grandfather, or in his absence the nearest male relative in the male line.[6] If for any reason this is not possible, then the *walī* has to be a representative of the public authority, i.e., a representative of the *qāḍī* under whose authority the legal contract was made (Schacht et al. 2012). This is the case in our document, where the *walī* was a dignitary who was not a relative of the bride, but was a representative of the judicial authority.

We learn in **48**r:12–13 that the *walī* ʾAbū ʿAlī Muḥammad ibn Ḥaydara ibn al-Ḥusayn ibn al-Ḥasan al-Ḥusaynī was the son of the judge responsible for jurisdiction in Aswan, ʾAbū Turāb

---

[6] There were slight differences of opinion in the various schools of law; see Alrudainy et al. (2024, 35).

Ḥaydara ibn al-Ḥusayn ibn al-Ḥasan al-Ḥusaynī, and that this judge authorised ʾAbū ʿAlī Muḥammad to act as *walī*. The document also indicates that the judge ʾAbū Turāb Ḥaydara ibn al-Ḥusayn was deputising for another son of his, the noble judge, leader of the Ṭālibids in the southern sector of Upper Egypt (بالصعيد الاعلى), ʾAbū ʿAbd Allāh Muḥammad ibn Ḥaydara ibn al-Ḥusayn ibn al-Ḥasan al-Ḥusaynī. According to Yāqūt (d. 626 AH/1229 AD; *Kitāb Muʿjam al-Buldān*, III:408), the southern sector of Upper Egypt was constituted by the region from Aswan to Ak̲mīm.

The names of these judges reflect their affiliation to prominent Shiʿite families. The *nisba* al-Ḥusaynī indicates descent from Ḥusayn ibn ʿAlī ibn ʾAbī Ṭālib, a grandson of the prophet Muḥammad. The Ṭālibids were descendants of ʾAbū Ṭālib, the father of ʿAlī, the prophet's cousin and son-in-law. The *kunya* ʾAbū Turāb (literally: Father of Dust), in the name of the judge presiding over Aswan, was attributed to ʿAlī ibn ʾAbī Ṭālib.[7]

The authorisation of ʾAbū ʿAlī Muḥammad to act as *walī* was validated by witnesses (شهد على ذلك 'that was witnessed' **48**r:13).

We learn from this that the marriage contract was drawn up within the jurisdiction of the judge of Aswan and not in Nubia. Although the judge authorised (*ʾad̲ina*, literally 'permitted' **48**r:12) the appointment of ʾAbū ʿAlī Muḥammad as *walī*, the bride formally appointed him as her *walī* and this act of appointment (*tawkīl*) was witnessed (**48**r:8).

---

[7] See *Ṣaḥīḥ Muslim*, https://sunnah.com/muslim:2409, accessed 8 March 2024.

The contract closes with eight witness clauses. Marriage contracts frequently have more witness clauses than are usual in other types of contract, as is the case here. A marriage contract published by Abbott (1941) dated 336 AH/948 AD had 77 witnesses!

5.7. Document 48 Verso: Acknowledgement (21st Šaʿbān 516 AH/25th October, 1122 AD)

The verso of **48** contains an acknowledgement (*ʾiqrār*) by the son of the bridegroom of the marriage in the contract recorded on the recto. The son, who is called ʿAbd al-Ḥusayn, acknowledges that he has received from his father four and a half dīnārs, "this being everything that is apportioned to him by right of his inheritance from his mother... of the postponed portion of her bridal gift, which is certified as being owed to her by his father on the recto" (**48**v:4–5). The *ʾiqrār* closes with five witness clauses. Three of the witnesses have the name al-Ḥusayn ibn al-Ḥasan al-Ḥusaynī in their genealogy and so belong to the family of the *walī* mentioned on the recto.

The *ʾiqrār* was written in 516 AH/1122 AD, thirty-two years after the contract on the recto, which was written in 484 AH/1091 AD. The reference to "the postponed portion of her bridal gift, which is certified as being owed to her by his father" indicates that the groom never paid this to his wife, although he undertook to do so in the contract on the recto five years after the date of the contract. Rapoport (2000) has drawn attention to the fact that medieval Egyptian documents show that husbands frequently did not pay the postponed portions of the bridal gift.

He argues that the specific dates for the deadline of payment mentioned in contracts are legal fictions intended to prevent the marriage from being nullified on the grounds of formal irregularities. In practice, it seems, women did not demand the postponed portion until the termination of the marriage contract. The practice of postponing, therefore, is likely to have had the purpose of deterring husbands from unilateral divorces. Further evidence for this is adduced from Fatimid documents of marriage by Alrudayny et al. (2023, 31).

The son in our document receives from his father four and a half dīnārs from the total of the postponed payment, which was fifteen dīnārs. The marriage gift was deemed to be the property of the wife and was part of her estate after her death. As remarked, in practice, women did not demand the postponed payment until the termination of the contract. With the death of the woman the contract was terminated and, in the case of the situation reflected by our document, it is the son, her heir, who has demanded the postponed payment. According to the document, this is "everything that is apportioned to him by right of his inheritance from his mother." It is not clear how the son's inheritance right to four and a half dīnārs from the fifteen dīnārs of the original postponed payment was calculated. According to Islamic law, the husband would have had the right to receive one quarter of his deceased wife's estate, since there was a living son (Qurʾān 4:12).

5.8. Document 49 Recto: Document concerning Division of Property after Divorce (Muḥarram 429 AH/October–November 1037 AD)

The recto of **49** contains a document relating to a divorce between Qērqe ibn Yuḥannis and Maryam ibnat Yuḥannis. This is the first of a series of documents relating to the turbulent marital affairs of Maryam ibnat Yuḥannis (**50**, **51**, **52**, **53**). It is specified in some of the other documents that the two parties named in **49** recto were Nubians. The name Qērqe (قيرقة) appears to be an attempt to represent the Nubian name Georgi, a shortened form of Georgios.[8] Maqrīzī in his *al-Muqaffā al-Kabīr* (IV:227) refers to a Nubian called قيرقي, which indicates that a name with this form was in use elsewhere. In **49** verso, his name is spelt قيورقة, which represents the medial /o/. In **50**, the name is represented as جريج Jurayj, which is an Arabicised form of the same name. The documents were drawn up under the jurisdiction of a Muslim *qāḍī*, presumably in Aswan or its vicinity.

Unfortunately, the right side of the document has been torn away and this makes the interpretation of the full contents of the document difficult.

At the top there is a note that indicates that the parties recognised "in my presence," i.e., the presence of the presiding judge, everything that is in the document (اعترفوا عندى جميعا بجميع ما فى هذا الكتاب). The judge's name is given as Hibat Allāh ibn Makīn ibn Hibat Allāh ibn Fāris ibn Ḥammād ibn Suwayd. A

---

[8] See http://www.medievalnubia.info/dev/index.php/Names, accessed 8 March 2024.

similar note appears at the top of the marriage contract **51** recto, which was made before the same judge.

The opening formula of the document is missing in the lacuna on the right side, but it is likely that the document was a testimony (*šahāda*) opening [شهد الشهود المسمون اخر هذا] الكتاب 'The witnesses named at the end of this document have borne testimony'. The word الكتاب is extant after the lacuna. At the end of the document only one witness clause has been preserved, but presumably others were written on the right side that is now lost. Several medieval documents of divorce that have been published are testimonies, e.g., Vienna: National Library 15311 (ed. Thung 2006, 31), National Library 32302 (ed. Thung 2006, 27–28), National Library 3165 (ed. Grohmann and Khoury 1993, 42).

It is recorded in the document that an argument and dispute (مشاجرة ومنازعة) had occurred and then after a lacuna there is reference to a divorce (طلاق).

Qērqe ibn Yuḥannis made two claims against his wife. One of these (**49**r:8–9) relates to dīnārs. This presumably related to the bridal gift (*ṣadāq*, *mahr*). According to Islamic law, the bridal gift is the property of the wife. If her husband divorces her, it remains with her and the husband is obliged to pay her any of the postponed payment that he has not yet paid. The basis of this is Qurʾān 4:20: "If you want to take a wife in place of the one (you have), and you have given her plenty of wealth, then do not take any of it back."

If the man divorces a wife before the marriage has been consummated, he must leave half of the bridal gift with her (Qurʾān 2:236–37). In our document there is a reference to an infant girl (الطفلة الرضيعة, **49**r:12), which indicates that the marriage had been consummated.

The other claim of Qērqe related to clothing (*qišr*)[9] and the dowry (*raḥl*).[10] The dowry was given to the bride by the bride's family and typically consisted of a trousseau of clothes, textiles and household utensils. Dowries were not required by Islamic law and so were not recorded in Muslim marriage contracts, which registered only the bridal gift bestowed by the groom. According to Sunni inheritance law, daughters received half the share of their brothers. Families, therefore, used the custom of the dowry as a form of pre-mortem inheritance to compensate for this. The dowry remained under the woman's exclusive ownership and control throughout the marriage, and also through widowhood and divorce. Husbands, in principle, had no formal right over their wives' dowries (Rapoport 2005, 12–30). According to the document, however, Qērqe claimed that the dowry belonged to him and that Maryam should send it to him (**49**r:10–11).

These seemingly irregular claims of the husband indicate that the divorce was not a unilateral repudiation by the husband but rather a consensual separation, known as *ḵulʿ*. In a consensual separation a wife gave up some, or all, of her financial rights, including the postponed bridal price, in return for a divorce. In this type of divorce, the wife typically initiated the separation and returned the bride price by way of compensation to the husband. In some cases, the compensation may have been greater

[9] For the term *qišr* in the sense of clothing, see Lane (*Lexicon*, 2525).

[10] For the term *raḥl*, literally 'luggage', in the sense of dowry, see Goitein (1978, 124, 453).

than the bride price. Separation by *kul*ʿ was, in fact, more commonly practiced than unilateral repudiation, in which the husband forfeited all claims to the property of the wife (Rapoport 2005, 69, 72; Hallaq 2009, 66–67). Although the term *ṭalāq* appears in our document, this is found as a generic term for divorce in combination with the specific term *kul*ʿ in some medieval documents, e.g., Vienna: National Library 28011 (ed. Grohmann and Khoury 1993, 43–46): بطلقة واحدة خلع 'with a single act of repudiation of compensation'.

The document then mentions an infant girl (الطفلة الرضيعة) over whom there seems to have been a dispute. It is indicated, however, that they came to an agreement and separated, being in sound mind and body, not forced or coerced.

Document **50**, which was written one and a half years later, was an acknowledgement of this divorce. Document **49** recto, therefore, may have been a document of agreement of assignment of property before the divorce officially took place.

5.9. Document 49 Verso: Court Record relating to Divorce

On the verso of the divorce document **49** recto, there are two fragmentary documents.

One document is written on the top left side of the verso. Only the first few words of the lines of this are extant. It appears to be an instruction to a fellow judge recording a decision concerning the husband's claims recorded on the recto. It opens with the request: "My brother please attend... [ ] to the man who granted her the bride price (مصدقها)." The remainder of this instruction is largely obscure. There is a mention of 'his portion' (حصته) and the prohibition 'do not oblige him' (لا تحوجه), which may be indicating that he is not obliged to pay the postponed portion of the bride price to his wife.

The other document is a court record, the left side of which is missing. The document relates to the specific content of the dowry that the husband is claiming from his wife. In this document, the husband's name is spelt قيورقة Qēōrqe. It is stated that Qēōrqe ibn Yuḥannis and Maryam ibnat Yuḥannis attended (حضر) court and Qēōrqe had "this document," i.e., the document with the text on the recto, in his hand. He made a claim for clothes (*qišr*), presumably of Maryam's dowry, which included:

زنارين *zunnārayn* 'two belts'[11] (**49**v:10)
ملفة *milaffa* 'a head-cloth'[12] (**49**v:10)
مخدة *mikadda* 'a pillow' (**49**v:10)
منديل *mindīl* 'a kerchief' (**49**v:10)
الملاتين *al-malʾatayn* 'two cloaks'[13] (**49**v:10)
الردا *al-ridāʾ* 'mantle' (**49**v:11)
القطيفة *al-qaṭīfa* 'items of velvet' (**49**v:11–12)

In addition, Qēōrqe claims "what remains owed to him by her with regard to [...]."

11 According to Lane (*Lexicon*, 1258), the *zunnār* was a waist-belt worn by Christians.

12 According to Dozy (1845, 403), the *milaffa* was a piece of cloth that women placed on their head so that their veil was not moistened by the perfumed oil that they put on their hair.

13 This item of clothing had the variants forms *mulāʾa* and *milāya* (Dozy 1845, 408–11).

The document closes with a statement that any further claims by either party would be invalid.

There are no autograph witness clauses, but the simple statement شهد على ذلك *šuhida ʿalā ḏālika* 'that was witnessed'.

5.10. Document 50: Acknowledgement relating to Divorce (15th Jumādā II 430 AH/14th March 1039 AD)

This document, which is dated one and half years later than document **49** recto, is an acknowledgement (*ʾiqrār*) by the husband that he has divorced his wife. This, therefore, records the carrying out of the divorce. Here the husband has the Arabicised name Jurayj ibn Yuḥannis, rather than Qērqe or Qēōrqe.

The core content of the acknowledgement is as follows:

انه طلق زوجته مريم ابنت يحنس طلقة واحدة يملك بها نفسها وقوتها منه

> 'that he had divorced his wife, Maryam ibnat Yuḥannis with one act of repudiation, by which she acquired from him possession of herself and control of herself' (**50**:8–10)

The specification of *ṭalqa wāḥida* 'one act of repudiation' is significant, since in Islamic law a husband was allowed to take a wife back if he repudiated her once or twice. If he repudiated her three times, then he was not permitted to take her back unless she had subsequently been married to another man and this second marriage had terminated. Some extant medieval documents indicate that a divorce was made by a triple repudiation, e.g., Vienna: National Library 32302 (ed. Thung 2006, 27–28): طلق ثلث بتة 'he repudiated three times'.

A parallel to the phrase تملك بها نفسها ‘by which she acquired possession of herself’ is found in a divorce document from Damascus dated 490 AH/1097 AD (ed. Mouton et al. 2013, 121–123). Similar phraseology is found also in documents of manumission of slaves, e.g., وملكت نفسها ‘and she (the manumitted slave girl) took possession of herself’ (APEL 37, ed. Grohmann 1934, I:61–64).

As discussed in the commentary on **49**, the divorce must have been a consensual separation (*ḵulʿ*). The document Vienna: National Library 28011 (ed. Grohmann and Khoury 1993, 43–46), which is cited above, combines the phrase طلقة واحدة, which occurs in our document, with the term *ḵulʿ*: بطلقة واحدة خلع ‘with a single act of repudiation of compensation’.

The document closes with a confirmation that “the acknowledgement by the divorcer and the divorcee of all that was mentioned in it was witnessed.” This implies that Maryam also made a formal acknowledgement.

5.11. Document 51 Recto: Marriage Contract (Ṣafar 432 AH/October 1040 AD)

The recto of **51** contains a contract of a subsequent marriage of Maryam ibnat Yuḥannis. The groom is the Nubian Mariane ibn Īsū.

The formulary of the document is that of Muslim contracts of marriage.

The document opens, after the *basmala*, with the standard formula:

هذا ما اصدق فلان فلانة وبه تزوجها

'This is what so-and-so (the bridegroom) granted to so-and-so (the bride) and he married her by it.' (**51**r:4)

At the top of the document, there is a note indicating that "the two spouses and the guardian of the bride recognised all that is in this document." This is followed by a statement that "it was written by Hibat Allāh ibn Makīn on its date." This is the judge that appears in **49** recto and also the letter **53**.

The bride price, which is referred to by the term *mahr* (**51**r:5), was four dīnārs. Three dīnārs of this was paid in advance (*muʿajjal*) "before his having sexual intercourse with her and his deflowering of her" and the payment of the remaining one dīnār was postponed until the passage of one year. According to Islamic law, brides were not able to claim the full bride price until the marriage was consummated. According to the contract, Maryam was a virgin (**51**r:14). We learn in **49**r:12 that there was an infant girl (الطفلة الرضيعة) from Maryam's previous marriage. So the reference to her virginity seems to be part of a fossilised formulaic phraseology of marriage contracts that was not adapted to the reality of the situation.

The guardian of the bride was Kayl ibn Mariane (**51**r:13), who, judging by his name, was likewise a Nubian.

The contract closes with four witness clauses.

5.12. Document 51 Verso: Testimony (Ḏū al-Ḥijja 432 AH/August 1041 AD)

On the verso of the contract recording the marriage of Mariane ibn Īsū and Maryam ibnat Yuḥannis, there is a document, in a faded hand, that lists various items that the husband undertakes to give to the wife. These include:

اربع قسط زيت الجوز *ʾarbaʿ qisṭ zayt al-jawz* 'four measures of walnut oil' (**51**v:3)

الخل *al-ḵall* 'vinegar' (**51**v:3)

الملح *al-milḥ* 'salt' (**51**v:3)

الحصيرة *al-ḥaṣīra* 'straw mat' (**51**v:3)

القز *al-qazz* 'raw silk' (**51**v:3)

الحطب *al-ḥaṭab* 'fire wood' (**51**v:4)

المشاط *al-mišāṭ* 'combs' (**51**v:4)

الكمين *al-kummayn* 'two sleeves' (**51**v:4)

الملفة *al-milaffa* 'head-cloth' (**51**v:4)

النفقة ويبتى قمح لكل شهر استقبال ذلك *al-nafaqa waybatay qamḥ li-kull šahr istiqbāl ḏālika* 'an allowance of two waybas of wheat each month in the future' (**51**v:4–5)

The document opens

[هذا] ما اشهدنى مرينى بن يسو النوبى

'This is what Mariane ibn Īsū the Nubian called me to witness.' (**51**v:2)

The document, therefore, has the form of a testimony. It closes with the clause:

وكتب هبة الله بن مكين فى تاريخه

'It was written by Hibat Allāh ibn Makīn on its date.' (**51**v:6)

Hibat Allāh ibn Makīn was the judge who certified the contract on the recto.

It is dated Ḏū al-Ḥijja 432 AH/August 1041 AD. This was several months after the contract on the recto, which is dated Ṣafar 432 AH/October 1040 AD.

5.13. Document 52: Court Record relating to Marriage

This document is a court record relating to the marriage of Mariane ibn Īsū (spelt in one case in this document Īsūy) and Maryam ibnat Yuḥannis. It opens

حضر مرينى بن يسوى النوبى وزوجته مريم ابنت يحنس النوبى

> 'Mariane ibn Īsūy the Nubian and his wife Maryam ibnat Yuḥannis the Nubian attended (court)' (**52**:2)

The document records that a dispute had arisen between the husband and wife since the husband had not fulfilled the full obligations of the marriage contract. The wife produced the contract dated Ṣafar of the year 432 AH/October 1040 AD (i.e., **51** recto), indicating that the husband was obliged to pay in advance three dīnārs but she had received only two dīnārs. This statement of hers was certified by witnesses:

اشهدت على نفسها انها قبضت منه دينارين

> 'She called witnesses to certify that she had received from him two dīnars.' (**52**:8–9)

The court record indicates that the husband agreed to pay the remaining debt of a dīnār in six months' time, this being Ḏū al-Ḥijja of the year 432 AH/August–September 1041 AD. It is indicated that this undertaking of his was witnessed:

شهد على ذلك

'That was witnessed.' (**52**:12)

The court record closes with three witness clauses.

It is significant that the document written on the verso of the marriage contract between Mariane ibn Īsū and Maryam ibnat Yuḥannis (**51**) is dated Ḏū al-Ḥijja of the year 432. This was the date that Mariane undertook in the court record to pay the debt of one dīnār. The fact that it was written on the verso of the contract and written by the judge who certified the marriage contract suggests that the delivery of the various commodities by Mariane to his wife that is recorded in **51** verso was intended to be in lieu of a cash payment of the debt of one dīnār.

5.14. Document 53: Letter relating to a Marital Dispute

This document is a letter that records a further episode in the troubled marriage of Mariane ibn Īsū and Maryam ibnat Yuḥannis. It is a letter written by the judge Hibat Allāh ibn Makīn, who certified their marriage contract (**51** recto) and the divorce document (**49** recto). We learn from the address that he is writing from al-Marāġa, a town in Upper Egypt north of Aswan. His title of *qāḍī* is explicitly indicated in the address (**53**v, left, 1). The letter was addressed to a certain ʾAbū al-Ḥasan Zuhayr, who, although his title is not specified in the address, appears to have been another judge.

The writer Hibat Allāh indicates that the bearer of the letter is Mariane ibn Īsū. Hibat Allāh goes on to report that a long time ago he had authorised a divorce between a man known as Qērqe (i.e., the Qērqe ibn Yuḥannis appearing in the documents relating to divorce **49** and **50**) and Maryam ibnat Yuḥannis. Then, a year ago, he had authorised the marriage of Mariane ibn Īsū to Maryam ibnat Yuḥannis. Recently, however, Qērqe had taken Maryam out of the house of Mariane, claiming that she was his wife. Hibat Allāh requests the addressee to arrest Qērqe and send this man to him together with Maryam and Mariane so that he "can act with them according to the requirements of the law," since he (Hibat Allāh) wrote Maryam's divorce document and her marriage document.

The letter, therefore, requests the extradition of parties to the dispute to the jurisdiction of Hibat Allāh. The dispute must be resolved by the judge who certified the divorce and the marriage.

On the verso of the letter, Hibat Allāh indicates that Mariane had gone to the judge in Aḵmīm, situated near to al-Marāġa between Aswan and Asyūṭ, but this judge sent him to Hibat Allāh, since he wrote the marriage contract. This indicates that these events took place in Upper Egypt.

6. COINAGE

The standard unit of currency mentioned in the letters is the dīnār and various fractions of it. The term *qīrāṭ* is used to refer to the 24th part of a dīnār. Letter **29**r:16 mentions "a quarter of a dīnār, in the form of a small coin (*tikk*)." Silver dirhams are also frequently mentioned.

The accounts (**42** and **43**) list the costs of commodities in dirhams, *waraq* (i.e., 'black dirhams'; **42**r, left, 10), dīnārs and the fractions of dīnārs, *qīrāṭ* (1/24) and *ḥabba* 'grain' (1/72; **42**r, left, 10).

When interpreting references to monetary amounts in the documents, one must be aware that in some cases the terms used may have been referring to money of account rather than physical coins, i.e., a notional standard rather than a medium of exchange (Grierson 1978, 10). This must have applied to fractions of a dīnār such as a *qīrāṭ* or a *ḥabba* 'grain'. Such amounts would have been paid in silver dirham coins according to the going exchange rate. It is possible that references to payments in full dīnārs in the documents also did not involve in reality gold dīnār coins but rather were made with the equivalent value of silver dirhams.

Payments of monetary amounts that are recorded in legal documents are in dīnār coins. The documents specify that the dīnār coins are of the standard weight and alloy, and also that they are 'in cash' (*ʿaynan*), e.g.,

 https://doi.org/10.11647/OBP.0391.06

ثلاثة دنانير مثاقيل ذهبا عينا وازنة صحاحا امرية مصرية جيادا

'three dīnārs, of standard weight, in gold, in minted coin of full weight, valid Egyptian coins of al-ʾĀmir, of good alloy' (**44**:5–6)

خمسة عشر دينارا مثاقيل ذهبا عينا وازنة صحاحا عاضدية مصرية جيادا

'fifteen dīnārs, of standard weight, in gold, in minted coin of full weight, valid Egyptian coins of al-ʿĀḍid, of good alloy' (**45**:10–11)

بدينار واحد متقال من الذهب العين الوازن الصحيح الوازن الحافظى المصرى الجيد

'for one dīnār, of standard weight, of gold, in minted coin, valid full weight, according to the Egyptian weight of al-Ḥāfiẓ, of good alloy' (**46**v:14–16)

دينار واحد والنصف دينار الذهب العين الوازن الامرى المصرى الجيد

'one dīnār and half a dīnār, gold, minted coin, full weight, in the Egyptian coinage of al-ʾĀmir, of good alloy' (**47**r:4–5)

ربع دينار وثمن الذهب العين الوازن الامرى

'a quarter of a dīnār and an eighth of gold, in coins of full weight, of al-ʾĀmir' (**47**v:3–4)

ثلا[ثة] وعشرين دينارا مثاقيل ذهبا عينا وازنة صحاحا مستنصرية مصرية جيادا

'twenty-three dīnārs, of standard weight, gold, in valid minted coins of full weight, Egyptian (dīnārs) of al-Mustanṣir, of good alloy' (**48**r:3–4)

اربعة دنانير ونصف دينار من العين الوازن الجيد

'four and a half dīnārs, coins of full weight and good alloy' (**48**v:3–4)

اربعة دنانيرا ذهبا عينا مستنصرية جيادا

> 'four dīnārs, gold, of minted coin, of al-Mustanṣir, of good alloy' (**49**r:5–6)

These various terms reflect the value of the amount indicated corresponding to the standard coinage that was controlled by the ruler. The attribution of coins to particular Fatimid rulers in the formulas indicates that the coins must be those minted in the current ruler's name, since rulers sometimes changed the standard weight (*miṯqāl*). Again, however, it is possible that these formulas were only money of account and the actual payments may have been made by an equivalent in debased coinage.

During the Fatimid period, the gold dīnār was the standard of currency. At the beginning of the Ayyubid period, however, due to the shortage of gold, Saladin made the silver dirham the standard and the dīnār was considered only as a commodity (Balog 1961a). Many coins of debased alloy and less than full weight were in circulation in medieval Egypt (Bates 1991).

The merchants frequently refer to dīnārs (gold coins) and dirhams (silver coins) in the letters of the corpus without any specification of their quality. Letter **9** refers to 'pieces' of dirhams:

> I have sent to you dirhams, two pieces in cash (*ḥaqq ʿayn qiṭʿatayn*), two boxes, a leather bag and bitumen. (**9**v:19–20)

The documents attest to considerable fluctuations in the exchange rate of dirhams to the dīnār. We learn from the following statement in letter **9** that there were 160 dirhams to a dīnār:

> He bought for a dīnār four balls of sugar, at a price of forty dirhams each. (**9**r:14–15)

In the account **42** it is stated:

> The total in black dirhams: three hundred and sixteen. Its exchange value in (gold) coinage: eight dīnārs and a half, minus a grain and a *qīrāṭ*. (**42**r, left, 7–11)

This would be roughly 40 dirhams to the dīnār.

Fluctuations to the dīnār are mentioned in the following passage:

> Let them send to me in this final hour of mine these nineteen dīnārs and eight dirhams, at the rate of five for every dīnār. I have made inquiries about the exchange rate on my side and I found it to be seven, but I traded them at the better rate of six and a half. If I do not go ahead with this transaction, the exchange will be more, and you will lose due to a higher exchange rate.... Cash is something that we cannot control (i.e., we have no control over its value). (**25**r, margin–v:5)

The value of a coin in relation to coins of other metals was not fixed (Bates 1991, 59–60). The rate of exchange of dīnārs and dirhams was in constant fluctuation in Fatimid Egypt. Some of the reasons for this include the deterioration of the silver content of dirhams, the shortage of silver in Egypt necessitating the import of most silver dirhams, the hoarding of dirhams, political crises and varying degrees of economic hardship.

Wide fluctuations are attested in the Genizah documents, which are contemporary with the Qaṣr Ibrīm corpus (Goitein 1967, 368–92). The average exchange rates listed by Goitein in his study of the Genizah documents datable to the Fatimid period range from approximately 30 to 40 dirhams to the dīnār.

The rate of 40 dirhams to the dīnār in the account **40** would be compatible with this. The rates of 160 to the dīnār (**9**) and five to the dīnār (**25**), on the other hand, are noteworthy.

Balog (1961b) has shown that in the late Fatimid period huge quantities of debased dirhams, known as *waraq* 'black dirhams', were struck due to the shortage of silver. These were small, roughly square chunks, cut carelessly from narrow ribbons of low-grade silver. Assays of some extant *waraq* dirhams have shown that they contain no more than 25 to 30 percent pure silver. The cut 'pieces' (*qiṭʿatayn*) of dirhams mentioned in **9**v:19–20 are likely to be referring to the cut-up black dirhams. An exchange rate of 140 to the dīnār could be due to such a pronounced debasement of the silver content of dirhams in the late Fatimid period.

An exchange rate in the range of 30–40 dirhams to the dīnār itself reflects a certain debasement of the silver content of the dirhams. The rate in pure silver dirhams, known as *nuqra*, would be at least three times less. One finds statements in the Genizah letters such as the following (CUL Or. 1080J.130):

> I received from the people ten dīnārs, three of which were coins of poor alloy (*bahārij*) and seven were in dirhams at a rate (*ṣarf*) of 3½ while the rate was 4[1]

Here the writer indicates that seven of the ten dīnārs that he received were paid to him in silver dirhams, so the term dīnār refers to money of account rather than coins. The rate is the rate of the debased silver coins that he received to pure silver coins,

---

[1] This translation of mine is somewhat more accurate than the one given by Goitein (1967, 388).

not to the rate of silver to gold, i.e., 3½ of the dirhams corresponded to one *nuqra*. It is feasible, therefore, to intepret the statement in **25** cited above in this light. When the writer said "Let them send to me in this final hour of mine these nineteen dīnārs and eight dirhams, at the rate of five for every dīnār," he possibly meant nineteen dīnārs in silver, as in the passage from the Genizah document, the dīnārs being money of account rather than gold coins. So, the statement "at the rate of five for every dīnār" would mean for each dīnār in debased silver dirhams, five of the dirhams would correspond to one pure silver *nuqra*. This is more than the rates of debased silver coins to a single pure silver coin that are specified in or inferrable from the Genizah documents. These range from three to four (Goitein 1967, 388–90). The rates of five, six and a half and seven that are mentioned in **25** presumably reflect the dramatic debasement of the silver content of coins in the late Fatimid period that was identified by Balog.

Letter **35** refers to dirhams paid in pure coins (*quḥaḥ*):

> As for other matters, O brother, what he needed has been conveyed from what remained from the price of the two baskets of cotton, which were with our brother Mufliḥ, namely thirty-two dirhams. If he has brought pure coins (*quḥaḥ*), then receive them and convey to me a share. If you cannot obtain pure coins, then send to me their value. (**35**r:4–6)

The term *quḥaḥ* here is apparently used as an equivalent to the more common term *nuqra*. The term *quḥḥ* appears also in the fragment 1978_B09_01A-02, which has not been included in the edited corpus: بقا قح ثلثة دراهم من اثنين دينارين 'There remains three pure dirhams from two dīnārs'.

Ruffini (2012b, 171–206; 2019) has presented evidence from the medieval Nubian documents discovered at Qaṣr Ibrīm that the Nubian economy had been monetised with Egyptian Islamic minted coinage at exchange rates of gold and silver values directly in keeping with those current in medieval Egypt. This is reflected by the many references to dīnārs and dirhams in documents relating to transactions between Nubians. Lists of payments in gold and silver reflect an exchange rate of around 40 silver dirhams to a gold dīnār. It is significant that Old Nubian borrowed the word dirham but not the word dīnār. According to Rufini (2012b, 177), this was probably because payments were more frequently made in silver dirham coins in Lower Nubia than in gold dīnārs. This would be evidence in support of the hypothesis discussed above that dīnārs mentioned in the Arabic letters of merchants may have been money of account rather than coins and actual payments may have often been made with the corresponding value of silver coins.

Relatively few Islamic coins dating before the Mamluk period have been found in archaeological excavations between the first and second cataracts. Those discovered at Qaṣr Ibrīm and identifiable are datable to the Mamluk and Ottoman periods.[2] Glass coin weights from the Fatimid period have been found at Qaṣr Ibrīm. These include a Nubian weight bearing the title of 'Eparch of Nobadia'. A glass weight has also been found in Soba

---

[2] These are listed in a log of coin discoveries in Qaṣr Ibrīm, which was shown to me by Pamela Rose.

from this period. This provides further evidence that the Nubians were dealing in coins south of the second cataract (Edwards 2019, 969). Ruffini (2019) has argued that the lack of archaeological finds of coins can be explained by the hypothesis that currency originating from Egypt circulated in Nubia but eventually returned to Egypt by various means, such as the frequent travel of Nubian kings and members of the elite to Egypt.

7. TAXES

Letter **32** refers to the payment of *jizya* 'poll-tax' apparently by non-Muslims. This was conveyed to the Fatimid ruler by the Kanz al-Dawla:

> If the ruler, may God strengthen his victory, has validly received their poll-tax (*jizyatahumā*), through the services of the Pride of the Arabs, Kanz al-Dawla, may God cause his elevation to endure. (**32**:2)

Letter **36** refers to the payment of *maks* (customs tax):

> I have sent the customs tax (*al-maks*). (**36**r:9)

There is a reference to *maks* in the legal document **45**, which records the hire of a boat by Muslims to sail from Bilāq (Philae) into Nubia to conduct trade:

> Duty (*maks*) was not liable on it (cargo) going upstream, but was liable on it going downstream, in accordance with customary practice. (**45**r:15–16)

This indicates that the Fatimid government, through its representative the Kanz al-Dawla, controlled trade with Nubia and taxed imported goods. When the Ayyubids took control of Egypt, Saladin abolished the *maks* taxes, which had become the perquisites of Fatimid dignitaries, such as the Kanz al-Dawla, with the intention of undermining the power of these dignitaries (Sartain 1993, 27).

 https://doi.org/10.11647/OBP.0391.07

8. LISTS OF COMMODITIES

8.1. Arabic–English

ʿarʿar juniper (**9**r:18)

ʿasīl al-riyāḥ extract of fragrant herbs (**42**r, right, 13)

ʿimāmatayn bi-juḥūf two turbans in a bucket (**4**r:5)

ʿūd aloes, aromatic wood (**29**r:14, **36**v:4)

ʿuṣfur safflower, carthamus tinctorius L., a yellow dye (**42**r, right, 2)

barrāya pen-knife (**31**v:1)

bunāk nascaphthon (**15**v:5)

burd striped or variegated garment (**21**r, margin, 1)

damk sayr thong of twisted leather (**37**v:1–2)

faras mare | *farasan jayyidatan* ‘a mare of excellent quality’ (**22**r:17)

firāš bed, mattress (**29**r:10, v:6) | *firāšayn ʿamal ʿIrāq* ‘two beds of Iraqi workmanship’ (**2**v:1)

ġarz sprigs (**29**r:15)

ġilāla tunic | two tunics (*al-ġilālatayn*) for half a dīnār (**29**r:11, **29**v:2), two tunics (*al-ġilālatayn*) for twenty-four dirhams (**42**r, left, 3)

ġirbāl al-ʿuṣfur sieve for safflower (**42**r, right, 4)

hāl cardamon (**9**r:16; **43**v:7)

ḥalāwa sweets | *sallat ḥalāwa* small basket of sweets (**13**v:5–6)

ḥallat šarb basket drinking vessel (**13**v:5)

ḥalqa ḏahab ring, gold (**36**r:5)

ḥaraš cloth, coarse (**34**r:8)

 https://doi.org/10.11647/OBP.0391.08

ḥaṣīra straw mat (**51**v:3)

ḥaṭab fire wood (**51**v:4)

ḥiṣān horse (**9**v:12)

ḥitta cloth, piece (**31**r:10)

jubba sleeved garment (**37**r:18)

kāfūr camphor (**9**r:16)

kimāmāt muzzles (**23**r:4, 5)

kummayn sleeves (**51**v:4)

kurkum Indian saffron (**43**r, middle, 6)

ḵall vinegar (**15**v:3; **51**v:3)

ḵaraz beads (**29**r:14, 16; **37**v:1)

ḵarīṭa bag (**9**v:20; **37**v:3)

ḵayl horses (**22**r:6, 9, 18; **23**r:14, 19; **33**:16)

ḵayyāṭa verbena nodiflora (**42**r, right, 14)

ḵūḏa helmet (**31**v:1; **37**r:19)

kurūk pieces of calico (**5**r, margin, 5)

lāḏan laudanum (**9**r:16)

lubān frankincense (**43**r, right, 4)

majlis seat (**4**r:5)

malʾa cloak (**49**v:10)

maqāṭiʿ pieces of cloth (**2**r:6; **13**v:5; **42**r, left, 1)

marsīn myrtle (**9**r:17)

maṣṭakī mastic tree gum (**9**r:16)

mayʿa storax (**43**r, middle, 1)

mayʿat ward rose liquid (**9**r:17)

miḵadda pillow (**49**v:10)

milaffa head-cloth (**49**v:10; **51**v:4)

milḥ salt (**9**r:18; **51**v:3)

mindīl kerchief (**49**v:10)
mišāṭ combs (**51**v:4)
muʾnat al-miṣbāḥ supplies for a lamp (**42**r, right, 9)
murr myrrh (**43**r, right, 9)
musaqqaʿ dyed garment (**36**v:2)
nuʿmā mulawwan coloured luxury item (**29**r:13)
nuqūb veils (**34**r:10)
qamḥ wheat (**18**r:4, 8; **51**v:4)
qamīṣ shirt (**37**r:18)
qaṭīfa velvet (**49**v:11, 12)
qazz raw silk (**51**v:3)
qirbatayn water-skins (**37**r:21)
qirfa cinnamon (**9**r:17; **29**r:15)
qišr clothing (**49**r:10; **49**v:9)
qufl nuḥās lock, brass (**29**r:16)
qumāš fabric (**21**r:7)
qurṭum cartham seed (**43**v:1)
qurub scabbards (**31**v:1)
qusṭ, quṣṭ costus (aromatic plant) (**9**r:17; **43**r, right, 7)
quṭn cotton (**35**r:5)
ridāʾ mantle (**49**v:11)
riwā (= *riwāʾ*) rope for binding a load (**29**r:15)
rumḥ spear (**31**v:1)
rumm bedding (**37**r:19)
safaṭ basket (**43**v:3)
salla small basket (**13**v:5)
saqāʾ bi-rasm al-miṣbāḥ fuel for a lamp (**42**r, right, 7)
sukkar sugar (**9**r:15)

sunbul spikenard (**9**r:18; **15**v:3; **43**r, middle, 4)
šabba alum (**9**r:17)
šajara (odiferous) shrub (**43**r, right, 1)
šakka chain of gold coins (**31**v:6)
šamla lifāfa li-l-ṣūf cloak of wool (**43**r, middle, 8)
šumūʿ candles (**29**r:13)
šuqqa oblong piece of garment (**21**r, margin, 1)
ṣūf ʾazraq wool, blue (**34**r:8)
ṣūf ʿaskarī army wool (**43**v:4)
ṣuffāt saddle pads (**31**v:6)
ṣundūq box (**9**v:20)
ṯawb garment, clothing (**18**r:2–3; **31**r:10)
tawbayn (= *ṯawbayn*) *ḥarīr mumazzaj* garments of mixed silk (**2**r:5)
ṯiyāb qūṣī Qūṣī garments (**42**r, right, 11)
ṭarrāḥa mattress (**13**v:6)
ṭīb scented goods (**9**r:12; **15**r:14; **37**v:3)
wabar fur | *ṣāḥib al-wabar* fur merchant (**29**r:11)
wisb herbs (**29**r:15)
zabād perfume extracted from civet cats (**29**r:13)
zaʿfarān saffron (**29**r:12, 14)
zayt ṭīb aromatic oil (**9**r:18)
zayt al-jawz walnut oil (**51**v:3)
zift bitumen (**9**v:20; **20**r:4–5; **43**v:2)
zubda butter (**9**r:16)
zujāj glass (**29**v:2)
zunnār belt (**49**v:10)

8.2. English–Arabic

aloes (*ʿūd*) (**29**r:14; **36**v:4)

alum (*šabba*) (**9**r:17)

aromatic oil (*zayt ṭīb*) (**9**r:18)

bag (*al-ḵarīṭa*) (**37**v:3)

basket (*safaṭ*) (**43**v:3)

basket drinking vessel (*ḥallat šarb*) (**13**v:5)

beads (*ḵaraz*) (**29**r:14, 16; **37**v:1)

bed (*firāš*) (**29**r:10, v:6) | *firāšayn ʿamal ʿIrāq* 'two beds of Iraqi workmanship' (**2**v:1)

bedding (*al-rumm*) (**37**r:19)

belt (*zunnār*) (**49**v:10)

bitumen (*zift*) (**9**v:20; **20**r:4–5; **43**v:2)

box (*ṣundūq*) (**9**v:20)

butter (*zubda*) (**9**r:16)

calico (*kurūk*) (**5**r, margin, 5)

camphor (*kāfūr*) (**9**r:16)

candles (*šumūʿ*) (**29**r:13)

cardamon (*hāl*) (**9**r:16; **43**v:7)

cartham seed (*qurṭum*) (**43**v:1)

chain of gold coins (*al-šakka*) (**31**v:6)

cinnamon (*qirfa*) (**9**r:17; **29**r:15)

cloak (*malʾa*) (**49**v:10)

cloak of wool (*šamla lifāfa li-l-ṣūf*) (**43**r, middle, 8)

cloth, coarse (*ḥaraš*) (**34**r:8)

cloth, piece (*al-ḥitta*) (**31**r:10)

clothing (*al-ṯawb*) (**18**r:2–3; **31**r:10)

clothing (*qišr*) (**49**r:10; **49**v:9)

combs (*mišāṭ*) (**51**v:4)
costus (aromatic plant) (*qusṭ, quṣṭ*) (**9**r:17; **43**r, right, 7)
cotton (*quṭn*) (**35**r:5)
dyed garment (*musaqqaʿ*) (**36**v:2)
extract of fragrant herbs (*ʿasīl al-riyāḥ*) (**42**r, right, 13)
fabric (*qumāš*) (**21**r:7)
frankincense (*lubān*) (**43**r, right, 4)
fuel for a lamp (*saqāʾ bi-rasm al-miṣbāḥ*) (**42**r, right, 7)
fur (*wabar*) | *ṣāḥib al-wabar* fur merchant (**29**r:11)
glass (*zujāj*) (**29**v:2)
head-cloth (*milaffa*) (**49**v:10; **51**v:4)
helmet (*al-ḵūḏa*) (**31**v:1; **37**r:19)
herbs (*wisb*) (**29**r:15)
horse (*ḥiṣān*) (**9**v:12)
horses (*ḵayl*) (**22**r:6, 9, 18; **23**r:14, 19; **33**:16)
juniper (*ʿarʿar*) (**9**r:18)
kerchief (*mindīl*) (**49**v:10)
laudanum (*lāḏan*) (**9**r:16)
leather bag (*ḵarīṭa*) (**9**v:20)
lock, brass (*qufl nuḥās*) (**29**r:16)
luxury item, coloured (*nuʿmā mulawwan*) (**29**r:13)
mantle (*ridāʾ*) (**49**v:11)
mare (*faras*) | *farasan jayyidatan* 'a mare of excellent quality' (**22**r:17)
mastic tree gum (*maṣṭakī*) (**9**r:16)
mat of straw (*ḥaṣīra*) (**51**v:3)
mattress (*ṭarrāḥa*) (**13**v:6)
muzzles (*al-kimāmāt*) (**23**r:4, 5)

myrrh (*murr*) (**43**r, right, 9)

myrtle (*marsīn*) (**9**r:17)

nascaphthon (*bunāk*) (**15**v:5)

oblong piece of garment (*šuqqa*) (**21**r, margin, 1)

odiferous shrub (*šajara*) (**43**r, right, 1)

pen-knife (*al-barrāya*) (**31**v:1)

perfume extracted from civet cats (*zabād*) (**29**r:13)

pieces of cloth (*maqāṭiʿ*) (**2**r:6; **13**v:5; **42**r, left, 1)

pillow (*mik̲adda*) (**49**v:10)

Qūṣī garments (*ṯiyāb qūṣī*) (**42**r, right, 11)

ring, gold (*al-ḥalqa al-ḏahab*) (**36**r:5)

rope for binding a load (*riwā* = *riwāʾ*) (**29**r:15)

rose liquid (*mayʿat ward*) (**9**r:17)

saddle pads (*ṣuffāt*) (**31**v:6)

safflower (*ʿuṣfur*) (**42**r, right, 2)

saffron (*al-zaʿfarān*) (**29**r:12, 14)

saffron, Indian (*kurkum*) (**43**r, middle, 6)

salt (*milḥ*) (**9**r:18; **51**v:3)

scabbards (*qurub*) (**31**v:1)

scented goods (*al-ṭīb*) (**9**r:12; **15**r:14; **37**v:3)

seat (*majlis*) (**4**r:5)

shirt (*al-qamīṣ*) (**37**r:18)

sieve for safflower (*ġirbāl al-ʿuṣfur*) (**42**r, right, 4)

silk | garments of mixed silk (*tawbayn ḥarīr mumazzaj*) (**2**r:5)

silk, raw (*qazz*) (**51**v:3)

sleeves (*kummayn*) (**51**v:4)

sleeved garment (*al-jubba*) (**37**r:18)

spear (*al-rumḥ*) (**31**v:1)

spikenard (*sunbul*) (**9**r:18; **15**v:3; **43**r, middle, 4)
sprigs (*ġarz*) (**29**r:15)
storax (*mayʿa*) (**43**r, middle, 1)
striped garment (*burd*) (**21**r, margin, 1)
sugar (*sukkar*) (**9**r:15)
supplies for a lamp (*muʾnat al-miṣbāḥ*) (**42**r, right, 9)
sweets (*ḥalāwa*) | *sallat ḥalāwa* small basket of sweets (**13**v:5–6)
thong of twisted leather (*al-damk al-sayr*) (**37**v:1–2)
tunic (*ġilāla*) | two tunics (*al-ġilālatayn*) for half a dīnār (**29**r:11, v:2), two tunics (*al-ġilālatayn*) for twenty-four dirhams (**42**r, left, 3)
turban | two turbans in a bucket (*ʿimāmatayn bi-juḥūf*) (**4**r:5)
veils (*al-nuqūb*) (**34**r:10)
velvet (*qaṭīfa*) (**49**v:11, 12)
verbena nodiflora (*k̲ayyāṭa*) (**42**r, right, 14)
vinegar (*k̲all*) (**15**v:3; **51**v:3)
walnut oil (*zayt al-jawz*) (**51**v:3)
water-skins (*al-qirbatayn*) (**37**r:21)
wheat (*qamḥ*) (**18**r:4, 8; **51**v:4)
wood for fire (*al-ḥaṭab*) (**51**v:4)
wool, blue (*ṣūf ʾazraq*) (**34**r:8)
wool, army (*ṣūf ʿaskarī*) (**43**v:4)

Several of the aromatic herbs and substances among the commodities listed above originated in India and East Asia. These would have been imported to Egypt by the Red Sea trade, most likely through the port of ʿAyd̲āb. Aswan and Qūṣ were the main Nile terminals of import trade from ʿAyd̲āb. This Red Sea port also carried most of the pilgrim traffic from Egypt and other parts of Africa to the Ḥijāz, since the more northerly routes were threatened by the Franks (Sartain 1993, 6).

The commodities that were imported from India are mentioned in letters preserved in the Genizah of Jewish merchants who conducted trade in India and further east, e.g.,

ʿūd aloes, aromatic wood; cf. Goitein and Friedman (2007, 110).
hāl cardamon; cf. Goitein and Friedman (2007, 59, 61)
kāfūr camphor; cf. Goitein and Friedman (2007, 288).
qirfa cinnamon; cf. Goitein and Friedman (2007, 261)
ʿuṣfur safflower, carthamus tinctorius L., yellow dye; cf. Goitein and Friedman (2007, 562).

Some of the commodities are likely to have been imported from Arabia, such as frankincense (*lubān*) and myrrh (*murr*). Others were imported from the north, such as storax (*mayʿa*), which was an aromatic resin obtained from trees in Asia Minor, used in perfume and medicine.

9. TITLES OF OFFICIALS

9.1. *Sulṭān*

The term *al-sulṭān* 'the ruler' appears in various letters. The Fatimid caliphs and viziers were sometimes referred to as *sulṭān* in the medieval sources (Khan 1993a, 487). In the late Fatimid period, the viziers were in de facto control, so, since the letters of the corpus are datable to the late Fatimid period, it is likely that 'the ruler' that is referred to would have been the vizier.

The writer of **21**, ʿAbd Allāh ibn al-Qāḍī al-Rašīd ʿAlī ibn al-Zubayr, describes various missions of his family to the Nubian king on behalf of the ruler:

> My grandfather travelled to visit the just king Basil and my father travelled to visit the king Mūyis, the father of Mena Kurē (?), as a messenger from the ruler, may God strengthen his victory, to Soba. It is he who strove to make a peace treaty between the ruler and the king when the situation deteriorated in the days of King David. My cousin, the judge ʾAbū al-Faḍl travelled to visit King Mūyis as a messenger of the ruler to Soba. (**21**r:9–13)

The writer of **22**, who is the *ʾamīr* ʾAbū Manṣūr ʿAjīl, says that he has received instructions from the ruler to stop a shipment of horses to the eparch:

> As for your saying that the ships conveying the horses have stopped, I was intending to (send them) until the order of the ruler, may God make his reign eternal, reached me by the hand of his brother, the governor of our land, together with a letter to the king informing him (the king) that if he (the king) needed an army, he (the ruler) would send it to

 https://doi.org/10.11647/OBP.0391.09

> him, but he (the ruler) has prohibited me from sending to you the first instalment of the horses until these messengers (i.e., my slave boy and the slave boy of the ruler) arrive (at the king). (**22**r:5–9)

He received the instructions "by the hand of his brother, the governor of our land (*wālī bilādinā*)." This may have been the brother of the vizier Bahrām, who was the governor of Qūṣ, the key governor in Upper Egypt at that period. The ruler in question, therefore, would have been Bahrām, who served as vizier 529 AH/1135 AD–531 AH/1136 AD, during the reign of the caliph al-Ḥāfiẓ (al-Imad 1990, 109–17). The chain of command, therefore, was the ruler > governor of Qūṣ > local *ʾamīrs*.

Letter **6**, which reports the news of the killing of the vizier Šāwar by Šīrkūh, indicates that the *ʾamīr* has been summoned by the new vizier Šīrkūh.

Letter **32**, which is somewhat obscure, refers to the direct communication between the Kanz al-Dawla and the ruler with regard to the payment of poll-tax of some freedmen:

> If the ruler, may God strengthen his victory, has validly received their poll-tax, through the services of the Pride of the Arabs, Kanz al-Dawla… (**32**:2)

The legal document **44** records the lease of a plot of land from the estate (*ʾiqṭāʿ*) of the lessor, which was "assigned to him by the Office of the Ruler (*ʾiqṭāʿatihi min dīwān al-sulṭān*), may God strengthen his victory" (**44**:4).[1]

---

[1] A fragmentary letter discovered at Qaṣr Ibrīm, which is not in the edited corpus (1974_V09_08-08A), is addressed to the 'prosperous Office of Friday and Neighbourhood Mosques' (*dīwān al-jawāmiʿ*

9.2. *Wazīr*

The term *wazīr* 'vizier' is regularly used as a title of the eparch, who is referred to as 'vizier of the king' (*wazīr al-malik*; see §3.3). The term is not used to refer to the Fatimid vizier. As discussed above, the term *sulṭān* 'ruler' in the documents is likely to be intended to denote the Fatimid vizier. Letter **6**, which reports the killing of the vizier Šāwar by Šīrkūh, indicates that

> Šīrkūh, the military commander (*sallār*), may God protect him... has taken on the viziership to bear the burden of evil that is to come (*tawazzara šarr yakūn*). (**6**:7–8)

9.3. *ʾAmīr*

Many letters refer to a commander (*ʾamīr*). In several of the letters, an *ʾamīr* appears in the address, and his identity is sometimes specified. As has been discussed in §3.4 above, the *ʾamīr*s appearing in addresses include the Kanz al-Dawla (**1**, **8**, **26**), the son of the Kanz al-Dawla (**2**, **7**) and *ʾamīr*s who do not have a Kanzī *nisba*, including ʾAbū Manṣūr ʿAjīl (**22**) and Ḥiṣn al-Dawla ibn al-ʿAsqalānī (**28**). Letter **29** is addressed to ʾAbū al-Qāsim Hibat Allāh ibn Muḥammad ibn al-ʾAʿmā, who is identified in the opening of the letter as *al-ʾamīr ʾIbrīm* 'the commander (at) Ibrīm'. In letter **33** there is reference to 'the commander of the desert river'

---

w-al-masājid al-maʿmūra). This was a Fatimid government office (Khan 1993a, 162). It is possible that the office concerned was a local branch in Upper Egypt.

(*al-ʾamīr fī baḥr al-ṣaḥrāʾ*). Evidently different *ʾamīrs* were operating at different localities in the region.

Some *ʾamīrs* who acted as witnesses to legal transactions are named in the legal documents:

> Muḥammad son of the commander Kanz al-Dawla ʾAbū al-Makārim Hibat Allāh (**46**r:3)
>
> Mubārak, the freedman of the most powerful commander, Saʿd al-Dawla, witnessed (**46**v, witness, 6)
>
> ʿAlī ibn Muḥammad son of the commander Sabʿ (**48**r, witness, 15)

Within the body of the letters, there are some references to the *ʾamīr* Kanz al-Dawla, e.g., **12**r:4; **15**r, margin, 8; **29**r:5; **32**:2; **33**:2, 7, 8, 9. In many cases within the body of the letters, there is only an anonymous reference to *al-ʾamīr* 'the commander'. The identity of the *ʾamīr* in such references is not clear. Given the variety of the *ʾamīrs* mentioned in the corpus, an unnamed *ʾamīr* was not necessarily always the Kanz al-Dawla. The Kanz al-Dawla was the supreme commander in the border region. Other *ʾamīrs* were presumably subordinate to him, such as his son, who is mentioned in **2** and **7**. It is not clear, however, whether the *ʾamīrs* without a Kanzī *nisba* were subordinate to the Kanz al-Dawla. The Kanzī sender of letter **9**, Lāmiʿ ibn Ḥasan, complains bitterly that the *ʾamīr* Ḥiṣn al-Dawla ibn al-ʿAsqalānī had impeded his activities in the court of the Nubian king, suggesting that he was a rival to the Banū al-Kanz. When there is reference to an *ʾamīr* in the letters, the context often shows that he was itinerant and not always to be found in the same place.

The letters indicate that *ʾamīrs* were responsible for the execution of the instructions of the eparch. The Muslims, it seems, could not carry out the eparch's requests without the authorisation of an *ʾamīr*, as seen in passages such as the following:

> The commander has written that he will arrive and he will give instructions for your (the eparch's) sake and for the sake of the carrying out of your requests. (**2**r:13–14)

The passage below from letter **16** shows that the writer, Ḥusayn ibn Ḥasan al-Kanzī, has been instructed by the *ʾamīr* to forward to him letters received from the eparch, indicating that the writer himself was not authorised to act independently:

> The commander is expecting in great anticipation news to reach him from your honour. Ensure that your letters reach the commander. Your envoys are in contact with him all the time. He has instructed that "when a letter from the Master of the Horses arrives, they should send it to me with anybody who comes here." (**16**r:16, top margin, 3)

In **25**, we learn that the eparch has sent a letter to the *ʾamīr* requesting him to carry out the requests of the writer, showing that authorisation from the *ʾamīr* was needed. The writer is frustrated by the fact that the *ʾamīr* has not done so:

> You mentioned in it that you have sent to the commander a letter and also sent to the executive official a letter in order that my requests be carried out. As for the commander, I visited him one day and he said to me "We shall carry out your requests," but I have not seen him again since and they do not allow me to visit him. I have stayed in the district morning and evening and my request has not been carried out. (**25**r:5–7)

The writer is expecting the delivery of a slave (*raqīq*). Evidently the problem is that the eparch's letter does not contain clear instructions nor has a necessary payment been made:

> He (the *ʾamīr*'s slave boy) says concerning the writer who wrote the letter for the commander, "I do not know what he is writing. There is no instruction in it concerning the slave (*al-raqīq*), nor payment, only the mention of the commander and nothing else. So far no payment has been made for anything." (**25**r:11–12)

The writer needs to receive the slave so that he can travel to Nubia in order to deliver it to the Nubian king:

> Write your letter to the commander that this slave belongs to the king and that he should bring it down (the river) so that the requests of the king be fulfilled out of respect. Cold will be upon me (soon) and I shall not be able (to carry out my business) and the Marīsī wind will not allow me to arrive. So, tell them to hurry up to carry out my requests and deliver the slave to me. (**25**r:12–15)

Letter **29** is sent to somebody addressed as *al-ʾamīr ʾIbrīm*, referring to a commander based in Ibrīm. The writer indicates that he requested the *ʾamīr* Kanz al-Dawla to send him a consignment in Ibrīm, evidently since the writer himself did not have the authority to send it himself:

> I inform you, my son, that I had sent you the advance consignment immediately after asking the commander, Kanz al-Dawla, may He cause his power to endure (to dispatch it), and he sent it with a reliable person indicating that he would meet ʿAbd al-Bāqī and deliver it to him. (**29**r:4–6)

In letter **30**, which is written to a dignitary of some kind, the writer laments that he is unable to pursue some runaway servants into the land of Nubia without the authorisation of the *ʾamīr*, but he is currently unable to obtain this since the *ʾamīr* is absent on a journey:

> Then I learnt that they (the runaway servants) had gone to Ibrīm. You did not give instructions for any power to be granted to me so that I could go there to exercise this and overcome my current inability to act until the time of the arrival of the commander from his journey there. I have informed you of this so that you know that I have asked him to respond quickly. Whatever he replies to you, give instructions to ʾAbū al-Wālid ibn Ḥāḍir to inform me of the decision of our lord (the commander), may you be granted success, if God wills. (**30**v:3–5)

The writer of **12**, Lāmiʿ ibn al-Ḥasan al-Kanzī, states that the letter has been presented to the eparch by the agency (*ʿalā yad*) of the *ʾamīr* Kanz al-Dawla, indicating that he was in control of communications with the eparch:

> I inform the Ikšīl… that my letter has been presented to him (i.e., you) through the agency of (*ʿalā yad*) my master, Kanz al-Dawla. I inform him (i.e., you) that my slaves are travelling to the king, may God cause him to live. (**12**r:2–4)

Letter **33** refers to the need to receive instructions from an *ʾamīr*. The *ʾamīr* is described as "the commander of the desert river:"

> My father commanded me that when I needed any instructions, we should write to your father, the commander of the desert river (*al-ʾamīr fī baḥr al-ṣaḥrāʾ*). (**33**:2–3)

An ʾ*amīr* was responsible for ensuring the protection of the Muslim merchants in Nubia and also had responsibility to protect the Nubian kingdom:

> He also mentions (the need) to safeguard the subjects and protect the merchants who are travelling to you from among the merchant community (and mentions) the country of the king and its guarding and protection. (**2**r:14–16)

The ʾ*amīr* was responsible for the "guarding and protection" of the king's country by virtue of being a representative of the Fatimid ruler. This can be linked to the situation described in letter **22**, which mentions a complaint by the eparch that the supply of horses (*ḵayl*) for the Nubian army by the Fatimid authorities has stopped. This indicates that the Fatimid ruler was supporting the Nubian army.

As has already been discussed, letter **9** indicates that the Muslim writer, Lāmiʿ ibn Ḥasan al-Kanzī, swore to an agreement between himself and the eparch in the presence of the bishop, the terms of which include service to the king and protection of the eparch's companions:

> Does not the Master of the Horses think that what has brought me and you together close in the presence of the bishop is that I provide him with provisions and I remain in the service of the king and the protection of your companions? (**9**r, margin, 11–v:1)

The protection of the eparch's companions is likely to be referring to the protection of Nubians crossing the border into Egypt. It is clear from the following passage from the same letter that the writer, Lāmiʿ ibn Ḥasan al-Kanzī, was working closely with an ʾ*amīr* and, presumably, representing him:

> I said to him that a messenger would reach you. I have sent the horse to you together with Maḥmūd, the slave boy of the commander (*al-ʾamīr*). When he reaches you, write to me a reply to this letter and read my letter to the bishop. For there have been good relations between us. My slave boy has come for the sake of good relations. The king should not allow Ibn al-ʿAsqalānī to sour his relationship with me or the commander. (**9**v:12–16)

Protection of the eparch's subjects in Egypt, therefore, was also the responsibility of the *ʾamīr*.

The *ʾamīr* was responsible for punishing misconduct of other officials, as seen in **16**:

> On account of this call for help in the land, the commander (*al-ʾamīr*) has come down and reprimanded the lieutenant (*al-ḵalīfa*) and forbidden him to do wrong to anybody. (**16**r:8–9)

The following passage from letter **30** indicates that an *ʾamīr* had a lieutenant (*ḵalīfa*):

> I hired a muleteer and travelled to the person who is his (the commander's?) lieutenant (*ḵalīfatuhu*) and he met with the Head of all of us (*rayīs kullinā*), presiding over everything, whose decision is the (supreme) decision and it is fixed. If you make a decision, it is (likewise) fixed. (**30**v:6)

Letter **6**, which reports the news of the killing of the vizier Šāwar by Šīrkūh, indicates that the *ʾamīr* has been summoned by the new vizier Šīrkūh. The *ʾamīr* in this case was presumably the Kanz al-Dawla.

> He (the new vizier Šīrkūh) has summoned the commander (*al-ʾamīr*) to him, and the commander is determined to

> travel to Egypt for the sake of his (Šīrkūh's) expeditions and his aid, while I am staying in the country (of Nubia). (**6**r:8–9)

Letter **4** refers to military action in which the *ʾamīr* Kanz al-Dawla has been involved:

> The commander Treasure of the Dynasty (*Kanz al-Dawla*) arrived after victory, slaughter and God's victory. (**4**v:2–3)

The writer of **15** indicates that the *ʾamīr* Kanz al-Dawla had set off on a journey:

> The reason I have delayed sending my letters to you is only that I travelled to say farewell to the commander, Kanz al-Dawla, may God establish his good omen and his glory, so that he may carry out all his tasks successfully. (**15**r, margin, 6–11)

Letter **32** refers to the payment of *jizya* apparently by non-Muslims. This was conveyed to the Fatimid ruler by Kanz al-Dawla:

> If the ruler, may God strengthen his victory, has validly received their poll-tax (*jizyatahumā*), through the services of the Pride of the Arabs, Kanz al-Dawla, may God cause his elevation to endure... (**32**:2)

9.4. *Šadīd, Šādd*

Letter **25** mentions an official who is variously referred to as *al-šadīd* and *al-šādd*, which I have translated 'executive officer'.

Such officers are mentioned in other sources in connection with the Fatimid administration. They assisted local staff to carry out their duties, especially in the collection of taxes; cf. al-Maqrīzī (*Ḵiṭaṭ*, I:107, 405); Stern (1964, decree no. 10, line

31); Rabie (1972, 66–67); Khan (1993a, 447). They were military officers, classified by al-Qalqašandī as belonging to the *ʾarbāb al-suyūf* 'masters of the sword' (Björkman 1928, 99, 102, 162, 164).

In **25**, the executive officer is presented as working together with the *ʾamīr* to carry out the requests of the writer:

> You (the eparch) mentioned in it (your letter) that you have sent to the commander (*li-l-ʾamīr*) a letter and also sent to the executive officer (*li-l-šadīd*) a letter in order that my requests be carried out. (**25**r:5)

> I do not need to order you (i.e., remind you) to write a letter to the commander regarding what concerns us and also the executive officer (*al-šadīd*). (**25**v:9)

> I told them he has instructed that I should only sell them (the slaves) in Egypt. So, send two letters concerning them, one letter to the commander and one letter to the executive officer (*al-šadīd*). (**25**v:13–14)

9.5. *Šarīf*

The term *al-šarīf* 'the noble one' occurs in letters **16** and **32**:

> I inform my honourable lord, the Master of the Horses... of the arrival of a letter by the hand of your slave boy Ipisi on the matter of the place that was discussed previously with the *šarīf*. (**16**r:2–3)

> May he (the addressee) undertake this and what is appropriate and customary, with our thanks and out of respect for the sons of the *šarīf* in our district (*bi-l-nāḥiya*). (**32**:7–8)

The term *šarīf* denotes somebody who claims distinguished rank because of his descent from illustrious ancestors. In Fatimid

Egypt this would be expected to refer to descent from ʿAlī, the prophet's cousin and son-in-law (ʿAlids), or ʿAlī's father ʾAbū Ṭālib (Ṭālibids).

Various judges in the marriage contract **48** have the epithet *šarīf*, including the noble judge, leader of the Ṭālibids in the southern sector of Upper Egypt (*al-šarīf al-qāḍī naqīb al-ṭālibiyyīn bi-l-Ṣaʿīd al-ʾAʿlā*), ʾAbū ʿAbd Allāh Muḥammad ibn Ḥaydara ibn al-Ḥusayn ibn al-Ḥasan al-Ḥusaynī (**48**r:12–13). The legal document no. 36 (407 AH/1017 AD) in the Genizah corpus (Khan 1993a, 210) refers to 'the glorious *šarīf*, a leader of the Ṭālibids' (*al-šarīf al-jalīl naqīb min nuqabāʾ al-ṭālibiyyīn*).

The *šarīf* mentioned in documents **16** and **32** in the present corpus must have had an influential social status in the Muslim community and possibly a *qāḍī* such as the one mentioned in **48** is intended.

9.6. *Mutawallī*

The Arabic term *mutawallī* 'administrator, governor' is used in sources relating to Fatimid administration as a title of the head of government offices and institutions (Khan 1993a, 106, 107, 175, 342, 358, 416, 434).

We have seen (§3.3) that the term regularly appears in the title of the eparch in the addresses of letters, in phrases such as *mutawallī bilād Marīs wa-ʾaʿmālihā* 'the governor of the land of Marīs and its districts' (**21**v, address, right, 2), *mutawallī ʾaʿmāl bilād al-Marīs* 'the governor of the districts of the land of al-Marīs' (**21**r:2), *mutawallī ʾal-qalʿa al-ʾibrīmiyya wa-bilād Marīs* 'the governor of the fortress of Ibrīm and the land of Marīs' (**7**v, address, right, 2).

The term is used in various other contexts in the corpus. It appears in the title *mutawallī al-bāb* 'administrator of the gate' in **8**r:4. The holder of this post was responsible for supervising the northern border between Egypt and Nubia (§3.5.5). The use of the term *mutawallī* indicates that this was a government office.

Letter **24** refers to a *mutawallī* in the entourage of the eparch:

> His slaves (i.e., the writers) [kiss the ground] before him and report to him that it has not been concealed from him (the eparch) that his slaves (the writers) were dependent on the administrator in his presence without being in financial partnership (*bi-dūn al-qarīḍa*). (**24**r:4–6)

The term *qarīḍa* here seems to be a variant of the form *qirāḍ*, which is used in medieval sources to denote a financial partnership. The intention seems to be that the trade activities of the writers were controlled by the administrator although he has not contributed capital to this trade, which would have given him a clearer right to have a say in how the trade was conducted. The Nubian *mutawallī* here, therefore, had some role in controlling trade.

9.7. *Wālī*

The term *wālī* in the definite singular is used to refer to a governor of a locality. In letter **22**, the writer refers to *wālī Qūṣ* 'the governor of Qūṣ' (**22**r:14) and *wālī bilādinā* 'the governor of our land' (**22**r:7), probably also meaning the governor of Qūṣ, who was the most powerful governor in Upper Egypt.

Letter **31** refers to business conducted with the *wālī*:

> By God, take for me the price of the five portions (*ašqāq*), which are owed to me by the governor (*al-wālī*). (**31**v:7–8)

9.8. *Wulāh*

The plural الولاة 'the governors' is mentioned in letter **14**:

> He has a right to your customary protection, so that he is able to have access to the administrators (*al-wulāh*) and others of your slaves and servants (*ʿabīdihā wa-ḵadamatihā*). (**14**r:5–6)

Here the term seems to be used in the sense of administrators of various government offices of the eparch and so has the same meaning as *mutawallī* (§9.6).

Letter **16** mentions الولا, evidently a variant form of الولاة, also referring to the eparch's administrators:

> I would like a letter to be sent to all the administrators (*al-wulā*) requesting them to protect the places of Lāmiʿ and his slaves and likewise my places and my slaves. (**16**r:13–14)

9.9. *Qāʾid*

Various people with the title *al-qāʾid* 'the leader' are mentioned in the letters. A *qāʾid* appears to have been of high rank and to have had important responsibilities. In letters **3** and **8**, *qāʾids* are mentioned who had honorific titles:

> The bearer (of this letter), the leader (*al-qāʾid*) Saʿāda, may God decree his abundant good health, the relative of the noble leader (*al-qāʾid al-najīb*), Humām al-Dawla ('Hero of

> the Dynasty') Ḥāmid, may God decree for him abundant good health, has departed. (**3**r, margin, 1–3)
>
> The bearer of (this letter), who has travelled (to you), is the leader (*al-qāʾid*) Ḥasan, the son of the leader (*al-qāʾid*) Šujāʿ al-Dawla ('the Courage of the State') ʾIsḥāq, the administrator of the gate (*mutawallī al-bāb*). His status with me is firmly established and his rank is well-known, may God decree his safety and cause him to have good company. (**8**r:3–6)

Honorific titles such as Humām al-Dawla and Šujāʿ al-Dawla, which were bestowed by the Fatimid régime, reflect the fact that the bearers had some kind of affiliation to a government office. For the origin of such titles, see Rosenthal (2012). The leader Ḥāmid is also described as *najīb* 'noble'. The leader Saʿāda is mentioned in several places in the corpus (**1**r:3; **3**r, margin, 1; **3**v:3; **10**r:4). 'Saʿāda' is most likely a personal name; cf. al-Ḏahabī (d. 748 AH/1348 AD), *Siyar ʾAʿlām al-Nubalāʾ*, XXIII:64. These passages also suggest that the office of *qāʾid* was hereditary.

In the passage in **8**, it is not clear whether the role of 'the administrator of the gate' (*mutawallī al-bāb*) describes Šujāʿ al-Dawla ʾIsḥāq or his son Ḥasan. The 'gate' is likely to be the entrance to Nubia at the town of al-Qaṣr, just south of Aswan. Al-ʾAswānī describes this town as *bāb ʾilā balad al-nūba* 'a gate into the land of the Nubians' (al-Maqrīzī, *Ḵiṭaṭ*, I:352). In this place there was an armed garrison (*maslaḥa* or *musallaḥa*) post (al-Maqrīzī, *Ḵiṭaṭ*, I:307), which is mentioned in **19** of the corpus. This suggests, therefore, that the *qāʾid* ʾIsḥāq or the *qāʾid* Ḥasan was responsible for controlling traffic passing in and out of Nubia and, presumably, supervising the garrison post. It is possible that both had this role. Borders facing non-Muslim territory (*ṯuġūr*) were controlled by a military commander with the title of *qāʾid* (Brauer 1995, 16). The men called *qāʾid* in our documents were clearly military officers.

The letters record that the leader Saʿāda made several trips to Nubia. Ṭalāʾiʿ ibn Ruzzīk, who was governor in Upper Egypt and subsequently vizier in the twelfth century, owned a powerful black *mamlūk* called Saʿāda (al-Maqrīzī, *ʾIttiʿāẓ al-Ḥunafāʾ* III, 257). Sartain (1993, 28) speculates that this could be the *qāʾid* Saʿāda who appears in our documents.

Letter **10** indicates that the leader Saʿāda was sent on a mission by the writer, Ḥāmid al-Kanzī, to carry out various tasks. This indicates that the duties of a *qāʾid* were varied:

> My companion, the leader Saʿāda, has set off. I have sent him to carry out various tasks that I have commissioned him to do. The Ikšīl is requested to send to specify the identity of the matters that need to be dealt with and send a request regarding them so that I am made grateful to the Ikšīl (for having the opportunity of carrying them out). (**10**r:4–7)

Letters **1** and **3** request the eparch to ensure the protection of the leader Saʿāda, who is the bearer of the letters, on various trips to Nubia:

> I inform the Ikšīl… that the leader Saʿāda has set off on the ship travelling to (meet) him. What I would like to request from the Ikšīl is to give him the status of the people belonging to my servants who have been granted freedom, like my other freedmen and servants. The Ikšīl cannot show them opposition in anything small or big, but should

> show honour to the aforementioned leader and care for him and for his companions who are travelling with him. (**1**r:2–7)
>
> The bearer (of this letter), the leader Saʿāda, may God decree his abundant good health... has departed.... So, please arrange for his (i.e., the eparch's) letter to be sent to me with authorisation for me to offer the leader Saʿāda respectful treatment until it (his work) is finished. (**3**r, margin, 1–3; **3**v:3–4)

The sender of letter **1** was the Kanz al-Dawla, which is a further indication of the high rank and military responsibilities of the *qāʾid*.

9.10. *Nāʾib*

The term *nāʾib* 'deputy' is used in various contexts in the corpus. As we have seen in §3.3, it is frequently used in the phrase *al-nāʾib ʿan al-malik* 'the deputy of the king' in titles of the eparchs in the addresses of letters. In **26**, the term refers to the deputy of the eparch Darmā, i.e., the vice-eparch.

Letter **16** reports to the eparch that people in the 'southern land', i.e., Muslims operating in Marīs, have complained about various officials, including a *nāʾib* of the Qūsa:

> As for the southern land, people have been arriving from there complaining about the lieutenant (*al-ḵalīfa*), the Master of the Shipmasts (*ṣāḥib al-sawārī*), and a deputy of the Qūsa (*nāʾib li-l-Qūsa*). (**16**r:7–8)

The Qūsa were a clan from Upper Egypt; cf. al-Maqrīzī (d. 845 AH/1441 AD), *Rasāʾil*, 136; al-Qalqašandī (d. 821 AH/1418 AD), *Nihāyat al-ʾArab fī Maʿrifat ʾAnsāb al-ʿArab*, 156. Members of this clan were evidently operating in Marīs under the authority of a deputy.

In the same letter there is reference to a *nāʾib al-ḥaḍra* called Ibn ʿImrān. This appears to be the deputy of the eparch. He is asked to pay for the salary of a visiting Muslim official:

> The agent (*al-ḵalīfa*) mentioned that he has instructions and he adhered to all of these. He wrote to Ibn ʿImrān, the deputy (*nāʾib*) of your honour asking him about his salary and he gave him his usual salary. (**16**r:14–16)

The writer of letter **21**, ʿAbd Allāh ibn ʿAlī ibn al-Zubayr, requests the eparch to grant privileges to his children through 'his deputies':

> May the Master of the Horses, may God cause his power to endure, instruct his deputies (*nuwwābahu*) in Erkinun concerning my children. (**21**r, margin, 2)

This suggests that the eparch had more than one *nāʾib* and these served as executive administrators.

The term 'deputy' is also used in letter **9** to refer to the loyalty and allegiance of the Muslim writer, Lāmiʿ ibn Ḥasan al-Kanzī, to the Nubian king:

> I am the servant of the king and his deputy (*ḵādim al-malik wa-nāyibuhu*), and the one who fulfills his needs, but, by God, I experience from people only pleasure in my suffering. (**9**r:27–margin, 2)

9.11. *Ḵalīfa*

The word *ḵalīfa* denotes somebody who substitutes or deputises for a superior, which I generally translate 'lieutenant' to distinguish it from *nāʾib*, which I translate 'deputy'. People with this title are mentioned in several letters.

In letter **30** and the marriage contract **48** the term is used to refer to a deputising judge:

> He is the son of the Kanzī judge deputising for him (*walad ḵalīfa li-l-qāḍī al-kanzī*). (**30**r, margin, 17)

> deputy for his son (*ḵalīfat waladihi*), the noble judge, leader of the Ṭālibids (**48**r:12)

In letter **30**, the term is also used in a context where it seems to be referring to the lieutenant of an absent *ʾamīr*:

> I hired a muleteer and travelled to the person who is his (the commander's?) lieutenant (*ḵalīfatuhu*) and he met with the Head of all of us (*rayīs kullinā*; i.e., the *ʾamīr*), presiding over everything, whose decision is the (supreme) decision and it is fixed. If you make a decision, it is (likewise) fixed. (**30**v:6)

In **16**, the writer reports that the *ʾamīr* reprimanded the lieutenant (*al-ḵalīfa*). This may have been his own lieutenant, though the context does not make this clear:

> As for the southern land, people have been arriving from there complaining about the lieutenant (*al-ḵalīfa*), the Master of the Shipmasts (*ṣāḥib al-sawārī*), and a deputy (*nāʾib*) of the Qūsa. On account of this call for help in the land, the commander (*al-ʾamīr*) has come down and reprimanded the lieutenant (*al-ḵalīfa*) and forbidden him to do wrong to anybody. (**16**r:7–9)

Elsewhere in the corpus, the function of the *ḵalīfa* is less clear. In **16**, a statement about a *ḵalīfa* follows a general request for the eparch to protect the writer's property and servants:

> I would like a letter to be sent to all the administrators requesting them to protect the places of Lāmiʿ and his servants (*ʿabīdihi*) and likewise my places and my servants (*ʿabīdī*). You know that they all perform good services to the king and to you. The lieutenant (*al-k̲alīfa*) mentioned that he has instructions and he adhered to all of these. He wrote to Ibn ʿImrān, the deputy of your honour (*nāʾib al-ḥaḍra*) asking him about his salary and he gave him his usual salary. (**16**r:13–16)

This may indicate that the *k̲alīfa* was a servant of senior rank. Dozy (*Supplément* I:397), indeed, notes that the term was used to designate slaves or servants in the court of the Umayyads in Spain. The reference in the passage above to the *k̲alīfa* requesting his salary from "the deputy of your honour," i.e., from the deputy of the eparch, suggest that he was based in Nubia.

The writer of letter **36** reports that the letter of a lieutnenant (*al-k̲alīfa*) has arrived "by the hand of his servants." It seems, therefore, that a *k̲alīfa* could have his own servants:

> The letter of the lieutenant Mašal Ankara, may God keep him safe, has reached me by the hand of his servants (*ʿabīdihi*). I dealt with their business and they departed. (**36**r:2–3)

In letter **18**, which was apparently written by the eparch Uruwī to a Muslim merchant, we read:

> As for the seeds of wheat, I have delivered to your slave six irdabbs minus a third without any waste. Your slave boy has received them. These garments are for you. The lieutenant (*al-k̲alīfa*) has nothing (from me). (**18**r:4–6)

The fact that the eparch states that the garments are for the Muslim recipient and not the *ḵalīfa*, suggests that the *ḵalīfa* was working for the Muslim rather than the eparch.

The writer of **27**, which is addressed to the secretary of the eparch Uruwī, refers to a *ḵalīfa* with the Nubian name Peti (if this is the correct reading). From the context, he appears to have held a responsible position in Nubia and had to be disabused of malicious gossip against the writer:

> The slave (the writer) requests his honour to write a letter to the slave (the writer) so that it be in his hand and mention in it the lieutenant Peti and the Master of the Shipmasts (asking them) not to listen to anybody saying things like "Have we triumphed over his slave in the (trading) places?" (**27**r:8–11)

9.12. *Ṣāḥib al-Sawārī*

An official with this title is mentioned in several letters of the corpus. The usual orthography of the second word is سوارى with a final *yā*ʾ. This is most easily interpreted as the plural of سارية *sāriya* 'shipmast'. I translate the title, therefore, 'Master of the Shipmasts'. This was presumably a title of an official responsible for shipping. It would correspond to the Greek title *ναυάρχης* 'Master of Ships', which is attested in several Greek inscriptions from the Nubian region (Hendrickx 2011, 317).[2] In letters **16** and **18**, the second word of the Arabic title is spelt without a final *yā*ʾ: صاحب السوار (**16**r:7–8; **18**r:1–3). This orthography is likely to

[2] For further references, see http://www.medievalnubia.info/dev/index.php/Offices_and_Titles, accessed 8 March 2024.

reflect the shortening of the final unstressed long *-ī* in vernacular speech.[3]

In letter **18**, which appears to have been sent by the eparch Uruwī, the Master of the Shipmasts is said to be conveying merchandise from the Muslim recipient to the eparch:

> The letter of the Master of the Shipmasts has reached me. He says that he will take for me from you three garments. He has taken [ ] two garments in your name. The Master of the Shipmasts has received them. (**18**r:1–3)

We learn also from letter **27**, which was sent to the secretary of the eparch Uruwī, that the Master of Shipmasts acted as purveyor of items from a Muslim merchant to the eparch:

> The slave will ask my master the elder ʿUbayd Allāh to encourage him (the secretary) to draft a letter for me and send it to me with the Master of the Shipmasts. This is what I need the most from my master (the eparch). In the days of his father, my master the Master of the Horses, nobody opposed me in anything.... I have sent (this letter) to him with the Master of the Shipmasts and we shall request him to pay one dīnār as cash commission to my master the elder ʿUbayd Allāh. (**27**r:17–v:8)

In **16**, the writer reports that a complaint has been made about the Master of Shipmasts and some other officials:

---

[3] In Classical Arabic, the form السوار would be more easily read as the word *suwār* 'bracelet'. ʾAbū al-Makārim (d. 1208 AD; *Taʾrīḵ al-Kanāʾis wa-l-ʾAdyira*, 323) mentions that *al-suwār al-ḏahab* 'the golden bracelet' was part of the apparel of a Nubian eparch. The interpretation of the title as 'Master of the Shipmasts', corresponding to the Greek title ναυάρχης, is, however, the preferable one.

> As for the southern land, people have been arriving from there complaining about the lieutenant (*al-ḵalīfa*), the Master of the Shipmasts, and a deputy (*nāʾib*) of the Qūsa (clan). On account of this call for help in the land, the commander (*al-ʾamīr*) has come down and reprimanded the lieutenant and forbidden him to do wrong to anybody. (**16**r:7–9)

The sender of letter **23** to an eparch is the Master of the Shipmasts. In the letter, he tells the eparch that a Nubian called Merki had behaved incorrectly in Aswan and that he has attempted to stop it:

> He entered Aswan and gathered the slaves of Darmā and brought me to them and said to me that "the Master of the Horses has ordered me to take over the administrative office." I said to him, "Who has endowed you with the office before I come to take over from you the office?" (**23**r:9–11)

The Master of the Shipmasts requests further instructions from the eparch:

> If you command me, I shall finish (my business here) and come (to you). Write and let me know. If you would like to tell me to come to you and return, write and let me know. (**23**r:17–18)

From these various passages it appears that the Master of the Shipmasts had the responsibility of liaising between the Muslim community in Aswan and the eparch and conveying goods, letters and money from the Muslims to the eparch.

9.13. *Simsār*

Letter **9** refers to a middleman called a *simsār* 'broker':

> When your slave boy informed me that you needed the goods (*al-ḥawāʾij*), I delivered him (the slave) to the broker (*al-simsār*) and he auctioned him and acquired (the offer of) five dīnārs. I then went to your slave boy and consulted him concerning his sale and sold him for five dīnārs, on the grounds that there is nobody in the land and none of the people have anything. (**9**r:7–11)

As can be seen, the job of this broker involved holding an auction. The Genizah documents refer to the activities of *simsārs*. In many cases, they specialised in specific commodities (Goitein 1967, 160). It is possible that the *simsār* mentioned in **9** was a slave broker.

9.14. *Kātib*

Letter **27** is addressed to *al-kātib* 'the secretary', whose master is the eparch Uruwī:

> The slave asks my honourable master (*ḥaḍrat mawlāya*), the sublime elder (*al-šayḵ al-ʾajall*), the secretary (*al-kātib*), may God cause his strength to endure, to kiss the hands of my sublime master, the Master of the Horses, (U)ruwī, the son of my sublime master [Īsū]. (**27**r:2–3)

The honorifics used in the address indicate that the secretary was regarded as being a person of high rank. It appears that the eparch was absent from Ibrīm and the writer, therefore, asks the secretary rather than the eparch to draft a letter for him that will put an end to malicious gossip. This demonstrates that the secretary, in principle, had the authority to issue correspondence of his own accord.

The term *kātib* is found also in letter **25**, where it refers to the secretary of an *ʾamīr*:

> He says concerning the secretary (*al-kātib*) who wrote the letter for the commander "I do not know what he is writing." (**25**r:11)

9.15. *ʾUsquf*

The bishop (*al-ʾusquf*), presumably of Ibrīm, is mentioned several times in letter **9**, in the context of the writer's complaint about the incorrect treatment of his slave boy at the court of the king at the hands of a certain Ibn ʿAsqalānī. The writer refers to the code of behaviour between himself and the eparch that has been sanctioned "in the presence of the bishop:"

> Does not the Master of the Horses think that what brings me and you together close in the presence of (*bi-ḥuḍūr*) the bishop is that I provide him with provisions and I remain in the service of the king and the protection of your companions? (**9**r, margin, 11–v:1)

As discussed above (§3.5.5), the phrase "in the presence of the bishop" gives the act of 'coming close' a legal sanction, just as a legal act is frequently stated in medieval Arabic legal documents to have been conducted in the presence of witnesses or of a judge. The bishop, therefore, played a role in establishing the working relationship between the Muslim merchants and the Nubians.

The writer indicates that he has written a letter to the bishop complaining of Ibn ʿAsqalānī's behaviour. Again, the bishop appears to have a quasi-legal role, in this case the role of arbitrating a dispute:

> I sent a messenger, after I had informed the bishop about my suffering due to his (Ibn ʿAsqalānī's) shocking

> behaviour, I said to him that a messenger would reach you. I have sent the horse to you together with Maḥmūd, the slave boy of the commander. When he reaches you, write to me a reply to this letter and read my letter to the bishop. (**9**v:10–14)

9.16. *ʿAqīd*

The sender of letter **38**, Danī ibn Kannān, has the title *al-ʿaqīd*. In the lease document **44**, the same man leases some of his land in "ʾAbū Fāris to the west of the border of Nubia, which is administered in his estate (*ʾiqṭāʿatihi*) assigned to him by the Office of the Ruler" (**44**:3–4). The term *ʿaqīd* has the basic meaning of somebody who is 'bound by a contract or treaty'. According to Dozy (*Supplément*, II:151), the word has the sense of 'military leader' in some sources. By the late Fatimid period in Egypt, grantees of an *ʾiqṭāʿ* were mainly professional army officers, so 'military leader' is likely to be the meaning of the term in **38**.

In Fatimid Egypt, an *ʾiqṭāʿ* typically consisted of agricultural land leased to a military grantee (*muqṭaʿ*) for a sum of money payable to the treasury, which, in turn, paid the soldiers a contractual supplement to their payment, called *qabāla*. The grantee (*muqṭaʿ*) was not necessarily resident on the property; cf. Cahen (2012), Rabie (1972, 26–29).

9.17. *Mukārī*

The term *mukārī* 'muleteer' is mentioned in letter **30**:

> I hired a muleteer (*mukārī*) and travelled to the person who is his (the commander's?) lieutenant (*k̲alīfatuhu*). (**30**v:6)

9.18. *Ṣāḥib al-Ḥarba*

The term *ṣāḥib al-ḥarba* 'master of the spear' is mentioned in letter **13**, where it seems to refer to a high-ranking military officer in the entourage of the king of Nubia. The writer is keen to reassure the eparch, to whom the letter is addressed, that his association with this officer should not be interpreted as sedition. This reflects the tension surrounding visits of the Muslims to the king:

> As for their saying that I am the slave boy of the Master of the Spear (*ṣāḥib al-ḥarba*)—I am only a merchant. I was the guest of the king and I lodged with the Master of the Spear like the (other) merchants. Not everybody who lodges with a person is his slave boy. (13r:9–11)

9.19. *Muʿaddī*

This term is mentioned in letter **20**:

> I put [the bitumen in them] and I loaded them on a ship of the purveyor of merchandise (*markaban li-l-muʿaddī bi-l-tijāra*). (**20**r:9–10)

It appears from this that the person called *muʿaddī* was responsible for porterage by ship. The participle is used in **22** as an adjective qualifying the noun *markab*:

> As for your saying that the ships conveying the horses (*al-marākib al-muʿaddiya li-l-ḵayl*) have stopped… (**22**r:5–6)

9.20. *Qāḍī*

There are numerous references to a judge (*qāḍī*) in the documents of the corpus.

Letter **19** was sent by a judge with the *nisba* al-Ḥusaynī, whose name appears in the address:

> the judge ʾAbū al-Faḍl Muḥammad ibn al-Fātiḥ ibn ʿAbd Allāh al-Ḥusaynī, the prosperous and just judge, Trust of the Kingdom (**19**v, address, left, 1–3)

The writer of **21** was the son of a judge ("ʿAbd Allāh, son of the rightly-guided judge ʿAlī ibn al-Zubayr," **21**v, address, left, 2–3) and several members of his family were judges, including his cousin, the judge ʾAbū al-Faḍl. The legal acknowledgement **47**r, which is dated 515 AH/1121 AD (during the reign of the caliph al-ʾĀmir), also mentions a judge from the Banū Zubayr:

> Merki ibn Abrām, the freedman of the rightly-guided, prosperous, just judge, Light of the Kingdom, ʾAbū al-Ḵayr ʾIbrāhīm ibn Muḥammad ibn al-Ḥusayn ibn Muḥammad ibn al-Zubayr (**47**r:3–4)

Al-Maqrīzī (d. 845 AH/1441 AD) mentions this judge in his *al-Muqaffā al-Kabīr*, I:181. He indicates that he had the *nisba* of al-ʾAswānī and was the judge of Qūṣ, who "was alive (*kāna ḥayyan*) in the year 471 AH (1078–79 AD)."

We learn from letter **30** that a certain judge called Nūr al-Dīn was a member of a partnership (*šarika*). Presumably a 'business partnership' is intended:

> Inform the Master of the Horses about the person who is with you and tell him that he (the person with you) is the son of the sister of the judge, Nūr al-Dīn, and he is a member of the partnership (*al-šarika*) of which Nūr al-Dīn is a member. (**30**r:15–16)

The same letter refers to the deputy (*ḵalīfa*) of a judge:

> So, talk to him and inform him that the author of the letter brought by Ṭāʿī is an elder sent by the judge. He is the son of the Kanzī judge deputising for him (*walad kalīfa li-l-qāḍī al-kanzī*). (**30**r, margin, 15–17)

The marriage contract **48** mentions two judges:

> the noble judge ʾAbū Turāb Ḥaydara ibn al-Ḥusayn ibn al-Ḥasan al-Ḥusaynī, deputising for his son, the noble judge, leader of the Ṭālibids in the southern sector of Upper Egypt, ʾAbū ʿAbd Allāh Muḥammad ibn Ḥaydara ibn al-Ḥusayn ibn al-Ḥasan al-Ḥusaynī (**48**r:12–13)

Documents **49**, **51–53** concerning marital affairs were drawn up under the authority of "the judge Hibat Allāh ibn Makīn." Within the body of letter **53**, there is reference to the judge of Akmīm:

> He (the bearer of this letter) went to the judge in Akmīm, may God cause his strength to endure, and he sent him to me. (**51**v:4)

9.21. *Raʾīs/Rayīs*

Letter **26**, which is addressed to the deputy of the eparch Darmā, mentions an official with the title *al-raʾīs* 'the Head':

> (I inform) that the bearer of these lines is the Head (*al-raʾīs*), may God decree his safety, and he must be shown favour and respect. (**26**r:3–5)

The sender of the letter was the Kanz al-Dawla, which suggests that 'the Head' was of high rank.

The writer of letter **30** mentions "the Head of all of us," who is presented as being equipollent with the eparch:

> I hired a muleteer and travelled to the person who is his (the commander's?) lieutenant (*ḵalīfatuhu*) and he met with the Head of all of us (*rayīs kullinā*), presiding over everything, whose decision is the (supreme) decision and it is fixed. If you (the eparch) make a decision, it is (likewise) fixed. (**30**v:6)

It is not completely clear what the status of this 'Head' was. He may have been a senior *ʾamīr*, though judging from **26** this was not the Kanz al-Dawla. Some Nubian documents refer to a chief called *ouran*, which literally means 'head', e.g., P. QI III 34.

9.22. *Šarīk*

Letter **30** mentions a 'partner' (*šarīk*), who is presumably a 'business partner':

> Moreover, I would not have desisted from travelling to Ibrīm in the current situation, but I did not know whether I had a friend or acquaintance in it (Ibrīm) after you departed from it upriver and Ṭāʿī was absent. So I desisted from coming to the partner (*al-šarīk*), because I did not dare, and, moreover, he could not have helped me (anyhow). (**30**r:10–11)

The same letter refers to a business parntership (*šarika*, **30**r:16).

10. SLAVES AND SERVANTS

10.1. *Raqīq, Riqq*

The terms *raqīq* and *riqq* are used to refer to slaves in bondage who were delivered by the eparch to the Muslims. The words are typically used as collective terms and specific individuals are expressed by the numerical classifier *raʾs* 'head':

> As for slaves (*al-raqīq*), there is nothing in Aswan. (**37**v:4–5)

> Then I wrote to you concerning the condition of the two slaves (*al-raʾsayn al-raqīq*) that my debtor ʾAbū al-Ḍubāʿ (should have) sent me, but he has not sent them to me. (**4**r, margin, 3–5)

> Your servant has seen the two slaves (*al-raʾsayn al-raqīq*). If it were not for the fact that he has stayed and the people would hear that I had returned them, I would have sent them to you. (**9**r, margin, 8–10)

Letter **24** refers to a *raqīq* that the eparch bestowed (*ʾanʿamathu*) upon the writers, but they complain that she was sick. This indicates that the slaves were given in an exchange of diplomatic gifts, which the Muslims expected would reciprocate the value of the goods that they delivered to the eparch:

> They inform him that the slave (*al-raʾs al-raqīq*) whom he bestowed (*ʾanʿamathu*) upon his slaves (*mamālīkihā*, i.e., the writers of this letter) through the agency of Bazilī was sick (*marīḍa* sg.f), and that his slaves (*mamālīkihā*, i.e., the writers) wanted to return her. (**24**r:6–8)

 https://doi.org/10.11647/OBP.0391.10

The feminine gender agreement of *al-raʾs al-raqīq* in the preceding passage indicates that the term referred to a female slave.

Letter **24** also contains a reference to a *riqq* whom the eparch could send to the north on an errand:

> But you know that you do not have any slaves (*al-riqq*) to send to the northern land to receive news. (**24**v:3–4)

10.2. *Waṣīf* (m.), *Waṣīfa* (f.)

These terms are used in the letters to refer to individual slaves that were delivered by the eparch to the Muslims. In all cases, a single slave is mentioned, not groups of slaves. As with the *raqīq/riqq*, slaves designated with these terms were received by the Muslims in exchange for the delivery of goods to the eparch and subsequently sold by the Muslims for cash:

> The letter of the Master of the Horses and vizier of the king… has arrived and another letter for the elder ʾAbū al-Ṭāhir ibn Tarīk, in both of which you mention the dispatch of the slave (*waṣīf*) and his sale. When your servant informed me that you needed the goods, I delivered him (the slave) to the broker and he auctioned him and acquired (the offer of) five dīnārs. (**9**r:2–9)

> He (the eparch) stated that he has sent to me a female slave (*waṣīfa*)… she has not reached me in his consignment so that I may take possession of her, my honour, Master of the Horses, and I shall not correspond with you nor give you consignments of cloth as gifts until what you send is at my disposal. (**4**r:3–8)

> Your two companions have seen my (the eparch's) messenger (*rasūlī*) whom I sent in connection with the slave (*al-waṣīfa*). (**17**r:9–10)

The terms *waṣīf* and *waṣīfa* designated slaves who were destined for domestic service, including child slaves (Goitein 1967, 131; Rāġīb 2006, II:23–25). Bridal dowries in the Genizah sometimes include one or more *waṣīfa*. Perry (forthcoming) suggests that the term in such a context should be translated 'lady-in-waiting' and that it designated a less menial role than that of a *jāriya*. Ibn Buṭlān (d. 458 AH/1066 AD), in his work on slaves and slave girls (*Risāla*, 376), stated that Nubian women made devoted domestic servants.

10.3. *Ġulām*

People referred to by the term *ġulām* (pl. *ġilmān*) are frequently encountered in the letters of the corpus.

The following passage refers to a *ġulām* who was the son of a slave girl, so the *ġulām* would also have had the status of a slave:

> They (the writers) inform him (the eparch) that… the slave girl (*al-jāriya*) and her son, Rāhim, your slave boy (*ġulāmaka*), were examined before purchase three times but she and her son have died. (**24**r:6–10)

When the name of the *ġulām* is mentioned, this is always a personal name (Arabic: *ism*) without any indication of genealogy, which is the normal naming practice of slaves in medieval Arabic letters:

Bišr (**20**r:4)
Ipisi (**14**r:8; **16**r:3)
Jawhar (**4**r:4)
Kablām (**9**r:24)
Mārīk̲ura (**4**v:1; **6**r:4; **9**v:19)
Munʿim (**2**r:4)
Ramaḍān (**30**r, margin, 7)
Šarīf (**7**r:4)
Yaḥyā (**22**r:18, v:8)

I, therefore, translate all occurrences of *ġulām* as 'slave boy'. The term *ġulām* is used in medieval sources with the sense of both free servants and slave servants (Sourdel et al. 2012). Many sources, however, treat *ġilmān* as the male equivalent of *jawārī* 'slave girls', e.g., al-Jāḥiẓ (d. 255 AH/869 AD), *Muqaddimat Mufāk̲arat al-Jawārī wa-l-Ġilmān* 'Introductory Treatise on the Vaunting Contest of Slave Girls and Slave Boys' (see Ayalon 1985). Although I translate the term *ġulām* as 'slave boy' to distinguish it from other terms for slaves and servants, it is important to note that it was used to refer to males of all ages, not only young men, just as the term *jāriya* was used to refer to women of all ages (Rāġīb 2006, II:24).

Slave boys (*ġilmān*) were working slaves and are not referred to as items of diplomatic or commercial exchange. They were sent by merchants to convey goods and letters:

> The bearer of this letter, who is (called) Munʿim, one of my slave boys (*ġilmānī*), has come to you carrying two garments of mixed silk and four pieces of cloth for the Master of the Horses. (**2**r:4–6)

> I have sent my slave boy (*ġulāmī*) Mārīḵura. Deliver to him the two slaves who are for ʾAbū al-Ḍubāʿ. (**4**v:1)
>
> The bearer of this (letter) is my loyal and respectful companion, Oua, who is my servant (*ḵādim*). I have sent him with my slave boy (*ġulāmī*) Mārīḵura. (**6**r:3–4)
>
> I have sent my slave boy (*ġulāmī*), who is called Šarīf, with a brown camel to his honourable presence. (**7**r:3–4)
>
> Send the slave boys of mine (*ġirmānī*, a phonetic variant of *ġilmānī*) who have my goods, namely ʾAbū ʿAbd Allāh and Mārīḵura, send (them) by the road. (**9**v:18–19)

In letter **18**, the eparch indicates that the slave boy of the Muslim recipient has received goods:

> As for the seeds of wheat, I (the eparch) have delivered to your slave (*ʿabdika*) six irdabbs minus a third without any waste. Your slave boy (*ġulāmuka*) has received them. (**18**r:5)

This passage also refers to *ʿabdika* 'your slave', which designates a person in the service of the writer. It appears that the *ʿabd* was based in Ibrīm and the *ġulām* was travelling between the eparch and the writer.

Letter **9** refers to the sending of a *ġulām* to carry out business in the court of the king:

> What I wish to inform the Ikšīl of is that my slave boy Kablām has arrived at the court of the king, but he (the king) has shown little gratitude for what I have undertaken for him. I am owed by the king two horses. He has sent me two good-for-nothing, aged servant women and six dīnārs. (**9**r:23–26)

Letters **14** and **20** refer to a *ġulām* of the eparch:

> A letter has reached me by the hand of your slave boy (*ġulāmihā*) Ipisi and I wrote a reply to it. (**14**r:7–8)

> His slave boy (*ġulāmuhu*), Bišr, arrived on Wednesday as I was leaving for the land of Nubia. I found in it (the letter) that the Master of the Horses sent three dīnārs and I asked on your behalf for bitumen to be bought for you before I left the land. (**20**r:4–6)

10.4. *Jāriya*

The term *jāriya* is used to denote a female slave who was delivered to the Muslims in exchange for goods. A *jāriya* in the corpus was not exactly the feminine equivalent of a *ġulām*, who was a working slave and not an item of exchange. I translate the term *jāriya* 'slave girl'. It did not necessarily, however, designate only young girls, as the following passage from letter **9** shows (cf. Rāġib 2006, II:23):

> I am owed by the king two horses. He has sent me two good-for-nothing, aged slave women (*jāriyatayn ʿajāyiz*) and six dīnārs. (**9**r:25–26)

They were considered to be a different category of slave from a *waṣīfa*, since the two terms are sometimes used in coordination as in the following passage:

> I have taken note of it and the fact that he stated that he has sent to me a female slave (*waṣīfa*), and has sent to me a slave girl (*jāriya*) with Jawhar, and that I have only been able to send to him two turbans with difficulty and a seat. (**4**r:3–5)

This passage and the following passage indicate clearly the practice of exchanging slaves for goods.

> I have sent a slave girl (*jāriya*) with ʾIbrāhīm (as payment) for what is owed together with her two children. (**17**r:5–6)

The writer of letter **31** says that he has arrived in Aswan and instructs the addresee to convey to him a slave girl from Nubia:

> When you come down the river, bring with you the slave girl (*al-jāriya*) to me. (**31**v:3)

The writer of letter **37** reports that there are no slaves in the markets in Aswan and instructs the recipient to bring a slave girl downriver:

> As for slaves, there is nothing in Aswan, or only a few. By God, bring your slave girl (*jāriyataka*) with you. (**37**r:4–6)

Slaves and slave girls can be vulnerable to loss by illness, as seen in **24**:

> They (the writers) inform him (the eparch) that... the slave girl (*al-jāriya*) and her son, Rāhim, your slave boy (*ġulāmaka*), were examined before purchase three times but she and her son have died. (**24**r:6–10)

10.5. *ʿAbd*

In the corpus the term *ʿabd* (pl. *ʿabīd*) is not used to refer to a slave that was an item of diplomatic or commercial exchange, but rather to designate people who are subordinate to a master and typically work as his functionaries. Most references to the *ʿabīd* of Muslim merchants imply that they are based in Nubia:

> I wrote to you concerning the condition of my slaves (*ʿabīd*) but you did not reply. (**4**r, margin, 2)

> I would like a letter to be sent to all the administrators requesting them to protect the places (*mawāḍiʿ*) of Lāmiʿ and his slaves (*wa-ʿabīdihi*) and likewise my places and my slaves (*ʿabīdī*). (**16**r:13–14)

The writer of letter **8** requests the eparch to grant 'the leader' (*qāʾid*) Ḥasan, the son of the leader Šujāʿ al-Dawla, the same status as his *ʿabīd* with regard to protection:

> The Ikšīl does not need my recommendation with regard to him (the bearer of the letter) or my reassurances to show him respect and treat him well, and grant him the status of those of my personal slaves (*ʿabīdī al-ḵaṣīṣīn*) that are similar to him with regard to care, guardianship, supervision and protection. (**8**r:8–11)

As discussed in §10.3, the passage below from letter **8** suggests that the *ʿabd* of the Muslim writer that is referred to was based in Nubia, whereas the *ġulām* was a travelling functionary:

> As for the seeds of wheat, I (the eparch) have delivered to your slave (*ʿabdika*) six irdabbs minus a third without any waste. Your slave boy (*ġulāmuka*) has received them. (**18**r:5)

It is possible that both the *ʿabd* and the *ġulām* had the status of working slaves and the distinction in terminology reflects their different functions. By the Fatimid period, the term *ʿabd* was applied specifically to black slaves (Goitein 1967, 131; Pipes 1981, 195; Rāġīb 2006, II:24), so this may also be a factor in the distinction in the terminology here.

Some letters refer to functionaries of the eparch by the term *ʿabīd*:

> He has a right to your customary protection, so that he is able to have access to the administrators (*al-wulāh*) and others of your slaves and servants (*ʿabīdihā wa-ḵadamatihā*). (**14**r:5–6)

> He entered Aswan and gathered the slaves of Darmā (*jamīʿ ʿabīd Darmā*; i.e., the people in the service of Darmā). (**23**r:9)

In letter **16**, there is a reference to the slaves (*ʿabīd*) of the Master of the Horses, but since the writer is asking for their protection, it appears that they are the staff of the Muslim writer who are subject to the authority and protection of the eparch:

> As for the slaves (*ʿabīd*) of the Master of the Horses, please take care of them and provide them with their needs. (**16**r:10–11)

The term *ʿabd* is also used as a term of politeness by writers when they refer to themselves in letters to people of superior rank. A conspicuous example of this practice is letter **27** to the secretary of Uruwī, e.g.,

> The slave (*al-ʿabd*) asks my honourable master, the sublime elder, the secretary, may God cause his strength to endure, to kiss the hands of my sublime master, the Master of the Horses, (U)ruwī the son of my sublime master [Īsū] (the slave writing the letter being) his (the eparch's) slave and the slave of his father (*ʿabduhu wa-ʿabd ʾabūhu*) before him, and informs him (the secretary) that the letter of your honour has reached his slave (*ʿabdihi*) and he has read it. (**27**r:2–5)

10.6. *Ḵādim*

The term *ḵādim* (pl. *ḵadama, ḵuddām*) is used in the letters to refer to functionaries of Muslims or of the eparch. They had greater responsibilities than functionaries called *ʿabīd* and were higher in rank, as is seen from the following passages:

> I have sent my slave boy (*ġulāmī*), who is called Šarīf, with a brown camel to his honourable presence.... So take the camel and do not cause him (i.e., Šarīf, my slave boy) to be delayed by a single day. Send him to Papa, my servant (*ḵādim*), who carries out my business (*qāḍī ḥawāʾijī*), for I shall be cut off from him, if there is a delay. (**7**r:3–9)

> The bearer of this (letter) is my loyal and respectful companion, Oua, who is my servant (*ḵādimī*). I have sent him with my slave boy (*ġulāmī*) Mārīḵura. (**6**r:3–4)

Letter **4** refers to the *ḵādim* of the eparch:

> I wrote to you concerning the condition of my slaves (*ʿabīdī*; i.e., my subordinate staff) but you did not reply. Then I wrote to you concerning the condition of the two slaves (*al-raʾsayn al-raqīq*) who are to be sent to my creditor ʾAbū al-Ḍubāʿ, but you have not sent them to me and I do not know whether your servant (*ḵādimuka*) has given us a share. (**4**r, margin, 3–v:1)

Letter **14** refers to the *ḵadama* 'servants' of the eparch together with his *ʿabīd*:

> He has a right to your customary protection, so that he is able to have access to the administrators (*al-wulāh*) and others of your slaves and servants (*ʿabīdihā wa-ḵadamatihā*). (**14**r:5–6)

In medieval Arabic sources, the term *k̲ādim* is often used to designate eunuchs, either those enslaved or those that have been freed (Ayalon 1985). This may be the basis of the distinction between *k̲adama* and *ʿabīd,* i.e., eunuch and non-eunuch servants respectively.

The writer of letter **30** reports that he has pursued two of his servants (*k̲ādimayn*) who had run away from Aswan to Nubia, heading for Soba. This may reflect their status as slaves that the writer regarded as being his property. It also suggests that they were Nubians, and so acquired as items of exchange:

> I have sent in advance a first letter to the Master of the Horses, the vizier of the king, with Ṭāʿī concerning two servants (*k̲ādimayn*) who fled from me there to Ibrīm, (where you are) during your trip, heading for Soba in the middle of Nubia. I did my utmost to pursue them until I crossed the waters of Kurkur. (**30**r:5–7)

When the name of a *k̲ādim* is mentioned, this is always an *ism* without any indication of geneaology, which is the normal naming practice of slaves in medieval Arabic letters:

Oua (**6**r:4)
Papa (**7**r:8)

The term *k̲ādim* is also used, however, to refer to a person who is loyal to the king and so, metaphorically, in his service:

> I have been wronged, although I am the servant of the king (*k̲ādim al-malik*). (**9**v:5)

> As for what you have said with regard to the service (*k̲idmat*) of the king, we are all his servants (*k̲uddāmuhu*). (**22**r:4–5)

> I am his (i.e., the king's) slave (*mamlūkuhu*) and servant (*ḵādimuhu*). (**13**r:9)

10.7. *Mamlūk*

The term *mamlūk* (pl. *mamālīk*) 'slave' (literally 'possessed as property') is, in most cases, used metaphorically as a term of politeness to express obedience and allegiance to the eparch or king:

In several letters, the term is used to refer to Muslims who become subjects of the Nubian king:

> I sent them (my sons) to be at the disposition of the king and (stay) in his land until God permits. I shall convey to them cloth for them to send to the king, may God preserve his life, and so that they can see his crown (i.e., have an audience with him) and become his slaves (*mamālīkihi*). (**21**r:6–8)

> As for what you have said with regard to the service (*ḵidmat*) of the king, we are all his servants (*ḵuddāmuhu*) and slaves of the crown (*mamālīk al-tāj*; i.e., his subjects). (**22**r:4–5)

> I am his (i.e., the king's) slave (*mamlūkuhu*) and servant (*ḵādimuhu*). (**13**r:9)

In letter **23**, which is addressed to an eparch, the writer, the Master of the Shipmasts, refers to himself as a *mamlūk* in the opening formula and in the address:

> The slave (*al-mamlūk*) kisses the ground and what he wishes him to know is that… (**23**r:3–4)

> His slave, the Master of Shipmasts (**23**v, address, left)

Likewise, the writers of letter **24** refer to themselves throughout as *mamālīkuhā* 'your slaves' (the 3sg.f pronominal suffix refers to the term *al-ḥaḍra* 'honourable presence', which is used to denote the eparch).

In one passage in letter **24**, the term *mamālīk* seems to be referring to functionaries of the eparch:

> Please arrange for your command to be issued to some of your slaves (*mamālīkihā*) to extract forcibly from him what is appropriate, God willing. (**24**v:9–7)

Likewise, letter **31** refers to a *mamlūk* who appears to be acting as a functionary in the service of the merchant writer:

> Do not leave them. Take their price. By God, convey (to me) half by means of the small slave (*al-mamlūk al-ṣaġīr*)... [ ] quickly, quickly, quickly! (**31**v:8–9)

10.8. *Mawlā*

A number of documents in the corpus refer to men termed *mawlā* 'freedman'.

The following passage in **31** suggests that a *mawlā* was used as a family servant:

> As for the freedman (*al-mawlā*), we brought him for the sake of the young girl (*bi-rasm al-ṣaġīra*). Do not leave him, but bring him with you. (**31**v:4–6)

In **35**, the writer sends greetings to a *mawlā*, indicating he is treated as part of the family:

> Best wishes to you and to our brother Ḥusayn greetings and to our brother the freedman (*mawlā*) greetings. (**35**r:10)

In the legal document **46**, a freedman acts as a witness:

> Mubārak, the freedman of the most powerful commander, Saʿd al-Dawla, witnessed… (**46**v, witness, 6)

In the legal document **47**, a *mawlā* is a creditor:

> ʿUbayd Allāh ibn Ḥasan, the trader, acknowledged… that he owes, has in his possession, is in debt to Merki ibn Abrām, the freedman of the rightly-guided, prosperous, just judge, Trust of the Kingdom, ʾAbū al-Ḵayr ʾIbrāhīm ibn Muḥammad ibn al-Ḥusayn ibn Muḥammad ibn al-Zubayr…. (**47**r:2–4)

In the document on the verso of **47**, another *mawlā* pays the debt to the creditor:

> Merki ibn Abrām, the freedman of the rightly-guided, prosperous, just judge, Light of the Kingdom, ʾAbū al-Ḵayr ʾIbrāhīm ibn Muḥammad ibn al-Ḥusayn ibn al-Zubayr, while he was in health, while his acts were legal, and he acted willingly, asked me to tesify that he has received in full from ʿAbd Allāh, a freedman (*mawlā*), substituting for his father. (**47**v:7–8)

10.9. *Rasūl*

Men referred to by the term *rasūl* (pl. *rusul*) 'messenger' were sent on various errands, conveying merchandise and letters and buying goods. These activities of a *rasūl* appear to overlap largely with those of a *ġulām* 'slave boy'. The difference between the *rasūl* and the *ġulām*, presumably, was that the former was free whereas the latter was a slave:

> I was intending to send a messenger (*rasūl*) to the king with the merchandise that I have bought for him for ten dīnārs and the horse that I have prepared for him, and equipment that he requested from me, but my slave boy (*ġulāmī*)

arrived, humiliated and wronged by Ibn al-ʿAsqalānī. I sent the messenger (*al-rasūl*), after I had informed the bishop about my suffering due to his (Ibn ʿAsqalānī's) shocking behaviour. I said to him that a messenger (*rasūl*) would reach you. (**9**v:7–12)

So, I sent your slave boy (*ġulāmaka*) together with my messenger (*rasūlī*) to the market and he bought… (**9**r:14)

The commander is expecting in great anticipation news to reach him from your honour. Ensure that your letters reach the commander. Your messengers (*rusuluhā*) are in contact with him all the time. (**16**r:16–margin, 2)

Your two companions have seen my messenger (*rasūlī*) whom I sent in connection with the slave (*al-waṣīfa*). (**17**r:9–10)

I [request that you arrange for] the dispatch of a messenger (*rasūl*) to it (Aswan?) afterwards. Please ensure that he proceeds safely to his colleagues, and take care of this colleague of mine and protect him, and also his colleagues in the armed garrison post, in order that his letter may reach me, thankfully, here (Aswan). (**19**r:4–6)

If my messenger (*rasūlī*) delays sending what should be sent, do not omit to send me a letter containing the mention of your news. (**32**:9–10)

The writers of letter **24** report that a *rasūl* who was accompanying a sick slave became ill himself:

They (the writers) inform him that the slave (*al-raʾs al-raqīq*) whom he bestowed upon his slaves (*mamālīkihā*, i.e., the writers of this letter) through the agency of Bazilī was sick, and that his slaves (*mamālīkihā*, i.e., the writers) wanted to return her, but the messenger (*al-rasūl*) whom she accompanied became ill. (**24**r:6–9)

The writer of letter **25** asks the eparch not to delay returning the writer's messenger:

> If you would (kindly) send my messenger (*rasūlī*) to them from your place, then please do so, for time has run out for me. (**25**r:15)

The term *rasūl* is used in letter **21** to refer to an envoy from the Fatimid ruler:

> My grandfather travelled to visit the just king Basil and my father travelled to visit the king Mūyis the father of Mena Kurē (?), as a messenger (*rasūl*) from the ruler, may God strengthen his victory, to Soba. (**21**r:9–11)

10.10. *Mutaḥammil*

The term *mutaḥammil* 'carrier, bearer' is frequently used in the correspondence of the corpus to refer to the bearer of the letter who delivers it to the addressee:

> When the bearer of this letter (*mutaḥammil hāḏā al-kitāb*) reaches you, release him and send him away quickly. (**2**r:6–7)

> I have sent with the bearer of this letter (*mutaḥammil hāḏā al-kitāb*) also two beds of Iraqi workmanship. (**2**v:1)

> The bearer of these lines (*mutaḥammil hāḏihi al-suṭūr*) is the Head, may God decree his safety, and he must be shown favour and respect. (**26**r:4–5)

A common phrase in the letters is *mutaḥammiluhā*. The 3sg.f suffix most likely has an inanimate plural sense. It may be referring to the lines (*suṭūr*) of the letter; cf. *mutaḥammil hāḏihi al-suṭūr* (**26**r:4). Alternatively it may be referring to the letter and associated items, e.g., enclosed accounts, goods, or possibly also other letters delivered in the same batch.

> The bearer of this letter (*mutaḥammiluhā*) is my loyal and respectful companion, Oua, who is my servant. (**6**r:3–4)

> The bearer of this letter (*mutaḥammiluhā*), who has travelled (to you), is the leader Ḥasan, the son of the leader Šujāʿ al-Dawla ('the Courage of the State') ʾIsḥāq, the administrator of the gate. (**8**r:3–4)

> (I report) the arrival of the bearer of this letter (*mutaḥammiluhā*) to the land of the Nubians, together with a horse in order to seek his livelihood by selling it. (**14**r:3–4)

> So, we have sent the carrier of this letter (*mutaḥammiluhā*) Bazilī. (**24**v:4)

> I have sent with the bearer of the letter (*mutaḥammilihā*) a dyed garment in place of the payment in cash. (**36**v:2–3)

> The bearer of this letter (*mutaḥammiluhā*), the leader Saʿāda, may God decree his abundant good health, the relative of the noble leader, Humām al-Dawla ('Hero of the Dynasty') Ḥāmid, may God decree for him abundant good health, has departed. (**3**r, margin, 1–3)

The second occurrence of *mutaḥammil* in the following passage from letter **2** refers to the carrier of goods:

> I have sent with the bearer of this letter (*mutaḥammil hāḏā al-kitāb*) also two beds of Iraqi workmanship. Please accept what he has sent you and send on the carrier of them (i.e., the goods; *mutaḥammilahum*) as quickly as possible, if God wills. (**2**v:1–3)

In the two passages from **24** below, the 3sg.f suffix of *mutaḥammil* refers to the eparch, the feminine agreement being with the honorific term *ḥaḍra* 'honourable presence'. The intention may be the carrier of the letter or the carrier of the goods, as in **2**v:3:

> ...for your carrier (*mutaḥammiluhā*) has absconded. (**24**v:5)
>
> Your carrier (*mutaḥammiluhā*) has arrived, grateful for your kindness and the good that you have done. (**24**v, margin, 1–2)

11. THE SOCIO-ECONOMIC SITUATION REFLECTED BY THE DOCUMENTS

Here I shall bring together various strands in the foregoing descriptions of the contents of the documents with the purpose of summarising what the corpus reflects with regard to the society and economy of Lower Nubia.

There is some confirmation in the corpus of the description given by al-ʾAswānī of an open trade zone for Muslim merchants in Lower Nubia between the first and second cataracts. This applies especially to document **45**, which indicates that Muslim traders were not permitted to navigate in their hired boat beyond the second cataract. One should be cautious, however, of comparing this zone in Lower Nubia with the 'port of trade' in Dahomey described by Polanyi (1966), as several historians of Nubia have done, without qualification.

The phenomenon of the Dahomey port of trade has a generic parallel with the open trade zone of Lower Nubia. The corpus, however, indicates that the boundary between Egypt and Lower Nubia was more porous on various levels than the Polanyi model would suggest. Rather, this boundary appears not to have been a sharp transition from one political entity to the next, but rather a gradual interpenetration of the adjoining communities on the social, economic, linguistic and indeed political levels. This, in fact, was typical for boundaries in the medieval Islamic world (Hourani 1992, 145; Brauer 1995, 13).

 https://doi.org/10.11647/OBP.0391.11

We have seen that the documents reflect the settlement of Nubians in Upper Egypt and the settlement of Muslims in Lower Nubia. Nubians were in the service of Muslim merchants operating in Nubia, reflected in particular by the Nubian names of the merchants' slaves. The legal document **47** refers to a Nubian *mawlā* 'freedman, client' of a prominent Muslim judge, who appears to have been based in Aswan.

Muslims, moreover, appear to have worked in the service of the eparch in Qaṣr Ibrīm. One clear example is the secretary (*kātib*) of the eparch Uruwī, who, according to letter **27**, had the Muslim Arabic name ʿUbayd Allāh ʿAlī.

Document **44** refers to a Nubian resident in Lower Nubia who served as a Fatimid military officer with an estate (*ʾiqṭāʿ*) in Upper Egypt.

As we have discussed, however, in various places above, there was not a clear binary division between service and allegiance to the representatives of the Muslim government, on the one hand, and service and allegiance to the Nubian eparch and king, on the other. Rather, Muslims operating in Nubia appear to have served and owed allegiance to both the Muslim and the Nubian authorities. In addition to the evidence for this that has been cited already, this situation seems to be reflected by passages such as the following:

> As for the slaves of the Master of the Horses (*ʿabīd ṣāḥib al-ḵayl*), please take care of them and provide them with their needs. (**16**r:10–11)

Here a Muslim merchant is asking the eparch to protect people who are apparently in the merchant's service, but they are simultaneously described as the 'slaves of the Master of the Horses'.

Another case that can only be understood on the assumption that there was dual allegiance is that of the Nubian called Merki whose activities are described in **23**. As far as can be established from the letter, Merki is working with the Muslim writer of the letter to supply the eparch with military equipment but he has also taken upon himself the responsibility of operating as an agent of the Nubian authorities in the suppression of a rebellion.

This dual allegiance is likely to have applied also to the Nubian Fatimid military officer mentioned in **44**. He had an *ʾiqṭāʿ* in Upper Egypt, near the border with Nubia, but originated from a village in Lower Nubia. The fact that the document was found in Qaṣr Ibrīm suggests, moreover, that he was resident in Nubia. The Shiʿite Fatimid dynasty appointed Christian Nubians to important positions in the Fatimid court and army (Vantini 1981, 129–30; Lev 1987; Zouache 2019; Tsakos 2021, 18). This is likely because the régime felt vulnerable within the population of Egypt, the majority of the Muslims of which were Sunni (den Heijer et al. 2015, 334). They also needed new alliances to counterbalance the traditionally Sunni régimes of the Middle East.

Some of the Muslims working for the eparch may have been converts. Although the name of the eparch Uruwī's secretary, ʿUbayd Allāh ʿAlī, suggests that he was a Muslim, the letters issued by Uruwī (**17** and **18**), which were presumably written by this secretary, are carelessly written with many oddities in the Arabic. It appears that the writer did not have a good knowledge of Arabic nor was he schooled in epistolary style that was used by educated Muslims in the Fatimid period (see §12.4). This correlates with the statement of al-ʾAswānī that the Muslim residents in Lower Nubia that he met during his travels did not speak good Arabic (al-Maqrīzī, *Ḵiṭaṭ*, I:352). The Muslim settlers in Nubia evidently underwent a cultural and linguistic assimilation to the environment in which they lived.

There was economic integration between Egypt and Nubia through the extension of the Egyptian monetary system into Nubia (Ruffini 2019). There are references in the corpus to the use of money in transactions and, in some cases, in gift exchanges (§6).

Document **46** recto records a legal partnership between Kanzī Muslims, at least one of whom was a resident of Lower Nubia, and a Nubian woman in the ownership of landed property in Lower Nubia. It is not clear where the document was drawn up, but the fact that it was discovered in Qaṣr Ibrīm suggest that the parties were resident in Nubia. The document on the verso of **46** records the purchase of property in Lower Nubia by a Kanzī resident of Lower Nubia. The dossier of documents relating to the marital affairs of the Christian Nubian Maryam ibnat Yuḥannis (**49–53**) shows that her marriages with Nubian men were administered legally in Muslim courts in Upper Egypt. The documents, however, were found in Qaṣr Ibrīm, suggesting that, at least in later life, she was a resident of Nubia. This juridical administration of Christian Nubian affairs by Muslim courts is reminiscent of the way Jews made contracts of various kinds in Muslim courts in medieval Fusṭāṭ, as we see in the Genizah documents (Khan

1993a). One of the motivations for Jews to carry out their legal affairs in Muslim courts was to strengthen the legal force of their cases. We know that in some circumstances they used both Muslim and Jewish courts for double security. There may have been a similar motivation for the Nubian Maryam to apply to Muslim courts. The same applies to the drawing up by a Muslim notary of the documents in **46** relating to property, including a partnership between Muslims and a Nubian. All this reflects a merger rather than a sharp separation of Muslim and Nubian spheres of juridical authority.

It is significant that some of the witnesses of the Arabic document of sale **46** verso have Nubian names. In order to avoid exposing documents drawn up by Muslim notaries to the danger of invalidation due to the rejection of the suitability of the witnesses, the institution of a permanent body of professional accredited witnesses (*ʿudūl*) arose in Islamic law. The suitability of these witnesses was verified by a Muslim judge and their testimonies and depositions could not be rejected.[1] It is not clear, however, whether this requirement was strictly applied outside the main urban centres. Medieval Arabic legal documents from peripheral areas were often witnessed by men with non-Muslim names. One clear case of this is the Khurasan corpus of documents (Khan 2007), many of which mention witnesses with local Iranian names. Some of these Iranian witnesses, moreover, appear also in the contemporary corpus of Bactrian documents from the region.

---

[1] This institution was established in Egypt in 174 AH/790 AD by the *qāḍī* Ibn Fuḍāla (al-Kindī, *Kitāb al-Wulāh*, 386, 612).

The question arises, therefore, whether the Nubian witnesses in **46** verso had been accredited as *ʿudūl* by a Muslim judge. One possibility is that the Arabic document was drawn up in Nubia by a Muslim notary and local Nubians who would have been in principle acceptable as witnesses of Nubian documents were called to witness it. This would be a further case of the integration of Muslim and Nubian juridical practice.

The Nubian partner in **46** is a woman, Pāpāy, the daughter of Ampātā. Numerous medieval Arabic documents written in Egypt record the purchase of property by women, e.g., APEL 56 (Edfū 239 AH/854 AD), in which a woman buys a house from her husband. The Arabic Papyrology Database contains many more examples. There are many references in the Genizah documents to women owning property, usually as a secure source of income from rent (Goitein 1983, 85). Several extant Nubian documents record land sales in which one or more parties are women (Ruffini 2012b, 61, 77, 125, 236, 237).

At the end of letter **17** (r:13) sent by the eparch Uruwī, there is a note that conveys greetings to the addressee from Uruwī's 'two wives'. If my reading and interpretation are correct, then this indicates that Uruwī practiced polygamy, which was a Muslim practice but was not, as far as I am aware, customary in Nubia. Perhaps this is a reflection of convergence of Nubian and Muslim legal practice.

Document **30** alludes to a business partnership between Muslims and Nubians:

> I have brought into partnership with him my wife and my slave boy, Ramaḍān and Rāšid, the mariner, who is with

> him and those of the Nubians [ ] upon them the greeting of Jaʿfar. (**30**r, margin, 6–9)

Several of the letters of the corpus reflect an economic crisis that affected Lower Nubia. Allusions to this are found in the letters of the Kanzī merchant Lāmiʿ ibn Ḥasan, e.g.,

> The lofty, most glorious and munificent presence, may God establish his happiness, has graciously released the boats, in the knowledge of what the country is undergoing with regard to the rising of prices, for the travellers have experienced hardship and (the prices) have risen to the disadvantage of the merchants, so that they have acquired goods at high prices. (**3**r:5–8)

> This year the people from the port (of Aswan) were hindered in two ways. One of these is the injustice done to them by the people of the land and the other is the lack of produce. So, I took some hair-cutters (and opened sacks of produce) and gave relief to the people and the first of them were the people in your land. If it was not for me, they (i.e., our people) would not have found produce, nor did anybody dare send (produce). (**5**r:5–11)

> The lack of produce this year has not been concealed from you and the condition of the people. No ship would have been sent this year, had I not opened the store and sold to the people of your land. (**36**r:6–8)

> I then went to your slave boy and consulted him concerning his sale and sold him for five dīnārs, on the grounds that there is nobody in the land and none of the people have anything. (**9**r:9–11)

Lāmiʿ ibn Ḥasan and the other merchants of the corpus were writing in the late Fatimid period, which was characterised by economic hardship. As we have seen, the economic weakness is reflected by the severe debasement of coinage at this period, which is attested in some letters (§6).

One cause of this was the political instability arising from power struggles of Egyptian viziers and the threat of invasion by the Crusaders and external Muslim forces. Political instability impacted also on Upper Egypt. Al-Maqrīzī, for example, reports in his *ʾItti‘āẓ al-Ḥunafāʾ* that in the year 556 AH/1161 AD "The King of the Nubians marched against Aswan in twelve thousand horsemen and massacred a great multitude of Muslims" (Beshir 1975, 21).

Such instability in the region is alluded to in letter **24**:

> If it was not for the news we have heard from the north and the strife of the land, your slaves (i.e., the writers) would have made sure to present ourselves before you to kiss the ground and to perform their obligations. (**24**v:1–3)

Another cause was the incidence of recurrent famines due to the impact on agriculture of excessively high or excessively low Nile floods at this period (Hassan 2007). When the Nile flood was sub-optimal, famines could occur because of predictions of a bad harvest in the next year, which created a buyers' market and drove the prices of grain up beyond the reach of many (Lev 2013).

Famines could be relieved by government intervention and the control of government grain stores, if well-managed (Shoshan 1981; Lev 2013). In the citations from letters **5** and **36** above, Lāmi‘ ibn Ḥasan states that he responded to shortages in grain experienced by people in the land of the eparch by opening grain stores. Letter **3** alludes to the release of boats to ameliorate economic hardship. So, both the Kanzī Lāmiʿ ibn al-Ḥasan and the eparch assumed responsibility for relieving grain shortages in Lower Nubia. There are several extant Nubian documents containing disbursement orders of grain issued by the eparch (e.g., P. QI II 23, P. QI III 49, P. QI IV 94), which were apparently from public stores or the eparch's personal store (Adams 1996, 226–27). The passages cited above from our corpus indicate that the supply of grain to Lower Nubia was also administered by the Banū al-Kanz, reflecting shared responsibilities of economic administration in this region of Nubia.

The corpus also shows that there was not a hard boundary for Muslims at the second cataract. According to al-ʾAswānī, this could be passed with authorisation of the eparch as far as Maqs al-ʾAʿlā and travel beyond this required permission from the king (al-Maqrīzī, *Ḵiṭaṭ*, I:353). Several letters refer to the travel of Muslims or their slaves to the king's court in Dongola or to Soba. In such cases the main purpose of the visits appears to be the supply of military equipment for the Nubian army or for diplomatic missions. Moreover, there is evidence of a Muslim community in Dongola and Soba in the Fatimid period (§1, §4.3). This reflects another level of integration of Egypt and Nubia.

12. SCRIPT AND LAYOUT

12.1. Preliminary Remarks

The documents in the corpus exhibit a number of variations in the form of their script and the layout of the script on the writing support.

As is generally the situation in medieval Arabic documents, it is difficult to match the form of script in the documents of our corpus with the names of specific script styles that appear in medieval literary sources. This is not only because of the lack of specific descriptive details in the literary sources but also because the script of the documents was typically not carefully executed according to a specfic standard (*muḥaqqaq*) but rather was a non-official, poorly executed script, current for popular purposes (*muṭlaq*).[1]

Diacritical dots on the consonants are written only sporadically. There are numerous unconventional ligatures between letters within words and sometimes across words.

12.2. Cursive Tendencies

Letter shapes are often simplified by cursive tendencies. These include:

[1] For this distinction, see al-Qalqašandī (d. 821 AH/1418 AD), *Ṣubḥ al-ʾAʿšā*, III: 26; Khan (1992, 44–46).

 https://doi.org/10.11647/OBP.0391.12

The writing of *sīn* and *šīn* without teeth, e.g.,

Figure 7: سير 'he has sent' (**4**r:4), left, and شر 'evil' (**6**r:8), right

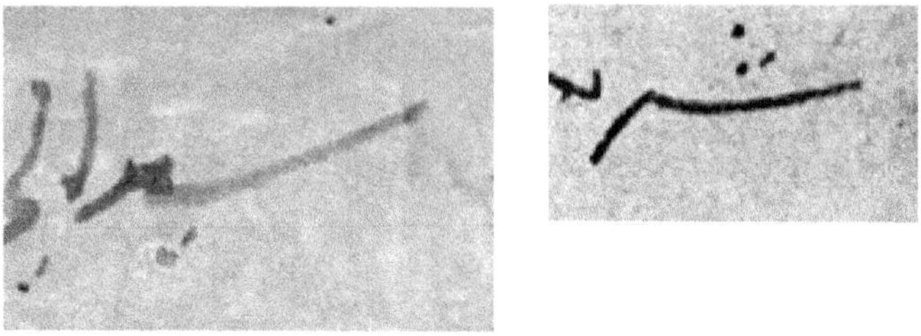

The contraction of the loop in *fā*ʾ and *qāf*:

Figure 9: وصيفة 'a female slave' (**4**r:4)

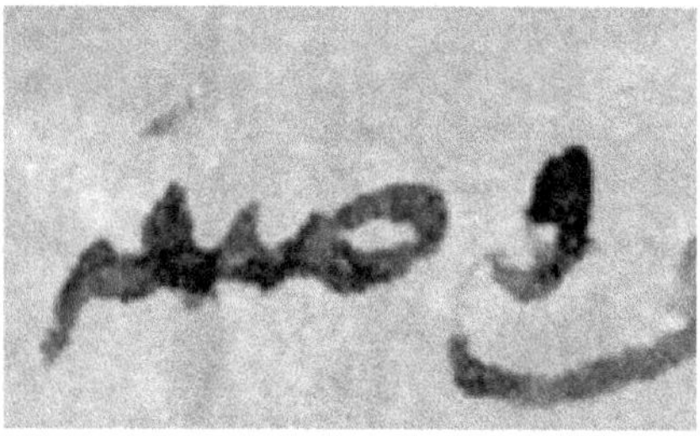

Levelling of distinctions between letter forms, e.g.,

Figure 10: الدولة 'the dynasty' (**8**r:4), left, والانفاذ 'and the sending' (**10**r:5), middle, هذا 'this' (**45**:2), right

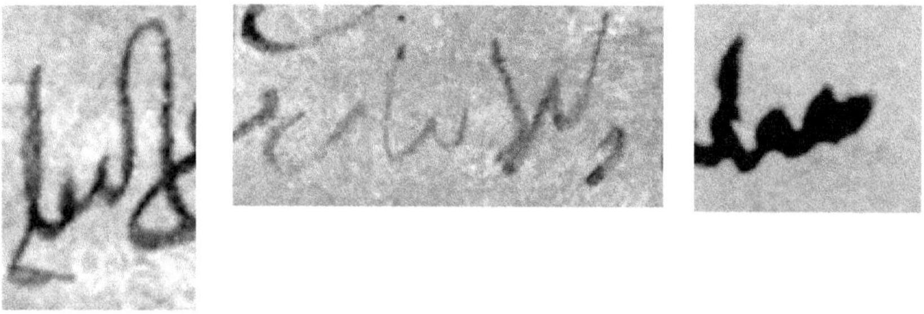

12.3. Writing Line

The documents show some differences with regard to the orientation of the writing lines.[2]

It is common for the line of the script to be level throughout most of the line and then to slant upwards at the end of lines, often stacking words to allow them to be inserted in the remaining space before the left margin, e.g.,

Figure 13: **2**r:5–7

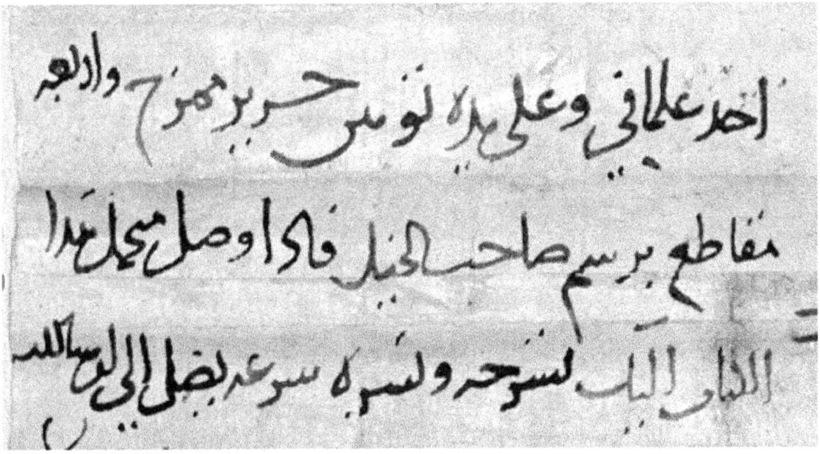

[2] I am using the term writing line to refer to the overall writing line upon which words are placed. This differs from the baseline, which refers to the invisible line upon which single characters within a word are placed. For this distinction, see Grob (2013).

Figure 14: **4**r:2–5

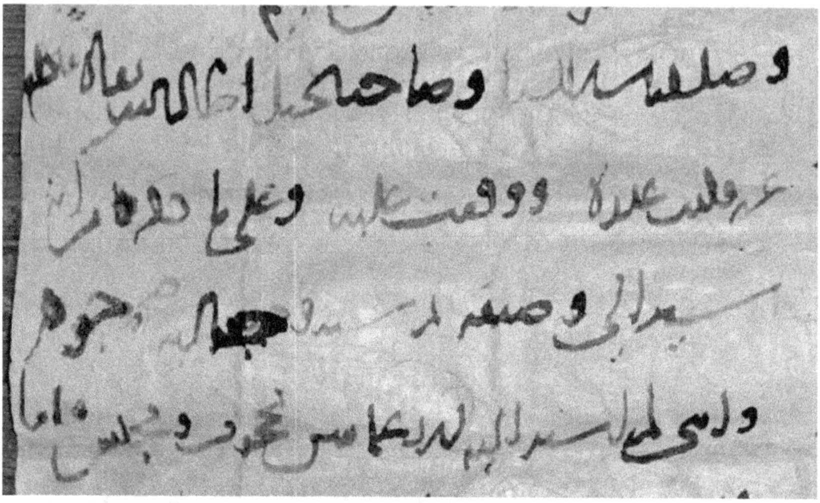

In some documents, the writing line slants downwards in most of the line and then is moved upwards at the end with the same angle of downwards slant, e.g.,

Figure 15: **3**r:1–4

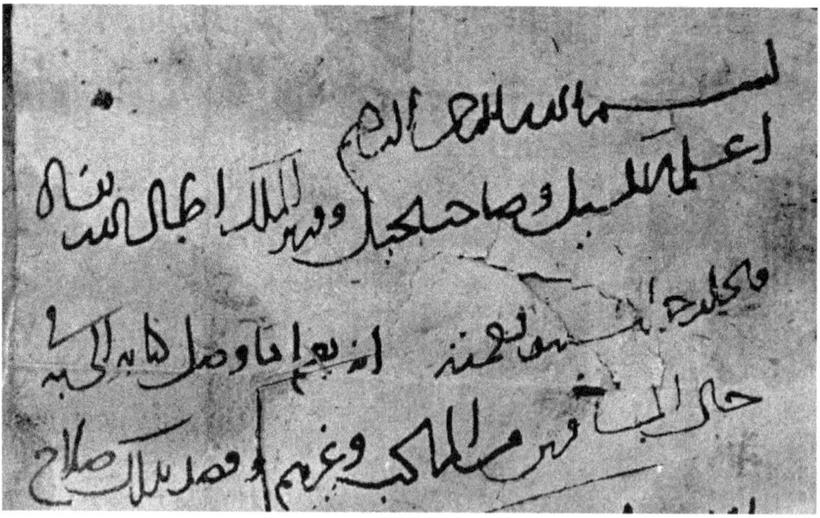

12.4. Line Spacing

In many of the letters, especially those to the eparch, the spacing between the lines is generous, which ensures that the descenders and ascenders of letters do not clash. This can be seen in the samples given above. Other clear examples of this feature are the following:

Figure 16: **6**r:1–5

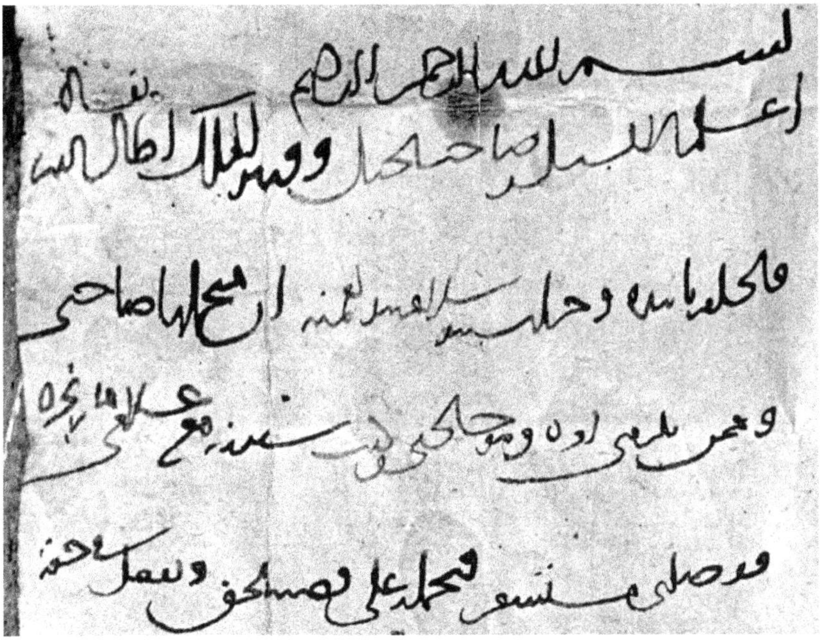

Figure 17: **8**r:1–5

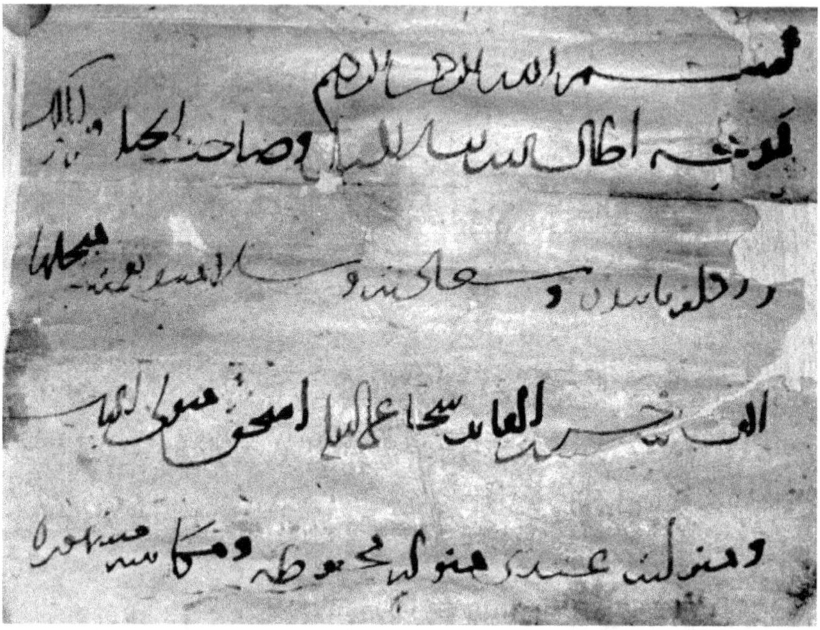

Note that the *basmala* is not followed by a large line space here and elsewhere.

In the following letter to a deputy of the eparch, the wide line spacing is combined with the vertical extension of the *hastae* of some of the letters, especially in the *basmala* and the first line of the letter:

Figure 18: **26**r:1–4

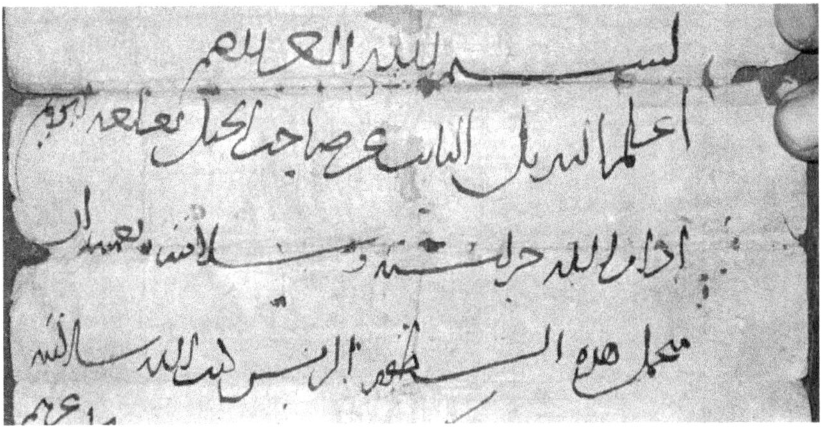

Wide line spacing is a characteristic feature of letters written to addressees of high social status in the Fatimid period. It is found in petitions to the chancery and letters to dignitaries. It is also found in dispositive documents issued by the chancery, such as decrees.[3] The fact that letters in our corpus that are addressed to the eparch and his deputy have this feature reflects the fact that the writers addressed them as dignitaries with a high social status.

In letters that are not addressed to an eparch or dignitary the line spacing is often narrower, e.g.,

[3] For plates of petitions to the Fatimid chancery, see Khan (1993a). For plates of Fatimid decrees, see Stern (1964). For an example of an Arabic letter with wide spacing to a Karaite dignitary, which has been preserved in the Genizah, see Khan (1993b). For more on the layout and production of Fatimid chancery documents, see Rustow (2020).

Figure 19: **38**r:1–6

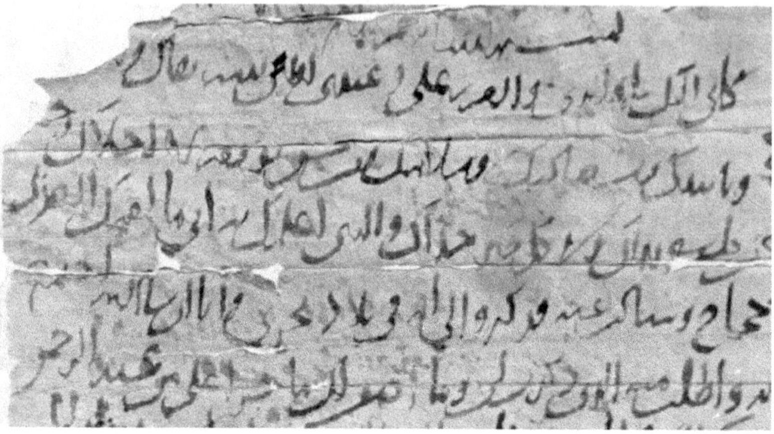

The letters sent by the secretary of Uruwī also do not exhibit conspicuously wide line spacing. This suggests that the secretary was not schooled in Fatimid epistolary étiquette to the same extent as the Egyptian writers of letters, which may reflect that he was a Nubian, e.g.,

Figure 20: **17**r:1–7

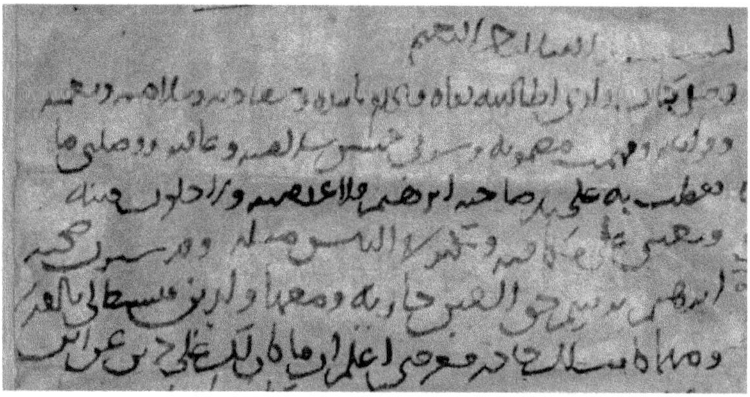

The line spacing of the legal documents is generally not conspicuously wide, but the spacing in the large marriage contract **48** is slightly wider than other documents:

Figure 21: **48**r:1–6

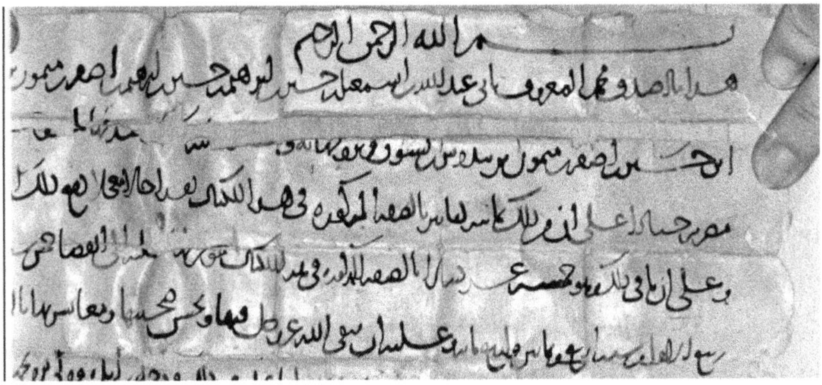

12.5. Width of the Document

Documents to eparchs and other dignitaries are typically written with a wide format. Letters to addressees of lower social rank are sometimes written on narrower sheets, e.g., Figure 22.

Figure 22: **37** recto

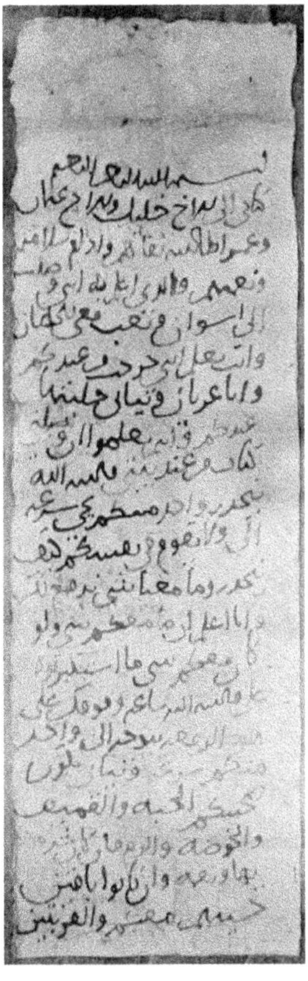

12.6. Thickness of the Pen

The samples given above of line spacing in letters also show that those letters written to the eparch and his deputy with wide line spacing tend to be written with a finer pen than those with narrower line spacing.

12.7. Margins

In both letters and legal documents, a wide space is typically left at the top before the beginning of the text and in the right margin, whereas the text is written up to the left margin, e.g., Figures 23 and 24.

Figure 23: **7r**:1–6

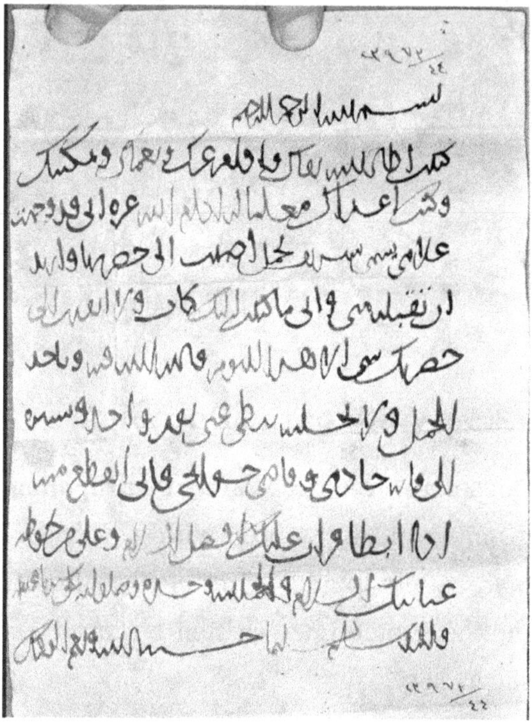

Figure 24: **45**:1–8

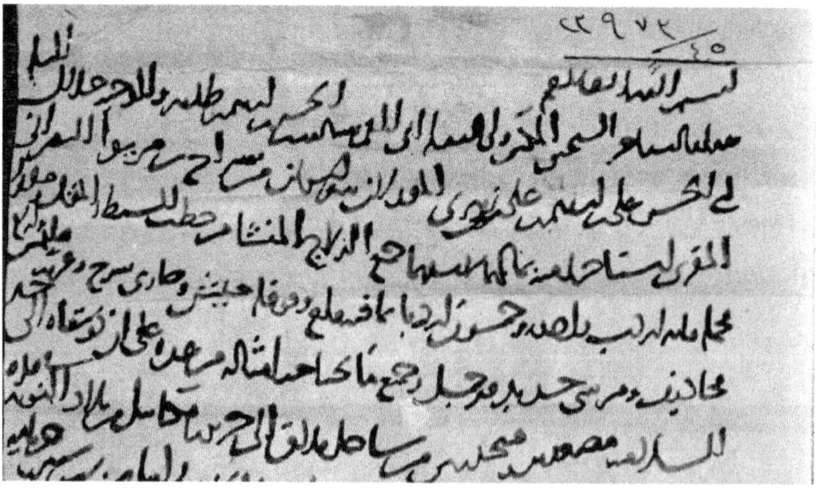

In letters, the text is generally continued from the bottom of the sheet into the right margin before the writer turns to the verso of the sheet. This practice does not occur in legal documents.

When text is added to the right margin in letters, this may be written as a single line perpendicular to the main text, e.g., Figure 25.

More often, however, the added text in the margin is written as a series of short lines arranged diagonally in relation to the main text. The first of these short lines is written nearest to the end of the main text at the bottom of the sheet and the following lines are written below, filling the margin to the top of the sheet, e.g., Figure 26.

Figure 25: **2** recto

Figure 26: **4** recto

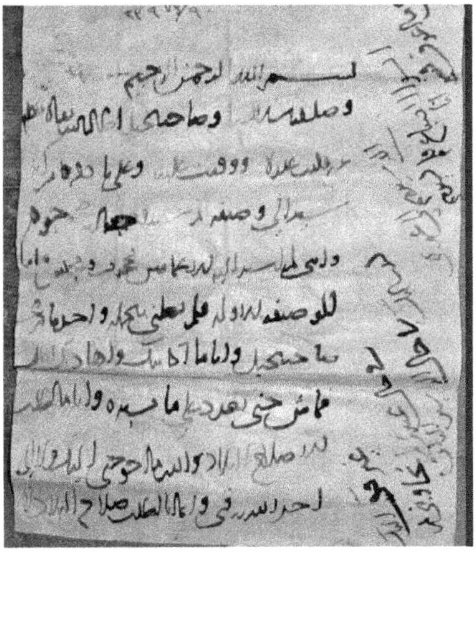

Figure 27: **11** recto

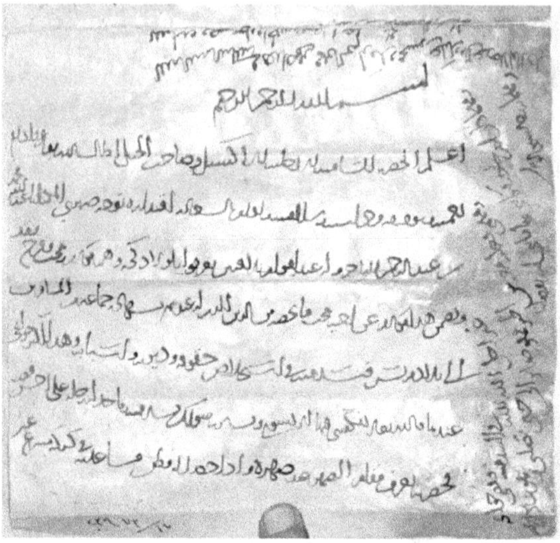

The marginal text occasionally continues into the top margin, written at approximately 180 degrees relative to the main text, e.g., Figure 27.

Figure 28: **16** recto

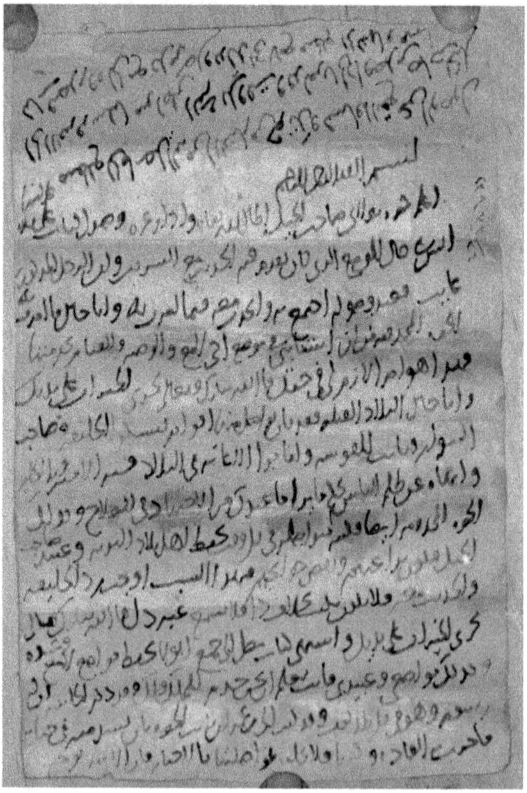

In some cases, the text continues directly from the bottom of the letter into the upper margin. This appears to be because not enough space was left in the right margin to contain text, e.g., Figure 28.

12.8. Text on the Verso

When an address is written on the verso of a letter and there is no continuation of the text of the letter onto the verso, the sheet is turned around the vertical axis and the address is written on the top, e.g.,

Figure 29: **6** recto (left) and **6** verso (right)

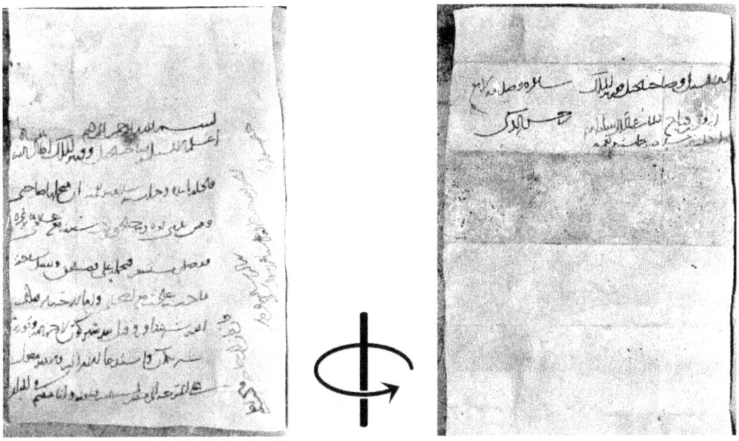

Figure 30: **11** recto (left) and **11** verso (right)

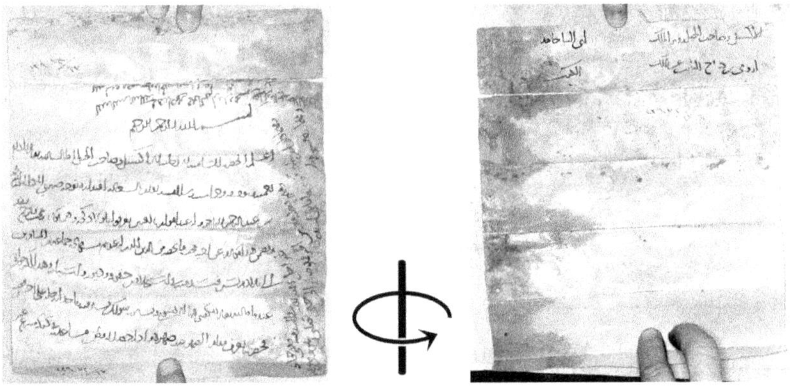

When the text of the recto of the letter continues onto the verso, the sheet is turned around the horizontal axis and the text of the letter is written from the top. The address is then added by

turning the verso 180 degrees, so that the address is up-side-down relative to the text of the verso, e.g.,

Figure 31: **4** recto (left) and **4** verso (right)

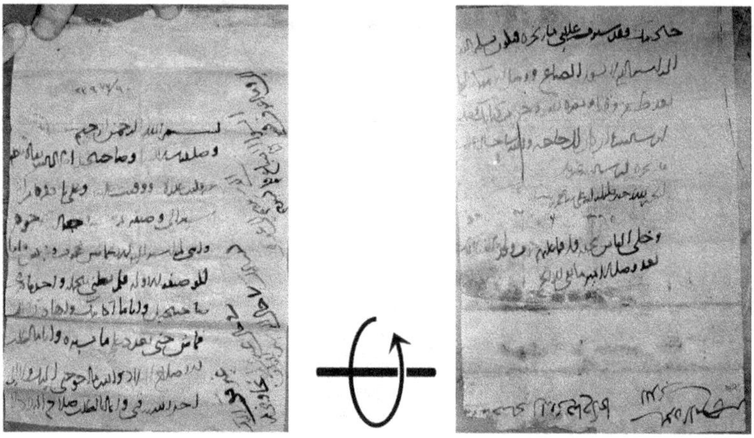

Figure 32: **5** recto (left) and **5** verso (right)

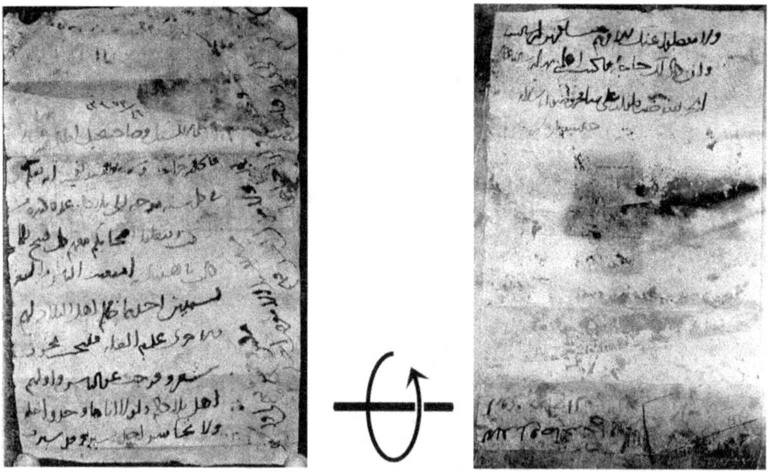

As far as I can establish from the photographs, legal documents were turned on both axes.

13. LANGUAGE

The Arabic language of the documents occasionally exhibits deviations from Classical Arabic usage, often due to interference from the spoken vernacular language.

13.1. Phonology and Orthography

13.1.1. Loss of Interdental Consonants

The diacritics of *tāʾ* are often written where Classical Arabic would have the interdental consonant *ṯāʾ*, e.g.,

تبات ‘a record’ (**9**r:22 < ثبات)
ويحدتك ‘and he will tell you’ (**22**r:14 < ويحدثك)
وتبت عليه ‘and he persisted’ (**23**r:12 < وثبت عليه)
وتلتة ‘and three’ (**25**v:12 < وثلثة)
متقال ‘standard weight’ (**46**v:14 < مثقال)
حدت ‘it was discussed’ (**49**r:12 < حدث)

A related phenomenon is the occasional replacement of Classical Arabic *ẓāʾ* by *ḍād*, e.g.,

النضر ‘looking’ (**38**r:4 < نظر)

13.1.2. *Tafḵīm*

In a few cases, an emphatic consonant *ṣād, ṭāʾ* or *ḍād* is written where Classical Arabic has a plain *sīn, tāʾ, dāl* or *ḏāl*, reflecting suprasegmental pharyngealisation (*tafḵīm*). This is attested in the environment of *rāʾ* and the labial vowel /*ū*/, both of which induce pharyngealisation in spoken vernacular Arabic, e.g.,

https://doi.org/10.11647/OBP.0391.13

قراط عليك افضل السلام 'I send you best wishes.' (**29**v:3 < قرات *qaraʾtu* literally: 'I have read')

الخوضة 'the helmet' (**37**r:19 < خوذة *ḵūḏa*)

13.1.3. Devoicing

The devoicing of a voiced consonant in contact with a following voiced consonant is reflected in the following orthography:

اتفو 'Edfu' (**38**r:9 < ادفو)

13.1.4. Loss of *hamza*

Word-medial and word-final *hamza* are often omitted in the orthography, e.g.,

ادام الله علاه 'may God cause to endure his ascendance' (**30**r:3 < عَلَاءَهُ)

بقضاها 'by carrying them out' (**30**r:5 < بِقَضَائِهَا)

The diacritics of *yāʾ* are often written where *hamza* on *yāʾ* would be expected in Classical Arabic, reflecting the loss of *hamza* in this environment in vernacular speech, e.g.,

القايد 'the leader' (**3**v:3 < القَائِد)

حوايج 'needs' (**9**r:11 < حَوَائِج)

غايب 'absent' (**16**r:4 < غَائِب)

In the following, a *yāʾ* is written where a *hamza* without a seat between two vowels would be expected in Classical Arabic:

احيا الله الملك وزريه 'May God keep the king and his viziers alive.' (**23**r:6 < وُزَرَاءَهُ)

Alternatively, it may be that the singular form وزيره 'his vizier' was intended, but the scribe metathesised the *yāʾ* and the *rāʾ* when writing the word.

The orthography sometimes reflects the elision of word-initial *hamzat al-qaṭʿ* after a word ending in a vowel, e.g.,

ماعرف ايش يكتب 'I do not know what he is writing.' (**21**r:10)

13.1.5. Shortening of a Final Long Vowel

The omission of final *yāʾ* in the following orthography appears to reflect the shortening of unstressed final long vowels in vernacular speech:

ولدين من اولاد 'two boys from my boys', i.e., two of my boys (= sons; **21**r:3 < اولادى *ʾawlā́dī*)

13.1.6. Assimilation to a Cliticised Prepositional Phrase

The following orthography appears to reflect the assimilation of the final *bāʾ* of the verbal form to the *lām* of the following prepositional phrase:

وكاتل لى 'and write to me' (**29**v:4 < وكاتب لى *wa-kātib lī*)

13.1.7. Final *yāʾ* Written for Final *ʾalif*

ما انا الى شاكر لله 'I am only grateful to God.' (**35**r:9)

Here the word الى corresponds to الا in Classical Arabic orthography.

In the following example, a final *ʾalif* is written where Classical Arabic has final short /*a*/:

فعن ايش تكلمت فيا ‘and (I know) what you have spoken about me (< *fiyya*).’ (**17**r:8)

13.1.8. Non-Classical Plene Orthography

Occasionally, long *ā* is represented by *ʾalif* where Classical Arabic has defective orthography, e.g.,

ذالك ‘that’ (**35**r:4; Classical Arabic ذٰلِكَ)

13.1.9. Two *ʾalifs* Represent Word-Initial *ʾā*

االجله ‘its postponed portion’ (**48**r:7)

This is an unconventional orthography for آجِله.

13.1.10. Interchange of *ḍād* and *ẓāʾ*

يقبظوها ‘they cause to acquire’ (**38**r, margin, 3)
لمعظلةٍ ‘to a misfortune’ (**41**:76)

In Classical Arabic orthography, these words are spelt with a *ḍād*, viz. يُقَبِّضُوهَا, مُعْضِلَةٌ.

13.2. Morphology

13.2.1. Interrogative Pronoun *ʾayš*

In several cases, writers use the inanimate interrogative pronoun ايش rather than ما or ماذا, e.g.,

فعن ايش تكلمت فيا ‘and (I know) what you have spoken about me.’ (**17**r:8)
فايشما كان لك من حاجة ‘and whatever request you have’ (**20**r:11)
ماعرف ايش يكتب ‘I do not know what he is writing.’ (**21**r:10)

13.2.2. Morphology of Fifth Form Verbs

An *ʾalif* is written before the *tāʾ* in the fifth form in the following, reflecting vernacular morpho-phonology:

اتسلموا 'they have received' (**38**r, margin, 2; Classical Arabic تَسَلَّمُوا)

13.2.3. Particle

The word سا is found in **23**r:4, which I am interpreting as a vernacular form meaning 'now, immediately', derived from ساعة.

13.3. Syntax

13.3.1. Independent Genitive Exponent

The independent genitive exponent *mtāʿ* is attested in the following, where it is written connected to the preceding word in the orthography.

والقوساmتاع درمس 'and the Qūsa (clan) of (the town of) Darmus' (**18**r:7)

The *ʾalif* before متاع presumably reflects an epenthetic vowel (*wa-l-Qūsa imtāʿ Darmus*).

13.3.2. Non-Classical Usages of the Negator *lam*

On a few occasions, the use of the negative particle *lam* has been extended beyond the Classical Arabic construction of *lam* + jussive and is used with past suffix-conjugation verbs and future prefix-conjugation verbs. This is more characteristic of non-standard written Arabic of the Ottoman period than medieval Arabic (Lentin 1997, 764–67; Wagner 2010, 141–50):

فانى لم لقينا 'and I have not found' (**9**v:20–21—Note that in this example the first person singular and plural pronominal subject indexes are interchanged.)

فان العسكر لم ينتظر 'for the army will indeed not wait' (**22**r:12)

In the last example, it seems that the negation is emphatic, which is a usage of *lam* that is still retained in Modern Egyptian Arabic (Rosenbaum 2002).

13.3.3. Non-Classical Usage of First Person Pronouns

In the following, a 1pl pronoun serves as the subject of a verb with a 1sg inflection:

لانا اريد 'because I want' (**2**r:8)

13.4. Lexical Items

The documents attest to a few lexical items that have forms or meanings that are not attested in the dictionaries, as far as I can establish:

بناك 'nascaphthon (aromatic root)' (**15**v:5): This is the meaning given by Dozy (*Supplément*, I:119) for the word *bunk*, also pronounced *bunak*. The orthography بناك may be a variant form of this word.

الغسيسن 'beauty' (**17**r:11): This appears to be a variant of the adjective غَيْسَانِيّ/غَسَّانِيّ 'beautiful' (Ibn Manẓūr, *Lisān al-ʿArab*, 3259; Hava, *Dictionary*, 517).

قريضة (**24**r:6): This may be a variant of the term قِرَاض, which was used in the context of medieval commerce to refer to a business commenda type of partnership.

نعمى *nuʿmā* (**29**r:13): literally 'pleasure, happiness', but here the word apparently has the sense of luxury goods. Dozy (*Supplément*, II:691) records a similar meaning for the related form النِعَم 'objects d'une grande valeur'.

تستثابُوا 'they gape' (**41**:18): This is the 3sg.f prefix conjugation form of the root *ṯ-ʾ-b*, although the dictionaries do not list the tenth form for this verb. The use of the tenth form is presumably a poetic licence for the sake of the metre. The final inflectional vowel would be short according to the rules of Classical Arabic (*tastaṯʾibu*), but has been lengthened for metrical purposes.

14. MAPS

Figure 33: Map of Nubia

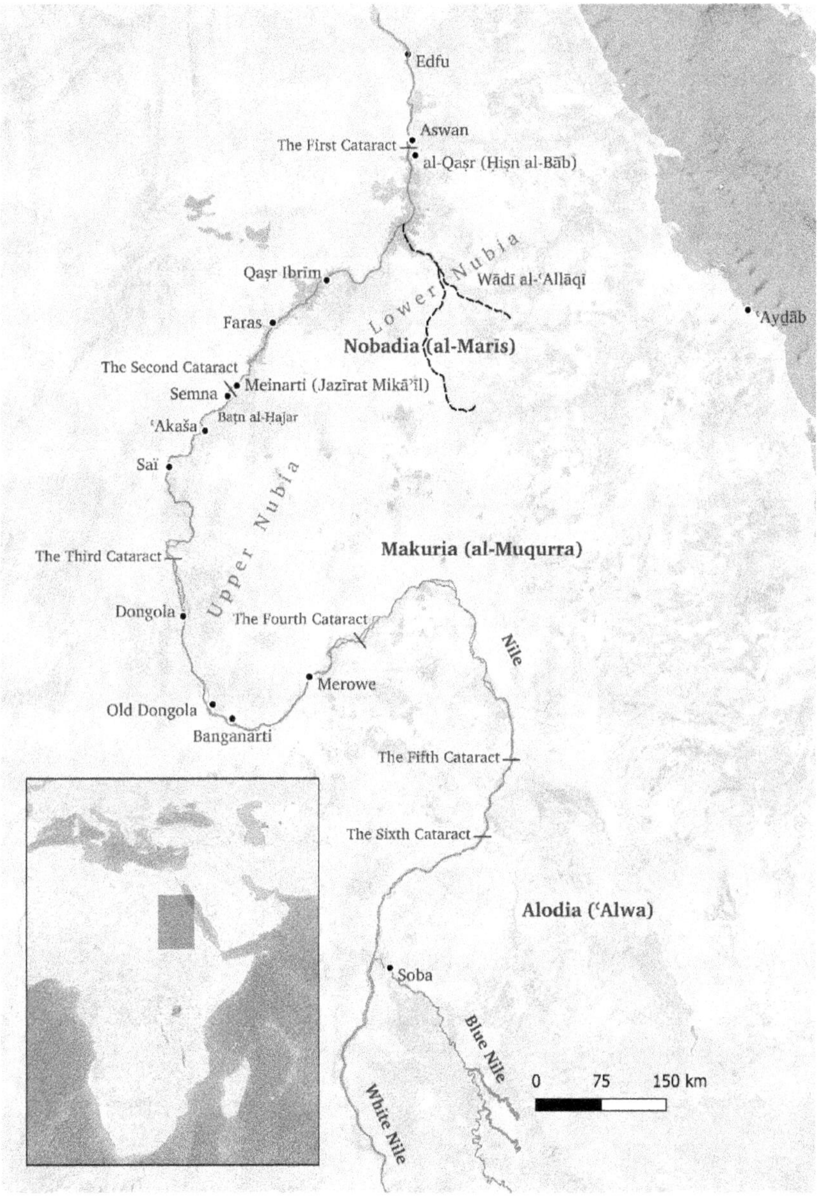

https://doi.org/10.11647/OBP.0391.14

Figure 34: Map of Lower Nubia

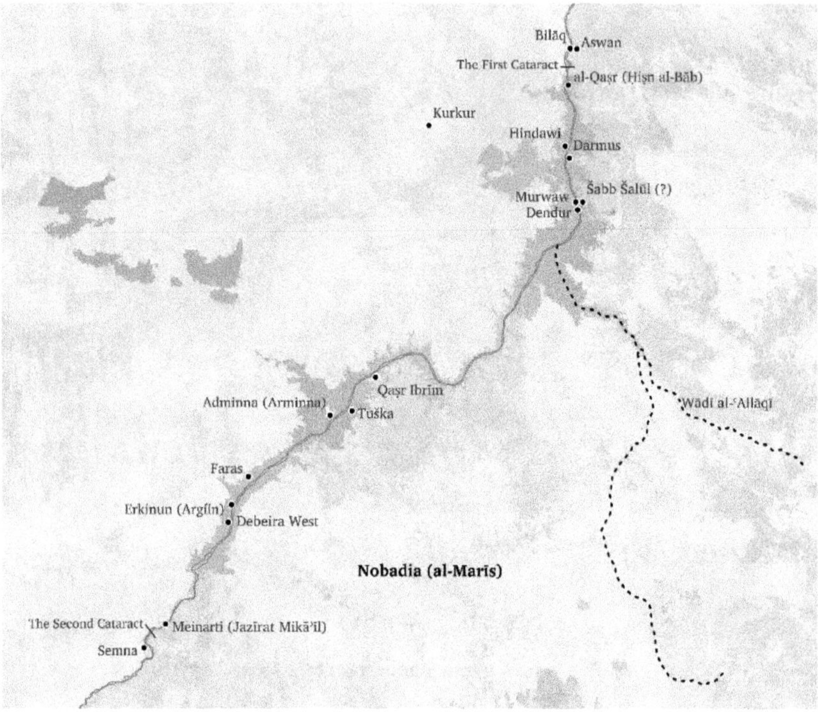

DOCUMENTS AND TRANSLATIONS

METHOD OF EDITING

The documents are transcribed into Arabic with full consonantal diacritics for the sake of clarity, although consonantal diacritics are marked only sporadically in the documents. The marking of the diacritics is occasionally referred to in the textual notes, especially when they help with the reading of an obscure word, when they reflect deviation from Classical Arabic or when they appear to be the result of scribal error. Medial *hamza* is marked on *yāʾ* unless the *yāʾ* has diacritical dots of *yāʾ* indicating that it has been weakened. Diacritical dots are marked on final *yāʾ* only where they are written in the documents.

Sporadically, Arabic vowel signs are marked in the documents. In such cases they are reproduced in the edition. The poem in **41** is exceptional in that it is fully vocalised in the original document. Vowel signs that do not appear in the documents are not added to the edition.

The following bracket system has been employed in the edition:

[ ] single square brackets indicate sections where the text is obliterated or missing owing to a *lacuna* in the document.

[[ ]] double square brackets enclose erasures.

( ) round brackets indicate the solution of abbreviations.

< > angular brackets enclose words or phrases that the writer omitted by mistake and are supplied as a correction.

{ } curly brackets enclose words and phrases that were written by mistake and should be omitted in reading the passage, e.g. dittographies.

..... dots are printed in place of letters that are visible but too faint to read.

1 LETTER TO THE EPARCH URUWĪ

Museum of Islamic Art inventory number: 23973.66

Excavation photograph numbers and image numbers:

Recto: 1966A_P06_18A-19 (image: 050308_106_o)

Recto: 1968_04_10–10A (image: 050308_690_u)

Verso: 1966A_P06_17A-18 (image: 050308_106_u)

Verso: 1968_04_11–11A (image: 050308_691_u)

Registration number: 66A/111 (?)

Paper. 28 cm × 19.5 cm

Text

Recto

1 بسم الله الرحمن الرحيم

2 اعلم الاكشيل وصاحب الخيل ووزير الملك اطال الله بقاه

3 وادام حراسته ونعمته توجه القائد سعادة على المركب

4 المتوجه عليه والذى اوثره من الاكشيل اجرايه مجرى

5 القوم المنتمين الى عبيدى المجرين فى العتق مجرى امثالهم

6 من موالى وعبيدى ولا يمكن الاكشيل من اعتراضهم فى شى قل

7 ولا جل واكرام القائد المذكور ورعايته واصحابه المتوجهين صحبته

8 ويصلنى كتابه بما اعتمده معه فانى المعتمد له بذلك والشاكر له عليه

Margin

1 ان شا الله عز وجل

2 الحمد لله وحده وصلواته على سيدنا محمد نبيه واله وسلام

3 حسبنا الله ونعم الوكيل

Verso

Address

Right Column

1 [للاكـ]ـشيل صاحب الخيل ووزير الملك

2 اروى بن خياخ النائب عن الملك بقلعة ابريم

3 ادام الله سلامته وحراسته ونعمته

Left Column

1 من الامير المخلص السعيد عضد الخلافة

2 نصر الملك تاج الدولة فخر العرب

3 كنز الدولة وعمدتها كفى البحريين حسام

4 امير المومنين ابو منصور متوج

5 العاضدى الجيوشى

Translation

Recto

1. In the name of God, the Merciful and Compassionate.
2. I inform the Ikšīl, Master of the Horses, vizier of the king—may God prolong his life

3. and cause his protection and wellbeing to endure—that the leader Saʿāda has set off (to him) on the ship
4. travelling to (meet) him. What I would like to request from the Ikšīl is to give him the status
5. of the people belonging to my slaves that have been granted freedom, like
6. my other freedmen and slaves. The Ikšīl cannot show them opposition in anything small
7. or big, but should show honour to the aforementioned leader and care for him and for his companions who are travelling with him.
8. So may his (the Ikšīl's) letter be dispatched to me with (instructions) for me to execute for his sake, for I am ready to execute that for him. I am grateful to him for this,

Margin

1. if God wills, the Mighty and Magnificent
2. Praise be to God alone, and His blessings be upon our lord Muḥammad, His prophet, and his family, and peace.
3. Our sufficiency is God. What a fine keeper is He!

Verso

Address

Right Column

1. To the Ikšīl, Master of the Horses, vizier of the king,
2. Uruwī ibn Ḵiyāḵ, the deputy of the king in the citadel of Ibrīm,

3. may God cause his health, his protection and wellbeing to endure.

Left Column

1. From the sincere commander, the blissful, the powerful arm of the caliphate,
2. the Victory of the Kingship, Crown of the Dynasty, Pride of the Arabs,
3. Treasure of the Dynasty (*Kanz al-Dawla*) and its support, protector of sailors, the Sword
4. of the Commander of the Faithful, ʾAbū Manṣūr Mutawwaj,
5. affiliated to al-ʿĀḍid, commander of the armies.

2 LETTER TO THE EPARCH URUWĪ

Museum of Islamic Art inventory number: 23973.65

Excavation photograph numbers and image numbers:

Recto: 1966A_P06_09A-10 (image 050308_103_u)

Recto: 1968_04_05–05A (image 050308_691_o)

Verso: 1966A_P06_10A-11 (image 050308_104_u)

Verso: 1966A_P06_11A-12 (image 050308_105_u)

Verso: 1968_04_09–09A (image 050308_689_u)

Registration number: 66A/111 (?)

Paper. 48 cm × 17 cm

Text

Recto

1 بسم الله الرحمن الرحيم
2 اعلم الاكشيل ووزير الملك وصاحب الخيل
3 اطال الله بقاه وادام عزه وهلك عدوه
4 وضده توجه موصل هذا الكتاب وهو منعم
5 احد غلماني وعلى يده توبين حرير ممزج واربعة
6 مقاطع برسم صاحب الخيل فاذا وصل متحمل هذا
7 الكتاب اليك تسرحه وتسيره سرعة يصل الى ان شا الله
8 لاننا اريد ان اسيره الى بحرى ليقضى حوائج لى وما
9 يحتاج صاحب فى هذا الامر وصية ولا تاكيد
10 ولا مرادده فى حقه وانا اعلم محبة صاحب الخيل

11 فى وقضى حوائجى عنده ومهما كانت له من حاجة

12 فتكتب الى وتعرفنى لامر بقضائها فاننى انا نائب [[عند]] عن

13 اخى   وسواه وان كتب الامير يصل وهو يوصى فيك

14 وقضى حوايجك ويذكر ايضا تضمين الرعية وحفظ التجار

15 السايرين اليكم من اهل التجارة وحفظهم ومراعتهم وبلاد الملك

16 وحفظها <ومراعتها> وما تحتاج فى موصل هذا الكتاب تجيب تسيرهُ

17 سرعة الي والسلام عليك وعلى من تحوط به عنايتك السلام

Margin

1 الحمد لله وحده وصلواته على سيدنا محمد نبيه واله وسلام   حسبنا الله ونعم الوكيل

Verso

1 وقد سيرت على يد متحمل هذا الكتاب ايضا فراشين عمل العراق

2 فتتفضل فى قبول ما سيره اليه وتسير متحملهم سرعة

3 سرعة ان شا الله والتجار فما يحتاج صاحب الخيل فى حالهم

4 منى وصية وسمعتك خيرة عند الناس وتسير منعم

5 سرعة فاننى اريد ان اسيره الى عند اخي ولو لا علمى ان حوائجى عندك

6 مقضية لم اسير اليك رسول وانا اعلم محبتى عندك والسلم

7 الحمد لله وحده وصلواته على سيدنا محمد نبيه واله وسلامه

8 حسبنا الله ونعم الوكيل

Address

Right Column

1 للاكشيل صاحب الخيل

2 ووزير الملك ابى الخير

3 اروى متولي بلاد مريس

4 واعمالها ادام الله عزه

Left Column

1 من الامير المنتخب سما الملك

2 تاج العرب اسد الدولة

3 ابو الفتوح تنوير بن الامير

4 كنز الدولة ابى اسحاق ابرهيم بن على

5 بن متوج ابن ابى يزيد الحنفى

Textual Notes

Recto

14. الرعية: This appears to be a mistake for الرعاية.

16. <ومراعتها>: MS: وماراعتها.

تسيرهُ: The final *hāʾ* is written with high vertical extensions of the strokes. In order to avoid confusion with the ligature لا, the writer has added a *ḍamma* vowel above the letter, reflecting the vocalism of the pronominal suffix *-hu*.

Verso

Address, Left Column

3. تنوير: The reading of this name is not certain.
5. الحنفى: This is the preferable reading of this *nisba*. The Banū al-Kanz claimed descent from the tribe of the Banū Ḥanīfa. The *nisba* al-Ḥanafī is attested in inscriptions from Aswan relating to Kanzī ʾ*amīr*s.

Translation

Recto

1. In the name of God, the Merciful and Compassionate.
2. I inform the Ikšīl, vizier of the king, Master of the Horses—
3. may God prolong his life, cause his strength to endure, and cause his enemy
4. and opponent to perish—that the bearer of this letter, who is (called) Munʿim,
5. one of my servants, has set off (to you) carrying two garments of mixed silk and four
6. pieces of cloth for the Master of the Horses. When the bearer of this letter reaches
7. you, release him and send him away quickly, so he can reach me, if God wills,
8. because I want to send him to the north to carry out some errands for me.

9. The Master (of the Horses) does not need in this matter instruction, ratification or
10. repetition with regard to what should be done. I am aware of the love of the Master of the Horses
11. for me and for carrying out my requests to him. Whatever request you may have,
12. write and inform me of it, so that I can give an order for it to be carried out. I am deputising
13. for my brother. On another matter, the commander has written that he will arrive and he will give instructions for your sake and for the sake of
14. the carrying out of your requests. He also mentions (the need) to safeguard the subjects and protect the merchants
15. who are travelling to you from among the merchant community (and mentions) the country of the king
16. and its guarding and protection.[1] Please give whatever reply you need to the bearer of this letter and send him
17. quickly to me. Best wishes to you and best wishes to those whom your care encompasses.

---

[1] The meaning may be that the commander is stating that the Ikšīl should both protect the foreign merchants and also ensure that the country and its people where they are travelling be protected. Alternatively, there may be an allusion here to a quid pro quo, whereby the Ikšīl is asked to protect the merchants in exchange for the protection by the Muslims of the land of the Ikšīl.

Margin

1. Praise be to God alone and His blessings be upon our lord Muḥammad, His prophet, and his family, and peace. Our sufficiency is God. What a fine keeper is He!

Verso

1. I have sent with the bearer of this letter also two beds of Iraqi workmanship.
2. Please accept what he has conveyed to you and send on the carrier of them (i.e., the goods) as quickly
3. as possible, if God wills. As for the merchants, the Master of the Horses does not require
4. instruction from me regarding their situation. Your reputation is good among the people. Send Munʿim
5. quickly, because I want to send him to my brother. If I had not known that my requests from you
6. would be carried out, I would not have sent you a messenger. Moreover, I know how I am loved by you. Greetings.
7. Praise be to God alone and His blessings be upon our lord Muḥammad, His prophet, and his family, and His peace.
8. Our sufficiency is God. What a fine keeper is He!

Address

Right Column

1. To the Ikšīl, Master of the Horses
2. vizier of the king, ʾAbū al-Ḵayr

3. Uruwī, the governor of the land of Marīs
4. and its districts, may God cause his power to endure.

Left Column

1. From the chosen commander, Firmament of the Kingdom,
2. Crown of the Arabs, Lion of the Dynasty
3. ʾAbū al-Futūḥ, Tanwīr, son of the commander
4. Treasure of the Dynasty (*Kanz al-Dawla*), ʾAbū ʾIsḥāq ʾIbrāhīm son of ʿAlī,
5. son of Mutawwaj, son of ʾAbū Yazīd, al-Ḥanafī.

3 LETTER TO THE EPARCH URUWĪ

Sartain inventory number: Add. 01

Excavation photograph numbers and image numbers:

Recto: 1966A_P06_15A-16 (image: 050308_108_o)

Verso: 1966A_P06_16A-17 (image: 050308_107_o)

Registration number: 66A/111 (?)

Paper. No measurements available

Text

Recto

1 بسم الله الرحمن الرحيم

2 اعلم الاكشيل وصاحب الخيل ووزير الملك اطال الله بقاه

3 وادام حراسته ونعمته   انه يعلم ما وصل كتابه الى به فى

4 حال المسافرين من المراكب وغيرهم وقصد بذلك صلاح

5 الاحوال وتفضلت الحضرة السامية الاجلية الكريمة ثبت الله سعدها

6 واطلقت المراكب عن علم منها بما كان امر البلد عليه

7 من غلو الاسعار فتكلفت المسافرين المشقة وتغلوا

8 على التجار الى ان جمعوا اليهم اموالهم باسعار غالية

9 وحاجة الاكشيل داعية الى حفظهم ومراعاتهم فى حق

10 نفوسهم فكيف حال من حقه واجب وخدمته فرض لازم

Margin

1 وقد توجه متحملها القائد سعادة كتب الله

2 سلامته قرابة للقائد النجيب همام الدولة

3 حامد وكتب الله سلامته والاكشيل

4 يعلم ما يجب من حفظ اصحابه والزامهم

5 ومنع من يتعرض اليه باذية ومضرة

6 او مستخدم يعترضه فى

Verso

1 تسعير او غيره وما حملنى على ذلك الا ما يلزمنى فى حق صاحب

2 الخيل وقصدى بشهادة الله استجذاب قلوب الناس كلهم

3 له وما يخفى عنه ذلك فيصلنى كتابه بما اعتمده مع القايد سعادة

4 من الاكرام الى حين انقضااه شاكرا ان شا الله عز وجل وجوابه [ ]

5 يعدل بها عنى مع عبيده وخدمته ان شا الله عز وجل

6 الحمد لله وحده وصلواته على سيدنا محمد نبيه واله وسلام

7 حسبنا الله ونعم الوكيل

Address

Right Column

1 للاكشيل وصاحب الخيل ووزير الملك

2 اروى بن خياخ النائب عن الملك بقلعة ابريم

3 ادام الله سلامته وحراسته ونعمته

Left Column

1 ضل ثقته وشاكر بركته

2 لامع بن حسن الكنزى

Textual Notes

Verso

4. الى حين انقضاءه: This is presumably referring to the completion of the work of the leader Saʿāda.

Translation

Recto

1. In the name of God, the Merciful and Compassionate.
2. I inform the Ikšīl, the Master of the Horses, the vizier of the king—may God prolong his life,
3. and cause his protection and wellbeing to endure—that his letter to me has referred to
4. the condition of the travellers from the boats and of others and that he has striven to ameliorate
5. this situation and the lofty, most glorious and munificent presence, may God establish his happiness, has graciously
6. released the boats,[1] in the knowledge of what the country is undergoing
7. with regard to the rising of prices, for the travellers have experienced hardship and (the prices) have risen
8. to the disadvantage of the merchants, so that they have acquired goods at high prices.

---

[1] This is apparently an allusion to the eparch's intervention to alleviate an economic crisis by granting permission for the shipment of supplies.

9. The Ikšīl, therefore, needs to protect them and care for them in accordance with
10. their rights, and all the more so since they belong to those whose right (to protection) is obligatory and the service of whom is a compulsory requirement.

Margin

1. The bearer (of this letter), the leader Saʿāda, may God decree his abundant
2. good health, the relative of the noble leader, Hero of the Dynasty,
3. Ḥāmid, may God decree for him abundant good health, has departed. The Ikšīl
4. knows what is required with regard to the restraint of his (the Ikšīl's) companions and the imposition upon them of obligations
5. and the prevention of those who oppose him (Saʿāda) with harm and damage
6. or a clerk who hinders him (Saʿāda) with regard to

Verso

1. pricing or anything else. I have been motivated (to write) this only by my obligation for the sake of the Master
2. of the Horses and my intention, as witnessed by God, to draw the hearts of all the people
3. to him, so that this is not hidden from him. So, please arrange for his (the eparch's) letter to be sent to me with authorisation for me to offer the leader Saʿāda

4. respectful treatment until it (his work) is finished, for which I would be grateful, if God, the Powerful and Glorious, wills.[2] His reply [ ]
5. would ensure that he would be treated justly in these matters through me[3] by his (the eparch's) slaves and servants, if God, the Powerful and Glorious, wills.
6. Praise be to God alone, and His blessings be upon our lord Muḥammad, His prophet, and his family, and peace.
7. Our sufficiency is God. What a fine keeper is He!

Address

Right Column

1. To the Ikšīl, Master of the Horses, vizier of the king,
2. Uruwī ibn Ḵiyāḵ, the deputy of the king in the citadel of Ibrīm,
3. may God cause his health, his protection and his wellbeing to endure.

Left Column

1. Shadow of his trust and one grateful for his blessing,
2. Lāmiʿ ibn Ḥasan al-Kanzī.

---

[2] The writer has no executive authority. The Ikšīl has the executive authority. He is expected and invited to exercise this by sending a letter.

[3] I.e., I would be empowered to ensure that he was treated correctly.

4 LETTER TO THE EPARCH URUWĪ

Museum of Islamic Art inventory number: 23973.90

Excavation photograph numbers and image numbers:

Recto: 1966A_P06_19A-20 (image: 050308_107_u)

Recto: 1968_01_02–02A (image: 050308_630_o)

Verso: 1966A_P06_20A-21 (image: 050308_108_u)

Verso: 1968_01_01–01A (image: 050308_629_o)

Registration number: 66A/111 (?)

Paper. No measurements available

Text

Recto

1 بسم الله الرحمن الرحيم

2 وصل كتاب الاكشيل وصاحب الخيل اطال الله بقاه وادام

3 عزه وكبت عدوه ووقفت عليه وعلى ما ذكره من انه

4 سير الي وصيفة ثم سير [[وصيفة]] جارية صحبة جوهر

5 واننى لم اسير اليه الا عمامتين بجحوف ومجلس واما

6 الوصيفة الاولة فلم تصلنى بمحمله واخذها كرمى

7 صاحب الخيل وانا ما اكاتبك واهاديك احمال

8 قماش حتى تعدد على ما تسيره وانا ما اطلب

9 الا صلاح البلاد والله ما احوجنى اليك ولا الى

10 احد الله رزقنى وانما انا اطلب صلاح البلاد لا

Margin

1 غير وكتبت اليك
2 في حال عبيدى لم تجاوبنى ثم
3 كتبت اليك فى حال الراسين الرقيق
4 الذى سيرهم الى غريمى
5 ابوا الضباع ولم تسيرهم
6 الي وما اعرف قسم لنا

Verso

1 خادمك فقد سيرت غلامي ماريخرة فتكون تسلم اليه
2 الراسين الذى لابوا الضباع ووصل الامير كنز الدولة
3 بعد ظفر وقتل ونصرة الله وجواب كتابك يصل
4 ان شا الله وان كان لك حاجة والله فى جالبة غلامى
5 ماريخرة ان شا الله عز وجل
6 الحمد لله وحده وصلواته على سيدنا محمد نبينا وسلامه

CHECK MARK

7 وخلى الناس ينحدروا فما عليهم خوف وقد اطلقنا الناس
8 بعد وصل الامير ما بقى الا الخير

Address

Right Column

1 صاحب الخيل اروى خياخ...

Left Column

1 شاكره لامع بن حسن
2 الكنزى

Textual Notes

Verso

1, 5. ماريخرة: It is possible to interpret this as a variant of the attested Nubian name Marikouda.[1] If this is correct, the *k* and the *d* of the name would have undergone lenition to *k̲* and *r* respectively, i.e., Mārīk̲ura. There is a diacritical dot over the *k̲ā*ʾ. For a discussion of these sound shifts, see §3.3.

Address, Right Column

There is a group of letters after the name خياخ that I was not able to decipher. These are apparently an incomplete word, which the writer has written incorrectly.

Translation

Recto

1. In the name of God, the Merciful and Compassionate.
2. The letter has arrived from the Ikšīl and the Master of the Horses, may God prolong his life, cause his
3. power to endure and crush his enemy. I have taken note of it and the fact that he stated that he
4. has sent to me a female slave, and has sent to me a slave girl with Jawhar,[2]

---

[1] DBMNT / TM Nam 33354: DBMNT NamVar 300149 (ⲙⲁⲣⲓⲕⲟⲩ̀ⲇ́), 301474 (ⲙⲁⲣⲓ̀ⲕ́).

[2] The name of a slave boy (*ġulām*).

5. and that I have only been able to send to him two turbans with difficulty and a seat. As for
6. the first (i.e., the aforementioned) female slave, she has not reached me in his consignment so that I may take possession of her, my honour,
7. Master of the Horses, and I shall not correspond with you nor give you consignments
8. of cloth as gifts until what you send is at my disposal. I seek
9. only the wellbeing of the land. God has not made me needful of you nor of
10. anybody else. God has provided for me. I only seek the wellbeing of the land and not

Margin

1. anything else. I wrote to you
2. concerning the condition of my slaves but you did not reply. Then
3. I wrote to you concerning the condition of the two slaves
4. who are to be sent to my creditor
5. ʾAbū al-Ḍubāʿ, but you have not sent them
6. to me and I do not know whether your servant has given us a share,

Verso

1. and I have sent my slave boy Mārīḵura. Deliver to him
2. the two slaves who are for ʾAbū al-Ḍubāʿ. The commander Treasure of the Dynasty (*Kanz al-Dawla*) arrived

3. after victory, slaughter and God's victory. Your response will arrive (soon),
4. if God wills. If you need anything, then of course (take) from the goods conveyed by my slave boy
5. Mārīḵura, if God, the Mighty and Glorious, wills.
6. Praise be to God alone and His blessings on our lord Muḥammad, our prophet, and His peace.

CHECK MARK

7. Let the people go down (the river) without fear. We have released the people.[3]
8. After the commander arrived, all was well.

Address

Right Column

1. The Master of the Horses, Uruwī Ḵiyāḵ …

Left Column

1. The one grateful to him, Lāmiʿ ibn Ḥasan
2. al-Kanzī.

---

[3] Apparently meaning: we have authorised them to travel.

5 LETTER TO THE EPARCH URUWĪ

Museum of Islamic Art inventory number: 23973.49

Excavation photograph numbers and image numbers:

Recto: 1966A_P06_21A-22 (image: 050308_109_u)
Recto: 1968_02_17A-18 (image: 050308_659_o)
Verso: 1966A_P06_22A-23 (image: 050308_110_u)
Verso: 1968_02_19A-20 (image: 050308_655_u)

Registration number: 66A/111 (?)

Paper. 25.5 cm × 17 cm

Text

Recto

1 [بسم الله الرحمن الرحيم]
2 [ا]علم الاكشيل وصاحب الخيل اطال الله بقاه
3 وادام حراسته وسلامته ونعمته انه يعلم ان
4 فى كل سنة تتوجه الى بلادكم عدة كبيرة من
5 المراكب ويفعلوا اصحابكم معهم كل قبيح ولما
6 كان فى هذه السنة امتنعت الناس من الثغر
7 بسببين احدها ظلم اهل البلاد لهم
8 والاخرى عدم الغلة ففتحت مجزز
9 شعر وفرجت عن الناس واولهم
10 اهل بلادكم ولولا انا ما وجدوا غلة
11 ولا تجاسر احد يسير وقد سيرت

Margin

مركبين وجميع ما فيهم لي واشتهى
من الاكشيل الا يعرض احد
اليهم ولا ينزل احد فيهم
وحقوقهم وان احتاجوا
الى كروك فياخذهم
لهم

Verso

ولا يتفضلوا عنك الا وهم شاكرين ان شا الله
وان كان لك حاجة فاكتب الى بها ان شا الله عز وجل
الحمد لله وحده وصلواته على سيدنا محمد نبيه وسلامه
حسبنا الله ونعم الوكيل

Address

Right Column

للاكشيل وصاحب الخيل ووزير الملك
اروى بن خياخ النائب عن الملك

Left Column

شاكره
لامع بن حسن الكنزى

Textual Notes

Recto

4, 5. اصحابكم, بلادكم: The 2pl pronominal suffixes are apparently used to refer to the eparch and his community.

Margin

5. كروك: The reading of this word is not certain due to the faded state of the text. The first and last letters have a diagonal stroke over them and appear to be *kāfs*. The form could be interpreted as a plural of the word *kirka* 'calico, type of blue cloth' (Dozy, *Supplément*, II:458).

Translation

Recto

1. In the name of God the Merciful and Compassionate.
2. I inform the Ikšīl and Master of the Horses—may God prolong his life
3. and cause his protection, safety and wellbeing to endure—that he knows that
4. every year a large number of boats travel to your land
5. and your colleagues badly mistreat them. This year
6. the people from the port (of Aswan) were hindered
7. in two ways. One of these is the injustice done to them by the people of the land

8. and the other is the lack of produce. So, I took[1] some hair-cutters (and opened sacks of produce)
9. and gave relief to the people and the first of them
10. were the people in your land. If it was not for me, they (i.e., our people) would not have found produce,
11. nor did anybody dare send (produce). I have sent

Margin

1. two boats and everything in them is mine. I would like
2. the Ikšīl to ensure that nobody obstructs
3. them and that nobody diminishes
4. what is rightly theirs, and if they need
5. pieces of calico cloth, then please undertake to provide these
6. for them.

Verso

1. They will not receive a favour from you without being grateful, if God wills.
2. If you have any need, write to me concerning it, if God, the Mighty and Glorious, wills.
3. Praise be to God alone, His blessings be upon our lord Muḥammad, His prophet, and His peace.
4. Our sufficiency is God. What a fine keeper is He!

---

[1] Literally: opened.

Address

Right Column

1. To the Ikšīl, Master of the Horses, vizier of the king
2. Uruwī ibn Ḵiyāḵ, the deputy of the king.

Left Column

1. One grateful to him,
2. Lāmiʿ ibn Ḥasan al-Kanzī.

6 LETTER TO THE EPARCH URUWĪ

Museum of Islamic Art inventory number: 23973.50

Excavation photograph numbers and image numbers:

Recto: 1966A_P04_29A-30 (image: 050308_080_o)

Recto: 1968_02_20A-21 (image: 050308_656_u)

Verso: 1966A_P04_30A-31 (image: 050308_075_u)

Verso: 1968_02_21A-22 (image: 050308_657_u)

Registration number: 66A/111 (?)

Paper. 26 cm × 17 cm

Text

Recto

1 بسم الله الرحمن الرحيم

2 اعلم الاكشيل وصاحب الخيل ووزير الملك اطال الله بقاه

3 وادام تاييده وحراسته وسلامته ونعمته ان متحملها صاحبى

4 وممن يكرمنى اوه وهو خادمى وكنت سيرته مع غلامى مارخرة

5 فوصلنى متسفر فتجمله على قضية الحق وتفضل فى حقه

6 فاحسبه على ثم مع اصحابى واما الاخبار فقد كفى

7 الله شر شاور وقتل بيد شيركوه سالار حرسه الله وتوزر

8 شر يكون واستدعا الامير اليه والامير معول

9 على المتوجه الى مصر لمسيراته وعونه وانا مقيم فى البلد

Margin

1 فان كان لك حاجة فاكتب اعلمنى

2 بها ان شا الله عز وجل

3 الحمد لله وحده وصلواته على سيدنا محمد نبيه واله وسلامه

4 حسبنا الله ونعم الوكيل

Verso

Address

Right Column

1 للاكشيل وصاحب الخيل ووزير الملك

2 اروى خياخ النائب عن الملك بـ{قـ}قلعة ابريم

3 ادام الله سلامته وحراسته ونعمته

Left Column

1 شاكره وصديقه لامع

2 بن حسن الكنزى

Textual Notes

Recto

4. اوه: This can be identified as the Nubian name Oua (ⲟⲩⲁ), which is attested in P. QI III 34 i, l. 34.

Translation

Recto

1. In the name of God, the Merciful and Compassionate.
2. I inform the Ikšīl and Master of the Horses, the vizier of the king—may God prolong his life
3. and cause his support, protection, safety and wellbeing to endure—that the bearer of it (this letter?)[1] is my
4. loyal and respectful[2] companion, Oua, who is my servant. I have sent him with my slave boy Mārīḵura.
5. He came to me on his travels. Please treat him well and correctly and provide him with his requirements,
6. and I shall reckon it as my debt and that of my companions. As for the news, God
7. has protected us from the evil of Šāwar and he has been killed by the hand of Šīrkūh, the military commander, may God protect him, and he (Šīrkūh) has taken on the viziership to bear the burden
8. of evil that is to come. He (Šīrkūh) has summoned the commander to him, and the commander is determined
9. to travel to Egypt for the sake of his (Šīrkūh's) expeditions and his aid, while I am staying in the country (of Nubia).

---

[1] The 3sg.f pronoun *-hā* could also be referring to the goods that he is carrying; see §10.10.

[2] Literally: one who honours me.

Margin

1. If you have any need, write to me and let me know
2. about it, if God, the Exalted and Majestic, wills it.
3. Praise be to God alone and His blessings be upon our lord Muḥammad, His prophet, and his family, and His peace.
4. Our sufficiency is God. What a fine keeper is He!

Verso

Address

Right Column

1. To the Ikšīl and Master of the Horses, the vizier of the king,
2. Uruwī Ḵiyāḵ, the deputy of the king in the fortress of Ibrīm,
3. may God cause his safety, protection and wellbeing to endure.

Left Column

1. The one who is grateful to him and his friend, Lāmiʿ
2. ibn Ḥasan al-Kanzī.

7 LETTER TO THE EPARCH URUWĪ

Museum of Islamic Art inventory number: 23973.44

Excavation photograph numbers and image numbers:

Recto: 1968_02_04A-05 (image: 050308_652_o)

Verso: 1968_02_05A-06 (image: 050308_653_o)

Paper. 25 cm × 17 cm

Text

Recto

1 بسم الله الرحمن الرحيم

2 كتبت اطال الله بقاك وادام عزك ونعماك وتمكينك

3 وكبت اعداك معلما له ادام الله عزه انى قد وجهت

4 غلامى يسمى شريف بجمل اصهب الى حضرتها واريد

5 ان تقبله منى وانى ما كتبت اليك كتاب ولا انفذت الى

6 حضرتك شى الا هذا اليوم فاحمد الله فيه وتاخذ

7 الجمل ولا تخليه يبطى عنى يوم واحد وتسيره

8 الى فابه خادمى وقاضى حوائجى فانى انقطع منه

9 اذا ابطا قرات عليك افضل السلام وعلى من تحوطه

10 عنايتك السلام والحمد لله وحده وصلواته على سيدنا محمد نبيه

11 واله وسلم تسليما حسبنا الله ونعم الوكيل

Verso

Address

Right Column

1 الاكشيل ووزير الملك وصاحب خيله

2 متولى القلعة الابريمية وبلاد مريس ابى الخير اروى

Left Column

1 الامير نصر بن الامير

2 كنز الدولة

Textual Notes

There are several shifts in person and gender in this letter. It begins by addressing the eparch in the second person, then shifts to addressing him in the third masculine singular (recto, line 3). In recto, line 4 he is addressed by the phrase حضرتها with a third feminine singular pronominal suffix. Subsequently the writer shifts back to addressing the eparch in the second person singular.

9. There is a horizontal stroke over the final *kāf* of عليك, which appears to be a mistake.

Translation

Recto

1. In the name of God, the Merciful and Compassionate.
2. I have written—may God prolong your life and cause your strength, your wellbeing and your power to endure,
3. and suppress your enemies—informing him, may God cause his strength to endure, that I have sent
4. my slave boy, who is called Šarīf, with a brown camel to his honourable presence. I want
5. you to receive it from me. I have not written you a letter or sent
6. to your presence anything before today, and I praise God for that. So take
7. the camel and do not cause him (i.e., Šarīf, my servant) to be delayed by a single day. Send him
8. to Papa, my servant, who carries out my business, for I shall be cut off from him,
9. if there is a delay. I send to you warmest greetings and also to those
10. within your care greetings. Praise be to God alone, His blessings be upon our lord Muḥammad, His prophet,
11. and his family, and save him. Our sufficiency is in God. What a fine keeper is He!

Verso

Address

Right Column

1. The Ikšīl and vizier of the king and the Master of his Horses,
2. governor of the fortress of Ibrīm and the Land of Marīs, ʾAbū al-Ḵayr Uruwī.

Left Column

1. The commander Naṣr son of the commander
2. Treasure of the Dynasty (*Kanz al-Dawla*).

8 LETTER TO THE EPARCH URUWĪ

Museum of Islamic Art inventory number: 23973.60

Excavation photograph numbers and image numbers:

Recto: 1968_03_31–31A (image: 050308_680_u)

Recto: 1968_03_32–32A (image: 050308_681_u)

Verso: 1968_03_33–33A (image: 050308_682_u)

Paper. 52 cm × 21 cm

Text

Recto

1 بسم الله الرحمن الرحيم

2 توجه اطال الله بقا الاكشيل وصاحب الخيل وزير الملك

3 وادام تاييده وسعادته وسلامته ونعمته متحملها

4 القائد حسن بن القائد شجاع الدولة اسحق متولى الباب

5 ومنزلته عندى منزلة محفوظة ومكانته مشهورة

6 كتب الله سلامته واحسن صحابته والذى ... [ ]

7 اليك حسن السمعة وجميل الاحدوثة وهى التى

8 يقضى بكثرة من يفد عليه ويسير اليه والاكشيل غير

9 محتاج الى ما كنت وصيته فى بابه ولا موكد عليه فى اكرامه

10 واعزازه وتنزيله منزلة امتاله من عبيدى

11 الخصيصين في وكلانه وحفظه ومراعاته والاشتمال

12 عليه الى حين انتضار شاكر الاكشيل ومهما فعله

13 معه من جميل او خير فانا المعتد له به والشاكر عليه

14 فكتاب الاكشيل ولا تخلينى منه بقضا حوائجه وما يتجدد

15 من الاخبار فيه ان شا الله عز وجل

16 الحمد لله وحده وصلواته على سيدنا محمد نبيه واله وسلامه

17 حسبنا الله ونعم الوكيل

Verso

Address

Right Column

1 للاكشيل وصاحب الخيل ووزير الملك

2 اروى بن خياخ النائب عنه بقلعة ابريم

3 ادام الله سلامته ونعمته

Left Column

1 من الامير المخلص المنصور [ ]

2 نصر الملك تاج الدولة فخر [العرب]

3 كنز الدولة وعمدتها اخو البحريين [حسام]

4 امير المومنين ابو منصور [متوج]

5 العاضـ[ـدى الجيوشى]

Textual Notes

Recto

15. After فيه there is a faint stroke of an *ʾalif*. This is followed by the word ان in bold ink. It appears that the writer wrote the first letter of ان, then re-inked the pen and started the word again.

Translation

Recto

1. In the name of God, the Merciful and Compassionate.
2. May God prolong the life of the Ikšīl, the Master of the Horses, the vizier of the king,
3. and cause his support, happiness, safety and wellbeing to endure. The bearer of this letter, who has travelled (to you),[1]
4. is the leader Ḥasan, the son of the leader Šujāʿ al-Dawla ('the Courage of the State') ʾIsḥāq, the administrator of the gate.[2]
5. His status with me is firmly established and his rank is well-known,
6. may God decree his safety and cause him to have good company. The one who [.....]

---

[1] Literally: Its bearer, Ḥasan… has travelled.

[2] The 'gate' is likely to be the entrance to Nubia at the town of al-Qaṣr, just south of Aswan. Al-ʾAswānī (al-Maqrīzī, *Ḵiṭaṭ*, I:352) describes this town as باب الى بلد النوبة 'a gate into the land of the Nubians'.

7. to you, has a good reputation and is well spoken of, and these are qualities that
8. are abundantly exhibited by those who come to him (i.e., you, the Ikšīl) and are sent to him. The Ikšīl does not
9. need my recommendation with regard to him or my reassurances to show him respect
10. and treat him well, and grant him the status of those of my personal slaves that are similar to him
11. with regard to care, guardianship, supervision and protection
12. until the time of waiting for the one who is grateful to the Ikšīl.[3] Whatever
13. kindness and good he (the Ikšīl) does in his (the bearer of the letter's) regard, I shall appreciate and be thankful for.
14. So, may the Ikšīl (send) a letter and do not omit to ask me in it to carry out his needs and to let me know in it
15. the latest news, if God, the Mighty and Glorious, wills it.
16. Praise be to God alone and His blessings on our lord, Muḥammad, His prophet, and his family, and His peace.
17. Our sufficiency is God. What a fine keeper is He!

---

[3] I.e., until such time as I, the writer, who is grateful to him, will indicate in the future.

Verso

Address

Right Column

1. To the Ikšīl, Master of the Horses and vizier of the king,
2. Uruwī ibn Ḵiyāḵ, his deputy in the fortress of Ibrīm,
3. may God cause his safety and wellbeing to endure.

Left Column

1. From the sincere and victorious commander [ ]
2. the Victory of the Kingship, Crown of the Dynasty, Pride [of the Arabs],
3. Treasure of the Dynasty (*Kanz al-Dawla*) and its support, brother of the northerners, [the Sword]
4. of the Commander of the Faithful, ʾAbū Manṣūr [Mutawwaj],
5. affiliated to al-ʿĀḍid, [the commander of armies].

9 LETTER TO THE EPARCH URUWĪ

Museum of Islamic Art inventory number: 23973.62

Excavation photograph numbers and image numbers:

Recto: 1966A_P04_31A-32 (image: 050308_076_u)

Recto: 1966A_P04_32A-33 (image: 050308_077_u)

Recto: 1968_03_34–34A (image: 050308_683_u)

Recto: 1968_03_35–35A (image: 050308_684_u)

Verso: 1966A_P04_33A-34 (image: 050308_078_u 73,62v)

Verso: 1966A_P04_34A-35 (image: 050308_079_u 73,62v)

Verso: 1968_03_36–36A (image: 050308_685_o)

Verso: 1968_03_37–37A (image: 050308_686_o)

Registration number: 66A/111 (?)

Paper. 49.5 cm × 17 cm

Text

Recto

1 بسم الله الرحمن الرحيم

2 وصل كتاب صاحب الخيل ووزير الملك اطال الله

3 بقاه وادام تاييده وسعادته وسلامته ونعمته وكتاب

4 اخر الى الشيخ ابو الطاهر بن تريك تذكر فيهما

5 تسفير الوصيف وبيعه وشرا الحوائج الذى

6 ذكرتها فالنفق عينه للشيخ ابو الطاهر فما هممت

7 ان ارد الوصيف فلما عرفني غلامك انك محتاج

8 الى الحوائج سلمته للسمسار فنادى عليه فبلغ

9 خمسة دنانير فحضرت غلامك وشاورته على بيعه

10 فبعته بخمسة دنانير بحكم ان البلد ما فيه احد

11 والناس جميعهم ما معهم شى وتقضينا على حوايج

12 الطيب فليس لقينا فى البلد منها شى يحسب عينه

13 التجار عين السوق فالنفق من الحوائج ما ضفرنا

14 بها فسيرت غلامك مع رسولى الى السوق وشرا

15 بدينار سكر اربع كرات سعر اربعين درهم الفرد

16 وزبدة وكافور خمسة عشرين درهم ومصطكى ولاذن وهال

17 وشبة وميعة ورد وقصط وقرفة ومرسين وشملة الحوائج

18 وسنبل دينار زيت طيب ملح عرعر بثمن الوصيف وهى

19 خمسة دنانير وان غليت الحوايج ما شريناها للاجين

20 البيوت عند النسا بحسب النما ما بقي فى السوق

21 من الحوائج شى وصار تمن كل ما ذكرته مضاعف من

22 العطر الذى فى السوق وتبات الحوائج وشراهم

23 باطن كتابى هذا نزل برقعة بكلما خرج والذي اعلم

24 به الاكشيل ان وصل غلامي كبلام عند الملك وهو قليل الشكر

25 لما اعتمد به معه ولى عند الملك حصانين سير الى جاريتين

26 عجايز ما يسو وستة دنانير وما علمت ان بن العسقلانى

27 هو الملك الذى جرى على غلامى منه كل قبيح وانا

Margin

1 خادم الملك ونايبه وقاضى

2 حوائجه والله ما لى الا شماتة الناس

3 الذى سمعوا ان الملك فعل مع

4 غلامى كل خير ووصل على قضية

5 الناس كلهم كرامة

6 مقاربة فانا افسدت

7 لك والملك يفعل مع غلامى هذا

8 القبيح وقد شاهد غلامك الراسين

9 الرقيق ولولا انه مكث ويسمعوا

10 الناس انى رديتهم كنت انفذهم اليك

11 ولكن هو حظي ولا يعتقدها صاحب

12 الخيل ان الذي تقرب بينى

13 وبينك بحضور الاسقف

Verso

1 اننى اغيره وانا باقى علي خدمة الملك وحفظ اصحابك
2 ولكنك اكتب الى الملك وعرفه ما جرى على غلامى
3 من بن العسقلانى وما استخفيت على الملك ولا عليك
4 ولا على اخوان بهون بن العسقلانى غلامى واخذ منه
5 فى المصلحة تومن وانا مغبون وخادم الملك ولكنى انا اخذ
6 النوبيين احسن اخذهم ان شا الله والله ما لى الا شماتة
7 الناس الذى شمتوني فكنت معول على تسيير رسول
8 الى الملك بتجارة الذى شريتها له بعشرة دنانير والحصان
9 الذى كنت عتدته له وجهزة طلبها مني ووصل غلامي
10 مخضوع مهون من بن العسقلانى فوجهت الرسول
11 بعد ان كنت عرفت الاسقف فى تنكالى عند روعه ذلك
12 وقلت له ان رسول يصل اليك وقد سيرت الحصان اليك
13 صحبة محمود غلام الامير وهو واصل اليك فتكتب الى
14 جواب هذا الكتاب وقرى كتابى على الاسقف فقد
15 كان تقرب بينى وبينكم حديث وقد وصل غلامي على قضية
16 مقاربة والملك ما يبقى مع الامير ولا معي يفسد بن العسقلانى
17 حاله اذا كان بن العسقلانى ملك فنحن فاتيه ومواسليه
18 والعمد اليه سير غرمانى الذى لى عندهم مالى وهم ابو عبد الله

19 وماريخرة سير الطريق فاكتب الى بحوائجك و قد سيرت اليك

20 دراهم حق العين قطعتين صندوقين وخريطة وزفت فانى لم

21 لقينا فى البلد شيا نشتريه لك وسير الى بخبرك

22 والحمد لله وحده صلواته على سيدنا محمد نبيه واله وسلامه

23 حسبنا الله ونعم الوكيل

Address

Right Column

1 للاكشيل وصاحب الخيل ووزير الملك

2 اوى بن خياخ النائب بقلعة ابريم

Left Column

1 صديقه وشاكره

2 لامع بن حسن الكنزى

Textual Notes

Recto

22. تبات: This is a derivative of the root *ṯ-b-t*, which is used in the sense of 'to register' in medieval Arabic documents (Khan 1993a, 100). There are two diacritics of *tāʾ* over the first letter, reflecting the dialectal pronunciation of the interdental *ṯ* as a stop *t*. This is a feature that is found in many places in this letter.

Verso

3. استخفيت: Several redundant diacritical dots have been written over this word, but this seems to be the intended reading.
9. وجهزة: This can be interpreted as the plural form *ʾajhiza* ‘equipment’ with the elision of the initial *ʾalif*.
18. غرمانى: The spelling غلمانى is expected, but the reading seems to be *rāʾ* rather than *lām*. It is perhaps the result of a phonetic interchange of /*l*/ and /*r*/.
20–21. فانى لم لقينا: The phrase uses the negator *lam* with a past verb in the *qatala* form. This is more characteristic of later non-standard written Arabic (Lentin 1997, 764–67; Wagner 2010, 141–50). The first person singular and plural pronominal subject indexes are interchanged.

Translation

Recto

1. In the name of God, the Merciful and Compassionate.
2. The letter of the Master of the Horses and vizier of the king—may God prolong
3. his life and cause his support, happiness, safety and well-being to endure—has arrived and also another letter
4. for the elder ʾAbū al-Ṭāhir ibn Tarīk, in both of which you mention
5. the dispatch of the slave (*waṣīf*) and his sale. As for the purchase of the goods that

6. you mentioned (in your letter), allocate the expenditure to the elder ʾAbū al-Ṭāhir. I do not intend
7. to return the slave (*waṣīf*). When your slave boy informed me that you needed
8. the goods, I delivered him (the slave) to the broker and he auctioned him[1] and acquired (the offer of)
9. five dīnārs. I then went to your slave boy and consulted him concerning his sale
10. and sold him for five dīnārs, on the grounds that there is nobody in the land
11. and none of the people have anything. We have dealt with the orders
12. for scented goods. We did not find in the land anything of these that
13. the merchants reckoned to be at market prices. Moreover we did not find the (sufficient) outlay for the goods.
14. So, I sent your slave boy together with my messenger to the market and he bought
15. for a dīnār four balls of sugar, at a price of forty dirhams each,
16. and butter and camphor for twenty-five dirhams, and gum of the mastic tree, laudanum, cardamon,
17. alum, rose liquid, costus, and cinnamon, and myrtle, some small items,
18. spikenard, a dīnār of aromatic oil, salt, juniper, for the price of the slave (*waṣīf*), which

---

[1] Literally: made an appeal for him.

19. is five dīnārs. If the goods become more expensive, we will not sell them to those taking refuge
20. in the houses with the women due to the inflation.[2] No goods
21. remain in the market. The price of all the spices in the market that I have mentioned
22. has doubled. A record of the goods and their purchase
23. is enclosed in this letter of mine. It has been inserted with a note of all expenditure. What I wish to inform
24. the Ikšīl of is that my slave boy Kablām has arrived at the court of the king, but he (the king) has shown little gratitude
25. for what I have undertaken for him. I am owed by the king two horses. He has sent me two good-for-nothing, aged
26. slave women and six dīnārs. I did not know that Ibn al-ʿAsqalānī
27. is the king from whom my slave boy suffered such abuse. I

Margin

1. am the servant of the king and his deputy, and the one who fulfills
2. his needs, but, by God, I experience from people only pleasure in my suffering.

---

[2] The meaning is apparently that the writer and his servants will not attempt to sell the expensive goods to those who do not come to the market but stay at home.

3. They have heard that (in the past) the king has done
4. great good to my slave boy and shown
5. to all the people respect
6. and friendliness, but (now) my relationship with you has been spoiled
7. since the king treats my slave boy
8. in such a bad way. Your slave boy has seen the two
9. slaves (*raqīq*). If it were not for the fact that he has stayed and the people would hear
10. that I had returned them, I would have sent them to you.
11. But that is my fate. Does not the Master
12. of the Horses think that what brings me
13. and you together close in the presence of the bishop

Verso

1. is that I provide him with provisions and I remain in the service of the king and the protection of your companions?
2. But write to the king and inform him what happened to my slave boy
3. at the hands of Ibn al-ʿAsqalānī. I have not concealed from the king, or from you,
4. or from brothers the disgrace inflicted by Ibn al-ʿAsqalānī on my slave boy, and I shall request
5 reparations from him, believe me. I have been wronged, although I am the servant of the king. But I shall treat the Nubians

6. in the best possible way, God willing. By God, I suffer only the gloating
7. of people, who have gloated (over my suffering). I was intending to send a messenger
8. to the king with the merchandise that I have bought for him for ten dīnārs and the horse
9. that I have prepared for him, and equipment that he requested from me, but my slave boy arrived
10. humiliated and wronged by Ibn al-ʿAsqalānī. I sent the messenger,
11. after I had informed the bishop about my suffering due to his (Ibn ʿAsqalānī's) shocking behaviour.
12. I said to him that a messenger would reach you. I have sent the horse to you
13. together with Maḥmūd, the slave boy of the commander. When he reaches you, write to me
14. a reply to this letter and read my letter to the bishop. For
15. there have been good relations between us. My slave boy has come for the sake
16. of good relations. The king should not allow Ibn al-ʿAsqalānī to sour his relationship with me or the commander.
17. For is Ibn al-ʿAsqalānī the king and we his slaves and his grovellers?
18. He is the one guilty of initiating this. Send the servants of mine who have my goods, namely ʾAbū ʿAbd Allāh
19. and Mārīḵura, send (them) by the road. Write to me concerning your requirements. I have sent to you

20. dirhams, two pieces in cash, two boxes, a leather bag and bitumen. I have not found
21 anything in the land to buy for you. Send me your news.
22. Praise be to God alone. His blessings be upon our lord Muhammad, His prophet, and his family, and His peace.
23. Our sufficiency is God. What a fine keeper is He!

Address

Right Column

1. To the Ikšīl, Master of the Horses and vizier of the king,
2. U(r)uwī ibn Ḵiyāḵ, the deputy in the citadel of Ibrīm.

Left Column

1. His friend and one who thanks him,
2. Lāmiʿ ibn Ḥasan al-Kanzī.

10 LETTER TO THE EPARCH URUWĪ

Museum of Islamic Art inventory number: 23973.63

Excavation photograph numbers and image numbers:

Recto: 1966A_P04_27A-28 (image: 050308_078_o)

Recto: 1968_04_01–01A (image: 050308_687_o)

Verso: 1966A_P04_28A-29 (image: 050308_079_o)

Verso: 1968_04_02–02A (image: 050308_688_o)

Registration number: 66A/111 (?)

Paper. 20 cm × 28 cm

Text

Recto

1 بسم الله الرحمن الرحيم

2 توجه اطال الله بقا صاحب الخيل ووزير الملك

3 واكشيله اطال الله بقاه وادام سعادته وسلامته

4 ونعمته و{ل}حراسته صاحبى القائد سعادة وبعثته لقضى

5 حوائج حملتهم اياه والانفاذ من الاكشيل من عينهم

6 خواصيهم على قضى حوائجهم وتسييره مطلبهم

7 الى ان يكوننى شاكر من الاكشيل ولا سماحا

8 يتحققه الاكشيل مما فعله الاكشيل مما يلزم

9 من الاكرام والاجمال من موانس القرابية من القائد سعادة

Margin

1 والاكشيل غير محتاج
2 من حاجة
3 اوصا قضاه شاكر
4 ان شا الله عز وجل
5 الحمد لله وحده وصلواته على سيدنا محمد نبيه وسلامه

Verso

Address

Right Column

1 للاكشيل ووزير الملك
2 وصاحب الخيل اروى متولى بلاد مريس واعمالها

Left Column

1 شاكره
2 حامد الكنزى

Translation

Recto

1. In the name of God, the Merciful and Compassionate.
2. May God prolong the life of the Master of the Horses, the vizier of the king
3. and his Ikšīl, may God preserve his life and cause his happiness, his safety,

4. his wellbeing and protection to endure. My companion, the leader Saʿāda, has set off. I have sent him to carry out
5. various tasks that I have commissioned him to do. The Ikšīl is requested to send to specify
6. the identity of the matters that need to be dealt with and send a request regarding them
7. so that I am made grateful to the Ikšīl (for having the opportunity of carrying them out). There is no greater generosity
8. performed by the Ikšīl than what the Ikšīl will have done with regard to the duty of
9. showing respect, kindness and polite hospitality for the leader Saʿāda.

Margin

1. Is the Ikšīl not in need
2. of something?
3. Let him give instruction for it to be carried out and I would be grateful (for the opportunity to do the service),
4. if God, the Mighty and Magnificent, wills.
5. Praise be to God alone. His blessings be upon our lord Muḥammad, His prophet, and His peace.

Verso

Address

Right Column

1. To the Ikšīl, vizier of the king,
2. and Master of the Horses, Uruwī, the governor of the land of Marīs and its districts.

Left Column

1. The one grateful to him,
2. Ḥāmid al-Kanzī.

11 LETTER TO THE EPARCH URUWĪ

Museum of Islamic Art inventory number: 23973.67

Excavation photograph numbers and image numbers:

Recto: 1966A_P06_01A-02 (image: 050308_101_o)
Recto: 1968_04_12–12A (image: 050308_692_u)
Verso: 1966A_P06_02A-03 (image: 050308_102_o)
Verso: 1968_04_13–13A (image: 050308_693_o)

Registration number: 66A/111 (?)

Paper. 24 cm × 21.5 cm

Text

Recto

1 بسم الله الرحمن الرحيم

2 اعلم الحضرة السامية الاجلية الاكشيل وصاحب الخيل اطال الله بقاه وادام

3 نعمته وتوفيقه وحراسته وسلامته وادام بالسعادة اقتداره توجه صهرى المكنا ابا عبد الله محمد

4 بن عبد الرحمن التاجر وله عند اقوام تلافيين يعرفوا باولاد كجة وهم مكارم ومحب وفرج فقد

5 وتضمن هذا مكارم عن اخيه محب ما يخصه من الدين الذى له عندهم بشهادة جماعة من المسافرين

6 الى بلاد مريس فيسد منه فى استخلاص حقوقه وديونه واسبابه وهذا اكبر حوائجى

7 عندها والله تعالا يكفينى فيها الاسوى وسيرته سواك تسد منه وتاخذ له رجله على احسن قضية

8 فحضرته تعرف مقام الصهر عند صهره واذا حصل له قطر مساعدته فى كركبه مسرع غير

Margin

1 غير اجل الله الله فى السد فيه وقضى حوائجه

2 ومهمى فعلته معرض الخير وهو صابر الى حتى تصلنى وهو شاكر ان شا الله

3 ومهما كان له من حاجة فيكاتبنى بها فاننى اسر بقضاها

4 ومهما به تحتسب كثر او قل

5 الله الله ثم الله الله فى هذا صهرى وهو اليوم لزمك ومحسوب عليك ومالى عند جلالها ادام

6 الله تاييده وصيتى سواه والحمد لله وحده وصلواته على سيدنا محمد نبيه واله وسلامه

Verso

Address

Right Column

1 الاكشيل وصاحب الخيل ووزير الملك

2 اروى بن خياخ النائب عن الملك

Left Column

1 ابى الثنا حامد

2 الكنزى

Textual Notes

Recto

4. كجة: This appears to be an Arabic name. It is attested in Nubian texts in the compounds Kajiŋŋal (ⲕⲁϭⲅ̄ⲅⲁⲗ; P. QI III 35, l. 12) and Kajjiŋa (ⲕⲁϭϭⲏⲅⲁ; Łajtar 2014) 'son of Kaj(j)i'.

8. كركبه 'his predicament': cf. Egyptian Arabic *karkib* 'to throw into confusion, to be apprehensive' (Hinds and Badawi, *A Dictionary of Egyptian Arabic*, s.v.).

Translation

Recto

1. In the name of God the Merciful and Compassionate.
2. I inform the exalted and glorious presence, the Ikšīl and Master of the Horses—may God prolong his life and cause
3. his wellbeing, success, protection and safety to endure, and cause his power to endure in happiness—that my son-in-law, who is called ʾAbū ʿAbd Allāh Muḥammad
4. ibn ʿAbd al-Raḥmān, the merchant, has set off (to you). He has suffered the loss of a debt owed to him by some spendthrift people known as the sons of Kajja, namely Makārim, Muḥibb and Faraj.
5. This Makārim stood guarantor for his brother Muḥibb with regard to his part of the debt that was owed to him (my son-in-law) by them with the testimony of a group of travellers

6. to the land of Marīs and undertook to pay his debt for him and reclaim from him what he owes, his debts and his possessions. This is the greatest of my requests
7. to you.[1] May God, the Exalted, grant me in you the fairest arbiter. I have sent him to you, please pay his debt and help him stand on his own feet in the best possible way.
8. You know the importance of a son-in-law for his father-in-law. If he could have a little help in his predicament, quickly without

Margin

1. delay, by God, to pay his debt and deal with his needs,
2. whatever you do would be a kindness. He is waiting for you to get back to me, and will be most grateful, if God wills.
3. Whatever need you have, write to me concerning it and I shall be happy to carry it out.
4. Whatever charity you could consider, be it much or little,
5. oh God, God, God, God, for this son-in-law of mine [please do], for you have an obligation to him, for my money is with your majesty, may
6. God cause his support to endure, [and this is] my instruction to you. Praise be to God alone. His blessings be upon our lord Muḥammad, His prophet, and his family, and His peace.

---

[1] Literally: it (sg.f), i.e., the presence (*ḥaḍra*) of the eparch.

Verso

Address

Right Column

1. The Ikšīl, Master of the Horses, vizier of the king,
2. Uruwī ibn Ḵiyāḵ, deputy of the king.

Left Column

1. ʾAbū al-Ṯanāʾ Ḥāmid
2. al-Kanzī.

12 LETTER TO THE EPARCH URUWĪ

Museum of Islamic Art inventory number: 23973.69

Excavation photograph numbers and image numbers:

Recto: 1966A_P04_24A-25 (image: ren 050308_075_o)

Recto: 1968_04_17–17A (image: 050308_697_o)

Verso: 1966A_P04_25A-26 (image: 050308_076_o)

Verso: 1968_04_18–18A (image: 050308_698_o)

Registration number: 66A/111 (?)

Paper. 24.5 cm × 17 cm

Text

Recto

1 بسم الله الرحمن الرحيم

2 اعلم الاكشيل وصاحب الخيل ووزير الملك اطال

3 الله بقاها وادام سعادته وسلامته ونعمته ان

4 كتابى تقدم اليه على يد مولاى كنز الدولة اعلمه ان عبيدى

5 سايرين الى الملك احياه الله وعرفته

6 ان كتبت على ايديهم كتاب الى الملك ما انا اعتمده

7 مع رغبة الملك وفى بلاده وتعرفه ان يتقدم

8 بحفظ عبيدى ومراعاتهم والاشتمال عليهم

9 وان ما جسر احد يخرج سواهم والناس

10 متواصلين الى بلاد الملك وما يطلبوا غير

11 العدل وفعل الخير وقد توجهوا عبيدى

Margin

1 كيلا وعالى بقماشى فالانسان
2 اذا حفظ الغلام وفعل معه خير
3 انما يفعله مع مولاه وهذه لك
4 وصيتى اليك والله كتب سلامتهم
5 اعزازا لهم واكراما من الملك

Verso

1 الحمد لله وحده وصلواته على سيدنا محمد نبيه واله وسلامه
2 حسبنا الله ونعم الوكيل

Address

Right Column

1 للاكشيل وصاحب الخيل ووزير الملك
2 اروى بن خياخ نائب الملك بقلعة ابريم
3 ادام الله سلامته وحراسته ونعمته

Left Column

1 شاكره وصديقه
2 لامع بن الحسن الكنزى

Translation

Recto

1. In the name of God, the Merciful and Compassionate.
2. I inform the Ikšīl, Master of the Horses and vizier of the king—
3. may God prolong his life and cause his happiness, safety and wellbeing to endure—that
4. my letter has been presented to him (i.e., you) through the agency of my master, Treasure of the Dynasty (*Kanz al-Dawla*). I inform him (i.e., you) that my slaves
5. are travelling to the king, may God cause him to live. I have informed him (i.e., you)
6. that I have had a letter written by them to the king, indicating I shall carry out
7. the wish of the king in his land. Please ask him to commit
8. to protecting my slaves, to making provision for them and to caring for them,
9. and to ensure that nobody has had the audacity to be hostile to them. These people
10. have friendly relations with the land of the king and request
11. only justice and kindness. My slaves

Margin

1. Kaylā and ʿĀli have travelled with my fabrics. If somebody
2. cares for the slave boy and does good to him,

3. he does it to his master. This is
4. my instruction to you. May God decree their protection,
5. and the king receive them with kindness and honour.

Verso

1. Praise be to God alone, and His blessings be upon our lord Muḥammad and his family, and His peace.
2. Our sufficiency is God. What a fine keeper is He!

Address

Right Column

1. To the Ikšīl, Master of the Horses, vizier of the king,
2. Uruwī ibn Ḵiyāḵ, the deputy of the king in the citadel of Ibrīm,
3. may God cause his health, his protection and his wellbeing to endure.

Left Column

1. One who is grateful to him and his friend
2. Lāmiʿ ibn al-Ḥasan al-Kanzī.

13 LETTER TO THE EPARCH URUWĪ

Museum of Islamic Art inventory number: 23973.21

Excavation photograph numbers and image numbers:

Recto: 1968_05_10–10A (image: 050308_710_u)

Verso: 1968_05_11–11A (image: 050308_711_u)

Paper. 25 cm × 17.5 cm

Text

Recto

1 بسم الله الرحمن الرحيم
2 وَصل كتاب مولاي الاكشيل صاحب الخيل اطال الله بقاه
3 وادام نعماه وكبت اعداه   ووقفت عليه وقوف مسرور بوروده
4 مبتهج بوفوده واما ما ذكر من حال التوجه الى
5 الملك وقوله انما عليه خوف فانا بحمد الله تعالى ما انا جندى
6 من جند الملك فاخاف انا رجل تاجر عبد من احسن اليّ
7 وما انا ابا من الدخول الى الملك حفضه الله تعالى كنت قد سرت
8 اولا اليه وانعم علي وسرحني واحسن اليّ واوعدنى بالرسالة
9 وانا فمملوكه وخادمه والسمعة عنه جميلة واما قولهم اننى غلام
10 صاحب الحربة ما انا الا تاجر وكنت ضيف الملك ونازلت صاحب
11 الحربة متل التجار ما كل من نازل احد كان غلامه ويحسن ضيوف
12 احسان من احسن الى التجار سارعوا اليه وانت ياكشيل

Margin

1 باحسانك الى الناس والتجار هم يسارعوا اليك وانت مشكور فى بلاد المسلمين

2 فما تركت المسير الى الملك الا تحكم ان شهر رمضان شهر ضيق خوفا من المسير

Verso

1 فى الطريق فافطر وانا ان شا الله بعد العيد اسير طالبا الى الملك

2 واسل تفضلها بان تكتب كتاب الى عبد الملك بان يوفي لي بالرسالة

3 الذى اوعدنى بها ويكون هذا الامر على يديك وانا ما كان يمكنى ان

4 اسير اليك جواب كتابك بلا حق عين وما كان عندى الا وصيف واحد

5 يسقينى الما وقد سيرته اليك وصحبته خمسة مقاطع وحلة شرب وسلة

6 حلاوة وطراحة برسمك وهذ اشيا لك وبرسمك وانت فلم تعرفنى

7 قط وما كان يمكنى ان تسير الي كتاب وانفذ لك جوابه بلا حق عين

8 واريد ان تسير الى غلامى سرعة فوحق الله لولا سفرى الى عند

9 الملك ما كنت اسير اليك هذا القليل فلا تخلى الغلام يقيم يوم واحد

10 وتسيره لى صحبة غلامك حتى اسير انا واياه ان شا الله حضرته مخصوصة بالسلام

11 والخير بكم ان شا الله وتخص الملك بالسلام وتعلمه اننى ان شا الله واصل اليه

12 وما اقدر اسير حتى يصلنى والحمد لله وحده

13 غلامى فسيره سرعة سرعة

Margin

1 وتسير الى كتابك ان جماعة من التجار يدخلوا معى فانك من قبل العيش تحسن

2 اليهم فيه فيصلنى كتابك سواهم

Address

Right Column

1 يصل هذا الكتاب الى مولاى الاكشيل

2 صاحب الخيل اروى اطال الله بقاه

Left Column

1 مملوكه

2 حصن الدولة بن العسقلانى

Textual Notes

Recto

2. وَصل: A *fatḥa* vowel is written over the *wāw*.
7. وما انا ابا من الدخول الى الملك: The form ابا appears to be the *faʿʿāl* form of the root *ʾ-b-y* to refuse, i.e., 'one who (customarily) refuses'.
   كنت قد سرت: There is a diacritical dot of *bāʾ* under the last letter of كنت but the reading كنت seems to be what is intended judging by the context.
8. بالرسالة: For the meaning 'consignment of goods', see Blau, *Dictionary*, 248.

10. صاحب الحربة 'Master of the Spear': This apparently refers here to a high-ranking military officer in the king's entourage. An official in Abbasid Iraq with the title *ṣāḥib al-ḥirāb* 'Master of the Spears' who is the second-in-command of the *šurṭa* is mentioned by al-Yaʿqūbī, *Kitāb al-Buldān*, 41.

Verso

6. وهذ اشيا: One would have expected وهذه اشيا.
12. والحمد لله وحده: This was written to close the text of the preceding line, then the writer wrote a note to the right of it beginning وما اقدر اسير....

Translation

Recto

1. In the name of God, the Merciful and Compassionate.
2. The letter of my master the Ikšīl, Master of the Horses—may God prolong his life
3. and cause his wellbeing to endure, and suppress his enemies—has arrived and I have read it, happy at its arrival
4. and delighted at its delivery. As for what he has (i.e., you have) mentioned about the situation of the journey to
5. the king and his (i.e., your) saying that he is (i.e you are) afraid, well, praise be to God the Exalted, I am not a soldier
6. of the king's army that I should be feared. I am a man who is a merchant, the slave of one who had done good to me.
7. Moreover, I am not one who refuses to have an audience with the king, may God preserve him. I travelled

8. previously to him and he showed me favour, facilitated my affairs, did good to me and promised me a consignment.
9. I am his slave and his servant. He has an excellent reputation.[1] As for their saying that I am the slave boy
10. of the Master of the Spear—I am only a merchant. I was the guest of the king and I lodged with the Master of
11. the Spear like the (other) merchants. Not everybody who lodges with a person is his slave boy. He treats guests
12. well. When somebody treats the merchants well, they rush (to stay) with him. You, Ikšīl,

Margin

1. when you treat people and merchants well, they rush to (stay with) you, and you are (greatly) thanked in the land of the Muslims.
2. I have desisted from journeying to the king only in consideration of the fact that Ramaḍān is a difficult month and I am anxious about travelling

Verso

1. on the road before breaking the fast. If God wills, I shall travel to the king after the festival.
2. I ask for your[2] kindness to write a letter to the slave of the king requesting him to deliver to me the consignment

---

[1] I.e., he is greatly respected by me.

[2] Literally: her, referring to the feminine honorific title *ḥaḍra*.

3. that he promised me. Please could this be done through your agency. I could not
4. send you a reply to your letter without cash payment. I only had a single slave (*waṣīf*)
5. who supplied water for me. I sent him to you together with five pieces (of fabric), a large basket drinking vessel, a small basket of
6. sweets and a mattress for you. These were things for you and for you alone. But you never let me know (whether you received them).
7. I could not send you a reply to a letter you sent without cash payment.
8. I want you to send me my slave boy quickly. By God's truth, if it were not for my journey to
9. the king, I would not have sent you this little (gift). Do not make the slave boy delay a single day,
10. but send him to me with your slave boy, so that I can go (to the king) together with him, if God wills. Greetings to you
11. and good wishes, if God wills. Give the king my greetings and inform him that, if God wills, I shall be coming to him.
12. Praise be to God alone. But I cannot travel until
13. my slave boy arrives, so send him quickly, quickly!

Margin

1. Send your letter to me, so that a group of merchants can enter (to see the king) with me, for you would thereby help
2. them in their livelihood. So, I would like your letter for them to reach me.

Address

Right Column

1. May this letter reach my lord, the Ikšīl,
2. Master of the Horses, Uruwī, may God prolong his life.

Left Column

1. His slave,
2. Stronghold of the Dynasty (*Ḥiṣn al-Dawla*) ibn al-ʿAsqalānī.

14 LETTER TO THE EPARCH URUWĪ

Museum of Islamic Art inventory number: 23973.22

Excavation photograph numbers and image numbers:

Recto: 1968_05_12–12A (image: 050308_712_u)

Verso: 1968_05_13–13A (image: 050308_713_o)

Paper. 24 cm × 17 cm

Text

Recto

1 بسم الله الرحمن الرحيم

2 <اعلم> حضرة مولاى الاجل صاحب الخ{لد}يل ووزير الملك اطال الله بقاه واحسانه

3 وادام عز[ه] وحـ[ـسـ]ـن نعمته وصول متحملها الى بلاد النوبة وصحبته فرس

4 لطلب المعاش فى بيعه وهو ممن يتعين على حقه و حفظه ومراعته

5 واستحق حفظها كما لم تزل حفظا بالتقدم الى الولاة وغيرهم

6 من عبيدها وخدمتها بان بالحضرة تعين الحفظ والرعاية

7 الى ان يعود شاكر كما لم تزل سمعته جميلة وقد وصل كتاب الى على يد

8 غلامها ابس وكتبت اليه جوابه واما الاخبار البحرية فلم يصل فيها بعد توجه

9 الحضرة السامية الكبيرية الا ما متيسرها والامور بحمد الله على قضية حقه

10 ولم ينحدر خدمتها فاكتب به الينا والسلام الحمد لله وحده وصلواته على سيدنا محمد النبى واله والسلام

11 وحسبنا الله ونعم الوكيل

Verso

Address

Right Column

1 حضرة مولاى الاكشيل صاحب الخيل ووزير <الملك> اروى

2 متولى بلاد مريس واعمالها

3 <اطال> الله بقاه وادام عزه

Left Column

1 شاكره حسين بن حسن

2 الكنزى

Textual Notes

Recto

2. The verb اعلم appears to have been omitted in the opening formula by mistake.
8. ابس: This name, also attested in **16**r:3, may possibly be identified with the attested Nubian names ⲉⲓⲡⲥⲓ (Lepsius 1846–56, VI [plates], XI, pl. 11, 58 [upper]) and ⲉⲓⲡⲓⲥⲓ (Łajtar 2020, no. 693). The vowel digraph ⲉⲓ was pronounced as short [i] or long [i:] in Nubian (Van Gerven Oei 2021, 34–38). So ⲉⲓⲡⲥⲓ and ⲉⲓⲡⲓⲥⲓ could represent the pronunciation Ipsi and Ipisi, and this would be compatible with the Arabic orthography ابس without *mater lectionis yāʾ*.
10. واله والسلام: These words are written below the end of the line.

Translation

Recto

1. In the name of God the Merciful and Compassionate.
2. <I inform> the presence of my majestic lord, the Master of the Horses and vizier of the king—may God prolong his life and the good He does to him,
3. and cause his strength and good fortune to endure—of the arrival of the bearer of this letter to the land of the Nubians, together with a horse
4. in order to seek his livelihood by selling it. He is somebody who should be treated correctly, protected and cared for.
5. He has a right to your[1] customary protection,[2] so that he is able to have access to the administrators and others
6. of your slaves and servants, because it is incumbent upon your honour to protect and care for him
7. in your customary way[3] until he returns—for which he will be grateful—since he has a good reputation. A letter has reached me by the hand
8. of your slave boy Ipisi and I wrote a reply to it. As for news from the north, since

---

[1] The 3sg.f pronoun refers to the feminine singular honorific title *ḥaḍra* 'presence', which is explicitly mentioned in line 6.

[2] Literally: as you have not ceased protecting.

[3] Literally: as you have not ceased.

9. the exalted and great honourable presence left,[4] only what was easily available has reached us. Affairs are all in order, God be praised.
10. Your servants have not come downriver. Write to us about it. Greetings. Praise be to God alone and His blessings be upon our lord Muḥammad, the prophet, and his family, and His peace.
11. Our sufficiency is God. What a fine keeper is He!

Verso

Address

Right Column

1. My honourable master, the Ikšīl, Master of the Horses and vizier <of the king> Uruwī,
2. governor of the land of Marīs and its districts,
3. may God prolong his life and cause his strength to endure.

Left Column

1. One who is grateful to him, Ḥusayn ibn Ḥasan
2. al-Kanzī.

---

[4] It is not clear to whom this title is referring, possibly the Kanz al-Dawla.

15 LETTER TO THE EPARCH URUWĪ

Museum of Islamic Art inventory number: 23973.25

Excavation photograph numbers and image numbers:

Recto: 1968_05_18–18A (image: 050308_718_o)

Verso: 1968_05_19–19A (image: 050308_713_u)

Paper. 25 cm × 16.5 cm

Text

Recto

1 بسم الله الرحمن الرحيم
2 وصلتنى كتب حضرة مولاى الاكشيل وزير الملك ثبت الله
3 سعادته وحرس من غير الزمان مكانته وكبت حسدته
4 وعداته ووقفت عليها واحطت علما بما لديها وشكرت
5 الله تعالي على سلامته وعافيته وسالته المزيد
6 لديها وتخليد التنعيم عليها   فاما ما ذكره الاكشيل ادام
7 الله تاييده من حال اننى غفلت عن مكانته والسوال
8 عنه فليس الامر كذلك بل اننى معترف بفضله باق
9 على وُدّه وشكره فى كل محضر واما حال المتاجر
10 اذا طلبته حضرته فاننى لما وصلت الى البلد سالت عن
11 ذلك فلم الق منه شيأً وما امكننى ان اهمل الحال الى
12 ان سيرت الى قوص من يشتريه وانا ارجوا ان وصلنى
13 مع سلامة الله سيرته اليه مع كل من يصل وبالله اقسم
14 ما وصلنى من المكارم من الطيب شى فاسيره اليه بل

Margin

1 انا منتظر وصول
2 المكارم واسير ما ينفق من وجوده
3 وقد كانت حضرته طلبت خبره وانا
4 متطلب لها فان انفق وجودها
5 سيرتها اليه مع ما يصلح
6 لها وما سبب تاخر كتبى
7 عنها الا توجهى لوداع
8 الامير كنز الدولة ثبت
9 الله سعده وفخره
10 ويجرى بالتوفق جملة
11 توفقاته

Verso

1 والماثور من تفضل الاكشيل ان يواصلنى بكتبه مضمنة
2 ما لعله يسنح من مهماتها وخدمها وقد سيرت مع موصل
3 هذه الاحرف حق عين وهو رطل {د}خل ووقية سنبل
4 برسم صاحبة الدار وقد كنت سيرت اليها متقدما
5 اوقيتين بناك مع احد غلمانها عرفها كذلك وانا اخص
6 مجلس صاحب الخيل باتم سلام وازكى محبة والاكرام
7 وبخير يكون ان شا الله

Address

Right Column

1 حضرة الاكشيل صاحب خيل

2 الملك ووزيره متولى بلاد

3 المقرة والمريس ابو الخير اروى

4 ادام الله عزه ونعمته

Left Column

1 شاكر تفضله

2 محمد بن رمضان الحاج

Textual Notes

Recto

In this letter, pronominal references to the eparch, who is the addressee, are 3sg.m or 3sg.f, the latter agreeing with the title *ḥaḍra* '(honourable) presence'. Both are translated as 'he/him' below.

Verso

3. {د}خل: There is a stroke over the first letter, which seems to be a deletion mark. The writer apparently intended the word خل 'vinegar'.
5. بناك: I am interpreting this as an aromatic root known as nascaphthon. This is the meaning given by Dozy (*Supplément*, I:119) for the word *bunk*, also pronounced *bunak*. The orthography بناك may be a variant form of this word.

Translation

Recto

1. In the name of God, the Merciful and Compassionate.
2. The letters of my honourable lord the Ikšīl, vizier of the king—may God establish
3. his happiness and protect his status forever and suppress those who hate him
4. and his enemies—have reached me and I have read them and taken note of their contents. I thank
5. God, the Exalted, for his safety and health, and I request Him to increase these
6. for him and grant him eternal wellbeing. As for the statement of the Ikšīl, may
7. God cause his support to endure, that I have shown neglect for his status and have not inquired
8. about him, the situation is not like that. I recognise his eminence, and am steadfast
9. in my love for him and my gratitude to him in all circumstances. As for the situation of the trade consignment,
10. since your honour requested it, when I reached the land, I asked about
11. it, but did not find any of it. I did not want to[1] neglect this and so I
12. sent somebody to Qūṣ to buy it. I promise when he has reached me

[1] Literally: I was not able to.

13. safely I shall send it to him (i.e., you) with anybody who arrives.[2] I swear by God
14. that no perfumes have arrived from al-Makārim that I could send to him (i.e., you), rather

Margin

1. I am waiting for the arrival of
2. al-Makārim so that I can send (to you) what he has managed to find and trade.
3. Your honour has asked about his news and I
4. am making inquiries for you. If he manages to find such merchandise,
5. I shall send it to him (i.e., you) to his (i.e., your)
6. satisfaction. The reason I have delayed sending my letters
7. to him (i.e., you) is only that I travelled to say farewell
8. to the commander Treasure of the Dynasty (*Kanz al-Dawla*), may
9. God establish his good omen and his glory,
10. so that he may carry out all his tasks
11. successfully.

Verso

1. I request the Ikšīl kindly to send me his letters containing
2. what tasks or services he may have (for me to carry out). I have sent with the conveyor

---

[2] I.e., I shall send it with any messenger who comes and is available to carry it.

3. of these words (i.e., this letter) a payment, which consists of a *raṭl* of vinegar and an ounce of spikenard
4. for the housekeeper. I had already sent him (i.e., you) an advance
5. of two ounces of nascaphthon roots with one of his (i.e., your) messengers who indeed knew her (the housekeeper). I send
6. the honourable Master of the Horses warmest greetings, the purest love and respect,
7. wishes for future good, if God wills.

Address

Right Column

1. The honourable Ikšīl, Master of the Horses
2. of the king and his vizier, the governor of the land
3. of Makuria and Marīs, ʾAbū al-Ḵayr Uruwī,
4. may God cause his strength and wellbeing to endure.

Left Column

1. One who is grateful for his munificence,
2. Muḥammad ibn Ramaḍān, the pilgrim.

16 LETTER TO THE EPARCH URUWĪ

Museum of Islamic Art inventory number: 23973.26

Excavation photograph numbers and image numbers:

Recto: 1968_05_20–20A (image: 050308_714_u)

Verso: 1968_05_21–21A (image: 050308_715_u)

Paper. 25.5 cm × 17 cm

Text

Recto

1 بسم الله الرحمن الرحيم

2 اعلم حضرة مولاى صاحب الخيل اطال الله بقاه وادام عزه وصول كتاب على يده غلامها

3 ابس فى حال الموضع الذى كان تقدم فيه الحديث مع الشريف وان الرجل المذكور

4 غايب فعند وصوله اجتمع به واتحدث معه فيما اعرف به واما حال ما اعرف به

5 الحضرة المخدومة فهو ان اسبابى فى موضع اخى لامع والوصية والقيام بخدمتها

6 فهذا هو امرا لازم لى فى حقك فاالله تبارك وتعالى يجرى الخيرات على يديك

7 واما حال البلاد القبلية فقد كان تواصل منها اقوام يشتكوا الخليفة وصاحب

8 السوار ونائب للقوسة واما هذا الاغاتة فى البلاد فنزل <ا>لامير ونكر الخليفة

9 وانهاه عن ظلم الناس كلهم فايرا ما عندك من الاجتهاد فى الصلاح وكذلك

10 الحضرة المخدومة ايضا وكتبه متواصلة فى كل وقت بحفظ اهل بلاد النوبة وعبيد صاحب

11 الخيل فتكون تراعيهم وتقضى حوايجهم وهذا السبب اوجب رد الخليفة

12 والحديث معه فلا تكون تكتب بخلاف دا فلا تسمع غير دل فاالله تبارك وتعالى

13 يجرى الخيرات على يديك واشتهى كتاب يصل الى جميع الولا بحفظ مواضع لامع وعبيده

14 وكذلك مواضعى وعبيدى فانت تعلم ان تحسن خدم الملك ولك وقد ذكر الخليفة ان له

15 رسوم وهو فى كل ذلك وقف وقد كتب الى بن عمران نائب الحضرة بان يسل منه فى جرايته

16 فاجرى به العادة وكتبها فلا تخلفنى بمواصلتها بالاخبار فان الامير توجه

Top Margin

1 متطلع الى ما يصل اليه من الاخبار من حضرتك وكتبها ولا تمنع عن الوصول

2 الى الامير فرسلها متواصلين اليه فى كل وقت وقد اعرف ان اذا وصل من صاحب الخيل

3 كتاب فيصدروه الى مع كل من يصل وكذلك اخى لامع متطلع الى كتبها {ومهما}

Verso

1 ومهما كان للحضرة الاجلية من الحوائج فانني موقوف برسم قضى حوائ<ـجـ>ـها

2 وامتثال امرها والسلام والحمد لله وحده ونعم الوكيل

Postscript

3 وقد وقف محسن برسم حق العين لان كان كتب الكتاب

4 فى وقتها لا يقدر على سوق البزازين فاسل حضرته بسط

5 العذر فى ذلك ورسولى فهو يصلك بعد كتابى هذا

Address

Right Column

1 حضرة مولاى الاكشيل صاحب الخيل ووزير الملك اروى

2 متولى بلاد مريس واعمالها

3 اطال الله بقاه وادام عزه

Left Column

1 شاكر تفضلها

2 حسين بن حسن الكنزى

Textual Notes

Recto

2. يده: The writer first wrote ‘by his hand’ and then wrote above this غلامها ‘your slave boy’.

9. فايرا: By this orthography the writer seems to have intended to represent *fa-yarā* ‘and he sees’.

Translation

Recto

1. In the name of God, the Merciful and Compassionate.
2. I inform the presence of my lord, the Master of the Horses—may God prolong his life and cause his strength to endure—of the arrival of a letter by the hand of your slave boy
3. Ipisi on the matter of the place that was discussed previously with the *šarīf*. The man mentioned (the *šarīf*?)
4. is absent. When he arrives, I shall meet with him and talk to him concerning what I know. What I would like to tell
5. my honourable lord is that my goods are in the place of my brother Lāmiʿ. Following instructions and undertaking your service
6. is an obligatory duty for me for your sake. May God, the Blessed and Exalted, bring bounty to you.
7. As for the southern land, people have been arriving from there complaining about the lieutenant (*al-ḵalīfa*),[1] the Master of
8. the Shipmasts, and a deputy (*nāʾib*) of the Qūsa.[2] On account of this call for help in the land, the commander has come down and reprimanded the lieutenant (*al-ḵalīfa*)

---

[1] The *ḵalīfa* appears to be an official in charge of the Muslims in the ‘southern land’ (*al-bilād al-qibliyya*), i.e., *al-Marīs* (§3.3).

9. and forbidden him to do wrong to anybody. He recognises your efforts to do good and likewise,
10. also my honourable lord.[3] His (the commander's) letters are arriving all the time giving instructions to protect the people of Nubia. As for the slaves of the Master
11. of the Horses, please take care of them and provide them with their needs.[4] This matter necessitated the repudiation of the lieutenant (*al-ḵalīfa*)
12. and reprimanding him.[5] Do not write in opposition to this and do not listen to anybody except them.[6] May God, the Blessed and Exalted,
13. give you bounty. I would like a letter to be sent to all the administrators requesting them to protect the places[7] of Lāmiʿ and his servants
14. and likewise my places and my servants. You know that they all perform good services to the king and to you. The lieutenant (*al-ḵalīfa*) mentioned that he has

---

[2] The Qūsa were a clan from Upper Egypt; cf. al-Maqrīzī (d. 845 AH/1441 AD), *Rasāʾil*, 136; al-Qalqašandī (d. 821 AH/1418 AD), *Nihāyat al-ʾArab fī Maʿrifat ʾAnsāb al-ʿArab*, 156.

[3] This seems to be referring to the king.

[4] The reference here may be to the Muslims operating in Nubia.

[5] Literally: talking to him.

[6] I.e., listen to these Muslims operating in Nubia and not to the lieutenant.

[7] This is likely to be referring to landed property owned by Muslims in Nubia.

15. instructions and he adhered to all of these. He wrote to Ibn ʿImrān, the deputy (*nāʾib*) of your honour, asking him about his salary
16. and he gave him his usual salary. Do not delay sending letters to me about your news. The commander is expecting

Top Margin

1. in great anticipation news to reach him from your honour. Ensure that your letters reach
2. the commander.[8] Your envoys are in contact with him all the time. He has instructed that "when
3. a letter from the Master of the Horses arrives, they should send it to me with anybody who comes here." Likewise my brother Lāmiʿ is expecting your letters.

Verso

1. Whatever needs your illustrious honour has, I am committed to carrying out your needs
2. and obeying your instruction. Farewell. Praise be to God alone. What a fine keeper is He!

Postscript

3. Muḥsin has been delayed in delivering what is owed. He has just written a letter

[8] Literally: Do not prevent your letters from reaching the commander.

4. saying that he cannot make it to the market of the cloth-merchants. I ask your honour to grant
5. forgiveness for that. My messenger will reach you after this letter of mine.

Address

Right Column

1. My honourable lord, the Ikšīl, Master of the Horses and vizier of the king, Uruwī,
2. governor of the land of Marīs and its districts,
3. may God preserve his life and cause his strength to endure.

Left Column

1. One who is grateful for his kindness,
2. Ḥusayn ibn Ḥasan al-Kanzī.

17 LETTER FROM THE EPARCH URUWĪ

Museum of Islamic Art inventory number: 23973.36

Excavation photograph numbers and image numbers:

Recto: 1968_05_00–00A (image: 050308_706_o)

Verso: 1968_05_01–01A (image: 050308_707_o)

Paper. 15.5 cm × 17 cm

Text

Recto

1 بسم الله الرحمن الرحيم
2 وصل كتاب ولدى اطال الله بقاه وادام تاييده وسعادته وسلامته ونعمته
3 وقراته وفهمت مضمونه وسرنى حسن سلامته وعافية ووصلنى ما
4 تفضلت به على يد صاحبه ابرهيم ولا عدمته ولا خلوت منه
5 وتعين على مكافته ويكثر فى الناس مثله   وقد سيرت صحبة
6 ابرهيم برسم حق العين جارية ومعها ولدين فبسط لى بالعذر
7 ومهما كانت لك حاجة فعرفنى اعلم ان ما كان لك على دين عن اننى
8 الجارية قد بعتها بخيارى فعن ايش تكلمت فيا وانا ان شا الله
9 اسيرها لك وقد راى صاحبيك رسولى الذى سيرته بسبب
10 الوصيفة فلا تكون على قليل هم فالخير يكون ان شا الله وكانها
11 الغسيسن جوهر كانت صاحب الخيل يقبل يدها الكريمة ويسال
12 عن حضرته والمسول من مولاى يتفضل وينعم على عبدها قروه
13 امرتيها بخير فلا زالت حضرته متفضلة

Margin

والحمد يكون لوحده
حسبنا الله ونعم الوكيل

Verso

ولا يضيق صدرك عن السراج الذى سيرته لوالدتك كانت على
السفر وما كان بيدها فالامور تصلك كما يجب ويختار ويصلك
سراج جيد من عبدها ان شا الله فلا تكون على قبل هم فادعى لها بالسلام
ودفعت لصاحبك ابرهيم جارية كفوا لنفسه

Address

Right Column

حضرة ولدى الشيخ ابو الطاهر
اطال الله بقاه وادام سلامته ونعمته

Left Column

شاكر بفضله صاحب الخيل
ووزير الملك اروى متولى بلاد
مريس

Textual Notes

Recto

In this letter there is a confusing interchange of 3sg.m, 3sg.f and 2sg.m references to the addressee.

2. ولدى 'my son': This is a polite term that the eparch uses to refer to the addressee, who is unlikely to be his son in reality. The fact that he uses the term 'my son' rather than والدى 'my father', which is also used as a term of politeness, suggests that the addressee is younger than the eparch.

11. الغسيسن 'beauty': This appears to be a variant of the adjective غَيْسَانِيّ/غَسَّانِيّ 'beautiful' (Ibn Manẓūr, *Lisān al-ʿArab*, 3259; Hava, *Dictionary*, 517).

Translation

Recto

1. In the name of God, the Merciful and Compassionate.
2. The letter of my son—may God prolong his life and cause his support, his happiness, his safety and wellbeing to endure —has arrived
3. and I have read it and noted its contents. I was pleased to hear that you are well and in good health. I have received
4. what you have graciously given me by the hand of your companion ʾIbrāhīm. May I not be deprived of him or left alone without him.
5. He should be rewarded. May there be many like him among the people. I have sent a slave girl with
6. ʾIbrāhīm (as payment) for what is owed together with her two children. Forgive me (for the delay).
7. Let me know whatever you need. I know that I owe you a debt arising from the fact that

8. I sold the slave girl of my own accord (without consulting you)[1] and (I know) what you have spoken about me. God willing,
9. I shall send her to you. Your two companions have seen my messenger whom I sent in connection with
10. the slave (*al-waṣīfa*). Do not have any worries. All will be well, God willing. She (the slave girl)
11. is a beauty who is like a jewel. The Master of the Horses kisses your honourable hand and makes a request to
12. your honour. What is requested from my lord is that you do goodness and kindness to your slave (the Master of the Horses).
13. His (i.e., of the Master of the Horses) two wives send their best wishes. You are always so kind.

Margin

1. Praise be to the One alone
2. Our sufficiency is God. What a fine keeper is He!

Verso

1. Do not be anxious about the lantern, which I sent to your mother. She was on
2. a journey and she did not have it with her (and so could not send it to you). Everything will reach you as required and as is appropriate. A

---

[1] Literally: through my choice.

3. fine lantern will be conveyed to you by her slave, God willing. Do not be concerned. I send you greetings.
4. I have given a slave girl to your companion ʾIbrāhīm who suits him well.

Address

Right Column

1. My honourable son, the elder ʾAbū al-Ṭāhir,
2. may God preserve his life and cause his safety and wellbeing to endure.

Left Column

1. One who is grateful for his kindness, the Master of the Horses
2. and vizier of the king, Uruwī, governor of the land of
3. Marīs.

18 LETTER FROM THE EPARCH URUWĪ

This is written in the same hand as **17** and contains similar formulaic phrases. It is likely, therefore, that it was also written by the secretary of Uruwī, though it does not contain an address.

Museum of Islamic Art inventory number: 23973.23

Excavation photograph numbers and image numbers:

Recto: 1968_05_14–14A (image: 050308_714_o)

Verso: 1968_05_15–15A (image: 050308_715_o)

Paper. 18.5 cm × 17 cm. The beginning of the letter on the recto is missing. Some of the letters at the end of the lines on the recto have been truncated due to the fact that the left margin has been cut.

Text

Recto

1 [و]هلك عدوه وضده .... يا مولاى ان ووصلنى [كتاب صاحب]

2 السوار وهو يذكر لى ان ياخذ لى منك ثلثة ثوب وقد اخذ

3 .. ثوبين على اسمك وقد تسلمهم صاحب السوار وهم يتعملوا

4 مع اصحاب البلاد تعملا ما هو جيد وحبائب القمح فقد سلمت لعبدك

5 ست ارادب الا ثلث من دون تافه وقد تسلمهم غلامك وهذه الثياب

6 لك فان الخليفة ما له شى ويا مولاى ازداد اعلى الناس زائد ثلثة

7 امداد والقوسامتاع درمس لما حبوا القرطمى حبوا له حقه

8 فى ايام بابه فلما اخذ رسمه رجع بابى دفعه ويتى قمح وثوب ثوب

9 وهذا شى ما جرت به عادة يا مولا صاحب هذا الكتاب يفعل معه خير

10 فانا اذا جا اخر من عندك حرمته وهذا الرجل هو صاحبى وهو رجل

11 جيدة فاسئل ما فعلته معه وقد وصلنى يا مولاى انى من جا

12 على اسمك انا اطلبه اكرام لك عبدها يقبل يدها ورجليها

13 وعلى الكتاب متاع الحضرة افضل السلام والحمد لله وحده

Verso

1 ومهما كان شى ابكرك ياخذوا ويجوا الى عندك وانا اسيرها فعلوا

2 انا اكتب اعرفك وانا عب<د>ك فى البلاد

Textual Notes

Recto

1. يا مولاى ان: Several letters of this phrase are only barely visible due to the damaged state of the document.
7. والقوسامتاع درمس: This is a construction containing the vernacular genitive exponent *mtāʿ*, which is written bonded to the head noun in the orthography. The first half of the phrase may be referring to the Qūsa clan, who are mentioned in **16**r:8 (see the references in the note there). The word درمس could be identified with Darmus, a town in Lower Nubia that is attested in Nubian documents and Arabic sources (see Seignobos 2015, 562–63). So the whole phrase is probably referring to a section of the clan of the Qūsa who had settled in Lower Nubia.

القرطمي al-Qirṭimī: This *nisba* may relate to *qirṭim* 'safflower seed' and so denote somebody who sells safflower; cf. Ibn al-ʾAṯīr, *al-Lubāb fī Tahḏīb al-ʾAnsāb*, III:26.

11. جيدة: The word has feminine inflection although it refers to a man.

Translation

Recto

1. and may (God) destroy his enemy and opponent [ ] my Lord, that [the letter of
2. the Master of] the Shipmasts has reached me. He says to me that he will take for me from you three garments. He has taken
3. [ ] two garments in your name. The Master of the Shipmasts has received them. They[1] are working together with
4. the people of the land in an excellent collaboration. As for the seeds of wheat, I have delivered to your slave
5. six irdabbs minus a third without any waste.[2] Your slave boy has received them. These garments are
6. for you. The lieutenant has nothing (from me). My master, the debt of the people has risen by three

[1] It is not clear to whom this 3pl pronoun is referring. One possibility is that it is referring to the staff of the Muslim merchant, including the Master of the Shipmasts, and the point is that they are working well with the local Nubian officials.

[2] I.e., of good quality.

7. measures.[3] As for the Qūsa clan of Darmus, when they showed favour to al-Qirṭimī, they granted him his right
8. in the days of his father. When he received his mandate, my father reinstated the payment of two *waybas* of wheat and many garments.
9. This is what is customary. Master, the bearer of this letter will do you good service.
10. When another man came (to me), I shunned him. This man, however, is my companion. He is
11. an excellent man. Ask him what I did with him when he came to me. My master, I shall request the presence of anybody
12. who comes in your name out of respect for you. Your slave (i.e., the writer) kisses your hand and legs,
13. and warmly welcomes a letter from your honour. Praise be to God alone.

Verso

1. Whatever it may be (that you need), I shall hasten to ensure that people take it and come to you, and I shall send it—they will do it.
2. I shall write to keep you informed. I am your slave in the land.

[3] The meaning of this is not clear. It appears to be referring to some kind of economic hardship of the Nubian people.

19 LETTER TO THE EPARCH ĪSŪ

Violet MacDermot's photograph number: 27 in a circle[1]
Excavation photograph numbers and image numbers:

Recto: 1974_V10_03A-04 (image: 170308_283_u)
Verso: 1974_V10_04A-05 (image: 170308_284_u)

Registration number: 74/12
Paper. 25 cm × 17 cm. The letter is damaged and there are several lacunae.

Text

Recto

1 بسم الله الرحمن الرحيم

2 اعلم صاحب الخيل [ووزير الملك] اطال الله بقاه وادام تاييده وحراسته

3 وسلامته ورفعته وصولى الى ثغر اسوان حماه الله [ ] واعتمد على

4 وصول موصل كتابى هذا [من ...] ناحيتى هبة الله بن ابرهيم بن عبد الرحمن القلزمى وانا

5 [ت]خلى انفاذ رسولا اليها بعد ذلك وليسلم ان يتقدم الى اصحابه مراعات

[1] The numeral 27 has been written on the recto and verso of the document in a circle. This is in western numerals and not in the Arabic numerals that are used to write the inventory numbers of the Museum of Islamic Art on other documents. These appear to relate to numberings allocated by Violet MacDermot (see §2.5.3).

6 صاحبى المذكور وحمايته واصحابه فى المسلحة ايضًا بذلك حتى يصلنى كتابه شاكرا لها فانا الشاكر

7 له على ذلك والمكافى وكتابه واسل ويخلينى منه مضمو[ن ال]شكر اخباره واحواله فانى اسر

8 بذلك وابتهج ان شا الله

9 والحمد لله وحده وصلواته على محمد ومن خلفه وصحبه وسلم تسليما وسلامه

10 حسبنا الله ونعم الوكيل

Verso

Address

Right Column

1 لصاحب الخيل ووزير الملك ابى الخير يسوا

2 متولى بلاد مريس مكن واعمالها

3 اطال الله بقاه وادام سلامته

Left Column

1 من القاضى ابى الفضل محمد بن الفاتح

2 ابن عبد الله الحسينى القاضى

3 الموفق السديد ثقة الملك

Textual Notes

Recto

6. المسلحة *al-maslaḥa* or *al-musallaḥa* ‘armed garrison post’ for observing the enemy (see Lane, *Lexicon*, 1403). This could be identified with the medieval armed garrison in al-Qaṣr (= Ḥiṣn al-Bāb), in the region of the first cataract on the eastern bank of the Nile, which is referred to by al-ʾAswānī (al-Maqrīzī, *Ḵiṭaṭ*, I:352).

Verso

Address

Right Column

1. يسوا: For the form and orthography of the name, see §3.2.3. In the fragmentary document 1974_V08_24–24A (not included in this corpus), diacritical dots of *yāʾ* are written below the first letter of the name.
2. مكن: The reading of this word is tentative. It would seem to be an Arabic transcription of the topographic element *migin* in the title *migin soŋoj* ‘the eparch of Nobadia’. The word occurs also in **22**v, address, right, 2, where the reading is certain. See §3.3.

Translation

Recto

1. In the name of God, the Merciful and Compassionate.
2. I inform the Master of the Horses [and vizier of the king]—may God prolong his life, cause his support, his guardianship,
3. his safety and his high office to endure—of my arrival at the border of Aswan, may God protect it, [ ] and I trust that
4. the conveyor of this letter of mine from me, Hibat Allāh ibn ʾIbrāhīm ibn ʿAbd al-Raḥmān al-Qulzumī, has arrived. I
5. [request that you arrange for] the dispatch of a messenger to it (Aswan?) afterwards. Please ensure that he proceeds safely to his colleagues, and take care of
6. this colleague of mine and protect him, and also his colleagues in the armed garrison post, in order that his letter may reach me, thankfully, here (Aswan). I thank
7. him for that and shall requite him. I request that he writes—for which I would be most grateful—concerning his news and his situation. I would be glad
8. of that and delighted, if God wills.
9. Praise be to God alone, and His blessings be upon Muḥammad, those who succeeded him and companions, and may He save (them), and His peace.
10. Our sufficiency is God. What a fine keeper is He!

Verso

Address

Right Column

1. To the Master of the Horses and vizier of the king, ʾAbū al-K̲ayr Īsū,
2. the governor of the land of Marīs Migin and its districts,
3. may God prolong his life and cause his safety to endure.

Left Column

1. From the judge ʾAbū al-Faḍl Muḥammad ibn al-Fātiḥ
2. ibn ʿAbd Allāh al-Ḥusaynī, the
3. prosperous and just judge, Trust of the Kingdom.

20 LETTER TO THE EPARCH ĪSŪ

Violet MacDermot's photograph number: 25 in a circle
Excavation photograph numbers and image numbers:

Recto: 1974_V09_36–36A (image: 170308_280_u)
Verso: 1974_V09_37–37A (image: 170308_281_u)

Registration number: 74/12
Paper. 26 cm × 18 cm. The letter is damaged with lacunae in places.

Text

Recto

بسم الله الرحمن الرحيم
وصل كتاب صاحب الخيل ووزير الملك اطال الله بقاه وادام
عزه وسلامته وحراسته   ووقفت عليه وسررت بوصوله
ووصل غلامه بشر يوم الثلثة خروجى الى بلد النوبة ووجدت فى ذلك
ان صاحب الخيل انفذ ثلثة دنانير فطلبتهم منه ليشترى له الزفت قبل
خروجى من البلد فجمعت ثلثة درهم حقا حتى يشترى له الزفت
وبعد ان خرجت الى بلد النوبة [يوم ال]ثلثة [ب]عث صاحـ[ـبى ......]
اليه عشرين قيراط يشترى له عشرو[ن ....]
اليه قربتين من عندى يجعل فيها الزفت وقد جعـ[ـلت الزفت فيها]
وحملتها واركبت مركب للمعدى بالتجارة وبالله لقد سررت
بكتابه فايشما كان لك من حاجة فاكتب الى فانى اقضيها
له وافعل له ما يلزمنى صغيرة كانت او كبيرة فلا يقطع

Margin

1 لانابة عنى بالتجارة وحاجاته وللخير

2 الحمد لله وحده وصلواته

3 تكون ان شا الله عز وجل

4 على محـ[ـمد ومن] خلفه وصحبه وسلم تسليما وسلامه

5 حسبنا الله ونعم [الوكيل]

Verso

1 اعذرنى فانى كتبت هذا الكتاب من دندور فلو كنت باسوان لكنت

2 انفذ اليه حق عين حتى تدارك الصداقة بما يقول هذا ان شا الله

Address

Right Column

1 [لصاحب الخيل وو]زير الملك

2 [اب]ى الخير ايسوا

3 اطال الله بقاه وادام سعادته

Left Column

1 الحسين بن محمد [ ] بن نصر [ ]

Textual Notes

Recto

4. يوم الثلثة خروجى الى بلد النوبة: This appears to mean that the eparch's messenger Bišr arrived on Wednesday as the writer was leaving for the land of Nubia. The writer states

that he had received the letter, so the messenger must have arrived before the writer left.

Verso

1. دندور: I am interpreting this as the place name Dendur, between Aswan and Qaṣr Ibrīm (Pierce 2017, 53), but the reading is not completely certain.

Address, Right Column

2. ايسوا: An additional *ʾalif* is added before the *yāʾ* of the name Īsū.

Translation

Recto

1. In the name of God the Merciful and Compassionate.
2. The letter of the Master of the Horses and vizier of the king—may God prolong his life and cause
3. his strength, safety and guardianship to endure—has arrived, and I have taken note of it and am pleased with its arrival.
4. His slave boy, Bišr, arrived on Wednesday as I was leaving for the land of Nubia. I found in it (the letter)
5. that the Master of the Horses sent three dīnārs and I asked on your behalf for bitumen to be bought for you before
6. I left the land. I collected three dirhams commission in order for him to buy for him (i.e., the Master of the Horses) the bitumen.

7. When I left for the land of the Nubians on Wednesday, my colleague sent [ ]
8. to him twenty *qīrāṭs* in order to buy for him twenty [ ]
9. to him two water skins from me, in which the bitumen could be put, and I put [the bitumen in them]
10. and I loaded them on a ship of the purveyor of merchandise. By God, I was delighted
11. with his letter. Whatever request you have, write to me, and I shall carry it out
12. and perform my duty, whether it be small or large. May he (the Master of the Horses) not cease

Margin

1 to allow me to act as his agent in trade, to carry out his needs and for any service.
2. Praise be to him alone. May His blessings
3. be—if God, the Almighty and Exalted, wishes—
4. upon Muḥammad [and those who] succeeded him, and his companions, and may He save (them), and His peace.
5. Our sufficiency is God. What a fine keeper is He!

Verso

1. I ask forgiveness, since I have written this letter from Dendur. If I were in Aswan, I would have

2. sent him cash, so that trusting friendship may accompany what this (letter) says,[1] if God wills.

Address

Right Column

1. To the Master of the Horses and vizier of the king
2. ʾAbū al-Ḵayr Īsū,
3. may God prolong his life and cause his happiness to endure.

Left Column

1. Al-Ḥusayn ibn Muḥammad [ ] ibn Naṣr [ ]

---

[1] I.e., so that you may have trust in what he (the conveyer of the message) says.

21 LETTER TO AN EPARCH

Museum of Islamic Art inventory number: 23973.48

Excavation photograph numbers and image numbers:

- Recto: 1966A_P06_12A-13 (image: 050308_111_o)
- Recto: 1966A_P06_13A-14 (image: 050308_110_o)
- Recto: 1968_02_14A-15 (image: 050308_656_o)
- Recto: 1968_02_15A-16 (image: 050308_657)
- Verso: 1966A_P06_14A-15 (image: 050308_109_o)
- Verso: 1968_02_16A-17 (image: 050308_658_o)

Registration number: 66A/111 (?)

Paper. 51 cm × 17 cm

Text

Recto

1 بسم الله الرحمن الرحيم
2 اعلم الاكشيل صاحب الخيل ووزير الملك متولي اعمال بلاد المريس
3 اطال الله بقاه وادام نعماه اننى سيرت ولدين من اولاد وهما قاسم
4 وابو عبد الله الى اركنون ليقيموا فيها وهم ضيفانك وضيفان
5 الملك احياه الله وما سيرتهم لتجارة ولا لفائدة في بيع ولا
6 شرى وانما سيرتهم ليكونوا فى حسب الملك وفى بلاده الى ان
7 يفرج الله وانفذ لهم قماش يسيروا به الى الملك احياه الله وينظروا
8 تاجه ويصيروا من جملة مماليكه كما ابي القاضى الرشيد وربما سمعت به
9 وجدي وابن عمي القاضى ابو الفضل وسافر جدى الى الملك العادل

باسيل وسافر والدي الي الملك مويس أبو مينه كري رسول من السلطان اعز الله نصره الى سوبة وهو الذى سعى فى الصلح بين السلطان وبين الملك لما فسدت الاحوال في ايام الملك داوود وسافر ابن عمى القاضى ابو الفضل الى الملك مويس رسول السلطان الى سوبة وسافرت انا مع ابن عمى وانا صبى الى سوبة الى الملك مويس ولقيت منه كل خير وسافر ولدى هبة الله الى الملك العادل مويس وهو فى دنقلة ولقى منه كل خير واخلع عليه واهلى وابى واجدادى معروفين بخدمة الملوك المتقدمين وكل خير عندنا من عندهم واملاكنا الذى نعيش منها فى بلادهم وانا اشتهى من صاحب الخيل ان يكون بينى وبينه معرفة وصداقة للزمان وقد سيرت اولادى مقدمة قبل وصولى اليه وقبل دخولى الى بلاد الملك فان تفضل بكتاب الى الملك احياه الله يعرفه جميع ما ذكرته ورغبتى فى الوصول الى بلاده فيفعل وياخذ لي منه كتاب يكون من الملك الى صاحب الخيل اليك بان يفعل معى ومع اولادى كل خير ويجرينى على رسوم اجدادي ويامرك فيه بان تجعل لى بيت فى ابريم وبيت في ادمنا وبيت في اركنون ابنيهم واسكن انا واولادى فى بيت اشتهيت منهم ويكون على الكتاب علامته ان شا الله عز وجل الحمد لله وحده وصلواته على سيدنا محمد نبيه

Margin

1 سيرت برسم حق عين شقة برد عراقى فبسط بالعذر
2 ويوصى صاحب الخيل ادام الله عزه نوابه فى اركنون باولادى
3 ويقيموا الى ان يصل اليهم كتابى ان شا الله

Verso

Address

Right Column

1 يصل هذا الكتاب الى الاكشيل صاحب الخيل
2 ووزير الملك متولي بلاد المريس واعمالها
3 اطال الله بقاه وادام حراسته ونعمته

Left Column

1 محبه وشاكره
2 عبد الله بن القاضى الرشيد
3 على بن الزبير

Textual Notes

Recto

3. ولدين من اولاد: The syntax of this phrase suggests that اولاد should be read *ʾawlādī* ‘my boys’. The lack of a final *mater lectionis* is likely to reflect a shortening of the final unstressed vowel, which is a feature of vernacular speech.

4. اركنون Erkinun (?): The location and identity of this place name are not clear. The first three letters could be the Old Nubian word for village *erk-*, modern Nubian *irki* (Browne, *Old Nubian Dictionary*, 61). This may possibly be identified with the place name Arginī/Argini/Arginē, which is attested in medieval Nubian sources (Pierce 2017, 43), and the village pronounced Argíin in modern Nobíin, in Lower Nubia on the west bank of the Nile just north of Wādī Ḥalfa, coordinates: 21.999140 31.350410 (Ṣabbār and Bell 2017, 27; Salvoldi and Geus 2017, 82).

10. مينه كري: This may be a variant of the Nubian name Menakouda, i.e., Menakure. The consonant *d* sometimes interchanges with *r* in Nubian names, e.g., Menakourra < Menakouda (Łajtar and Ochała 2017, 246–47), Maššoura < Maššouda (P. QI III 54).

25. ادمنا: This can be identified with the Nubian place name Adminna, which is also attested with the variant phonetic forms Adminne, Adiminnen, Adiminne, Arminne and Arminna, the latter two reflecting the sound shift *d* > *r* (Pierce 2017, 42); cf. the Nubian texts P. QI III 38, 60, IV 77, 78, 79, 123 (see DBMNT). It is situated just south of Ibrīm in Lower Nubia, coordinates: 22.458850 31.836860 (Pierce 2017, 78). Edward Lane, who visited it in the nineteenth century, refers to it as Arminna (Lane 2000, 492). In modern spoken Nobíin, it is pronounced Armínney (Ṣabbār and Bell 2017, 27).

Margin

1. شقة برد: A *šuqqa* is an oblong piece of a garment. The word *burd* is used to designate a striped or variegated garment (Lane, *Lexicon*, 184).

Translation

Recto

1. In the name of God, the Merciful and Compassionate.
2. I inform the Ikšīl, Master of the Horses, vizier of the king, the governor of the districts of the land of al-Marīs—
3. may God prolong his life and cause his wellbeing to endure—that I sent two of my sons, called Qāsim
4. and ʾAbū ʿAbd Allāh to Erkinun in order for them to dwell there, as your guests and the guests
5. of the king, may God preserve his life. I did not send them for trade nor for benefit through selling and
6. buying. Rather, I sent them to be at the disposition of the king and (stay) in his land until
7. God permits. I shall convey to them cloth for them to send to the king, may God preserve his life, and so that they can
8. see his crown (i.e., have an audience with him) and become his slaves, like my father the rightly-guided judge—perhaps you have heard of him—
9. and my grandfather, and my cousin, the judge ʾAbū al-Faḍl. My grandfather travelled to visit the just king

10. Basil and my father travelled to visit King Mūyis, the father of Mena Kurē (?), as a messenger
11. from the ruler, may God strengthen his victory, to Soba. It is he who strove to make a peace treaty between
12. the ruler and the king when the situation deteriorated in the days of King David.
13. My cousin, the judge ʾAbū al-Faḍl travelled to visit King Mūyis as a messenger of the ruler
14. to Soba. I myself travelled with my cousin when I was young to Soba to visit King
15. Mūyis. I was received by him very well. My son, Hibat Allāh, travelled to the just king
16. Mūyis, while he was in Dongola, and was received very well by him and he bestowed gifts of honour upon him.
17. My children, my father and my forefathers are known for their (court) service of the previous kings and we have
18. been treated very well by them. Our property, from which we have a livelihood, is in their country. I would
19. like to express my wish to the Master of the Horses that there be a long-term acquaintance and friendship between the two of us.
20. I have sent my sons as harbingers before I reach him and before I enter the country
21. of the king. If you would do the kindness of sending a letter to the king, may God preserve his life, informing him of everything
22. I have mentioned and my wish to come to his country, then please do so. Also obtain for me from him

23. a letter from the king to the Master of the Horses /to you/ instructing that he treats me
24. and my sons well and treats me in the same way as my forefathers, and instruct you
25. in the letter to provide me with a house in Ibrīm, a house in Adminna and a house
26. in Erkinun, so that I can build them and I can live in whichever of these houses I wish together with my sons.
27. Let his (the king's) signature be on the letter, if God, the Mighty and Glorious, wills.
28. Praise be to God alone, and His blessings be upon our lord Muḥammad, His prophet.

Margin

1. I have sent a piece of an Iraqi striped garment in lieu of a cash payment. Please forgive me.
2. May the Master of the Horses, may God cause his power to endure, instruct his deputies in Erkinun concerning my children,
3. and let them wait for the arrival of my letter, if God wills.

Verso

Address

Right Column

1. This letter should reach the Ikšīl, Master of the Horses
2. the vizier of the king, governor of the land of Marīs and its districts,

3. may God prolong his life and cause his protection and wellbeing to endure.

Left Column

1. One who loves him and is grateful to him,
2. ʿAbd Allāh, son of the rightly-guided judge
3. ʿAlī ibn al-Zubayr.

22 LETTER TO AN EPARCH

Museum of Islamic Art inventory number: 23973.59

Excavation photograph numbers and image numbers:

Recto: 1966A_P04_18A-19 (image: 050308_069_u)
Recto: 1966A_P04_19A-20 (image: 050308_070_u)
Recto: 1966A_P04_20A-21 (image: 050308_071_u)
Recto: 1966A_P04_21A-22 (image: 050308_072_u)
Recto: 1968_03_28–28A (image: 050308_683_o)
Recto: 1968_03_29–29A (image: 050308_684_o)
Verso: 1966A_P04_22A-23 (image: 050308_073_u)
Verso: 1968_03_30–30A (image: 050308_679_u)

Registration number: 66A/111 (?)

Paper. 14 cm × 20.5 cm

Text

Recto

بسم الله الرحمن الرحيم
وصل كتاب حضرة مولاي صاحب الخيل اطال الله بقاها وادام
تاييدها وعلاها ورفعتها وسناها وتمكينها وكبت بالذل المهين
كافة حسدتها واعداها اما ما ذكرته عن خدمة الملك فنحن جميعنا
خدامه ومماليك التاج واما ما ذكرته انك توقف المراكب <ا>لمعدية
للخيل فانني كنت معول الى ان وصلني امر السلطان خلد الله ملكه
على يدى اخوه والى بلادنا وكتاب الى الملك يعلمه ان كان يحتاج

8 الى عسكر يسيره اليه وعاقني انا الى ما يصل هاده الرسل واسير

9 مقدم الخيل اليكم وقد توجه ايضا غلام السلطان صحبة

10 غلامى الى الملك والله الله تنفذهم بعد اكرامهم واعزازهم

11 الى الملك وتوصيه فى كتابك لا يعيقهم ساعة واحدة

12 فان العسكر لم ينتظر الا وصول الرسل الذي توجهت اليكم

13 وججري يتحدث معك وكبان بما شاهدوه وقد حضر كبان الى

14 والى قوص وسمع حديته وهو يستجمع معك ويحدتك بما عاينه

15 شفاها والوصية جميعها انك توكد على الملك انه لا يخلي

16 الغلمان يقيموا فانت تعلم انني ما اقول هادا جميعه الا في

17 حق الملك وانا مملوكه وخادمه وقد سيرت فرسا جيدة

18 من خيلي تصلح لك على يد غلامى يحيى فتنعم بقبولها ومهما كان لها من حاجة

Margin

1 تسرنى بقضائها والحمد لله وحده وصلواته على سيدنا محمد النبى واله وسلم تسليما وحسبى الله ونعم الوكيل

Verso

Address

Right Column

1 الى الاخ صاحب الخيل

2 متولى ابريم وبلاد مكن

3 ادام الله سلامته

Left Column

1 من الامير الموفق السعيد الاكرم

2 ناصر الدين سيف امير المومنين

3 ابى منصور محمد بن الامير الناصح هلال

4 الدولة شيخنا كنز الدين

Textual Notes

Recto

5. The phrase انك توقف المراكب is difficult to construe syntactically. From the context it seems that the eparch had complained that the supply of horses to Nubia had stopped. If this is the case, then the 2sg.m pronoun in *ʾannaka* cannot be the subject of the verb, but must be in extraposition without resumption. The subject is *al-marākib* 'the ships'.

12. لم ينتظر: This negator *lam* here appears to express a denial of a future action rather than a past action, as would be expected according to Classical Arabic grammar. The generalised use of *lam* as a negator for all tenses is a feature of non-standard written Arabic of the Ottoman period (Lentin 1997, 764–67; Wagner 2010, 141–50). This is an early example of such usage. It is likely that the writer used it to express an emphatic denial, a usage that it has still retained in Modern Egyptian Arabic (Rosenbaum 2002).

13. جحرى: Diacritical dots of *jīm* are written under the first two letters.

كبان: This name could be identified with the Nubian name Kapenē, which is attested as the name of the scribe of the Old Nubian documents P. QI III 35, l. 22 and 37, l. 29, dated to the end of the twelfth century.

Verso

Address

A symbol in the shape of a cross is written between the two columns of the address.

Right Column

2. مكن: The form would seem to be an Arabic transcription of the topographic element *migin* in the title *migin soŋoj* 'the eparch of Nobadia', which is attested in Nubian sources (Ruffini 2012b, 34). The form *migin* is a genitive form *migi-*.

Translation

Recto

1. In the name of God, the Merciful and Compassionate.
2. The letter of your honour, my lord, the Master of the Horses—may God prolong his life and cause
3. his support, exaltation, supremacy, resplendence and power to endure and suppress in abject humility
4. all his enviers and enemies—has arrived. As for what you have said with regard to the service of the king, we are all

5. his servants and slaves of the crown (i.e., his subjects). As for your saying that the ships conveying
6. the horses have stopped, I was intending to (send them) until the order of the ruler, may God make his reign eternal, reached me
7. by the hand of his brother, the governor of our land, together with a letter to the king informing him (the king) that if he (the king) needed
8. an army, he (the ruler) would send it to him, but he (the ruler) has prohibited me from sending to you
9. the first instalment of the horses until these messengers (i.e., my slave boy and the slave boy of the ruler) arrive (at the king). For the slave boy of the ruler has set off together
10. with my slave boy to the king. Please, please allow them passage, after showing them due honour and respect,
11. to the king, and request him in your letter not to delay them for a single hour,
12. for the army will indeed wait for only the arrival of the messengers who have travelled to you.
13. Jajrī will speak with you, together with Kabān, concerning what they have seen. Kabān has visited
14. the governor of Qūṣ and heard what he said. He (Kabān) will meet you and tell you in person what he witnessed.
15. The full instruction (for you) is that you emphasise to the king that he should not make
16. the servants stay. You know that I say all this only

17. in the interest of the king. I am his slave and servant. I have sent you a mare of excellent quality
18. from my horses for your personal benefit by the hand of my slave boy Yaḥyā. Be so kind as to accept it. Whatever need you have,

Margin

1. you would please me by allowing me to carry it out. Praise be to God alone and blessings be upon our lord Muḥammad, the prophet, and his family, and may He save (them). My sufficiency is God. What an excellent keeper is He!

Verso

Address

Right Column

1. To the brother, Master of the Horses,
2. the governor of Ibrīm and the land of Nobadia,
3. may God cause to endure his good health.

Left Column

1. From the prosperous, auspicious and most gracious commander,
2. Victor of the Religion, Sword of the Commander of the Faithful,
3. ʾAbū Manṣūr Muḥammad, son of the sincere commander Crescent
4. of the Dynasty (*Hilāl al-Dawla*), our elder Treasure of the Religion (*Kanz al-Dīn*).

23 LETTER TO AN EPARCH

Museum of Islamic Art inventory number: 23973.24

Excavation photograph numbers and image numbers:

Recto: 1968_05_16–16A (image: 050308_716_o)

Verso: 1968_05_17–17A (image: 050308_717_o)

Paper. 26 cm × 16.5 cm

Text

Recto

1 بسم الله الرحمن الرحيم

2 عبد حضرة مولاى الاكشيل ووزير الملك اطال الله بقاها وادام تاييدها

3 وعلاها ورفعتها وسناها وتمكينها وكبت حسدتها واعداها المملوك

4 يقبل الارض والذى يريد علمه ان مركى يقول كمامات اسير سا

5 انا اخلى عبيد صاحب الخيل جميعهم يمتن كمامات اسير سا وقلنا

6 له احيا الله الملك وزريه ما واصل الله عليهم فما يصل بنا شر وقال

7 نجمنا يظهر قريب ان شا الله لما سمعوا ان النوبة نافقوا على

8 الملك قتلهم فقال فعبيد صاحب الخيل الذى هم فى هذه البلاد اين

9 لهم موضع يدخلوا فيه ودخل اسوان وجمع عبيد درما

10 واحضرنى عندهم وقال لى ان صاحب ا<ل>خيل امرنى ان اخذ الوالية

11 فقلت له من دفع لك ولاية حتى اجى اخذ من عندك ولاية

12 وتبت عليه كل ما ذكر الى فى هذا الكتاب وهو جاى اليك لما سمع

13 انى احب انهب بيته فخاف وجا اليك فلا تقبل منه وانا فما اعدم

14 عنده ما يجب ا<ل>خمسة اروس خيل انت تريد الكثير او القليل فلا تقبل

15 منه شى حتى احضر اواقفه وهذا الكلام ما هو من قديم وانا هو

16 ما تكلم الا فى هذا الوقت القريب ما هو حديث كان قديم وانما هو فى

17 هذه الشهرين فان امرتنى انهيه واجى اكتب عرفنى وان قلت لى

18 حتى اجيك وارجع فاكتب عرفنى وجميع الكلام قد حضر حامل هذا

19 الكتاب كان حاضر <ا>ساله عن خيلك فانا ما استانى غير جواب هذا الكتاب

Verso

Address

Right Column

1 يصل هذا الكتاب الى حضرت مولاى الاكشيل ووزير الملك

2 اطال الله بقاها وادام عزها ونعماها

Left Column

1 مملوكه

2 صاحب السوارى

Textual Notes

Recto

4. يريد علمه: The upper strokes of the *yā*ʾ and the *dāl* in يريد are unusually elongated. The reading, however, is clear since the formula occurs elsewhere, e.g., **25**r:4.
مركى: This can be identified with the attested Nubian name Merki or Merkē.[1] The name is also attested in **46**r, witness, 12 and **47**r:3, v:1, 7.
سا: I am interpreting this as a vernacular form meaning 'now, immediately', derived from ساعة.

6. وزريه: This may reflect a vernacular form of the Classical Arabic plural form *wuzarāʾahu* with weakening of the *ʾalif*. Alternatively, it may be that the singular form وزيره 'his vizier' was intended but the scribe metathesised the *yā*ʾ and the *rā*ʾ when writing the word.
يصل: The reading is tentative, since the stroke of the final *lām* has a truncated descending stroke.

7. نافقوا: 'rebelled'. For this meaning of the third form of this verb see Dozy (*Supplément*, s.v.) and Blau (*Dictionary*, s.v.).

10. الوالية: This appears to be a scribal error for الولاية.

12. وتبت عليه: This corresponds to وثبت عليه. The two diacritical dots of *tā*ʾ are written over the first letter of the verb, indicating that the *ṯā*ʾ was pronounced as a stop /t/, as in vernacular Egyptian Arabic.

---

[1] DBMNT / TM Nam 10598 (Merkourios): DBMNT NamVar 301566 (ⲙⲉⲣⲕⲏ), 301569 (ⲙⲉⲣⲕⲓ).

15. وانا هو: There is a stroke descending from the *hā*ʾ, which appears to be that of a *mīm*. It seems that the writer first wrote وانا هم and then changed it to وانا هو.
19. سااله: I am interpreting this as the imperative with an elided initial *ʾalif*. Only the three teeth of a *sīn* are distinguishable. In principle, however, it could be read as a 2sg.m prefix conjugation تساله, which would mean 'you may ask him', or the like.

There are some words in the top margin written inverted relative to the main text. These appear to be pen exercises rather than coherent text. The words can be read as المملوك يقبل الارض 'the slave kisses the ground', والاخ 'and the brother'.

Translation

Recto

1. In the name of God, the Merciful and Compassionate.
2. The slave of my honourable lord, the Ikšīl and vizier of the king—may God prolong his life and cause his support,
3. his elevation, his loftiness, his magnificence and his power to endure, and suppress his haters and his enemies—the slave
4. kisses the ground and what he wishes him to know is that Merki[2] says, "I shall send the muzzles[3] immediately.

[2] From the following context it appears that this person was a Nubian in the service of the eparch and also the Muslim merchant.

[3] The muzzles may have been accoutrements of horses for military purposes.

5. I shall make all of the slaves of the Master of the Horses grateful (for the service, since) I shall send the muzzles immediately." We said
6. to him, "May God keep the king and his vizier alive. May God not bring upon them or upon us any evil." He said,
7. "Our star will rise soon, if God wills." When they heard that the Nubians had rebelled against
8. the king, he (Merki) killed them[4] and said, "The slaves of the Master of the Horses who are in this land—wherever
9. they have a place, they enter into it."[5] He entered Aswan and gathered the slaves of Darmā[6]
10. and brought me to them and said to me that "the Master of the Horses has ordered me to take over the administrative office."
11. I said to him, "Who has endowed you with the office before I come to take over from you the office?"
12. But he persisted. Everything that he said to me is in this letter. He decided to come[7] to you, when he heard

---

[4] This is referring to a rebellion by the Nubians who had settled in the Aswan region against the Nubian king. The 3pl pronoun 'they heard' is probably impersonal without any specific reference, i.e., 'when it was heard'.

[5] The term 'place' here is likely to be referring to residential property and the meaning is that the Nubians have settled in Upper Egypt wherever they could.

[6] I.e., those in Darmā's service.

[7] Literally: he is coming.

13. that I wanted to plunder his house. He was afraid and came to you. Do not accept (anything) from him. I am not
14. owed by him what is needed with regard to the five head of horses.[8] Whatever you want,[9] do not accept
15. from him anything until I come and take a stand against him. What he says is not old.
16. He has only spoken (these things) in recent times. What is new was something old,[10] but it was only
17. in these last two months. If you command me, I shall finish (my business here) and come (to you). Write and let me know. If you would like to tell me
18. to come to you and return, write and let me know. The bearer of this letter has brought you the full report.
19. When he is present (with you), ask him about your horses. I am only waiting for the reply to this letter.

Verso

Address

Right Column

1. May this letter reach my honourable lord the Ikšīl and vizier of the king,

---

[8] Literally: I do not lack with him what is required—the five head of horses.

[9] Literally: (whether) you want much or little.

[10] Perhaps this means that the reported words and behaviour of Merki are recent, but they are a continuation of old habits.

2. may God prolong his life and cause his strength and well-being to endure.

Left Column

1. His slave,
2. the Master of the Shipmasts.

24 LETTER TO AN EPARCH

Museum of Islamic Art inventory number: 23973.95

Excavation photograph numbers and image numbers:

> Recto: 1966A_P06_03A-04 (image: 050308_103_o)
> Recto: 1968_01_09–09A (image: 050308_631_u)
> Verso: 1966A_P06_04A-05 (image: 050308_104_o)
> Verso: 1968_01_10–10A (image: 050308_632_u)

Registration number: 66A/111 (?)

Paper. Measurements are not available. There is a tear at the top of the letter and there is a small lacuna on the right side.

Text

Recto

بسم الله الرحمن الرحيم
سبب اصدار هذه المناجاة اطال الله بقاه حضرة مولاى
الاكشيل صاحب الخيل وزير الملك وادام تاييده وعلاه ورفعته
[و]سناه وسموه وارتقاه وكبت بالذل حسدته واعداه مماليكها
[يقبلون الارض بي]ن يديها وينهون اليها انها ما خفى عنها ان مماليكها
كانوا معولون على المتولى بين يديها بدون القريضة ويعلموها ان
الراس الرقيق الذى انعمته علي مماليكها على يد بزلي انها كانت
مريضة وان مماليكها ارادوا يردوها وان الرسول الذى كانت
علي يده مرض وان الجارية وولدها راهم غلامك مشورة تلات

10 دفوع وانها توفيت هى وولدها ومماليكها فهى اخبر باحوالهم
11 وانهم ما طلبوا قربها الا بحسب ما ينهى عنها من التنا الحسن
12 والذكر بجميل والدعا الصالح فابقينا على ما الناس عليه من الشكر

Margin

1 شاكرين نحشر
2 لها والتنا عليها والناس ما يبتغوا المنيل
3 الا يطلبوا فضله ونحن فقد خسرنا

Verso

1 ولولا ما تسمع من الاخبار البحرية واختلاف البلاد والا فكانوا
2 مماليكها معولين علي المثول بين يديها لتقبيل الارض وادا ما يلزمهم
3 من الفرض ولكنها تعلم ان ما لك الرق توجههم الى البلاد البحرية لاخذ
4 الاخبار وقد سيرنا متحملها بزلي فتفعل معه ما يليق بشاكلتها
5 وما هي اهله وكان متحملها قد خرج على اقدام قطن فيكون يخرج
6 امرها الى بعض مماليكها فى الشد منه واستخراج ما له مثال ان
7 شا الله ومماليكها منتظرين تفضلها وانفاقها كما لم يزل تمتعهم
8 بتفضلها ان شا الله عز وجل
9 الحمد لله وحده وصلواته على سيدنا محمد {و}نبيه واله وسلم تسليما

Margin

1 ووصل متحملها شاكر لتفضلها وما فعلت
2 الخير فنحن الشاكرين لها عليه والمعينين لها به ان شا الله

Address

1 [ابو] الخير[متولى بلاد]
2 مريس واعمالها] [

Textual Notes

Recto

6. The term قريضة is obscure. The two diacritical dots of *qāf* are clearly written over the first letter. I am interpreting it as a variant of the term *qirāḍ*, which was used in the context of medieval commerce to refer to a business commenda type of partnership. This would have involved one partner putting capital into a transaction and the other partner doing the work. The meaning of the sentence is apparently that the writers are dependent on the goodwill of the eparch's director of adminstration (*mutawallī*) without the latter putting capital into business transactions.
7. The name بزلي is not clear. There are two dots under the first letter, but the one on the left is much bolder than the one on the right. It is possible that the one on the right is a mark on the paper and was not intended as a diacritic. It is most likely to be read as Bazilī, which would be a variant of the Nubian name Basileios. This is attested in Nubian texts with various spellings, e.g., ⲃⲁⲥⲓⲗⲉⲓ (ostracon from Debeira West, tenth century; Shinnie and Shinnie 1978, 97, no.149), ⲃⲁⲥⲓⲗⲏ (Ruffini 2012b, 207–12, no. J), and ⲡⲁⲥⲓⲗⲏ (P. QI IV 116).

9. مشورة: I am interpreting this as an inflection of the verb *šawwara* 'to try before buying'.

Verso

9. محمد {و}نبيه: The *wāw* before نبيه is a scribal error.

Translation

Recto

1. In the name of God, the Merciful and Compassionate.
2. The reason for sending this message, may God prolong his life, my honourable lord,
3. the Ikšīl, Master of the Horses, vizier of the king, may God cause his support, his exaltedness, his ascendance,
4. his splendour, his loftiness and his elevation to endure, and crush in humility his enviers and his enemies, his slaves
5. [kiss the ground] before him and report to him that it has not been concealed from him[1] that his slaves
6. were dependent on the administrative director in his presence without being in financial partnership. They inform him that
7. the slave whom he bestowed upon his slaves (i.e., the writers of this letter) through the agency of Bazilī was
8. sick, and that his slaves (i.e., the writers) wanted to return her, but the messenger whom

[1] I.e., we are reminding you of this unsatisfactory situation, which you are aware of.

9. she accompanied became ill, and that the slave girl (*al-jāriya*) and her son, Rāhim, your slave boy (*ġulāmaka*), were examined before purchase three
10. times, and that she and her son have died. As for his slaves (i.e., the writers of this letter), he is best informed about their circumstances,
11. and that they only demand from him according to what is reported about him with regard to high praise,
12. kind words and pious prayer,[2] so put us in a position to be grateful to him, as other people are,

Margin

1. thankful to be gathered
2. into his (favour) to praise him. People only seek to obtain something
3. through asking your favour. But we have lost this.

Verso

1. If it was not for the news we have heard from the north and the strife of the land, your
2. slaves (i.e., the writers) would have made sure to present ourselves before you to kiss the ground and to perform their
3. obligations. But you know that you do not have any slaves (*al-riqq*) to send to the northern land to receive

[2] I.e., we are not asking more than his customary kindness.

4. news. So, we have sent the bearer of this message, Bazilī. But do with him what is appropriate for your manner (of conducting affairs)
5. and what you are in a position to do, for your carrier has absconded.[3] Please arrange for
6. your command to be issued to some of your slaves to extract forcibly from him what is appropriate,
7. God willing. Your slaves expect your kindness and munificence, as they have unceasingly enjoyed
8. your kindness, if God, the Mighty and Glorious, wills.
9. Praise be to God alone and His blessings be upon our lord Muḥammad, His prophet, and his family, and may He save (them).

Margin

1. Your carrier has arrived, grateful for your kindness and the good
2. that you have done. We also are grateful to you for this and would like to help you with regard to it, if God wills.

Address

1. [ʾAbū] al-Ḵayr [the governor of the land]
2. of Marīs and its districts [ ]

[3] Literally: has left on feet of cotton, i.e., secretly.

25 LETTER TO AN EPARCH

Museum of Islamic Art inventory number: 23973.5

Excavation photograph numbers and image numbers:

Recto: 1966A_P06_23A-24 (image: 050308_111_u)
Recto: 1968_02_33A-34 (image: ren 050308_663_u)
Verso: 1966A_P06_24A-25 (image: ren 050308_112_o)
Verso: 1968_02_34A-35 (image: ren 050308_664_u)

Registration number: 66A/111 (?)

Paper. 18 cm × 17 cm. Text is missing from the top of the recto of the letter.

Text

Recto

1 [بسم الله الرحمن الرحيم]

2 مملوك الحضرة السامية ال[ا]جلية الكريمة

3 ثبت الله قواعد مجدها ووطد سعدها واهلك عدوها وضدها يقبل الارض

4 بين يديها وينهى اليها حرس الله معاليها الذى يريد علمه ان وصلنى كتابك وقراته

5 وفهمت ما فيه وذكرت فيه انك سيرت للامير كتاب وللشديد كتاب تقضى حوائجى

6 اما الامير فاننى دخلت له فرد يوم فقال لى نقضى حوائجك ولم ارجع لنظره الى

7 الان ولا يتركونى ادخل اليه وصرت ملازم الربع بكرة وعشية فلم تقضى لى حاجة

8 اكثر ما يقول لى قم اطلع معى دار الامير فاطلع معه مثل ما اطلع ارجع انزل

9 ما تقضى لى حاجة قال لى اذا جاني كتاب صاحب الخيل انا اقضى حوائجك وقد اتعبني

10 ولم يردنى الا مطال وكلمه يوسوا طريق على طريق فما له جواب الا ان نقول له نعم

11 نعم وذكر عن الكاتب التي كتب الكتاب للامير ماعرف ايش يكتب وما فيه وصية عن الرقيق

12 ولا دفعة غير ذكر الامير ولا غيره والى الان لم يدفعوا لا ذا ولا ذا فتكتب كتابك

13 للامير وتقول له ان هذا الرقيق للملك ينحدر به يقضى به حوائج الملك احتراما

14 يدخل على البرد فما اقدر والريح المريسى ما تقدرني اصل فيها فتعجلهم فى قضى حوائجى

15 وتسليم الرقيق الى وان سيرت اليهم رسولى من عندك فافعل فقد حال على الوقت

Margin

1 [ ] .. يرسـ<ـلـ>ـوا الى اخر ساعتى هذه تسعة عشر دينارا وثمانية دراهم على صرف خمسة كل دينار

Verso

1 واستقصيت عن الصرف بجهتى ولقيته سبعة فقد اصطرفتها

2 بستة ونصف اخيرا ما اوديها يكون الصرف اكثر تخسر فيها زايد

3 الصرف وقد صارت معى دنانير ذهب وقد سيرت وقته بريده صحبة

4 يوسوا حق عين فما ثم شى يوافقك ولو كانت خيرة حاضرة او غائبة كنت سيرتها

5 لكن العين ما لا نقدر عليه ولا لقينا شاد وعجل علي بالجواب والشديد

6 ما فى له فانت تعرف ان الانحدار هين والصعود صعب اعلمت الحضرة ذلك

7 والجارية استعرضت دفع فيها عشرة دنانير لقيوها مقعدة ردوها وقد ابعتها

8 لمرة باثنا عشر دينارا وسبعة دراهم خارج عن الافريز واستدركنا الثوب اخذناه

9 منها وما احتاج اوصيك بان تكتب كتاب للامير ايضا فيما يخصنا وكذلك [[...]] الشديد

10 فقد انضريت فى حالى واريد كل يوم نفقة عظيمة واما هذا الكتاب فاننى كتبته على سبيل

11 ان يوسوا مسافر اليك واذا قضيت حوائجى اعلمتك ما يكون والراسين التى عندهم دفعوا

12 لى فيهم اثنين وثلاثين دينارا صرف ستة وثلاثين كل دينار وهم دفعوا ايضا اكثر بدينار واثنين وتلتة

13 وما مكنونى فيهم فقلت لهم ما امرنى ان ابيعهم الا بمصر فسير كتابين فى معناهم كتاب للامير وكتاب

14 للشديد فقد حال على الوقت قبضت لهما دينار ونصف الجملة عشرين دينارا ونصف وربع صرف خمسة وثلثين

15 الحمد لله وحده وصلواته على سيدنا محمد نبيه واله وسلامه حسبنا الله [ونعم الوكيل] والله والله العجل العجل العجل

Textual Notes

Recto

2. الحضرة السامية ال[ا]جلية الكريمة: This formula occurs also in 3r:5.

10. يوسوا: This is a personal name, which may be a variant or shortened form of the attested Nubian names Iesou and Isou.[1] Alternatively, it could perhaps be a shortened form the Arabic name Yūsuf.[2]

11. ماعرف: This reflects a contraction resulting from the elision of a *hamza* < ما اعرف.

15. وان سيرت اليهم رسولى من عندك فافعل: This conditional construction is used to express a polite request; see Khan (1990).

Verso

4. حاضرة او غائبة: 'here or elsewhere', literally: present or absent.

8. اخذناه: The final 3sg.m pronominal suffix is a correction of an original 3sg.f suffix (*-hā*). A *ḍamma* vowel is written above it to make it clear that it is to be read as the 3sg.m suffix *-hu*.

12. دفعوا: A word has been deleted after this word.

بدينار واثنين وتلتة: This obscure phrase appears to be referring to the rate at which a sale was offered. The diacritics in

[1] DBMNT / TM Nam 3410 (Iēsous): DBMNT NamVar 300288 (ιηcoγ), 300218 (ιcoγ), 301143 (ι̅c̅oγ), 300907 (ειcoγ), 300984 (εc̅oγ).

[2] I am grateful to Krisztina Szilagyi for this suggestion.

تلتة reflect the replacement of interdental /ṯ/ by the stop /t/ in vernacular pronunciation.

Translation

Recto

1. [In the name of God, the Merciful and Compassionate.]
2. The slave of the lofty, most glorious and munificent presence—
3. may God establish the foundations of his glory, consolidate his good fortune, and destroy his enemy and opponent—kisses the ground
4. before him and reports to him, may God protect his exalted position, that what he wishes him to know is that your letter has arrived and I have read it
5. and I have understood what is in it. You mentioned in it that you have sent to the commander a letter and also sent to the executive officer a letter in order that my requests be carried out.
6. As for the commander, I visited him one day and he said to me, “We shall carry out your requests,” but I have not seen him again
7. since and they do not allow me to visit him. I have stayed in the district morning and evening and my request has not been carried out.
8. The most he (the executive officer?) says to me is, “Come up with me to the house of the commander,” and I go with him, but just as I go up, I come down again

9. without any request of mine being carried out. He (the commander) said to me, "When the letter comes from the Master of the Horses, I shall carry out your requests." He wore me out
10. and replied to us only with delay. Yūsū talked to him in all kinds of ways, but we can only reply to him, "Yes,
11. yes." He says concerning the secretary who wrote the letter for the commander, "I do not know what he is writing. There is no instruction in it concerning the slave (*al-raqīq*),
12. nor payment, only the mention of the commander and nothing else. So far no payment has been made for anything." Write your letter
13. to the commander that this slave belongs to the king and that he should bring him (the slave) down (the river) so that the needs of the king be carried through him out of respect.
14. Cold will be upon me (soon) and I shall not be able (to carry out my business) and the Marīsī wind will not allow me to arrive. So, tell them to hurry up to carry out my requests
15. and deliver the slave to me. If you would (kindly) send my messenger to them from your place, then please do so, for time has run out for me.

Margin

1. [ ] let them send to me in this final hour of mine these nineteen dīnārs and eight dirhams, at the rate of five for every dīnār.

Verso

1. I have made inquiries about the exchange rate on my side and I found it to be seven, but I traded eventually them (at the better rate)
2. of six and a half. If I do not go ahead with this transaction, the exchange will be more, and you will lose due to a higher
3. exchange rate. I have acquired gold dīnārs. I have sent at the time (of the transaction) a mail relating to it
4. with Yūsū as payment of the amount in coin. But there is nothing that would suit you. If there were anything good at all, here or elsewhere, I would have sent it to you.
5. However, cash is something that we cannot control (i.e., we have not been able to acquire it or we have no control of its value) and we have not found an executive officer. Reply to me quickly. But what would I have for the executive officer (in the way of payment)?
6. You know that going downriver is easy and going upriver is difficult. This is what I have to say to your honour.
7. The slave girl was inspected and the price paid for her was ten dīnārs, but they found that she was crippled and they returned her. I had offered her for sale
8. to a woman for twelve dīnārs and seven dirhams in a private transaction[3] and I resolved the issue of the clothing and took it back

---

[3] Literally: outside of the cornice.

9. from her (the slave girl). I do not need to order you (i.e., remind you) to write a letter to the commander regarding what concerns us and also the executive officer,
10. for I have suffered harm and I need to make a large expenditure every day. As for this letter, I have written this because
11. Yūsū is travelling to you. When my needs have been fufilled, I shall inform you what the situation is. As for the two slaves who are with them, they paid
12. to me for them thirty-two dīnārs, for an equivalent exchange of thirty-six, each dīnār (having this exchange value). They have also paid more, at a rate of a dīnār, two and three.
13. They have not, however, given me control over them. I told them he has instructed that I should only sell them in Egypt. So, send two letters concerning them, one letter to the commander and one letter
14. to the executive officer. In the end,[4] I accepted for them one dīnār and a half, in total twenty dīnārs and a half and a quarter, at a rate of thirty-five.
15. Praise be to God alone and His blessings be upon our lord Muḥammad, His prophet, and his family and His peace. Our sufficiency is God. [What a fine keeper is He!] By God, by God, be quick, be quick, be quick!

---

[4] Literally: The time for me came.

26 LETTER TO AL-BAZĪL, THE DEPUTY OF THE EPARCH DARMĀ

Museum of Islamic Art inventory number: 23973.46

Excavation photograph numbers and image numbers:

Recto: 1968_02_11A-12 (image: 050308_653_u)

Recto: 1968_02_12A-13 (image: 050308_654_o)

Verso: 1968_02_10A-11 (image: 050308_652_u)

This document also contains letter **35**.

Paper. 21 cm × 19 cm. Text is missing from the bottom of the letter.

Text

Recto

1 بسم الله الرحمن الرحيم

2 اعلم البزيل النائب عن صاحب الخيل بقلعة ابريم

3 ادام الله حراسته وسلامته ونعمته ان

4 متحمل هذه السطور الرئيس كتب الله سلامته

5 فيجب اعزازه واكرامه وحماية خيانته ومن يتعد من تجار وغريم

6 وكف اسباب المضار عنهم حتى ينكفوا عنها وهم شاكرين ان شا الله

7 والحمد لله وحده وصلواته على سيدنا محمد النبى واله الطاهرين

Verso

Address

Right Column

1 البزيل النائب عن صاحب الخيل

2 ووزير الملك واكشيله ابى الخير درما

3 ادام الله حراسته وسلامته ونعمته

Left Column

1 من الامير السعيد المخلص المنصور عضد الخلافة

2 عز الملك تاج الامرا فخر العرب كنز الدولة

3 وعمدتها ذو الفخر وحسام امير المومنين

4 العاضدى الجيوشى

Textual Notes

The document was reused at some point to write another letter. The second letter, which is private in nature, is **35** in the corpus.

Translation

Recto

1. In the name of God, the Merciful and Compassionate.
2. I inform al-Bazīl, the deputy of the Master of the Horses in the fortress of Ibrīm—
3. may God cause his protection, safety and wellbeing to endure—that

4. the bearer of these lines is the Head, may God decree his safety,
5. and he must be shown favour and respect, and be protected from breach of trust and from unjust treatment by merchants and competitors,
6. and the means of harm should be removed from them until they willingly desist from causing such harm, if God wills.
7. Praise be to God alone and His blessings be upon our lord Muḥammad, the prophet, and his pure family.

Verso

Address

Right Column

1. Al-Bazīl, the deputy of the Master of the Horses
2. and vizier of the king and his Ikšīl, ʾAbū al-Ḵayr Darmā,
3. may God cause his protection, safety and wellbeing to endure.

Left Column

1. From the auspicious, devoted and victorious commander, the Power of the Caliphate,
2. the Might of the Kingdom, Crown of Commanders, Pride of the Arabs, Treasure of the Dynasty (*Kanz al-Dawla*)
3. and its Support, the Glorious One, Sword of the Commander of the Faithful,
4. al-ʿĀḍid, Commander of the Armies.

27 LETTER TO THE SECRETARY OF THE EPARCH URUWĪ

Excavation photograph numbers and image numbers:

Recto: 1974_P04_08A-09 (image: 170308_647_u)
Verso: 1974_P04_09A-10 (image: 170308_648_u)

Object number: 74.1.29/11.7
Paper. Measurements are not available.

Text

Recto

1 بسم الله الرحمن الرحيم
2 العبد يسل حضرة مولاى الشيخ الاجل الكاتب ادام الله عزه
3 قبول يدى مولاى الاجل صاحب الخيل روى بن مولاى الاجل [يسو]
4 عبده وعبد ابوه قبله ويعلمه توصل كتاب حضرته الى عبده
5 ووقفه عليه وما يمنع العبد ان يكتب الى حضرته كتاب
6 الا انه لم يبق مع عبده شى فينفذه مع الله وسلامته
7 فهو الذى اوجب باخير كتاب عبده اليه حق يمتع
8 له فى العدن والعبد يسل حضرته ان تكتب كتاب
9 لـ{لـ}عبد يكون بيده تذكر فيه الخليفة بتى
10 وصاحب السوارى ان لا يسمعوا قول احد
11 كذا هل فزنا على عبده فى المحال والخفى عليك
12 اصحاب ذلك القول وممن يانس سو كذا هو واريد

13 من مولاى فى الكتاب يذكر فيه الى عقيل العجمانى
14 تعرف فيه فى مواضعى وفى عبيدى وحراثين الذين
15 لى وتعرف بتى الخليفة وصاحب السوارى فى حالى
16 حتى يرجع مولاى ان شا الله من سفره فريت
17 انا اصعد اليه ان شا الله والعبد يسل
18 مولاى الشيخ عبيد الله ان يحرضه باخذ لى كتاب
19 وينفذه الى مع صاحب السوارى

Verso

1 فهو اكبر حاجة لى عند مولاى وانا قد كنت فى
2 ايام والده مولاى صاحب الخيل ما تعرض احد
3 الى فى شى وانا عزيز والقدوم ليسل حضرة مولاى
4 ان يجرينى على ما كان والده اجرانى عليه ورعيتم
5 منى الدعا الصالح المشا وحسن الشاكر ان يصل
6 مع السلامة وقد انفذت اليه مع صاحب
7 السوارى سنخرجه احد دينار حق عين
8 لمولاى الشيخ عبيد الله والسلام عليك
9 وحسبنا الله ونعم الوكيل

Address

Right Column

1 حضرته مولاى الكاتب عبيد الله
2 على كاتب صاحب الخيل

Left Column

1 من عبده

2 ابرهيم بن عبد الرحمن

Textual Notes

Recto

3. روى بن مولاى الاجل: The text is faint in the photograph and the reading of this phrase is not completely certain. A possible alternative reading is وزير مولاى الملك 'the vizier of my lord the king'. The reference to the father of the eparch later in the letter, however, supports the reading offered in the edition.

   [يسو]: For the reconstruction of the name in the lacuna here as Īsū, see §3.2.3.

4. عبده وعبد ابوه قبله: This appears to be in apposition to the subject of the verb in line 2 (العبد يسل) referring to the writer's obeisance to the eparch and his father, i.e., 'he (the slave writing the letter) being his (the eparch's) slave and the slave of his father'.

9. بتى: the diacritical dots of the initial *bāʾ* and the medial *tāʾ* are visible. This could be identified with the attested Nubian name Peti.[1]

Verso

7. The reading احد دينار is not certain.

---

[1] DBMNT / TM Nam 27685: DBMNT / TM NamVar 60012 (ⲡⲉⲧⲓ).

Address, Left Column

2. The reading of عبد الرحمن is not certain. A man called ʾIbrāhīm ibn ʿAbd al-Raḥmān occurs in the name Hibat Allāh ibn ʾIbrāhīm ibn ʿAbd al-Raḥmān in **19**r:4.

Translation

Recto

1. In the name of God the Merciful and Compassionate.
2. The slave asks my honourable master, the sublime elder, the secretary, may God cause his strength to endure,
3. to kiss the hands of my sublime master, the Master of the Horses, (U)ruwī, the son of my sublime master [Īsū],
4. (the slave writing the letter being) his (the eparch's) slave and the slave of his father before him, and informs him (the secretary) that the letter of your honour has reached his slave (the writer)
5. and he has read it. The only thing preventing the slave (the writer) from sending your honour a letter (earlier)
6 is that the slave (the writer) no longer had the means to send it safely.[2]
7. He (the secretary) is the one most deserving of the best letter of the slave (the writer), which would give him (the secretary) the right to enjoy

---

[2] Literally: Nothing remained with the slave in order that he send it with God and His safekeeping.

8. Eden. The slave (the writer) requests his honour to write a letter
9. to the slave (the writer) so that it be in his hand and mention in it the lieutenant Peti
10. and the Master of the Shipmasts (asking them) not to listen to anybody saying
11. things like “Have we triumphed over his slave in the (trading) places?” It has been hidden from you who
12. the people saying this are. It is like somebody with malicious intent. I request
13. my master (to write) a letter in which this is mentioned to ʿUqayl al-ʿAjmānī
14. in which you inform him of my situation, my slaves, and my cultivators
15. and you inform the lieutenant Peti and the Master of the Shipmasts about my situation
16. before my master (the eparch) returns from his journey, God willing. I have decided
17. to go up to meet him, God willing. The slave will ask
18. my master, the elder ʿUbayd Allāh, to encourage him (the secretary) to draft a letter for me
19 and send it to me with the Master of the Shipmasts.

Verso

1. This is what I need the most from my master (the eparch).
2. In the days of his father, my master, the Master of the Horses, nobody opposed

3. me in anything. I am well respected and (request) that he goes to ask my honourable master (the eparch)
4. to treat me in the same way that his father treated me. Please be aware
5. that I pray sincerely and with kind gratitude that it (the letter)
6. will arrive safely. I have sent (this letter) to him with the Master of
7. the Shipmasts and we shall request him to pay one dīnār as cash commission
8. to my master the elder ʿUbayd Allāh. Greetings to you.
9. Our sufficiency is God. What a fine keeper is He!

Address

Right Column

1. My honourable master, the secretary, ʿUbayd Allāh
2. ʿAlī, the secretary of the Master of the Horses.

Left Column

1. From his slave
2. ʾIbrāhīm ibn ʿAbd al-Raḥmān.

28 LETTER TO A COMMANDER

Excavation photograph numbers and image numbers:

Recto: 1974_P03_34–34A (image: 170308_643_u)

Verso: 1974_P03_35–35A (image: 170308_644_u)

Object number: 74.1.29/11.2

Paper. Measurements are not available. The beginning of the letter is missing and pieces are missing in the top and bottom corners.

Text

Recto

1 [الا]مير الاجل حصن الدولة اطال الله بقاها وادام تاييدها و[كبت]

2 [حسدت]ها واعداها تعلم مودتى اياها وايثارى لمشاهدتها وملاحظتها

3 ومشافهتها وما انا عليه من الفزة الى سعد طلعتها والتعجل بالنظر اليها

4 وانى ممن لا يشك فى مصافاتها ولا يرتاب باخوتها فاسل من الله المشية ان يمتعنى

5 ببقاها ولا يعدمنى حياتها ويجعل عليها واقية باقية ويزي[د] سعادتها

6 ولا يحط باسرتها ويبلغها باهلها ويظفرها باعداها نقما الى كل مارقيها

7 [ ] الغلب بها وبما طرى تعدى لها فينادى من طيب اخبارها فاشكر الله

8 [ ] اسله اشد انعمه اليه ليزيد سعده لى وشكره لمن خلفى وانا مطلع

9 [ ] سعادتها

Margin

1 تعرف كل صادفهم بايجاب

2 وابو الدر ان يقدم محبته والسلم

Verso

1 ....

2 كما حسن للصديق وتكتب اعذر وانا منرجى خبرا

3 من الملك ثبت الله سعادته والخير يكون ان شا الله

4 والحمد لله وحده وصلواته على سيدنا محمد واله وسلامه

Translation

Recto

1. […] the glorious commander, Ḥiṣn al-Dawla,[1] may God extend his life and cause his support to endure, [and suppress]
2. his [haters] and his enemies. You know my love for you and my desire to meet you, to see you
3. and to speak to you, and how ardently I long for the good fortune of your appearance and how impatient I am to see you.
4. I am one who does not doubt his sincerity nor is uncertain about his brotherliness. I ask God to have the will to grant me the enjoyment

[1] This is the title of Ibn al-ʿAsqalānī in **13**.

5. of the continuation of your existence and not to deprive me of your life and to give you lasting protection, and increase your happiness,
6. not to diminish his family, but to allow his family to live to maturity, and cause him to triumph over his enemies, avenging all those who desert him,
7. [attempting] to overcome him and with unexpected hostility. May he announce his good news. I thank God
8. and ask him (God) to grant him the most robust favours so that his good fortune increases for my sake and his gratitude to those after me. I am looking out eagerly
9. [ ] his happiness.

Margin

1. Inform (me) of everything that befalls them as a matter of duty.
2. [ ] and ʾAbū al-Durr (asks) for his love to be sent in advance. Farewell.

Verso

1. .....
2. as it is good for a friend and write, forgive me, for I am hoping for news
3. from the king, may God establish his happiness. All will be well, God willing.
4. Praise be to God alone and His blessings be upon our lord Muḥammad and his family, and His peace.

29 LETTER TO A COMMANDER

Excavation photograph numbers and image numbers:

Recto: 1974_P03_32–32A (image: 170308_641_u)

Verso: 1974_P03_33–33A (image: 170308_642_u)

Object number: 74.1.29/11.1

Paper. Measurements are not available.

Text

Recto

1 بسم الله الرحمن الرحيم

2 كتبت اليك يا ولدى العزيز على الامير ابريم اطال الله بقاك وادام عزك

3 وتاييدك وسعادتك وسلامتك كتبت عن حال سلامة وعافية

4 لله الحمد على ذلك اعلمك يا ولدى انى كنت قد انفذت اليك

5 العينة اول مرة بعد ان سالت الامير كنز الدولة ادام عزه

6 وانفذها مع امين انسان على انه يلتقى بعبد الباقى و<يسلمها> له

7 فمشى الى بعض الطريق ورجع وبقيت عندنا الى يومنا

8 هذا وقد انفذت بها اليك مع عبد الباقى وفيها تسعة

9 ارطال لكنى ارجو ان وفيها ارجو ان نقمى وارجو ان احضر واخصكم

10 بتسعة ارطال ونصف بدينار وقد بعت الفراش بدينار ونصف

11 والغلالتين بنصف دينار صار الجميع دينارين فسلمت الى صاحب الوبر

12 ثلاثة دنانير وانفذت بها اليك واخذ له بدينارين الزعفران واخذ

13 بدينار نعمى ملون واخذت لك زباد بقيراطين واخذت شموع بقيراط

واخذت بقيراط عود وقيراطين زعفران واخذت بقيراطين خرز
واخذت بقيراط ونصف قرفة واخذت بقيراط غرز ووسب وروى
بقيراط ونصف وعينة وقفل نحاس ربع دينار وهو تك وخرز
سدس دينار وقد دفعت الى عبد الباقى سدس دينار غير اجرة
العينة الباقى عندك من ثمن دينار احبت اعلامك ذلك
لتقف عليه وما كانت لك من حاجة فاكتب اليه بها تجاز اسل

Verso

واولادك و<ا> بيك من الله فى كل عافية وقد دفعت اليه
على يد ابو الحسين النحاس الغلالتين والزجاج احببت اعلامك
ذلك قراط عليك افضل السلام ولدى يخصك بالسلام
وكاتل لى ان قد وصل من سو كل فتحرص ان حاجة لى تقضا شى
والا فاعلمنى حتى اصعد اليه وتسل لى عن ان التبان يقال
له مسلم الفراش لى عنده وفيه ذهب قيل لى انه طلع
على الرابح والسلام وحسبنا الله ونعم الوكيل

Address

Right Column

لولدى العزيز على ابو القاسم هبة الله
بن محمد بن الاعمى
اطال الله بقاه وادام عزه وتاييده

Left Column

1 من عبد الكريم بن الحسن

2 بن داود

3 الى ابريم ان شا الله

Textual Notes

Recto

6. ويسلمها: The *lām* and *mīm* are mistakenly written in reverse order, thus: ويسملها.
9. ارجو ان وفيها ارجو ان نقمى وارجو ان: These appear to be several false starts of the sentence beginning وارجو ان 'I hope that'.
13. نعمى *nuʿmā*: literally 'pleasure, happiness'. Here this may have the sense of luxury goods; cf. Dozy (*Supplément*, II:691 s.v. *al-niʿam* 'objects d'une grande valeur').
    زباد *zabād*: perfume extracted from civet cats.
15. وروى: I am interpreting روى as رِوَاء 'rope for binding a load'.

Verso

1. و<ا>بيك: The omission of the *ʾalif* may reflect a vernacular form of the word.
3. قراط: This reflects the form قرات *qaraʾtu* pronounced with *tafḵīm* spreading to the verbal suffix (*qaṛaʾṭu*).
4. وكاتل لى: This appears to reflect the phrase وكاتب لى (*wa-kātib lī*) with assimilation of the final *bāʾ* of the verbal form to the *lām* of the following prepositional phrase (*wa-kātil lī*).

Address, Left Column

3. ابريم: The reading is not certain.

Translation

Recto

1. In the name of God, the Merciful and Compassionate.
2. I have written to you, my son, who is dear to me, the commander (at) Ibrīm, may God prolong your life and cause your strength,
3. your support, your happiness and your good health to endure. I am writing to you in a state of wellness and good health,
4. praise be to God for that. I inform you, my son, that I had sent you
5. the advance consignment immediately after asking the commander, Treasure of the Dynasty (*Kanz al-Dawla*), may He cause his power to endure, (to dispatch it)
6. and he sent it with a reliable person indicating that he would meet ʿAbd al-Bāqī and deliver it to him.
7. He went on part of the way, but then returned, and it (the advance consignment) has remained with us until
8. this day. I have (now) sent it to you with ʿAbd al-Bāqī. It contains nine
9. *raṭls*. I hope I shall come and assign to you
10. nine and a half *raṭls* for a dīnār. I have sold the mattress for a dīnār and a half

11. and the two tunics for half a dīnār. This made a total of two dīnārs. I handed over to the fur merchant
12. three dīnārs and sent them to you. He took for himself the saffron for two dīnārs. He also took
13. for a dīnār a coloured luxury item, and I took for you civet perfume for two *qīrāṭs*. I took candles for a *qīrāṭ*.
14. I took for a *qīrāṭ* aloes and for two *qīrāṭs* saffron. I took for two *qīrāṭs* beads.
15. I took for a *qīrāṭ* and a half cinnamon. I took for a *qīrāṭ* sprigs and herbs, and a rope for binding a load
16. for a *qīrāṭ* and a half, and a sample, and a brass lock, a quarter of a dīnār, in the form of a small coin, beads,
17. a sixth of a dīnār. I paid to ʿAbd al-Bāqī a sixth of a dīnār apart from the fee for
18. the credit that would remain with you of an eighth of a dīnār. I wanted to inform you of this
19. so that you are aware of it. If you have any requests, write to him concerning them and they will be carried out. I pray to God

Verso

1. that your children and your father are in good health. I have paid to him (ʿAbd al-Bāqī?)
2. through ʾAbū al-Ḥusayn, the coppersmith, the two tunics and the glass. I wanted to tell you
3. that. I send you best wishes. My son sends you wishes.
4. Write to me if anything untoward comes up and you want some request to be carried out.

5. Indeed let me know so that I can deal with it. You ask concerning the straw-dealer called
6. Muslim "Is my bed, which has gold in it, with him?" I have been told that he has come
7. upon something lucrative. Best wishes. Our sufficiency is God. What a fine keeper is He!

Address

Right Column

1. My son, who is dear to me, ʾAbū al-Qāsim Hibat Allāh
2. ibn Muḥammad ibn al-ʾAʿmā,
3. may God prolong his life and cause his power and strength to endure.

Left Column

1. From ʿAbd al-Karīm ibn al-Ḥasan
2. ibn Dāʾūd
3. to Ibrīm, if God wills.

30 LETTER TO A DIGNITARY

Excavation photograph numbers and image numbers:

Recto: 1974_P04_01A-02 (image: 170308_646_o)

Verso: 1974_P04_00A-01 (image: 170308_645_o)

Object number: 74.1.29/11.3

Paper. Measurements are not available. There are some lacunae in the letter.

Text

Recto

1 بسم الله الرحمن الرحيم وصلواته على سيدنا محمد واله وسلم تسليما

2 كتابى الى حضرة مولاى الشيخ الاجل اطال الله بقاه وادام عزه وعلاه ورفعته وسناه وتمكينه

3 وكبت بالذل حسدته واعداه   اعلمه ادام الله علاه اننى كثير الشوق الى حضرته المحروسة

4 متطلع الى الطريق فى كتب اخباره وسايل عنه كثيرا وهو يعلم حرس الله عزه انه عندى مقام

5 الوالد وانه ان يشتهى منى بحاجة ولا يستخدمنى شيا فاسر بقضاها وقد كنت قدمت الى صاحب

6 الخيل وزير الملك كتاب اول صحبة طاعى فى معنا خادمين قد هربا من عندى هناك الى ابريم عند مسيركما

7 متوجهين الى سوبة في مركز النوبة وانهيت عزمى وراهما الى ان تعديت امياه كركر واعلمت انكما لم تكونا

8 بالقلعة المعروفة بابريم ولما انبئت وصولهما الى بلده رجعت عنهما وعلمت ان ما لى نفقته الا عند عودته وقد

9 كان سير جمعيته الحالين حمدان وبن عمتى صلح باثر ذلك العبدين والناقة لو سا ظنك فلا عدمت اهتمامك ولا

10 خلوت خيرك وما تركت الوصول الى ابريم عند ذلك الا انى لم اعلم ان لى بها صديق ولا معرفة بعد

11 صعودك منها وطاعى غائب فمسكت بفسى عن الوصول الى الشريك لانى لم اجرء ولا عنده من نصرته بى

12 وبعد ذلك فقد بلغنى ان الشريك انفذ الثلاثة خدم الهاربان الى اسوان وباعهما ولم اصحح ذلك

13 الا بعد وصول كتابك الى علمت فيه ما تريد احياك الله بكثرة همتك وترك الغفلة عن ذلك فانت تعلم اننى من

14 جماعة لا يعجزوا عن حقهم وانت اخبر الناس بى وبوالدى فلا تهمل الامر وكاتبنى بالجواب بسرعة بصحبة ما ظهر لك

15 وتعلم صاحب الخيل من عندك وتذكر له انه ابن اخت القاضى نور الدين وهو صاحب

16 الشركة التى نور الدين فيها

Margin

1 وعرضت عليه وبركنا بحالة ثقة وشان

2 لانه اكرم ثقة منى والان

3 فما يحتاج وكتبت فى ذلك

4 لتعلم من هو الثقة فانت تعلم

5 وتعلم ان لى كل [ ] ولديه

6 اشركت للزوجة ولغلامى

7 رمضان وراشد البحار

8 الذى صحبته والذين من النوبة

9 [ ] عليهم تحية جعفر السلام

10 والامير ما اعجز عن مكافاته المكرمة

11 ومكافاتك باكرام سعيد فقد كنت

12 اشتهى لو تعيد لى اكرام وجالبة كريمة

13 [ ]لها كله فهان على حبى اخذ حلاوة

14 الظفر وانت اخير بحلاة اليوم

15 فتخاطبه وتعلمه ان صاحب الكتاب

16 المنفذ مع طاعى شيخ بعثه القاضى

17 وهو ولد خليفة للقاضى الكنزى

18 وتعرفه يكافى ما يفتح لك شى

19 ان اشكل على انا عليك جميعا

20 هو [ ]كريم

Verso

1 وما تركت الوصول اليكم بعد وصولكم الا لصيام رمضان عند اهلى وانا انفا ارحل طاعى يجى

2 بجواب كتابى وكان بعد هروب الخادم ركبت جملا نوبى بحر يوم وليلة ر[كبـ]ـت ولم اتكل على احد

3 من الغلمان ليتخذوا فى البحث عليهم فركبت الى جهت كركر فرجعت منها وعلمت انهم رحلوا الى ابريم

4 ولم تكن تامر حق شى فاصل اليه اقضى من حقى امكن قصرى الى حين وصول الامير من السفر اليه وقد عرفته لك لتعلم

5 انى سالته الجواب سرعة ومهما جاوب لك تامر لابى الوالد بن حاضر فيطالعنى بما راى سيدنا موفقا ان شا الله

6 اجرت مكارى ووصلت الى من خليفته ولقى برييس كلنا فى الكل رايه الراى وقر وان رايت قر فخذ منى

7 هذا الخادم فتعلمه انه قادر على نهب قريتين ثلاثة من قرا بلدك ادا ليد غلمانه لانى وجهت عبد

8 موالى وهو صحيح لا تترك له فسحة فان خاننى يهينون القوم منك وان ضيعهم التبديل فتشترى مثلهم

9 تسيرهم لى وله ثلث ثمنهم ان شا حجتى وان فعل معى جميل كما افعله مع غيرى يمكنه الله فى سببه

10 انا قادر على بيعه وضمنه جميل الصافى والموالى والقاضى واكثر لانى من اهل البلد وحكمت فى البلد

11 تحكمى اكثر منهم من بنى عم واخوان وجماعة عرفته ذلك وانا اسير اكرا الخادمين بمزيدهم يكونوا جماعة

12 [ ] ... والسلام عليك برحمته وجميع من حضرتك المحروسة تحيى افضل اكثر التحيات وعلى من يحرس

13 حياتك ... والحمد لله وحده حسبنا الله نعم الوكيل

Margin

1 والزوجة وجهت سلامها ....

Address

Right Column

1 حضرة مولاى الشيخ ابو محمد عيسى بن محمد بن حسن

2 حرسها الله من حسدتها وكبت اعداها بالذل الحقير ليصل ابريم

Left Column

1 منصور مويدها بن شاكره لامع بن

2 حسن بامر من خليفة بن حسن

Textual Notes

Recto

7. انكما لم تكونا: This reflects a pseudo-classical use of the dual.
امياه كركر: 'the waters of Kurkur'. This is likely to be referring to the Wādī Kurkur, situated in the western desert approximately 60 km west of Aswan, or the oasis of Kurkur, situated high in the Wādī Kurkur in the northeastern end of the Sinn al-Kaddab escarpment. The oasis of Kurkur was the hub of several ancient roads linking the first and second cataract region, including one leading to Qaṣr Ibrīm (Paprocki 2019, 242).
12. الثلاثة خدم الهاربان: It is not clear why three rather than two fugitive slaves are now referred to. The dual on the adjec-

tive and subsequent pronouns suggests that 'three' is a mistake.

15. نور الدين: The first element in this name could also be read as بدر (*badr*).

Verso

2. الخادم: A plural sense is required in the context. This appears, therefore, to be a mistake, possibly conditioned by the similar-sounding plural form *ḵadam*.

Translation

Recto

1. In the name of God, the Merciful and Compassionate. His blessings be upon our lord Muḥammad, and his family, and may He save (them).
2. (This is) my letter to my honourable lord, the most illustrious elder, may God prolong his life and cause his strength, his ascendance, his elevation, his splendour and his power to endure,
3. and crush in humility his enviers and his enemies. I inform him, may God cause his ascendance to endure, that I long greatly for his presence, may he be protected,
4. and am looking out on the road for letters conveying his news, and I often ask about him. He knows, may God protect his power, that he has the status
5. of a father for me and that if he wants me to do a task or needs my service for anything, then I would be happy to

carry it out. I have sent in advance a first letter to the Master

6. of the Horses, the vizier of the king, with Ṭāʿī concerning two servants who fled from me there, to Ibrīm, (where you are) during your trip,
7. heading for Soba in the middle of Nubia. I did my utmost to pursue them until I crossed the waters of Kurkur. I was told that you were not
8. in the citadel known as Ibrīm. When I was notified that they had arrived in his (the eparch's) land, I turned back (from my pursuit of) them. I have been informed that I shall not have my wages from him (the addressee) until when he returns.
9. Your current group, Ḥamdān and the son of my aunt, Ṣāliḥ, has sent in pursuit of those two servants and the camel (they fled on). If you had felt concern, I would not have been deprived of your attention,
10. nor would I have lacked your kindness. Moreover, I would not have desisted from travelling to Ibrīm in the current situation, but I did not know whether I had a friend or acquaintance in it (Ibrīm)
11. after you departed from it upriver and Ṭāʿī was absent. So I desisted from coming to the partner, because I did not dare, and, moreover, he could not have helped me (anyhow).
12. It has subsequently been reported to me that the partner had sent the three fugitive servants to Aswan and has sold them there, but I was not able to verify this

13. until your letter arrived, in which I was informed what you, may God preserve your life, wish, in your great solicitude and care[1] for this matter. You know that I am from
14. among those who are capable of obtaining their rights and you know me and my father best. Do not neglect the matter, but write to me with a response quickly together with what is new in your place.[2]
15. Inform the Master of the Horses about the person who is with you and tell him that he (the person with you) is the son of the sister of the judge Nūr al-Dīn and that he is a member
16. of the partnership of which Nūr al-Dīn is a member.

Margin

1. I explained (the affair) to him (Nūr al-Dīn?) and we were blessed with his trust and support,
2. for he offers me very kind support. Now,
3. this is what is needed. I have written concerning this
4. so that you know who is a trustworthy support
5. and you know that I have every [ ] and
6. I have brought into partnership with him my wife and my slave boy,
7. Ramaḍān and Rāšid, the mariner,
8. who is with him and those of the Nubians
9. [ ] upon them the greeting of Jaʿfar.

---

[1] Literally: lack of neglect.

[2] Literally: what has appeared to you.

10. The commander was able to recompense him generously
11. and also recompense you with great generosity. I had hoped
12. that you would return such generosity to me and generous merchandise
13. all [ ] and my love (for you) makes me unwilling to take the sweet reward
14. of victory, when you are more worthy of reward today.
15. So, talk to him (the Master of the Horses?) and inform him that the author of the letter
16. brought by Ṭāʿī is an elder sent by the judge.
17. He is the son of the Kanzī judge deputising for him (the judge).
18. Let him (the Master of the Horses?) know and he will recompense you with anything available for you,
19. if either of us have difficulties.
20. He is [ ] generous.

Verso

1. The only reason I did not come to you after you arrived was that I wanted to spend the fast of Ramaḍān with my family. I will immediately send Ṭāʿī to bring back
2. the reply to my letter. After the flight of the servants,[3] I rode a Nubian camel throughout the day and night and I did not rely on any

[3] The text has the singular form *al-ḵādim*.

3. of the servants to undertake the search for them. I rode in the direction of Kurkur and then returned from there. Then I learnt that they had gone to Ibrīm.
4. You did not give instructions for any power to be granted to me so that I could go there to exercise this and overcome my current inability to act until the time of the arrival of the commander from his journey there. I have informed you of this so that you know
5. that I have asked him to respond quickly. Whatever he replies to you, give instructions to ʾAbū al-Wālid ibn Ḥāḍir to inform me of the decision of our lord (the commander), may you be granted success, if God wills.
6. I hired a muleteer and travelled to the person who is his (the commander's?) lieutenant and he met with the Head of all of us, presiding over everything, whose decision is the (supreme) decision and it is fixed. If you make a decision, it is (likewise) fixed. So take from me
7. this servant and inform him that he is able to extract payment[4] from two or three villages of your district to deliver into the hand of his (the commander's?) slave boys. For I have sent the slave
8. of my freedmen. He is sound, but do not allow him any dispensation, and if he betrays me, the people will despise you. If he misses the opportunity for them to be exchanged, then buy similar ones

---

[4] Literally: loot.

9. and send them to me, and he should have a third of their price, if he wants my written certification. If he does me a good turn, as I do with others, let God enable him in his enterprise.
10. I can sell it and guarantee him a good net income, also the freedmen, the judge and more, because I am from among the people of the town and I get my way in the town.
11. I get my way more than cousins and brothers and family. I have informed him and I shall bring about the increase of the servants, and through this increase they will become a group.
12. [......] and greetings to you, with his mercy, and everybody in you presence, may it be protected, greet with the best greetings, and those who protect
13. your life. .... Praise be to God alone. Our sufficiency is God. What a fine keeper is He!

Margin

1. And the wife has sent her greetings.

Address

Right Column

1. My honourable lord, the elder ʾAbū Muḥammad ʿĪsā ibn Muḥammad ibn Ḥasan,
2. may God protect him from his enviers and crush his enemies in vile humiliation. It should go to Ibrīm.

Left Column

1. Manṣūr, his supporter, son of the one grateful to him, Lāmiʿ ibn
2. Ḥasan, by the order of Ḵalīfa ibn Ḥasan.

31 LETTER TO A DIGNITARY

Sartain inventory number: Add. 03

Excavation photograph numbers and image numbers:

Recto: 1966A_P06_25A-26 (image: 050308_113_o)

Recto: 1966A_P06_26A-27 (image: 050308_114_o)

Registration number: 66A/111 (?)

Paper. Measurements are not available.

Text

Recto

1 بسم الله الرحمن الرحيم

2 اعلم حضرة مولاي الشيخ الاجل اطال الله بقاها وادام تاييدها

3 وعلاها ورفعتها وسناها وسموها وارتقاها وكبت بالذل

4 المهين حسدتها واعداها وسوا ذلك فانى خرجت ورا

5 المريس فوصلت الى [[ابريم]] اسوان وحصانى مغبر كثير وجمعت

6 المريس جميعهم وهم جاياين اليكم وطلبت المجى معهم

7 فما عاقنى غير ثمن الحمل وما يصلح اصعد واخلى ثمن الحمل

8 ورائى وقد وصل قاسم الى عندكم وكان جمع بينى وبين

9 اقوام انهم يخلصونى وما خلصونى الى الان فالله الله

10 سيروا لى الحتة والثوب وكتاب جا وراى من البيت

Margin

1 [ف]عسى اتخلى عمر او خليل او واحد منكم يجينى الى اسوان

2 [با]لصناعات الذى لى عند غلامى والى فارس الا نكافى

3 وهم جميع باسوان

Verso

1 وان لقيت من يشترى الخوذة والبراية والثلاث قرب والرمح

2 فبيعهم والله الله تحرض واحد منكم يجى الى فان حصانى ضعيف

3 ما اقدر اجى اليكم واذا انحدرتوا فجيبوا الجارية لى معكم

4 فما ثم الا الخير ولا تسمعوا من كلام الناس والخر والمولى

5 كان جيبناه برسم الصغيرة لا تسيبوه جيبوه معكم

6 والشكة الذى تكون فى يد النسا جيبها معك والصفات

7 عند عجلان الدباغ خذها منه والله الله خذوا لى ثمن الخمس

8 اشقاق الذى لى عند الوالى لا تخلوها خذوا ثمنها والله الله

9 بلغوا النصف عن المملوك الصغير ما ...... بسرعة سرعة

Margin

1 وان كان ما يجينى واحد منكم والا انا اكون اروح

2 خصوا انفسكم باتم السلام وعلى جميع اصحابنا السلام مثلكم

3 والحمد لله وحده وصلواته على سيدنا محمد نبيه

4 وحسبى الله ونعم الوكيل

Textual Notes

Recto

6. جايايين: This appears to be what is written, though the second *yāʾ* has lost graphic distinctness. It corresponds to Classical Arabic *jāʾiʾīn* (pl.m active participle of *j-y-ʾ*).

Margin

1. اتخلى *itkalli*: 'allow!' with a prosthetic vowel.
2. فارس 'Fāris': This may be identified with the place name Fāris listed by Ramzī (1963, IV:228) as being situated between Aswan and Ibrīm on the east bank of the Nile. It may be the same place as the one called *Serg el Farras* on the map by Jacotin (1818).

Verso

1. البراية: pen-knife, for drawing and paring, Classical Arabic *barrāʾa* (Lane, *Lexicon*, 198).
   قرب *qurub*: plural of *qirāb* 'scabbard'.
4. الخر: literally 'excrement'.
6. الشكة *šakka*: 'chain of gold coins'.

Translation

Recto

1. In the name of God, the Merciful and Compassionate.
2. I inform my honourable master, the most illustrious elder, may God prolong his life and cause his strength,

3. his exaltedness, his ascendance, his splendour, his loftiness and his elevation to endure, and crush in vile humility
4. his enviers and enemies. As for other matters, I journeyed beyond
5. al-Marīs and arrived at Aswan. My horse was covered in dust (and exhausted).
6. All the people of al-Marīs have gathered and they are coming to you. I asked (them to allow me) to come with them
7. and all that has prevented me is the cost of the transport. It is not appropriate for me to go up (the river) and leave the cost of the transport
8. behind me (i.e., without paying it). Qāsim has arrived at your place and he had made an arrangement
9. with people that they should finish their business with me (and let me go), but they have still not finished their business with me. By God,
10. send me the piece (of cloth) and the clothing. Also a letter has come after me (i.e., has been sent after me) from home.

Margin

1. Perhaps you could have ʿUmar or Ḵalīl or one of you to come to me in Aswan
2. with my goods that I have with my slave boy and (also come) to Fāris. If not, we shall manage.
3. They are all in Aswan.

Verso

1. If you find somebody who will buy the helmet, the penknife, the three scabbards and the spear,
2. then sell them. For God's sake, encourage one of your group to come to me, for my horse is weak
3. and I cannot come to you. When you come down (the river), bring with you the slave girl to me.
4. Everything is fine. Do not listen to the talk of people and the rubbish (they speak). As for the freedman,
5. we brought him for the sake of the young girl. Do not leave him, but bring him with you.
6. As for the chain of gold coins that will be in the possession of the women, bring it with you. As for the saddle pads
7. that are with ʿAjlān the tanner, take them from him. By God, take for me the price of the five
8. portions, which are owed to me by the governor. Do not leave them. Take their price. By God,
9. convey (to me) half by means of the small slave .. [ ] quickly, quickly, quickly!

Margin

1. If none of you comes to me, I shall go.
2. Best wishes to you and likewise to all our companions.
3. Praise be to God alone, and His blessings be upon our lord Muḥammad, His prophet.
4. My sufficiency is God. What a fine keeper is He!

32 LETTER TO A DIGNITARY

Excavation photograph number and image number:

1974_P04_06A-07 (image: 170308_645_u)

Object number: 74.1.29/11.6

Paper. Measurements are not available. The top of the letter is missing and there are two horizontal tears in the middle.

Text

1 اعز الله نصره لا[ ]ى تملك الاحرار ويجب ان يعتمد بما ثبت فخرها وثبت سع[ادتها]

2 فان صح للسلطان اعز الله نصره عن جزيتهما اشتغالا من فخر العرب كنز الدولة ادام الله سموه

3 وهو يعلم ما ا[ع]تمده السلطان اعز الله نصره من اعاشتهما ممن باعهما وان السلطان

4 جبى ابنه اعالى الاجلية النجيبية السديدية العزيزية حرس اعادتهما ما يتمعش عليه ولا توخى

5 ما يحسن فعله فيه ومن اعادتهما ونكر مولاى الامتهما من بائعهما وتركهما لانفسهما

6 فاعرف ما يصلح له فيهما احرار وهو يعلم لهما عادة السبى القديم الى بلاد النوبة

7 السافية لـ[ـسنيـ]ـن ثم فى بلاد الاسلام المدة الطويلة وهو اسلم لله وسلامته يقوم الى ذلك

8 وما يتعين عـ[ـليه] ويجرى على العادة المشكورة منه وعطف عنه لبنى الشريف بالناحية

9 ان جا به وصل وان يتاخر رسولى عنه بما يصلح انفاذه فلا تخلينى من كتابه متضمنا ذكر

10 اخباره وساير حاجاته لابلغ فى ذلك غرضه ان شا الله

11 الحمد لله وحده وصلواته على حرمة من خلقه محمد نبيه واله الطاهرين سلامه

12 حسبنا الله ونعم الوكيل

Textual Notes

This document was a considerable challenge to decipher. It is fragmentary and written in a highly cursive script. The decipherment offered here is not always certain. Furthermore, the content of the letter is obscure in many places.

Translation

1. (the ruler), may God strengthen his victory [ ] reign over the free and whose pride and happiness must be established.
2. If the ruler, may God strengthen his victory, has validly received their poll-tax, through the services of the Pride of

the Arabs, Treasure of the Dynasty (*Kanz al-Dawla*), may God cause his elevation to endure,

3. he knows what the ruler, may God strengthen his victory, has undertaken to support the livelihood of the two from the one who sold them and
4. the ruler's son, the exalted, glorious, noble, rightly-guided and powerful presence, who safeguarded their return, gathered (funds) for supporting their families that could be lived off. Indeed I can
5. do what is appropriate concerning it and with regard to their return. My lord has decried the fact that they have been blamed by their seller and left to themselves.
6. Let me know what your preference is regarding them, now that they are free. He knows that they experienced being former captives, taken to the
7. dusty land of Nubia for years,[1] then (were captives) in the land of Islam for a long period. He has submitted to God and His safety. May he (the addressee) undertake this
8. and what is appropriate and customary, with our thanks and out of respect for the sons of the *šarīf* in our district.
9. If he brings it, it will arrive. If my messenger delays sending what should be sent, do not omit to send me a letter containing the mention
10. of your news and your other needs, so I can fulfil your wishes in that regard, God willing.

---

[1] If the reading is correct, this suggests that they were taken captive by Nubians raiding Upper Egypt.

11. Praise be to God alone and His blessings upon the sanctity of those whom he has created, Muḥammad, His Prophet, and his pure family, and His peace.
12. Our sufficiency is God. What a fine keeper is He!

33 LETTER TO A DIGNITARY

Verso of **32**.

Excavation photography number and image number:

1974_P04_07A-08 (image: 170308_646_u)

Object number: 74.1.29/11.6

Paper. Measurements are not available. The top of the letter is missing and there are two horizontal tears in the middle.

Text

1 والناس لما سمعوا تعرف به لنا ان شا الله اذا وصلت انت [ا]طلب منك جميع واخذ [ ]

2 الامير فخر العرب كنز الدولة فامه ... والدى وامرنى والدى ان اذا اردت حاجة اوامر نكتب الى والدك

3 الامير فى بحر الصحرا نكتب له كتابنا <ا>لساعة ليكون عنده علم خبرك ان شا الله وقد امتثلت جميع ما ذكره والدى واوامره

4 وانا ان شا الله اسير الى كنز الدولة عبيد افضل السلالة الجزيل الله عز و[جـ]ـل يحفظ الاخوة التى بينى وبينك

5 ذلك ليكون العلم عندك فلادخل لـ<ـلـ>ـلملك فاتوا لمولاى الملك

6 الولد من والده لانك مـ[ـسيـ]ـر كتابى الى والدى والى حضرة مولاى الملك انا ان شا الله اسير الى محل

7 الامير فخر العرب كنز الدولة ان شا الله اذا وصل والدى كنت تسمع منه خبرى فانفذ غلامك الى حتى سيرجع

8 على اخى مولاى الامير وعددت اقدم مسيرى الى حضرة الامير كنز الدولة عبيد واسوة فتوح وهو

9 .... مثل ما امر لى الامير فخر العرب كنز الدولة

10 ....

11 وانا يا اخى قد قدمت [م]سيرى اليك اعدد عددى تكتب لى وانا اعزم ان شا مولاى العزيز

12 فى اخر شهر مسرى هذا وصلت الى العرب كتبك وسمعت خ[برك] والكلام ان كان صحيح او غير صحيح

13 اليك ان شا الله عز وجل وقد انقذت اليك يا اخى مولاى الا[مير ا]خر شهر مسرى فاردت ان اعلمك

14 وقد سمعت يا اخى ما فيه عليه مع السافرين والنوبة الشاكرين .... خبرك بكتب

15 والسلام الحمد لله وحده وصلى الله على محمد واله وسلم تسليما وحسبنا الله ونعم الوكيل

16 اكثر الله خيرك تسمع لى والى النوبة خبر من احمال الخيول فاخرج لانك الوالد وهذا الذى سيرته حق عين فهو

17 لما اراد عبيد الله المسير الى نحوك سيرت هذا فيه اليك سرعة لفور العجلة وعرفته انى اقدم مسيرى اليك

Margin

1 [ ] لها والسلام اعلمك احياك الله ان الملك احياه الله جدد الولاية
لوالدى وقال له الملك لما فتح للرجل الواصل معه

Textual Notes

Like **32**, this document was a considerable challenge to decipher due to its fragmentary state and the high cursivity of its script. The decipherment offered here is not always certain. The content of the letter is obscure in many places.

5. This line appears to have been inserted as an afterthought in between the adjacent lines. It does not extend to the left edge of the paper like the other lines. The sense of line 4 continues in line 6.

9–10. Only the left side of line 9 is extant. The right side has been lost after the document was torn. There are traces of the bottom of the words of line 10, but none of the words are decipherable. It appears that lines 9 and 10 began in the middle of the sheet, which suggests that they were written as an afterthought.

12. مسرى Mesra: This is one of the Coptic months, known as Mesori in Coptic.

Translation

1. and when the people have heard, inform us about it. God willing, when you arrive, I shall ask you about everything. He took [ ]

2. the commander, pride of the Arabs, Treasure of the Dynasty (*Kanz al-Dawla*),… my father and my father commanded me that when I needed any instructions, we should write to your father,
3. the commander of the desert river, that we should write to him our letter immediately so that he be informed of your news, God willing. I have followed all that my father advised and instructed,
4. and I, God willing, shall go to Treasure of the Dynasty (*Kanz al-Dawla*) ʿUbayd, the Greatest of the Progeny, the Noble One. May God, the Mighty and Glorious, preserve the brotherhood that is between us,
5. (This is so that you be aware of it so that I can have an audience with the king. Please bring us to my lord the king.)
6. as a son in relation to his father, for you are the conveyor of my letter to my father and to my honourable lord the king. God willing, I shall travel to the residence
7. of the commander Pride of the Arabs, Treasure of the Dynasty (*Kanz al-Dawla*). God willing, when my father arrived, you would have heard from him my news. Send your slave boy to me by the time
8. my brother ʿAlī, my lord the commander, returns. I have made preparations to bring forward my journey to his honour the commander Treasure of the Dynasty (*Kanz al-Dawla*) ʿUbayd, and Model of Victories. He
9. [................] as the commander, Pride of the Arabs, Treasure of the Dynasty (*Kanz al-Dawla*), commanded me
10. [................................]

11. My brother, I have brought forward my journey to you. I am making my preparations. Write to me. I am intending (to come), if my great lord wishes,
12. at the end of this month of Mesra (Mesori). Your letters have reached the Arabs and I have heard your news, and the talk, whether it be true or not true,
13. will reach you, if God, the Mighty and Magnificent, wills. I have sent to you, my brother, the commander at the end of the month of Mesra (Mesori). I wanted to inform you of this.
14. I have heard, my brother, what the situation is with the travellers and the Nubians, who are grateful [Send me] your news by letters.
15. Greetings. Praise be to God alone and the blessings of God be upon Muḥammad and may He save (him). Our sufficiency is God. What a fine keeper is He!
16. May God give you abundant blessings. Let me and the Nubians know about the transport of the horses, so that I can leave, for you are the father. What I have sent is a cash payment. This is because,
17. when ʿUbayd Allāh decided to travel to you, I sent this enclosed with it for you quickly in haste, and I informed him that I shall put forward my journey to you

Margin

1. [ ] to it. Greetings. I inform you, may God give you life, that the king, may God give him life, has renewed the governorship of my father. The king said (this) to him- when he admitted the man arriving with him.

34 LETTER TO A DIGNITARY

Museum of Islamic Art inventory number: 23973.94

Excavation photograph numbers and image numbers:

Recto: 1968_01_07–07A (image: 050308_629_u)

Verso: 1968_01_08–08A (image: 050308_630_u)

Paper. Measurements are not available.

Text

Recto

1 بسم الله الرحمن الرحيم

2 بسم الله الرحمن الرحيم

3 كتابى الى حضرة مولاى وولى واخى على اطال الله بقاها وادام سموها

4 وسناها وتمكينها وكبت حسدتها وعداها اسل الله تعالى يقرب

5 اجتماع بها على اسر حال بمنه وكرمه انه على ما يشا قدير وما

6 احسن اصف كُلَ ما لقيت لك من الوحشة الله تعالى يقضى

7 كل بخيره منه وَكرمه وغير ذلك فقد سيرت اليك على موصل

8 هذا الكتاب رطل صوف ازرق الى خان فتح الصباغ وحرش

9 لا توضع عني كتبت مع كل من يصل اليك بهم وان قررت تسيير شى سيره

10 وعرف ولدى محمود انى سيرت اليه كتاب اعرفه ما يوصل له من النقوب وانه

11 جعل له ان يكون شاهد نصوص واما احسن اصف لك ما جعله معه

12 الشيخ المكنى ابو عبد الله بن رائق الوراق من الخير الحمد لله على ذلك خص نفسك باتم

13 السلام وجميع في المنزل باتم السلام اشوف ذلك

Margin

1 وتعرف عينى اخى وبن امى السلام وجميع من عنده وعرف الشيخ ابو اسحق

2 انى انفذت اليه كتاب وفى طيته حجتين عَلى بني فروة وعرفه ان ولده ابو لطافة على جملة السلام الحمد لله على ذلك

3 جميع الاهل على جملة السلام

Verso

1 وعلى ولدى الشيخ جليل الدولة ابو نعم السلام وعرفه

2 ان جميع من عند بن ولده على جملة السلام وعلى ولدى محمود السلام

3 الحمد لله وحده وصلى على سيدنا محمد النبى وسلم تسليما

4 وحسبنا الله نعم الوكيل

5 وكان وصل الى كتاب من عند محمود وهو

6 يشكر فيه الشيخ جليل الدولة ابو نعم وما

7 يفعل معه من الخير الله تعالى يخيره عنى

8 بالخير وعنك على شكره والحمد لله عز وجل

Note written at a right angle to the previous note

1 ست تخصك باتم السلام

2 زكية تخصك باتم السلام

3 وجميع من فى الدار يخصك باتم السلام

Address

Right Column

1 يصل هذا الكتاب اخى ابو الحسن على

2 بن الشيخ الداعى ابو <ا>لطاهر عبيد الله بن ابى ترعة

Left Column

1 من اخوه جعل فديه

2 محمد بن عبيد الله بن الحسن بن على

Textual Notes

Recto

1. A *basmala* written in large script, which is apparently a pen exercise, appears above the *basmala* of the letter.

10. النقوب: I interpret this as a plural of نقاب 'veil'.

Verso

3. There are some random words written in a large hand around this line, which do not seem to be connected to the text.

Translation

Recto

1. In the name of God, the Merciful and Compassionate.

2. In the name of God, the Merciful and Compassionate.
3. (This is) my letter to my honourable master, my friend and brother, ʿAlī, may God prolong his life and cause his exaltedness,
4. his splendour and his power to endure, and crush his enviers and enemies. I ask God, the Exalted One, to make close
5. a most joyful meeting with him through His graciousness and kindness. He is able to carry out what He wishes, and
6. I could describe in detail all the desolation I feel in your absence. May God, the Exalted, bring about
7. everything in his goodness, graciousness and kindness. On another matter, I have sent to you by the conveyer of
8. this letter a *raṭl* of blue wool to the caravanserai of Fatḥ the dyer, and coarse cloth.
9. Do not lower the price of this for me. I sent letters concerning these items with everybody who was travelling to you. If you would (kindly) determine to send something, then please send it,
10. and inform my son Maḥmūd that I have sent to him a letter informing him about the veils that will reach him and that

11. arrangements have been made for him to be witness of documents. It gives me pleasure to describe to you the goodness that was done to him by
12. the elder called ʾAbū ʿAbd Allāh ibn Rāʾiq, the paper-merchant. Praise be to God for that. Warmest greetings to you
13. and everybody in the house. Let me see that.[1]

Margin

1. Convey to my dear brother, the son of my mother, greetings, and to everybody with him. Tell the elder ʾAbū ʾIsḥāq
2. that I have sent to him a letter, in which are enclosed two deeds against the Banū Farwa. Inform him that his son, ʾAbū Liṭāfa, is in the best of health—praise be to God for that.
3. All the folk are in the best of health.

Verso

1. Greetings to my son, the elder Jalīl al-Dawla ʾAbū Nuʿm. Inform him
2. that everybody in the home of the son of his son is in the best of health. Greetings to my son Maḥmūd.
3. Praise be to God alone and bless our lord Muḥammad, the prophet, and may He save (him).
4. Our sufficiency is God. What a fine keeper is He!

---

[1] I.e., I want you to do as I say.

5. A letter has arrived from Maḥmūd and he
6. thanks the elder Jalīl al-Dawla ʾAbū Nuʿm and
7. as for the good that he does to him, may God the Exalted grant him good on my behalf
8. and on your behalf, with his thanks. Praise be to God, the Mighty and Glorious

Note written at a right angle to the previous note

1. Sitt sends you warmest greetings.
2. Zakiyya sends you warmest greetings.
3. Everybody in the house sends you warmest greetings.

Address

Right Column

1. May this letter reach my brother ʾAbū al-Ḥasan ʿAlī,
2. son of the elder, the preacher, ʾAbū al-Ṭāhir ʿUbayd Allāh ibn ʾAbī Turʿa.

Left Column

1. From his brother, may he be made his ransom,
2. Muḥammad ibn ʿUbayd Allāh ibn al-Ḥasan ibn ʿAlī.

35 LETTER

Museum of Islamic Art inventory number: 23973.46

Excavation photograph numbers and image numbers:

Recto: 1968_02_09A-10 (image: 050308_651_u)

Recto: 1968_02_10A-11 (image: 050308_652_u)

Verso: 1968_02_11A-12 (image: 050308_653_u)

This document also contains letter **26**.

Paper. 21 cm × 19 cm

Text

Recto

1 بسملة

2 كتابى الى اخى وسيدى واعز الخلق على وعندى اطال <الله> بقاه وادام تاييده وعلاه

3 ورفعته وسناه وعن شوق الى شديد اسل الله فيه الاجتما ع

4 قريب واما غير ذالك ياخى ما احتاج اوصل فى ما فضل من ثمن القفتين

5 القطن الذى كانت صحبة الاخ مفلح هو اثنين وثلثين درهم ان كان جاب

6 قحح قبضته وحصل لى قطعه وان لم تقدر على قحح فانت سير لى باجرهم ولكن

7 تستوثقنى وخليه لى غير ذلك فانى حين اصل بعد الشقة ارتحل

8 فمتى استحصلته عندك فان عندك وانت تعرف ما لنا فيه من الرى

9 ما انا الى شاكر لله تعالى وكانت سنة متلايمة على وسفر متلايم

10 خص نفسك باتم السلام وعلى الاخ حسين السلام وعلى الاخ مولى السلام

Verso

Address

1 الى حضرة موالى الاخ ابو فنجان البياع بن فكة من اخوه على بن مصعب

2 من ابريم الى تشكة

Textual Notes

Recto

1. بسملة: The writer did not write the *basmala* in full.
2. واعز الخلق على وعندى: Literally 'the dearest person to me and with me'.
3. الى: This appears to be a mistake for اليه.
6. فانت سير: These two words are joined by a ligature.
9. ما انا الى: The word الى corresponds to الا in Classical Arabic orthography.

Verso

Address

Unlike most addresses, the address here does not seem to be arranged in clear columns.

1. مولى الاخ: The left stroke of the ligature لا has been overwritten by the letter خ. The first word could be read as a plural of majesty, i.e., *mawālī* (singular *mawlā*), used to refer to a single person.
2. ابريم Ibrīm: The reading is not completely certain. If this is the correct reading, the *bā*ʾ is horizontally extended. The letter was sent from Ibrīm.
   تشكة Tuška. This location, which is the destination of the letter, is situated a short distance south of Ibrīm, just north of Arminna, coordinates: 22.497340 31.882830 (Salvoldi and Geus 2017, 78; Pierce 2017, 53).

Translation

Recto

1. *Basmala* (i.e., in the name of God, the Merciful and Compassionate).
2. (This is) my letter to my brother and my lord, the dearest person to me, may God prolong his life and cause his strength, his elevation,
3. his ascendance and his splendour to endure. I have great longing for him and I, therefore, ask God that we shall meet
4. soon. As for other matters, O brother, what he needed has been conveyed from what remained from the price of the two baskets
5. of cotton, which were with our brother Mufliḥ, namely thirty-two dirhams.

6. If he has brought pure coins, then receive them and convey to me a share. If you cannot obtain pure coins, then send to me their value. But
7. trust me and leave it to me. On another matter, when I arrive from my long journey, I shall set off again,
8. and when I collect it at your place, if it is with you—you know what my view is about this.
9. I am grateful only to God, the Exalted. It was a terrible year for me and a terrible journey.
10. Best wishes to you and to our brother Ḥusayn greetings and to our brother the freedman greetings.

Verso

Address

1. To the honourable lord and brother ʾAbū Finjān the merchant, the son of Fakka. From his brother ʿAlī ibn Muṣʿab
2. From Ibrīm to Tuška

36 LETTER

Museum of Islamic Art inventory number: 23973.64

Excavation photograph numbers and image numbers:

Recto: 1966A_P06_06A-07 (image: ren 050308_100_u)

Recto: 1968_04_03–03A (image: 050308_689_o)

Verso: 1966A_P06_07A-08 (image: 050308_101_u)

Verso: 1968_04_04–04A (image: 050308_690_o)

Registration number: 66A/111 (?)

Paper. 25 cm × 16.5 cm

Text

Recto

بسم الله الرحمن الرحيم

كان كتاب الخليفة مشل انكرة سلمه الله وصلنى على

يد عبيده وقضيت حوائجهم وتوجهوا ولم اكتب

لهم كتاب من كثرة اشغالى قسط عذرى

ووصلنى الحلقة الذهب وما سيرت لك حق عين

وما خفى عنك فى هذه السنة قلة الغلة وما

الناس عليه وما كان ثم مركب يسير فى هذه السنة

لولا انا فتحت مخزن وبعت لاهل بلادكم

وسيرت مكس ومما عماد وبابا وقد

10 كتبت الى صاحب الخيل لا يمكن احد يوذيهم
11 ولا يتعرض لهم ويحفظهم الى ان يصلوا

Margin

1 شاكرين ان شا الله وعرفنى حجاج
2 ولد مسرد انك راغب الى المجى
3 والدخول اسوان فان رغبت تدخل
4 فتصل وانت مكرم طيب العيش
5 وقد بلغنى جميلك فالله يجزيك
6 ويعيننى على مكافاتك

Verso

1 وقد علم الله اننى انا ايضا ما اطلب الا صلاح البلاد
2 وقد سيرت صحبة متحملها ثوب مسقع برسم
3 حق عين بسط عذرى وسيرت لكنونة
4 زوجتك خرقة فيها خمس قطيعات عود
5 وان كان لك حاجة فاكتب اعلمنى بها ان شا الله عز وجل
6 الحمد لله وحده وصلواته على سيدنا محمد نبيه واله وسلامه
7 حسبنا الله ونعمة الوكيل

Address

Right Column

1 لصديقى القرطمق مشل الفريك
2 سلمه الله وتولاه

Left Column

1 شاكره لامع بن حسن

2 الكنزى

Textual Notes

Recto

2. مشل انكرة: The name Mašal (ⲙⲁϣⲁⲗ) is attested in P. QI III 38 (Appendix, l. 5). The second name may be a variant of the Nubian name attested with the form Ankarou (ⲁⲛⲕⲁⲣⲟⲩ) in an inscription from Banganarti (Łajtar 2020, no. 478).
9. بابا: The final *ʾalif* has been added as an afterthought, after the writer had written the *bāʾ* with the word-final form of the letter.

Translation

Recto

1. In the name of God the Merciful and Compassionate.
2. The letter of the lieutenant Mašal Ankara, may God keep him safe, has reached me by
3. the hand of his servants. I dealt with their business and they departed. I did not write
4. a letter for them (to take) due to my many work commitments. Accept my apologies.
5. The gold ring has arrived. I have not sent you cash.
6. The lack of produce this year and the condition

7. of the people have not been concealed from you. No ship would have been sent this year,
8. had I not opened a store and sold to the people of your land.
9. I have sent the customs tax and logistic support.[1] I have
10. written to the Master of the Horses (stating that) nobody should harm them
11. or obstruct them, but that he should protect them until they arrive,

Margin

1. for which they will be grateful, if God wills. Ḥajjāj,
2. the son of Misrad, has informed me that you want to come
3. and enter Aswan. If you want to enter,
4. you would be given a warm welcome.[2]
5. Your kindness has come to my attention. May God reward you
6. and help me return the kindness to you.[3]

Verso

1. God knows that I wish for only what is good for the land.
2. I have sent with the bearer of the letter a dyed garment in place of

---

[1] Literally: pillar and door.

[2] Literally: you would arrive and you would be honoured with the good of life.

[3] Literally: recompense you.

3. the payment in cash. Please forgive me. And I have sent to Kanūna,
4. your wife, a bundle in which are five pieces of aloeswood.
5. If you need anything, write and let me know about it, if God, the Mighty and Magnificent, wills.
6. Praise be to God alone. His blessings be upon our lord Muḥammad, His prophet, and his family, and His peace.
7. Our sufficiency is God. What a fine keeper is He!

Address

Right Column

1. To my friend al-Qarṭamaq Mašal al-Farīk,
2. may God keep him safe and take care of him.

Left Column

1. The one who is grateful, Lāmiʿ ibn Ḥasan
2. al-Kanzī.

37 LETTER

Sartain inventory number: Add. 02

Excavation photograph numbers and image numbers:

Recto: 1966A_P06_27A-28 (image: 050308_115_o)

Verso: 1966A_P06_28A-29 (image: 050308_116_o)

Registration number: 66A/111 (?)

Paper. Measurements are not available.

Text

Recto

بسم الله الرحمن الرحيم
كتابى الى الاخ خليل وللاخ عثمان
وعمر اطال الله بقاهم ادام سلامتهم
ونعمتهم والذى اعلم به اننى وصلت
الى اسوان وتعب معى الحصان
وانت تعلم اننى خرجت من عندكم
وانا عريان وتيابى خليتها
عندكم وانتم تعلموا ان وصلنى
كتاب من عند بيتى والله الله
ينحدر واحد منكم يجي سرعة
الى ولا يقوم فى نفسكم كيف
ينحدر وما معنا شى ندفع لك

13 وانا اعلم ان ما معكم شى ولو
14 كان معكم شى ما استكبرتوه
15 على والله الله ساعة وقوفك على
16 هذه الرقعة يتوجه الى واحد
17 منكم سرعة وتيابى تكون
18 صحبتكم الجبة والقميص
19 والخوضة والرم وان كان شروهم
20 بها ونعمة وان كانوا باقين
21 تجيبهم معكم والقربتين

Verso

1 والخرز متاع الصغار والدمك
2 السير متاع النسي الذى فيه
3 الطيب فهو في الخريطة مع
4 الخرز تجيبه معك والرقيق
5 ما فى اسوان شى فهو قليل والله
6 الله تجيب جاريتك معك ولا
7 تجى الا فى مركب ولا تجيب فرس
8 واذا انحدرت انت تاخذ فرسى
9 وتصعد والله الله يجى واحد منكم
10 سرعة سرعة ولو كان لكم الف
11 شغل والله الله اخى خليل
12 رجل محتشم فلا ضير من الخلع الذى

دفعها له فلا تخلوه يمشى الى موضع
ويا اخى خليل اين ابونا واين
اصحابنا وما بقى الا انا وانت
والله لا تسمع من كلام احد وتمشى
فى القلعة من مكان الى مكان وان
ما فيه خير والسلام عليكم
والله الله انتم تلاتة وكونوا
رجال مع بعضكم بعض والسلام
احق بك

Address

Right Column

الى الاخوا خليل وعمر
وعثمان سلمهم الله

Left Column

من اخوهم
جامع

Textual Notes

Recto

19. الخوضة: I am interpreting this as خوذة *ḵūḏa* 'helmet' with *tafḵīm*.
الرم *al-rumm*: 'house furniture', i.e., bedding and matting.

Verso

1. الدمك *al-damk*: ‘twisting’, < *damaka* ‘to twist (rope), to compact’.
2. السير *al-sayr*: ‘leather, thong’.

Translation

Recto

1. In the name of God, the Merciful and Compassionate.
2. (This is) my letter to my brother Ḵalīl and my brother ʿUṯmān
3. and ʿUmar, may God prolong their life, and cause their good health
4. and wellbeing to endure. What I wish to inform you of is that I have arrived
5. in Aswan and both I and the horse are exhausted.[1]
6. You know that I departed from you
7. without (additional) clothes,[2] and I left my clothes
8. with you. You know that I received
9. a letter from my family.[3] By God,
10. please could one of you come downriver quickly
11. to me. Do not (hesitate to) consider how one would come downriver.

---

[1] Literally: the horse has become tired with me.

[2] Literally: naked.

[3] The letter from his family presumably was the reason he left in haste.

12. We do not have anything to pay you.
13. I know that you do not have anything and if
14. you had anything, you would not regard it as being too generous
15. to give it to me. By God, the minute you read
16. this note, one of you please come to me
17. quickly, taking my clothes
18. with you—the sleeved garment, the shirt
19. the helmet and bedding. If they have sold them,
20. that is fine.[4] If they still remain,
21. then bring them with you as well as the two water-skins

Verso

1. and the beads for the children. As for the twisted
2. leather thong for the women, in which
3. there is scent, this is in the bag together with
4. the beads. Bring it (the thong) with you. As for slaves,
5. there is nothing in Aswan, or only a few. By God,
6. bring your slave girl with you.
7. Come only in a boat. Do not bring a horse.
8. When you come downriver, take my horse
9. and go back upriver. By God, one of you please come
10. quickly, quickly, even if you have a thousand
11. things to do. By God, oh my brother Ḵalīl,
12. (who are) a decent man, there is no harm from the gifts that

[4] Literally: (that is) brightness and wellbeing.

13. he has paid to him. Do not let him go anywhere.[5]
14. Oh my brother Ḵalīl, where is our father and where
15. are our companions? Only I and you remain.
16. By God, do not listen to what anybody says and do not go
17. from place to place in the citadel (listening to gossip), for
18. there is no good in it. Greetings to you.
19. By God, you are three! Behave like
20. men with each other. Greetings.
21. That is more worthy of you.

Address

Right Column

1. To the brothers Ḵalīl, ʿUmar
2. and ʿUṯmān, may God give them good health.

Left Column

1. From their brother
2. Jāmi.ʿ

[5] I.e., we need his help.

38 LETTER

Excavation photograph numbers and image numbers:

Recto: 1974_P04_02A-03 (image: 170308_647_o)

Verso: 1974_P04_03A-04 (image: 170308_648_o)

The verso also contains the document of lease **44**.

Object number: 74.1.29/11.4

Paper. Measurements are not available. A piece is missing from the top left of the recto (top right of the verso).

Text

Recto

1 بسم الله الرحمن الرحيم

2 كتابى اليك يا والدى والعزيز على وعندى اطال الله بقاك وا[دام عزك]

3 وتاييدك وسعادتك وسلامتك وثبت حسن توفيقه لا اخلاك وجـ[علنى]

4 من كل سو فداك وفى كل خير جداك والذى اعلمك به انى ما امسكت النضر الى

5 حجاج وسالت عنه وذكروا لى انه فى بلاد بحرى وانا ان شا الله اجتمع

6 به واطلب منه الذى ذكرت لى وما اصف لك ما جرا على من عبد الرحمن

7 حراثك الذى فى الجزيرة طرد الرجل الذى جعلته انت وخاف لنا

8 من لا نبيع منصور واتو الخبر واجروا المحراث من الجريزة ومروا

9 به الى بلد اتفو وخروا علينا وما انا معهم فى حال قليل ولك فى ذلك

10 علو الراى والله والله ثم الله ان كان عندكم من يطلب المجى الى الكسب

11 فلا توخروا ساعة واخذه فى الزرع اسبوعين وهو ينحصد فى خمسة عشرة

12 من شهر برمهات فلا توخروا الا تجريها والسلام

Margin

1 وعلى من سال عنا السلام وعلى ابو شاكر السلام

2 واما شان المرض تقدم دوا بعد ما اتسلموا عينه

3 [ ] الذى اخذه لعبيد الله بن عزام طلب حاجة له يقبظوها والسلام

Verso

Address

Right Column

1 [بلا]د المريس ...... الى العقيد دنى بن كنان

2 اطال الله بقاه

Left Column

1 من ولده محمد بن ابو حى

2 جعل فداه

Textual Notes

Recto

4. النضر: A *ḍād* is written in place of a *ẓā*ʾ (Classical Arabic النَظَر).
9. اتفو: There are diacritic dots over the *tā*ʾ and the *fā*ʾ. I am interpreting this as a variant of the place name ادفو Edfu.

The orthography would reflect the devoicing of the */d/* before the unvoiced */f/*.

Margin

2. اتسلموا: This is a dialectal form of *tasallamū*.
3. يقبظوها *yuqabbiẓūhā*: The *ẓāʾ* replaces the *ḍād* of the Classical Arabic form.

Verso

Address, Right Column

1. دنى: This can be identified as the Nubian name Dani (ⲆⲀⲚⲒ), which is attested in P. QI IV 85 (recto, l.1, verso, l. 1) and IV 109 (verso, ll. 15–16).

Translation

Recto

1. In the name of God, the Merciful and Compassionate.
2. (This is) my letter to you, my father, who is dear to me, may God prolong your life and cause your power,
3. your support, your happiness and your good health to endure, may He establish His granting of prosperity, may He not leave you alone, may He make me
4. your redemption from all evil and may He bestow upon you every goodness. What I (write to) inform you of is that I have not ceased looking out for
5. Ḥajjāj. I have asked about him and people have told me that he is in a town in the north. God willing, I shall

6. meet him and shall request from him what you mentioned to me. I would like to describe to you[1] what has happened to me due to ʿAbd al-Raḥmān,
7. your plougher, who is in the island. He has dismissed the man whom you yourself appointed and Manṣūr feared
8. that we could not sell. They gave notification and moved the plough from the island and took it
9. to the town of Edfu. They shat upon us. I am not with them in any way. Please could you make
10. the authoritative decision with regard to this. By God, by God, by God, if you have somebody with you who would like to come to earn a wage,
11. do not delay for a moment and engage him in cultivation for two weeks. The harvest will be on the fifteenth
12. of the month of Baramhāt. Do not delay carrying it out. Greetings.

Margin

1. Greetings to those who have asked after us. Greetings to ʾAbū Šākir.
2. As for the matter of the illness, bring medicine after they have received cash for it
3. [ ] which he has taken for ʿUbayd Allāh ibn ʿAzzām. He asked him to arrange for some requested item to be given to him. Greetings.

---

[1] Literally: What I (wish to describe) to you is...

Verso

Address

Right Column

1. [The land] of Marīs… to the leader Danī ibn Kannān,
2. may God grant him a long life.

Left Column

1. From his son, Muḥammad ibn ʾAbū Ḥayy,
2. may he be his redemption.

39 LETTER

Excavation photograph numbers and image numbers:

Recto: 1974_P04_04A-05 (image: 170308_649_o)
Verso: 1974_P04_05A-06 (image: 170308_650_o)

Object number: 74.1.29/11.5

Paper. Measurements are not available. A piece from the top right of the letter is missing and there is a small lacuna in the middle.

Dated 10th Šawwāl 485 AH/18 November 1092 AD.

Text

Recto

1 بسم الله الرحمن الرحيم

2 كتابى اليك يا والدى والعزيز على اطال الله بقاك وادام عزك وتاييدك وسعـ[ـادتك]

3 وسلامتك ونعمتك وعن شوقى اليك شديد جمع الله بيننا على اسر حال بمنه وكرمه

4 [انه ولـ]ـى ذلك والقادر عليه ان شا الله والذى اعلمك يا والدى ان وصلنا الى سوبة

5 سالمين فى كل عافية وما عدمت من الله بمنه الكريم الا النظر الى طلعتك الكريمة

6 ولا عدمتها ولا خلوت منها وما بطاعتنا الا نافصة مطلوبة واحرصوا ان

7 تنفذوا لنا اخباركم مع من اتفق سفره الى بلد النوبة فنسر بها ونقف على

8 رسم علمه من احوالكم وما نحن الا متفقين مع بعضنا بعض ولو كان لحقنا

9 الملك فى سوبة لما كنا نقعد فى البلد اكثر من شهر او شهرين لكنهم ه ومع

10 المتاع الذى معنا على الملك وعلى جنده وانما لحقنا البلد ما فيه الا اليسير

11 ونحن فى كل عافية ووصلنا الى سوبة فى العشر الاخر من شهر رمضان فى سنة

12 خمس وثمانين واربع ماة وكتبت هذا الكتاب يوم العاشر من شوال قرات عليك

13 افضل السلم وعلى والدتى السلم وعلى اولادى واهلي السلم وعلى اخى ابو در

14 السلم وعلى جدتى وخالى السلم وعلى ابو القاسم ومحمد السلم وعلى ابو الحسن

15 وصبيرة السلم وعلى يحيى وقائد السلم وعلى الشيخ على السلم

Verso

1 وعلى ابو جعفر وعلى السلم وعلى جيراننا كلهم السلم وعلى جميع من يسال عنا

2 وصهرى يبلغكم كلهم السلم

Address

Right Column

1 يصل هذا الكتاب من ع ..... ومن صهرى

2 [و]من صاحبى ....

Left Column

1 ....

2 يبلغ بو حسن

Textual Notes

Recto

9. The writer first wrote لكنهم ‘but they’ and then wrote after it a letter ه, which seems to be intended as a correction to لكنه ‘but he’. After this the writer appears to have missed out some text by mistake.

Translation

Recto

1. In the name of God, the Merciful and Compassionate.
2. (This is) my letter to you, my father, who is dear to me—may God prolong your life and cause your strength, your support, your happiness,
3. your safety and your wellbeing to endure—and (I have written this) while missing you greatly, may God bring us together in the happiest circumstances in his kindness and grace.
4. He has the power over that and is able to do it, God willing. What I wish to inform you of, my father, is that we have arrived in Soba
5. safe and sound. I lack nothing by the gracious kindness of God except the opportunity to see your gracious face.

6. I wish we did not lack it or were not bereft of it. All we have in our power is something missing that is longed for. Please make an effort to
7. send us your news with whomsoever may happen to travel to the land of Nubia. We would be happy about that and be able
8. to be informed about what he knows about your situation. We are only meeting one another by chance. If the king had
9. come to us in Soba, we would not have stayed in the country more than a month or two months, but they/he— (We are) with
10. the merchandise that we have for the king and his army, but we have found that there is only little (business) in the land.
11. We are in good health. We arrived in Soba in the last ten days of the month of Ramaḍān in the year
12. four-hundred and eighty-five (25th October–3rd November 1092 AD). I am writing this letter on the tenth day of Šawwāl (13th November 1092 AD). I send you
13. warmest greetings. Greetings to my mother. Greetings to my children and my family. Greetings to my brother ʾAbū al-Durr.
14. Greetings to my grandmother and maternal uncle. Greetings to ʾAbū al-Qāsim and Muḥammad. Greetings to ʾAbū al-Ḥasan
15. and Ṣabīra. Greetings to Yaḥyā and Qāʾid. Greetings to the elder ʿAlī.

Verso

1. Greetings to ʾAbū Jaʿfar and ʿAlī. Greetings to all our neighbours. Greetings to everybody who asks after us.
2. My brother-in-law sends you greetings.

Address

Right Column

1. May this letter arrive from ..... and from my brother-in-law
2. and from my companion ....

Left Column

1. ....
2. May it reach Bū Ḥasan.

40 LETTER

Museum of Islamic Art inventory number: 23973.54

Excavation photograph numbers and image numbers:

1966A_P06_05A-06 (image: 050308_105_o)

1968_03_23–23A (image: 050308_678_u)

Registration number: 66A/111 (?)

Paper. 24 cm × 16.5 cm

Text

1 بسم الله الرحمن الرحيم

2 اسال عن اخباركم فيسرنى سماعى لما اختار منها واطلب

3 اذا كنتم فى نعمة وسلامة فما انا الا فيهما اتفلت

4 ما المهجور بعد الوصال ولا الظمان المشتاق الى الما الزلال

5 ولا ام خشف فارقت خشفها ولا ذات طوق عدمت

6 الفها باشوق منى الى حضرة مولاي سيدي اطال الله

7 بقاه وادام تاييده وعلاه ورفعته وسناه وسموه وارتقاه

8 وكبت حسدته واعداه ومن حسن التوفيق لا اخلاه

9 جمع الله بيننا على اسر حال بمنه وكرمه وخفى لطفه والقادر

10 عليه ان شا الله عز وجل

Translation

1. In the name of God, the Merciful and Compassionate.
2. I (write to) ask about your news, for it would make me happy to hear something of this that I would treasure. I request (to know)
3. whether you are in a good condition and in good health, for I am indeed so. I am longing (for you).
4. One who is abandoned after being connected, the thirsty man who yearns for cool water,
5. the mother of a young gazelle that has left her young, the ringed pigeon who has lost
6. her friend, none are more desirous than I am for my honourable master, my lord, may God prolong
7. his life and cause his strength, his exaltedness, his loftiness, his splendour, his elevation and his ascendance to endure,
8. crush his enviers and enemies, and not cause him to cease achieving glorious success.
9. May God bring us together in a most joyful state, through His generosity and benevolence, and His hidden kindness. He is able to do
10. this, if God, the Mighty and Exalted, wills.

41 POEM OF A TRAVELLER

Museum of Islamic Art inventory number: 23973.47

Excavation photograph number and image number:

1968_02_13A-14 (image: 050308_655_o)

Paper. 25.5 cm × 18 cm

Text

1 وما توفيقى الا بالله

2 يقول الناسُ فى الأسفار ذُلٌّ ومَصْعَبةٌ وَهُونٌ واغترابُ

3 سواى فاننى فيها تهيّت لى اللّذاتُ والعَيشُ اللّبابُ

4 كَسَبت بها وداد اخٍ رئيسُ له مَجدٌ واخلاقٌ رِحابُ

5 نماه سادةٌ عز كرام لهم في ذِرْوةِ العَلْيا قبابُ

6 مُروَّتُه دعتهُ الي اخاي وبُعْد الدار كان لنا اِنتسَاب

7 دعاني للمسير الي بلاد بها امنُ وعيشٌ يستَطَابُ

8 ركبت مطيّةً حَسُنت وفاقت تمرّ بنا كَما مر السَحابُ

9 نُشِرن قلوعها للسير زهوًا كما نَشرتْ جناحيها العقابُ

10 وقد ضَمّت من الاخيار قومًا لهم فى موْرد الكُرم انصبابُ

11 واخلاقٌ خُلِقن لكُلِ جُودٍ وافعالٌ تهون بها الصعابُ

12 عُبَيدُ وعابد الرحمن كلا عن الاحسان ليس لهم حجابُ

13 غمرنى من جميلهم ايادٍ يقصر عن تعاطيها الصحابُ

14 فلو اني استطعْتُ لكان خِدّي اذا وطيوا التراب لهم تراب

15 وربان لها فطن خبير له راىٌ يُقادُ به الصوابُ

16 عجبنا من تصَرّفه وخِلنا بانّ لهُ الي نوح انتسابُ
17 واعوان له غلبٌ شِدادٌ اذا نُودُوا لمعظلةٍ اجابوا

Margin

18 كانهم اذا نهضُوا لامرٍ ليوثٌ للفَرايس تستثابُوا
19 محمد فيهم شمس مضى وسيد للأملّ نجم لا يغابُ
20 وبدرٌ بدرهُم وابو حبيبٍ سما لهُم ومحبوبٌ شهابُ
21 وبو العيد الحليم لهم سما واسماعيل زينه الشباب

Textual Notes

4. رئيسُ: One would expect *tanwīn kasra* according to the conventions of Classical Arabic, since this is an indefinite noun in apposition to اخٍ.
7. امنُ: One would expect *tanwīn ḍamma* according to the conventions of Classical Arabic.
13. ايادٌٍ: The writer wrote both *tanwīn kasra*, which is the vocalisation of Classical Arabic, and also *tanwīn ḍamma*.
17. لمعظلةٍ: In Classical Arabic orthography this word is spelt with a *ḍād*, viz. مُعْضِلَةٌ 'misfortune'.
18. تستثابُوا 'they gape': This is the 3sg.f prefix conjugation form of the root *ṯ-ʾ-b*, although the dictionaries do not list the tenth form for this verb. The use of the tenth form is presumably a poetic licence for the sake of the metre. The final inflectional vowel would be short according to the rules of Classical Arabic (*tastaṯʾibu*), but has been lengthened for metrical purposes.

19. للأملّ: A *šadda* is written over the word, which I interpret as being intended to mark the gemination of the final *lām*. The word, therefore, would be an elative *ʾafʿal* form of the adjective مَلّ 'wearied', from the root *m-l-l*.
يغاب: There is a diacritical dot under the second letter, but the proposed reading, a passive of أغَابَ, i.e., يُغَابُ 'it is caused to be absent', seems to be what was intended.

Translation[1]

1. Any achievement of mine is due to God's help alone.
2. People say that in journeys there is ignominy, difficulty, humiliation and homesickness.
3. Not me, for on my journey pleasures and good living were made possible for me.
4. I won the friendship of a brother, a leader of distinction and generous character,
5. One raised by esteemed and noble leaders of men, whose status towered above the peaks of excellence.
6. His magnanimity led him to treat me as a brother; distance from home made us kin.
7. He invited me to travel to a land of safety and comfort.
8. I mounted a superb steed which bore us along as a cloud scuds along.
9. Its sails were spread in splendour as it moved, like an eagle spreads its wings.

---

[1] A translation of this poem that was made by Elizabeth Sartain appears in Adams (2010, 254). My translation reproduces much of this, but differs from it and supplements it in a number of places.

10. On board were a company of good men, all brimming over with generosity.
11. Their natures were created for every kind of liberality, their deeds by which difficulties were made insignificant,
12. ʿUbayd and ʿĀbid al-Raḥmān, neither of them secluded from excellence.
13. The benefits of their kindness overwhelmed me; even old friends could not have given as much.
14. If I could, I would have made my cheek the dust of the ground they trod.
15. The ship's captain was astute and skilled; his wise decisions guided good judgment itself.
16. We admired his conduct, and imagined him a descendant of Noah.
17. His men were tough and strong; when summoned (to help) with a problem, they instantly obeyed,

Margin

18. Jumping to work like lions, gaping (to consume) their prey.
19. Muḥammad among them was a sun that continued to shine. Sayyid was for the wearied traveller an ever-present star.
20. Badr was their full moon, ʾAbū Ḥabīb their sky and Maḥbūb a bright meteor.
21. The mild Bū al-ʿĪd was their heaven and the ornament of Ismāʿīl was youth.

42 ACCOUNT

Excavation photograph numbers and image numbers:

Recto: 1974_V10_31A-32 (image: 170308_301_o)
Verso: 1974_V10_32A-33 (image: 170308_297_u)

Object number: 74.1.29/7

Paper. 18.5 cm × 5 cm, 7.5 cm × 5 cm, 16 cm × 5 cm. The document consists of three narrow strips. Text is missing on what is designated here the verso of the strips, suggesting that these constituted the original recto of a larger document from which the strips were cut.

Text

Recto

Right Piece

1 خمسة وعشرين درهم

2 عصفر

3 ثلثين درهما

4 غربال العصفر

5 ثلثة دراهم

6 ونصف

7 سقا برسم المصباح

8 درهمين

9 مونة المصباح

10 خمسة دراهم

11 ستة ثياب قوصى

12 اربعة وثمانين درهم

13 عسيل الرياح

14 وخياطة

15 درهمين

16 حمولة الثياب

17 نصف [در]هم

Middle Piece

1 الخاص

2 ثمن العدل

3 احد عشر د[رهما]

4 ونصف

5 بسم الله ا[لرحمن الرحيم]

6 ثبت———

7 المشترى من اسـ[ ]

8 افلح حسبى

Left Piece

1 اربعة مقاطع

2 ماية درهما

3 غلالتين

4 اربعة وعشرين درهما

5 حمولة عدل

6 درهمين

Written perpendicularly to lines 1–6 with six check marks through the text:

7 الجملة

8 ورقا ثلثة ماية وست عشرة

9 صرفها عينا

10 ثمانية دنانير ونصف الا حبة

11 وقيراط

Written perpendicularly to lines 7–11:

12 نقص الذهب

13 ستة دراهم

14 وبيد ابو الطاهر

15 دينارين

16 سوا

Verso

Right Piece

1] [.

2]]ين

3]]حبتين

4] الـ]عدل

5] [.

6]]. وعشرين درهما

Middle Piece

1]]ه

2]]تسليمه

3]].. عينا

4]].. غرمها

Left Piece

1 ونصف و..]   [
2 دينا]ر   [
3 النامى من ثمن الـ]   [

Textual Notes

Recto

Middle Piece

7. [   ]المشترى من اسـ: The word after من could perhaps be reconstructed as اسوان 'Aswan'.[1]

Translation

Recto

Right Piece

1. Twenty-five dirhams

2. Safflower
3. thirty dirhams

4. Sieve for safflower
5. three dirhams

[1] This was suggested to me by Krisztina Szilagyi (personal communication).

6. and a half

7. Fuel[2] for a lamp
8. two dirhams

9. Supplies for a lamp
10. five dirhams

11. Six Qūṣī garments
12. eighty-four dirhams

13. Extract of fragrant herbs
14. and verbena nodiflora
15. two dirhams

16. Porterage of garments
17. half a dirham

Middle Piece

1. Special
2. The price of a sack
3. eleven dirhams
4. and a half

5. In the name of God the Merciful and Compassionate.
6. It has been registered.

---

[2] Literally: irrigation.

7. The purchaser from As[wan]
8. My calculation has been completed successfully

Left Piece

1. Four pieces of cloth
2. one hundred dirhams
3. Two tunics
4. twenty-four dirhams

5. Porterage of a sack
6. two dirhams

7. The total
8. in black dirhams: three hundred and sixteen.
9. Its exchange value in (gold) coinage:
10. eight dīnārs and a half, minus a grain
11. and a qīrāṭ.

12. Minus the gold
13. six dirhams
14. and in the hand of ʾAbū al-Ṭāhir
15. two dīnārs
16, apart from

Verso

Right Piece

1. [ ]
2. [ ]
3. [ ] two grains
4. [ ] the sack
5. [ ]
6. [ ] twenty-[ ] dirhams

Middle Piece

1. [ ]
2. [ ] its delivery
3. [ ] in coinage
4. [ ] its debt

Left Piece

1. a half and [ ]
2. dīnār [ ]
3. the increase of the price of

43 ACCOUNT

Violet MacDermot's photograph number: 10 in a circle
Excavation photograph numbers and image numbers:

Recto: 1974_V09_01–01A (image: 170308_264_o)
Verso: 1974_V09_04–04A (image: 170308_263_u)

Registration number: 74/12
Paper. 17.5 cm × 11 cm. The bottom of the sheet has been torn away.

Text

Recto

Right Column

1 ثلثة ارطال شجرة

2 اربعة دراهم

3 ونصف

4 رطل لبان

5 اربعة دراهم

6 ونصف

7 رطل وربع قسط

8 ثمن دينار

9 رطل ونصف مر
10 ثمن دينار

Middle Column

1 ثلثة ارطال ميعة
2 اربعة دراهم
3 ونصف

4 ربع من سنبل
5 ربع دينار

6 رطل من كركم
7 ثمن دينار

8 شملة لفافة للصوف
9 درهمين

Left Column

1 بسم الله [الرحمن الرحيم]
2 الدنانير الواصد[ة]

3 منها ما خرج ..
4 ومنها ما وكس ...

Verso

1 وعن اربعة عشر ويبة قرطم ثلثى دينار
2 وعن اثنى عشر رطل ونصف زفت ثلثى دينار
3 وعن سفط ياتى ذكره
4 والقراط الزائد على ثمن الصوف العسكرى دينارين
5 وثلث دينار
6 تفصيلها
7 هال نصف[ ]

Translation

Recto

Right Column

1. Three *raṭls* of (odiferous) shrub
2. four dirhams
3. and a half

4. A *raṭl* of frankincense
5. four dirhams
6. and a half

7. A *raṭl* and a quarter of costus (aromatic plant)
8. an eighth of a dīnār

9. A *raṭl* and a half of myrrh
10. an eighth of a dīnār

Middle Column

1. Three *raṭls* of storax
2. four dirhams
3. and a half

4. A quarter of spikenard
5. a quarter of a dīnār

6. A *raṭl* of Indian saffron
7. an eighth of a dīnār

8. An enveloping cloak made of wool
9. two dirhams

Left Column

1. In the name of God, the Merciful and Compassionate.
2. The dīnārs that are income [ ]

3. Those that have been disbursed [ ]
4. and those that have been lost [ ]

Verso

1. and for fourteen *waybas* of cartham seed: two thirds of a dīnār
2. and for twelve *raṭls* and a half of bitumen: two thirds of a dīnār
3. and for a basket (the contents of which) are mentioned below
4. The additional *qīrāṭ* is for the price of the army wool:[1] two dīnārs
5. and a third of a dīnār
6. The details of its contents
7 cardamon half [ ]

---

[1] This was presumably intended for blankets or the like for the Nubian army.

44 LEASE OF LAND (RAJAB 518 AH/ AUGUST 1124 AD)

Excavation photograph number and image number:

1974_P04_03A-04 (image: 170308_648_o)

Object number: 74.1.29/11.4

This document also contains the letter **38**, the address of which appears at the top of the sheet.

Paper. Measurements are not available. The top left corner is damaged.

Text

1 بسم الله الرحمن الرحيم

2 استاجر رحمة بن سعيد من دنى بن كنان الشخريابى استاجر منه صفقة واحدة وعقدا واحدا ثلاث اسهم

3 من اربعة وعشرين سهما كملا مشاعا من جميع اراضى الجزيرة المعروفة بابى فارس بالغرب من حد النوبة

4 الجارية فى اقطاعته من ديوان السلطان اعز الله نصره بجميع حدود ذلك وحقوقه وحروفه ومرافقه فى

5 الجزيرة المذكورة فى مدة سنة اولها كيهك سنة ثمان عشرة وخمس مائة باجرة مبلغها ثلاثة دنانير مثاقيل

6 ذهبا عينا وازنة صحاحا امرية مصرية جيادا ودفع المستاجر الى الاجر المسمى معه جميع الثمن

7 الثمن المذكور وقبضه منه تاما وافيا وابراه منه براة قبض واستيفا وسلم اليه ما اجره اياه

8 من الجزيرة المذكورة وجعل اليه قسطا الى ما يحضر النصيب المذكور مشاهرة بغلة لشهر فى سلخه

9 الى انقضا السنة المذكورة فما ادرك المستاجر المذكور من درك من ديوان السلطان اعز الله نصره

10 او من احد من الناس كلهم كان على هذا دنو بن كنان خلاصه والخروج اليه ما يلزمه حكم شروط

11 المسلمين وضمانهم وبذلك اتفقا وتراضيا فى صحة منهما وجواز امر فى العشر الاول من رجب سنة ثمان عشرة

12 وخمس مائة

Textual Notes

2. دنى بن كنان: Danī ibn Kannān is mentioned in the address of **38**v, right, 1. The gentilic al-Šaḵriyābī relates to Wādī al-Šaḵriyābī, which was in the district of Ibrīm (Hinds and Sakkout 1986, document no. 27).

5. فى مدة سنة اولها: This is a tentative reading. If it is correct, some of the letters are misshapen and truncated.
كيهك: The name Kīhak is a variant name of the Coptic month name Koiak (10th December–8th January), which is also spelt كياك in Arabic.

8. وجعل اليه قسطا: The reference to instalments contradicts the statement in line 7 that the lessor received the sum in full. The phraseology referring to receipt in full must be a slavish use of a fixed formula that was not appropriate in this

particular case. A similar contradiction of a formula expressing full receipt with the reality of only a partial receipt is found in the acknowledgement document **47**v.

Translation

1. In the name of God, the Merciful and Compassionate.
2. Raḥma ibn Saʿīd leased from Danī ibn Kannān al-Šak̲riyābī—he leased from him with one clapping (of the hand) and with one contract three shares
3. from twenty-four shares in total, held in common, of the lands of the island known as ʾAbū Fāris to the west of the border of Nubia,
4. which is administered in his estate assigned to him by the Office of the Ruler, may God strengthen his victory, with all its boundaries, rights and amenities in
5. the said island for a period of a year, beginning in (the month of) Kīhak of the year five-hundred and eighteen (December 1124 AD) with a rent of three dīnārs, of standard weight,
6. in gold, in minted coin of full weight, valid Egyptian coins of al-ʾĀmir, of good alloy. The lessee paid the lessor named with him all the price,
7. the said price and he received it from him in total and in full and released him from it with a release customary on the receipt in full.
8. He delivered to him what he leased to him with regard to the said island. He allowed him to pay in instalments until

the aforementioned amount is delivered, monthly with the produce of a month at its end,

9. until the completion of the said year. Whatever claim comes upon the aforementioned lessee from the Office of the Ruler, may God strengthen his victory,

10. or from anybody, it is the duty of Danī ibn Kannān to clear it and pay him what is required by the law of the legal instruments of

11. the Muslims and their warranty. They agreed and consented to this while they were in sound health and able to conduct their affairs in the first ten days of Rajab of the year

12. five-hundred and eighteen (August 1124 AD).

45 LEASE OF A BOAT (566 AH/1170 AD)

Museum of Islamic Art inventory number: 23973.45

Excavation photograph numbers and image numbers:

1968_02_06A-07 (image: 050308_648_u)

1968_02_07A-08 (image: 050308_649_u)

Paper. Measurements are not available.

Text

1 بسم الله الرحمن الرحيم

2 هذا ما استاجر الشيخين المكين ولى الدولة ابى العمر هبة الله بن الحسن بن ابرهيم بن طلعة والوجيه جلال الدولة

3 ابى الحسين على بن ابرهيم بن على بن نهرى المعدلان بثغر اسوان من سراج بن مريوا النصرانى

4 المقرى استاجرا منه بمالهما لانفسهما جميع الزلاج المنشا من حطب السنط والمقل ومقدار

5 محمله مائة اردب واحدة وخمسون اردبا بما فيه قلع وفوقانه خيش وصارى بسرج وعرشة وصلبيس واربع

6 مجاديف ومرسى حديد قد حبل وجميع ما تحتاجه امثاله من عدة على ان يوسقاه الى حد

7 السلامية مصعدين ومنحدرين من ساحل بلاق الى جزيرة مكائيل من بلاد النوبة فى مدة

8 اولها كيهك واخرها اخر يوم من امشير من شهور القبط الجارى فى اثنا سنة ستة وستين وخمس مائة

9 على ان يكون انحدارهم من جزيرة مكائيل فى اول يوم من برمهات من شهور القبط الجارى اثنا

10 السنة المذكورة باجرة مبلغها عن المدة المذكورة خمسة عشر دينارا مثاقيل ذهبا عينا وازنة

11 صحاحا عاضدية مصرية جيادا دفع الشيخان المستاجران الى الاجر لهما المسمى معهما فيه جميع

12 الاجرة المذكورة وهى خمسة عشرة دينار بالصفة المذكورة فيه فقبض ذلك منهما تاما وافيا وابراهما من

13 ذلك براة صحيحة براة قبض واستيفا وسلم لهما الزلاج المذكور على انهما ان اقاما فى جزيرة مكائيل

14 يوم او ايام من برمهات كان عليهما بحساب ذلك من الاجرة واشترط عليهما الاجر

15 الثلث بمحمل عشرة مصعدا وبما يبتاعه بها منحدرا ولم يلزمه فى صعوده مكس وعليه

16 منحدرا اسوة امثاله فتسلما الزلاج المذكور على ما قد شرح وعقدا ذلك بينهما عقدا صحيحا

17 بعد ان تخاطبوا عليه شهد على اقرار الاجر والشيخين ولى الدولة وجلال الدولة المستاجرين

18 المسمين في الكتاب بجميع ما نسب اليهم فيه بصحة عقولهم وابدانهم وجواز امورهم طائعين غير مكرهين

19 ولا مجبرين وذلك بثغر اسوان فى اليوم العشرين من شهر ربيع الاول من سنة
ست وستين وخمسمائة وشهد على ذلك

Witness Clauses

1 شهد احمد بن نصر بن هبة الله بن حسين بن احمد على اقرار
2 الاجر والشيخان الخطيب جلال الدولة
3 والمكين ولى الدولة المستاجران المسمين فيه بما فيه بتاريخه
فى تاريخه (؟)

4 شهد على بن عبيد الله بن على بن شريك على اقرار الاجر
5 والشيخان الخطيب الوجيه جلال الدولة والمكين ولى الدولة
6 المستاجرين المسمين فى هذا الكتاب بجميع ما نسب اليهما فيه بتاريخه
فى تاريخه (؟)

Textual Notes

3. سراج بن مريوا: The name Sirāj is Arabic, whereas the name Mario (ⲙⲁⲣⲓⲟ) is Nubian, which is attested in P. QI III 31, l. 13 and IV 80 (Ochała 2020, no. 2). In the last attestation the name refers to a woman.
5. عرشة: This is a possible reading, although the *šīn* is horizontally contracted. For this term designating part of a boat, see the list of names of parts of boats in the modern Kuwaiti dialect presented by Johnstone and Muir (1964, 315), where it means 'screen erected over the poop as a sunshade; a fixed cabin top in launches' or an 'awning'.

صلبيس: I am interpreting this as a term related to the word *salbīs* in the list of Johnstone and Muir (1964, 312), which denotes the 'deck shelf, the stringer on which the deck-beams rest'. The first letter in the document appears to be a *ṣād* rather than a *sīn*, which would have developed by pharyngealisation (*tafḵīm*), presumably induced by the following /*l*/ and /*b*/, which are liable to pharyngealisation.

6. قد حبل *qad ḥubila*: 'which was made fast with rope'.

17. The scribe first wrote تخاطبا 'they (two) discussed together', then subsequently corrected it to تخاطبوا by adding a *wāw*.

Witness Clauses

3. المستاجران: It appears that a *yāʾ* has been added after the *rāʾ* in an attempt to correct the nominative dual to an oblique dual.

Under each of the witness clauses there is a cipher which can be tentatively read as فى تاريخه 'on its date'. These marks may have been 'secondary witnessing' to strengthen the validity of the witness clauses (see §5.2, §5.3).

Translation

1. In the name of God, the Merciful and Compassionate.
2. This is what the two elders, the notable Guardian of the Dynasty ʾAbū al-ʿUmar Hibat Allāh ibn al-Ḥasan ibn ʾIbrāhīm ibn Ṭalʿa, and the dignitary Glory of the Dynasty

3. ʾAbū al-Ḥusayn ʿAlī ibn ʾIbrāhīm ibn ʿAlī ibn Nahray, the two certified witnesses in the border town of Aswan, hired from Sirāj ibn Mario, the Christian,
4. al-Muqurrī. They hired from him with their money, for themselves, all of the 'gliding' boat, made of acacia wood and Theban palm wood,[1] the capacity
5. of its load being one hundred and fifty irdabbs, with a sail, the upper part of which is coarse cloth, a mast with a saddle, an awning, a deck shelf, four
6. oars, an iron anchor, which is made fast with rope, all that such boats need in the way of equipment. (They hired the boat) for the purpose of loading (and transporting) goods to
7. the border of the region where Muslims have the right to travel (*al-islāmiyya*), travelling up- and downstream, from the coast of Bilāq to the Island of Michael in the Land of the Nubians, in a period
8. beginning in Kīhak and ending on the last day of ʾAmšīr of the Coptic months, within the year five-hundred and sixty-six (December–March 1170–71 AD),
9. with the stipulation that they sail downstream from the Island of Michael on the first day of Baramhāt, the Coptic month, within

[1] The Theban palm tree (*muql*), also known as bdellium, is mentioned by al-ʾAswānī in his description of the trees growing in the region (al-Maqrīzī, *Ḵiṭaṭ*, I:353).

10. the aforementioned year, for a rent whose amount for the aforementioned period is fifteen dīnārs, of standard weight, in gold, in minted coin of full weight,
11. valid Egyptian coins of al-ʿĀḍid, of good alloy. The two elders who were the lessors paid to the one leasing to them, who is named together with them in it (the document), all
12. the aforementioned rent, namely fifteen dīnārs with the aforementioned properties. And he received that from them, completely and in full, and he released them from
13. that with a valid release, a release of receipt in full. And he handed over to them the aforementioned gliding boat, on the condition that if they stay on the Island of Michael
14. for a day or several days of Baramhāt, they would be liable to (the payment of additional) rent in consideration of this. The lessor fixed the cost for them at
15. three in every ten parts of the cargo going upstream and what was bought with it going downstream. Duty was not liable on it going upstream, but was liable on it
16. going downstream, in accordance with customary practice. They received the aforementioned gliding boat in accordance with what was stipulated. They contracted that between them with a valid contract
17. after they discussed it together. Testimony was borne to the acknowledgement by the lessor and the two elders, Guardian of the Dynasty and Glory of the Dynasty, the lessees

18. named in the document, of everything that is attributed to them in it, while being in sound mind and body, legally capable of conducting their affairs, willingly, not coerced
19. nor forced. This was in the border town of Aswan on the 20th day of the month of Rabīʿ I of the year five-hundred and sixty-six (12th December 1170 AD). Testimony was borne to this.

Witness Clauses

1. ʾAḥmad ibn Naṣr ibn Hibat Allāh ibn Ḥusayn ibn ʾAḥmad bore witness to the acknowledgement
2. by the lessor and the two elders, the preacher Glory of the Dynasty
3. and the notable Guardian of the Dynasty, the two named lessees in it of what is in it on its date.

On its date (?)

4. ʿAlī ibn ʿUbayd Allāḥ ibn ʿAlī ibn Šarīk bore witness to the acknowledgement by the lessor
5. and the two elders, the preacher and dignity Glory of the Dynasty
6. and the notable Guardian of the Dynasty, the two lessees named in this document of everything attributed to them in it on its date.

On its date (?)

46 DOCUMENT OF TESTIMONY AND DOCUMENT OF SALE

Museum of Islamic Art inventory number: 23973.1

Excavation photograph numbers and image numbers:

Recto: 1968_02_22A-23 (image: 050308_658_u)
Recto: 1968_02_23A-24 (image: 050308_659_u)
Recto: 1968_02_24A-25 (image: 050308_660_o.jpg)
Verso: 1968_02_25A-26 (image: ren 050308_661_o)
Verso: 1968_02_26A-27 (image: ren 050308_662_o)
Verso: 1968_02_27A-28 (image: ren 050308_663_o)

Paper. 53 cm × 11 cm. Text is missing from the left side of the recto.

Recto: Document of Testimony

Text

بسم الله الرحمن الرحيم
شهد الشهود المسمون فى هذا الكتاب [ ]
محمد بن الامير كنز الدولة ابى المكارم هبة الـ[ـله]
من اهل دندور قرية من القرى السبع انـ[ـهما اقرا واشهدا]
على انفسهما فى صحة عقولهما وابدانهما وجـ[ـواز امورهما]
فيه عندهما ولا عند احدهما على جميع ما . [ ]
لغليون بن سليمان بن غليون المسمى في هذا الكـ[ـتاب]
سهمان اثنان من ثلثة اسهم وباقى ذلك [وهو الثلث سهم واحد]

من ثلثة اسهم لفافاى ابنة امفاتا النصرانية الـ[ ]
الذى طوله تسعة اذرع بذراع العمل . [ ]
وانحرف الى بلد النوبة فى الغرب . [ ]
الى النيل حده القبلى ينتهى الى موضع [ ]
وحدها البحرى ينتهى الى موضع ارض محمد [ ]
الى النيل وحده الغربى ينتهى الى الصحرا [ ]
القرية المعروفة بهنداو المعروف قديما [ ]
بن حسن بن الحسين وحده البحرى ينتهى الى [ ]
نافذ وحده الشرقى ينتهى الى منزل يعرف بعـ[ ]
اسوان البحرى المعروف بربض البجة فى ا[ ]
حده القبلى ينتهى الى منزل يعرف بنسيبة مـ[ ]
ينتهى الى منزل يعرف بمونسة النصرانية وحـ[ـده]
وحده الغربى ينتهى الى الحفرة المطـ[ ]
ومرتفعة وارض به وبياض وبحر وكل ورد[ ]
وجرف وبنا وسفل وعلو الى الهوى .. [ ]
من ذلك فيه ومنه من حقوقه وكل حق هو لكل[واحد منهم داخل]
وشرب ما له من ذلك شرب من بئر مائه التى يسـ[ـقى منها من قليل]
وكثير والممر الى ذلك كله مسلما فى حقوقه ومنه جميع [ ]
الذى منهم اربعة بقرات وثورين وجميع الـ[ ]
الاربعين راس دواب الذى منهم عشرون [ ]
معرفة صحيحة حتى لم يخف عليهما ولا على احـ[ـد]
على ما تقدم ذكره على ان الذى لغليون بن سلـ[ـيمان]

31 ثلثة اسهم وباقى ذلك وهو الثلث سهم واحد [ ]

32 فيه شركة صحيحة ماضية نافذة على انه مهما ... [ ]

33 تسليم نصيبه من ذلك وبيعه والتصرف فيه [ ]

34 وكل ذلك بايديهما جميعا فمتى ادعا احدهما [ ]

35 ويدعى ذلك له وعنه فى حياته او بسببه بعـ[ ]

36 او فى شى منه يرى وفى كل وسعه فى الدنيا والا[خرة]

37 الكتاب ما نسب اليه فيه من الاقرار والشركة والـ[ ]

38 [ ] الشاركين المسمـ[ـين فى هذا الكتاب]

Witness Clauses

Margin

1 شهد عبد الله بن عبد الله بن الحسين بن معبد على اقرار البائع والمشتري بجميع ما نسب اليهما فيه كتبه <بـ>خطه فى تاريخه

2 شهد كامل بن خميس بن ابرهيم على اقرار البائع والمشترى بجميع ما نسب

3 اليهما فيه وكتب عنه وبحضرته فى تاريخه

4 شهد قلادى بن مولى على اقرار البائع والمشترى بجميع ما فيه

5 وكتب عنه وبحضرته فى تاريخه

Textual Notes

4. دندور 'Dendur': This village was situated on the west bank of the Nile between Ibrīm and Aswan (Pierce 2017, 53).
قرية من القرى السبع: The phrase 'seven villages' as a designation of a cluster of villages in this region of the Nile is mentioned in the Mamlūk chronicle of ʿIzz al-Dīn ibn Šaddād (d. 684 AH/1285 AD; Seignobos 2015, 559).

8. وهو الثلث سهم واحد: This reconstruction is based on the phraseology in line 30.

9. لفافاى ابنة امفاتا: The name فافاى could be identified as a variant of the attested Nubian names Papa and Papi.[1] The reading of the second name is not clear. The letters at the beginning of the name are bunched together. One possible reading is امفاتا, which is given in the edition above. Two diacritical dots are written over the letter that I am reading as *tāʾ*. This could be related to the Nubian name Ampapa (ⲁⲙⲡⲁⲡⲁ), which is attested in Banganarti (Łajtar 2020, nos. 434 and 696).

10. طوله 'its length': It is not clear what this dimension relates to in the fragmentary text.

15. هنداو: This may possibly be identified with the village Hindawī, on the west bank of the Nile between Aswan and Ibrīm (Salvoldi and Geus 2017, 70), coordinates: 23.658720 32.874570. The place name with the orthog-

---

[1] DBMNT / TM Nam 34870 (Papas): DBMNT / TM NamVar 54656 (ⲡⲁⲡⲁ), 54658 (ⲡⲁⲡⲁⲥ); DBMNT Nam 201836 (Papi): DBMNT NamVar 301836 (ⲡⲁⲡ), 302853 (ⲡⲁⲡⲓ).

raphy هنداو occurs also in the Mamlūk chronicle of ʿIzz al-Dīn ibn Šaddād (Seignobos 2015, 559).

22. بياض: According to Lane (*Lexicon*, 283), بياض الارض is 'that part of land wherein is no cultivation nor population and the like'.
23. وجرف: The جرف *jurf* was a fertile slope of the riverbank that is naturally irrigated by the flood.

Margin

1. معبد 'Maʿbad': The name could also be read as معيد 'Muʿayd'.

Translation

1. In the name of God, the Merciful and Compassionate.
2. The witnesses named in this document bore testimony [ ]
3. Muḥammad son of the commander Treasure of the Dynasty (*Kanz al-Dawla*) ʾAbū al-Makārim Hibat Allāh [ ]
4. from the people of Dendur, one of the seven villages, that they [acknowledged and called witnesses to testify]
5. to their actions while healthy in mind and body and legally capable [of conducting their affairs,]
6. in it in the possession of them both, not in the possession of one of the two of them, [the witnesses bore testimony] to all that [ ]
7. belonging to Ġalyūn ibn Sulaymān ibn Ġalyūn, who is named in this document [ ]

8. two shares, two from three shares, and the remainder of that [which is the third of one share]
9. of three shares to Pāpāy the daughter of Ampātā, the Christian woman [ ]
10. the length of which is nine cubits, according to (the length of) cubit that is in current use [ ]
11. and bordered on the land of Nubia in the west [and in the east bordered]
12. on the Nile. Its southern boundary extends to the place of [ ]
13. Its northern boundary extends to the place of the land of Muḥammad [ ]
14. to the Nile. Its western boundary extends to the desert [ ]
15. the village known as Hindāw, which was known formerly [ ]
16. ibn Ḥasan ibn al-Ḥusayn. Its northern boundary extends to [ ]
17. thoroughfare. Its eastern boundary extends to a house known as . [ ]
18. Aswan in the north, known as the dwelling place of the Beja in [ ]
19. Its southern boundary extends to a house known as (that of) Nasība [ ]
20. extends to a house known as (that of) Mu'nisa the Christian woman. Its [northern] boundary [ ]
21. Its western boundary extends to the hollow ... [ ]

22. high, and (cultivated) land in it and uncultivated land, and a river and every watering place [ ]
23. and riverbank, and a building, with a lower floor and an upper floor in the open air .. [ ]
24. [all that] is in and appertains to that with regard to its rights. Every right belongs to every [one of them inside]
25. and drinking what belongs to him with regard to that, drinking from the well of its water, by which it is irrigated, [whether this be little]
26. or much.[2] The passage to all that safely is included in its rights all [ ]
27. which includes four cows and two bulls and all [ ]
28. forty head of riding animals, twenty of which [ ]
29. with a valid recognition, so that it was not hidden from them nor from [one]
30. according to what was mentioned previously, on the condition that what belongs to Ġalyūn ibn Sulaymān [ ]
31. three shares, and the remainder of that, which is a third of one share [ ]
32. in it, with a valid, effective, operative partnership, on the condition that whatever [ ]
33. delivery of his portion of that, its sale, and the disposition of it [ ]
34. All of that is in their hands. Whenever one of them claims [ ]

[2] I.e., whatever right there is.

35. and claims that for him and on his behalf in his lifetime, or through his disposal, after [ ]
36. or in some visible part thereof, and in all his power in this world and the [next]
37. document, the acknowledgement and partnership that are attributed to him and [ ]
38. [ ] those entering into partnership [named in this document]

Witness Clauses

Margin

1. ʿAbd Allāh ibn ʿAbd Allāh ibn al-Ḥusayn ibn Maʿbad witnessed the acknowledgement by the seller and the buyer of everything that has been attributed to them in it. He wrote it with his own writing on its date.

2. Kāmil ibn Ḵamīs ibn ʾIbrāhīm witnessed the acknowledgement by the seller and the buyer of everything that has been attributed
3. to them in it. It was written on his behalf and in his presence on its date.

4. Qilādī ibn Mawlā witnessed the acknowledgement by the seller and the buyer of everything that is in it.
5. It was written on his behalf and in his presence on its date.

Verso: Document of Sale (Rajab 535 AH/February 1141 AD)

Text

1 بسم الله الرحمن الرحيم

2 هذا ما اشترى غليون بن سليمن الكنزى من

3 فخر بن فريج بن مينا الاسمناوي اشترى منه

4 صفقة واحدة وعقد واحد سبعة اذرع

5 بذراع المرفق مشاعا من جميع ارض الموضع المعروف

6 بشب شلول فى الشرق قبالة القرية المعروفة

7 بمروا وحده القبلى ينتهى <الى> بقعة عرفت بالمشترى

8 المذكور حديثا وحده البحرى ينتهى الى بيت

9 عون ومحمد وعبيد الله بنى عبد الله بن معبد واشراكهم

10 والحد الشرقى ينتهى الى الصحرا والحد الغربى ينتهى

11 الى النيل بجميع حقوق ذلك من قليل وكثير وشرب

12 ذلك من بئر مائها التى يسقى منها وكل حق هو لذلك

13 داخل فيه وكل حق هو لذلك خارج منه والممر الى

14 ذلك كله مسلما فى حقوقه بدينار واحد متقال

15 من الذهب العين الوازن الصحيح الوازن الحافظى المصرى

16 الجيد شرى لا شرط فيه يفسده ولا عدة فيه

17 تبطله فتسلم ذلك منه وحازه وصار فى يده

18 وحوزه وقبضه وملكه بالشرى المذكور

19 وسلم اليه الثمن المذكور بوزنه وصفته وابراه

20 من ذلك برا قبض واستيفا على ما يوجبه شرط

21 بيوع المسلمين وضمانهم وشروطهم شرا نافذا ماضيا

22 صحيحا وذلك بعد ان تراضيا وامضياه

23 على انفسهما وانفذاه منهما فى صحة عقولهما

24 وابدانهما وجواز امورهما طائعين غير مكرهين

25 وذلك العشر الاول من شهر رجب سنة خمس وثلثين

26 وخمس مائة

Witness Clauses

1 شهد اماكى

2 بن ابرام على

3 اقرار البائع والمشترى

4 بجميع ما نسب اليهما فيه

5 وكتب عنه بمحضره فى تاريخه

6 شهد مبارك مولى الامير الاقدر

7 سعد الدولة على اقرار البائع

8 والمشترى بجميع ما نسب اليهما فيه وكتب

9 عنه وبامره وبمحضره فى تاريخه

10 شهد شدا بن ابرام على اقرار البائع

11 والمشترى المسمى معه فيه بجميع ما نسب اليهما فيه وكتب عنه وبمحضره

12 شهد انغشور بن مركى على اقرار البائع والمشترى
13 المسمى معه بجميع ما نسب اليهما فيه وكتب عنه وبمحضره فى تاريخه

14 شهد اندريا بن استرسكرا على اقرار البائع
15 والمشترى بجميع ما نسب اليهما فيه وكتب عنه وبمحضره فى تاريخه

Textual Notes

3. الاسمناوى: This may be a *nisba* relating to the place called Semna, which was situated between the second and third cataracts (Pierce 2017, 50; Salvoldi and Geus 2017, 86).
7. مروا: This may perhaps be identified with the village of Murwaw (Salvoldi and Geus 2017, 70), situated between Aswan and Ibrīm, coordinates: 23.412870 32.925800. This was on the west bank of the Nile, whereas the property described in the document was on the east bank of the Nile. So ‘opposite Murwā’ could have meant opposite Murwā across the river.
9. معبد: A diacritical dot is written under the *bā*ʾ in this name.
14. There are diacritics of *tā*ʾ on the second letter of متقال, indicating that the interdental *ṯā*ʾ was pronounced as the stop *tā*ʾ.

Between lines 18 and 19, some phrases are written perpendicularly to the text. One phrase can be read as يحيى بن على ‘Yaḥyā ibn ʿAlī’. The reading of the other phrase, which is enclosed in a circle, can tentatively be read as احمد الله ‘I praise God’.

Witness Clauses

10. شدا بن ابرام 'Šudā ibn ʾAbrām': The name Šouda is attested in the Old Nubian document 74.1.29/7b (unpublished), in an inscription from Faras (Łajtar and Ochała 2015, 84–87, no. 2) and at Banganarti (Łajtar 2020, nos. 109, 202, 338, 352, 439, 495, 837).
12. انغشور: This could possibly be identified with the Nubian name Angešouda. This name is attested in two Nubian documents from Qaṣr Ibrīm: P. QI III 39, l. 13 (landowner), IV 109 recto, ll. 16–19 (witness), and in a document of unknown provenance (Browne 1992, ll. 14 and 18) (two witnesses). The *ġayn* in انغشور would represent the Nubian *g*. The Nubian *d* has shifted to *r*, which is a common feature in the Arabic transcriptions of the Nubian names in the Arabic corpus.
14. اندريا بن استرسكرا 'Andrea ibn ʾIstaruskurā': If the reading is correct, the first name would presumably be a short form of the attested Nubian name Andreas.[3] The second name could be identified with the attested Nubian name Staurosinkouda.[4]

Translation

1. In the name of God, the Merciful and Compassionate.
2. This is what Ġalyūn ibn Sulaymān al-Kanzī bought from

[3] DBMNT / TM Nam 2024.

[4] DBMNT / TM Nam 34040: DBMNT / TM NamVar 65486 (ⲥⲧⲁⲩⲣⲟ ⲥⲓⲛⲕⲟⲩⲇⲁ).

3. Fak̲r ibn Furayj ibn Mīnā al-ʾIsamnāwī. He bought from him
4. with one clapping of the hands and one contract seven cubits,
5. (measured) in the cubit of the elbow, held in common, of all the land known as
6. Šabb Šalūl in the east opposite the village known
7. as Murwā. Its southern boundary extends to a piece of land known (by the name) of the aforementioned purchaser
8. recently. Its northern boundary extends to the house
9. of ʿAwn and Muḥammad and ʿUbayd Allāh, the sons of ʿAbd Allāh ibn Maʿbad, and their partners.
10. The eastern boundary extends to the desert. The western boundary extends
11. to the Nile. This includes all its rights, small and big, and the right to drink,
12. namely from its water well, by which it is irrigated, and every right relating to
13. to what is inside it, and every right relating to what is outside it; and the passage to
14. all of it safely is included in its rights. (He bought it) for one dīnār, of standard weight,
15. of gold, in minted coin, valid full weight, according to the Egyptian weight of al-Ḥāfiẓ,
16. of good alloy; a purchase without a condition that would invalidate it or a promise

17. that would make it void. He received it from him and took possession of it and it passed into his hand,
18. his ownership, his possession and his property, by the aforementioned purchase.
19. He delivered to him the aforementioned price, with its specified weight, and he released him
20. from that, a release of receipt in full, according to the requirements of the condition
21. of sale of the Muslims, and their warranties and stipulations, with an operative, effective
22. and valid sale; after the two had reached agreement and taken
23. upon themselves its obligation, and put it into effect, while in sound mind
24. and body, legally capable of conducting their affairs, acting willingly, not forced.
25. This was in the first ten days of the month of Rajab, the year five-hundred and thirty-five (February 1141 AD).

Witness Clauses

1–2. ʾAmākī ibn ʾAbrām witnessed
3. the acknowledgement by the seller and buyer
4. of all that is attributed to them in it.
5. It was written on his behalf in his presence on its date.

6. Mubārak, the freedman of the most powerful commander, Saʿd al-Dawla, witnessed
7. the acknowledgement by the seller

8. and buyer of all that is attributed to them in it. It was written
9. on his behalf, by his instruction and in his presence on its date.

10. Šudā ibn ʾAbrām witnessed the acknowledgement by the seller
11. and the buyer mentioned with him of all that is attributed to them in it. It was written on his behalf in his presence.

12. Angešoura ibn Merki witnessed the acknowledgement by the seller and the buyer
13. named with him of all that is attributed to them in it. It was written on his behalf in his presence on its date.

14. Andrea ibn ʾIstaruskurā witnessed the acknowledgement by the seller
15. and the buyer of all that is attributed to them in it. It was written on his behalf in his presence on its date.

47 AN ACKNOWLEDGEMENT OF A DEBT AND TESTIMONIES

Excavation photograph numbers and image numbers:

Recto: 1974_P04_11A-12 (image: 170308_650_u)
Verso: 1974_P04_10A-11 (image: 170308_649_u)

Object number: 74.1.29/11.8

Paper. Measurements are not available. There are tears horizontally along the folds.

Recto: Acknowledgement (Ramaḍān 515 AH/ November 1121 AD)

Text

1 بسم الله الرحمن الرحيم

2 اقر عبيد الله بن حسن الجلاب واشهد على نفسه فى صحة عقله وبدنه وجواز امره طائعا

3 غير مكره ان عليه وعنده وقبله لمركى بن ابرام مولى القاضى الرشيد الموفق السديد

4 ثقة الملك ابى الخير ابرهيم بن محمد بن الحسين بن محمد بن الزبير دينار واحد والنصف دينار الذهب العين الوازن الامرى

5 المصرى الجيد دينا ثابتا وحقا واجبا لازما صحيحا له عليه هو يقر انه ياتى بهذا الحق الذى اخذه قسط باسره

6 دينار ونصفه المذكور فى هذا الكتاب ويوصله اليه ويقوم له بذلك فى العشر الاول من ذى الحجة

7 سنة خمس عشرة وخمس مائة بغير مدافعة ولا ممانعة ولا يمين ولا تاول وذلك بامر حق واجب لازم صحيح عرفه له ولزمه

8 بلاقرار واقر بقبول ذلك بسبب حق منه على الاجل المذكور فيه بمخاطبة بينهما على ذلك شهد على اقرار المقر بالدين

9 والدائن المسمين فى هذا الكتاب بما نسب اليهما فيه فى صحة عقولهما وابدانهما وجواز امورهما طائعين غير مكرهين

10 وذلك فى العشر الاول من شهر رمضان سنة خمس عشرة وخمس مائة شهد على ذلك

Witness Clauses

1 شهد ابرهيم بن احمد بن ابرهيم بن نصر على

2 اقرار المقر بالدين بما نسب اليه فيه وكتب

3 بخطه بتاريخه

4 شهد احمد بن الحسين بن محمد بن منصور على اقرار

5 المقر بالدين والمقر له بما نسب اليهما فيه وكتب بخطه

6 بتاريخه

7 شهد بذلك وبالله تصحيح

Textual Notes

3. لمركى بن ابرام: If the reading is correct, these names can be identified with the attested Nubian names Merki[1] and Abrām.[2]

Translation

1. In the name of God the Merciful and Compassionate.
2. ʿUbayd Allāh ibn Ḥasan, the trader, acknowledged and called people to be his witnesses, in sound mind and body, legally capable of conducting his affairs, willing,
3. not forced that he owes, has in his possession, is in debt to Merki ibn Abrām, the freedman of the rightly-guided, prosperous, just judge,
4. Trust of the Kingdom, ʾAbū al-Ḳayr ʾIbrāhīm ibn Muḥammad ibn al-Ḥusayn ibn Muḥammad ibn al-Zubayr one dīnār and half a dīnār, gold, minted coin, full weight, in the Egyptian coinage of al-ʾĀmir,
5. of good alloy, an established debt, a valid binding right with legal force owed to him by him. He acknowledges that he will return this amount, which he has taken, its complete portion,

---

[1] DBMNT / TM Nam 10598 (Merkourios): DBMNT NamVar 301566 (ⲙⲉⲣⲕⲏ), 301569 (ⲙⲉⲣⲕⲓ).

[2] DBMNT / TM Nam 1707 (Abraham): DBMNT / TM NamVar 52589 (ⲁⲃⲣⲁⲁⲙ), 52593 (ⲁⲃⲣⲁⲙ).

6. a dīnār and a half mentioned in this document, and convey it to him and undertake this in the first ten days of D̲ū al-Ḥijja
7. of the year five-hundred and fifteen (10th–19th February 1122 AD), without delay, without obstruction, without an oath, without (a different) interpretation, this being by virtue of valid, binding right with legal force. He (the creditor) recognised it was owed to him and it became an obligation for him (the debtor)
8. through the acknowledgement; and he (the debtor) acknowledged the receipt of that, through which he (the creditor) would have a right with regard to the aforementioned due date, through a discussion between them regarding that. Witnesses witnessed the acknowledgement by the acknowledger of the debt
9. and the creditor who are named in this document of what relates to them in it, in sound mind and body, legally capable of conducting their affairs, willing, not forced.
10. That was in the first ten days of the month Ramaḍān in the year five-hundred and fifteen (13th–22nd November 1121 AD). It was witnessed.

Witness Clauses

1. ʾIbrāhīm ibn ʾAḥmad ibn ʾIbrāhīm ibn Naṣr witnessed
2. the acknowledgement by the acknowledger of the debt of what is attributed to him in it, and he wrote
3. with his own handwriting on its date.

4. ʾAḥmad ibn al-Ḥusayn ibn Muḥammad ibn Manṣūr witnessed the acknowledgement
5. by the acknowledger of the debt and the one to whom the acknowledgement was made of what was attributed to them in it, and he wrote with his own handwriting
6. on its date.

7. That was witnessed and by God (there is) a correction (in it).

Verso: Testimonies (Šawwāl 516 AH/December 1122 AD)

Text

1 اشهدنى مركى بن ابرام مولى القاضى الرشيد الموفق السديد ثقة الملك

2 المسمى باطنه انه قبض واستوفا دينا له من عبيد الله بن حسن

3 المسمى باطنه عن انه عبيد الله المذكور دفع ربع دينار وثمن الذهب

4 العين الوازن الامرى وابرا [[الغريم]] عبيد الله وشاكر المذكور من ذلك

5 براة قبص واستيفا وكتب محمد بن حسين بن على بخطه فى العشر

6 الاخر من شهر رمضان من سنة ستة عشرة وخمس مائة

7 اشهدنى مركى بن ابرام مولى القاضى الرشيد الموفق السديد ثقة الملك ابى الخير ابرهيم بن محمد بن الحسين

8 ابن الزبير على نفسه فى صحة منه وجواز امر طوعا انه قبض واستوفا من عبد الله مولى خليفة ابيه

9 ربع وسدس وثمن دينار عين من الذهب الامرى الوازن الجيد عن غريمه عبيد الله بن حسن

10 المسمى باطنه وابراه من ذلك براة قبض واستيفا وان الباقى له على غريمه ربع وسدسين

11 دينار عين وكتب على بن عبيد الله بن محمد بن تركى بخطه فى العشر الاخر

12 من شوال سنة ست عشرة وخمس مئة وذلك بعد ان استوفا الحكم عليه للباقى كتب عبد الله

13 بن محمد بن توفيق بن حسين فى العشر الاخر من شوال سنة ست عشرة وخمس مائة وكتب بخطه

14 وكان استيفائه الحكم عليه بالله الذى لا اله الا هو يمينا موكدة مستوفاة كما يحلف

15 امثاله من المسلمين فى شوال من سنة ست عشرة وخمسمائة وكتب بخطه

16 وكل ما اشهده مركى بن ابرام الشاهد الذى خطه باعلا

17 خطى هذا اشهدنى وحضرت استيفا الحكم عليه اليمين الموكدة

18 كما يحلف امثاله وذلك شوال من سنة ستة عشر وخمس مئة

19 وكتب محمد بن يحيا بن ابرهيم الانطاكى فى تاريخه

Textual Notes

4. الغريم: This word seems to have been crossed through by the scribe.

19. محمد: The reading is not certain.

Translation

1. Merki ibn Abrām, the freedman of the rightly-guided, prosperous, just judge, Trust of the Kingdom,
2. who is named on the recto, called me to witness that he has received in full a debt that he has from ʿUbayd Allāh ibn Ḥasan,
3. who is named on the recto, in that he, the aforementioned ʿUbayd Allāh, paid a quarter of a dīnār and an eighth of gold,
4. in coins of full weight, of al-ʾĀmir. The aforementioned (Merki) released the aforementioned ʿUbayd Allāh, [[the debtor]], who expressed his thanks,
5. a release of receipt in full. It was written by Muḥammad ibn Ḥusayn ibn ʿAlī in his hand, in the
6. last ten days of the month of Ramaḍān of the year five-hundred and sixteen (23rd November–2nd December 1122 AD).

7. Merki ibn Abrām, the freedman of the rightly-guided, prosperous, just judge, Trust of the Kingdom, ʾAbū al-Ḵayr ʾIbrāhīm ibn Muḥammad ibn al-Ḥusayn
8. ibn al-Zubayr, asked me to testify with regard to himself, while he was in health, while his acts were legal, and he acted willingly, that he has received in full from ʿAbd Allāh, a freedman, substituting for his father,
9. a quarter, a sixth and an eighth of a dīnār, in gold coinage of al-ʾĀmir, full weight, of good alloy, on behalf of his debtor ʿUbayd Allāh ibn Ḥasan,

10. who is named on the recto; and he released him from that with a release of full receipt; and that the remainder that is owed to him by his debtor is a quarter and two sixths
11. of a dīnār, in cash. It was written by ʿAlī ibn ʿUbayd Allāh ibn Muḥammad ibn Turkī in his own hand, in the last ten days
12. of Šawwāl, in the year five-hundred and sixteen (22nd–31st December 1122 AD). That was after he had received a legal injunction against him for the remainder, which was written by ʿAbd Allāh
13. ibn Muḥammad ibn Tawfīq ibn Ḥusayn in the last ten days of Šawwāl of the year five-hundred and sixteen (22nd–31st December 1122 AD). He wrote with his own hand.
14. His receipt of the legal injunction against him was by means of a full, ratifying oath sworn by God, other than whom there is no other God. He received it in the way
15. that other Muslims like him swear (oathes), in Šawwāl of the year five-hundred and sixteen (December 1122 AD). He wrote with his own hand.

16. Everything that Merki ibn Abrām asked the witness whose writing is above
17. this writing of mine to witness he made me (also) witness, and I was present at the receipt of the injunction against him (i.e., against the debtor), the ratifying oath,
18. as such similar (oaths) are sworn. This was in Šawwāl of the year five-hundred and sixteen (December 1122 AD).
19. It was written by Muḥammad ibn Yaḥyā ibn ʾIbrāhīm al-ʾAnṭākī on its date.

48 MARRIAGE CONTRACT AND ACKNOWLEDGEMENT

Museum of Islamic Art inventory number: 23973.61
Excavation photograph numbers and image numbers:

Recto: 1968_04_21–21A (image: 050308_695_u)
Recto: 1968_04_22–22A (image: 050308_696_u)
Recto: 1968_04_23–23A (image: 050308_697_u)
Recto: 1968_04_25–25A (image: 050308_699_o)
Recto: 1968_04_26–26A (image: 050308_700_o)
Verso: 1968_04_27–27A (image: 050308_701_o)

Paper. 38.5 cm × 37.5 cm

Recto: Marriage Contract (23rd Rabīʿ I 484 AH/ 15th May 1091 AD)

Text

1 بسم الله الرحمن الرحيم

2 هذا ما اصدق محمد المعروف بابى عبد الله بن اسمعيل بن حسين بن ابرهيم بن حسين {بن ابرهيم} بن اصفر بن ميمون بن بيدوس بن بسون ام الحسن ابنة على بن احمد بن حسين بن ابرهيم

3 ابن حسين بن اصفر بن ميمون بن بيدوس بن بسون وتزوجها به [ا]صدقها ثلا[ثة] وعشرين دينارا مثاقيل ذهبا عينا وازنة صحاحا مستنصرية

4 مصرية جيادا على ان من ذلك ثمانية دنانير بالصفة المذكورة فى هذا الكتاب نقدا حالا معجلا دفع ذلك اليها وقبضته منه تاما وافيا بوزنه وصفته وابراته منه براة قبض واستيفا

5 وعلى ان باقى ذلك وهو خمسة عشر دينارا بالصفة المذكورة فى هذا الكتاب موخر لها عليه الى انقضا خمس سنين متواليات كوامل اول اولهن اليوم [الث]ا[ث] والعشرين من شهر

6 ربيع الاول من سنة اربع وثمانين واربع مائة وعليه ان يتقى الله عز وجل فيها ويحسن صحبتها ومعاشرتها بالمعروف كما امر الله سبحانه فى كتابه وسنة نبيه محمد صلى الله عليه

7 وعلى اله الطاهرين وسلم تسليما وله عليها مثل الذى لها عليه من ذلك ودرجة زائدة فولى تزويجها اياه منه بهذا الصداق المذكور عاجله واجله فى هذا الكتاب

8 الشريف الخطيب ابو على محمد بن حيدرة بن الحسين بن الحسن الحسينى توكيلها اياه لذلك بشهادة من يذكر ذلك فى شهادته فى هذا الكتاب مع شهادتهم عليها بقبض معجل

9 مهرها المذكور وبتاجيل اجله الى اجله وهى يومئذ امراة بكر بالغ صحيحة العقل والبدن وقبل الزوج المسمى فى هذا الكتاب من الولى المسمى معه فيه هذا التزويج

10 المذكور فى هذا الكتاب على الصداق المذكور عاجله واجله فيه ورضى به بعد ان تخاطبا على ذلك وشهد على اقرار الزوجين والولى المسمين فى هذا الكتاب

11 بجميع ما فيه فى صحة عقولهم وابدانهم وجواز امورهم طائعين غير مكرهين وذلك فى شهر ربيع الاول من سنة اربع وثمانين واربعماية

12 وبعد ان اذن الشريف القاضى ابو تراب حيدرة بن الحسين بن الحسن الحسينى خليفة ولده الشريف القاضى نقيب الطالبين بالصعيد الاعلى ابى عبد الله محمد بن حيدرة بن الحسين بن

13 الحسن الحسينى على الحكم باسوان لولده الشريف الخطيب ابى على محمد بن حيدرة بن الحسين بن الحسن الحسينى الولى المسمى فى هذا الكتاب بعقد هذا النكاح بين الزوجين المذكورين فيه شهد على ذلك

14 فيه لحق بين سطرين مثاله على الحكم باسوان

Witness Clauses

1 شهد احمد بن محمد بن يحيى بن محمود بن الشريف على اقرار

2 الولى والزوج المسمين فى هذا الكتاب وكتب بخطه فى تاريخه

3 شهد الحسن بن محمد بن مهدى على اقرار

4 الولى والزوج بما فيه وكتب بخطه {بخطه} فى التاريخ

5 شهد الحسين بن محمد بن الحسين بن اسحق بن نصر على اقرار الولى والزوج المسمين فى هذا الكتاب بما نسب اليهما فيه وكتب بخطه فى التاريخ

6 شهد حيدرة بن على بن محمد على اقرار

7 الولى والزوج بما فيه وكتب بخطه فى تاريخه

8 شهد محمد بن على بن عبد الرحمن بن بى الخير
9 على اقرار الزوجين والولى بما فيه فى تاريخه

10 شهد عبد العزيز بن حسنون بن على على اقرار الزوجين
11 والولى المسمين فى هذا الكتاب بما نسب اليهم فى تاريخه

12 شهد الحسن بن على بن زيد على اقرار الولى والزوج
13 بما فيه وكتب بخطه فى التاريخ

14 شهد على بن محمد بن الربيع على اقرار
15 الولى والزوج بما فيه وكتب بخطه فى تاريخه

Textual Notes

2. حسين بن ابرهيم بن حسين {بن ابرهيم} بن اصفر: The second phrase بن ابرهيم, which is enclosed in curly brackets, does not occur in the genealogy of the bride or in that of the son of the bridegroom on the verso (**48**v:3). This indicates that it is a dittography.
بيدوس بن بسون: Diacritical dots are written under the *bāʾ* and the *yāʾ* of بيدوس and under the *bāʾ* of بسون. The name بيدوس Baydūs is likely to correspond to the Coptic name Paitos. It is found in the genealogies on Arabic gravestones from Aswan, e.g., CG VII, 100, no. 2627.[3]

---

[3] I am grateful to Stefanie Schmidt for drawing this to my attention and sending me the reference.

7. الاجله: This is an unconventional orthography for آجله.
13. على الحكم باسوان: This is written as an addition above the line.

Translation

1. In the name of God the Merciful and Compassionate.
2. This is what Muḥammad, known as ʾAbū ʿAbd Allāh ibn ʾIsmaʿīl ibn Ḥusayn ibn ʾIbrāhīm ibn Ḥusayn {ibn ʾIbrāhīm} ibn ʾAṣfar ibn Maymūn ibn Baydūs ibn Basūn, granted to ʾUmm al-Ḥasan ʾibnat ʿAlī ibn ʾAḥmad ibn Ḥusayn ibn ʾIbrāhīm
3. ibn Ḥusayn ibn ʾAṣfar ibn Maymūn ibn Baydūs ibn Basūn and married her with it [ ]. He granted to her twenty-three dīnārs, of standard weight, gold, in valid minted coins of full weight, Egyptian (dīnārs) of al-Mustanṣir,
4. of good alloy, on the understanding that eight dīnārs of that (sum) of the quality mentioned in this document will be a sum due for immediate payment. He paid that to her and she received it from him, completely and in full, according to its correct weight and quality. She released him from it with a release of receipt in full;
5. and on the understanding that the remainder of that, which is fifteen dīnārs of the quality mentioned in this document is postponed as a debt owed by him to her until the passing of five full consecutive years, the beginning of the first of which is the twenty-third day of the month
6. of Rabīʿ I of the year four-hundred and eighty-four (15th May 1091 AD). He is obliged to fear God, the Mighty and

Glorious, with regard to her, to act as a good companion and partner for her in kindness, as God, praise be to Him, has commanded in His Book, and the tradition of His prophet, Muḥammad, may God bless him

7. and his pure family, and may He save (them). Her duty to him is like his duty to her in this matter and one degree more. The carrying out of her marriage to him by this endowment from him, the amount that is immediately payable and the amount that is postponed, mentioned in this document, has been entrusted to

8. the noble preacher ʾAbū ʿAlī Muḥammad ibn Ḥaydara ibn al-Ḥusayn ibn al-Ḥasan al-Ḥusaynī. Her act of appointing him as her representative for this was by the testimony of those who declare this in their testimony in this document; together with their testimony that she received the immediate payment

9. of her aforementioned bride price and accepted to postpone the part that is to be postponed to the appointed time. On this day she is a virgin woman, legally of age, sound of mind and body. The groom named in this document accepted from the representative (of the bride) named with him in it the contract of marriage

10. mentioned in this document on the condition of the aforementioned endowment, the portion that is immediately payable of it and the portion that is postponed, and agreed to it, after they discussed the matter. Witnesses witnessed the acknowledgement by the two spouses and the bride's representative named in this document

11. of everything that is in it, in sound mind and body, legally capable of conducting their affairs, willingly, not forced. That was in the month of Rabīʿ I of the year four-hundred and eighty-four (May 1091 AD);
12. after the noble judge ʾAbū Turāb Ḥaydara ibn al-Ḥusayn ibn al-Ḥasan al-Ḥusaynī, deputising for his son, the noble judge, leader of the Ṭālibids in the southern sector of Upper Egypt, ʾAbū ʿAbd Allāh Muḥammad ibn Ḥaydara ibn al-Ḥusayn ibn
13. al-Ḥasan al-Ḥusaynī, responsible for jurisdiction in Aswan, gave permission to his son, the noble preacher, ʾAbū ʿAlī Muḥammad ibn Ḥaydara ibn al-Ḥusayn ibn al-Ḥasan al-Ḥusaynī, the bride's representative named in this document, to contract this marriage between the spouses mentioned in it. That was witnessed.
14. An insertion was made between two lines with the text 'over the jurisdiction in Aswan'.

Witness Clauses

1. Aḥmad ibn Muḥammad ibn Yaḥyā ibn Maḥmūd ibn al-Šarīf witnessed the acknowledgement
2. by the bride's representative and the groom named in this document. He wrote in his own hand on its date.

3. Al-Ḥasan ibn Muḥammad ibn Mahdī witnessed the acknowledgement
4. by the bride's representative and the groom of what is in it. He wrote in his own hand on the date.

5. Al-Ḥusayn ibn Muḥammad ibn al-Ḥusayn ibn ʾIsḥāq ibn Naṣr witnessed the acknowledgement by the bride's representative and the groom named in this document of what is attributed to them in it. He wrote in his own hand on the date.

6. Ḥaydara ibn ʿAlī ibn Muḥammad witnessed the acknowledgement
7. by the bride's representative and the groom of what is in it. He wrote in his own hand on its date.

8. Muḥammad ibn ʿAlī ibn ʿAbd al-Raḥmān ibn Bū al-Ḵayr
9. witnessed the acknowledgement by the two spouses and the bride's representative of what is in it on its date.

10. ʿAbd al-ʿAzīz ibn Ḥusnūn ibn ʿAlī witnessed the acknowledgement by the two spouses
11. and the bride's representative named in this document of what is attributed to them, on its date.

12. Al-Ḥasan ibn ʿAlī ibn Zayd witnessed the acknowledgement by the bride's representative and the groom
13. of what is in it. He wrote in his own hand on the date.

14. ʿAlī ibn Muḥammad ibn al-Rabīʿ witnessed the acknowledgement
15. by the bride's representative and the groom of what is in it. He wrote in his own hand on its date.

Verso: Acknowledgement (21st Šaʿbān 516 AH/ 25th October 1122 AD)

Text

1 بسم الله الرحمن الرحيم

2 اقر عبد الحسين بن محمد المعروف ببو عبد الله بن اسمعيل بن حسين بن اصفر واشهد على نفسه فى صحة عقله وبدنه وجواز

3 [امره] طائعا غير مكره انه قبض من والده محمد المعروف ببو عبد الله بن اسمعيل بن حسين بن اصفر اربعة دنانير ونصف دينار

4 من العين الوازن الجيد وذلك جميع ما يخصه بحق مورثه عن والدته ام الحسن ابنة على بن احمد بن حسين من موخر صداقها

5 المكتتب لها على والده باطنه وابراه من ذلك براة صحيحة واجبة لازمة براة قبض واستيفا ولم يبق له عليه ولا

6 عنده بسبب نصيبه من الموخر المذكور حق قليل ولا كثير ولا دعوى ولا طلبة بوجه ولا سبب وقبل منه

7 هذا الاقرار المقر له ورضى به بعد ان تخاطبا عليه شهد على اقرار المقر بالقبض المبرى والمقر له القابل

8 المسميين فى هذا الكتاب بجميع ما نسب اليهما فيه فى صحة منهما وجواز امر طوعا فى اليوم الحادى والعشرين من شعبان

9 سنة ست عشرة وخمس مائة

Witness Clauses

1 شهد محمد بن يحيا بن ابرهيم بن الـ... الحسينى على اقرار المقر بالقبض

2 المبرى والقابل بما فيه وكتب فى تاريخه

3 شهد احمد بن محمد بن حيدرة بن الحسين بن الحسن الحسينى على اقرار

4 المقر بالقبض المبرى والقابل المسمين فيه فى تاريخه

5 شهد حيدرة بن محمد بن حيدرة بن الحسين بن الحسن الحسينى على اقرار

6 المقر بالقبض المبرى والقابل المسمين فى هذا الكتاب بما فيه فى تاريخه

7 شهد على بن عبيد الله بن محمد بن شاكر على اقرار

8 المقر بالقبض المبرى والقابل المسمين فى هذا

9 الكتاب بما نسب اليهما فيه بتاريخه

10 شهد ابرهيم بن على بن محمد بن ابى جعفر على اقرار

11 المقر بالقبض المبرى والقابل المسمين فى هذا الكتاب

12 بما فيه وكتب بتاريخه

Translation

1. In the name of God the Merciful and Compassionate.
2. ʿAbd al-Ḥusayn ibn Muḥammad, known as Bū ʿAbd Allāh, ibn ʾIsmaʿīl ibn Ḥusayn ibn ʾAṣfar acknowledged and called witnesses to witness him, while he is healthy in mind and body and legally capable
3. of conducting his affairs, willing and unforced, that he has received from his father, Muḥammad, known as Bū ʿAbd

Allāh, ibn ʾIsmaʿīl ibn Ḥusayn ibn ʾAṣfar four and a half dīnārs,

4. coins of full weight and good alloy, this being everything that is apportioned to him by right of his inheritance from his mother, ʾUmm al-Ḥasan ʾibnat ʿAlī ibn ʾAḥmad ibn Ḥusayn, of the postponed portion of her bridal gift,

5. which is certified as being owed to her by his father on the recto; and he released him from that with a release that is valid, binding and has legal force, a release of receiving in full; and he (the son) was no longer owed by him (the father)

6. with regard to his share of the aforementioned postponed portion (of the dowry) any right, small or large, claim or demand, in any way; and the one acknowledged to (the father) accepted from him

7. this acknowledgement and was satisfied with it, after they had negotiated concerning it. Witnesses testified to the acknowledgement of the acknowledger of the receipt, who released (from liability), and of the one acknowledged to, who accepted it,

8. who are named in this document, with regard to everything that was attributed to them in it, they (the parties) being healthy, legally capable of conducting their affairs and willing, on the twenty-first day of Šaʿbān

9. of the year five-hundred and sixteen (25th October 1122 AD).

Witness Clauses

1. Muḥammad ibn Yaḥyā ibn ʾIbrāhīm ibn al-... al-Ḥusaynī witnessed the acknowledgement of the one acknowledging the receipt,
2. who released from liability, and the one accepting what it contained, and wrote this on its date.

3. ʾAḥmad ibn Muḥammad ibn Ḥaydara ibn al-Ḥusayn ibn al-Ḥasan al-Ḥusaynī witnessed the acknowledgement
4. of the one acknowledging the receipt, who released from liability, and the one accepting, who are named in it, on its date.

5. Ḥaydara ibn Muḥammad ibn Ḥaydara ibn al-Ḥusayn ibn al-Ḥasan al-Ḥusaynī witnessed the acknowledgement
6. of the one acknowledging the receipt, who released from liability, and the one accepting, who are named in this document, with regard to what is contained in it, on its date.

7. ʿAlī ibn ʿUbayd Allāh ibn Muḥammad ibn Šākir witnessed the acknowledgement
8. of the one acknowledging the receipt, who released from liability, and the one accepting, who are named in this
9. document, with regard to what was attributed to them in it, on its date.

10. ʾIbrāhīm ibn ʿAlī ibn Muḥammad ibn ʾAbī Jaʿfar witnessed the acknowledgement
11. of the one acknowledging the receipt, who released from liability, and the one accepting, who are named in this document,
12. with regard to what is contained in it, and he wrote on its date.

49 DOCUMENTS RELATING TO DIVORCE

Excavation photograph and image numbers:

Recto: 1978_B09_12A-13 (image: 070408_204_o)
Verso: 1978_B09_11A-12 (image: 070408_203_u)

Object number: 78.2.13/45A-E
Registration number: [78/]276
Paper. 26.9 cm × 9.6 cm. The text has been torn away on one side (right of the recto and left of the verso).

Recto: Document concerning Division of Property after Divorce (Muḥarram 429 AH/October–November 1037 AD)

Text

1 اعترفوا عندى جميعا بجميع ما فى هذا الكتاب

2 والحمد لله والاخر وكتب هبة الله بن مكين بن هبة

3 الله بن فارس بن حماد بن سويد بخطه وتاريخه

4 [بسم الله الرحمن الرحيم]

5 [شهد الشهود المسمون اخر هذا] الكتاب منهم من كتب بخطه ومنهم من كتب عنه بامره

6 [سنة تسـ]ـع وعشرين واربع ماية انهم خبروا قيرقة بن

7 [بن يحنس ومريم ابنت يحنـ]ـس وقد جرا بينهم مشاجرة ومنازعة فلم

8 [ ] طلاق وادعا عليها قيرقة بن يحنس

9 [ ] عنها من الدنانير واحضرت يوميذ مريم

10 [ابنت يحنس...] ادعا عليها بسبب قشر ورحل تسيره

11 [قيرقة بن يحـ]نس ان الرحل له فاستقر الامر بين قيرقة

12 [بن يحنس ومريم ابنت يحنس]. ان متا حدث على هذه الطفلة الرضيعة

13 [ ] جرى عليه المشاجرة لقيرقة بن يحنس دون

14 [ ] ذلك اتفقا وافترقا فى صحة عقولهما وابدانهما

15 [وجواز امورهما طائعن غير مكرهين ولا مـ]جبرين وذلك فى المحرم سنة تسع

16 [وعشرين واربع ماي]ة

Witness Clause

1 شهد ابرهيم بن حسن بن محمد على اقرار

2 المقرين بما فيه وكتب عنه بتاريخه

Textual Notes

3. فارس بن: The word بن is written as an extension of stroke of the final *sīn* of the word before it.

Translation

1. They all recognised in my presence everything that is in this document.
2. Praise be to God etc. It was written by Hibat Allāh ibn Makīn ibn Hibat
3. Allāh ibn Fāris ibn Ḥammād ibn Suwayd, in his handwriting and on its date.
4. [In the name of God, the Merciful and Compassionate.]

5. [The witnesses named at the end of this] document [have borne testimony,], some of them wrote with their own handwriting and some of them had it written for them by their command,
6. [the year] four hundred and twenty-nine that they know Qērqe ibn
7. [Yuḥannis and Maryam ibnat Yuḥann]is and that an argument and dispute had taken place between them and … not
8. [ ] divorce. Qērqe ibn Yuḥannis made a claim against her
9. [ ] from her with regard to the dīnārs. On this day Maryam [ibnat Yuḥannis] had brought
10. [ ] he made a claim against her with regard to clothing and the dowry requiring that she should send it
11. [Qērqe ibn Yuḥ]annis that the dowry belonged to him. The matter was decided between Qērqe
12. [ibn Yuḥannis and Maryam ibnat Yuḥannis] that when the infant girl was discussed
13. [ ] the dispute took place concerning it, belonged to Qērqe ibn Yuḥannis and not
14. [ ] that they agreed and separated in soundness of mind and body,
15. [legally capable of conducting their affairs, willing, not forced or] coerced. That was in Muḥarram of the year
16. [four-hundred and twenty] nine.

Witness Clause

1. ʾIbrāhīm ibn Ḥasan ibn Muḥammad witnessed the acknowledgement
2. of the two acknowledgers of what is in it. It was written on his behalf on its date.

Verso: Court Document relating to Divorce

Text

1 ليقف اخى وسـ[ـيدى [

2 على مصدقها] [

3 عنه وان وجه] [

4 حصته المذكـ]ـورة [

5 ولا تحوجه الـ] [

6 فى الناحية] [

7 بسم الله الرحمن الرحيم

8 حضر قيورقة بن يحنس ومريم ابنت يحـ]ـنس [

9 هذا الكتاب بيده وادعا بقشر فيها] [

10 وزنارين وملفة ومخدة ومنديل الملاتين] [

11 من القطيفة لقيورقة بن يحنس والردا] [

12 من القطيفة وما يبقا له عندها من الا] [

13 عليها او دعت عليه كان باطل وزور] [

14 شهد على ذلك

Textual Notes

8. قيورقة: This spelling of the name matches the Nubian form of the name Giorke (ⲅⲓⲟⲣⲕⲉ), which is found in an inscription from Sonqi Tino (Laisney 2012, 610, nos. 12–14).

Translation

1 My brother and master please attend [ ]
2. to the man who granted her the bride price [ ]
3. on his behalf and that he has sent [ ]
4. his aforementioned portion [ ]
5. do not oblige him [ ]
6. in the district [ ]

7. In the name of God the Merciful and Compassionate.
8. Qēōrqe ibn Yuḥannis and Maryam ibnat Yuḥannis attended (court) [ ]
9. this document in his hand and made a claim for clothes, including [ ]
10. two belts, a head-cloth, a pillow, a kerchief, two cloaks [ ]
11. of velvet, for Qēōrqe ibn Yuḥannis and a mantle [ ]
12. of velvet and what remains owed to him by her with regard to [ ]
13. against her or she claimed against him, it would be invalid and false. [ ]
14. This was witnessed.

50 ACKNOWLEDGEMENT RELATING TO DIVORCE (15TH JUMĀDĀ II 430 AH/ 14TH MARCH 1039 AH)

Excavation photograph number and image number:

1978_B19_05A-06 (image: 070408_384_o)

Object number: 78.2.13/45A-E

Registration number: [78/]276

Paper. 6 cm × 17.6 cm. Text is missing at the bottom.

Text

1 بسم الله الرحمن الرحيم

2 اقر جريج بن يحنس النوبى

3 واشهد على نفسه فى صحة

4 عقله وبدنه وجواز امره

5 طايعا غير مكره ولا مجبر

6 وذلك لاربعة عشر ليلة بقين

7 من جمادى الاخرة سنة ثلاثين وار

8 بعماية انه طلق زوجته مريم

9 ابنت يحنس طلقة واحدة تملك

10 بها نفسها وقوتها منه

11 شهد على اقرار المطلق والمطلقة

12 بجميع ما ذكر فيه فى صحة من عقولهما

13 وابدانهما وجواز امرهما طائعين غير

14 مكرهين ولا مجبرين وذلك فى جمادى

Translation

1. In the name of God, the Merciful and Compassionate.
2. Jurayj ibn Yuḥannis the Nubian acknowledged
3. and called people to witness himself, (he being) healthy
4. in mind and body and legally capable of conducting his affairs,
5. willingly, not forced or coerced,
6. this being when fourteen nights remained
7. of Jumādā II in the year four-hundred and thirty,
8. that he had divorced his wife, Maryam
9. ibnat Yuḥannis with one act of repudiation,
10. by which she acquired from him possession of herself, and control of herself.
11. The acknowledgement by the divorcer and the divorcee
12. of all that was mentioned in it was witnessed, they being in soundness of mind
13. and body, legally capable of conducting their affairs, willing,
14. not forced or coerced. That was in Jumādā.

51 MARRIAGE CONTRACT AND TESTIMONY

Excavation photograph numbers and image numbers:

Recto: 1978_A102_17–17A (image: 200308_101_u)
Verso: 1978_A102_18–18A (image: 200308_102_u)

Object number: 78.2.13/45A-E
Registration number: [78/]276
Paper. 18.1 cm × 27.1 cm

Recto: Marriage Contract (Ṣafar 432 AH/October 1040 AD)

Text

1 اعترفو اثنى الزوجين والولى بجميع ما فى هذا الكتاب

2 وكتب هبة الله بن مكين فى تاريخه صح

3 بسم الله الرحمن الرحيم

4 هذا ما اصدق مرينى بن يسو [النوبى] مريم ابنت يحنس النوبى وبه تزوجها اصدقها على كتاب

5 الله عز وجل وسنة نبيه صلى الله عليه وسلم وبذل لها من المهر المعجل والموجل اربعة

6 دنانيرا ذهبا عينا مستنصرية جيادا نقدها من ذلك قبل دخوله بها واصابته اياها ثلا

7 ثة دنانيرا ذهبا عينا واخرت عليه بقية مهرها وهو دينار واحد الى انقضى حجة

8 واحدة اولها صفر من سنة اثنين وثلاثين واربعمائة وعليه ان يتقى الله عز وجل

9 فيها ويحسن صحبتها ومعاشرتها بالمعروف كما امر الله عز وجل في كتابه

10 وسنة نبيه محمد صلى الله عليه وسلم على اله الطاهرين تسليما وله عليها متل

11 الذى لها عليه من ذلك ودرجة زائدة من افضل الد<ر>جات بكمال العفة

12 والصيانة والخضوع والقنوع وترك المفاضلة والله عليها شهيدا وكفى

13 بالله كفيلا وولى تزويجها اياه والقلد بعقدة نكاحها منه كيل بن مرينى امرها

14 ورضاها واشهادها له شاهدين حرين بعد ان سالته ذلك وهى يومئذ امراة بكر بالغ

15 صحيحة العقل والبدن جائزة الامر لها وعليه فازوجها مرينى بن يسو النوبى من وليها كيل بن مرينى

16 بما سمى ووصف فى كتابنا هذا عاجله واجله بمخاطبة منه اياها على ذاك شهد على اقرار الزوجين والولى

17 بجميع ما فى هذا الكتاب من اوله الى اخره فى صحة من عقلهم وابدانهم وجواز امر طائعين غير مكرهين ولا

18 مجبرين وذلك فى صفر من سنة اثنى وتلاتين واربعمائة

Witness Clauses

1 شهد حيدرة بن محمد بن جماعة بجميع ما فى هذا الكتاب وكتب بخطه

2 شهد مسلم بن جماعة على اقرار الزوجين والولى بجميع ما فى هذا الكتاب

3 وكتب عنه بامره ومحضره

4 شهد على ذلك حسن بن هبة الله بن طلاق

5 بن فارس بجميع ما فيه وكتب في تاريخه

6 شهد يوسف بن جماعة القلزمى على اقرار الزوجين

7 بجميع ما فى هذا الكتاب وكتب عنه بامره ومحضره

Textual Notes

4. مرينى: The word is pointed thus with diacritics in document **52**. This can be identified as the Nubian name Mariane.[1]

   يسو: This can be tentatively read Īsū. In document **50**r:2 the same name is written يسوى with a final *yā*ʾ, perhaps representing the pronunciation Īsūy.

11. The word that appears as الدجاث in the document is presumably a mistake for الدرجات ‘the degrees’, with the *rā*ʾ omitted and the final *tā*ʾ written hypercorrectly with the diacritics of *ṯā*ʾ.

13. القلد: One would expect التقليد.

15. كيل ‘Kayl’: This is a shortened form of the name Michael (Arabic: مكائيل).

Translation

1. The two spouses and the guardian of the bride recognised all that is in this document.

---

[1] DBMNT / TM Nam 7120 (Marianos): DBMNT / TM NamVar 66081 (ⲙⲁⲣⲓⲁⲛⲉ).

2. It was written by Hibat Allāh ibn Makīn on its date. Valid.
3. In the name of God, the Merciful and Compassionate.
4. This is what Mariane ibn Īsū the Nubian granted to Maryam ibnat Yuḥannis the Nubian, by which he married her. He granted it to her according to the Book
5. of God, the Mighty and Glorious, and the tradition of His prophet, may God bless him and save him. He gave to her a bride price, including the amount immediately payable and the amount whose payment is postponed, of four
6. dīnārs, gold, of minted coin, of al-Mustanṣir, of good alloy. He paid to her of that, before his having sexual intercourse with her and his deflowering of her,
7. three dīnārs, gold, of minted coin, and the remainder of the bride price was postponed as a debt owed by him, this being one dīnār, until the passage of one year,
8. beginning in Ṣafar of the year four-hundred and thirty-two (October 1040 AD). He is obliged to fear God, the Mighty and Glorious,
9. with regard to her, and to act as a good companion and partner for her in kindness, as God, the Mighty and Glorious, has commanded in His Book,
10. and the tradition of His prophet, Muḥammad, may God bless him and save his pure family. Her duty to him is like
11. his duty to her in this matter and one degree more, of the best degrees, in complete chastity
12. and modesty, obedience, contentment, and lack of contention, God being knowledgeable of her, and

13. in God there is sufficiency as a protector. Kayl ibn Mariane carried out her nuptial to him and undertook the contract of her marriage to him, by her command
14. and agreement, and by her calling two free witnesses to testify for him, after she asked him that, she being this day a virgin woman of (marriageable) age,
15. sound of mind and body, legally capable of conducting her affairs with regard to his obligation to her. He married her to Mariane ibn Īsū the Nubian, the one who represented her being Kayl ibn Mariane,
16. through what is named and described in this document of ours, the sum that is payable immediately and the sum that is postponed, by his negotiation with her concerning this. Witnesses witnessed the acknowledgement by the two spouses and the bride's guardian
17. of all that is in this document from its beginning until its end, in sound mind and body, legally capable of conducting their affairs, willingly, not forced
18. and not coerced. That was in Ṣafar of the year four-hundred and thirty-two (October 1040 AD).

Witness Clauses

1. Ḥaydara ibn Muḥammad ibn Jamāʿa witnessed with regard to all that is in this document and he wrote with his own hand.

2. Muslim ibn Jamāʿa witnessed the acknowledgement by the two spouses and the representative of the bride of all that is in this document;
3. and it was written on his behalf by his command and in his presence.

4. Ḥasan ibn Hibat Allāh ibn Ṭalāq
5. ibn Fāris witnessed that with regard to all that is in it and he wrote on its date.

6. Yūsuf ibn Jamāʿa al-Qulzumī witnessed the acknowledgement by the two spouses
7. of all that is in this document; it was written on his behalf by his command and in his presence.

Verso: Testimony (Ḏū al-Ḥijja 432 AH/August 1041 AD)

Text

1 بسم الله الرحمن الرحيم

2 [هذا] ما اشهدنى مرينى بن يسو النوبى للزوجة مريم ابنت يحنس

3 اربع قسط زيت الجوز والخل والملح والحصيرة والقز

4 والحطب والمشاط والكمين والملفة والنفقة ويبتى قمح

5 لكل شهر استقبال ذلك فى ذو الحجة سنة اثنين وثلاثين واربع مائة

6 وكتب هبة الله بن مكين فى تاريخه

Textual Notes

2. اشهدني: The document is faded and damaged at this point and the reading of this word is not certain. This is what the script seems to offer, but it is curious that there is no witness clause at the end of the document.

Translation

1. In the name of God, the Merciful and Compassionate.
2. This is what Mariane ibn Īsū the Nubian called me to witness for his wife Maryam ibnat Yuḥannis.
3. (He undertakes to give her) four measures of walnut oil, vinegar, salt, a straw mat, raw silk,
4. firewood, combs, two sleeves, a head-cloth, an allowance of two waybas of wheat
5. each month in the future. (This testimony was) in Ḏū al-Ḥijja of the year four hundred and thirty-two.
6. It was written by Hibat Allāh ibn Makīn on its date.

52 COURT RECORD RELATING TO MARRIAGE

Excavation photograph number and image number:

1978_A102_19–19A (image: 200308_103_u)

Object number: 78.2.13/45A-E

Registration number: [78/]276

Paper. 16.6 cm × 27 cm

Text

1 بسم الله الرحمن الرحيم

2 حضر مرينى بن يسوى النوبى وزوجته مريم ابنت يحنس النوبى

3 وقد جرا بينهم مشاجرة ومنازعة بسبب عطا وقظا والزام

4 مرينى بن يسو النوبى هذا نفسه العطا والقضا من ج[ـميـ]ع

5 ما يجب عليه لها بعد ان اظهرت كتاب بيدها تاريخه

6 صفر سنة اثنى وثلاثين واربعمائة ومبلغه دينار واحد

7 موخر الى انقضى حجة واحدة اولها صفر سنة اثنى وثلاثين

8 واربع مائة وثلاثة دنانير معجلة بعد ان اشهدت على

9 نفسها انها قبضت منه دينارين وازنين بقيها بدينار

10 واحد وامنها يخلى منه فى ستة اشهر فى الوقت

11 الذى كتب فى هذا الكتاب وهو ذو الحجة من سنة اثنى وثلاثين

12 واربعمائة شهد على ذلك وكتب شهادته فى خطه فى تاريخه

Witness Clauses

1 شهد محمد بن جماعة على اقرار المقرين بجميع ما سمى
2 ووصف فى هذا الكتاب وكتب عنه بامره ومحضره

3 شهد عبد الجليل بن هبة الله بن مكين
4 بجميع ما فى هذا الكتاب وكتب عنه فى تاريخه

5 شهد حيدرة بن محمد
6 بن جماعة بجميع ما فى
7 هذا الكتاب وكتب عنه

Translation

1. In the name of God, the Merciful and Compassionate.
2. Mariane ibn Īsūy the Nubian and his wife Maryam ibnat Yuḥannis the Nubian attended (court),
3. there having passed between them a quarrel and dispute regarding payment and fulfilment (of obligations), and the undertaking by
4. this Mariane ibn Īsū the Nubian to pay, to fulfill all
5. that which he owes to her, and after she showed a document in her hand dated
6. Ṣafar of the year four-hundred and thirty-two (October 1040 AD), (certifying that the payment of) the amount of one dīnār

7. was postponed until the end of one year, the beginning of which is Ṣafar, four-hundred and thirty-two (October 1040 AD)
8. and that three dīnārs were immediately payable, after she called witnesses
9. to certify that she had received from him two dīnārs of full weight and he had held back from her one
10. dīnār; and he reassured her that he would be cleared of it (i.e., its debt) in six months at the time
11. that is written in this document, this being Ḏū al-Ḥijja of the year four-hundred and thirty-two (August–September 1041 AD).
12. That was witnessed and he (the witness) wrote his testimony in his hand on its date.

Witness Clauses

1. Muḥammad ibn Jamāʿa witnessed the acknowledgement by the two acknowledgers of all that is named
2. and described in this document, and it was written on his behalf, by his instruction and in his presence.

3. ʿAbd al-Jalīl ibn Hibat Allāh ibn Makīn witnessed
4. all that is in this document and it was written on his behalf on its date.

5. Ḥaydara ibn Muḥammad
6. ibn Jamāʿa witnessed all that is in
7. this document and it was written on his behalf.

53 LETTER RELATING TO A MARITAL DISPUTE

Excavation photograph numbers and image numbers:

Recto: 1978_A102_16–16A (image: 200308_100_u)

Verso: 1978_A102_15–15A (image: 200308_099_u)

Object number: 78.2.13/45A-E

Registration number: [78/]276

Paper. 17.7 cm × 13.8 cm

Text

Recto

1 بسم الله الرحمن الرحيم

2 تصل هذه الاحرف ياخى العزيز على اطال الله بقاك وادام عزك وتاييدك وسعادتك ونعمتك

3 من يد مرينى النوبي وكان قد جا رجل يعرف بقيرقة بمرة وطلقها عندى

4 من مدة طويلة وجانى هذا الرجل موصل هذه الاحرف وكتبت له صداق

5 هذه الامراة منذ سنته فلما كان في هذا الوقت جا وعدا على زوجة هذا

6 الرجل واخرجها من بيته وادعا انها زوجته فعند وقوفك ياخى على هذه

7 الاحرف فتقبض على هذا الرجل وتعمل فى حاله ما يقتضيه الحق

8 وبعد اخذ حبسه انفذته الى والزوجة وزوجها موصل هذه الاحرف

9 لانى كتبت طلاقها وانا كتبت صداقها وتكاتبنى بجواب كتابى هذا لاعمل معهم ما يقتضيه الحق

10 تقرونا باخبارك وباحوالك وحاجاتك لابلغ فيها سارك ان شا الله

11 خصصتك بافضل سلام الله واطيبه   وحسبنا الله ونعم الوكيل

12 وصلى الله على محمد نبيه واله وسلم تسليما

Upper Margin

1 وبالاشارة انى وجدتك اول امس على

2 باب مولاى الامير

3 ادام الله علاه وقلت لك تحتاج الى

4 حاجة فعلت اريد بقاك

Verso

1 والله الله لا تدع ان تنفذ الي هذا الرجل والزوجة وزوجها بعد ان تاخذه

2 وتعمل معه ما يوجبه الحق لانه عدا على زوجة هذا الرجل

3 وتكشف حالهم على صح وتوقع فى ذلك ما اشكرك عليه ان شا الله

4 فقد دخل الى القاضى باخميم ادام الله عزه وانفذه الي لاني كتبت صداقها

5 وقد عرفتك ذلك لتعلمه ان شا الله

Address

Right Column

1 لاخى العزيز علي ابو الحسن زهير

2 اطال الله بقاه وادام عزه ونعمته

Left Column

1 من محبه القاضى هبة الله بن مكين

2 بالمراغة

Textual Notes

Recto

8. انفذته: The use of the *qatal* form here is somewhat unusual, but probably reflects some degree of hypotheticality on the model of conditional sentences, i.e., 'if you manage to detain him, then send him…' Alternatively, it could be a truncated form of the conditional politeness formula ان رايت انفذته 'If you see fit, send him', in which the *qatala* form is in the apodosis. For this construction, see Khan (1990).
9. لاعمل معهم ما يقتضيه الحق: These words are written above the line, apparently as an afterthought.
10. وباحوالك: The *bā*ʾ of the preposition *bi-* is written disconnected from the following *ʾalif*.

Verso

Address, Left Column

2. المراغة: al-Marāġa is a town in Upper Egypt in the modern Sohag Governorate.

Translation

Recto

1. In the name of God, the Merciful and Compassionate.
2. These lines[1] are arriving, my dear brother[2]—may God prolong your life and cause your strength, support,
3. happiness and wellbeing to endure—by the hand of Mariane the Nubian. A man known as Qērqe had come with a woman and divorced her in my presence
4. a long time ago. The man bringing (to you) these lines came to me and I wrote for him a marriage contract
5. for this woman a year ago. Recently[3] he (the former husband) came and acted wrongfully towards the wife
6. of this man and took her out of his house, claiming that she was his wife. When you, my brother, read these
7. lines, seize this man and do what is required by law with regard to him.
8. After he has been detained, send him to me together with the wife and her husband, the bearer of these lines,
9. since I wrote her divorce document and I wrote her marriage document. Reply to this letter of mine, so that I can act with them according to the requirements of the law.

---

[1] Literally: letters (of the alphabet).

[2] Literally: my brother dear to me.

[3] Literally: When it was in this time.

10. Tell us about your news, your circumstances and your needs, so I can bring about what pleases you with regard to them, God willing.
11. I send you the very best wishes for God's peace. God is our sufficiency. What a fine keeper is He!
12. May God bless Muḥammad, His prophet, and his family, and may He save (them).

Upper Margin

1. By the way, I met you the day before yesterday by
2. the door of my lord the commander,
3. may God cause his exaltation to endure, and I said to you "If you need
4. anything, I shall do it." I wish you long life.

Verso

1. By God, do not delay sending me this man, the wife and her husband after you detain him
2. and do to him what is required by law, because he acted wrongfully to the wife of this man.
3. Ensure that their correct legal situation is known and authorise that, God willing. I would be most grateful to you.
4. He (the bearer of this letter) went to the judge in Aḵmīm, may God cause his strength to endure, and he sent him to me, since I wrote her marriage contract.
5. I have informed you of this, so that you will know it, God willing.

Address

Right Column

1. To my dear brother ʾAbū al-Ḥasan Zuhayr,
2. may God prolong his life and cause his strength and his wellbeing to endure.

Left Column

1. From the one who loves him, the judge Hibat Allāh ibn Makīn,
2. in al-Marāġa.

REFERENCES

Abbreviations

ALAD = Khan, Geoffrey. *Arabic Legal and Administrative Documents in the Cambridge Genizah Collections*. Cambridge University Library Genizah Series 10. Cambridge: Cambridge University Press, 1993.

APEL = Grohmann, Adolf. *Arabic Papyri in the Egyptian Library*. 6 vols. Cairo: Egyptian Library Press, 1934–1974.

BAU = Abel, Ludwig. *Aegyptische Urkunden aus den koeniglichen Museen zu Berlin, herausgegeben von der Generalverwaltung. Arabische Urkunden*. Berlin: Weidmann, 1896–1900.

CG = Rached, Hussein, Hassan Hawary, and Gaston Wiet. *Catalogue Général du Musée Arabe du Caire: Stèles Funéraires*. 10 vols. Cairo: Imprimerie de l'Institut français d'archéologie orientale, 1932–1942.

DBMNT = Database of Medieval Nubian Texts (www.dbmnt.uw.edu.pl).

P. QI II = Browne, Gerald M. *Old Nubian Texts from Qaṣr Ibrīm II*. Texts from Excavations 10. London: Egypt Exploration Society, 1989.

P. QI III = Browne, Gerald M. *Old Nubian Texts from Qaṣr Ibrīm III*. Texts from Excavations 12. London: Egypt Exploration Society, 1991.

P. QI IV = Ruffini, Giovanni R. *The Bishop, the Eparch and the King: Old Nubian Texts from Qasr Ibrim (P. QI IV)*. The Journal of Juristic Papyrology Supplement Series 22. Warsaw: University of Warsaw, 2014.

RCEA = Combe, Étienne, Jean Sauvaget, and Gaston Wiet, eds. *Répertoire chronologique d'épigraphie arabe*. Publications de l'Institut français d'archéologie orientale du Caire. Cairo: l'Institut français d'archéologie orientale, 1931–1991.

Primary Sources

ʾAbū al-Makārim, *Taʾrīḵ al-Kanāʾis wa-l-ʾAdyira* = ʾAbū al-Makārim Saʿd Allāh ibn Jirjis ibn Masʿūd. تاريخ الكنائس والاديرة. Edited by Basil T. A. Evetts as *The Churches and Monasteries of Egypt and Some Neighbouring Countries: Attributed* [erroneously] *to Abû Ṣâliḥ, the Armenian*. Oxford: Clarendon Press, 1895.

al-ʾAnṭākī, *Kitāb al-Ḏayl* = al-ʾAnṭākī, Yaḥyā ibn Saʿīd ibn Yaḥyā. كتاب الذيل. Edited by I. Kratchkovsky and A. Vasilev as *Histoire de Yahya-ibn-Saʿïd d'Antioche continuateur de Saʿïd-ibn-Bitriq*. Fascicule II. Patrologia Orientalis 23, 345–520. Paris: Firmin-Didot, 1932.

al-Ḏahabī, *Siyar ʾAʿlām al-Nubalāʾ* = al-Ḏahabī, Šams al-Dīn Muḥammad ibn ʾAḥmad. سير أعلام النبلاء. 25 vols. Beirut: Muʾassasat al-Risāla, 1985.

al-ʾIdfūwī, *al-Ṭāliʿ al-Saʿīd* = al-ʾIdfūwī, ʾAbū al-Faḍl Kamāl al-Dīn Jaʿfar ibn Ṯaʿlab. الطالع السعيد الجامع أسماء نجباء الصعيد. Edited by Saʿd Muḥammad Ḥasan. Cairo: Al-Dār al-Miṣriyya li-l-Taʾlīf wa-l-Našr, 1966.

al-ʾIṣṭaḵrī, *Masālik al-Mamālik* = al-ʾIṣṭaḵrī, ʾAbū ʾIsḥāq ʾIbrāhīm ibn Muḥammad al-Fārisī. مسالك الممالك. Edited by Michael J. de Goeje. Leiden: Brill, 1870.

al-Jāḥiẓ, *Muqaddimat Mufāḵarat al-Jawārī wa-l-Ġilmān* = al-Jāḥiẓ, ʿAmr ibn Baḥr. الرسائل الأدبية: قدمة مفاخرة الجواري والغلمان. Beirut: Dār Maktabat al-Hilāl, 2002–2003.

al-Kindī, *Kitāb al-Wulāh* = al-Kindī, Muḥammad ibn Yūsuf. كتاب الولاة وكتاب القضاة. *The Governors and Judges of Egypt.* Edited by Rhuvon Guest. E. J. W. Gibb Memorial Series 19. Leiden; London: Brill; Luzac, 1912.

al-Maḵzūmī, *Kitāb al-Minhāj* = al-Maḵzūmī, ʾAbū al-Ḥasan ʿAlī ibn ʾUṯmān. كتاب المنهاج فى علم خراج مصر. Edited by Claude Cahen and Yūsuf Rāġib. Cairo: L'Institut français d'archéologie orientale, 1986.

al-Maʿarrī, *al-Lāmiʿ al-ʿAzīzī* = al-Maʿarrī, ʾAbū al-ʿAlāʾ ʾAḥmad ibn ʿAbd Allāh. اللامع العزيزي شرح ديوان المتنبي. Edited by Muḥammad Saʿīd al-Mawlawī. Riyadh: Markaz al-Malik Fayṣal li-l-Buḥūṯ w-al-Dirāsāt al-ʾIslāmiyya, 2008.

al-Maqrīzī, *al-Muqaffā al-Kabīr* = al-Maqrīzī, ʾAḥmad ibn ʿAlī. المقفى الكبير. 8 vols. Edited by Muḥammad al-Yaʿlāwī. Beirut: Dār al-Ġarb al-ʾIslāmī, 2006.

al-Maqrīzī, *al-Sulūk* = al-Maqrīzī, ʾAḥmad ibn ʿAlī. السلوك لمعرفة دول الملوك. 8 vols. Edited by Muḥammad ʿAbd al-Qādir ʿAṭāʾ. Beirut: Dār al-Kutub al-ʿIlmiyya, 1997.

al-Maqrīzī, *ʾIttiʿāẓ al-Ḥunafāʾ* = al-Maqrīzī, ʾAḥmad ibn ʿAlī. اتعاظ الحنفاء بأخبار الأئمة الفاطميين الخلفاء. 3 vols. Edited by Jamāl al-Dīn al-Šayyāl and Muḥammad Ḥilmī. Cairo: Lajnat ʾIḥyāʾ al-Turāṯ al-ʾIslāmī, 1973.

al-Maqrīzī, *Kiṭaṭ* = al-Maqrīzī, ʾAḥmad ibn ʿAlī. المواعظ والاعتبار بذكر الخطط والآثار. 4 vols. Beirut: Dār al-Kutub al-ʿIlmiyya, 1997–1998.

al-Maqrīzī, *Rasāʾil* = al-Maqrīzī, ʾAḥmad ibn ʿAlī. رسائل المقريزي. Cairo: Dār al-Ḥadīṯ, 1998–1999.

al-Marġīnānī, *al-Fatāwā al-Ẓahīriyya* = al-Marġīnānī, Ẓahīr al-Dīn ʾAbū al-Maḥāsin. الفتاوى الظهيرية. Part II. MS British Library Or. 4305.

al-Masʿūdī, *Murūj al-Ḏahab* = al-Masʿūdī, ʾAbū al-Ḥasan ʿAlī ibn Ḥusayn. مروج الذهب ومعادن الجوهر. Edited by Charles Barbier de Meynard and Abel Pavet de Courteille. Paris: Imprimerie impériale, 1861–1877.

al-Nuwayrī, *Nihāyat al-ʾArab* = Al-Nuwayrī, ʾAḥmad ibn ʿAbd al-Wahhāb. نهاية الأرب في فنون الأدب. 33 vols. Cairo: Dār al-Kutub w-al-Waṯāʾiq al-Qawmiyya, 2002–2003.

al-Qāḍī ʿIyāḍ, *Tartīb al-Madārik* = al-Qāḍī ʿIyāḍ, ʾAbū al-Faḍl ibn Mūsā al-Yaḥṣubī. ترتيب المدارك وتقريب المسالك. 8 vols. Al-Muḥammadiyya: Maṭbaʿat Faḍḍāla, 1965–1983.

al-Qalqašandī, *Nihāyat al-ʾArab fī Maʿrifat ʾAnsāb al-ʿArab* = al-Qalqašandī, ʾAbū al-ʿAbbās ʾAḥmad. نهاية الأرب في معرفة أنساب العرب. Edited by Ibrāhīm al-ʾIbyārī. Beirut: Dār al-Kuttāb al-Lubnāniyyīn, 1980.

al-Qalqašandī, *Ṣubḥ al-ʾAʿšā* = al-Qalqašandī, ʾAbū al-ʿAbbās ʾAḥmad. صبح الأعشى في صناعة الإنشاء. 14 vols. Beirut: Dār al-Kutub al-ʿIlmiyya, 2012.

al-Saraḵsī, *Kitāb al-Mabsūṭ* = al-Saraḵsī, Muḥammad ibn Aḥmad. كتاب المبسوط. 31 vols. Cairo: Maṭbaʿat al-Saʿāda, 1906–1907.

al-Ṭabarī, *Taʾrīḵ al-Rusul wa-l-Mulūk* = al-Ṭabarī, ʾAbū Jaʿfar Muḥammad ibn Jarīr. تاريخ الرسل والملوك. 11 vols. Edited by Muḥammad ʾAbū al-Faḍl ʾIbrāhīm. Cairo: Dār al-Maʿārif, 1967.

al-Yaʿqūbī, *Kitāb al-Buldān* = al-Yaʿqūbī, ʾAḥmad ibn ʾAbī Yaʿqūb. كتاب البلدان. Beirut: Dār al-Kutub al-ʿIlmiyya, 2001–2002.

al-Yaʿqūbī, *Taʾrīḵ* = al-Yaʿqūbī, ʾAḥmad ibn ʾAbī Yaʿqūb. تاريخ. Edited by Martijn Theodor Houtsma. Leiden: Brill, 1883.

al-Zubayr ibn Bakkār, *al-ʾAḵbār al-Muwaffaqiyyāt* = al-Zubayr ibn Bakkār ibn ʿAbd Allāh. الأخبار الموفقيات. Edited by Sāmī Makkī al-ʿĀnī. Beirut: ʿĀlam al-Kutub, 1996.

Bar Hebraeus, *Chronography* = Wallis A. Budge, ed. *The Chronography of Gregory Abû'l Faraj, Commonly Known as Bar Hebraeus*. 2 vols. London: Oxford University Press, 1932.

ibn ʿAbd al-Ḥakam, *Futūḥ Miṣr* = ibn ʿAbd al-Ḥakam, ʿAbd al-Raḥmān ibn ʿAbd Allāh. فتوح مصر والمغرب. Edited by Charles C. Torrey. *The History of the Conquest of Egypt, North Africa and Spain*. New Haven: Yale University Press, 1922.

ibn al-ʾAṯīr, *al-Kāmil fī al-Taʾrīḵ* = ibn al-ʾAṯīr, ʾ Abū al-Ḥasan ʿAlī ibn ʾAbī al-Karam. الكامل في التاريخ. 10 vols. Edited by ʿUmar ʿAbd al-Salām Tadmurī. Beirut: Dār al-Kitāb al-ʿArabī, 1997.

ibn al-ʾAṯīr, *al-Lubāb fī Tahḏīb al-ʾAnsāb* = ibn al-ʾAṯīr, ʾAbū al-Ḥasan ʿAlī ibn ʾAbī al-Karam. اللباب في تهذيب الأنساب. Beirut: Dār Ṣādir, 1972.

ibn al-Wardī, *Ḵarīdat al-ʿAjāʾib* = ibn al-Wardī, Sirāj al-Dīn ʾAbū Ḥafṣ ʿUmar ibn al-Muẓaffar. خريدة العجائب وفريدة الغرائب. Edited by ʾAnwar Maḥmūd Zanātī. Cairo: Maktabat al-Ṯaqāfa al-ʾIslāmiyya, 2008.

ibn Buṭlān, *Risāla* = ibn Buṭlān, ʾAbū al-Ḥasan ibn al-Ḥasan ibn ʿAbdūn. رسالة جامعة لفنون نافعة فى شرى الرقيق وتقليب العبيد. Edited by ʿAbd al-Salām Hārūn. Cairo: Muṣṭafā al-Bābī al-Ḥalabī, 1972.

ibn Ḥazm, *Jumal Futūḥ al-ʾIslām* = ibn Ḥazm al-Ẓāhirī, ʿAlī ibn ʾAḥmad ibn Saʿīd. رسائل ابن حزم الاندلسى. Edited by Iḥsān ʿAbbās. 2nd ed. Beirut: al-Muʾassasa al-ʿArabiyya li-l-Dirāsāt wa-l-Našr, 1987.

ibn Jinnī, *Ḵaṣāʾiṣ* = ibn Jinnī, ʾAbū al-Fatḥ ʿUṯmān. الخصائص. 3 vols. Cairo: al-Hayʾa al-Miṣriyya al-ʿĀmma lil-Kuttāb, 1990.

ibn Mākūlā, *al-Ikmāl* = ibn Mākūlā, ʾAbū Naṣr ʿAlī ibn Hibat Allāh. الإكمال في رفع الارتياب عن المؤتلف والمختلف في الأسماء والكنى والأنساب. 7 vols. Vols 1–6 edited by ʿAbd al-Raḥmān ibn Yaḥyā al-Muʿallamī al-Yamānī. Hyderabad: Dāʾirat al-Maʿārif al-ʿUṯmāniyya, 1962–1967. Vol. 7 edited by Nāʾif al-ʿAbbās. Beirut, n.d.

ibn Mammātī, *Kitāb Qawānīn al-Dawāwīn* = ibn Mammātī, al-Asʿad ibn al-Kaṯīr. *Kitāb Qawānīn al-Dawāwīn*. Edited by ʿAzīz Sūryāl ʿAṭiyya. Cairo: al-Jamʿiyya al-Zirāʿiyya al-Malakiyya, 1943.

ibn Manẓūr, *Muḵtaṣar Taʾrīḵ Dimašq* = ibn Manẓūr, Muḥammad ibn Mukarram. مختصر تاريخ دمشق لابن عساكر. 29 vols. Damascus: Dār al-Fikr li-l-Ṭibāʿa wa-l-Tawzīʿ w-al-Našr, 1984.

Pliny. *Natural History, Volume VI: Books 20–23*. Translated by William H. S. Jones. Loeb Classical Library 392. Cambridge, MA: Harvard University Press, 1951.

Strabo. *The Geography of Strabo. Vol. 8*. [Book XVII]. Translated by Horace L. Jones. London: William Heinemann, 1935.

Yāqūt, *Kitāb Muʿjam al-Buldān* = Yāqūt Shihāb al-Dīn ibn-ʿAbd Allāh al-Rūmī al-Ḥamawī. كتاب معجم البلدان. 6 vols. Edited by Ferdinand Wüstenfeld. Leipzig: Brockhaus, 1866–1871.

Dictionaries

Blau, *Dictionary* = Blau, Joshua. *A Dictionary of Mediaeval Judaeo-Arabic Texts*. Jerusalem: Academy of Hebrew Language, Israel Academy of Science and Humanities, 2006.

Browne, *Old Nubian Dictionary* = Browne, Gerald M. *Old Nubian Dictionary*. Leuven: Peeters, 1996.

Dozy, *Supplément* = Dozy, Reinhart P. A. *Supplément aux dictionnaires arabes*. 2nd ed. Leiden: Brill, 1927.

Hava, *Dictionary* = Hava, J. G. *Arabic English Dictionary*. Beirut: Catholic Press, 1899.

Hinds and Badawi, *A Dictionary of Egyptian Arabic* = Hinds, Martin, and el-Said Badawi. *A Dictionary of Egyptian Arabic: Arabic–English*. Beirut: Librairie du Liban, 1986.

ibn Manẓūr, *Lisān al-ʿArab* = ibn Manẓūr, Muḥammad ibn Mukarram. لسان العرب. Beirut: Dār Ṣādir, 1993–1994.

Lane, *Lexicon* = Lane, Edward William. *An Arabic–English Lexicon*. London: Williams & Norgate, 1863.

Secondary Sources

Abbott, Nabia. 1941. 'Marriage Contracts among Copts'. *Zeitschrift der Deutschen Morgenländischen Gesellschaft* 95: 59–81.

Adams, William Y. 1977. *Nubia: Corridor to Africa*. London: Allen Lane.

———. 1979. 'The "Library" of Qasr Ibrim'. *The Kentucky Review* 1: 5–27.

———. 1996. *Qaṣr Ibrîm: The Late Mediaeval Period*. London: Egypt Exploration Society.

———. 2003. *Meinarti IV and V: The Church and the Cemetery—The History of Meinarti, An Interpretive Overview*. London: The Sudan Archaeological Research Society.

———. 2010. *Qasr Ibrim: The Earlier Medieval Period*. London: Egypt Exploration Society.

Adams, William Y., and Nettie K. Adams. 1999. *Kulubnarti II: The Artifactual Remains*. London: Sudan Archaeological Research Society.

al-Imad, Leila S. 1990. *The Fatimid Vizierate (979–1172)*. Berlin: Klaus Schwarz Verlag.

al-Qaddūmī, Ghāda al-Ḥijjāwā. 1996. *Book of Gifts and Rarities (Kitāb al-Hadāyā wa al-Tuḥaf)*. Harvard: Harvard University Press.

Alrudainy, Reem, Mathieu Tillier, and Naïm Vanthieghem. 2024. 'The Silence of the Bride: A Fatimid Marriage Contract on Silk'. *Journal of Semitic Studies* 69 (1): 415–56.

Ashtor, Eliyahu, and John Burton-Page. 2012. 'Makāyil'. In *Encyclopaedia of Islam* (online), edited by Peri Bearman, Thierry

Bianquis, Clifford E. Bosworth, Emeri van Donzel, and Wolfhart P. Heinrichs. 2nd ed. Leiden: Brill. http://dx.doi.org/10.1163/1573-3912_islam_COM_0635

Ayalon, David. 1985. 'On the Term Khādim in the Sense of «Eunuch» in the Early Muslim Sources'. *Arabica* 32: 289–308.

Balog, Paul. 1961a. 'History of the Dirhem in Egypt from the Fāṭimid Conquest until the Collapse of the Mamlūk Empire'. *Revue Numismatique*, 6th ser., 3: 109–46.

———. 1961b. 'Notes on Some Fāṭimid Round-Flan Dirhems'. *The Numismatic Chronicle and Journal of the Royal Numismatic Society*, 7th ser., 1: 175–79.

Bates, Michael L. 1991. 'Coins and Money in the Arabic Papyri'. In *Documents de l'Islam médiéval: Nouvelles perspectives de recherche*, edited by Youssef Rāġib, 43–64. Cairo: Institut français d'archéologie orientale du Caire.

Bell, Herman. 1971. 'The Phonology of Nobíin Nubian'. *African Language Review* 9: 115–39.

Beshir, Beshir Ibrahim. 1975. 'New Light on Nubian Fāṭimid Relations'. *Arabica* 22: 15–24.

Björkman, Walther. 1928. *Beiträge zur Geschichte der Staatskanzlei im Islamischen Agypten*. Hamburg: de Gruyter.

Bloom, Jonathan M. 1984. 'Five Fatimid Minarets in Upper Egypt'. *Journal of the Society of Architectural Historians* 43: 162–67.

Bramoullé, David. 2012. 'The Fatimids and the Red Sea (969–1171)'. In *Navigated Spaces, Connected Places: Proceedings of Red Sea Project V Held at the University of Exeter, 16–17 September 2010*, edited by Dionisius A. Agius, John P. Cooper,

Athena Trakadas, and Chiara Zazzaro, 127–36. British Foundation for the Study of Arabia Monographs 12. Oxford: Archaeopress.

Brauer, Ralph W. 1995. 'Boundaries and Frontiers in Medieval Muslim Geography'. *Transactions of the American Philosophical Society* 85: 1–73.

Brett, Michael. 1969. 'Ifriqiya as a Market for Saharan Trade from the Tenth to the Twelfth Century AD'. *Journal of African History* 10: 347–64.

Browne, Gerald M. 1989. 'The Protocol of Griffith's Old Nubian Sale'. *Altorientalische Forschungen* 16: 216–19.

———. 1992. 'Griffith's Old Nubian Sale'. *Orientalia* 61: 454–58.

———. 1996. *Old Nubian Dictionary*. Leuven: Peeters.

Bruning, Jelle. 2020. 'Slave Trade Dynamics in Abbasid Egypt: The Papyrological Evidence'. *Journal of the Economic and Social History of the Orient* 63: 682–742.

Brunschvig, Robert. 1975. 'Ibn Abd Al-Hakam et la conquète de l'Afrique du Nord par les Arabes'. *Al-Andalus* 40: 129–79.

Cahen, Claude. 2012. 'Iḳṭāʿ'. In *Encyclopaedia of Islam* (online), edited by Peri Bearman, Thierry Bianquis, Clifford E. Bosworth, Emeri van Donzel, and Wolfhart P. Heinrichs. 2nd ed. Leiden: Brill. http://dx.doi.org/10.1163/1573-3912_islam_SIM_3522

Caillé, Alain. 2007. *Anthropologie du don*. Paris: La Découverte.

Crum, Walter E. 1939. *A Coptic Dictionary*. Oxford: Oxford University Press.

Cuoq, Joseph. 1986. *Islamisation de la Nubie chrétienne, viie–xvie siècles*. Paris: Geuthner.

Cutler, Anthony. 2001. 'Gifts and Gift Exchange as Aspects of the Byzantine, Arab, and Related Economies'. *Dumbarton Oaks Papers* 55: 247–78.

Daniels, Charles M., and Derek A. Welsby. 1991. *Soba: Archaeological Research at a Medieval Capital on the Blue Nile*. London: The British Institute in Eastern Africa.

Danys, Katarzyna, and Dobrochna Zielińska. 2017. 'Towards an Insight into the Aesthetics of the Kingdom of Alwa through the Painted Pottery Decoration'. *Sudan and Nubia* 21: 177–85.

Davies, W. Vivian, and Derek A. Welsby, eds. 2020. *Travelling the Korosko Road: Archaeological Exploration in Sudan's Eastern Desert*. Sudan Archaeological Research Society 24. Oxford: Archaeopress.

den Heijer, Johannes. 1996. 'Coptic Historiography in the Fāṭimid, Ayyūbid and Early Mamlūk Periods'. *Medieval Encounters* 2: 67–98.

den Heijer, Johannes, Yaacov Lev, and Mark N. Swanson. 2015. 'The Fatimid Empire and Its Population'. *Medieval Encounters* 21: 323–44.

Dozy, Reinhart P. A. 1845. *Dictionnaire détaillé des noms de vêtements chez les Arabes*. Amsterdam: Jean Müller.

Ducène, Jean-Charles. 2007. 'Le Darb al-Arbaʿīn à l'époque musulmane'. In *Pharaons noirs: Sur la piste des quarante jours*, edited by Marie Cécile Bruwier, 245–52. Mariemont: Musée royal de Mariemont.

Edwards, David N. 2004. *The Nubian Past: An Archaeology of the Sudan*. New York: Routledge.

———. 2011. 'Slavery and Slaving in the Medieval and Post-Medieval Kingdoms of the Middle Nile'. In *Slavery in Africa: Archaeology and Memory*, edited by Paul Lane and Kevin C. Macdonald, 79–108. Proceedings of the British Academy 168. Oxford: Oxford University Press.

———. 2019. 'Islamic Archaeology in Nubia'. In *Handbook of Ancient Nubia*, edited by Dietrich Raue, 965–84. Berlin: de Gruyter.

Forand, Paul. 1971. 'Early Muslim Relations with Nubia'. *Der Islam* 48: 111–21.

Frantz-Murphy, Gladys. 1988. 'A Comparison of the Arabic and Earlier Egyptian Contract Formularies, Part III: The Idiom of Satisfaction'. *Journal of Near Eastern Studies* 47: 105–12.

Frenkel, Miriam. 2017. 'The Slave Trade in Geniza Society'. In *Slavery and the Slave Trade in the Eastern Mediterranean (c. 1000–1500 CE)*, edited by Reuven Amitai and Christoph Cluse, 143–61. Turnhout: Brepols.

Fu'ād Sayyid, Ayman. 1983. *Passages de la chronique d'Égypte d'Ibn al-Ma'mūn*. Textes arabes et études islamiques 21. Cairo: Institut français d'archéologie orientale du Caire.

Gadallah, F. F. 1959. 'The Egyptian Contribution to Nubian Christianity'. *Sudan Notes and Records* 40: 38–43.

Garcin, Jean-Claude. 1976. *Un centre musulman de la haute-Égypte médiévale: Qūṣ*. Cairo: Institut français d'archéologie orientale du Caire.

Garcin, Jean-Claude, and Michel Tuchscherer. 2012. 'Uswān'. In *Encyclopaedia of Islam* (online), edited by Peri Bearman, Thierry Bianquis, Clifford E. Bosworth, Emeri van Donzel, and Wolfhart P. Heinrichs. 2nd ed. Leiden: Brill. http://dx.doi.org/10.1163/1573-3912_islam_COM_1314

Gascoigne, Alison L. 2008. 'Between the Two Dams: The Forgotten Medieval and Post-Medieval Archaeology of the First Nile Cataract'. *Al-ʿUṣūr al-Wusṭā* 20: 37–45.

Gascoigne, Alison L., and Pamela J. Rose. 2012. 'The Forts of Hisn Al-Bab and the First Cataract Frontier from the 5th to the 12th Centuries AD'. *Sudan & Nubia: The Sudan Archaeological Reearch Society* 16: 88–95.

Gerhards, Gabriel. forthcoming. 'A History of Arabs in the Nubian Kingdom of Alwa'.

Gizewski, Christian. 2006. 'Magister equitum'. In *Brill's New Pauly* (online), Antiquity volumes edited by Hubert Cancik and Helmuth Schneider, English edition edited by Christine F. Salazar. http://dx.doi.org/10.1163/1574-9347_bnp_e717010

Godlewski, Włodzimierz. 2008. 'Bishops and Kings: The Official Program of the Pachoras (Faras) Cathedrals'. In *Between the Cataracts: Proceedings of the 11th Conference for Nubian Studies*, edited by Włodzimierz Godlewski and Adam Łajtar, 263–82. PAM Supplement Series 2.1. Warsaw: Warsaw University.

———. 2010. 'Archbishop Georgios of Dongola: Socio-Political Changes in the Kingdom of Makuria in the Second Half of the 11th Century'. *Polish Archaeology in the Mediterranean* 22: 663–77.

Godlewski, Włodzimierz, and Stanisław Medeksza. 1987. 'The So-Called Mosque Building in Old Dongola (Sudan): A Structural Analysis'. *Archéologie du Nil moyen* 2: 185–205.

Goitein, Shlomo D. 1967. *A Mediterranean Society: The Jewish Communities of the Arab World as Portrayed in the Documents of the Cairo Geniza.* Vol. 1, *Economic Foundations*. Berkeley: University of California Press.

———. 1978. *A Mediterranean Society: The Jewish Communities of the Arab World as Portrayed in the Documents of the Cairo Geniza.* Vol. 3, *The Family*. Berkeley: University of California Press.

———. 1983. *A Mediterranean Society: The Jewish Communities of the Arab World as Portrayed in the Documents of the Cairo Geniza.* Vol. 4, *Daily Life*. Berkeley: University of California Press.

Goitein, Shlomo D., and Mordechai Akiva Friedman. 2008. *India Traders of the Middle Ages: Documents from the Cairo Geniza ('India Book')*. Jerusalem: Ben-Zvi Institute.

Greenfield, Jonas. 1992a. 'Some Arabic Loanwords in the Aramaic and Nabatean Texts from Naḥal Ḥever'. *Jerusalem Studies in Arabic and Islam* 15: 10–21.

———. 1992b. 'The "Defension Clause" in Some Documents from Naḥal Ḥever and Naḥal Seʿelim'. *Revue de Qumran* 15: 467–71.

Grierson, Philip. 1978. 'The Origins of Money'. In *Research in Economic Anthropology: An Annual Compilation of Research*, edited by George Dalton, 1–35. Greenwich, CT: Jai Press Inc.

Grob, Eva M. 2013. 'A Catalogue of Dating Criteria for Undated Arabic Papyri with "Cursive" Features'. In *Documents et histoire: Islam, viie–xvie siècle*, edited by Anne Regourd, 115–35. Hautes Études Orientales: Moyen et Proche-Orient 5. Geneva: Librairie Droz.

Grohmann, Adolf. 1934. *Arabic Papyri in the Egyptian Library*. Vol. 1. Cairo: Egyptian Library Press.

———. 1954. *Einführung und Chrestomathie zur arabischen Papyruskunde*. Československý Ústav Orientální v Praze: Monografie Archion Orientálního 13. Prague: Státní pedagogické nakl.

Grohmann, Adolf, and Raif Georges Khoury. 1993. *Chrestomathie de papyrologie arabe: Documents relatifs à la vie privée, sociale et administrative dans les premiers siècles Islamiques*. Handbuch der Orientalistik, Erste Abteilung: Nahe und der Mittlere Osten, Ergänzungsband 2, 2. Leiden: Brill.

Guo, Li. 2004. *Commerce, Culture, and Community in a Red Sea Port in the Thirteenth Century: The Arabic Documents from Quseir*. Islamic History and Civilization: Studies and Texts 52. Leiden: Brill.

Hallaq, Wael, B. 2009. *Sharīʿa: Theory, Practice, Transformations*. Cambridge: Cambridge University Press.

Halm, Heinz. 1998. 'Der Nubische Baqṭ'. In *Egypt and Syria in the Fatimid, Ayyubid and Mamluk Eras II: Proceedings of the 4th and 5th International Colloquium, Katholieke Universiteit Leuven, 1995–1996*, edited by Urbain Vermeulen and Daniel De Smet, 63–103. Leuven: Peeters.

Hassan, Fekri A. 2007. 'Extreme Nile Floods and Famines in Medieval Egypt (AD 930–1500) and Their Climatic Implications'. *Quaternary International* 173–74: 101–12.

Hellström, Pontus. 1970. *The Rock Drawings*. Vol. 1 of *The Scandinavian Joint Expedition to Sudanese Nubia*. Solna: Scandinavian University Books.

Hendrickx, Benjamin. 2011. 'The Lord of the Mountain: A Study of the Nubian Eparchos of Nobadia'. *Le Muséon* 124: 303–55.

Hinds, Martin, and Victor Ménage. 1991. *Qaṣr Ibrīm in the Ottoman Period: Turkish and Further Arabic Documents*. Texts from Excavations 11. London: Egypt Exploration Society.

Hinds, Martin, and Hamdi Sakkout. 1981. 'A Letter from the Governor of Egypt Concerning Egyptian–Nubian Relations in 141/758'. In *Studia Arabica et Islamica: Festschrift for Iḥsān ʿAbbās on His Sixtieth Birthday*, edited by Wadād al-Qāḍī, 209–29. Beirut: American University of Beirut.

———. 1986. *Arabic Documents from the Ottoman Period from Qaṣr Ibrīm*. Texts from Excavations 8. London: Egypt Exploration Society.

Hinz, Walther. 1955. *Islamische Masse und Gewichte*. Handbuch der Orientalistik, Ergänzungsband 1, 1. Leiden: Brill.

Holt, Peter M. 2012. 'Kanz, Banu ʾl'. In *Encyclopaedia of Islam* (online), edited by Peri Bearman, Thierry Bianquis, Clifford E. Bosworth, Emeri van Donzel, and Wolfhart P. Heinrichs. 2nd ed. Leiden: Brill. http://dx.doi.org/10.1163/1573-3912_islam_SIM_3876

Hourani, Albert. 1992. *A History of the Arab Peoples*. London: Faber and Faber.

Hudson, Michael. 2010. 'Entrepreneurs: From the Near Eastern Takeoff to the Roman Collapse'. In *The Invention of Enterprise*, edited by David S. Landes, Joel Mokyr, and William J. Baumol, 8–36. Princeton: Princeton University Press.

ʿĪsā, Mirfat Maḥmūd. 2000. 'عقد زواج من العصر الفاطمي'. *Majallat Markaz al-Dirāsāt al-Bardiyya wa-l-Nuqūš, Jāmiʿat ʿAyn Šams* 17: 259–91.

Jacotin, Pierre. 1818. *Carte géographique de l'Égypte et des pays environnans*. Paris: C. L. F. Panckoucke.

Jakobielski, Stefan, Małgorzata Martens-Czarnecka, Magdalena Łaptaś, Bożena Mierzejewska, and Bożena Rostkowska. 2017. *Pachoras Faras: The Wall Paintings from the Cathedrals of Aetios, Paulos and Petros*. Warsaw: University of Warsaw.

Johnstone, T. M., and J. Muir. 1964. 'Some Nautical Terms in the Kuwaiti Dialect of Arabic'. *Bulletin of the School of Oriental and African Studies* 27: 299–332.

Kapteijns, Lidwien, and Jay Spaulding. 1988. *After the Millennium: Diplomatic Correspondence from Wadai and Dar Fur on the Eve of Colonial Conquest, 1885–1916*. East Lansing: Michigan State University.

———. 1990. 'Gifts Worthy of Kings: An Episode in Dar Fur–Taqali Relations'. *Sudanic Africa* 1: 61–70.

Khan, Geoffrey. 1990. 'The Historical Development of the Structure of Medieval Arabic Petitions'. *Bulletin of the School of Oriental and African Studies* 53: 8–30.

———. 1992. *Arabic Papyri: Selected Material from the Khalili Collection.* Studies in the Khalili Collection 1. London: The Nour Foundation and Oxford University Press.

———. 1993a. *Arabic Legal and Administrative Documents in the Cambridge Genizah Collections.* Cambridge University Library Genizah Series 10. Cambridge: Cambridge University Press.

———. 1993b. 'On the Question of Script in Medieval Karaite Manuscripts: New Evidence from the Genizah'. *Bulletin of the John Rylands University Library of Manchester* 75: 133–41.

———. 1994. 'The Pre-Islamic Background of Muslim Legal Formularies'. *ARAM* 6: 193–224.

———. 2007. *Arabic Documents from Early Islamic Khurasan.* London: Nour Foundation in association with Azimuth Editions.

———. 2008. 'Remarks on the Historical Background and Development of the Early Arabic Documentary Formulae'. In *Documentary Letters from the Middle East: The Evidence in Greek, Coptic, South Arabian, Pehlevi, and Arabic (1st–15th c CE)*, edited by Eva M. Grob and Andreas Kaplony, 885–906. Asiatische Studien: Zeitschrift der Schweizerischen Asiengesellschaft = Études Asiatiques: Revue de la Société Suisse–Asie 62. Bern: Peter Lang.

———. 2013. 'The Medieval Arabic Documents from Qasr Ibrim'. In *Qasr Ibrim, between Egypt and Africa: Studies in Cultural Exchange (Nino Symposium, Leiden, 11–12 December 2009),* edited by Jacques Van der Vliet and J. L. Hagen, 145–56. Leuven: Peeters.

———. 2019. 'The Opening Formula and Witness Clauses in Arabic Legal Documents from the Early Islamic Period'. *Journal of the American Oriental Society* 139 (1): 23–39.

———. To appear 2024. 'An Arabic Document of Sale from Medieval Cairo Preserved in the Firkovitch Collection'. In *From the Battlefield of Books: Essays Celebrating 50 Years of the Taylor–Schechter Genizah Research Unit*, edited by Magdalen Connolly and Nick Posegay. Leiden: Brill.

Kheir, El-Hag H. M. 1989. 'A Contribution to a Textual Problem: *Ibn Sulaym al-Aswānī's Kitāb Akhbār al-Nūba wa-l-Maqurra wa-l-Beja wa-l-Nīl*'. *Arabica* 36: 36–80.

Kirzner, Israel M. 1979. *Perception, Opportunity, and Profit: Studies in the Theory of Entrepreneurship*. Chicago: University of Chicago Press.

Laisney, Vincent P.–M. 2012. 'Les inscriptions grecques et nubiennes de l'église de Sonqi Tino'. *Scienze dell'Antichità* 18: 601–13.

Łajtar, Adam. 2009. 'Varia Nubica XII–XIX'. *Journal of Juristic Papyrology* 39: 89–94.

———. 2014. 'A Survey of Christian Textual Finds from Gebel Adda in the Collections of the Royal Ontario Museum, Toronto'. In *The Fourth Cataract and Beyond: Proceedings of the 12th International Conference for Nubian Studies*, edited by Julie Anderson and Derek A. Welsby, 951–59. British Museum Publications on Egypt and Sudan 1. Leuven: Peeters.

———. 2020. *A Late Christian Pilgrimage Centre in Nubia: The Evidence of Wall Inscriptions in the Upper Church at Banganarti.* Journal of Juristic Papyrology Supplement 39. Leuven: Peeters.

Łajtar, Adam, and Tomasz Derda. 2019. 'Organization of the Church in Medieval Nubia in the Light of a Newly Discovered Wall Inscription in Dongola'. *Jahrbuch des Österreichischen Byzantinistik* 69: 135–54.

Łajtar, Adam, and Grzegorz Ochała. 2015. 'Two Wall Inscriptions from the Faras Cathedral with Lists of People and Goods'. In *Nubian Voices II: New Texts and Studies on Christian Nubian Culture*, edited by Adam Łajtar, Grzegorz Ochała, and Jacques Van der Vliet, 73–102. The Journal of Juristic Papyrology Supplement Series 27. Warsaw: Peeters.

———. 2017. 'Ase: A Toponym and/or a Personal Name (Notes on Medieval Nubian Toponymy 3)'. *Dotawo* 4: 241–56.

Lane, Edward William. 2000. *Description of Egypt: Notes and Views in Egypt and Nubia, Made during the Years 1825, -26, -27, and -28—Chiefly Consisting of a Series of Descriptions and Delineations of the Monuments, Scenery, &c. of Those Countries.* Cairo: American University of Cairo Press.

Lee, Doug. 2018. 'Armies, Roman'. In *The Oxford Dictionary of Late Antiquity* (online). Oxford: Oxford University Press. https://www.oxfordreference.com/view/10.1093/acref/9780198662778.001.0001/acref-9780198662778-e-452, accessed 1 March 2024.

Lentin, Jérôme. 1997. 'Recherches sur l'histoire de la langue arabe au Proche-Orient à l'époque moderne'. Ph.D. thesis, Paris: University of Paris III.

Lepsius, Karl R. 1846. *Denkmäler aus Ägypten und Äthiopien*. Berlin: Nicolaische Buchhandlung.

Lev, Yaacov. 1987. 'Army, Regime, and Society in Fatimid Egypt, 358–487/968–1094'. *International Journal of Middle East Studies* 19: 340–42.

———. 1998. *Saladin in Egypt*. Leiden: Brill.

———. 2013. 'Famines in Medieval Egypt: Natural and Man-Made'. *Leidschrift: Verraderlijke rijkdom—Economische crisis als historisch fenomeen* 28 (September): 55–65.

Lilie, Ralph Johannes, Claudia Ludwig, Beate Zielke, and Thomas Pratsch. 2013. *Prosopographie der mittelbyzantinischen Zeit Online*. Berlin: de Gruyter. https://doi.org/10.1515/pmbz

Lohwasser, Angelika. 2013. 'Tracks in the Bayuda Desert: The Project "Wadi Abu Dom Itinerary" (W.A.D.I.)'. In *Desert Road Archaeology in Ancient Egypt and Beyond*, edited by Frank Förster and Heiko Riemer, 425–43. Africa Praehistorica 27. Cologne: Heinrich-Barth-Institut.

Martindale, John R. 1980. *The Prosopography of the Later Roman Empire*. Vol. 2, *A.D. 395–527*. Cambridge: Cambridge University Press.

Mauss, Marcel. 2002. *The Gift: The Form and Reason for Exchange in Archaic Societies*. London: Routledge.

Michałowski, Kazimierz, and Georg Gerster. 1967. *Faras: Die Kathedrale aus dem Wüstensand*. Zürich: Benzinger.

Mills, A. J. 1982. *Cemeteries of Qasr Ibrim: A Report of the Excavations Conducted by W. B. Emery in 1961*. Excavation Memoir 51. London: Egypt Exploration Society.

Mina, Togo. 1942. *Inscriptions coptes et grecques de Nubie*. Cairo: Société d'archéologie copte.

Mouton, Jean-Michel, Dominique Sourdel, and Janine Sourdel-Thomine. 2013. *Mariage et séparation à Damas au Moyen Âge: Un corpus de 62 documents juridiques inédits entre 337/948 et 698/1299*. Paris: L'Académie des inscriptions et belles-letters.

Negru, Ioana. 2009. 'The Plural Economy of Gifts and Markets'. In *Economic Pluralism*, edited by Robert F. Garnett, Erik Olsen, and Martha Starr, 194–204. London: Routledge.

Obłuski, Artur. 2014. *The Rise of Nobadia: Social Changes in Northern Nubia in Late Antiquity*. Journal of Juristic Papyrology Supplement 20. Warsaw: University of Warsaw.

Ochała, Grzegorz. 2011. *Chronological Systems of Christian Nubia*. The Journal of Juristic Papyrology Supplement Series 16. Warsaw: University of Warsaw.

———. 2020. 'Nubica Onomastica Miscellanea V: Re-Edition of Two Old Nubian Lists of Names from Qasr Ibrim'. *Journal of Juristic Papyrology* 50: 233–61.

Osman, Ali. 1982. 'Medieval Nubia: Retrospects and Introspects'. In *New Discoveries in Nubia*, edited by Paul van Moorsel, 69–92. Leiden: Brill.

Paprocki, Maciej. 2019. *Roads in the Deserts of Roman Egypt: Analysis, Atlas, Commentary*. Oxford: Oxbow.

Perry, Craig. 2017. 'Historicizing Slavery in the Medieval Islamic World'. *International Journal of Middle East Studies* 49: 133–38.

———. 2019. 'An Aramaic Bill of Sale for the Enslaved Nubian Woman Naʿīm'. *Jewish History* 32: 451–61.

———. forthcoming. *Slavery in the Medieval Middle East: A History*. Princeton: Princeton University Press.

Pierce, Richard Holton. 2017. 'Nubian Toponyms in Medieval Nubian Sources'. *Dotawo: A Journal of Nubian Studies* 4: 35–55.

Pipes, Daniel. 1981. *Slave Soldiers and Islam: The Genesis of a Military System*. New Haven: Yale University Press.

Plumley, J. Martin. 1966. 'Qaṣr Ibrîm, 1966'. *Journal of Egyptian Archaeology* 52: 9–12.

———. 1975a. 'Qaṣr Ibrîm, 1974'. *Journal of Egyptian Archaeology* 61: 5–27.

———. 1975b. *The Scrolls of Bishop Timotheos*. Texts from Excavations 1. London: Egypt Exploration Society.

Polanyi, Karl. 1963. 'Ports of Trade in Early Societies'. *The Journal of Economic History* 23: 30–45.

———. 1966. *Dahomey and the Slave Trade: An Analysis of an Archaic Economy*. Seattle: University of Washington Press.

Rabie, Hassanein. 1972. *The Financial System of Egypt AH, 564–741/AD, 1169–1341*. London: Oxford University Press.

Rāġib, Yūsuf. 1993. 'Les marchés aux esclaves en terre d'Islam'. In *Mercati e mercanti nell'alto medioevo: L'area Euroasiatica e l'area Mediterranea—Settimane di studio del centro Italiano di studi sull'alto medioevo XL*, 721–66. Spoleto: Centro italiano di studi sull'alto medioevo.

———. 2006. *Actes de vente d'esclaves et d'animaux d'Égypte médiévale*. Vol. 2. Cairo: Institut français d'archéologie orientale du Caire.

Ramzī, Muḥammad. 1963. القاموس الجغرافى للبلاد المصرية. Vol. 4. Cairo: Dār al-Kutub Press.

Rapoport, Yossef. 2000. 'Matrimonial Gifts in Early Islamic Egypt'. *Islamic Law and Society* 7: 1–36.

———. 2005. *Money, Marriage and Divorce in Medieval Islamic Society*. Cambridge: Cambridge University Press.

Renault, François. 1989. *La traité des noires au Proche-Orient médiéval vii–xiv siècles*. Paris: Geuthner.

Renger, Johannes. 2000. 'Das Palastgeschäft in der Altbabylonischen Zeit'. In *Interdependency of Institutions and Private Entrepreneurs: Proceedings of the Second MOS Symposium (Leiden 1998)*, edited by A. C. V. M. Bongenaar, 153–83. Istanbul-Leiden: Nederlands Historisch-Archaeologisch Instituut te Istanbul–Nederlands Instituut voor het Nabije Oosten.

Richter, Tonio Sebastian. 2022. 'BnF Copte 132.5 f. 9, an Astrological Leaflet, among Other Coptic Technical Writings from the White Monastery'. In *The Rediscovery of Shenoute: Studies in Honor of Stephen Emmel*, edited by Anne Boud'hors, David Brakke, Andrew Crislip, and Samuel Moawad, 423–42. Leuven: Peeters.

Rilly, Claude. 2008. 'Enemy Brothers, Kinship and Relationship between Meroites and Nubians (Noba)'. In *Between the Cataracts: Proceedings of the 11th Conference for Nubian Studies,* Part 2, Fasc. 1, edited by Włodzimierz Godlewski and Adam Łajtar, 211–25. Warsaw: Warsaw University Press.

Rose, Pamela J. 2011. 'Qasr Ibrim: The Last 3000 Years'. *Sudan & Nubia: The Sudan Archaeological Research Society* 15: 1–9.

Rosenbaum, Gabriel. 2002. 'The Particles Mā and Lam and Emphatic Negation in Egyptian Arabic'. In *"Sprich doch mit deinen Knechten Aramäisch, Wir verstehen es!" 60 Beiträge zur Semitistik: Festschrift für Otto Jastrow Zum 60. Geburtstag,* edited by Werner Arnold and Hartmut Bobzin, 583–98. Wiesbaden: Harrassowitz.

Rosenthal, Franz. 2012. 'Dawla'. In *Encyclopaedia of Islam* (online), edited by Peri Bearman, Thierry Bianquis, Clifford E. Bosworth, Emeri van Donzel, and Wolfhart P. Heinrichs. 2nd ed. Leiden: Brill. http://dx.doi.org/10.1163/1573-3912_islam_SIM_1748

Ruffini, Giovanni R. 2012a. 'The Meinarti Phylactery Factory: Medieval Nubian Ostraka from the Island of Michael'. *The Journal of Juristic Papyrology* 42: 49–76.

———. 2012b. *Medieval Nubia: A Social and Economic History.* New York: Oxford University Press.

———. 2014. *The Bishop, the Eparch, and the King: Old Nubian Texts from Qasr Ibrim (p. QI IV).* The Journal of Juristic Papyrology Supplements 22. Warsaw: University of Warsaw.

———. 2016a. 'Documentary Evidence and the Production of Power in Medieval Nubia'. *Afriques* 7. https://doi.org/10.4000/afriques.1871

———. 2016b. 'Dotawo's Later Dynasties. A Speculative History'. In *Aegyptus et Nubia Christiana: The Włodzimierz Godlewski Jubilee Volume on the Occasion of His 70th Birthday*, edited by Adam Łajtar, Artur Obłuski, and Iwona Zych, 539–52. Warsaw: Polish Centre of Mediterranean Archaeology, University of Warsaw.

———. 2019. 'Monetization across the Nubian Border'. In *The Archaeology of Medieval Islamic Frontiers: From the Mediterranean to the Caspian Sea*, edited by A. Asa Eger, 105–18. Boulder: University Press of Colorado.

———. 2020. 'The History of Medieval Nubia'. In *The Oxford Handbook of Ancient Nubia*, edited by Geoff Emberling and Bruce Beyer Williams, 759–72. Oxford: Oxford University Press.

Ruffini, Giovanni R., and Robin Seignobos. 2020. 'Makouria'. In *Encyclopaedia of Islam* (online), edited by Kate Fleet, Gudrun Krämer, Denis Matringe, John Nawas, and Devin J. Stewart. 3rd ed. Leiden: Brill. http://dx.doi.org/10.1163/1573-3912_ei3_COM_36632

Rustow, Marina. 2020. *The Lost Archive: Traces of a Caliphate in a Cairo Synagogue*. Princeton: Princeton University Press.

Ṣabbār, ʿAbd al-Halīm, and Herman Bell. 2017. 'Endangered Toponymy along the Nubian Nile'. *Dotawo: A Journal of Nubian Studies* 4: 9–33.

Salvoldi, Daniele, and Klaus Geus. 2017. 'A Historical Comparative Gazetteer for Nubia'. *Dotawo: A Journal of Nubian Studies* 4: 57–182.

Sartain, Elizabeth M. 1993. 'Nubian Egyptian Relations in the Late Fatimid Period: The Sudan Trade'. Paper presented at the Annual Meeting of the Middle East Studies Association, Research Triangle Park, NC.

Savage, Elizabeth. 1992. 'Berbers and Blacks: Ibadi Slave Traffic in Eighth-Century North Africa'. *Journal of African History* 33: 351–68.

Säve-Söderbergh, Torgny, ed. 1987. *Temples and Tombs of Ancient Nubia: The International Rescue Campaign at Abu Simbel, Philae and Other Sites*. London: Thames & Hudson/UNESCO.

Schacht, Joseph, Aharon Layish, Ron Shaham, Ghaus Ansari, Jan M. Otto, Sebastiaan Pompe, Jan Knappert, and Jean Boyd. 2012. 'Nikāḥ'. In *Encyclopaedia of Islam* (online), edited by Peri Bearman, Thierry Bianquis, Clifford E. Bosworth, Emeri van Donzel, and Wolfhart P. Heinrichs. 2nd ed. Leiden: Brill. http://dx.doi.org/10.1163/1573-3912_islam_COM_0863

Seignobos, Robin. 2010. 'La frontière entre le bilād al-Nūba: Enjeux et ambiguïtés d'une frontière immobile (viie–xiie siècle)'. *Afriques* 2: 1–36.

———. 2015. 'La Liste des conquêtes nubiennes de Baybars selon Ibn Saddad (1217–1285)'. In *Aegyptus et Nubia Christiana: The Włodzimierz Godlewski Jubilee Volume on the Occasion of His 70th Birthday*, edited by Adam Łajtar, Atur Obłuski, and

Iwona Zych, 553–77. Warsaw: Polish Centre of Mediterranean Archaeology, University of Warsaw.

———. 2016. 'L'Égypte et la Nubie à l'époque médiévale: Élaboration et transmission des savoirs historiographiques (641–ca. 1500)'. Ph.D. Thesis, Paris: University of Paris I.

———. 2020. 'Émir à Assouan, souverain à Dongola: Rivalités de pouvoir et dynamiques familiales autour du règne nubien du Kanz al-Dawla Abū ʿAbd Allāh Muḥammad (1317–1331)'. *Médiévales* 79: 137–60.

———. 2021. 'L'Épigraphie arabe et la question de la présence musulmane en Nubie: Autour d'un fragment de stèle funéraire provenant de l'île de Saï (fin de vi[e]/xiie siècle)'. *Annales Islamologiques* 55: 329–42.

Sherwin-White, A. N., and Andrew Lintott. 2015. 'magister equitum'. In *Oxford Classical Dictionary* (online). Oxford: Oxford University Press. https://doi.org/10.1093/acrefore/9780199381135.013.3866

Shinnie, Peter L. 1961. *Excavations at Soba*. Khartoum: Sudan Antiquities Service.

Shinnie, Peter L., and Margaret B. E. Shinnie. 1978. *Debeira West: A Mediaeval Nubian Town*. Warminster: Aris & Phillips.

Shoshan, Boaz. 1981. 'Fāṭimid Grain Policy and the Post of the Muḥtasib'. *International Journal of Middle East Studies* 13: 181–89.

Sindzingre, Alice Nicole. 2017. 'Understanding the Concept of Gift in Economics: Contributions from Other Social Sciences'. *Eidos* 2: 4–20.

Smoor, P. 2006. 'The Yemen Connection in Cairo: A Case of Revenge?' In *Authority, Privacy and Public Order in Islam*, edited by B. Michalak-Piculska and A. Pikulski, 223–38. Leuven: Peeters.

Sourdel, Dominique, Clifford E. Bosworth, P. Hardy, and Halil İnalcık. 2012. 'G̲h̲ulām'. In *Encyclopaedia of Islam* (online), edited by Peri Bearman, Thierry Bianquis, Clifford E. Bosworth, Emeri van Donzel, and Wolfhart P. Heinrichs. 2nd ed. Leiden: Brill. http://dx.doi.org/10.1163/1573-3912_islam_COM_0237

Spaulding, Jay. 1995. 'Medieval Christian Nubia and the Islamic World: A Reconsideration of the Baqt Treaty'. *The International Journal of African Historical Studies* 28: 577–94.

———. 1998. 'Early Kordofan'. In *Kordofan Invaded: Peripheral Incorporation and Social Transformation in Islamic Africa*, edited by Endre Stiansen and Michael Kevane, 46–59. Leiden: Brill.

Spaulding, Jay, and Lidwien Kapteijns. 1994. *An Islamic Alliance: Ali Dinar and the Sanusiyya, 1909–1916*. Evanston: Northwestern University Press.

Stern, Samuel Miklos. 1964. *Fāṭimid Decrees: Original Documents from the Fāṭimid Chancery*. London: Faber.

Swanson, Mark N. 2007. *The Coptic Papacy in Islamic Egypt*. Vol. 2 of *The Popes of Egypt: A History of the Coptic Church and Its Patriarchs*. Cairo: The American University in Cairo Press.

Thung, Michael. 2006. *Arabische juristische Urkunden aus der Papyrussammlung der Österreichischen Nationalbibliothek*. Corpus Papyrorum Raineri Archeducis Austriae 26. Vienna: Österreichische Nationalbibliothek.

Trimingham, J. Spencer. 1965. *Islam in the Sudan*. London: Frank Cass & Co. Ltd.

Trivers, Robert L. 1971. 'The Evolution of Reciprocal Altruism'. *The Quarterly Review of Biology* 46: 35–57.

Troupeau, Gérard. 1954. 'La «Description de la Nubie» d'al-Uswānī (ive/xe siècle)'. *Arabica* 1: 276–88.

Tsakos, Alexandros. 2021. 'Medieval/Christian Nubia'. In *Oxford Research Encyclopedia of African History* (online), 1–30. Oxford: Oxford University Press.

———. 2023. 'Words on Warfare from Christian Nubia'. *Dotawo: A Journal of Nubian Studies* 8: 138–61.

Van Gerven Oei, Vincent W. J. 2011. 'The Old Nubian Memorial for King George'. In *Nubian Voices: Studies in Christian Nubian Culture*, edited by Adam Łajtar and Jacques Van der Vliet, 225–62. Supplements to the Journal of Juristic Papyrology 15. Warsaw: University of Warsaw.

———. 2021. *A Reference Grammar of Old Nubian*. Leuven: Peeters.

Vantini, Giovanni. 1970. 'Le Roi Kirki de Nubie à Baghdad: Un ou deux voyages?' In *Kunst und Geschichte Nubiens in christlicher Zeit*, edited by Erich Dinkler, 41–48. Recklinghausen: Aurel Bongers.

———. 1975. *Oriental Sources Concerning Nubia*. Heidelberg; Warsaw: Heidelberger Akademie der Wissenschaften; Polish Academy of Sciences.

———. 1981. *Christianity in the Sudan*. Bologna: EMI.

Vorderstrasse, Tasha. 2012. 'Coinage and the Monetary Economy in 7th Century Nubia'. In *Arab-Byzantine Coins and History*, edited by Tony Goodwin, 169–81. London: Archetype.

Wagner, Esther-Miriam. 2010. *Linguistic Variety of Judaeo-Arabic in Letters from the Cairo Genizah*. Leiden: Brill.

Wakin, Jeanette A. 1972. *The Function of Documents in Islamic Law: The Chapters of Sale from al-Ṭaḥāwī's Kitāb al-Šurūṭ al-Kabīr*. Albany: State University of New York Press.

Welsby, Derek A. 2002. *The Medieval Kingdoms of Nubia: Pagans, Christians and Muslims along the Middle Nile*. London: British Museum Press.

Wensinck, Arent J. 2012. 'Kunya'. In *Encyclopaedia of Islam* (online), edited by Peri Bearman, Thierry Bianquis, Clifford E. Bosworth, Emeri van Donzel, and Wolfhart P. Heinrichs. 2nd ed. Leiden: Brill. http://dx.doi.org/10.1163/1573-3912_islam_SIM_4526

Wiet, M. Gaston. 1971. *Catalogue général du Musée de l'art islamique du Caire: Inscriptions historiques sur pierre*. Cairo: Institut français d'archéologie orientale du Caire.

Williams, Bruce Beyer, and Geoff Emberling. 2020. 'Nubia, a Brief Introduction'. In *The Oxford Handbook of Ancient Nubia*, edited by Geoff Emberling and Bruce Beyer Williams, 1–4. Oxford: Oxford University Press.

Wojciechowski, Bartosz. 2011. 'The Old Nubian "Eparchal Archive" from Qasr Ibrim Reconsidered'. *Journal of Juristic Papyrology* 41: 265–92.

Yadin, Yigael, Jonas Greenfield, Ada Yardeni, and Baruch A. Levine. 2002. *The Documents from the Bar Kokhba Period in the Cave of Letters: Hebrew, Aramaic and Nabatean-Aramaic Papyri.* Jerusalem: Israel Exploration Society.

Yaron, Reuven. 1958. 'On Defension Clauses of Some Oriental Deeds of Sale and Lease from Mesopotamia and Egypt'. *Bibliotheca Orientalis* 15: 15–22.

Zarroug, Mohi el-Din Abdalla. 1991. *The Kingdom of Alwa.* Calgary: University of Calgary Press.

Zouache, Abbès. 2019. 'Remarks on the Blacks in the Fatimid Army, Tenth–Twelfth Century CE'. *Northeast African Studies* 19: 23–60.

Zieliński, Łukasz. 2015. 'New Insights into Nubian Archery'. *Polish Archaeology in the Mediterranean* 24 (1): 791–801.

Zyhlarz, Ernst. 1932. 'Neue Sprachdenkmäler des Altnubischen'. In *Studies Presented to F. Ll. Griffith*, 187–95. London: Egypt Exploration Society & Oxford University Press.

INDICES

Names of People (Referenced by Text and Line Number)

ʿAbd al-ʿAzīz ibn Ḥusnūn ibn ʿAlī (48r, witness, 10)
ʿAbd al-Bāqī (29r:6, 8, 17)
ʿAbd al-Ḥusayn ibn Muḥammad, known as Bū ʿAbd Allāh, ibn ʾIsmāʿīl ibn Ḥusayn ibn ʾAṣfar (48v:2)
ʿAbd al-Jalīl ibn Hibat Allāh ibn Makīn (52, witness, 3)
ʿAbd al-Karīm ibn al-Ḥasan (29v, address, left column, 1)
ʿAbd Allāh ibn ʿAbd Allāh ibn al-Ḥusayn ibn Maʿbad (46r, margin, 1)
ʿAbd Allāh ibn ʿAlī ibn al-Zubayr (2v, address, left column)
ʿAbd Allāh ibn Muḥammad ibn Tawfīq ibn Ḥusayn (47v:12–13)
ʿAbd al-Raḥmān (38r:6)
ʿĀbid al-Raḥmān (41:12)
ʾAbū ʿAbd Allāh (son of ʿAbd Allāh ibn ʿAlī ibn al-Zubayr) (21r:4)
ʾAbū ʿAbd Allāh ibn Rāʾiq the paper-merchant (*al-warrāq*) (34r:12)
ʾAbū ʿAbd Allāh Muḥammad ibn ʿAbd al-Raḥmān, the merchant, son-in-law (*ṣihr*) of the writer (ʾAbū al-Ṭanāʾ Ḥāmid al-Kanzī) (11r:3–4)
ʾAbū ʿAbd Allāh Muḥammad ibn Ḥaydara ibn al-Ḥusayn ibn al-Ḥasan al-Ḥusaynī (48r:8, 12, 13)
ʾAbū al-Ḍubāʿ (*ġarīmī* 'my creditor') (4r, margin; 4v:2)
ʾAbū al-Durr (28r, margin, 2)
ʾAbū al-Durr, my brother (39r:13)
ʾAbū al-Faḍl Muḥammad ibn al-Fātiḥ ibn ʿAbd Allāh al-Ḥusaynī, the prosperous and just judge, trust of the Kingdom (19v, address, left column)
ʾAbū al-Faḍl, judge, the cousin (*ibn ʿammī*) of ʿAbd Allāh ibn ʿAlī ibn al-Zubayr (21r:9, 13) | cf. ʾAbū al-Ḵayr ʾIbrāhīm ibn Muḥammad ibn al-Ḥusayn ibn Muḥammad ibn al-Zubayr, judge (47r:4)

ʾAbū al-Ḥasan (39r:14)
ʾAbū al-Ḥasan ʿAlī | son of the elder, the preacher ʾAbū al-Ṭāhir ʿUbayd Allāh ibn ʾAbī Turʿa (34v, address, right column, 1–2)
ʾAbū al-Ḥasan Zuhayr (53v, address, right column, 1)
ʾAbū al-Ḥusayn ʿAlī ibn ʾIbrāhīm ibn ʿAlī ibn Nahray (45:3)
ʾAbū al-Ḥusayn, the coppersmith (*al-naḥḥās*) (29v:2)
ʾAbū ʿAlī Muḥammad ibn Ḥaydara ibn al-Ḥusayn ibn al-Ḥasan al-Ḥusaynī, the noble preacher (*aš-šarīf al-ḵaṭīb*) (48r:8, 13)
ʾAbū al-Ḵayr ʾIbrāhīm ibn Muḥammad ibn al-Ḥusayn ibn Muḥammad ibn al-Zubayr, judge (47r:4; 47v:7–8)
ʾAbū al-Qāsim (39r:14)
ʾAbū al-Qāsim Hibat Allāh ibn Muḥammad ibn al-ʾAʿmā (29v, address, right column, 1–2)
ʾAbū al-Ṭāhir (17v, right column, 1)
ʾAbū al-Ṭāhir ibn Tarīk (9r:4, 6)
ʾAbū al-Ṭāhir ʿUbayd Allāh ibn ʾAbī Turʿa (34v, address, right column, 2) | father of ʾAbū Muḥsin ʿAlī
ʾAbū al-ʿUmar Hibat Allāh ibn al-Ḥasan ibn ʾIbrāhīm ibn Ṭalʿa (45:3)
ʾAbū al-Wālid ibn Ḥāḍir (30v:5)
ʾAbū Finjān the merchant, the son of Fakka (35v, address, right column, 1)
ʾAbū Ḥabīb (41:20)
ʾAbū ʾIsḥāq (34r, margin, 1)
ʾAbū Jaʿfar (39v:1)
ʾAbū Liṭāfa (34r, margin, 2)
ʾAbū Manṣūr Muḥammad (22v, left column, 3)
ʾAbū Manṣūr Mutawwaj, affiliated to al-ʿĀḍid, al-Ḥarasī (1v, left column, 4–5)
ʾAbū Muḥammad ʿĪsā ibn Muḥammad ibn Ḥasan (30v, address, right column, 1)
ʾAbū Nuʿm (34v:1, 6) | the elder Jalīl al-Dawla ʾAbū Nuʿm
ʾAbū Šākir (38r, margin, 1)

ʾAbū Turāb Ḥaydara ibn al-Ḥusayn ibn al-Ḥasan al-Ḥusaynī (48r:12)
ʾAḥmad ibn al-Ḥusayn ibn Muḥammad ibn Manṣūr (47r, witness, 4)
ʾAḥmad ibn Muḥammad ibn Ḥaydara ibn al-Ḥusayn ibn al-Ḥasan ibn al-Ḥasan al-Ḥusaynī (48v, witness, 3)
ʾAḥmad ibn Muḥammad ibn Yaḥyā ibn Maḥmūd ibn al-Šarīf (48r, witness, 1)
ʾAḥmad ibn Naṣr ibn Hibat Allāh ibn Ḥusayn ibn ʾAḥmad (45, witness, 1)
ʿAjlān (31v:7)
al-ʾĀmir (44r:6) | excellent and valid Egyptian gold coins of al-ʾĀmir
al-Bazīl, deputy of the eparch Darmā (26r:2; 26v, address, right column, 1)
al-Ḥasan ibn ʿAlī ibn Zayd (48r, witness, 12)
al-Ḥasan ibn Muḥammad ibn Mahdī (48r, witness, 3)
al-Ḥusayn ibn Muḥammad [ ] ibn Naṣr [ ] (20v, left column, 1)
al-Ḥusayn ibn Muḥammad ibn al-Ḥusayn ibn ʾIsḥāq ibn Naṣr (48r, witness, 5)
ʿAlī (33:8; 34r:3)
ʿAlī (39v:1)
ʿAlī ibn ʿUbayd Allāh ibn Muḥammad ibn Turkī (47v:11)
ʿAlī ibn Muḥammad ibn al-Rabīʿ (48r, witness, 14)
ʿAlī ibn Muṣʿab (35v, address, left column, 1)
ʿAlī ibn ʿUbayd Allāḥ ibn ʿAlī ibn Šarīk (45, witness clause, 2)
ʿAlī ibn ʿUbayd Allāh ibn Muḥammad ibn Šākir (48v, witness, 7)
ʿAlī, the elder (39r:15)
al-Makārim (15r:14)
al-nūba the Nubians (23r:7; 30r, side margin, 8)
al-Qarṭamaq Mašal al-Farīk (36v, address, right column, 1)
al-Qirṭimī (18r:7)
ʾAmākī ibn ʾAbrām (46v, witness clause, 1)
Andrea ibn ʾIstaruskurā (46v:14)
Angešoura ibn Merki (46r, witness, 12)

ʿAwn ibn ʿAbd Allāh ibn Maʿbad (46v:9)
Badr (41:20)
Banū Farwa (34r, margin, 2)
Basil (king) (21r:10)
Bazilī (24r:7; 24v:4)
Bišr (*ġulām*) (20r:4)
Bū al-ʿĪd (41:21)
Bū Ḥasan (39v, address, left column, 2)
Danī ibn Kinān (38v, address, right column, 1)
Danī ibn Kinān al-Šaḵriyābī (44r:2)
Darmā (23r:9; 26v, address, right column, 2)
David (king) (21r:12)
Faḵr al-ʿArab ʾIbrāhīm Kanz al-Dawla (28v, address, left column, 2)
Faḵr ibn Furayj ibn Mīnā al-ʾIsamnāwī (46v:3)
Faraj | one of the sons of Kajja (*ʾawlād Kajja*) (11r:4)
Ġalyūn ibn Sulaymān al-Kanzī (46v:2)
Ġalyūn ibn Sulaymān ibn Ġalyūn (46r:7)
Ḥajjāj (38r:5)
Ḥajjāj the son (*walad*) of Misrad (36r, margin, 1–2)
Ḥamdān (30r:9)
Ḥasan ibn Hibat Allāh ibn Ṭalāq ibn Fāris (51r, witness, 4–5)
Ḥasan ibn Šujāʿ al-Dawla ʾIsḥāq (8r:4)
Ḥaydara ibn ʿAlī ibn Muḥammad (48r, witness, 6)
Ḥaydara ibn Muḥammad ibn Ḥaydara ibn al-Ḥusayn ibn al-Ḥasan al-Ḥusaynī (48v, witness, 5)
Ḥaydara ibn Muḥammad ibn Jamāʿa (51r, witness, 1; 52, witness, 5–6)
Hibat Allāh ibn ʾIbrāhīm ibn ʿAbd al-Raḥmān al-Qulzumī (19r:4)
Hibat Allāh ibn Makīn (49r:2; 51r:2; 53v, address, left column, 1)
Ḥiṣn al-Dawla, *ʾamīr* (28r:1) | cf. Ibn al-ʿAsqalānī, Ḥiṣn al-Dawla (13v, address)
Ḥusayn (35r:10)

Ḥusayn ibn Ḥasan al-Kanzī (brother of Lāmiʿ)
Ibn al-ʿAsqalānī (9r:26; 9v:4, 5, 10, 16, 17)
Ibn al-ʿAsqalānī, Ḥiṣn al-Dawla (13v, address)
Ibn ʿImrān (16r:15)
ʾIbrāhīm (17r:4)
ʾIbrāhīm ibn ʿAbd al-Raḥmān (27v, address, left column, 2), the father of a *ḵalīfa*
ʾIbrāhīm ibn ʾAḥmad ibn ʾIbrāhīm ibn Naṣr (47r, witness, 1)
ʾIbrāhīm ibn ʿAlī ibn Muḥammad ibn ʾAbī Jaʿfar (48v, witness, 10)
ʾIbrāhīm ibn Ḥasan ibn Muḥammad (49r, witness, 1)
Ipisi (*ġulām*) (14r:8; 16r:3)
ʾIsmāʿīl (41:21)
Īsū (19v, address, right column, 1; 20v, address, right column, 2; 27r:3; 51r:4; 51v:2)
Īsūy (52:2, 5)
Jaʿfar (30r, side margin, 9)
Jajrī (servant) (22r:13)
Jalīl al-Dawla ʾAbū Nuʿm (34v:1, 6)
Jāmiʿ (37v, address, left column, 2)
Jawhar (*ġulām*) (4r:4)
Kabān (servant) (22r:13)
Kablām (*ġulām*) (9r:24)
Kajja | the sons of Kajja (*ʾawlād Kajja*) (11r:4)
Ḵalīfa ibn Ḥasan, by order of (30v, address, left column, 2)
Kāmil ibn Ḵamīs ibn ʾIbrāhīm (46r, margin, 2)
Kanz al-Dawla (1v, address, left column, 3; 2v, address, left column, 4; 4v:2; 7v, address, left column, 2; 8v, address, left column, 3; 12r:4; 15r:8; 26v, address, left column, 2; 29r:5; 32:2; 33:2, 4, 7, 8, 9; 46r:3) → ʾAbū Manṣūr Mutawwaj, Faḵr al-ʿArab, Naṣr
Kanūna (woman) (36v:3)
Kayl ibn Mariane (49r:13, 15)
Khalīl (37r:2; 37v:11, 14, address, right column, 1)

Lāmiʿ (16r:5; 33:1)

Lāmiʿ ibn Ḥasan (9v, address) | Manṣūr, son of Lāmiʿ ibn Ḥasan (30v, address, left column, 1–2; 36v, address, left column, 1–2)

Maḥbūb (41:20)

Maḥmūd (34r:10; 34v:2, 5)

Makārim | one of the sons of Kajja (*ʾawlād Kajja*) (11r:4)

Manṣūr (38r:7)

Manṣūr, son of Lāmiʿ ibn Ḥasan (30v, address, left column, 1–2)

Mariane ibn Īsū/Īsūy the Nubian (51r:4, 15; 52:2, 4)

Marīḵura (*ġulāmī*) (4v:1; 6r:4; 9v:19)

Maryam ibnat Yuḥannis the Nubian (49r:7, 9; 49v:8; 50:8–9; 51r:4; 51v:2; 52:2)

Mašal Ankara, the agent (*ḵalīfa*) (36r:2)

Mena Kurē, son of king Mūyis (21r:10)

Merki ibn Abrām (47r:3; 47v:1, 7)

Mubārak, the freedman of the most powerful commander, Saʿd al-Dawla (46v, witness clause, 6)

Mufliḥ (35r:5)

Muḥammad (39r:14; 41:19)

Muḥammad ibn ʿAbd Allāh ibn Maʿbad (46v:9)

Muḥammad ibn ʾAbū Ḥayy (38v, address, left column, 1)

Muḥammad ibn ʿAlī ibn ʿAbd al-Raḥmān ibn Bū al-Ḵayr (48r, witness, 8)

Muḥammad ibn Ḥusayn ibn ʿAlī (47v:5)

Muḥammad ibn Jamāʿa (52, witness, 1)

Muḥammad ibn Ramaḍān al-Ḥājj (15v, address, left column, 2)

Muḥammad ibn ʿUbayd Allāh ibn al-Ḥasan ibn ʿAlī (34v, address, left column, 2)

Muḥammad ibn Yaḥyā ibn ʾIbrāhīm al-ʾAnṭākī (47v:19)

Muḥammad ibn Yaḥyā ibn ʾIbrāhīm al-Ḥusaynī (48v, witness, 1)

Muḥammad, known as ʾAbū ʿAbd Allāh ibn ʾIsmāʿīl ibn Ḥusayn ibn ʾIbrāhīm ibn Ḥusayn ibn ʾIbrāhīm ibn ʾAṣfar ibn Maymūn ibn Baydūs ibn Basūn (48r:2, 48v:3)
Muḥibb | one of the sons of Kajja (*ʾawlād Kajja*) (11r:4)
Muḥsin (*ġulām* ?) (16v:3)
Munʿim (*ġulām*) (2r:4)
Muʾnisa the Christian woman (46r:19)
Muslim ibn Jamāʿa (51r, witness, 2)
Mūyis (king) (21r:10)
Muzakkī (servant ?) (23r:4)
Naṣr ibn al-ʾamīr Kanz al-Dawla (7v, address, left column, 1–2)
Nūr al-Dīn, judge (*al-qāḍī*) (30r:15–16)
Oua (*ḳādim*) (6r:4)
Papa (*ḳādim*) (7r:8)
Qāʾid (39r:15)
Qāsim (31r:8)
Qāsim (son of ʿAbd Allāh ibn ʿAlī ibn al-Zubayr) (21r:3)
Qerqe/Qeorqe/Jurayj ibn Yuḥannis (49v:6, 8, 11, 13; 50:2; 53r:3)
Qilādī ibn Mawlā (46r, margin, 4)
Raḥma ibn Saʿīd (44r:2)
Ramaḍān (*ġulāmī*) (30r, side margin, 7)
Rāšid (*al-baḥḥār*) (30r, side margin, 7)
Saʿāda (*al-qāʾid*) (1r:3; 10r:4, 9)
Ṣabīra (39r:15)
Ṣāliḥ (30r:9)
Šarīf (*ġulāmī*) (7r:4)
Sayyid (41:19)
Shīrkūh, the military commander (*sālār*) (6r:7)
Sirāj, son of Mario, the Christian, al-Muqurrī (45:3–4)
Sitt (34v, note 1)
Šudā ibn ʾAbrām (46v:10)
Ṭāʿī (30r:6, side margin, 16; 30v:1)

ʿUbayd (33:4) | I, God willing, shall go to ʿUbayd, Treasure of the Dynasty (Kanz al-Dawla), the Greatest of the Progeny, the Noble One
ʿUbayd (41:12)
ʿUbayd Allāh ibn ʿAbd Allāh ibn Maʿbad (46v:9)
ʿUbayd Allāh ibn ʿAzzām (38r, margin, 3)
ʿUbayd Allāh ibn Ḥasan, the trader (*al-jallāb*) (47r:2; 47v:2)
ʿUbayd Allāh, secretary of Uruwī (27r:18)
ʿUbayd Allāh ʿAlī (27v, address, right column, 1–2)
ʿUmar (37r:3; 37v, address, right column, 1)
ʾUmm al-Ḥasan ibnat ʿAlī ibn ʾAḥmad ibn Ḥusayn ibn ʾIbrāhīm ibn Ḥusayn ibn ʾAṣfar ibn Maymūn ibn Baydūs ibn Basūn (48r:2–3; 48v:4)
ʿUqayl al-ʿAjmānī (27r:13)
Uruwī (1v, address, right column, 2; 2v, address, right column, 3; 3v, address, right column, 2; 4v, address, right column, 1; 5v, address, right column, 2; 6v, address, right column, 2; 7v, address, right column, 2; 8v, address, right column, 2; 10v, address, right column, 2; 11v, address, right column, 2; 12v, address, right column, 2; 13v, address, right column, 2; 15v, address, right column, 3; 16v, address, right column, 1; 17v, address, left column, 2)
ʿUthmān (37r:2; 37v, address, right column, 2)
Yaḥyā (39r:15)
Yaḥyā (*ġulāmī*) (22r:18; 22v:8)
Yūsū (servant?) (25r:10; 25v:4, 11)
Yūsuf ibn Jamāʿa al-Qulzumī (51r, witness, 6)
Zakiyya (34v, note 2)

Names of Places (Referenced by Text and Line Number)

ʾAbū Fāris (island) (44r:3)
Adminna (21r:25)
Akmīm (53v:4)
al-Marāġa (53v, address, left column, 2)
Aswan (5r:6; 19r:3; 20v:1; 23r:9; 30r:12; 31r:5, margin, 1, 3; 36r:3; 37r:5; 37v:5; 45:19; 46r:18; 48r:12, 13)
baḥrī northern (2r:8; 24r:8; 24v:1) | *al-bilād al-baḥriyya, bilād baḥrī* northern land (24v:3; 38r:5)
Bilāq (45:7)
Darmus (18r:7)
Dendūr (20v:1; 46r:4)
Dongola (21r:16)
Edfu (اتفو) (38r:9)
Egypt (*Miṣr*) (6r:9; 25v:13)
Erkinun (21r:4)
Fāris (31r, margin, 2)
Hindāw (46r:15)
Ibrīm (1v, address, right column, 2; 3v, address, right column, 2; 7v, address, right column, 2; 8v, address, right column, 2; 9v, address, right column, 2; 12v, address, right column, 2; 21r:25; 22v, address, right column, 2; 25r:12; 26r:2; 29r:2; 29v, address, left column, 2; 30r:6, 8, 10; 30v:3, address, right column, 2; 35v, address, 2)
Island of Michael (*Jazīrat Mikāʾīl*) (45:7, 9)
ḵān caravanserai (34r:8, 10)
Kurkur (30r:7; 30v:3)
Marīs (2v, address, right column, 3; 7v, address, right column, 2; 10v, address, right column, 2; 11r:6; 14v, address, right column, 2; 15v, address, right column, 3; 16v, address, right column, 2; 17v, ad-

dress, left column, 3; 19v, address, right column, 2; 21r:2; 21v, address, right column, 2; 24v, address, 2; 31r:5, 6; 38v, address, right column, 1)
maslaḥa armed garrison post (19r:6)
Migin (Nubia) (19v, address, right column, 2; 22v, right column, 2)
Murwā (46v:7)
Nūba | *balad al-Nūba* the land of Nubia (20r:4, 7; 39r:7; 46r:11)
qalʿa citadel (1v, address, right column, 2; 3v, address, 3, 2; 9v, address, right column, 2; 12v, address, right column, 2; 30r:8; 37v:17)
qiblī southern | *al-bilād al-qibliyya* the southern land (16r:7)
Qūṣ (15r:12; 22r:14)
rabaḍ al-Beja the dwelling place of the Beja (46r:18)
Semna (46v:3)
Soba (21r:11, 14; 30r:7; 39r:4, 9, 11)
Šabb Šalūl (46v:6)
ṯaġr border (5r:6), *ṯaġr ʾAswān* border of Aswan (19r:3; 45:19)
Tuška (35v, address, 2)

General Index (Referenced by Page Number)

Abbasid, 9–10, 19, 85, 87, 150, 161, 364
ʿabd, 239, 241–243
ʿAbd al-Bāqī, 138, 210, 462–463
ʿAbd al-Ḥusayn, 170, 592
ʿAbd al-Karīm ibn al-Ḥasan, 132, 464
ʿAbd Allāh, 4–5, 5 n. 2, 72–76, 78, 83, 91–92, 94–96, 165, 167, 169, 205, 216, 222, 232, 239, 248, 344, 353, 401, 413, 416, 497, 566, 571, 581–582, 587, 589, 592
ʿAbd Allāh ibn al-Qāḍī al-Rašīd ʿAlī ibn al-Zubayr, 74–76, 91–92, 94–95, 165, 205, 222, 232, 416
ʿAbd Allāh ibn Saʿd ibn ʾAbī Sarḥ, 4–5
ʾAbū ʿAbd Allāh, 75–76, 91
ʾAbū ʿAbd Allāh Muḥammad, 72, 83, 169, 216, 353, 589

ʾAbū ʿAbd Allāh Muḥammad ibn ʿAbd al-Raḥmān, 83, 353
ʾAbū ʿAbd Allāh Muḥammad ibn Ḥaydara ibn al-Ḥusayn ibn al-Ḥasan al-Ḥusaynī, 169, 216, 589
ʾAbū al-Ḍubāʿ, 106, 112, 235, 239, 244, 312
ʾAbū al-Faḍl, 60, 73, 75–76, 78, 91, 205, 232, 401, 413–414
ʾAbū al-Faḍl Muḥammad ibn al-Fātiḥ ibn ʿAbd Allāh al-Ḥusaynī, 78, 232, 401
ʾAbū al-Faḍl Muḥammad ibn Ḥusayn, 75
ʾAbū al-Fatḥ Naṣr, 72
ʾAbū al-Ḥasan Zuhayr, 182, 622
ʾAbū al-Ḥasan ʿAlī, 74, 132, 498
ʾAbū al-Ḥasan ʿAlī ibn ʾAbū al-Ṭāhir ʿUbayd Allāh ibn ʾAbī Turʿa, 74, 132, 498
ʾAbū al-Ḥusayn ʿAlī, 72, 156, 555
ʾAbū al-Ḥusayn ʿAlī ibn ʾIbrāhīm ibn ʿAlī ibn Nahray, 156, 555
ʾAbū ʿAlī Muḥammad ibn Ḥaydara ibn al-Ḥusayn ibn al-Ḥasan al-Ḥusaynī, 168–169, 588–589
ʾAbū al-ʿIzz Mutawwaj, 72
ʾAbū al-Ḵayr, 54, 60, 77–78, 164–165, 232, 248, 300, 328, 378, 401, 407, 447, 577, 581
ʾAbū al-Ḵayr ʾIbrāhīm ibn Muḥammad ibn al-Ḥusayn ibn Muḥammad ibn al-Zubayr, 164, 232, 248, 577, 581
ʾAbū al-Makārim Hibat Allāh, 32, 72, 160, 208, 563
ʾAbū al-Qāsim Hibat Allāh ibn Muḥammad ibn al-ʾAʿmā, 132, 207, 464
ʾAbū al-Ṭāhir, 74, 78, 105–106, 119–120, 236, 340–341, 391, 498, 539
ʾAbū al-Ṭāhir ibn Tarīk, 74, 119, 236, 340
ʾAbū al-Ṭāhir ʿUbayd Allāh ibn ʾAbī Turʿa, 74, 498
ʾAbū al-Ṯanāʾ Ḥāmid, 73, 77, 355
ʾAbū al-ʿUmar Hibat Allāh ibn al-Ḥasan ibn ʾIbrāhīm ibn Ṭalʿa, 156, 554

ʾAbū al-Wālid ibn Ḥāḍir, 211, 474
ʾAbū Fāris, 133, 145, 230, 549
ʾAbū Finjān ibn Fakka, 132, 502
Abu Hamed, 3
ʾAbū Ḥanīfa, 152
ʾAbū Manṣūr ʿAjīl, 73–74, 78, 205, 207
ʾAbū Manṣūr Mutawwaj, 72, 77, 294
ʾAbū Muḥammad ʿĪsā ibn Muḥammad ibn Ḥasan, 132, 475
ʾAbū Rakwa, 32
ʾAbū Ṭālib, 169, 216
ʾAbū Turāb Ḥaydara ibn al-Ḥusayn ibn al-Ḥasan al-Ḥusaynī, 169, 233, 589
ʾAbū Yūsuf Yaʿqūb, 152
accusative, 58
acknowledgement, 46, 79, 148, 150, 160, 162, 164, 170, 175, 177–178, 232, 549, 556–557, 566, 572–573, 575, 578–579, 583, 588–591, 593–595, 600, 603–604, 609–610, 615
Adama, 67
Adiminne, 412
Adiminnen, 412
Adminna, 93, 412, 415
Adminne, 412
advance consignment, 131, 138, 210, 462
agent, 35, 38, 83, 94, 104, 222, 255, 406
ʿAkaša, 89
Akkadian, 153
Aḵmīm, 169, 183, 233, 621
al-ʿĀḍid, 50, 52, 54, 186, 294, 333, 447, 556
al-ʾAfḍal, 34, 97, 148
al-ʾĀmir, 75, 122–123, 186, 232, 549, 577, 581
al-ʾAswānī, 4–5, 5 n. 2, 8, 10–11, 13, 42, 61, 69, 75, 85–88, 111, 135, 219, 232, 253, 256, 261, 331 n. 2, 399, 555 n. 1
al-Bazīl, 51, 78, 117, 127, 445–447
al-bilād al-baḥriyya, 69
al-bilād al-qibliyya, 69, 382 n. 1
al-Ḥāfiẓ, 75, 186, 206, 571
al-Ḥākim, 32–33, 38
al-Ḥanafī, 72–73, 298, 301
al-Ḥusayn ibn Muḥammad, 74–75, 78, 164, 232, 248, 407, 577, 579, 590, 592
ʿAlī, 64, 72–78, 91–92, 130, 132, 142, 156, 165, 167–

169, 205, 208, 216, 222, 232, 254–255, 301, 416, 454, 490, 496, 498, 502, 524–525, 555, 557, 569, 581–582, 587–590, 593–595
ʿAlī ibn Muḥammad, 208, 590, 595
ʿAlī ibn Muṣʿab, 132, 502
al-islāmiyya, 86, 157, 555
al-jallāb, 164
al-Kanzī, 73, 77–78, 80, 85, 90, 130–132, 160, 163, 209, 211–212, 220, 222–223, 233, 307, 313, 319, 324, 345, 350, 355, 360, 372, 385, 507, 570
al-Maʾmūn, 85, 123
al-Marāġa, 182–183, 619, 622
al-Marġīnānī, 154
al-Muqurra, 4, 12, 12 n. 11, 68–70, 156
al-Mustanṣir, 186–187, 587, 608
al-Muʿtaṣim, 10, 87
Alodia, 3–4, 8, 12, 69–70, 98–101
aloes, 195, 199, 203, 463
al-Qāḍī al-Rašīd ʾAḥmad, 74, 92
al-Qarṭamaq Mašal al-Farīk, 132, 507
al-Qaṣr, 6 n. 3, 37, 86–87, 146, 219, 331 n. 2, 399
al-raʾīs, 82, 233
al-Šaḵriyābī, 145–146, 548–549
al-Saraḵsī, 154
al-Ṭaḥāwī, 152 n. 2, 153, 155, 162
alum, 104, 198–199, 341
ʿAlwa, 4–5, 5 n. 2, 6 n. 3, 8, 12, 44, 69–70, 99
ʾamīr, 5, 31, 64, 71–74, 76, 90, 112, 123, 129, 133, 205–215, 223, 227–228, 234, 298
ʿĀmir, 63
Ampapa, 562
Ampātā, 161, 258, 564
ʿAmr ibn al-ʿĀṣ, 4
ʾAmšīr, 157, 555
Andaandi, 34
Andrea ibn ʾIstaruskurā, 570, 573
Andreas, 570
Angešouda, 570
Ankarou, 505
ʿaqīd, 145, 230
Aramaic, 153
ʿarʿar, 195, 200

ʾ*arbāb al-suyūf*, 215
Argíin, 91, 412
Argîn, 91
Arginē, 412
Argini, 412
Arginī, 412
Arminna, 412, 501
Arminne, 412
Armínney, 412
army, 12, 34, 37, 37 n. 8, 45, 64–66, 89–90, 97, 99, 102, 134, 198, 202, 205, 212, 230, 255, 261, 282, 294, 333, 364, 421, 447, 524, 545, 545 n. 1
aromatic oil, 198–199, 341
Aroua, 4
Arqin, 91
Asouwil, 55
Assyrian, 153
Aswan, 1–3, 5–6, 6 n. 3, 8, 13, 16, 21, 23, 31–33, 35, 38, 44, 46, 52, 69–70, 73, 75, 85–86, 95, 105, 108, 110–111, 113, 116, 129, 137, 140, 156, 158, 160–161, 163, 168–169, 172, 182–183, 202, 219, 227, 235, 241, 243, 245, 249, 254, 259–260, 298, 317, 331 n. 2, 400, 405–406, 427, 427 n. 4, 469, 471, 479–480, 506, 512–513, 537, 555, 557, 562, 564, 569, 586, 589
Aswan High Dam, 16
Asyūṭ, 183
Atbara, 3
Athanasios, 19
auction, 228
ʿAyḏāb, 32, 202
Ayyubid, 12–13, 33, 187, 193
Babylonian, 153
Bactrian, 257
bag, 106, 187, 196, 199–200, 345, 513
bahārij, 189
Bahrām, 206
Banū al-Kanz, 32–34, 71–73, 76, 131, 208, 261, 298
Banū Ḥanīfa, 73, 298
baqṭ, 4–5, 7, 7 n. 4, 8–10, 10 n. 7, 11, 11 n. 8, 13, 19–20, 33–35, 37, 41–43, 65, 70, 85, 94, 104, 136
Baramhāt, 148, 157–158, 518, 555–556
barrāya, 195, 201
baseline, 265 n. 2
Basil, 51, 97–98, 98 n. 18, 205, 250, 414
Basileios, 433

basket, 190, 195, 197, 199, 202, 366, 501, 545
basmala, 115, 141, 148, 158, 166, 178, 268, 495, 500–501
Baṭn al-Ḥajar, 88–89
Baybars al-Bunduqdārī, 11
Baydūs, 167, 586–587
Bayuda, 100
beads, 196, 199, 463, 513
bed, 195, 199, 250–251, 300, 464
bedding, 197, 199, 511, 513
Beja, 4–5, 5 n. 2, 11, 32, 564
belt, 176, 176 n. 11, 198–199, 601
Bilāq, 86, 88, 146, 157, 193, 555
bishop, 19, 27, 93–94, 136, 212–213, 229–230, 249, 343–344
Bišr, 106, 238, 240, 404–405
Bīstū, 69
bitumen, 102, 106, 109, 138, 187, 198–199, 231, 240, 345, 405–406, 545
Blemmyes, 4
blessings, 115, 121, 123, 126, 143–144, 293, 300, 307, 313, 318, 324, 327, 332, 345, 349, 354, 360, 372, 400, 406, 415, 422, 436, 444, 447, 457, 470, 481, 486, 491, 507
Blue and White Niles, 1, 3, 99
boat, 46, 81, 84, 86, 88–89, 111, 113, 115, 129, 139–140, 156–157, 193, 253, 259–260, 305, 317–318, 513, 551, 553, 555–556
Bosnian, 17, 26, 26 n. 5, 27
box, 106, 187, 198–199, 345
brass, 197, 200, 463
bridal gift, 166–167, 170, 173–174, 593
broker, 105, 109, 227–228, 236, 341
Bū Ḥasan, 132, 525
bunāk, 195, 201
burd, 110, 195, 202, 413
butter, 108, 198–199, 341
Byzantine, 2–4, 9, 52, 66
Cairo, 21, 23–27, 37 n. 8, 151
Cairo Museum, 23–25, 27
calico, 196, 199, 317–318
caliph, 10, 32, 50, 75–76, 85, 87, 122–123, 205–206, 232
camel, 81, 102, 104, 111, 141, 239, 244, 327, 471, 473
camphor, 196, 199, 203, 341
candles, 198–199, 463
caravanserai, 141, 496

cardamon, 195, 199, 203, 341, 545
cartham seed, 138, 197, 199, 545
cash, 39, 84, 103–104, 106, 110, 139, 182, 185, 187–188, 226, 236, 251, 345, 366, 407, 415, 443, 454, 491, 505, 507, 518, 582
cataract, 1–3, 9, 14–15, 42–43, 64, 69, 85–89, 95, 111, 146, 151, 156–157, 191–192, 253, 261, 399, 469, 569
cathedral, 13, 17, 27, 98 n. 18
chain of gold coins, 198–199, 479, 481
Chalcedonian, 101
Christianity, 2–3
cinnamon, 197, 199, 203, 341, 463
civet cats, 198, 201, 461
cloak, 176, 196, 198–199, 544, 601
cloth, 30–31, 91, 108, 112, 176, 176 n. 12, 180, 195–196, 199–201, 236, 238, 246, 298, 312, 317–318, 413, 480, 496, 539, 555, 601, 611
cloth-merchants, 108
clothing, 174, 174 n. 9, 176 n. 13, 197–199, 443, 480, 599
combs, 180, 197, 200, 611
commission, 84, 109, 226, 405, 454
commodities, 14, 32, 35, 37, 40–41, 102, 104, 106, 108–110, 132, 136–138, 182, 185, 195–203, 228
consensual separation, 174, 178
Constantine, 66
Coptic, 2, 8, 9 n. 6, 13 n. 13, 15, 18–19, 21, 27, 29, 58, 68–69, 100–101, 147–148, 157, 489, 548, 555, 586
Coptic patriarchate, 2
costus (aromatic plant), 197, 200, 341, 543
cotton, 30, 138, 190, 197, 200, 436 n. 3, 501
credit, 138, 463
Crusaders, 12, 260
cubit, 161, 163, 564, 571
currency, 39, 44, 185, 187, 192
currency zone, 44
Dahomey, 42, 253
Damādim, 101
Damascus, 168, 178
damk, 195, 202, 512

Dani, 517
Danī ibn Kannān, 132–133, 145–146, 148, 151, 230, 519, 548–550
dār al-ḥarb, 5
dār al-ʾIslām, 5
Darfur, 2, 103
Darmā, 49, 51–52, 60, 78, 99, 127, 221, 227, 233, 243, 427 n. 6, 445, 447
Darme, 51–55
Darmus, 281, 394, 396
Dauti, 54
David, 43, 53–55, 92, 96–98, 100, 205, 414
Debeira West, 43, 433
debt, 36, 46, 83, 106, 153, 164–165, 181–182, 248, 323, 353–354, 389, 395, 540, 575, 577–579, 581, 587, 608, 615
Demotic, 18
Dendur, 110, 160, 405–406, 562–563
deputy, 32, 49, 51, 56, 61, 66, 78, 83, 93, 117, 127, 221–224, 227, 232–233, 268–269, 271, 293, 307, 319, 324, 333, 342, 345, 355, 360, 382, 384, 415, 445–447
digraph, 50, 56, 58, 370
ḏimmī, 6
dīnār, 84, 90, 103–106, 109–111, 114, 138, 157, 164–165, 167–168, 170–171, 173, 179, 181–182, 185–191, 195, 202, 226, 228, 236, 239–240, 248, 259, 341–342, 344, 405, 442–444, 454, 462–463, 539–540, 543–545, 549, 556, 571, 577–578, 581–582, 587, 593, 599, 608, 614–615
Diocletian, 2, 9
diplomatic relations, 33, 35, 41
dirham, 104–106, 109, 111, 138, 185, 187–191, 195, 202, 341, 345, 405, 442–443, 501, 537–540, 543–544
dīwān al-ʾiqṭāʿāt, 146
domestikos, 52, 69
Dongola, 3, 3 n. 1, 4, 8, 11, 13, 19, 32, 34, 42, 44–45, 61, 70, 88–89, 91, 95, 99–100, 111, 261, 414
Dongolawi, 34
Dotawo, 4, 101

dowry, 174, 174 n. 10, 176, 237, 593, 599
drinking vessel, 195, 199, 366
dual, 47, 255, 469, 554
dyed garment, 139, 197, 200, 251, 506
dyer, 141, 496
Egypt, 1–2, 4, 6, 10–12, 14–15, 17–20, 22 n. 3, 25, 31–32, 34–35, 38–39, 41, 44–47, 68, 97, 133, 145, 148, 151, 155, 169, 182–183, 187–188, 191–193, 202, 206–207, 212–217, 220–221, 230, 233, 253–256, 257 n. 1, 258, 260–261, 323, 383 n. 2, 427 n. 5, 444, 485 n. 1, 589, 619
Egypt Exploration Society, 17–18
Egyptian Arabic, 282, 353, 419, 425
Egyptian hieroglyphs, 18
eikšil, 56–57, 59, 88
entrepreneur, 13–14, 38–39
eparch, 9 n. 6, 13, 13 n. 13, 19, 29–32, 34–36, 38–47, 49–127, 129, 132–136, 143–144, 191, 205, 207, 209–213, 215–218, 220–226, 226 n. 3, 227–229, 231, 233–237, 239, 241–244, 246–247, 250–251, 254–255, 258, 260–261, 267–269, 271, 291, 295, 303, 305 n. 1, 306–307, 309, 315, 317, 321, 325–326, 329, 335, 347, 351, 354 n. 1, 357, 361, 369, 373, 375, 379, 387, 389, 393, 397, 399, 403–404, 409, 417, 419–420, 423, 426 n. 2, 431, 433, 437, 445, 449, 451–454, 471
eparchal house, 29
Eratosthenes, 2
Erkinun, 91, 93, 222, 412–413, 415
eunuch, 245
excavation, 12, 17–18, 21–27, 88, 134, 191, 291, 295, 303, 309, 315, 321, 325, 329, 335, 347, 351, 357, 361, 369, 373, 379, 387, 393, 397, 403, 409, 417, 423, 431, 437, 445, 449, 455, 459, 465, 477, 483, 487, 493, 499, 503, 509, 515, 521, 527, 529, 533, 541, 547, 551, 559, 575, 583, 597, 603, 605, 613, 617
fabric, 197, 200, 359, 366

Fakr al-ʿArab Hibat Allāh, 72
Fakr al-ʿArab ʾIbrāhīm, 72–73
Fakr ibn Furayj ibn Mīnā al-ʾIsamnāwī, 163, 571
Faras, 3, 69, 93 n. 14, 98 n. 18, 570
faras, 140, 195, 200
Fāris, 133, 145, 172, 230, 479–480, 549, 598, 610
Fatḥ, 72, 141, 496
Fatimid, 8, 11–12, 20–21, 32–35, 37–38, 41, 44, 46, 50, 64, 70–71, 74–76, 87–88, 90, 92–93, 95, 97, 102, 104, 122–123, 138, 145–149, 158–159, 164, 171, 187–191, 193, 205, 207, 212, 214–216, 219, 230, 242, 250, 254–256, 259, 261, 269, 269 n. 3, 270
firāš, 195, 199
fire wood, 180, 196
fragrant herbs, 195, 200, 538
frankincense, 196, 200, 203, 543
freedman, 137, 164–165, 206, 208, 220, 232, 247–248, 254, 293, 474–475, 481, 502, 572, 577, 581
funerary stelae, 15
fur, 198, 200, 463
Fusṭāṭ, 151, 155, 256
Ġalyūn ibn Sulaymān ibn Ġalyūn, 160, 163, 563, 565, 570
garrison, 15, 17, 20, 44, 80, 86–87, 108, 219–220, 249, 399–400
genitive, 59–60, 71, 281, 394, 420
Genizah, 37 n. 8, 38 n. 9, 188–190, 203, 216, 228, 237, 256, 258, 269 n. 3
Georgi, 172
Georgios, 172
Gezira, 3
gift, 7, 9, 35–36, 36 n. 7, 37–38, 40–43, 45–46, 99, 102, 104, 107–108, 111–112, 166–167, 170–171, 173–174, 235–236, 256, 312, 366, 414, 513, 593
gift exchange, 36, 36 n. 7, 37–38, 40–42, 45–46, 256
ġilāla, 195, 202
Giorke, 601
ġirbāl, 195, 201
glass, 102, 191, 198, 200, 463
gold, 32, 104, 106, 109, 111, 165, 185–188, 190–191, 195, 198–199, 201, 443, 464, 479, 481, 505, 539,

549, 556, 571, 577, 581, 587, 608
governor, 6, 10, 19, 32–35, 61, 66, 68, 70, 80, 90, 97, 116, 205–206, 216–218, 220, 301, 328, 350, 372, 378, 385, 391, 401, 413, 415, 421–422, 436, 481
gravestones, 43, 85, 586
Greek, 2–4, 8–9, 15, 18, 27, 32, 57, 67, 69, 88, 100, 153, 225, 226 n. 3
guardian, 156, 167–168, 179, 554, 556–557, 607, 609
ġulām, 47, 81, 89, 102, 137, 237–240, 242, 248, 311 n. 2
ḥabba, 185
hāl, 195, 199, 203
ḥalāwa, 195, 202
ḥallat šarb, 195, 199
ḥalqa, 195, 201
ḥamdala, 126, 144
Ḥāmid, 73, 77, 219–220, 251, 306, 350, 355
hamza, 278, 289, 440
hamzat al-qaṭʿ, 279
ḥaqq ʿayn, 104, 106, 110, 139, 187
ḥaraš, 195, 199
ḥarīr, 198, 201
Ḥasan al-Qāḍī al-Muhaḏḏab, 75–76
ḥasbala, 127, 144
ḥaṣīra, 180, 196, 200
ḥaṭab, 180, 196, 202
head-cloth, 176, 180, 196, 200, 601, 611
helmet, 65, 65 n. 8, 134, 196, 200, 278, 481, 511, 513
Heraclius, 7
herbs, 102, 108, 136, 138, 195, 198, 200, 202, 463, 538
Hibat Allāh, 32, 72, 75–76, 92, 99, 132, 156, 160, 172, 179–180, 182–183, 207–208, 233, 400, 414, 452, 464, 554, 557, 563, 598, 608, 610–611, 615, 622
Hibat Allāh ibn Makīn, 156, 172, 179–180, 182, 233, 598, 608, 611, 615, 622
Hibat Allāh ibn Makīn ibn Hibat Allāh ibn Fāris ibn Ḥammād ibn Suwayd, 172, 598
Ḥijāz, 203
Hilāl al-Dawla, 74, 422
Hilāl ibn Yaḥyā, 153
Hindāwī, 161
ḥiṣān, 140, 196, 200

Ḥiṣn al-Bāb, 87, 399
Ḥiṣn al-Dawla, 74, 77, 90, 129, 207–208, 367, 456
Ḥiṣn al-Dawla ibn al-ʿAsqalānī, 74, 77, 90, 129, 207–208, 367
historiographical sources, 10–11, 13, 20, 34, 41, 61, 104
ḥitta, 196, 199
horse, 52, 61–67, 77–80, 84, 90–94, 102–103, 106–107, 109–110, 112, 114–121, 126, 136–137, 140, 196, 200, 205–206, 209, 212–213, 215, 222, 226–232, 236, 238–240, 243, 245, 248, 251, 254–255, 292–293, 298–300, 305–307, 311–313, 317, 319, 323–324, 328, 331, 333, 340, 342–345, 348, 350, 353, 355, 359–360, 364, 367, 371–372, 378, 382–385, 390–391, 400–401, 405–407, 413–415, 419–422, 426 n. 3, 427–428, 428 n. 8, 434, 442, 446–447, 452–454, 471–473, 480–481, 491, 506, 512, 512 n. 1, 513
Huḏayl, 64
hudna, 5, 7, 9, 41, 46
Humām al-Dawla, 218–219, 251
Ḥusayn ibn Ḥasan, 73, 78, 209, 372, 385
Ḥusayn ibn ʿAlī ibn ʾAbī Ṭālib, 169
Ibn al-ʿAsqalānī, 74, 90, 129, 207–208, 213, 249, 343–344, 367, 456 n. 1
Ibn Fuḍāla, 257 n. 1
Ibn ʿImrān, 83, 222, 224, 384
Ibrīm, 3, 9 n. 6, 12–13, 13 n. 13, 15–25, 27, 29, 31–33, 35, 37, 39, 41–43, 45–47, 49, 56, 64, 68, 70–71, 83, 93, 93 n. 14, 100, 117, 129–130, 137, 140, 142, 145–146, 155–156, 160, 163, 188, 191, 191 n. 2, 206 n. 1, 207, 210–211, 217, 228–229, 234, 239, 245, 254–256, 293, 307, 324, 328, 333, 345, 360, 405, 412, 415, 422, 446, 462, 464, 469, 471, 474–475, 479, 501–502, 562, 569–570
ʾIbrāhīm, 72–73, 75–78, 107, 152, 156, 164–165, 167, 232, 241, 248, 301, 389, 391, 400, 452, 454, 554–

555, 566, 577–578, 581–582, 587, 594–595, 600
ʾIbrāhīm ibn Muḥammad ibn al-Ḥusayn ibn Muḥammad ibn al-Zubayr, 75, 164, 232, 248, 577, 581
ʾIbrāhīm ibn ʿAlī ibn Mutawwaj ibn ʾAbī Yazīd al-Ḥanafī, 72
Iēsou, 53, 440 n. 1
Ik̲šīdid, 11
ʾikšīl, 56–57, 59
ʿimāmatayn, 195, 202
ʿīna, 138
India, 202–203
interdental, 277, 339, 441, 569
Ipisi, 116, 215, 238, 240, 370–371, 382
ʾiqrār, 164, 170, 177
ʾiqṭāʿ, 46, 132, 145–147, 152, 206, 230, 254
Iraqi striped garment (*šuqqat burd ʿirāqī*), 110, 415
ʾirdabb, 104, 138
irki, 412
Island of Michael, 88, 157, 555–556
Īsū, 49, 53–55, 60, 78, 96, 99, 178–183, 228, 243, 397, 401, 403, 405, 407, 451–452, 607–609, 611, 614
Īsūy, 181, 607, 614
jabal al-janādil, 64
Jāmiʿ, 132
jāriya, 103, 107, 113, 237–238, 240–241, 435
Jawhar, 11, 107, 238, 240, 311
jazīrat Mikāʾīl, 88, 157
Jewish, 38 n. 9, 203, 257
Jews, 256–257
jizya, 9, 193, 214
Joasse, 55
jubba, 196, 201
juniper, 195, 200, 341
Jurayj ibn Yuḥannis, 172, 177, 604
Kablām, 114, 238–239, 342
k̲ādim, 81, 222, 239, 244–245, 473 n. 3
K̲ael, 67
kāfūr, 196, 199, 203
Kajja, 83, 353
k̲alāṣ, 153–156
k̲alīfa, 83, 213, 221–225, 227, 232–233, 382, 382 n. 1, 383
K̲alīfa ibn Ḥasan, 130, 476
K̲alīl, 132, 142, 480, 512–514
K̲alīl, ʿUmar and ʿUṯmān, 132, 142, 512, 514
k̲all, 180, 196, 202
k̲ān, 141

Kanz al-Dawla, 33, 35, 38–39, 46, 71–73, 77, 115, 131, 138, 160, 193, 206–208, 210–211, 213–214, 221, 233–234, 294, 301, 312, 328, 333, 359, 372 n. 4, 377, 447, 462, 485, 490, 563
Kanzī, 72–74, 77–78, 80, 85, 90, 130–132, 160, 163, 207–209, 211–212, 220, 222–223, 233, 256, 259, 261, 298, 307, 313, 319, 324, 345, 350, 355, 360, 372, 385, 473, 507, 570
Kapenē, 420
ḵarāj, 147
ḵaraz, 196, 199
ḵarīṭa, 196, 199–200
ḵartoularios, 53
kātib, 44, 78, 228–229, 254, 279, 461
Kayl, 179, 607, 609
ḵayl, 61–64, 66, 102, 196, 200, 212, 231, 254
Kayl ibn Mariane, 179, 607, 609
ḵayyāṭa, 196, 202
ḵeiakišši, 58
ḵeiakiššika, 58
keiakshshi, 58
Kenzi, 34
kerchief, 176, 197, 200, 601
Khartoum, 1, 3
Khurasan, 152, 257
kiak(i)šš(i)l, 58
Kīhak, 147, 157, 548–549, 555
kimāmāt, 65, 196, 200
king, 4–5, 8–9, 11–12, 12 n. 10, 13, 13 n. 13, 19, 32, 35, 38, 41–47, 51, 53–56, 66, 70, 74, 77–78, 80–81, 83, 86–96, 96 n. 15, 97–98, 98 n. 18, 99–100, 102–103, 110–121, 129, 132–134, 136, 192, 205–208, 210–213, 221–222, 224, 229, 231, 236, 239–240, 245–246, 248, 250, 254, 260–261, 278, 292–293, 298–300, 305, 307, 319, 323–324, 328, 331, 333, 340, 342–345, 348, 350, 355, 359–360, 364–367, 371–372, 376, 378, 383, 383 n. 3, 385, 391, 400–401, 405, 407, 413–415, 420–422, 426–427, 427 n. 4, 428, 434, 442, 447, 451, 457, 471, 490–491, 524
King George, 87, 98, 100
king's road, 100

k̠iyāk̠, 56, 58–61, 77, 293, 307, 313, 319, 324, 333, 345, 355, 360
Koiak, 147, 548
k̠oiak, 57–59, 88
k̠oiak-eikšil, 57, 59, 88
Kordofan, 2, 103
Kourte, 93 n. 14
k̠ūd̠a, 65, 134, 196, 200, 278, 511
k̠ulʿ, 174–175, 178
kummayn, 180, 196, 201
kurkum, 196, 201
Kurkur, 140, 245, 469, 471, 474
kurūk, 196, 199
Kushite, 1, 3, 100
lād̠an, 196, 200
Lake Nasser, 16
Lāmiʿ, 63, 73–74, 77, 80, 83, 85, 90, 130–132, 208, 211–212, 218, 222, 224, 242, 259-261, 307, 313, 319, 324, 345, 360, 382–384, 476, 507
Lāmiʿ ibn Ḥasan, 73–74, 77, 85, 90, 130–132, 208, 212, 222, 259–260, 307, 313, 319, 345, 507
lamp, 197, 200, 202, 538
lantern, 103, 390–391
Latin, 15, 18
laudanum, 196, 200, 341
lease, 46, 88, 133, 140, 145–150, 152, 155–159, 206, 230, 515, 547, 551
leather bag, 106, 187, 200, 345
Libyan desert, 1–2
lieutenant, 141, 143, 213, 221–225, 227, 230, 234, 382–383, 395, 453, 474, 505
loanword, 57–58
lock, 197, 200, 463
Lower Nubia, 1, 8, 13–15, 20, 32, 42–47, 64, 66, 68–70, 85, 91–92, 93 n. 14, 95, 104, 160, 191, 253–256, 259, 261, 286, 394, 412
loyalty, 41, 45, 47, 76, 94–95, 222
lubān, 196, 200, 203
luxury, 41, 103, 197, 200, 283, 461, 463
Maʿbad, 563, 566, 571
magister equitum, 66
Maḥmūd, 213, 230, 344, 496–498, 589
mahr, 166, 173, 179
majlis, 196, 201
maks, 158, 193

Makuria, 3–4, 8, 12, 34, 44, 66, 69–70, 98–101, 378
malʾa, 196, 199
malʾatayn, 176
Mamluk, 11, 13, 33, 191
mamlūk, 220, 246–247, 562–563
Manṣūr, 72–74, 77–78, 130, 132, 161, 205, 207, 294, 333, 422, 476, 518, 579
Manṣūr ibn Lāmiʿ ibn Ḥasan, 73, 130, 132, 476
mantle, 176, 197, 200, 601
maqāṭiʿ, 196, 201
Maqs al-ʾAʿlā, 88, 261
mare, 102, 195, 200, 422
margin, 39, 82–83, 93–94, 103, 106, 110, 112–114, 124–127, 131, 134, 136–137, 139, 188, 195–196, 198–199, 201–202, 208–209, 212, 214, 219, 221–223, 229, 233, 235, 238, 241, 244, 249, 251–252, 259, 265, 272–274, 280–281, 292–293, 296, 300, 304, 306, 310, 312, 316–318, 322, 324, 337, 342, 348–349, 352, 354, 358–359, 362–363, 365, 367, 374, 377, 380, 384, 388, 390, 393, 404, 406, 411, 413, 415, 418, 422, 426, 432, 435–436, 438, 442, 456–457, 466, 469, 472, 475, 478–481, 489, 491, 494, 497, 504, 506, 516–518, 530, 532, 561, 563, 566, 618, 621
Mariane ibn Īsū, 178–183, 607–609, 611, 614
Marikouda, 58, 311
Mārīḵura, 59, 238–239, 244, 311–313, 323, 344
Marīs, 4, 9, 68–70, 80, 86, 116, 140, 146, 216–217, 221–222, 301, 328, 350, 354, 372, 378, 382 n. 1, 385, 391, 401, 413, 415, 436, 480, 519
market, 36–37, 37 n. 8, 38, 40–42, 44–46, 105, 107–109, 111, 241, 249, 260, 341–342, 342 n. 2, 385
market economy, 40–41, 107
market exchange, 36–37, 40–42, 44–46, 111
marriage, 46, 100, 166–171, 173–174, 177–179, 181–183, 216, 223, 233, 256, 270, 583, 588–589, 605, 609, 613, 620–621

marsīn, 196, 201
Maryam ibnat Yuḥannis, 31, 172, 176–179, 181–183, 256, 599, 601, 604, 608, 611, 614
Mašal Ankara, 143, 224, 505
Masē, 51
Maššouda, 59, 412
Maššoura, 59, 412
mastaba, 29
maṣṭakī, 196, 200
Master of the Cavalry, 66
Master of the Horses, 52, 61–64, 66, 77–80, 84, 92–94, 106–107, 109, 112, 115–121, 126, 136–137, 209, 212, 215, 222, 226–229, 232, 236, 238, 240, 243, 245, 254–255, 292–293, 298–300, 305, 307, 311–313, 317, 319, 323–324, 331, 333, 340, 345, 348, 350, 353, 355, 359–360, 364, 367, 371–372, 378, 382, 384–385, 390–391, 400–401, 405–407, 413–415, 420, 422, 427, 434, 442, 446–447, 452–454, 472–473, 506
Master of the Mountain, 61–62, 64, 86
Master of the Shipmasts, 74, 78, 84, 221, 223, 225–226, 226 n. 3, 227, 246, 395, 395 n. 1, 429, 453
mastic tree gum, 196, 200
mat, 180, 196, 200, 611
Mattokki, 34
mattress, 195, 198, 200, 366, 462
mawlā, 137, 247–248, 254, 501, 566
mayʿa, 196, 202–203
mayʿat ward, 196, 201
Meinarti, 88, 157
meizoteros, 52
Mena Kurē, 205, 250, 414
Menakouda, 59, 412
Menakourra, 59, 412
merchant, 21, 31–32, 35–38, 38 n. 9, 39–47, 65 n. 8, 69, 79, 81, 83, 89–90, 94, 96, 99–111, 119–120, 129, 134, 139–141, 143, 187, 191, 198, 200, 203, 212, 224, 226, 229, 231, 238, 241, 247, 253–254, 259, 299, 299 n. 1, 300, 305, 341, 353, 364–365, 367, 395 n. 1, 426 n. 2, 447, 463, 502
Merkē, 425

Merki, 164–165, 227, 232, 248, 255, 425, 427, 428 n. 10, 573, 577, 581–582
Merki ibn Abrām, 164–165, 232, 248, 577, 581–582
Merkurios, 8
Meroe, 3, 100
Meroitic, 2, 15, 18
Mesori, 489, 491
Mesra, 489, 491
messenger, 89–91, 99, 102, 108, 113, 205–206, 213, 229–230, 237, 248–250, 300, 341, 344, 377 n. 2, 378, 385, 390, 400, 404–405, 414, 421, 434, 442, 485
Migi, 4, 71, 420
migin soŋoj, 70, 399, 420
mik̲adda, 176, 196, 201
milaffa, 176, 176 n. 12, 180, 196, 200
milāya, 176 n. 13
milḥ, 180, 196, 201
mindīl, 176, 197, 200
mišāṭ, 180, 197, 200
miṣbāḥ, 197, 200, 202
mit̲qāl, 187
Mograt Island, 3
monetary, 14, 36, 38–41, 44, 104–107, 110, 132, 138, 185, 256
Moses George, 51, 53–55, 96, 96 n. 15, 97–98, 98 n. 18, 99–101
mosque, 6 n. 3, 8, 17, 34, 87, 95, 206 n. 1
mourtin ŋod, 67
muʿaddī, 231
Muʿayd, 563
Mubārak, 208, 248, 572
Mufliḥ, 190, 501
Muḥammad ʾAbū ʿAbd Allāh ibn ʾIsmaʿīl ibn Ḥusayn ibn ʾIbrāhīm ibn Ḥusayn ibn ʾAṣfar ibn Maymūn ibn Baydūs ibn Basūn, 167, 587
Muḥammad ibn ʾAbū Ḥayy, 132, 146, 519
Muḥammad ibn Ramaḍān, 7, 74, 78, 80, 378
Muḥammad ibn Ramaḍān al-Ḥājj, 74
Muḥammad ibn ʿUbayd Allāh ibn al-Ḥasan ibn ʿAlī, 132, 498
muḥaqqaq, 263
mukārī, 141, 230
mulāʾa, 176 n. 13

muleteer, 141, 213, 223, 230, 234, 474
Munʿim, 238, 298, 300
muqṭaʿ, 145–146, 230
murr, 197, 201, 203
Murwā, 163, 569, 571
Murwaw, 163, 569
musaqqaʿ, 139, 197, 200
Museum of Islamic Art, 21, 24–25, 27, 291, 295, 309, 315, 321, 325, 329, 335, 347, 351, 357, 361, 369, 373, 379, 387, 393, 397 n. 1, 409, 417, 423, 431, 437, 445, 493, 499, 503, 527, 529, 551, 559, 583
mutaḥammil, 250–251
mutawallī, 68, 70–71, 101, 216–219, 433
mutawallī al-bāb, 217, 219
muṭlaq, 263
muwādaʿa, 5
Mūyis, 54, 96–97, 99, 205, 250, 414
muzzles, 65, 196, 200, 426 n. 3, 427
myrrh, 197, 201, 203, 544
myrtle, 196, 201, 341
Nabatean, 153
nāʾib, 51, 83, 221–224, 227, 382, 384
Napata, 100
nascaphthon, 195, 201, 282, 375, 378
Naṣr, 72–73, 77–78, 328, 407, 557, 578, 590
Naṣr ibn ʾIbrāhīm, 72–73, 77–78, 578
negator, 281, 340, 419
Nile, 1–3, 5, 5 n. 2, 13, 15, 32–33, 86, 88, 90–91, 99, 103, 146, 151, 160–161, 163–164, 202, 260, 399, 412, 479, 562, 564, 569, 571
nisba, 73, 146, 169, 207–208, 232, 298, 395, 569
Nobadia, 3–4, 8–9, 12–13, 15, 44, 50, 52, 66, 68–70, 88, 99, 191, 399, 420, 422
Nobates, 2, 9
North Temple Plaza, 27
Northeast Africa, 43
Noubai, 2
Nubian, 1–9, 9 n. 6, 10–12, 12 n. 10, 13, 15, 18–21, 21 n. 2, 27–29, 31, 33–35, 37, 37 n. 8, 38, 41–47, 49–51, 51 n. 1, 52–53, 53 n. 2, 54–55, 55 n. 5, 56–65, 65 n. 8, 66–67, 69–71, 74, 81–82, 85–88, 90–92, 94–104, 110, 117, 124, 129, 131–137,

141, 146–147, 157, 164, 172, 178–181, 191–192, 205, 208, 210, 212, 217, 219, 222, 225, 226 n. 3, 227, 229, 234, 237, 245–246, 251, 254–261, 270, 311, 322, 331 n. 2, 343, 353, 370–371, 394, 395 n. 1, 396 n. 3, 406, 412, 420, 425, 426 n. 2, 427, 427 n. 4, 427 n. 5, 433, 440, 451, 472–473, 485 n. 1, 491, 505, 517, 545 n. 1, 553, 555, 562, 570, 577, 601, 604, 607–609, 611, 614, 620
nuḥās, 197, 200
nuʿmā, 197, 200, 283, 461
nuqra, 189–190
nuqūb, 197, 202
Nūr al-Dīn, 137, 232, 472
ŋeshsh, 52
odiferous shrub, 201
Old Dongola (Dunqulā al-ʿAjūz), 3 n. 1
Old Nubian, 15, 18, 21, 27–29, 49–50, 51 n. 1, 58, 62, 191, 412, 420, 570
orthography, 49–51, 53, 55, 57, 143, 225, 277–282, 370, 375, 382, 394, 399, 500, 517, 530, 587
Ottoman, 15, 17–19, 25–26, 145, 191, 282, 419
Oua, 81, 115, 239, 244–245, 251, 322–323
Ourouwi, 49–50
Pachōras, 3
pact, 81, 94
Paitos, 586
Paḵōras, 52, 69
Papa, 81, 244–245, 327, 562, 562 n. 1
Papasa, 53
Pāpāy, 161, 258, 564
Papi, 562, 562 n. 1
papyrus, 10, 18–19, 69
partnership, 39, 101, 137, 160–163, 217, 232, 256–258, 283, 433–434, 472, 565–566
Patriarch Benjamin, 7
Patriarch Gabriel IV, 19
peace treaty, 92, 97, 205, 414
Pedeme, 15
pen-knife, 195, 201, 479
perfume, 198, 201, 203, 377, 461, 463
Peti, 225, 451, 453
Pharaonic, 15
pharyngealisation, 277, 554

Philae, 86, 88, 146, 157, 193
Phrim, 15
piece of garment, 198, 201
pieces of cloth, 196, 201, 238, 298, 539
pilgrim, 80, 202, 378
pillow, 176, 196, 201, 601
ports of trade, 42
preacher, 74, 168, 498, 557, 588–589
pre-industrial societies, 36, 42
pre-Islamic Near East, 153
Primis, 15
prosthetic, 479
qāḍī, 46, 63, 73–76, 91–92, 165, 168, 172, 182, 205, 216, 223, 231, 233, 244, 257 n. 1
qāʾid, 218–221, 242, 524
qāʾid Ḥasan, 119, 219, 242, 251, 331
qāʾid Saʿāda, 79, 82, 115, 218–221, 251, 293, 305–306, 349
qāʾid ʾIsḥāq, 119, 219, 251, 331
qamḥ, 103, 180, 197, 202
qamīṣ, 197, 201
Qarna, 63
Qāsim, 75–76, 91, 132, 207, 413, 464, 480, 524
Qaṣr Ibrīm, 3, 9 n. 6, 12–13, 13 n. 13, 15–25, 27, 29, 31–33, 35, 37, 39, 41–43, 45–47, 49, 64, 70–71, 93 n. 14, 100, 145–146, 155–156, 160, 163, 188, 191, 191 n. 2, 206 n. 1, 254–256, 405, 469, 570
qaṭīfa, 176, 197, 202
qazz, 180, 197, 201
Qēōrqe, 176–177, 601
Qērqe ibn Yuḥannis, 172–173, 177, 182–183, 599
qīrāṭ, 185, 188, 406, 463, 539, 545
qirbatayn, 197, 202
qirfa, 197, 199, 203
qirṭim, 395
qišr, 174, 174 n. 9, 176, 197, 199
qufl, 197, 200
quḥaḥ, 190
qumāš, 197, 200
qurṭum, 197, 199
qurub, 65, 134, 197, 201, 479
Qūṣ, 33, 75, 97, 108, 168, 202, 206, 217, 232, 376, 421
Quṣayr, 38
Qūṣī garments, 198, 201, 538
qusṭ, *quṣṭ*, 197, 200
quṭn, 197, 200

Rabīʿa, 32
Rāhim, 113, 237, 241, 435
raḥl, 174, 174 n. 10
Raḥma ibn Saʿīd, 145, 549
raʾīs, 82, 233
Ramaḍān, 7, 74, 78, 80, 111–112, 135, 137, 141, 164, 238, 258, 365, 378, 472–473, 524, 575, 578, 581
raqīq, 6, 35, 103, 105–107, 111–113, 137, 210, 235–236, 244, 249, 343, 442
Rāšid, 137, 139, 258, 472
rasūl, 113, 248–250
raṭl, 104, 138, 141, 378, 462, 496, 543–545
rayīs, 213, 223, 233–234
reciprocal gift exchanges, 40
reciprocation, 36
reciprocity, 35–36, 41, 43, 46, 107
Red Sea, 32–33, 38, 202
rent, 148–149, 157–158, 258, 549, 556
ridāʾ, 176, 197, 200
ring, 195, 201, 469, 505
riqq, 103, 235–236, 435
riwāʾ, 197, 201
riyāḥ, 195, 200
rope, 197, 201, 461, 463, 512, 554–555
rose liquid, 196, 201, 341
rumāt al-ḥadaq, 65 n. 8
rumḥ, 65, 134, 197, 201
rumm, 197, 199, 511
Saʿāda, 79, 82, 115, 218–221, 251, 293, 305–306, 349
Sabʿ, 208
Šabb Šalūl, 163, 571
šabba, 198–199
Saʿd al-Dawla, 208, 248, 572
ṣadāq, 166, 173
šādd, 214
saddle pads, 198, 201, 481
šadīd, 214–215
safaṭ, 197, 199
safflower, 195, 201, 203, 395, 537
saffron, 196, 198, 201, 463, 544
šahāda ʿalā šahāda, 159, 162, 166
ṣāḥib al-ḥarba, 231
ṣāḥib al-jabal, 61–62, 64
ṣāḥib al-ḵayl, 61–64, 66, 254
ṣāḥib al-sawārī, 74, 78, 221, 223, 225
Sahidic, 58
Sai, 93 n. 14
šajara, 198, 201
šakka, 198–199, 479
Saladin, 12, 187, 193

salary, 83, 222, 224, 384
sale, 38, 42, 46, 67, 105, 149, 152–155, 159–164, 228, 236, 257–259, 340–341, 440, 443, 559, 565, 567, 572
salt, 180, 196, 201, 341, 611
šamla, 198–199
Šams al-Dawla, 12
Šarīf, 81, 102, 117, 238–239, 244, 327, 589
šarīf, 168, 215–216, 382, 485
šarīk, 137, 234, 557
Šāwar, 50, 75, 92, 114, 206–207, 213, 323
sayr, 195, 202, 512
scabbards, 65, 134, 197, 201, 481
scented goods, 105, 108, 198, 201, 341
seat, 107, 123, 196, 201, 240, 278, 312
secretary, 44, 49, 55, 60, 78, 83–84, 118, 225–226, 228–229, 243, 254–255, 270, 393, 442, 449, 452–454
Seljuk Turks, 12
Semna, 569
servant, 52, 59, 81–82, 84, 89, 93, 95, 103, 106, 112–115, 133, 135, 141, 143, 211, 218, 220, 222–224, 235–252 298, 307, 312, 323, 327, 342, 342 n. 2, 343–344, 365, 371–372, 383, 421–422, 471, 473–475, 505
Shiʿite, 12, 169, 255
shirt, 197, 201, 513
sieve, 195, 201, 537
Silimi, 15
silk, 180, 197–198, 201, 238, 298, 611
silver, 104, 185, 187–191
simsār, 109, 227–228
Sinn al-Kaddab, 469
Sirāj ibn Mario, 156, 553, 555
Šīrkūh, 50, 114, 206–207, 213–214, 323
slave boy, 47, 81, 89–91, 102, 105–108, 113–114, 116–117, 137, 206, 210, 213, 215, 224, 228–231, 237–242, 244, 248–249, 258–259, 311 n. 2, 312–313, 323, 327, 341–344, 359, 365–366, 371, 381–382, 395, 405, 421–422, 435, 472, 474, 480, 490
slave girl, 103–105, 107, 113, 137, 178, 237–238, 240–

241, 311, 389–391, 435, 443–444, 481, 513
slaves, 5–7, 9, 9 n. 6, 10, 10 n. 7, 11, 14, 34–35, 37, 37 n. 8, 38–41, 43, 52, 65, 82–83, 85, 90–91, 93, 97, 101–107, 111–114, 118, 137, 178, 211, 215, 217–218, 224, 227, 235–252, 254–255, 260–261, 293, 307, 312, 332, 343–344, 359, 371, 383, 413, 421, 427, 434–436, 444, 453, 469, 513
sleeved garment, 196, 201, 513
sleeves, 180, 196, 201, 611
Soba, 3, 44–45, 70, 98–101, 134–135, 191, 205, 245, 250, 261, 414, 471, 523–524
Sohag, 619
Sonqi Tino, 601
soŋoj, 59, 62, 67, 70, 399, 420
Šouda, 570
spear, 65, 104, 134, 197, 201, 231, 364–365, 481
spikenard, 198, 202, 341, 378, 544
sprigs, 195, 202, 463
St Michael, 67
Staurosinkouda, 570
storax, 196, 202–203, 544
striped garment, 110, 202, 415
Šudā ibn ʾAbrām, 570, 573
Sudan, 1, 21 n. 2, 22 n. 3
ṣūf, 66, 141, 198–199, 202
ṣuffāt, 198, 201
sugar, 108, 138, 157, 187, 197, 202, 341
Šujāʿ al-Dawla, 119, 219, 242, 251, 331
sukkar, 197, 202
ṣulḥ, 5, 97
sulṭān, 145–146, 205–207
šumūʿ, 198–199
sunbul, 198, 202
ṣundūq, 198–199
Sunni, 12, 174, 255
šuqqa, 198, 201, 413
sweets, 195, 202, 366
tafḵīm, 277, 461, 511, 554
ṯaġr, 44–45
taḥwīl, 147–148
Ṭāʿī, 131, 137, 233–234, 245, 471, 473
Ṭalāʾiʿ ibn Ruzzīk, 220
Tanwīr, 72–73, 77, 301
Taqwā, 86
ṭarrāḥa, 198, 200
ṯawb, 198–199
taxation, 158

testimony, 150, 159–160, 162–165, 173, 179–180, 257, 353, 556–557, 559, 563, 575, 579, 588, 599, 605, 610–611, 615
thong of twisted leather, 195, 202
ṭīb, 198–199, 201
tikk, 185
Timotheos, 19
ṯiyāb qūṣī, 198, 201
trade zone, 14, 42–44, 46, 253
treaty, 4–5, 6 n. 3, 7, 7 n. 4, 8, 9 n. 6, 10–11, 19, 33, 70, 92, 97, 104, 136, 205, 230, 414
trousseau, 174
Ṭūlūnid, 11
tunic, 195, 202, 463, 539
turban, 107, 195, 202, 240, 312
Turkish, 18–20, 26
Tuška, 501–502
ʿUbayd Allāh, 74, 78, 84, 132, 164–165, 226, 248, 254–255, 453–454, 491, 498, 518, 571, 577, 581–582, 594
ʿUbayd Allāh ibn Ḥasan, 164–165, 248, 577, 581
ʿūd, 195, 199, 203
ʿUmar, 7, 132, 142, 156, 480, 512, 514, 554
ʿUmar ibn Šarḥabīl, 7
ʾUmm al-Ḥasan ibnat ʿAlī ibn ʾAḥmad ibn Ḥusayn ibn ʾIbrāhīm ibn Ḥusayn ibn ʾAṣfar ibn Maymūn ibn Baydūs ibn Basūn, 167, 587
Upper Egypt, 6, 11, 20, 31–32, 34–35, 46–47, 68, 97, 151, 155, 169, 182–183, 206–207, 216–217, 220–221, 233, 254–256, 260, 383 n. 2, 427 n. 5, 485 n. 1, 589, 619
Upper Nubia, 1, 44, 111
ʾūqiya, 104
Uruwī, 49–52, 55, 59–60, 71, 77–78, 80, 99, 103, 107, 118, 120, 125, 143, 224–226, 228, 243, 254–255, 258, 270, 291, 293, 295, 301, 303, 307, 309, 313, 315, 319, 321, 324–325, 328–329, 333, 335, 347, 350–351, 355, 357, 360–361, 367, 369, 372–373, 378–379, 385, 387, 391, 393, 449
ʿuṣfur, 195, 201, 203
ʾusquf, 229

ʿUṯmān, 132, 142, 512, 514
veil, 176 n. 12, 197, 202, 495–496
velvet, 176, 197, 202, 601
verbena nodiflora, 196, 202, 538
vernacular, 226, 277–279, 281, 411, 425, 441
vice-eparch, 51, 221
vinegar, 102, 104, 180, 196, 202, 375, 378, 611
vizier, 34, 50, 54, 56, 75, 80, 92, 96–97, 114–121, 123, 205–207, 213, 220, 236, 245, 260, 278–279, 292–293, 298, 300, 305, 307, 319, 323–324, 328, 331, 333, 340, 345, 348, 350, 355, 359–360, 371–372, 376, 378, 385, 391, 400–401, 405, 407, 413, 415, 425–428, 434, 447, 451, 471
wabar, 198, 200
Wādī al-ʿAllāqī, 32–33
Wādī al-Naṭrūn, 100
Wādī al-Šakriyābī, 145–146, 548
Wādī Ḥalfa, 3, 86, 88, 91, 412
Wādī Kurkur, 469
wages, 139, 471
walī, 156, 166–170
wālī, 6, 206, 217–218
walnut oil, 180, 198, 202, 611
waraq, 185, 189
warranty, 149–156, 159, 164, 550, 572
waṣīf, 38, 103, 236–237, 340–341, 366
waṣīfa, 38, 103, 236–237, 240, 249, 390
water-skins, 197, 202, 513
wayba, 138, 180, 396, 545, 611
West Africa, 42
wheat, 103–104, 138, 180, 197, 202, 224, 239, 242, 395–396, 611
wisb, 198, 200
witnesses, 20, 94, 150, 156, 159, 162, 164, 166, 169–170, 173, 181, 208, 229, 257–258, 555, 563, 570, 577–578, 588, 592–593, 599, 609, 615
wood for fire, 202
wool, 66, 138, 141, 198–199, 202, 496, 544–545
writing line, 265, 265 n. 2, 266
Yaḥyā, 102, 153, 238, 422, 524, 569, 582, 589, 594
Yarmūk, 7

Yemen, 75
Yūsuf, 152–153, 440, 610
Yūsuf ibn Ḵālid, 153
zabād, 198, 201, 461
zaʿfarān, 198, 201
zallāj, 140, 156–157
zayt al-jawz, 180, 198, 202
zayt ṭīb, 198–199
zift, 109, 198–199
zubda, 198–199
zujāj, 198, 200
zunnār, 176 n. 11, 198–199

Nubian Names in Nubian Script (Referenced by Page Number)

ⲁⲃⲣⲁⲁⲙ, 577 n. 2
ⲁⲃⲣⲁⲙ, 577 n. 2
ⲁⲙⲡⲁⲡⲁ, 562
ⲁⲛⲕⲁⲣⲟⲩ, 505
ⲃⲁⲥⲓⲗⲉⲓ, 433
ⲃⲁⲥⲓⲗⲏ, 433
ⲅⲓⲟⲣⲕⲉ, 601
ⲇⲁⲛⲓ, 517
ⲇⲁⲣⲙⲉ, 51–52
ⲇⲁⲩⲧⲓ, 54
ⲉⲓⲕⲱⲓⲗ, 56–57
ⲉⲓⲡⲓⲥⲓ, 370
ⲉⲓⲡⲥⲓ, 370
ⲉⲓⲥⲟⲩ, 53 n. 2, 440 n. 1
ⲉⲕ̅ⲱⲓⲗ, 56
ⲉⲗⲉⲓⲍⲁⲃⲉⲧ, 51 n. 1
ⲉⲗⲉⲓⲥⲁⲃⲉⲧ, 51 n. 1
ⲉⲥ̅ⲟⲩ, 53 n. 2, 440 n. 1
ⲍⲁⲏⲗ, 51 n. 1
ⲍⲓⲙⲉⲱⲛⲓ, 51 n. 1
ⲓⲏⲥⲟⲩ, 53, 53 n. 2, 440 n. 1
ⲓⲏⲥⲟⲩⲥ, 53 n. 2
ⲓⲥⲟⲩ, 53 n. 2, 440 n. 1
ⲕⲁⳝⳝⲏⲅⲁ, 353
ⲕⲁⳝ̅ⲅⲁⲗ, 353
ⲙⲁⲱⲁⲗ, 505
ⲙⲁⲣⲓⲁⲛⲉ, 607 n. 1
ⲙⲁⲣⲓⲕⲟⲩ`ⲇ´, 58 n. 7, 311 n. 1
ⲙⲁⲣⲓⲟ, 553
ⲙⲁⲣⲓⲥ, 68
ⲙⲁⲣⲓ`ⲕ´, 58 n. 7, 311 n. 1
ⲙⲉⲣⲕⲏ, 425 n. 1, 577 n. 1
ⲙⲉⲣⲕⲓ, 425 n. 1, 577 n. 1
ⲟⲩⲁ, 322
ⲟⲩⲣⲟⲩⲏⲗ, 50
ⲟⲩⲣⲟⲩⳟⲓ, 49–50
ⲡⲁⲡ, 562 n. 1
ⲡⲁⲡⲁ, 562 n. 1
ⲡⲁⲡⲁⲥ, 562 n. 1
ⲡⲁⲡⲓ, 562 n. 1
ⲡⲉⲧⲓ, 451 n. 1
ⲥⲁⲏⲗ, 51 n. 1
ⲥⲓⲙⲉⲱⲛⲓ, 51 n. 1
ⲥⲧⲁⲩⲣⲟⲥⲓⲛⲕⲟⲩⲇⲁ, 570 n. 4

ⲭⲉⲓⲁ̄ⲕⲱ̄ϣⲱⲓⲕⲁ, 58
ⲭⲓⲁϩⲉⲭ, 58
ⲭⲓⲁⲭ, 58
ⲭⲟⲓⲁⲕ, 57
ⲭⲟⲓⲁⲭ, 58

Inventory of Documents

Edition number: 1 (Letter to the Eparch Uruwī)

Museum of Islamic Art inventory number: 23973.66
Excavation photograph numbers and image numbers:
Recto: 1966A_P06_18A-19 (image: 050308_106_o)
Recto: 1968_04_10–10A (image: 050308_690_u)
Verso: 1966A_P06_17A-18 (image: 050308_106_u)
Verso: 1968_04_11–11A (image: 050308_691_u)
Registration number: 66A/111 (?)

Edition number: 2 (Letter to the Eparch Uruwī)

Museum of Islamic Art inventory number: 23973.65
Excavation photograph numbers and image numbers:
Recto: 1966A_P06_09A-10 (image 050308_103_u)
Recto: 1968_04_05–05A (image 050308_691_o)
Verso: 1966A_P06_10A-11 (image 050308_104_u)
Verso: 1966A_P06_11A-12 (image 050308_105_u)
Verso: 1968_04_09–09A (image 050308_689_u)
Registration number: 66A/111 (?)

Edition number: 3 (Letter to the Eparch Uruwī)

Sartain inventory number: Add. 01
Excavation photograph numbers and image numbers:
Recto: 1966A_P06_15A-16 (image: 050308_108_o)
Verso: 1966A_P06_16A-17 (image: 050308_107_o)
Registration number: 66A/111 (?)

Edition number: 4 (Letter to the Eparch Uruwī)

Museum of Islamic Art inventory number: 23973.90

Excavation photograph numbers and image numbers:

Recto: 1966A_P06_19A-20 (image: 050308_107_u)

Recto: 1968_01_02–02A (image: 050308_630_o)

Verso: 1966A_P06_20A-21 (image: 050308_108_u)

Verso: 1968_01_01–01A (image: 050308_629_o)

Registration number: 66A/111 (?)

Edition number: 5 (Letter to the Eparch Uruwī)

Museum of Islamic Art inventory number: 23973.49

Excavation photograph numbers and image numbers:

Recto: 1966A_P06_21A-22 (image: 050308_109_u)

Recto: 1968_02_17A-18 (image: 050308_659_o)

Verso: 1966A_P06_22A-23 (image: 050308_110_u)

Verso: 1968_02_19A-20 (image: 050308_655_u)

Registration number: 66A/111 (?)

Edition number: 6 (Letter to the Eparch Uruwī)

Museum of Islamic Art inventory number: 23973.50

Excavation photograph numbers and image numbers:

Recto: 1966A_P04_29A-30 (image: 050308_080_o)

Recto: 1968_02_20A-21 (image: 050308_656_u)

Verso: 1966A_P04_30A-31 (image: 050308_075_u)

Verso: 1968_02_21A-22 (image: 050308_657_u)

Registration number: 66A/111 (?)

Edition number: 7 (Letter to the Eparch Uruwī)

Museum of Islamic Art inventory number: 23973.44

Excavation photograph numbers and image numbers:

Recto: 1968_02_04A-05 (image: 050308_652_o)

Verso: 1968_02_05A-06 (image: 050308_653_o)

Edition number: 8 (Letter to the Eparch Uruwī)

Museum of Islamic Art inventory number: 23973.60

Excavation photograph numbers and image numbers:

Recto: 1968_03_31–31A (image: 050308_680_u)

Recto: 1968_03_32–32A (image: 050308_681_u)

Verso: 1968_03_33–33A (image: 050308_682_u)

Edition number: 9 (Letter to the Eparch Uruwī)

Museum of Islamic Art inventory number: 23973.62

Excavation photograph numbers and image numbers:

Recto: 1966A_P04_31A-32 (image: 050308_076_u)

Recto: 1966A_P04_32A-33 (image: 050308_077_u)

Recto: 1968_03_34–34A (image: 050308_683_u)

Recto: 1968_03_35–35A (image: 050308_684_u)

Verso: 1966A_P04_33A-34 (image: 050308_078_u 73,62v)

Verso: 1966A_P04_34A-35 (image: 050308_079_u 73,62v)

Verso: 1968_03_36–36A (image: 050308_685_o)

Verso: 1968_03_37–37A (image: 050308_686_o)

Registration number: 66A/111 (?)

Edition number: 10 (Letter to the Eparch Uruwī)

Museum of Islamic Art inventory number: 23973.63

Excavation photograph numbers and image numbers:

Recto: 1966A_P04_27A-28 (image: 050308_078_o)

Recto: 1968_04_01–01A (image: 050308_687_o)

Verso: 1966A_P04_28A-29 (image: 050308_079_o)

Verso: 1968_04_02–02A (image: 050308_688_o)

Registration number: 66A/111 (?)

Edition number: 11 (Letter to the Eparch Uruwī)

Museum of Islamic Art inventory number: 23973.67

Excavation photograph numbers and image numbers:

Recto: 1966A_P06_01A-02 (image: 050308_101_o)

Recto: 1968_04_12–12A (image: 050308_692_u)

Verso: 1966A_P06_02A-03 (image: 050308_102_o)

Verso: 1968_04_13–13A (image: 050308_693_o)

Registration number: 66A/111 (?)

Edition number: 12 (Letter to the Eparch Uruwī)

Museum of Islamic Art inventory number: 23973.69

Excavation photograph numbers and image numbers:

Recto: 1966A_P04_24A-25 (image: ren 050308_075_o)

Recto: 1968_04_17–17A (image: 050308_697_o)

Verso: 1966A_P04_25A-26 (image: 050308_076_o)

Verso: 1968_04_18–18A (image: 050308_698_o)

Registration number: 66A/111 (?)

Edition number: 13 (Letter to the Eparch Uruwī)

Museum of Islamic Art inventory number: 23973.21

Excavation photograph numbers and image numbers:

Recto: 1968_05_10–10A (image: 050308_710_u)

Verso: 1968_05_11–11A (image: 050308_711_u)

Edition number: 14 (Letter to the Eparch Uruwī)

Museum of Islamic Art inventory number: 23973.22

Excavation photograph numbers and image numbers:

Recto: 1968_05_12–12A (image: 050308_712_u)

Verso: 1968_05_13–13A (image: 050308_713_o)

Edition number: 15 (Letter to the Eparch Uruwī)

Museum of Islamic Art inventory number: 23973.25

Excavation photograph numbers and image numbers:

Recto: 1968_05_18–18A (image: 050308_718_o)

Verso: 1968_05_19–19A (image: 050308_713_u)

Edition number: 16 (Letter to the Eparch Uruwī)

Museum of Islamic Art inventory number: 23973.26

Excavation photograph numbers and image numbers:

Recto: 1968_05_20–20A (image: 050308_714_u)

Verso: 1968_05_21–21A (image: 050308_715_u)

Edition number: 17 (Letter from the Eparch Uruwī)

Museum of Islamic Art inventory number: 23973.36

Excavation photograph numbers and image numbers:

Recto: 1968_05_00–00A (image: 050308_706_o)

Verso: 1968_05_01–01A (image: 050308_707_o)

Edition number: 18 (Letter from the Eparch Uruwī ?)

Museum of Islamic Art inventory number: 23973.23

Excavation photograph numbers and image numbers:

Recto: 1968_05_14–14A (image: 050308_714_o)

Verso: 1968_05_15–15A (image: 050308_715_o)

Edition number: 19 (Letter to the Eparch Īsū)

Violet MacDermot's photograph number: 27 in a circle

Excavation photograph numbers and image numbers:

Recto: 1974_V10_03A-04 (image: 170308_283_u)

Verso: 1974_V10_04A-05 (image: 170308_284_u)

Registration number: 74/12

Edition number: 20 (Letter to the Eparch Īsū)

Violet MacDermot's photograph number: 25 in a circle

Excavation photograph numbers and image numbers:

Recto: 1974_V09_36–36A (image: 170308_280_u)

Verso: 1974_V09_37–37A (image: 170308_281_u)

Registration number: 74/12

Edition number: 21 (Letter to an Eparch)

Museum of Islamic Art inventory number: 23973.48

Excavation photograph numbers and image numbers:

Recto: 1966A_P06_12A-13 (image: 050308_111_o)

Recto: 1966A_P06_13A-14 (image: 050308_110_o)

Recto: 1968_02_14A-15 (image: 050308_656_o)

Recto: 1968_02_15A-16 (image: 050308_657)

Verso: 1966A_P06_14A-15 (image: 050308_109_o)

Verso: 1968_02_16A-17 (image: 050308_658_o)

Registration number: 66A/111 (?)

Edition number: 22 (Letter to an Eparch)

Museum of Islamic Art inventory number: 23973.59

Excavation photograph numbers and image numbers:

Recto: 1966A_P04_18A-19 (image: 050308_069_u)

Recto: 1966A_P04_19A-20 (image: 050308_070_u)

Recto: 1966A_P04_20A-21 (image: 050308_071_u)

Recto: 1966A_P04_21A-22 (image: 050308_072_u)

Recto: 1968_03_28–28A (image: 050308_683_o)

Recto: 1968_03_29–29A (image: 050308_684_o)

Verso: 1966A_P04_22A-23 (image: 050308_073_u)

Verso: 1968_03_30–30A (image: 050308_679_u)

Registration number: 66A/111 (?)

Edition number: 23 (Letter to an Eparch)

Museum of Islamic Art inventory number: 23973.24
Excavation photograph numbers and image numbers:
Recto: 1968_05_16–16A (image: 050308_716_o)
Verso: 1968_05_17–17A (image: 050308_717_o)

Edition number: 24 (Letter to an Eparch)

Museum of Islamic Art inventory number: 23973.95
Excavation photograph numbers and image numbers:
Recto: 1966A_P06_03A-04 (image: 050308_103_o)
Recto: 1968_01_09–09A (image: 050308_631_u)
Verso: 1966A_P06_04A-05 (image: 050308_104_o)
Verso: 1968_01_10–10A (image: 050308_632_u)
Registration number: 66A/111 (?)

Edition number: 25 (Letter to an Eparch)

Museum of Islamic Art inventory number: 23973.5
Excavation photograph numbers and image numbers:
Recto: 1966A_P06_23A-24 (image: 050308_111_u)
Recto: 1968_02_33A-34 (image: ren 050308_663_u)
Verso: 1966A_P06_24A-25 (image: ren 050308_112_o)
Verso: 1968_02_34A-35 (image: ren 050308_664_u)
Registration number: 66A/111 (?)

Edition number: 26 (Letter to al-Bazīl, the Deputy of the Eparch Darmā)

Museum of Islamic Art inventory number: 23973.46
Excavation photograph numbers and image numbers:
Recto: 1968_02_11A-12 (image: 050308_653_u)

Recto: 1968_02_12A-13 (image: 050308_654_o)
Verso: 1968_02_10A-11 (image: 050308_652_u)

Edition number: 27 (Letter to the Secretary of the Eparch Uruwī)

Excavation photograph numbers and image numbers:
Recto: 1974_P04_08A-09 (image: 170308_647_u)
Verso: 1974_P04_09A-10 (image: 170308_648_u)
Object number: 74.1.29/11.7

Edition number: 28 (Letter to a Commander)

Excavation photograph numbers and image numbers:
Recto: 1974_P03_34–34A (image: 170308_643_u)
Verso: 1974_P03_35–35A (image: 170308_644_u)
Object number: 74.1.29/11.2

Edition number: 29 (Letter to a Commander)

Excavation photograph numbers and image numbers:
Recto: 1974_P03_32–32A (image: 170308_641_u)
Verso: 1974_P03_33–33A (image: 170308_642_u)
Object number: 74.1.29/11.1

Edition number: 30 (Letter to a Dignitary)

Excavation photograph numbers and image numbers:
Recto: 1974_P04_01A-02 (image: 170308_646_o)
Verso: 1974_P04_00A-01 (image: 170308_645_o)
Object number: 74.1.29/11.3

Edition number: 31 (Letter to a Dignitary)

Sartain inventory number: Add. 03

Excavation photograph numbers and image numbers:

Recto: 1966A_P06_25A-26 (image: 050308_113_o)

Recto: 1966A_P06_26A-27 (image: 050308_114_o)

Registration number: 66A/111 (?)

Edition number: 32 (Letter to a Dignitary)

Excavation photograph number and image number:

1974_P04_06A-07 (image: 170308_645_u)

Object number: 74.1.29/11.6

Edition number: 33 (Letter to a Dignitary)

Verso of **32**

Excavation photography number and image number:

1974_P04_07A-08 (image: 170308_646_u)

Object number: 74.1.29/11.6

Edition number: 34 (Letter to a Dignitary)

Museum of Islamic Art inventory number: 23973.94

Excavation photograph numbers and image numbers:

Recto: 050308_629_u (image: 1968_01_07–07A)

Verso: 050308_630_u (image: 1968_01_08–08A)

Edition number: 35 (Letter)

Museum of Islamic Art inventory number: 23973.46

Excavation photograph numbers and image numbers:

Recto: 1968_02_09A-10 (image: 050308_651_u)

Recto: 1968_02_10A-11 (image: 050308_652_u)

Verso: 1968_02_11A-12 (image: 050308_653_u)

This document also contains letter **26**.

Edition number: 36 (Letter)

Museum of Islamic Art inventory number: 23973.64

Excavation photograph numbers and image numbers:

Recto: 1966A_P06_06A-07 (image: ren 050308_100_u)

Recto: 1968_04_03–03A (image: 050308_689_o)

Verso: 1966A_P06_07A-08 (image: 050308_101_u)

Verso: 1968_04_04–04A (image: 050308_690_o)

Registration number: 66A/111 (?)

Edition number: 37 (Letter)

Sartain inventory number: Add. 02

Excavation photograph numbers and image numbers:

Recto: 1966A_P06_27A-28 (image: 050308_115_o)

Verso: 1966A_P06_28A-29 (image: 050308_116_o)

Registration number: 66A/111 (?)

Edition number: 38 (Letter)

Excavation photograph numbers and image numbers:

Recto: 1974_P04_02A-03 (image: 170308_647_o)

Verso: 1974_P04_03A-04 (image: 170308_648_o)

The verso also contains the document of lease **44**.

Object number: 74.1.29/11.4

Edition number: 39 (Letter)

Excavation photograph numbers and image numbers:

Recto: 1974_P04_04A-05 (image: 170308_649_o)

Verso: 1974_P04_05A-06 (image: 170308_650_o)

Object number: 74.1.29/11.5

Edition number: 40 (Letter)

Museum of Islamic Art inventory number: 23973.54

Excavation photograph numbers and image numbers:

1966A_P06_05A-06 (image: 050308_105_o)

1968_03_23–23A (image: 050308_678_u)

Registration number: 66A/111 (?)

Edition number: 41 (Poem of a Traveller)

Museum of Islamic Art inventory number: 23973.47

Excavation photograph number and image number:

1968_02_13A-14 (image: 050308_655_o)

Edition number: 42 (Account)

Excavation photograph numbers and image numbers:

Recto: 1974_V10_31A-32 (image: 170308_301_o)

Verso: 1974_V10_32A-33 (image: 170308_297_u)

Object number: 74.1.29/7

Edition number: 43 (Account)

Violet MacDermot's photograph number: 10 in a circle

Excavation photograph numbers and image numbers:

Recto: 1974_V09_01–01A (image: 170308_264_o)

Verso: 1974_V09_04–04A (image: 170308_263_u)

Registration number: 74/12

Edition number: 44 (Lease of Land)

Excavation photograph number and image number:

1974_P04_03A-04 (image: 170308_648_o)

Object number: 74.1.29/11.4

This document also contains the letter **38**.

Edition number: 45 (Lease of a Boat)

Museum of Islamic Art inventory number: 23973.45

Excavation photograph numbers and image numbers:

1968_02_06A-07 (image: 050308_648_u)

1968_02_07A-08 (image: 050308_649_u)

Edition number: 46 (Document of Testimony and Document of Sale)

Museum of Islamic Art inventory number: 23973.1

Excavation photograph numbers and image numbers:

Recto: 1968_02_22A-23 (image: 050308_658_u)

Recto: 1968_02_23A-24 (image: 050308_659_u)

Recto: 1968_02_24A-25 (image: 050308_660_o.jpg)

Verso: 1968_02_25A-26 (image: ren 050308_661_o)

Verso: 1968_02_26A-27 (image: ren 050308_662_o)

Verso: 1968_02_27A-28 (image: ren 050308_663_o)

Edition number: 47 (An Acknowledgement of a Debt and Testimonies)

Excavation photograph numbers and image numbers:

Recto: 1974_P04_11A-12 (image: 170308_650_u)

Verso: 1974_P04_10A-11 (image: 170308_649_u)

Edition number: 48 (Marriage Contract and Acknowledgement)

Museum of Islamic Art inventory number: 23973.61

Excavation photograph numbers and image numbers:

Recto: 1968_04_21–21A (image: 050308_695_u)

Recto: 1968_04_22–22A (image: 050308_696_u)

Recto: 1968_04_23–23A (image: 050308_697_u)

Recto: 1968_04_25–25A (image: 050308_699_o)

Recto: 1968_04_26–26A (image: 050308_700_o)

Verso: 1968_04_27–27A (image: 050308_701_o)

Edition number: 49 (Documents relating to Divorce)

Excavation photograph and image numbers:

Recto: 1978_B09_12A-13 (image: 070408_204_o)

Verso: 1978_B09_11A-12 (image: 070408_203_u)

Object number: 78.2.13/45A-E

Registration number: 276

Edition number: 50 (Acknowledgement relating to Divorce)

Excavation photograph number and image number:

Recto: 1978_B19_05A-06 (image: 070408_384_o)

Object number: 78.2.13/45A-E

Registration number: 276

Edition number: 51 (Marriage Contract and Testimony)

Excavation photograph numbers and image numbers:

Recto: 1978_A102_17–17A (image: 200308_101_u)

Verso: 1978_A102_18–18A (image: 200308_102_u)

Object number: 78.2.13/45A-E

Registration number: 276

Edition number: 52 (Court Record relating to Marriage)

Excavation photograph number and image number:

1978_A102_19–19A (image: 200308_103_u)

Object number: 78.2.13/45A-E

Registration number: 276

Edition number: 53 (Letter relating to a Marital Dispute)

Excavation photograph numbers and image numbers:

Recto: 1978_A102_16–16A (image: 200308_100_u)

Verso: 1978_A102_15–15A (image: 200308_099_u)

Object number: 78.2.13/45A-E

Registration number: 276

PLATES

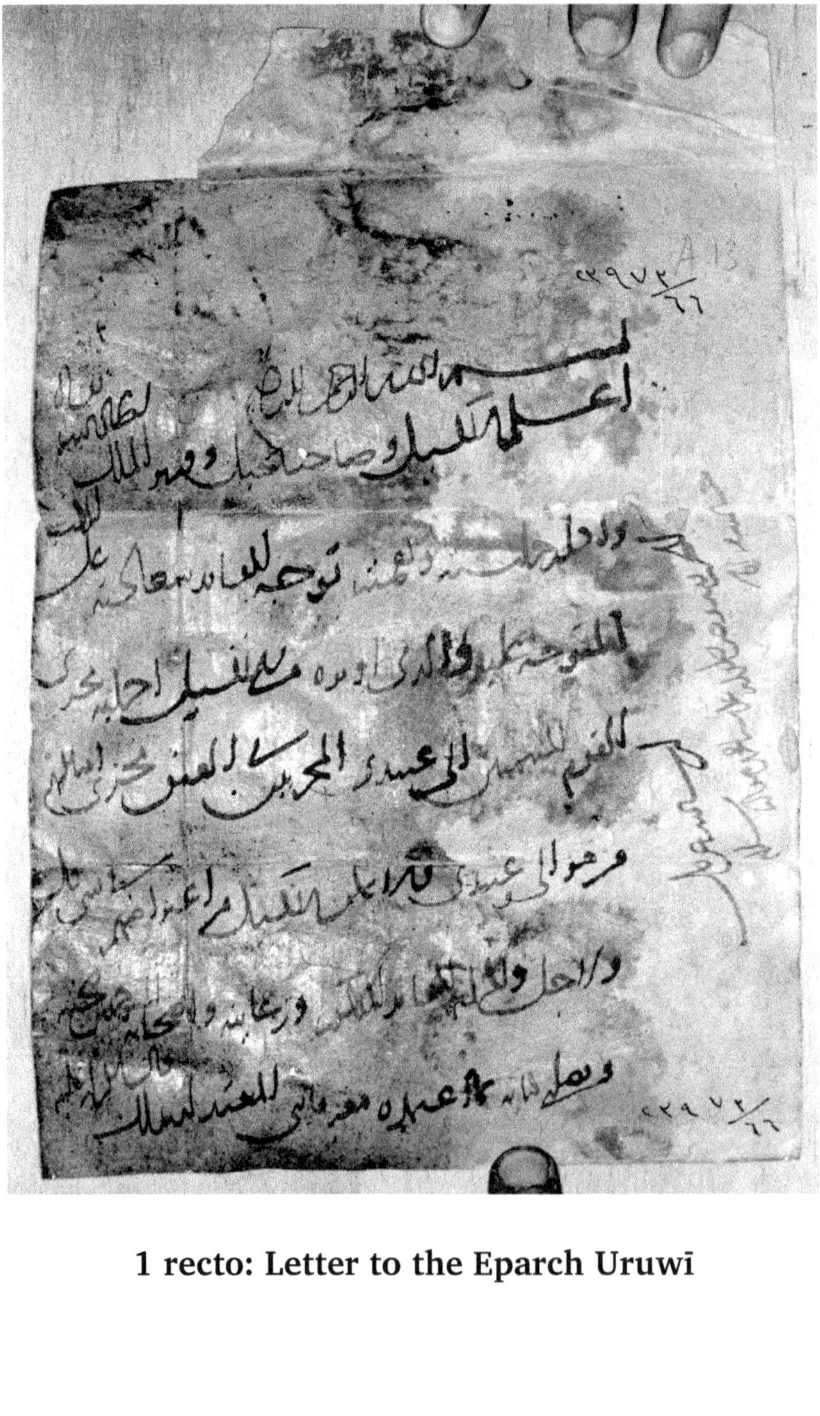

1 recto: Letter to the Eparch Uruwī

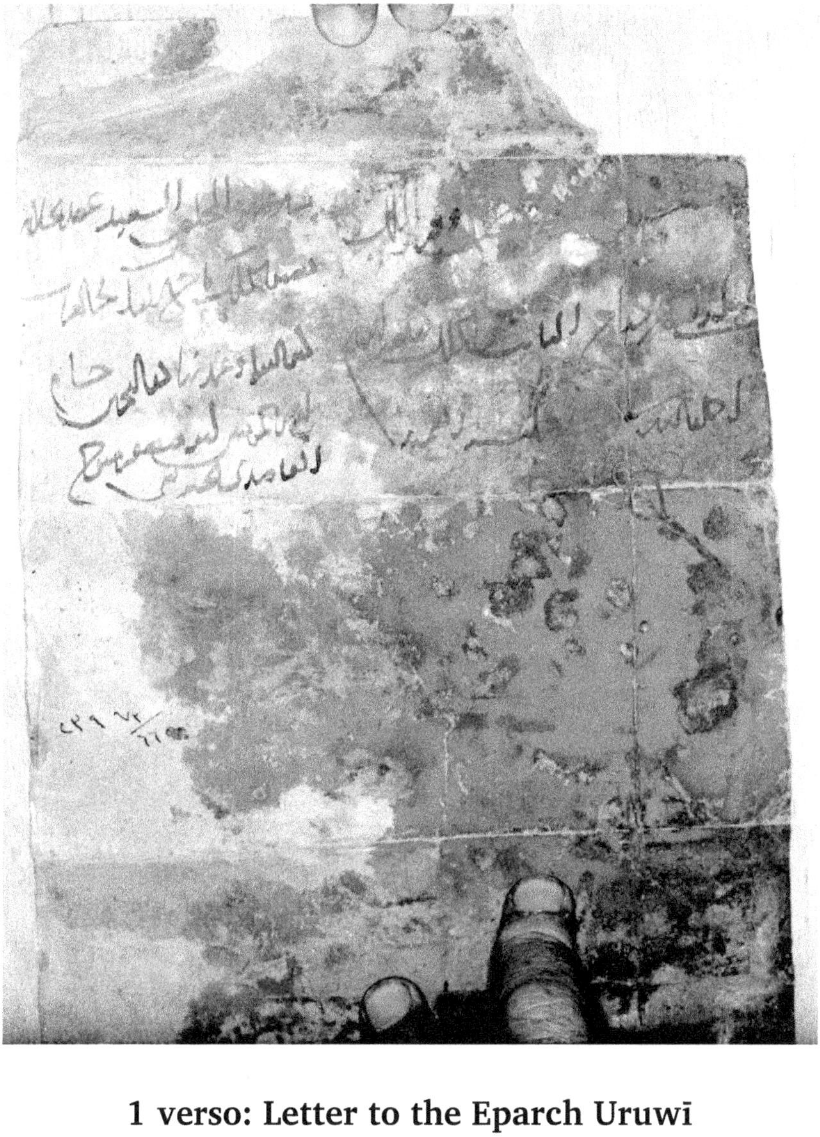

1 verso: Letter to the Eparch Uruwī

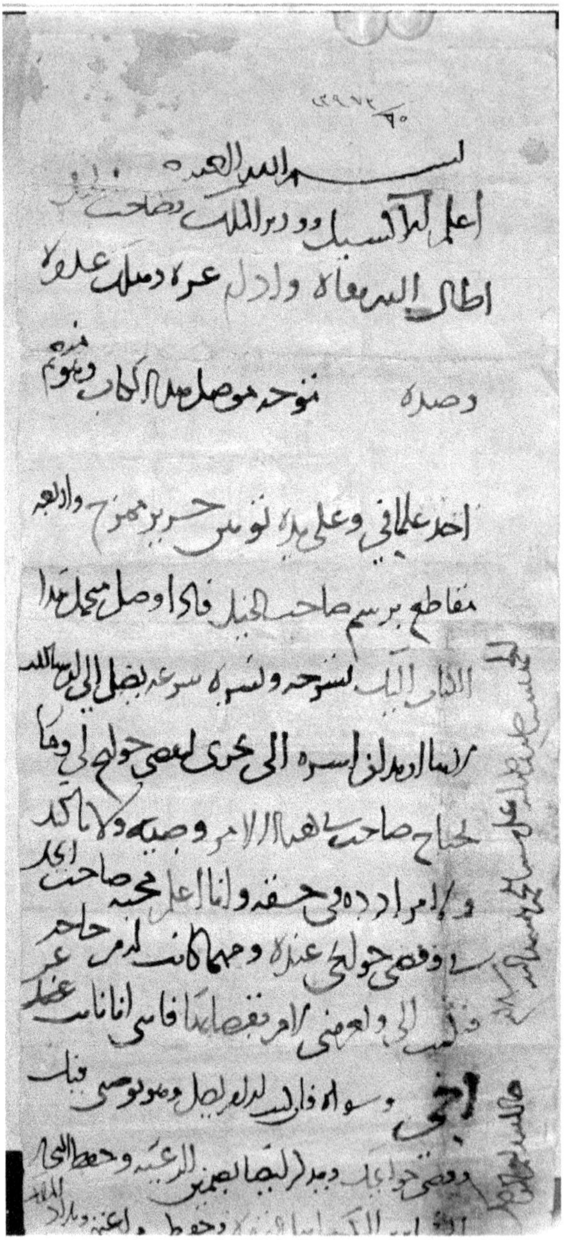

2 recto: Letter to the Eparch Uruwī

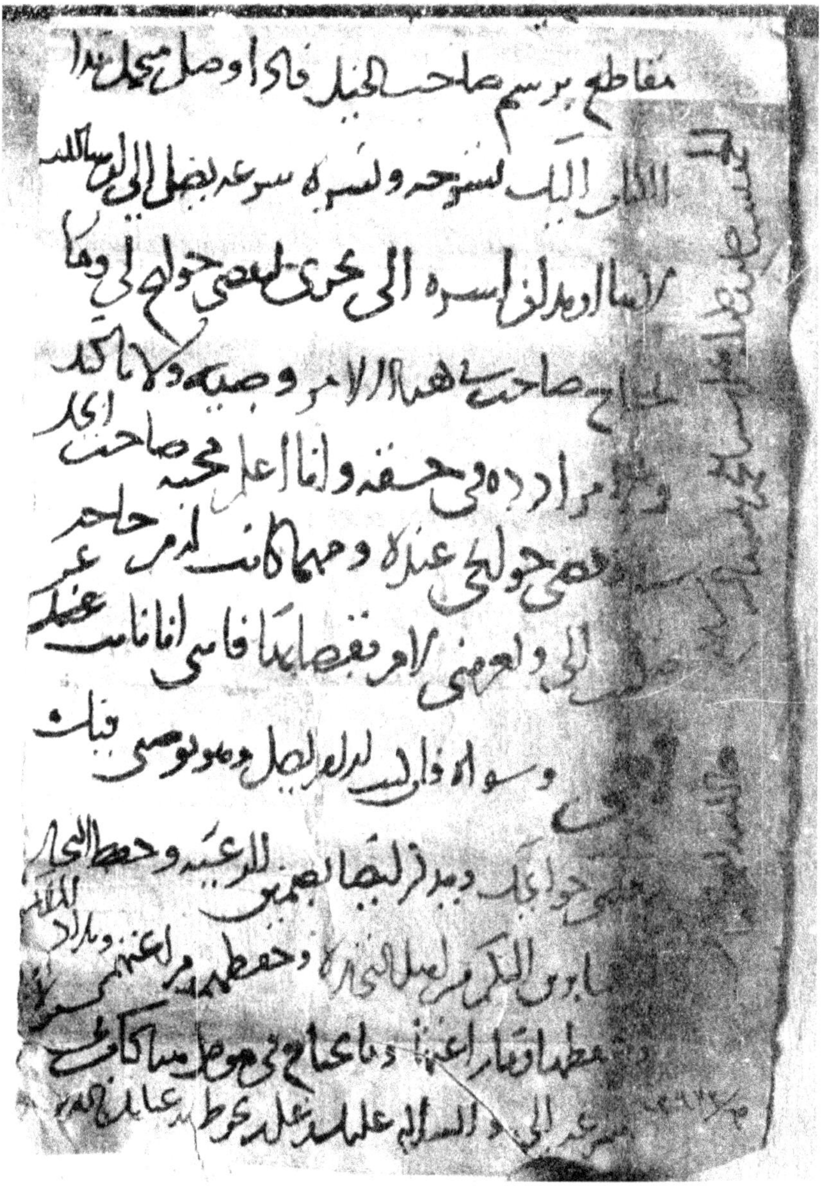

2 recto: Letter to the Eparch Uruwī

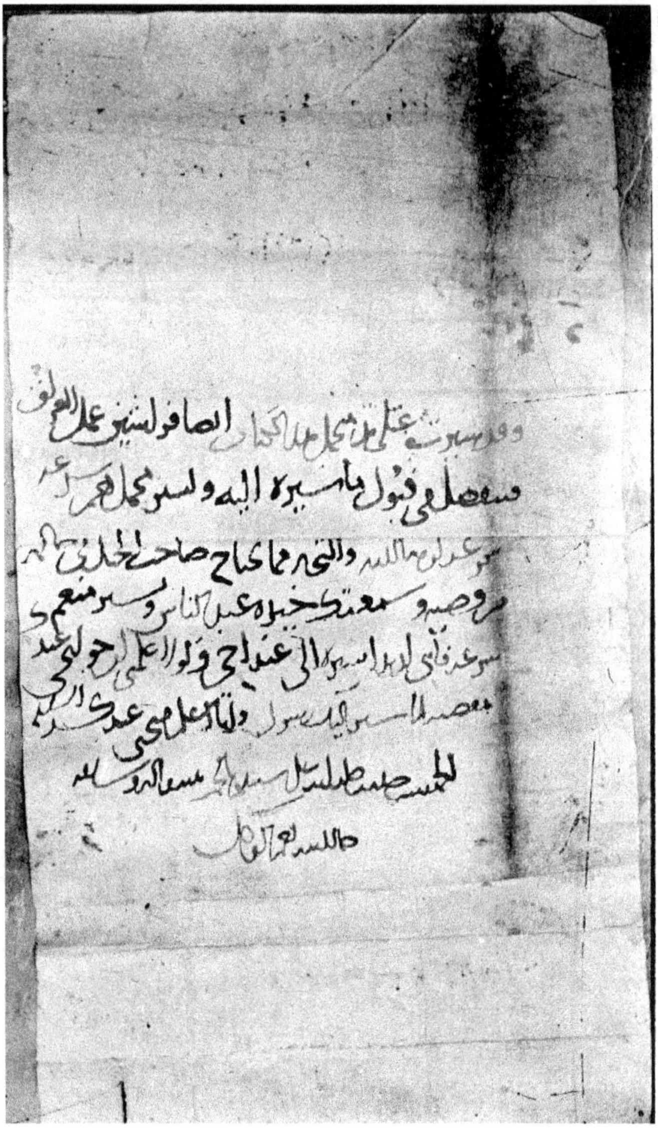

2 verso: Letter to the Eparch Uruwī

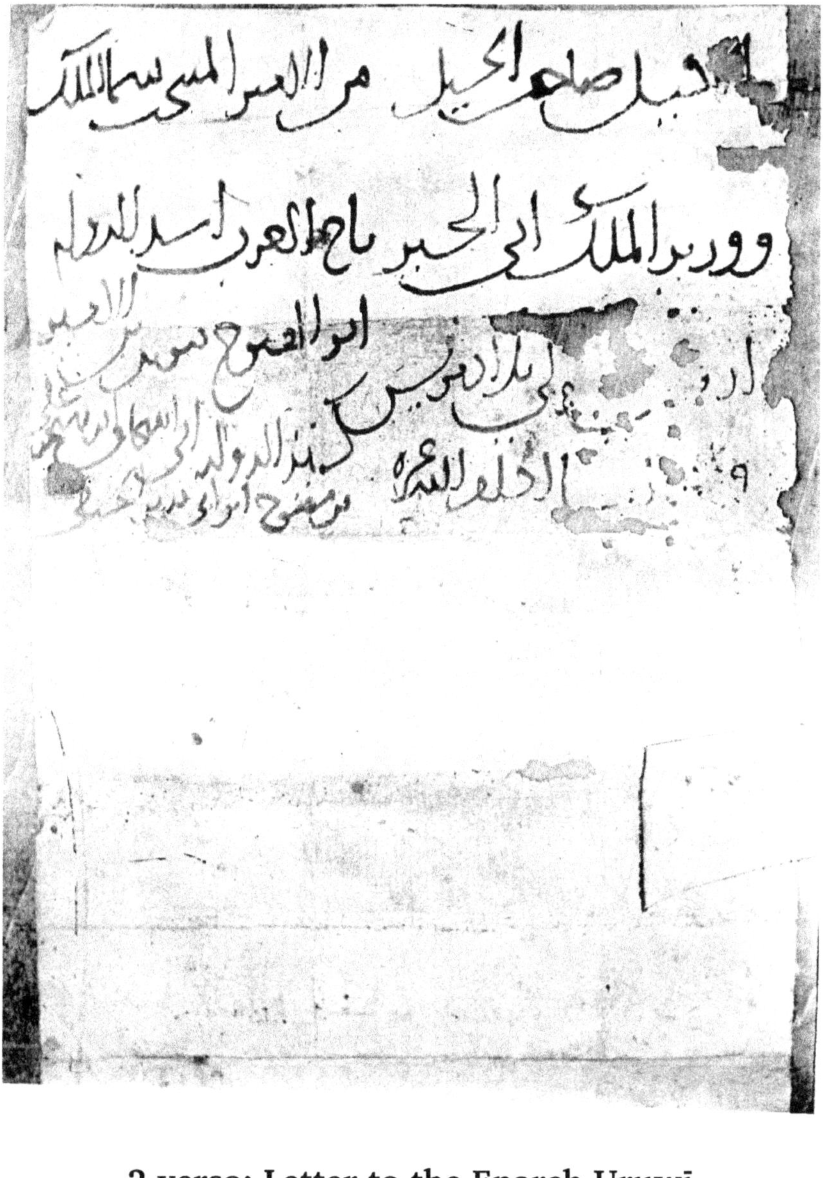

2 verso: Letter to the Eparch Uruwī

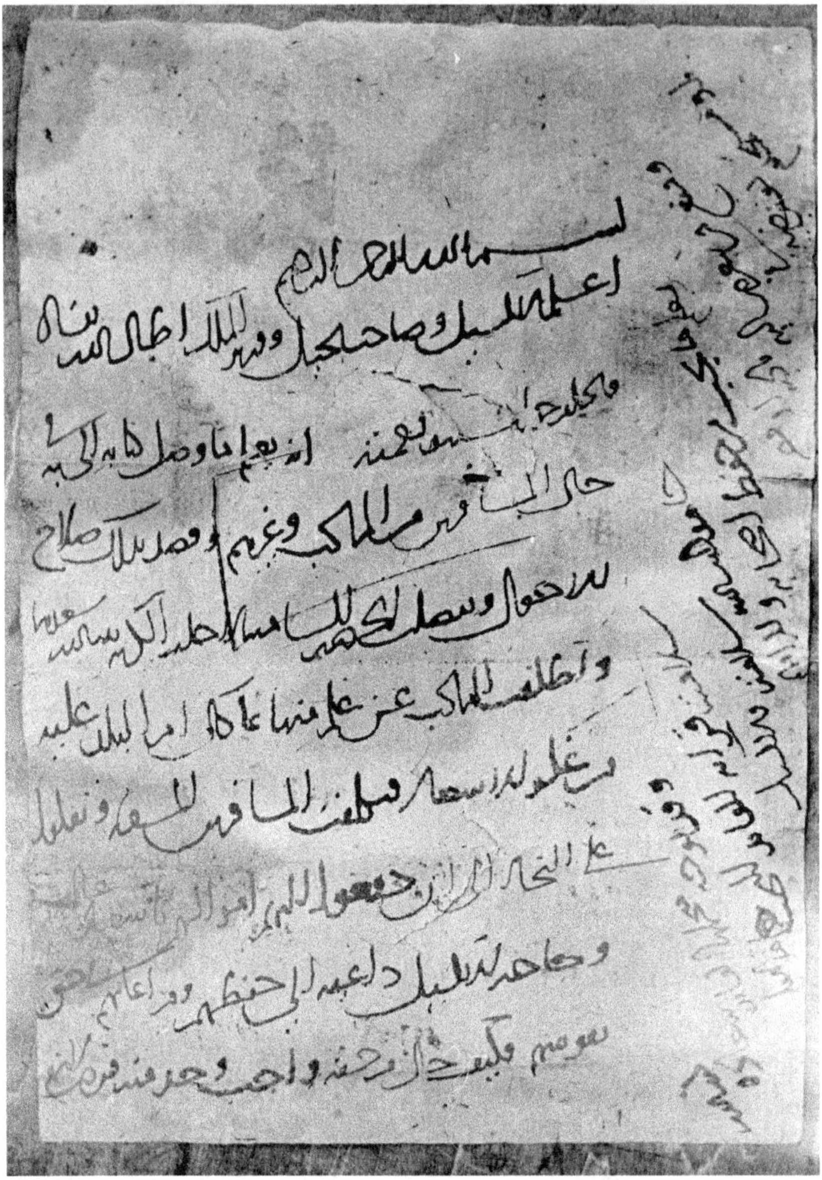

3 recto: Letter to the Eparch Uruwī

3 verso: Letter to the Eparch Uruwī

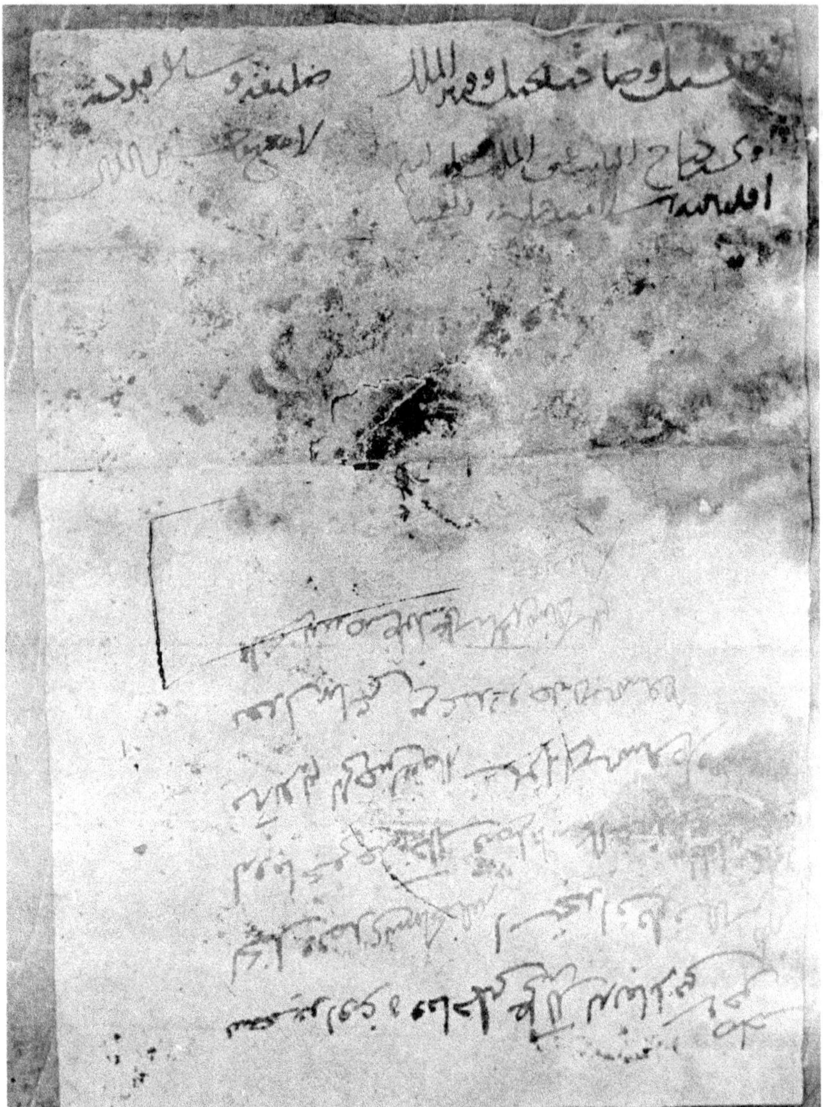

3 verso: Letter to the Eparch Uruwī

4 recto: Letter to the Eparch Uruwī

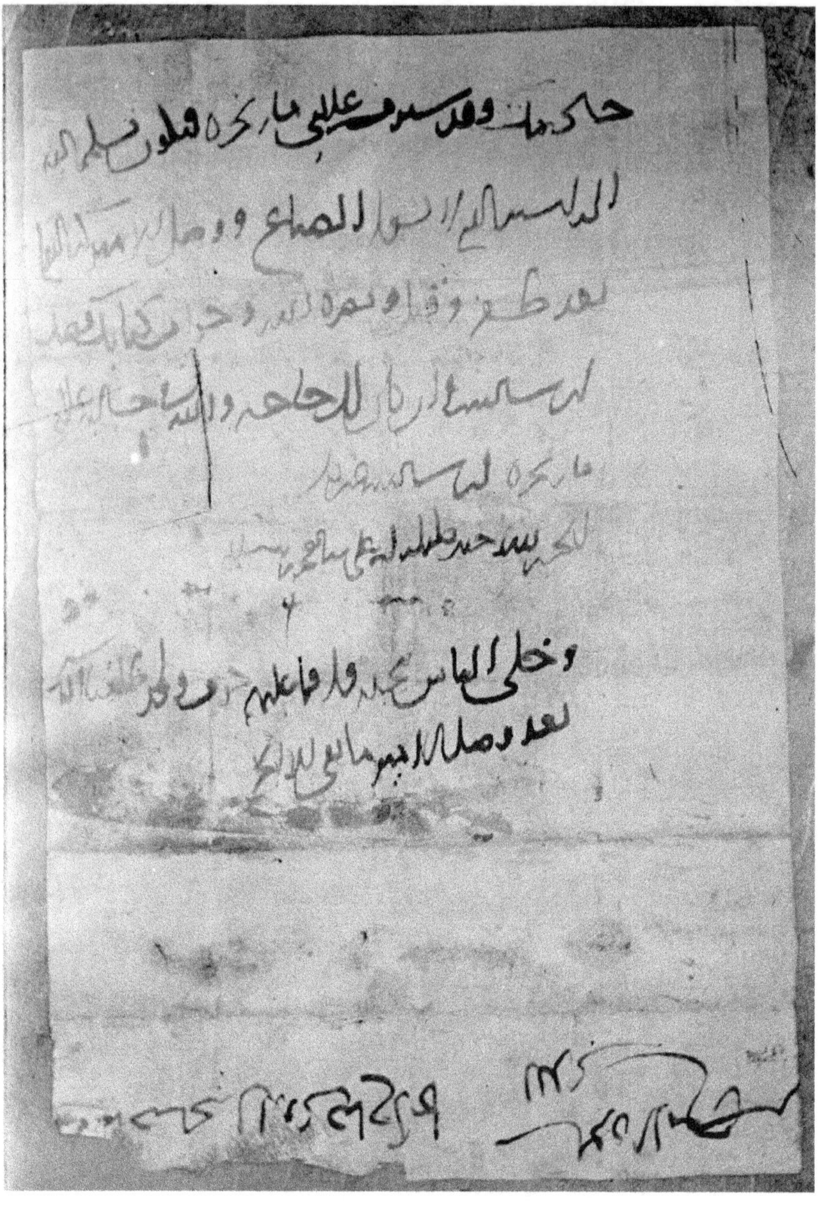

4 verso: Letter to the Eparch Uruwī

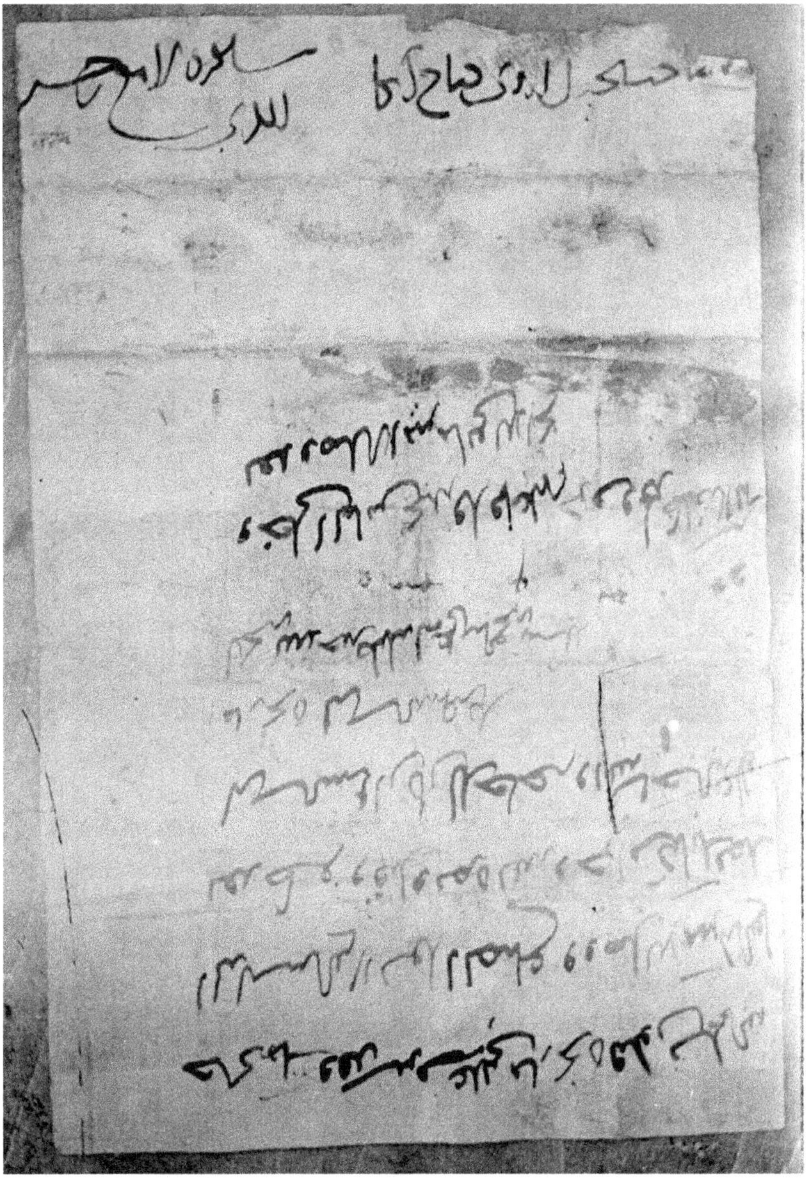

4 verso: Letter to the Eparch Uruwī

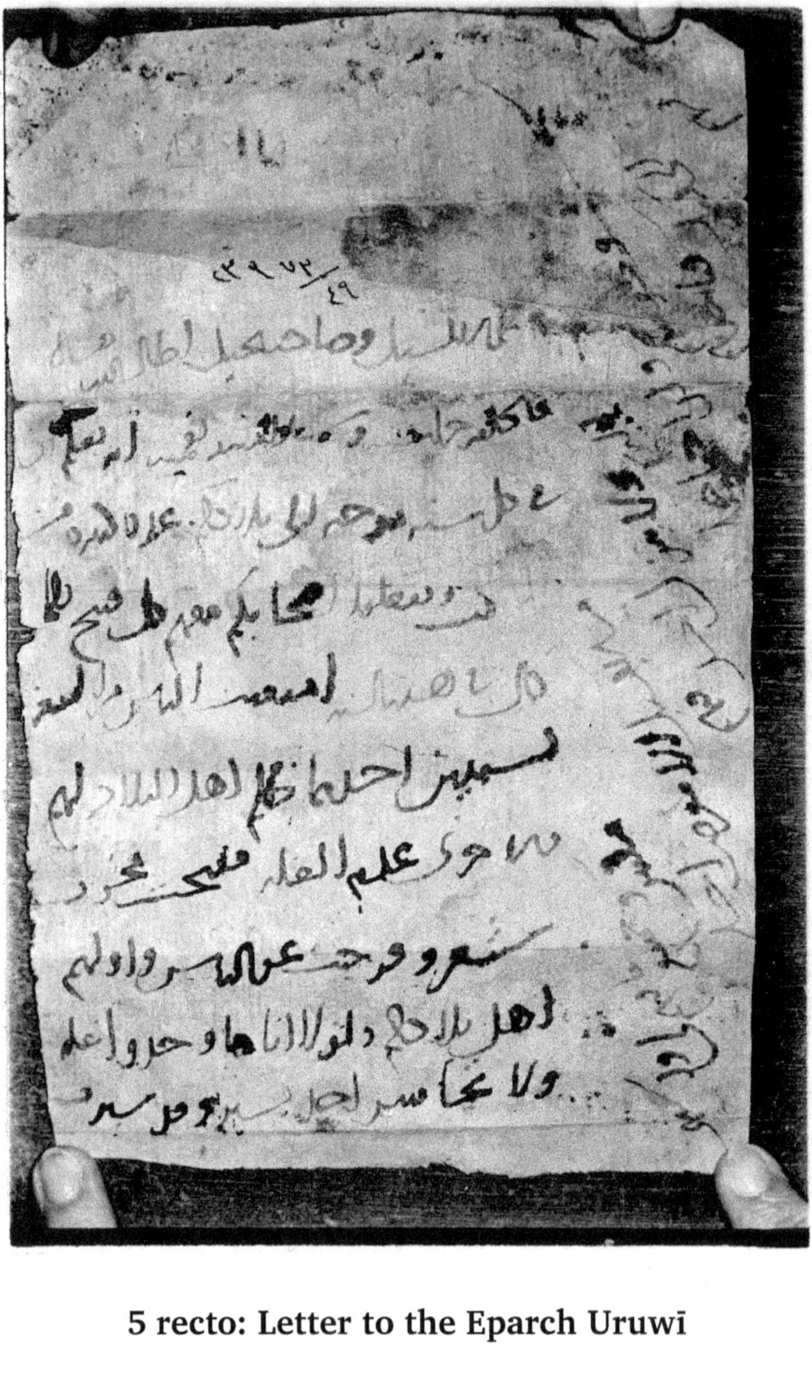

5 recto: Letter to the Eparch Uruwī

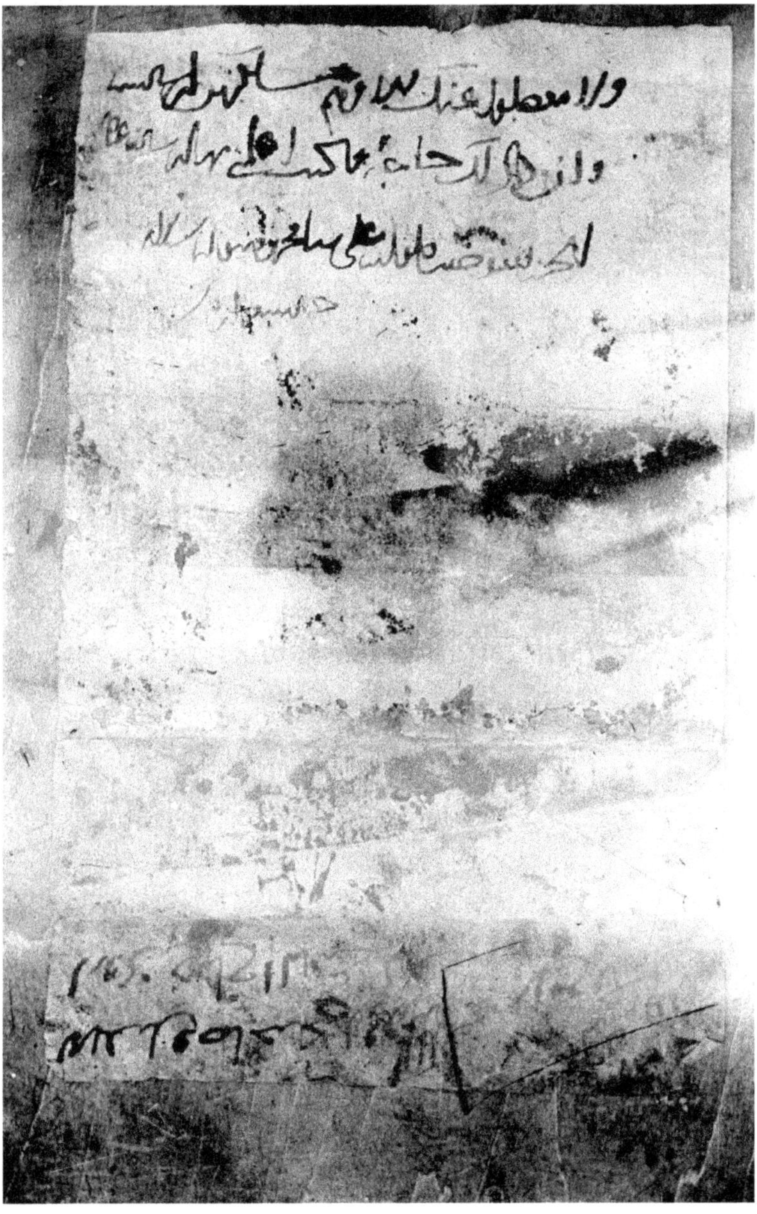

5 verso: Letter to the Eparch Uruwī

5 verso: Letter to the Eparch Uruwī

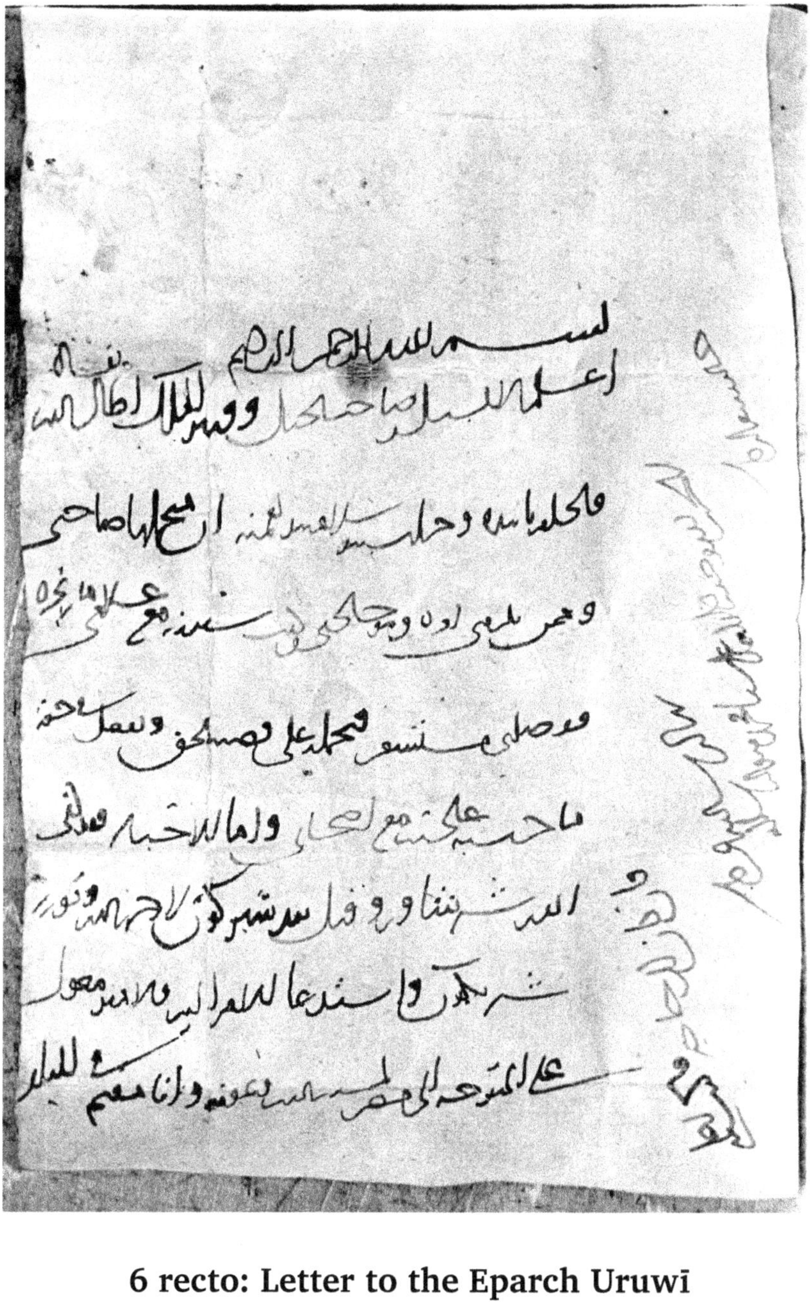
بسم الله الرحمن الرحيم

6 recto: Letter to the Eparch Uruwī

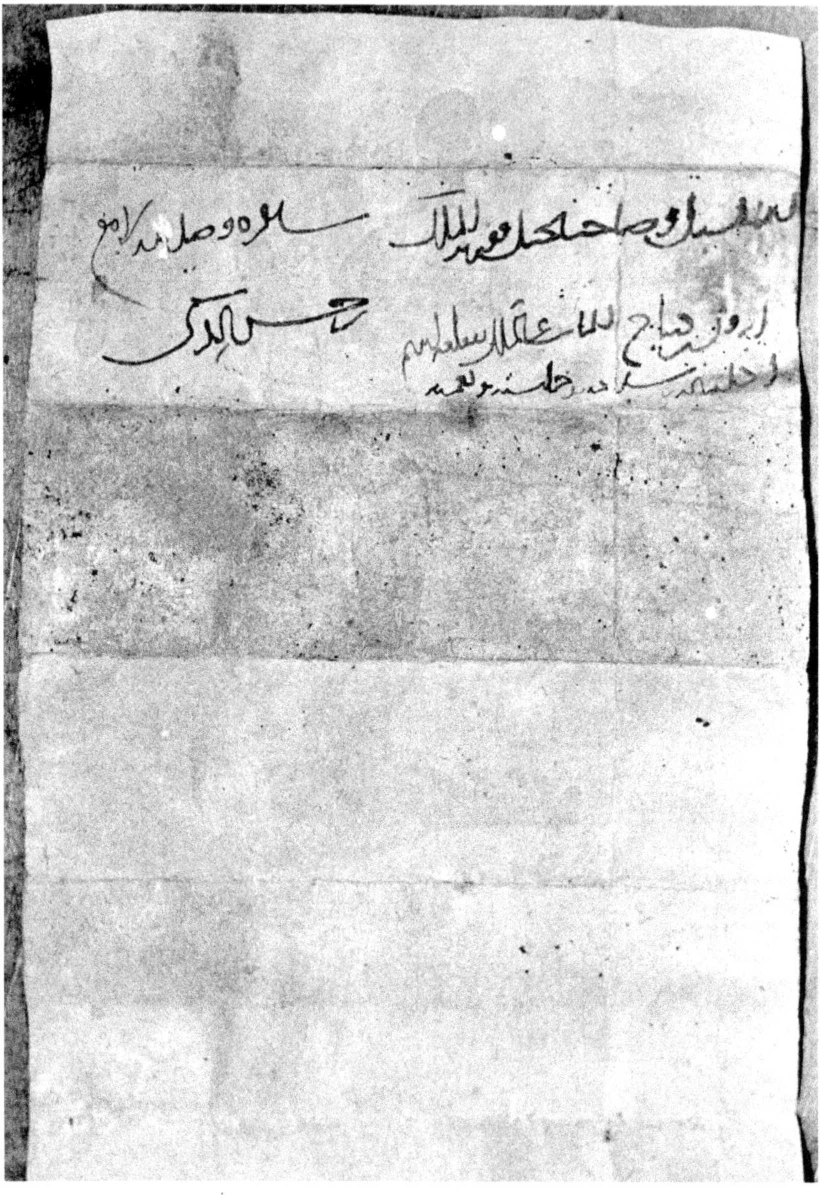

6 verso: Letter to the Eparch Uruwī

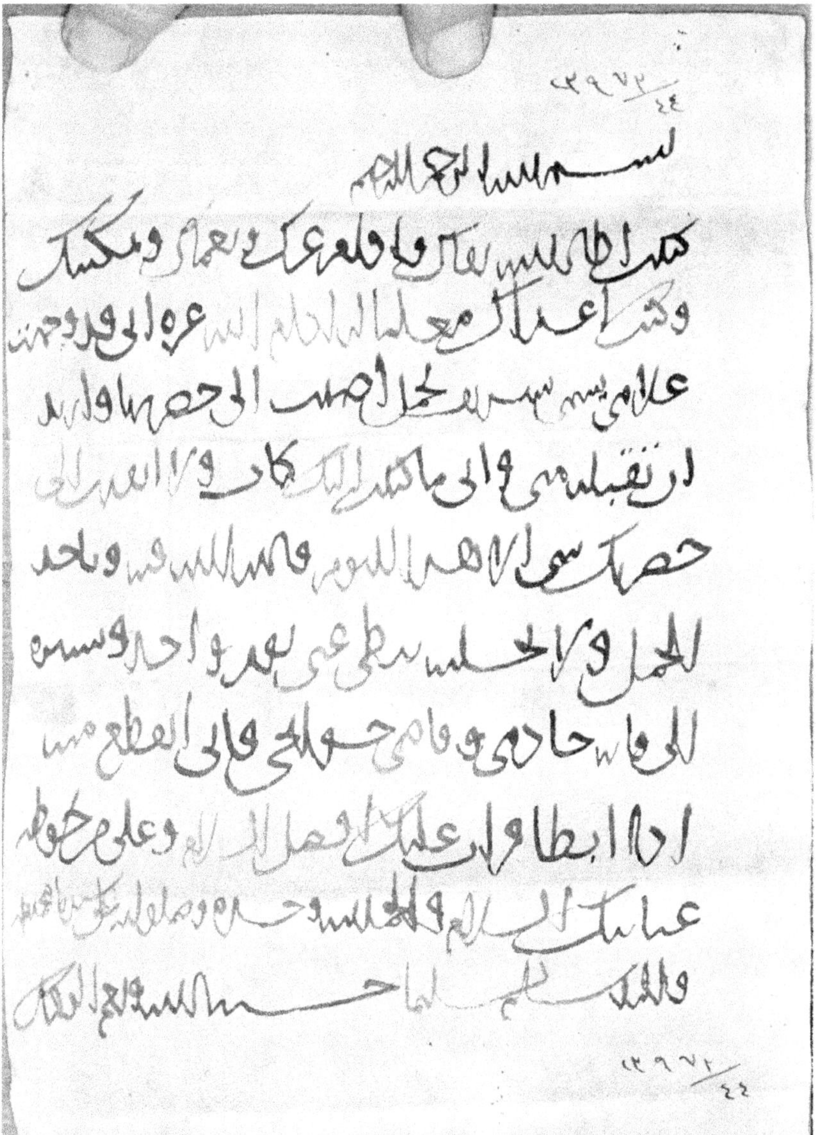
٢٩٧٢/٤٤

بسم الله الرحمن الرحيم

7 recto: Letter to the Eparch Uruwī

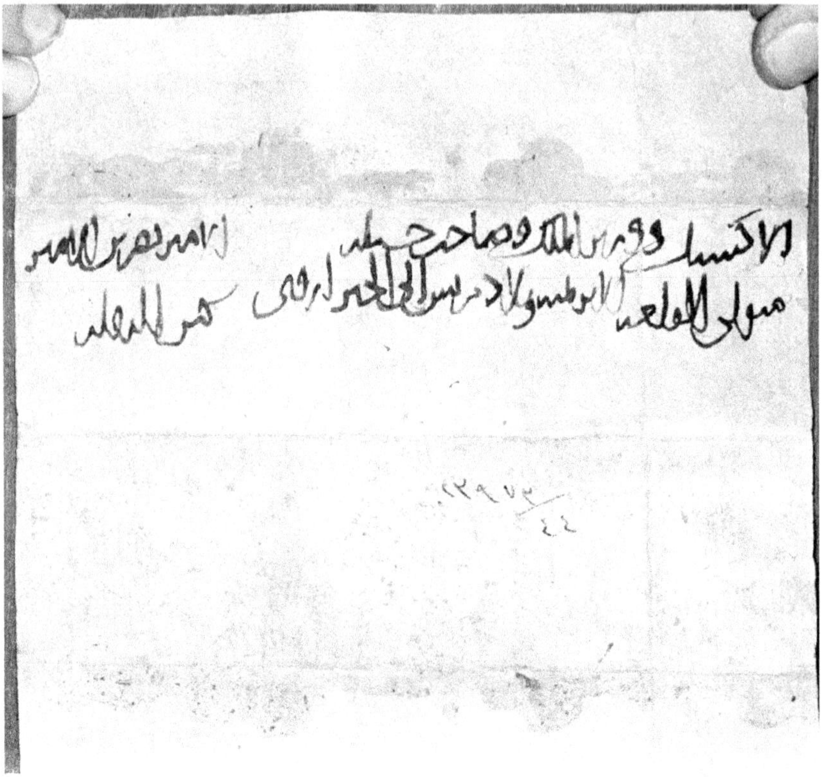

7 verso: Letter to the Eparch Uruwī

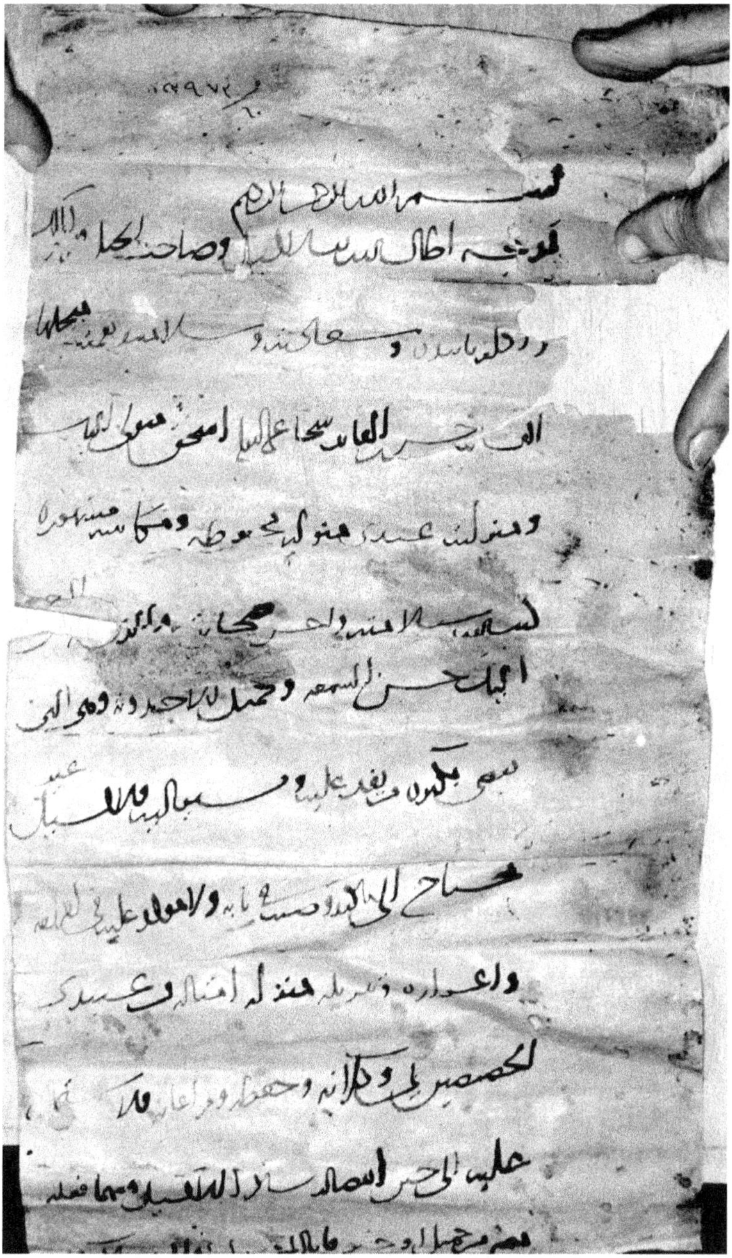

8 recto: Letter to the Eparch Uruwī

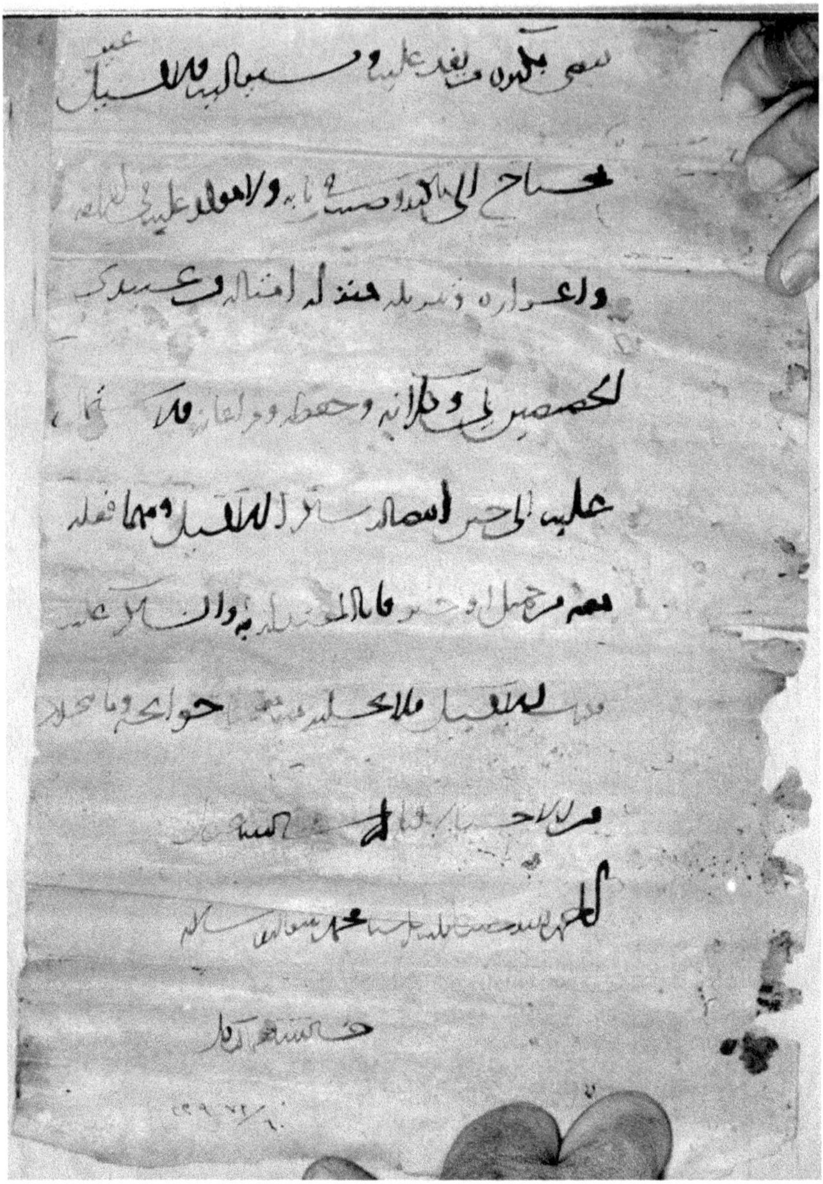

8 recto: Letter to the Eparch Uruwī

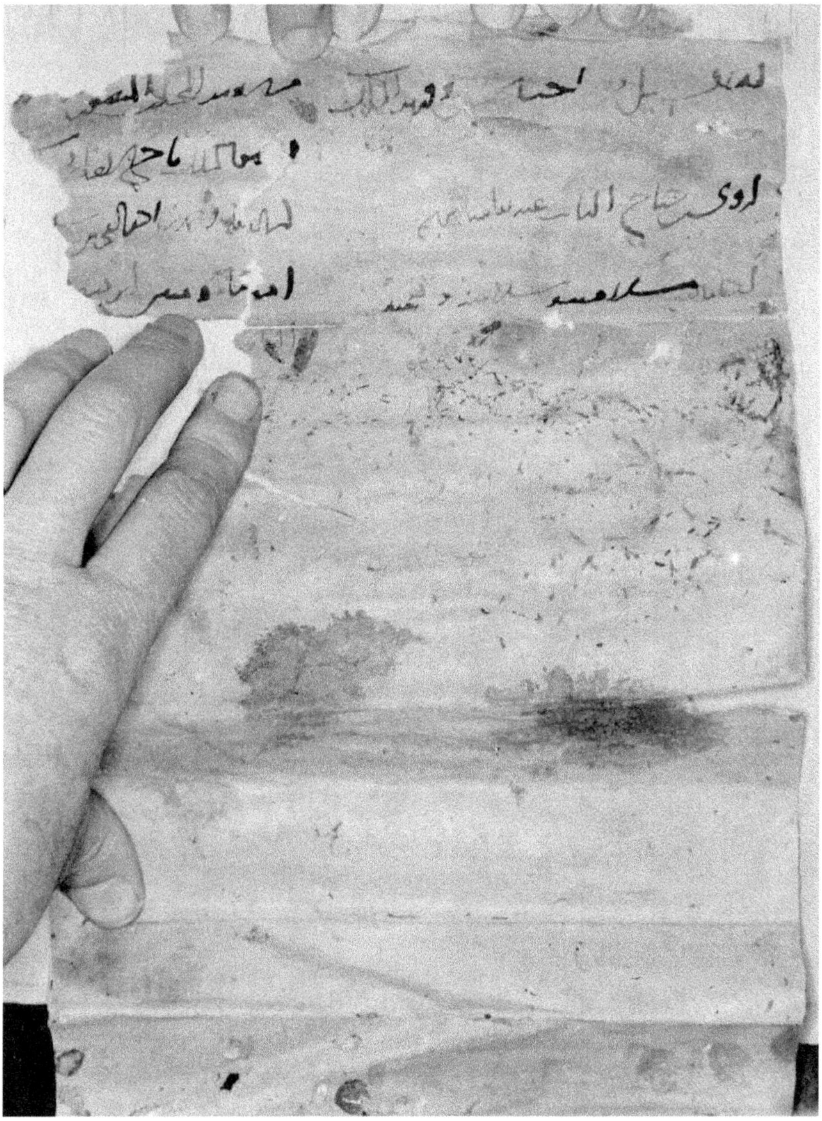

8 verso: Letter to the Eparch Uruwī

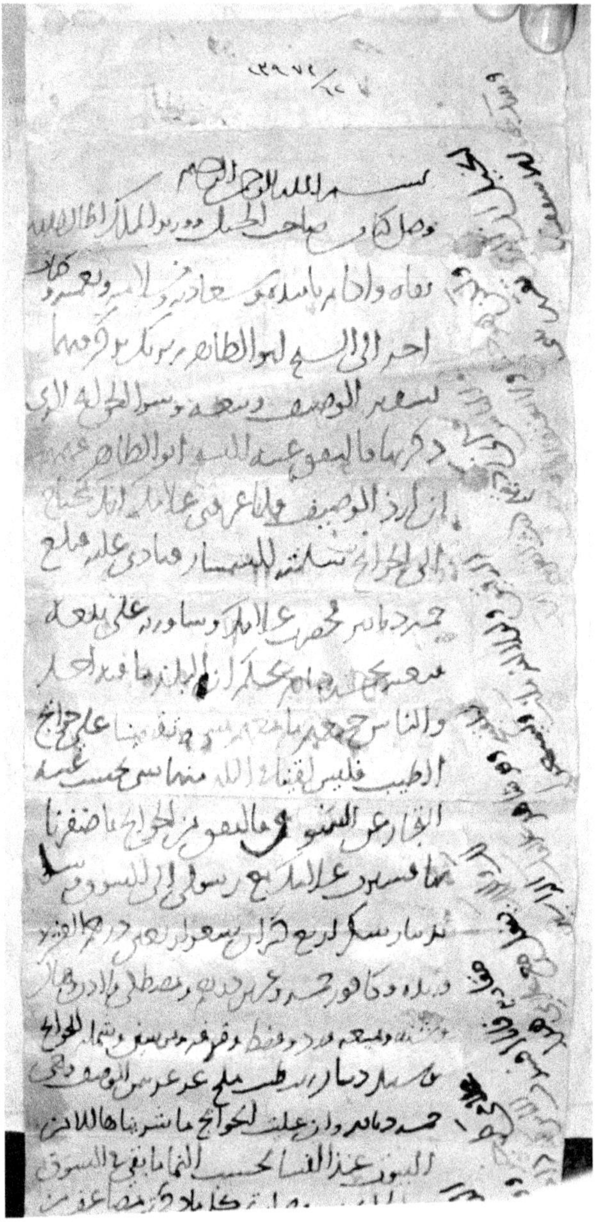

9 recto: Letter to the Eparch Uruwī

9 recto: Letter to the Eparch Uruwī

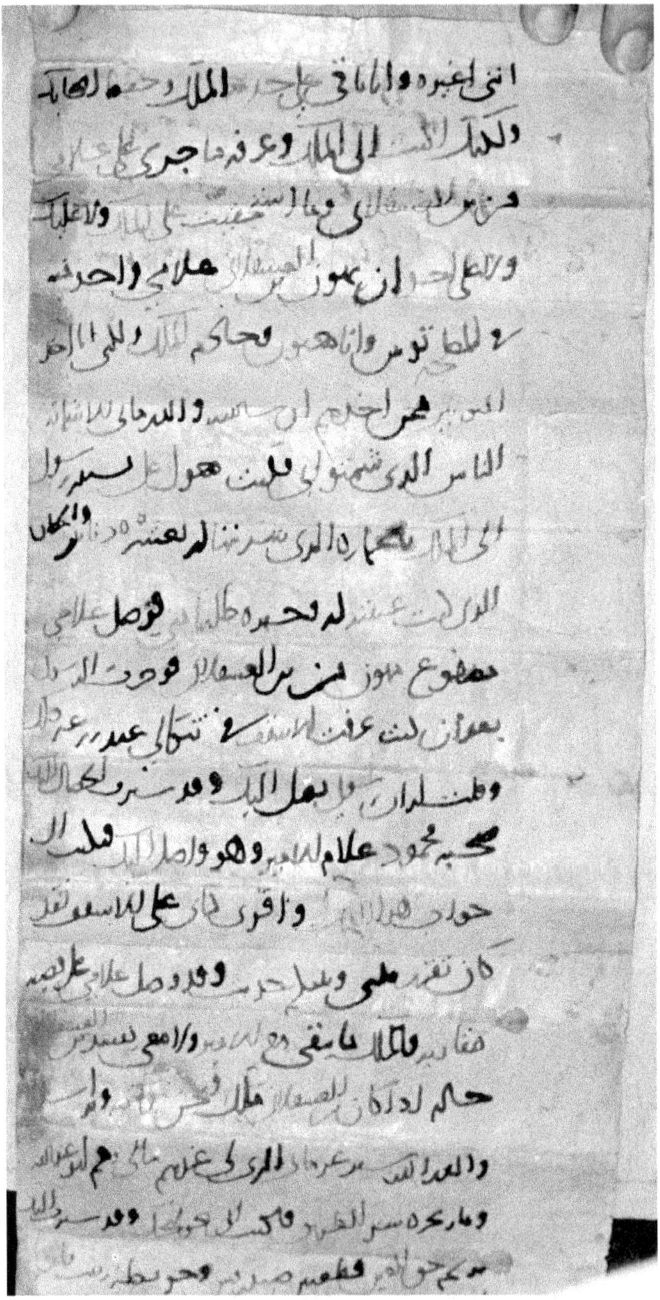

9 verso: Letter to the Eparch Uruwī

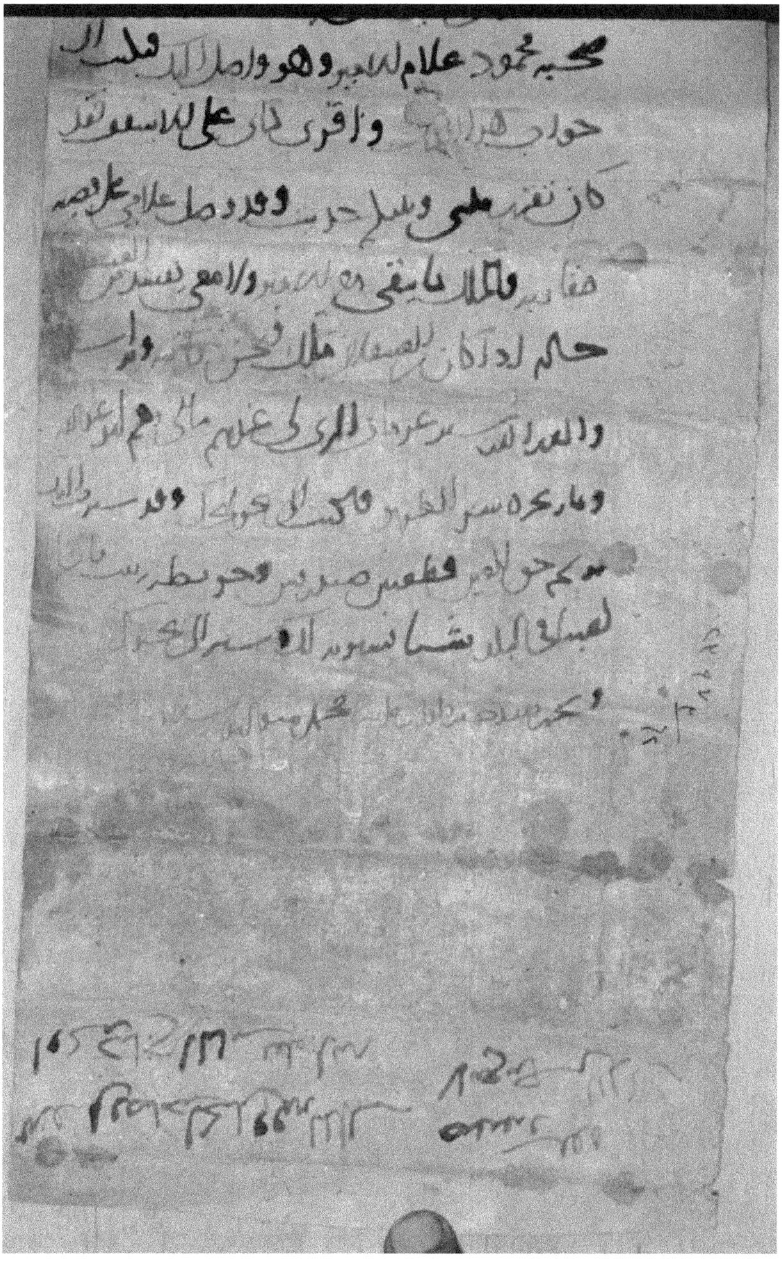

9 verso: Letter to the Eparch Uruwī

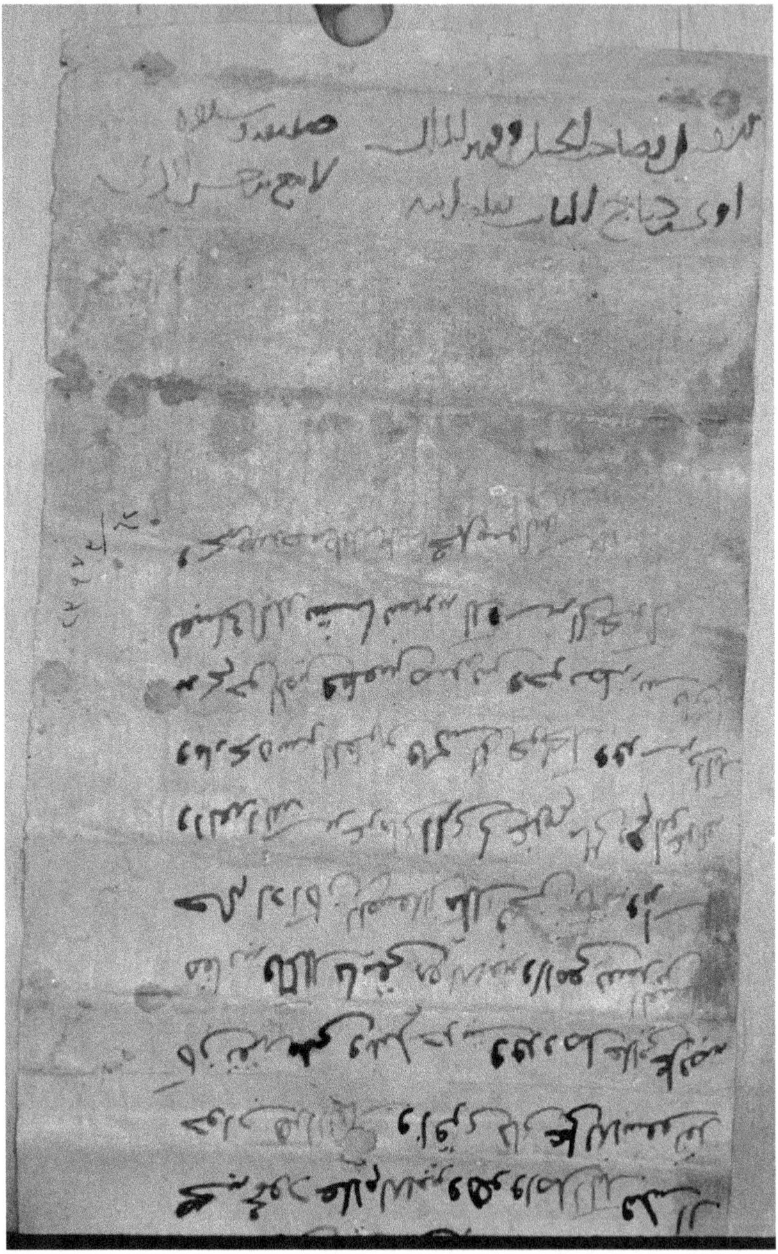

9 verso: Letter to the Eparch Uruwī

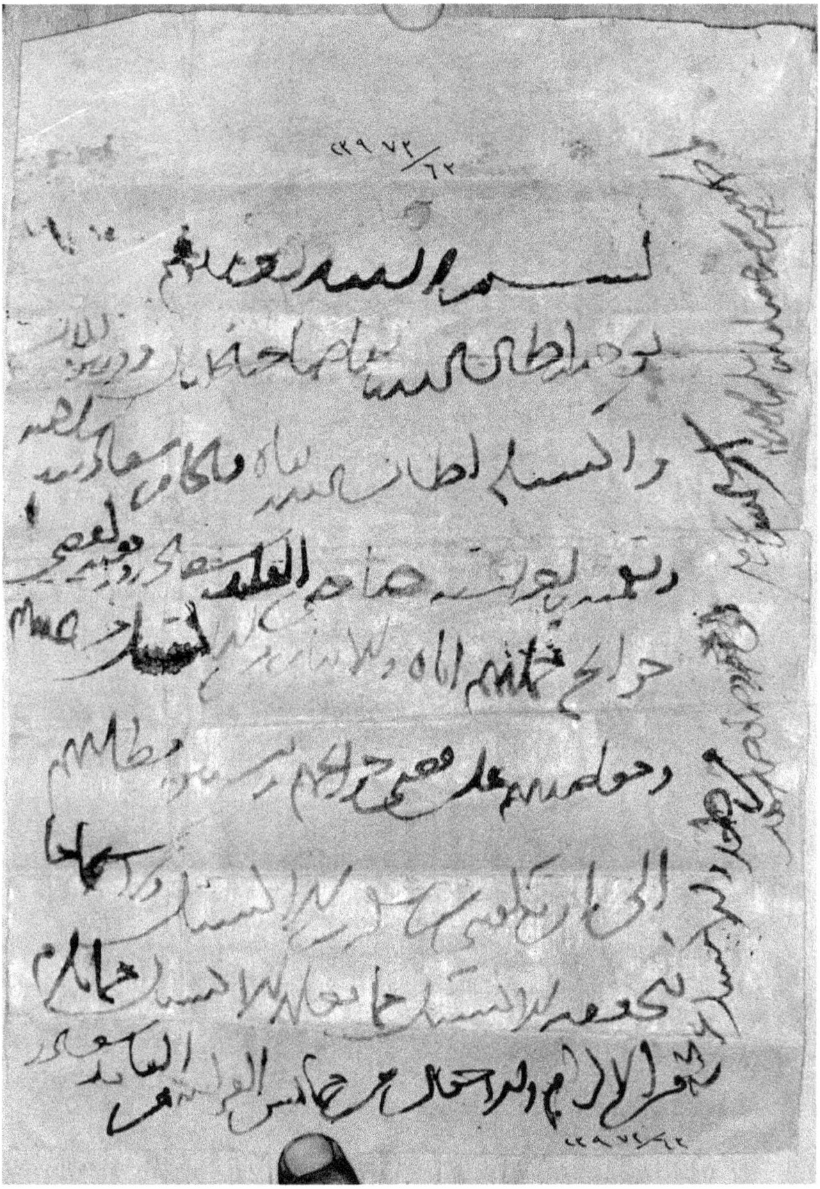

10 recto: Letter to the Eparch Uruwī

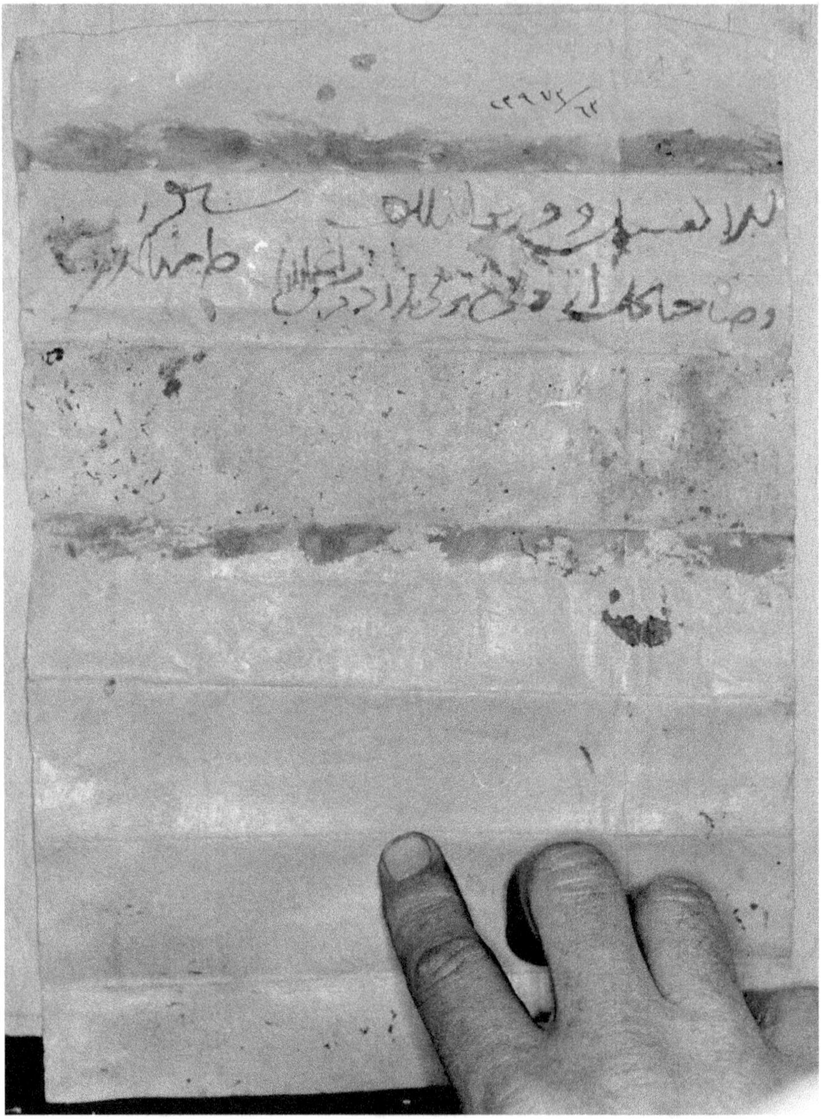

10 verso: Letter to the Eparch Uruwī

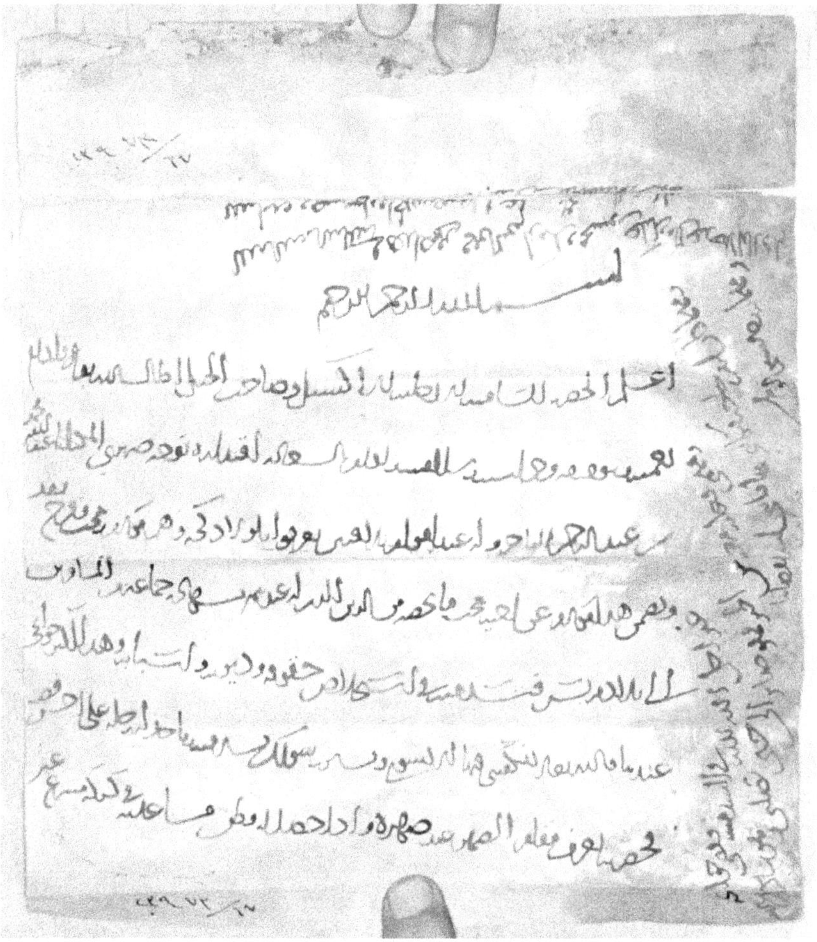

11 recto: Letter to the Eparch Uruwī

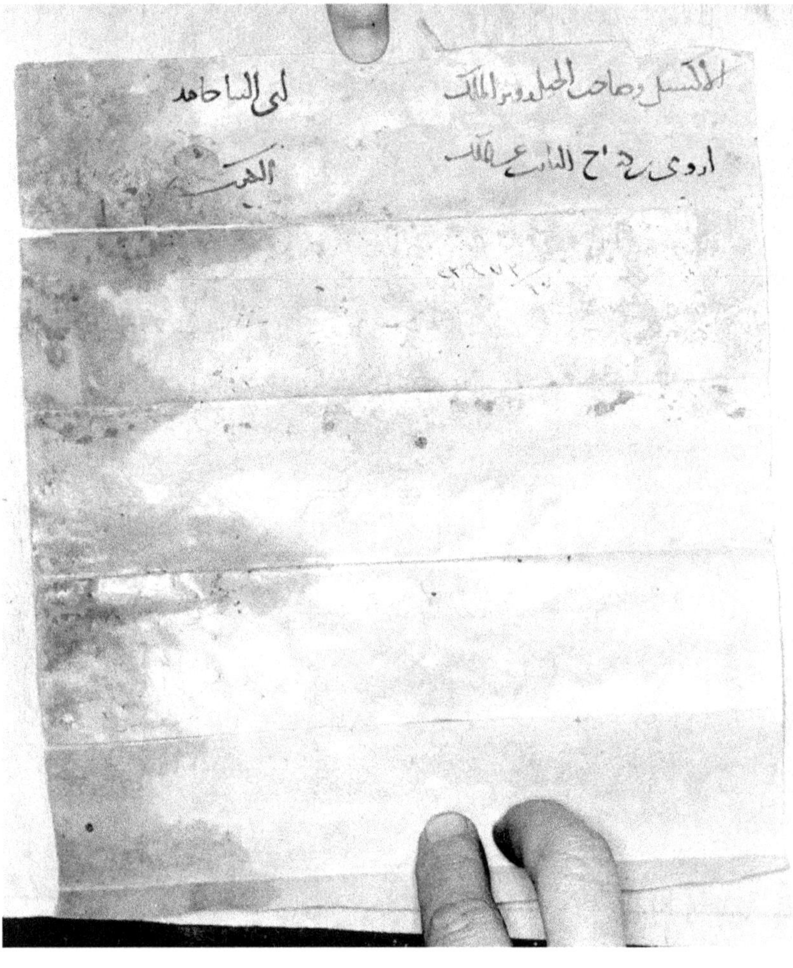

11 verso: Letter to the Eparch Uruwī

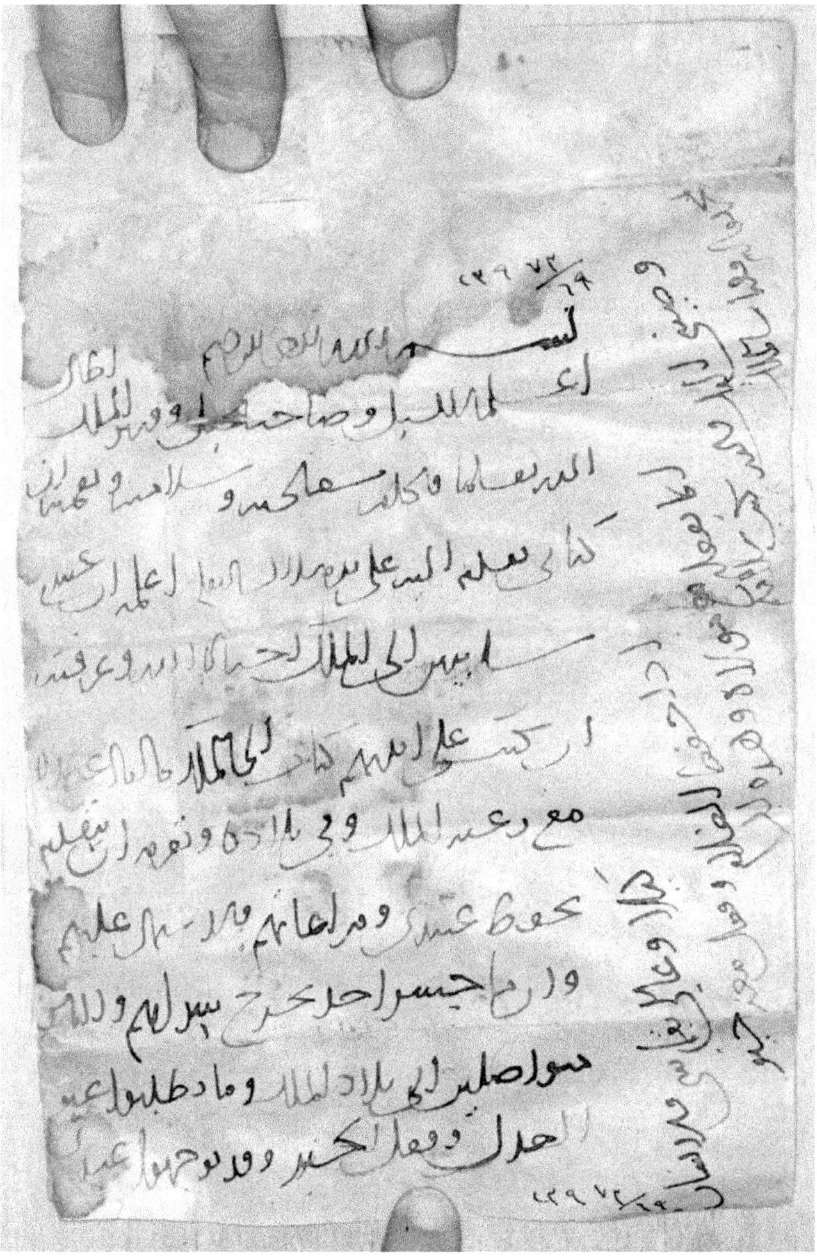

12 recto: Letter to the Eparch Uruwī

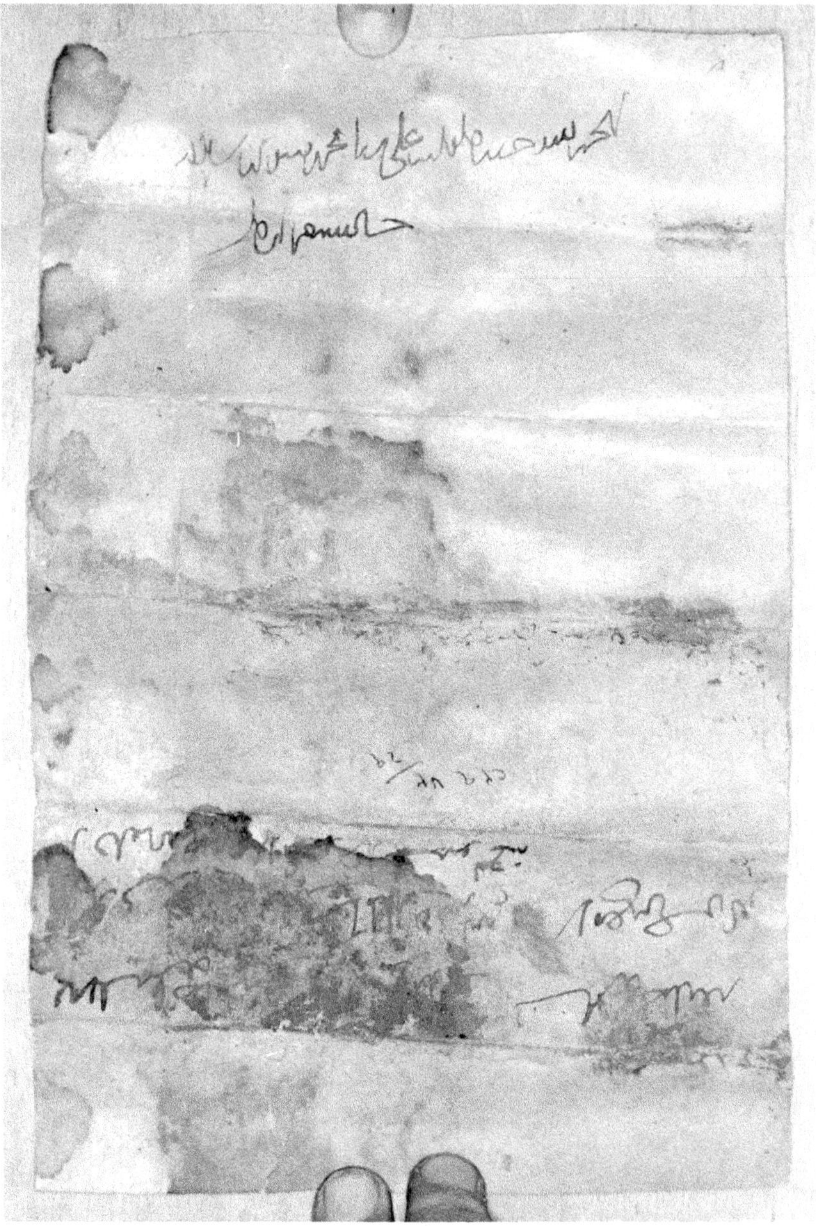

12 verso: Letter to the Eparch Uruwī

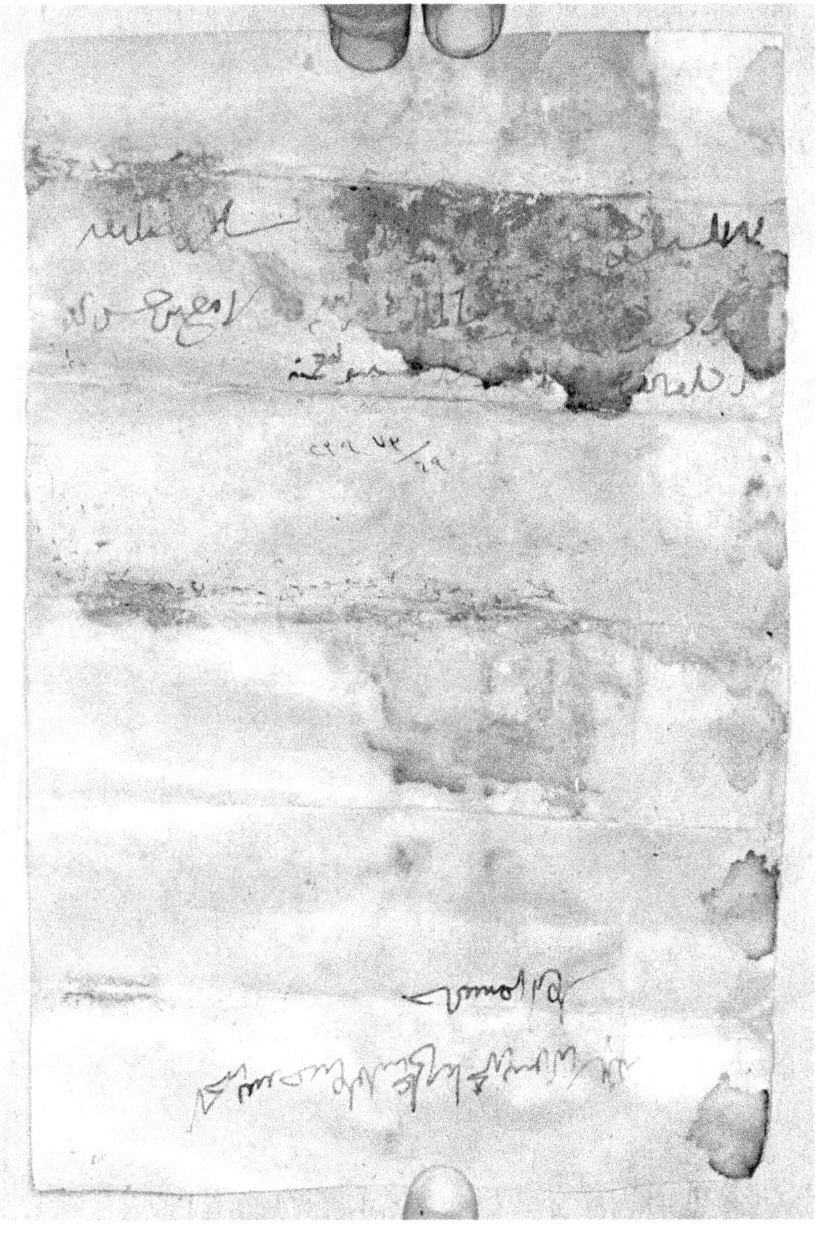

12 verso: Letter to the Eparch Uruwī

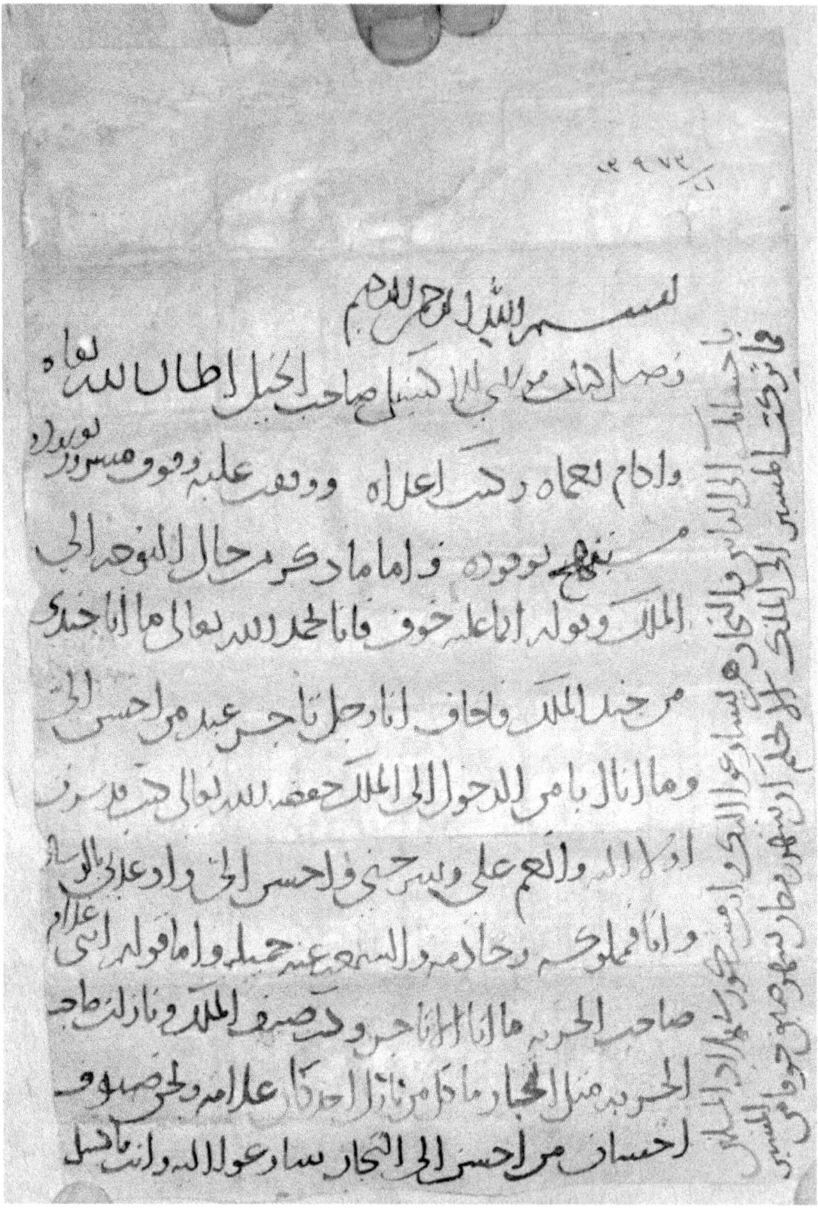

13 recto: Letter to the Eparch Uruwī

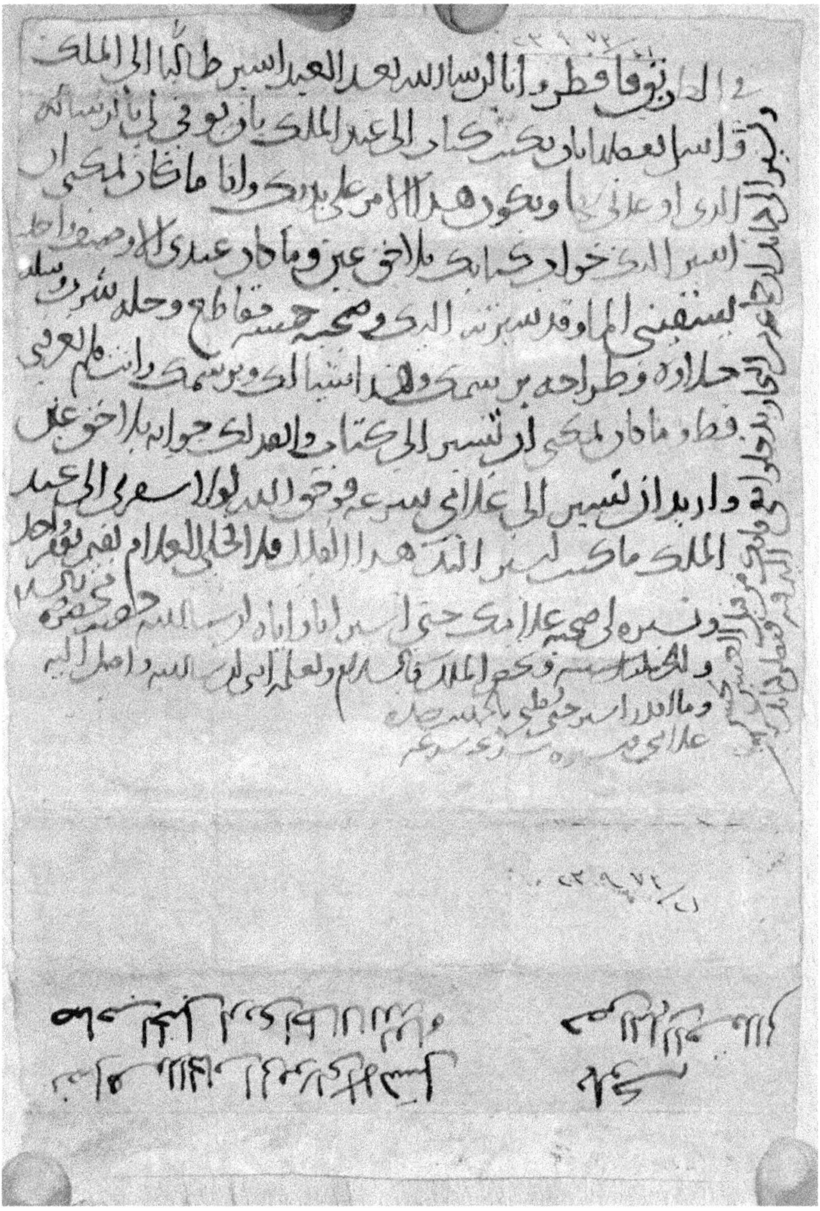

13 verso: Letter to the Eparch Uruwī

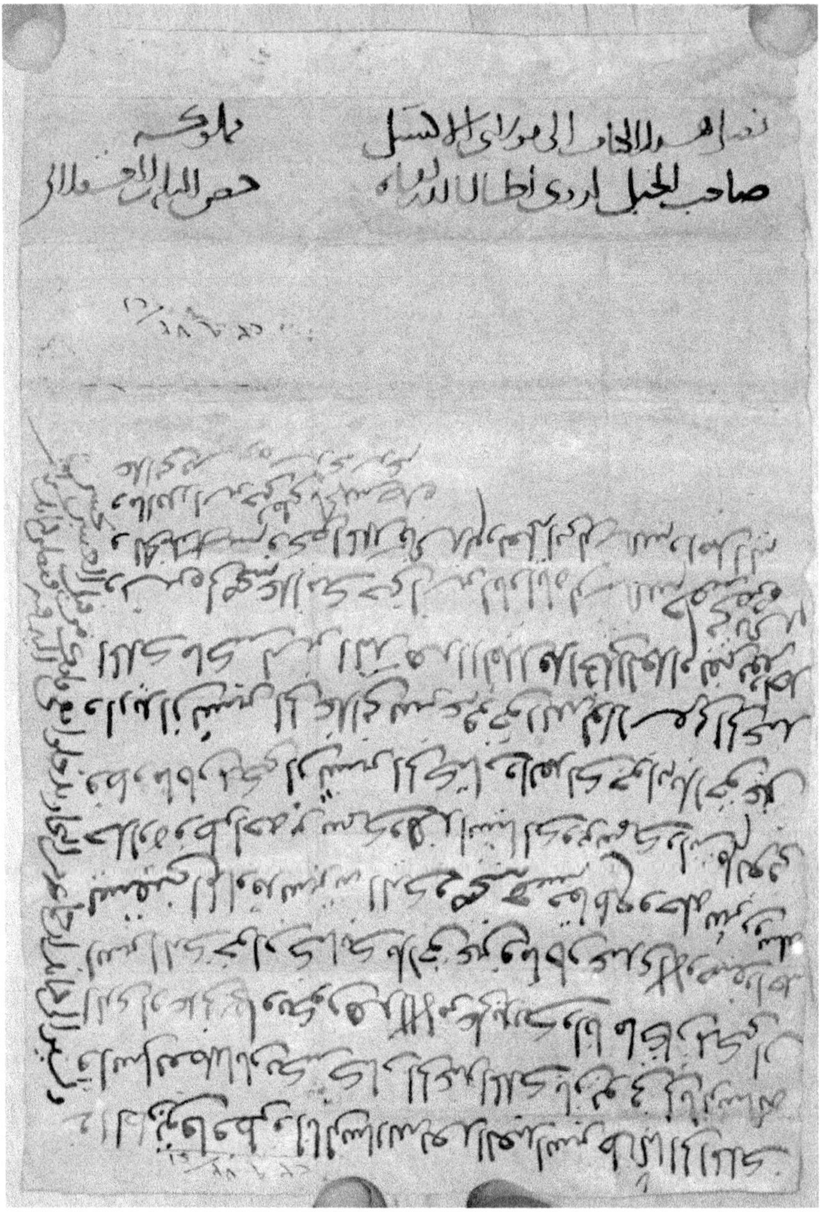

13 verso: Letter to the Eparch Uruwī

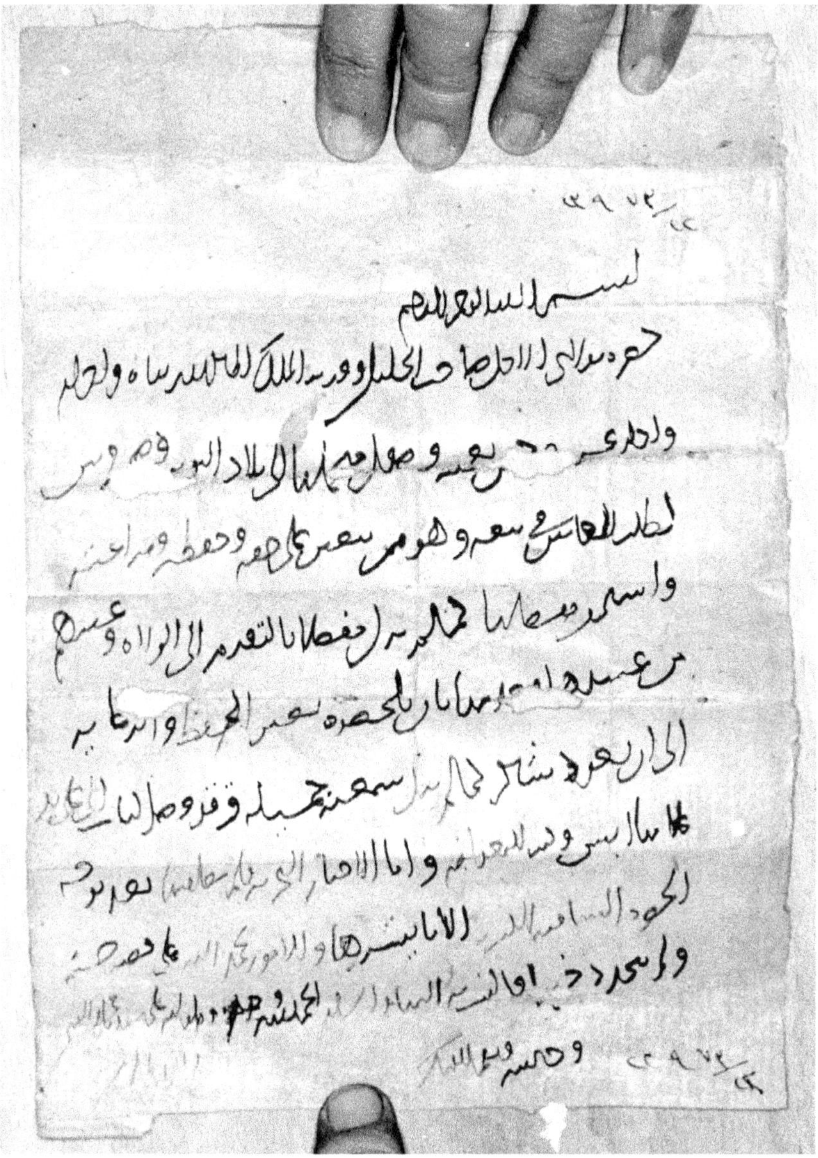

14 recto: Letter to the Eparch Uruwī

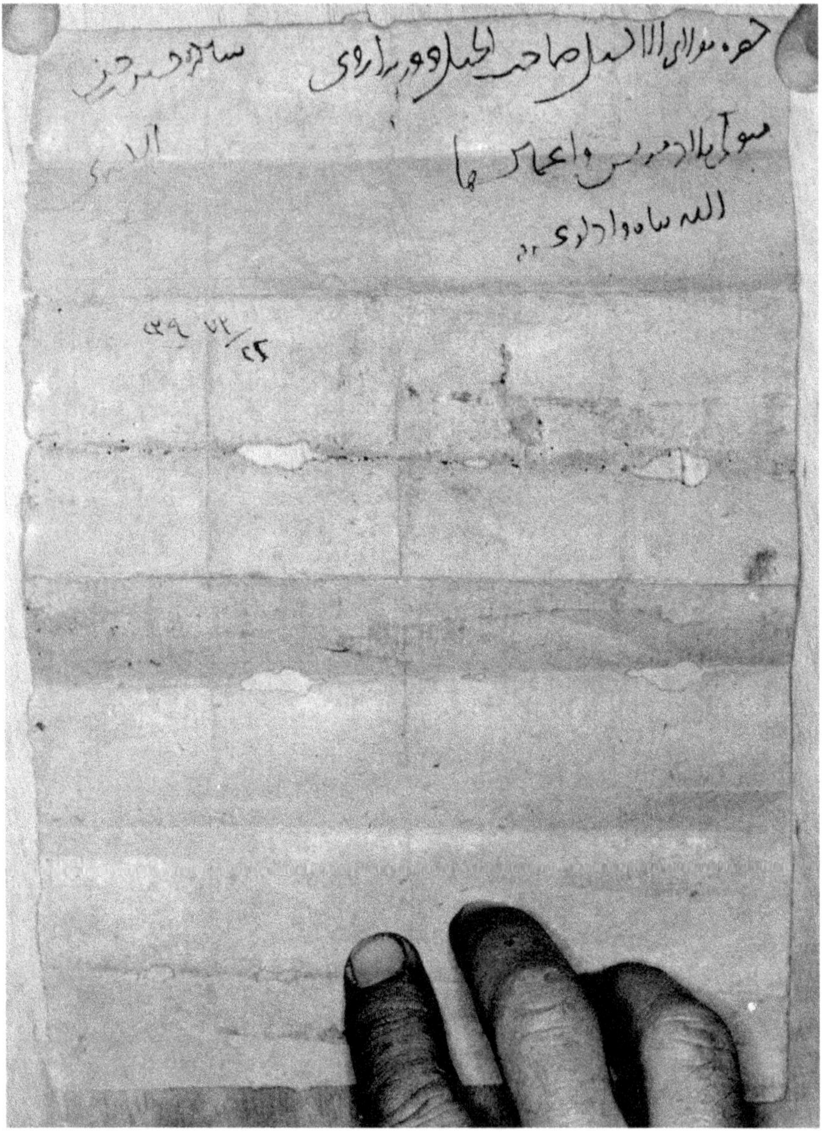

14 verso: Letter to the Eparch Uruwī

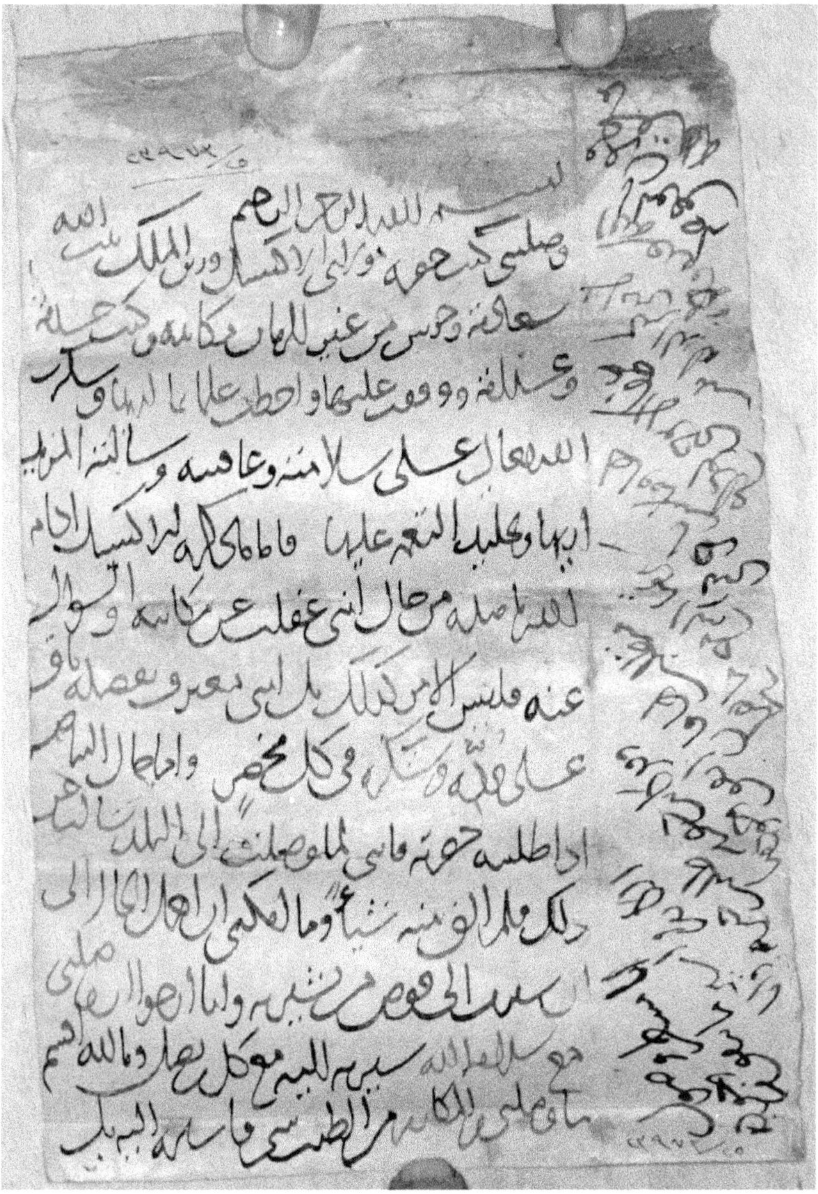

15 recto: Letter to the Eparch Uruwī

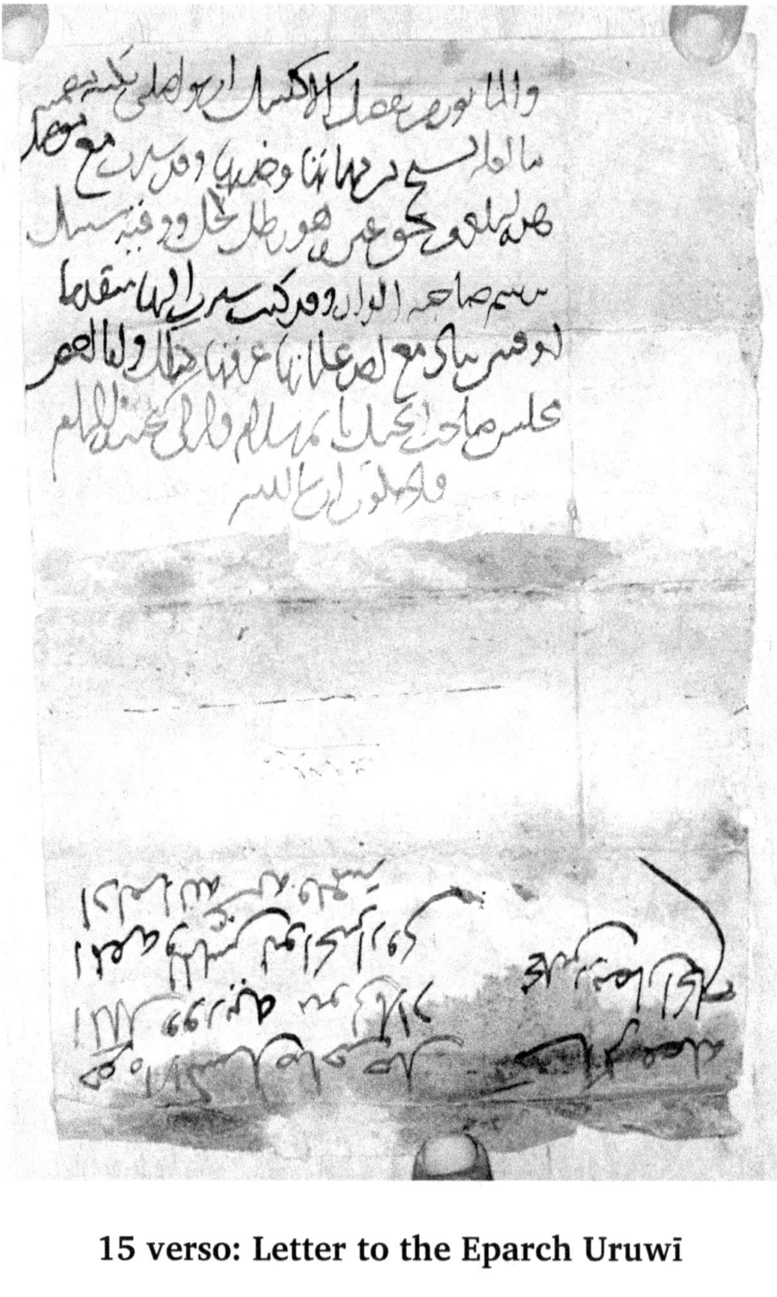

15 verso: Letter to the Eparch Uruwī

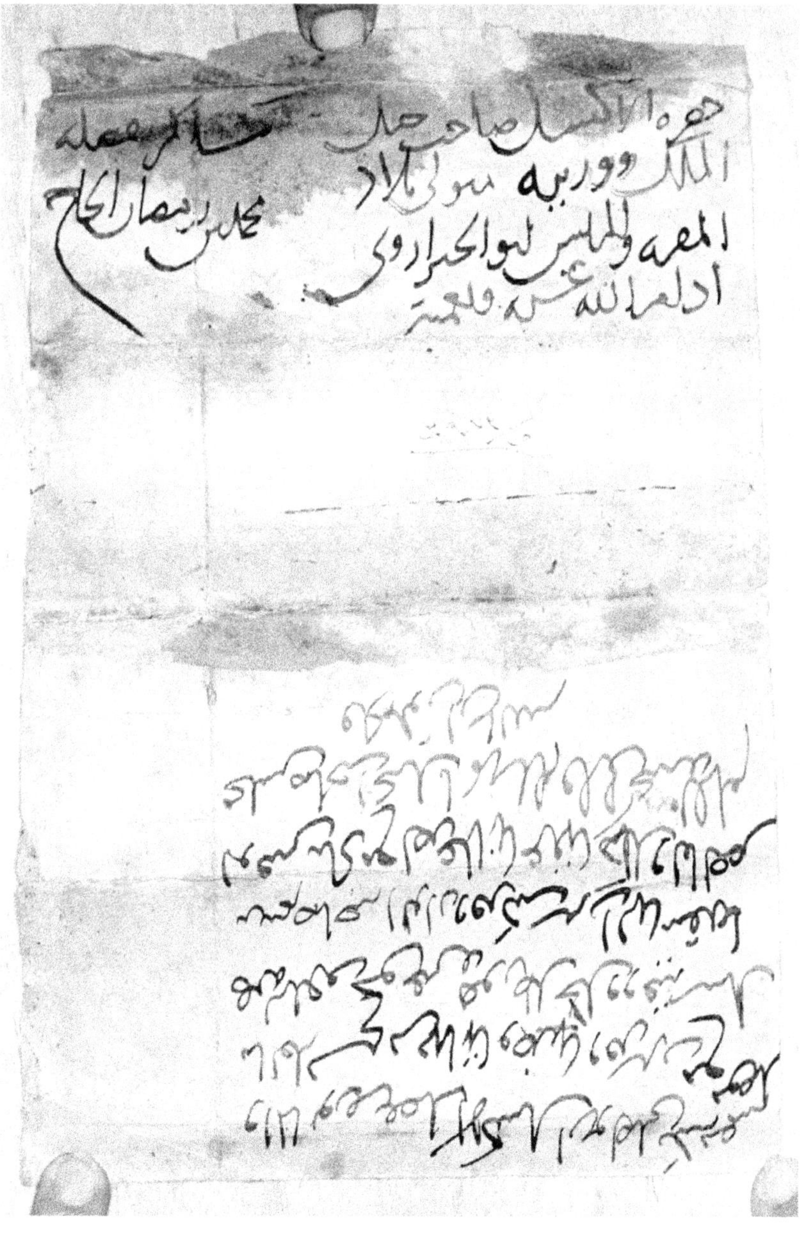

15 verso: Letter to the Eparch Uruwī

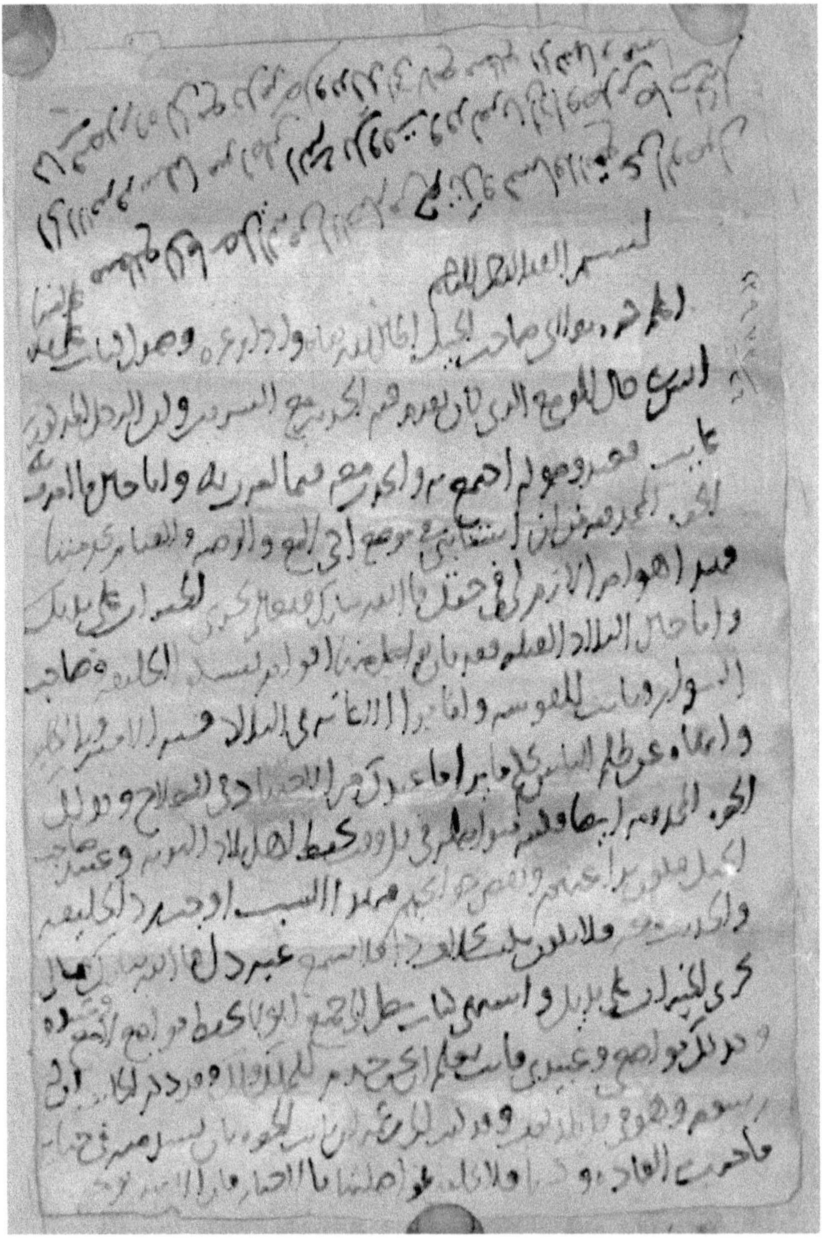

16 recto: Letter to the Eparch Uruwī

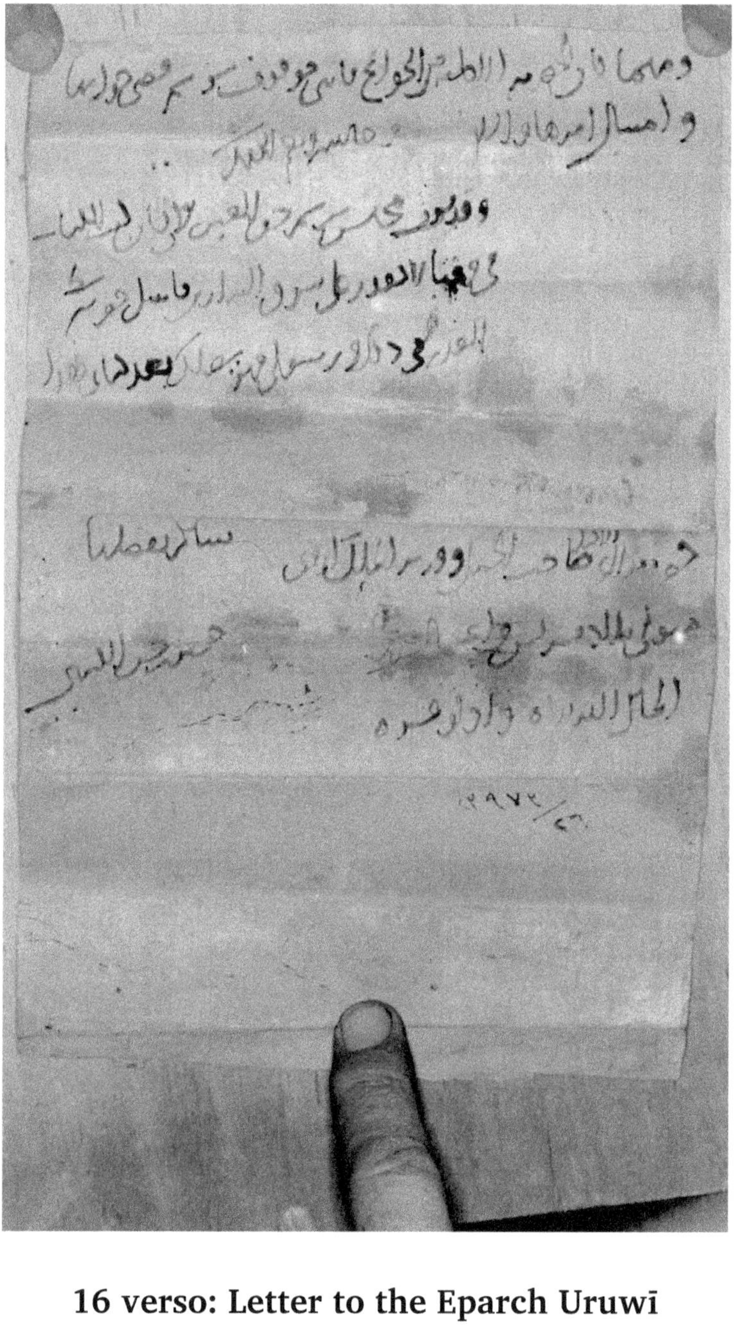

16 verso: Letter to the Eparch Uruwī

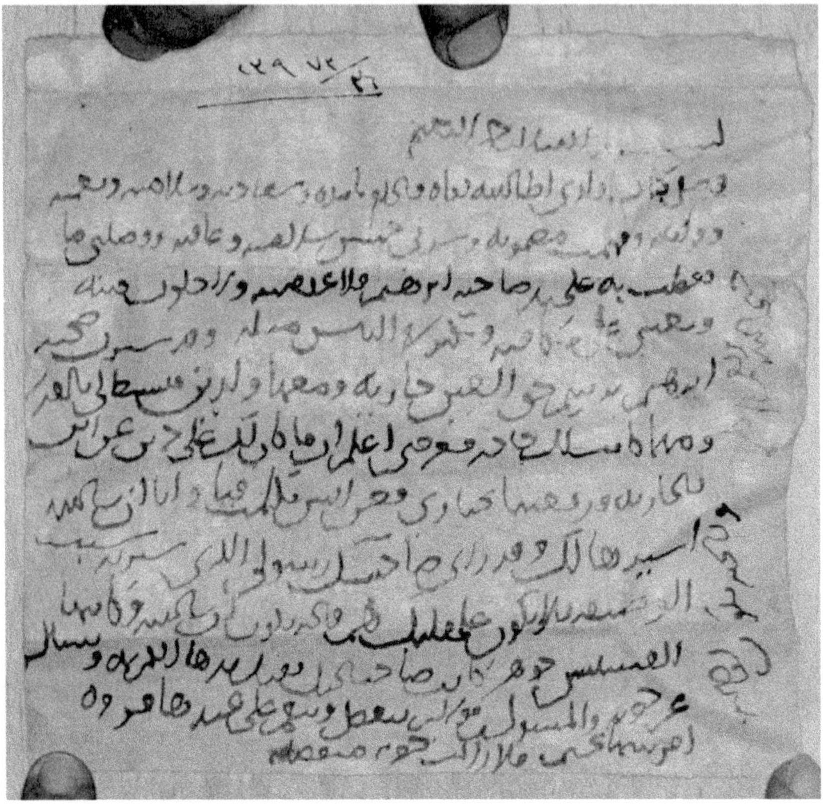

17 recto: Letter from the Eparch Uruwī

17 verso: Letter from the Eparch Uruwī

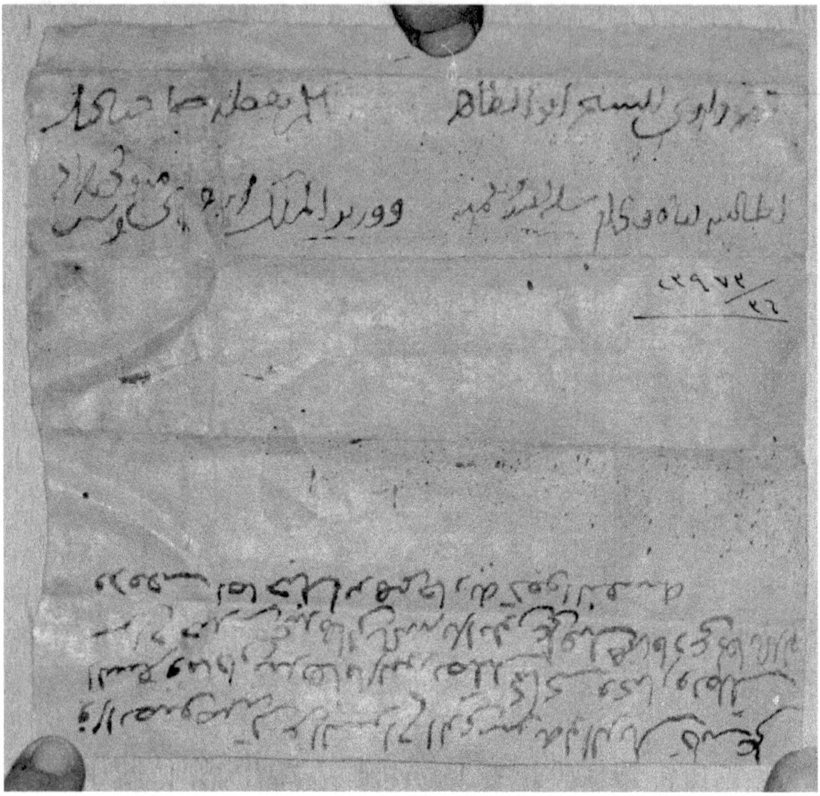

17 verso: Letter from the Eparch Uruwī

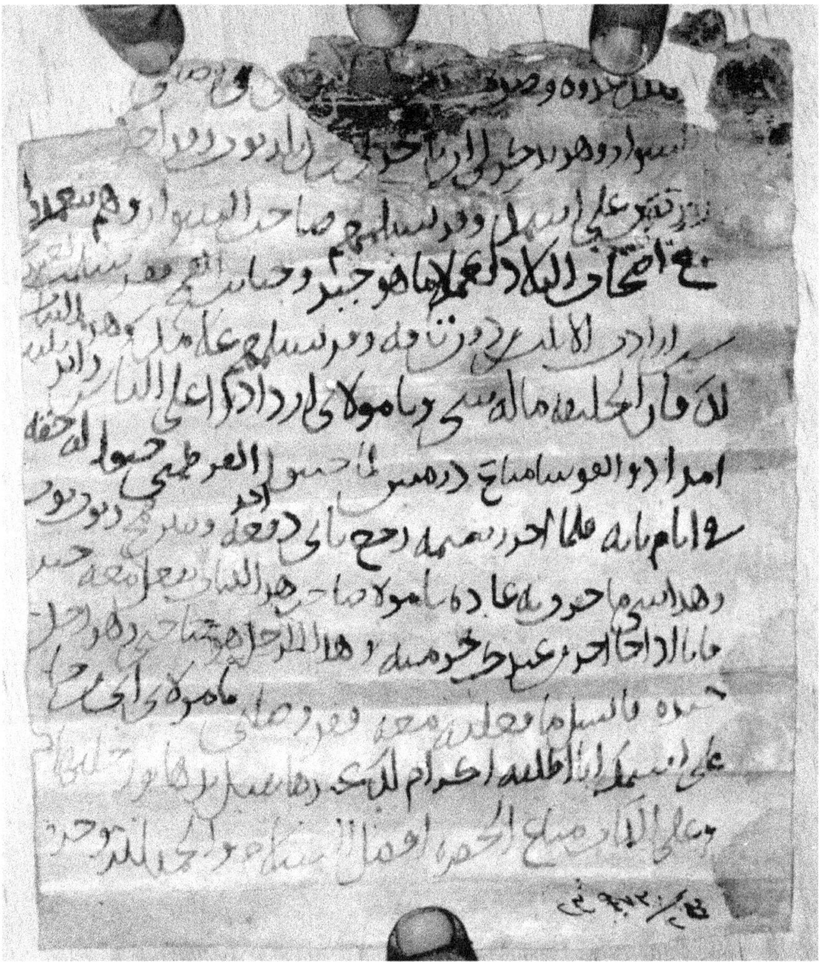

18 recto: Letter from the Eparch Uruwī (?)

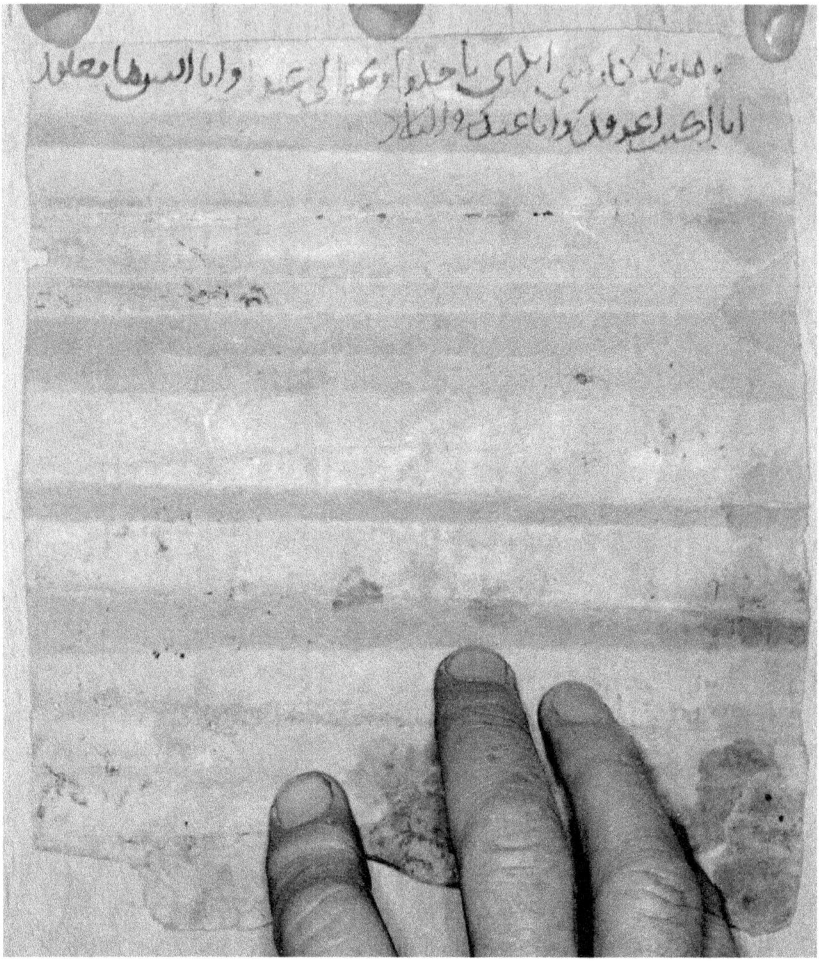

18 verso: Letter from the Eparch Uruwī (?)

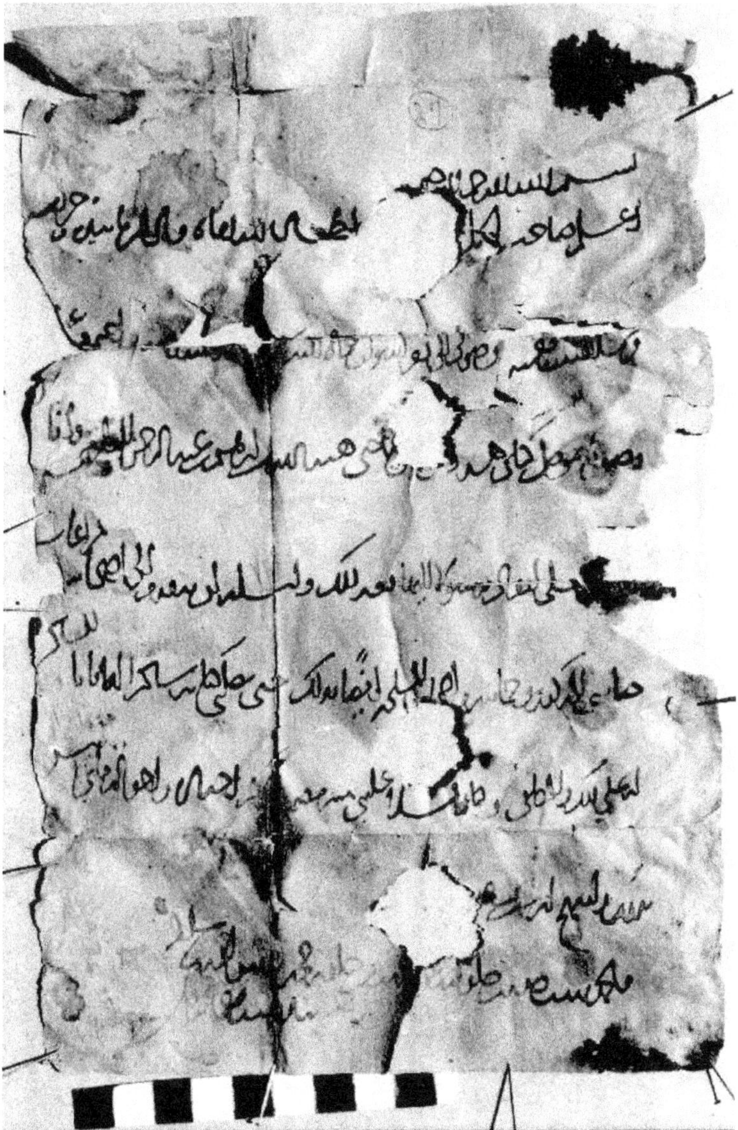

19 recto: Letter to the Eparch Īsū

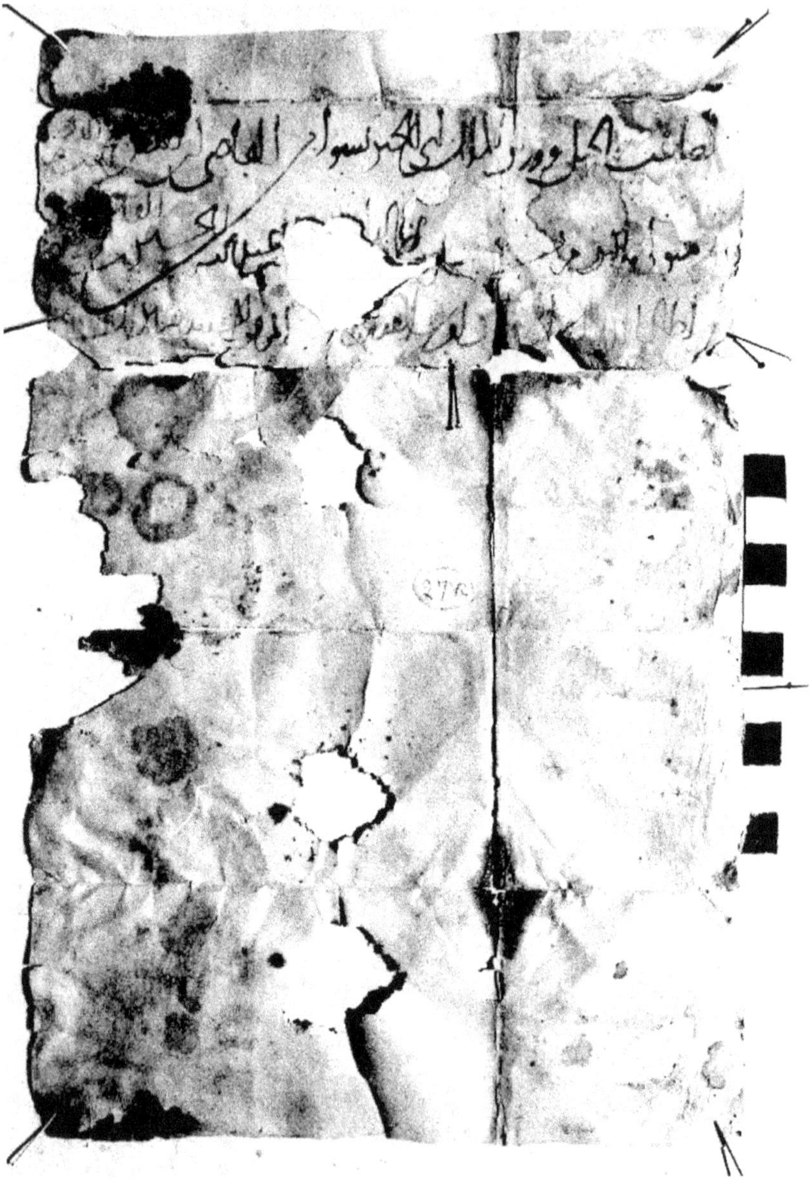

19 verso: Letter to the Eparch Īsū

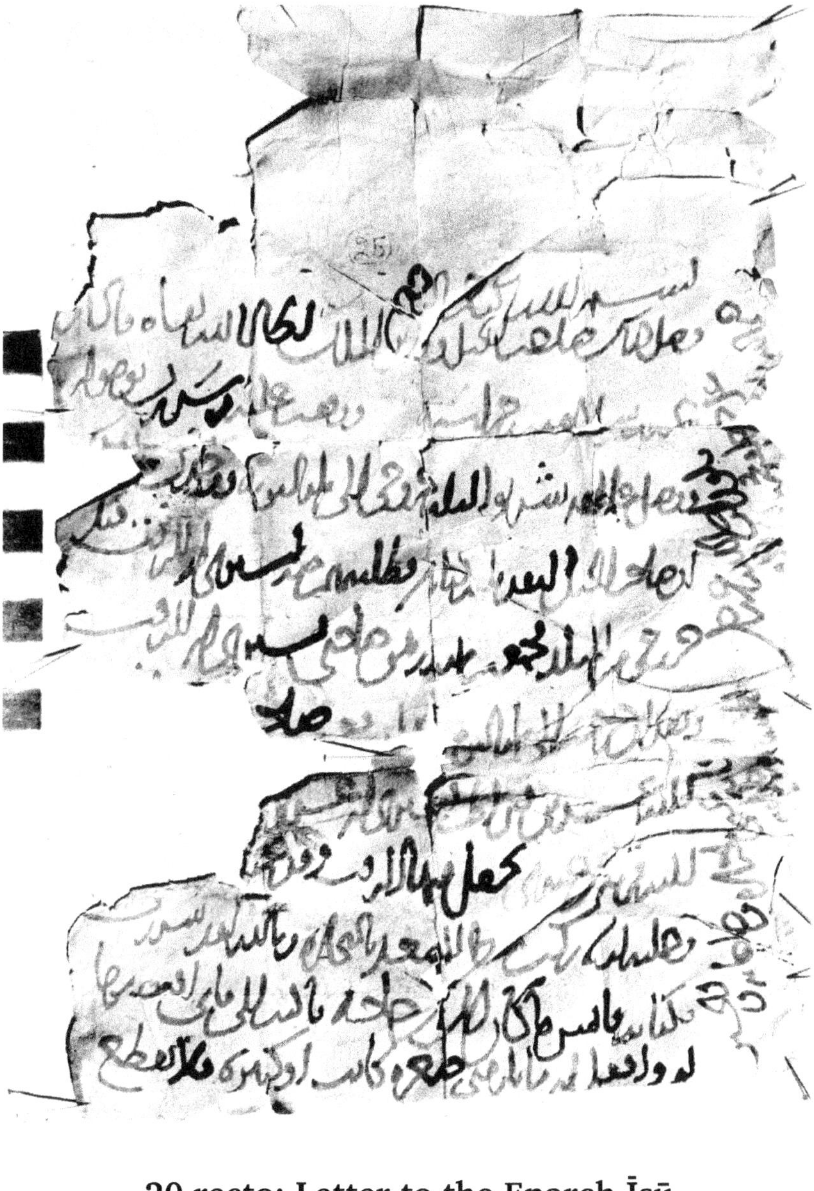

20 recto: Letter to the Eparch Īsū

20 verso: Letter to the Eparch Īsū

20 verso: Letter to the Eparch Īsū

21 recto: Letter to an Eparch

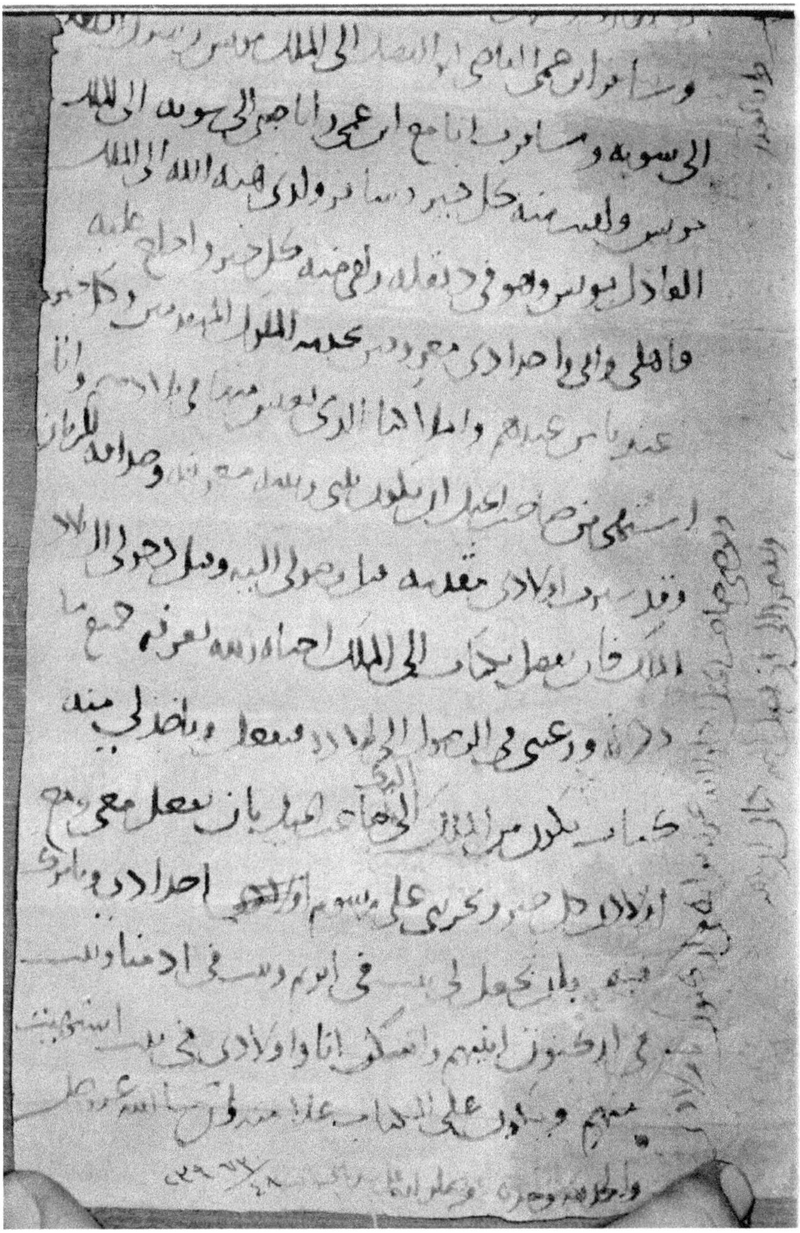

21 recto: Letter to an Eparch

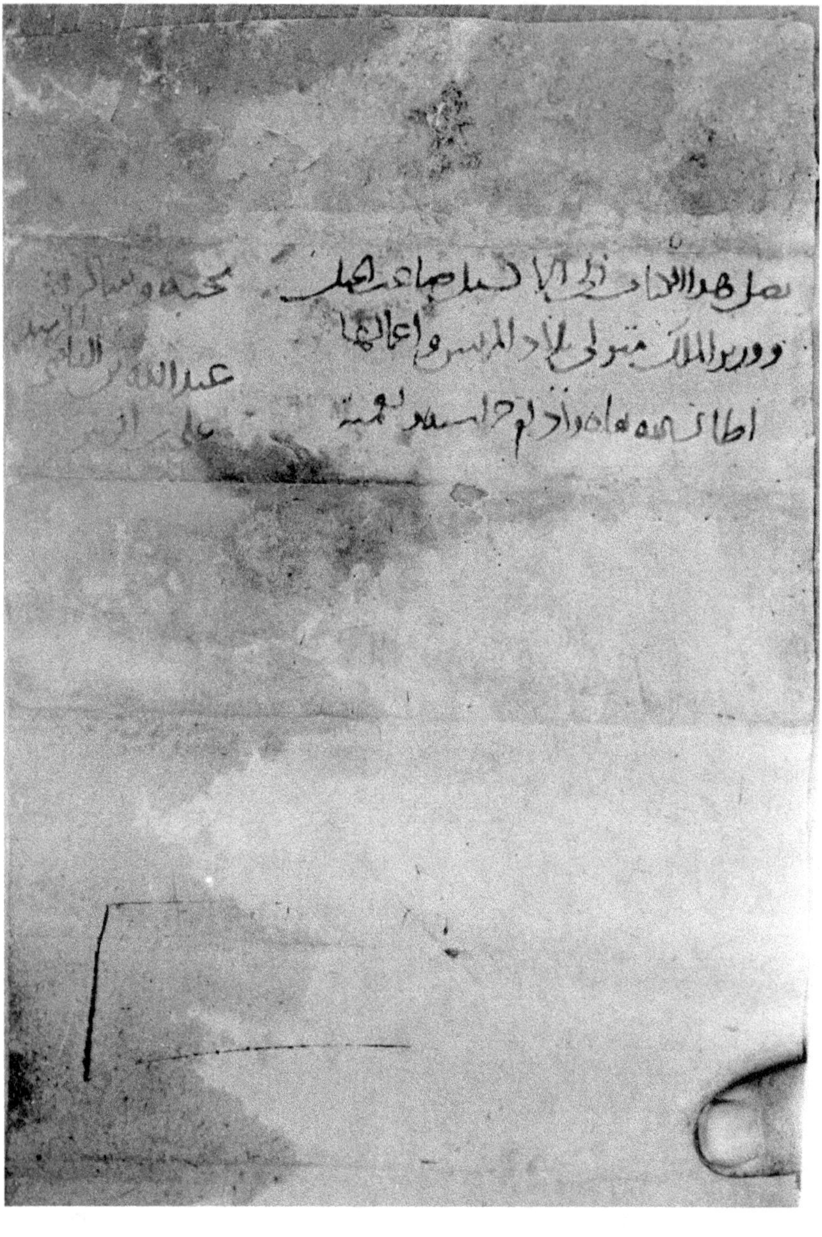

21 verso: Letter to an Eparch

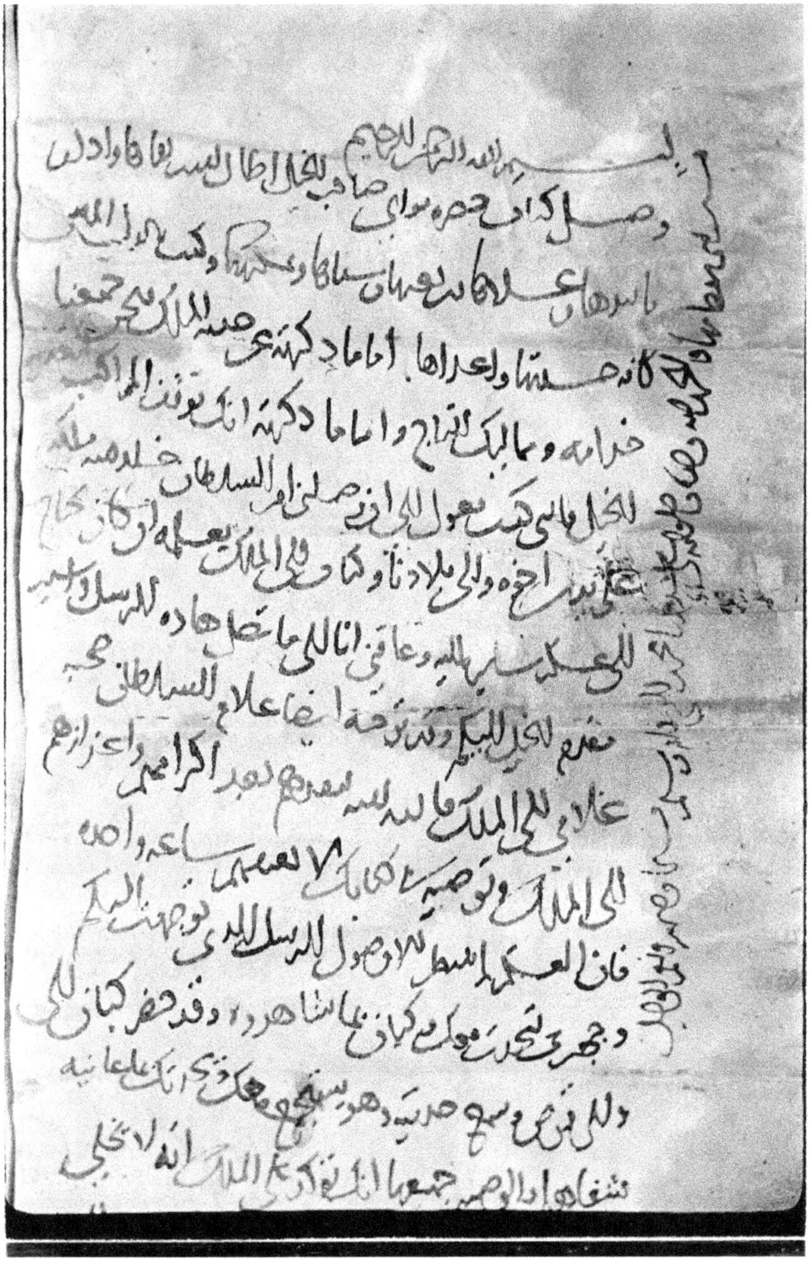

22 recto: Letter to an Eparch

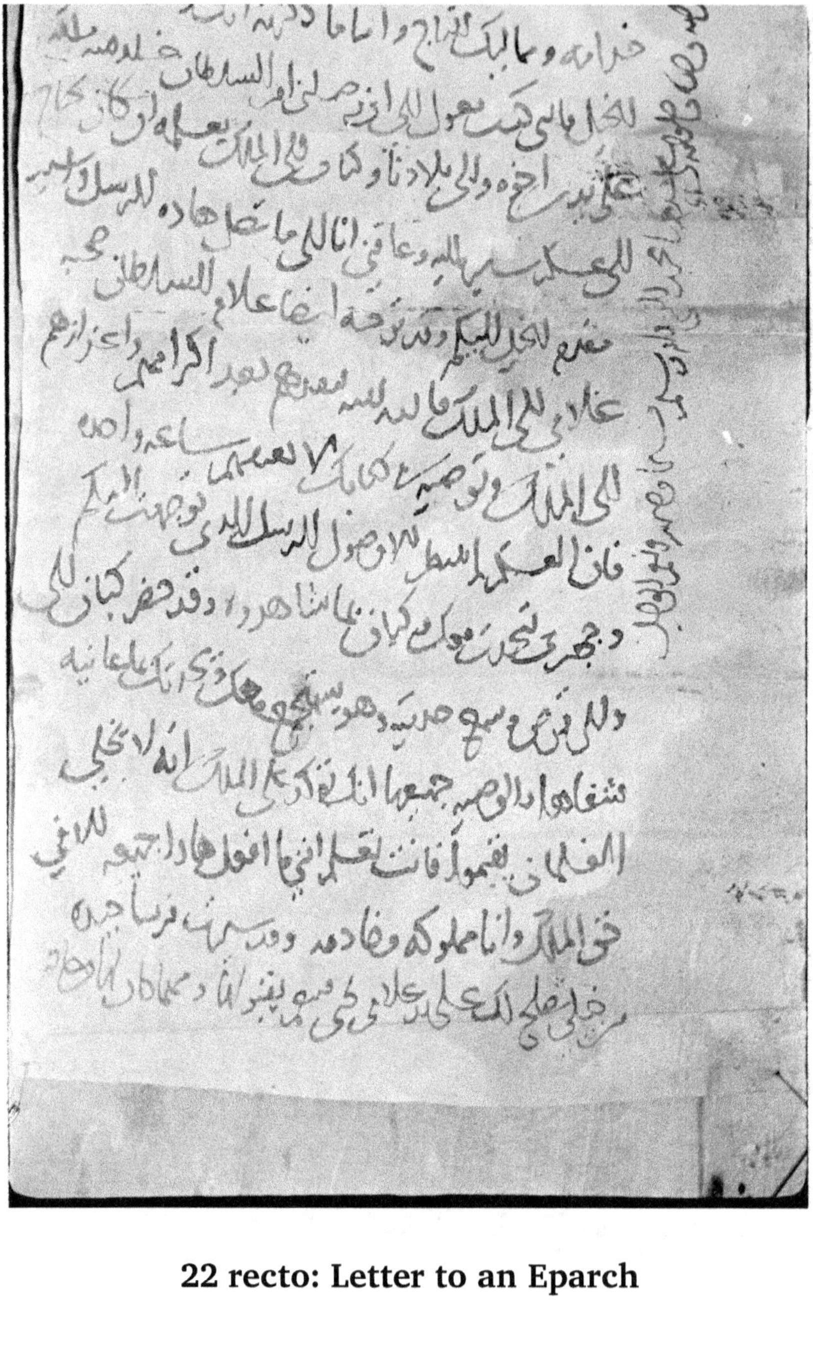

22 recto: Letter to an Eparch

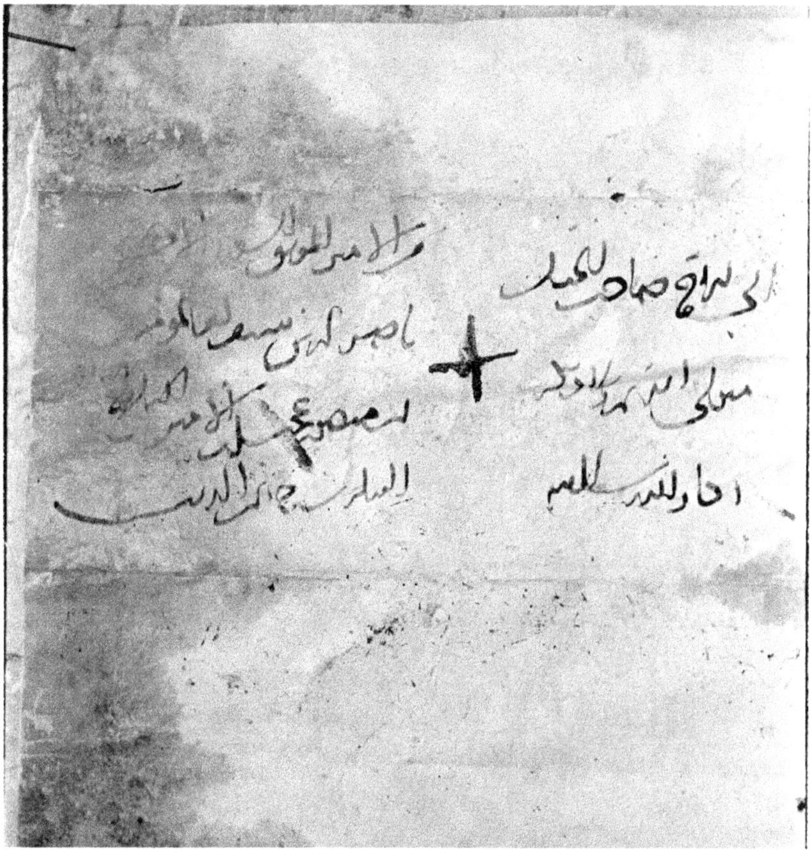

22 verso: Letter to an Eparch

23 recto: Letter to an Eparch

23 verso: Letter to an Eparch

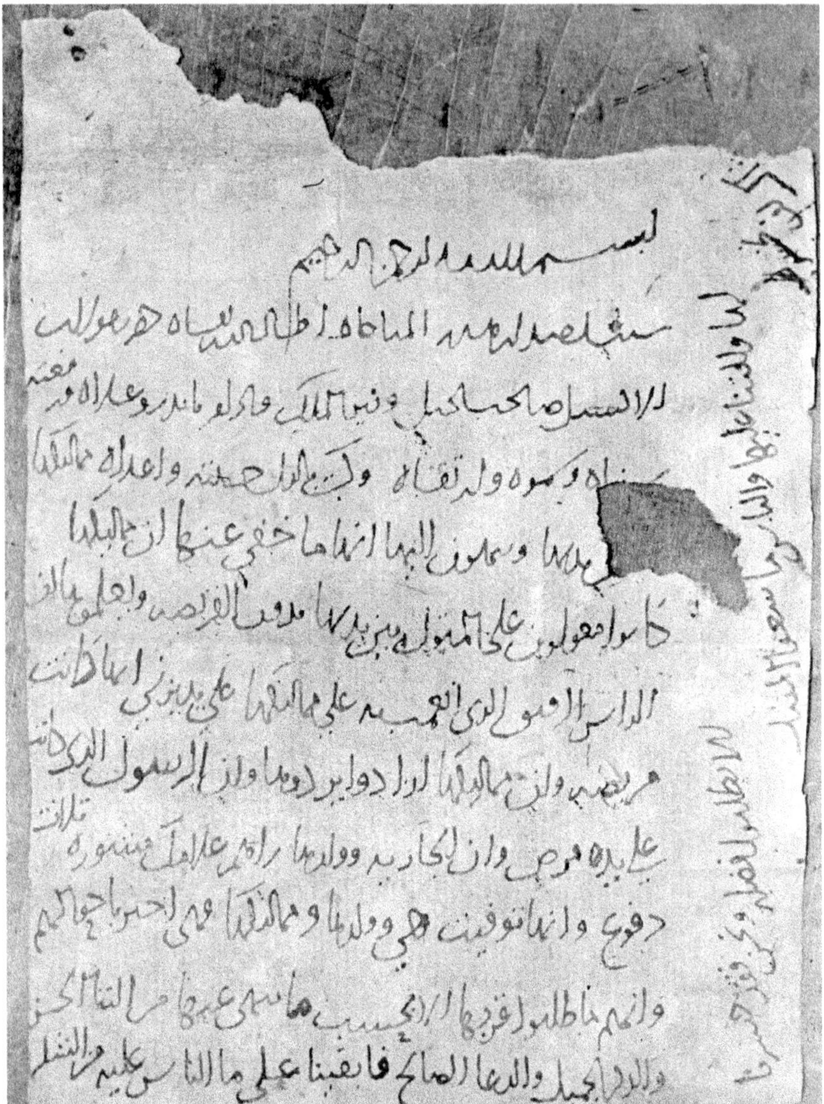
بسم الله الرحمن الرحيم

24 recto: Letter to an Eparch

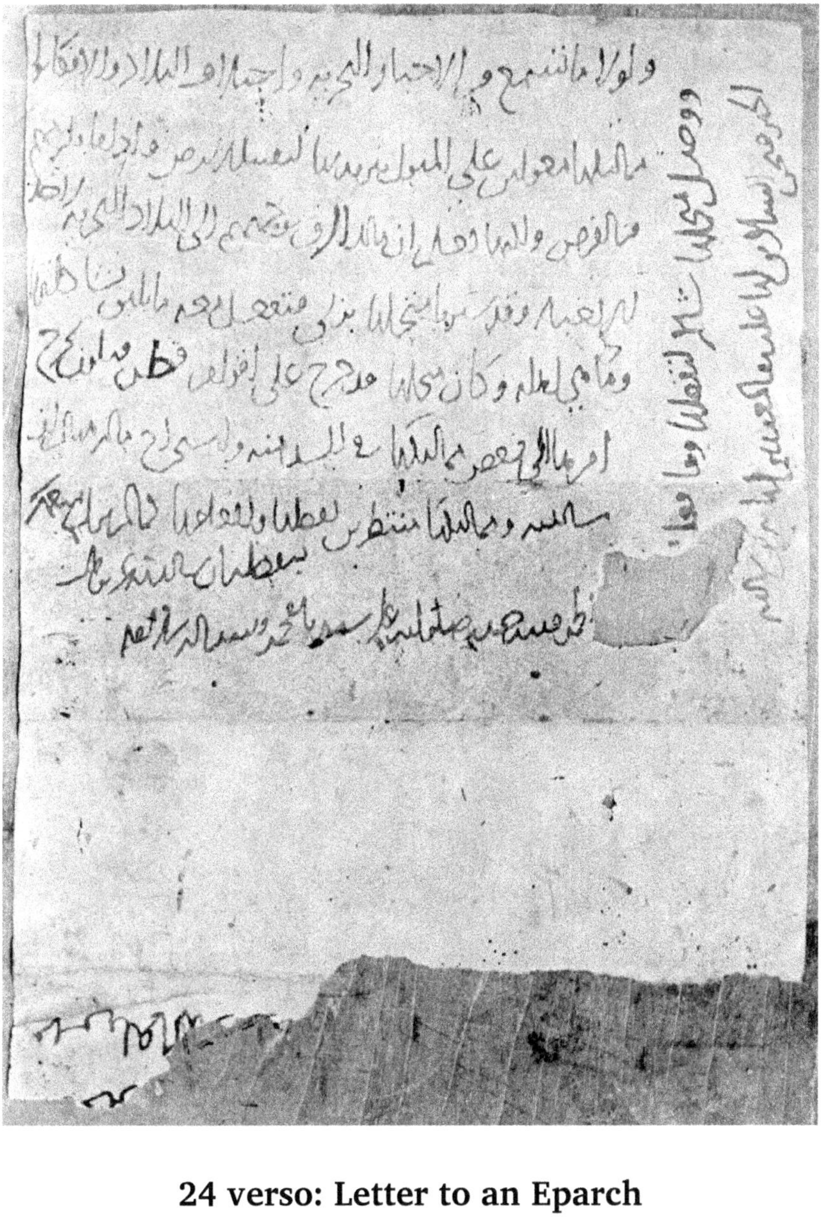

24 verso: Letter to an Eparch

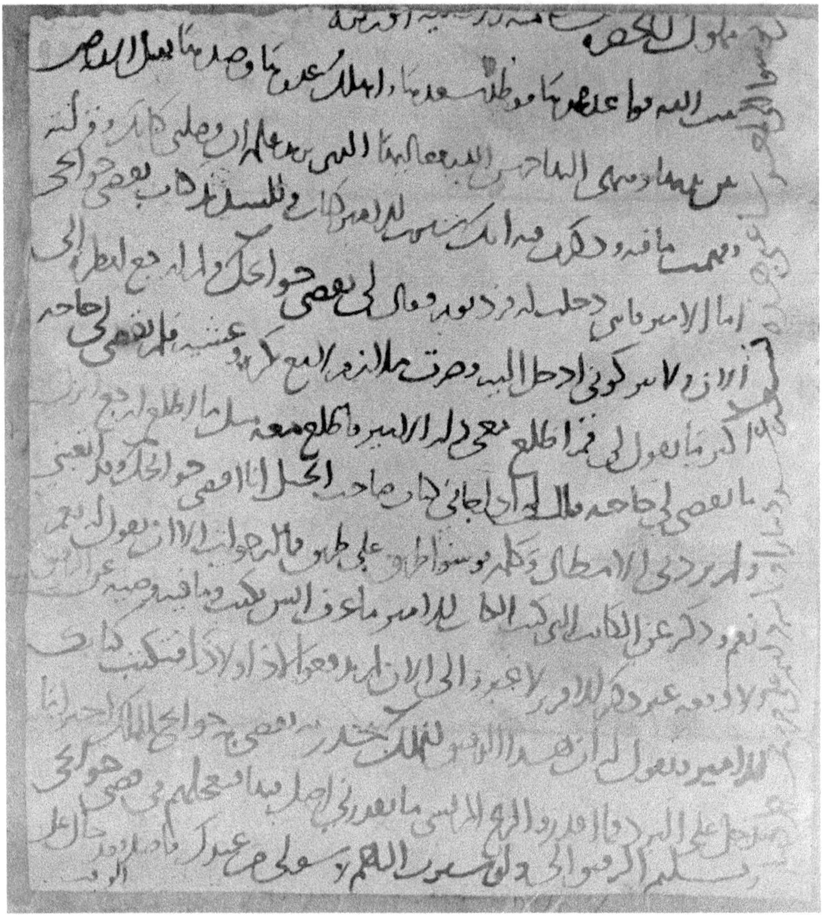

25 recto: Letter to an Eparch

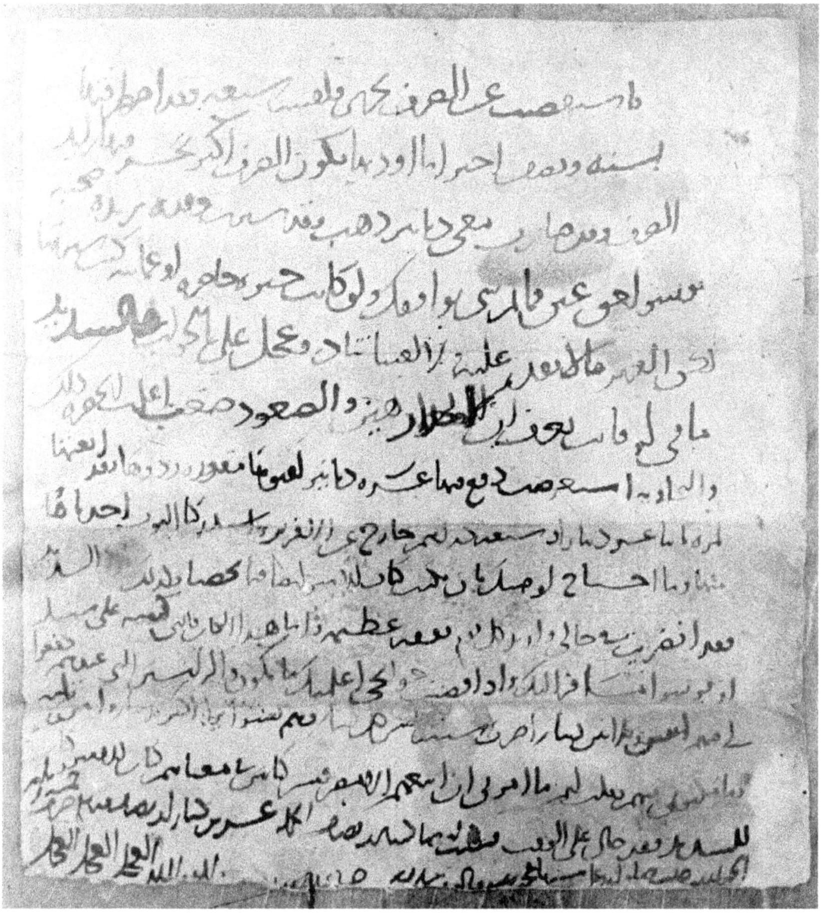

25 verso: Letter to an Eparch

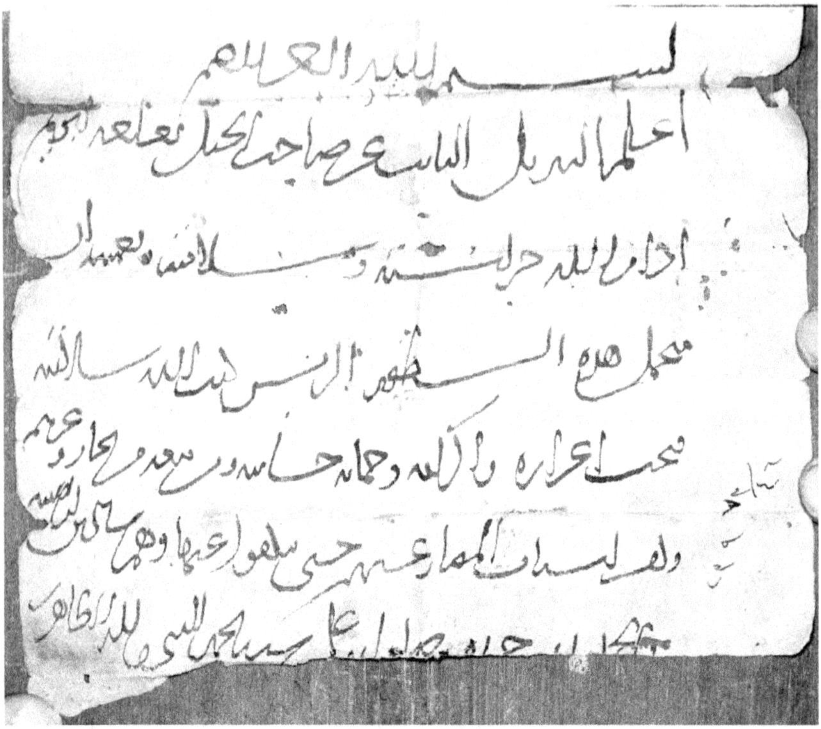

26 recto: Letter to al-Bazīl, the Deputy of the Eparch Darmā

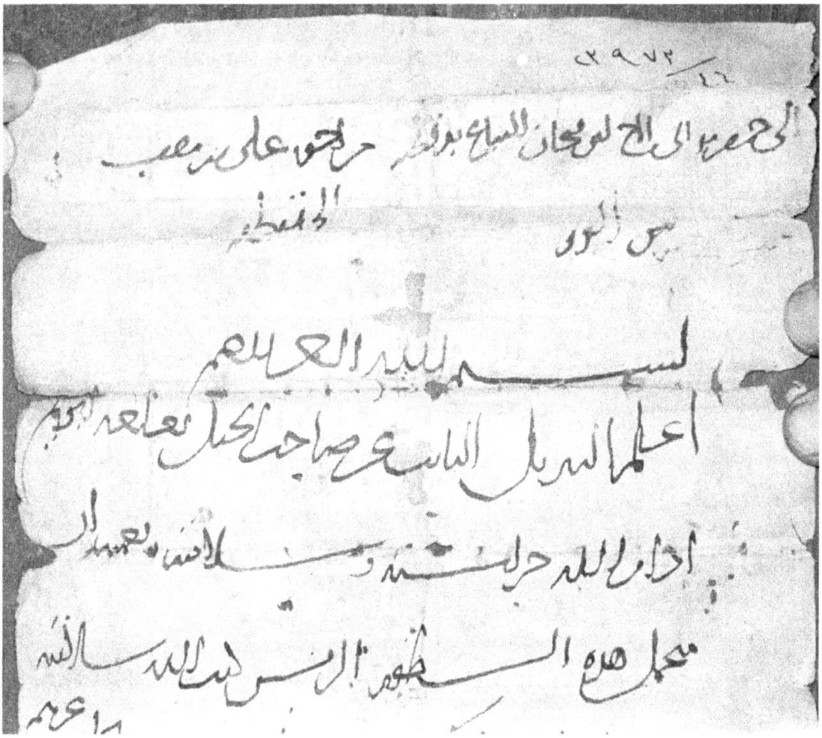

26 recto: Letter to al-Bazīl, the Deputy of the Eparch Darmā

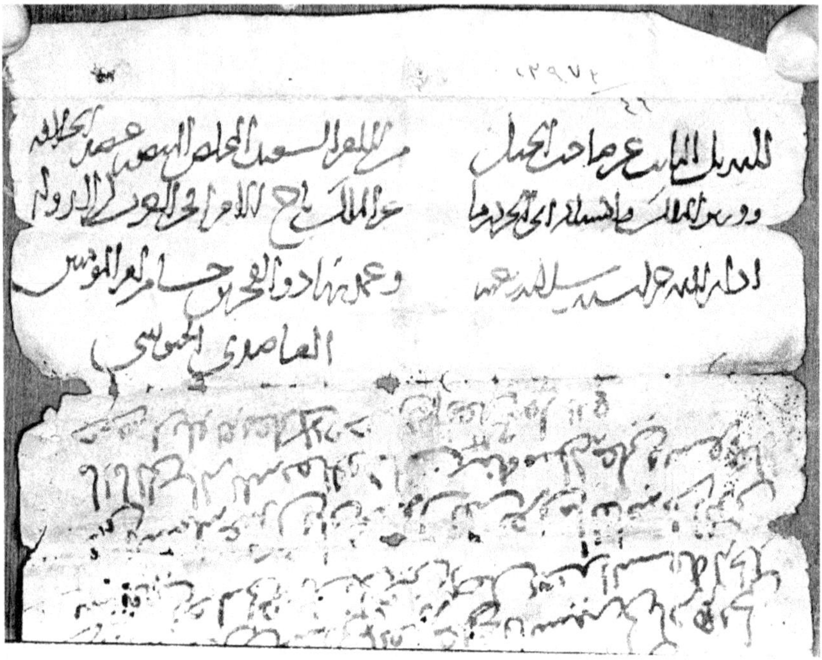

26 verso: Letter to al-Bazīl, the Deputy of the Eparch Darmā

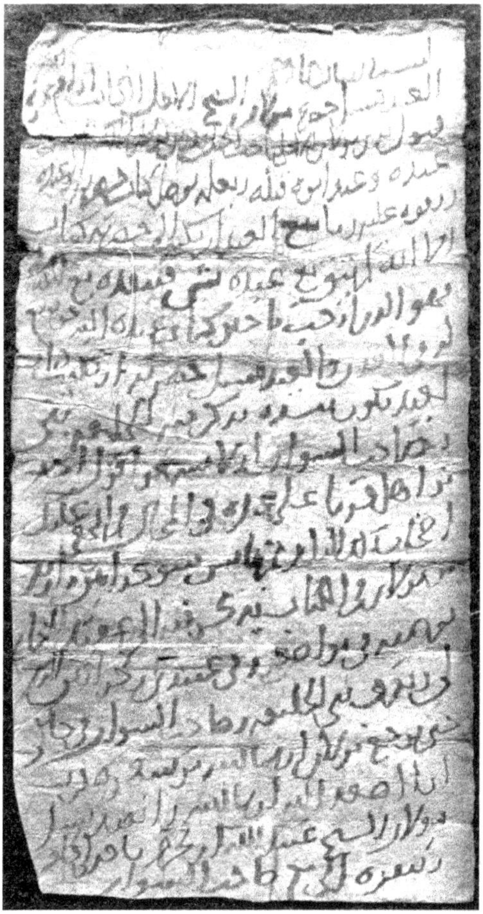

27 recto: Letter to the Secretary of the Eparch Uruwī

27 verso: Letter to the Secretary of the Eparch Uruwī

27 verso: Letter to the Secretary of the Eparch Uruwī

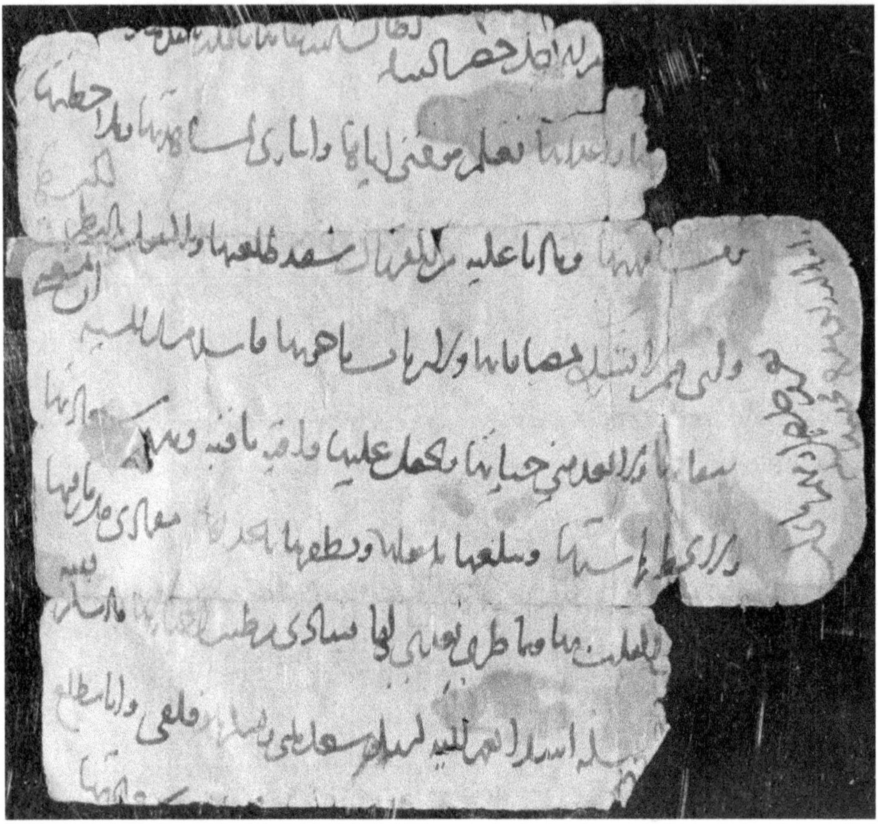

28 recto: Letter to a Commander

28 verso: Letter to a Commander

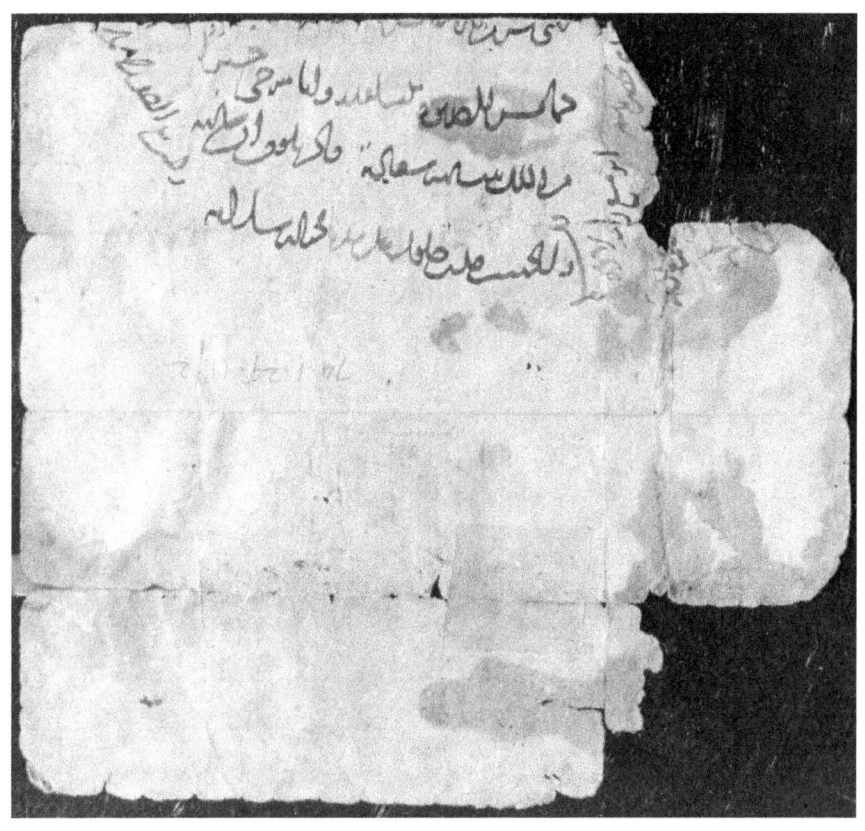

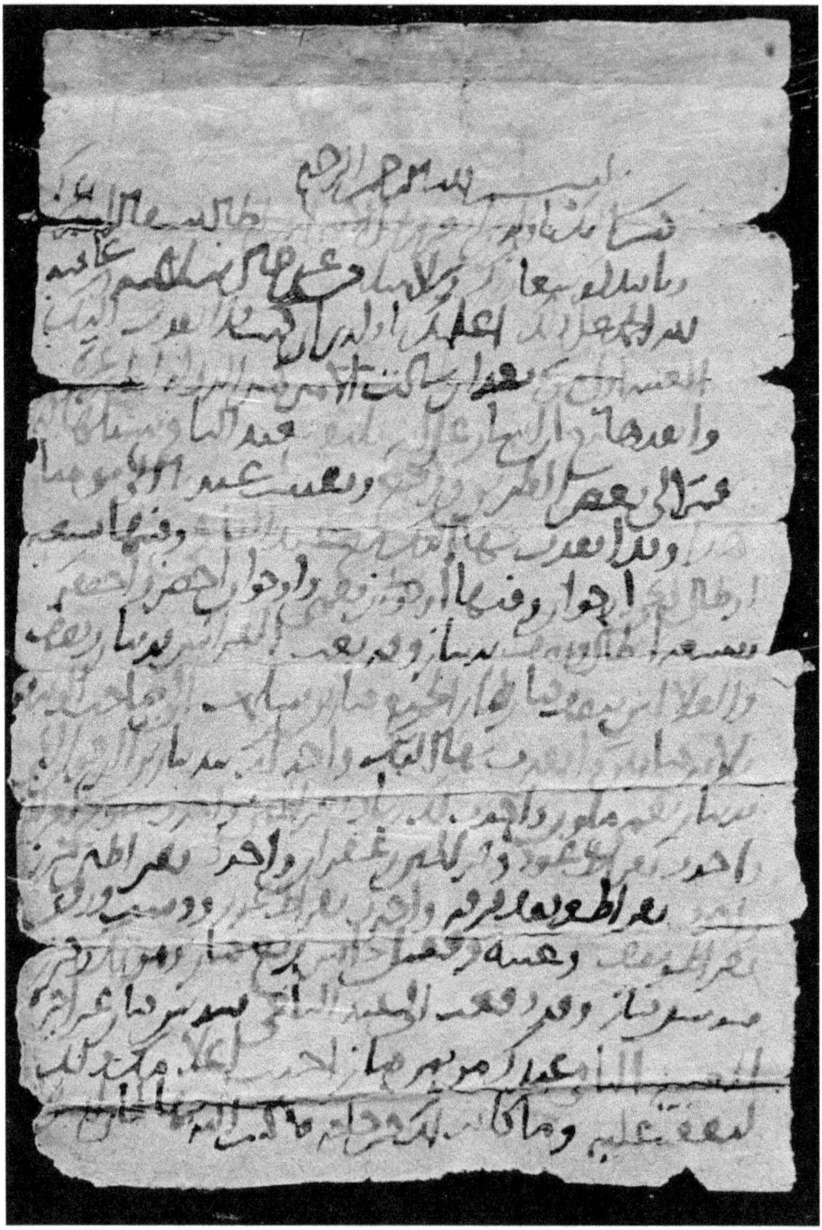

29 recto: Letter to a Commander

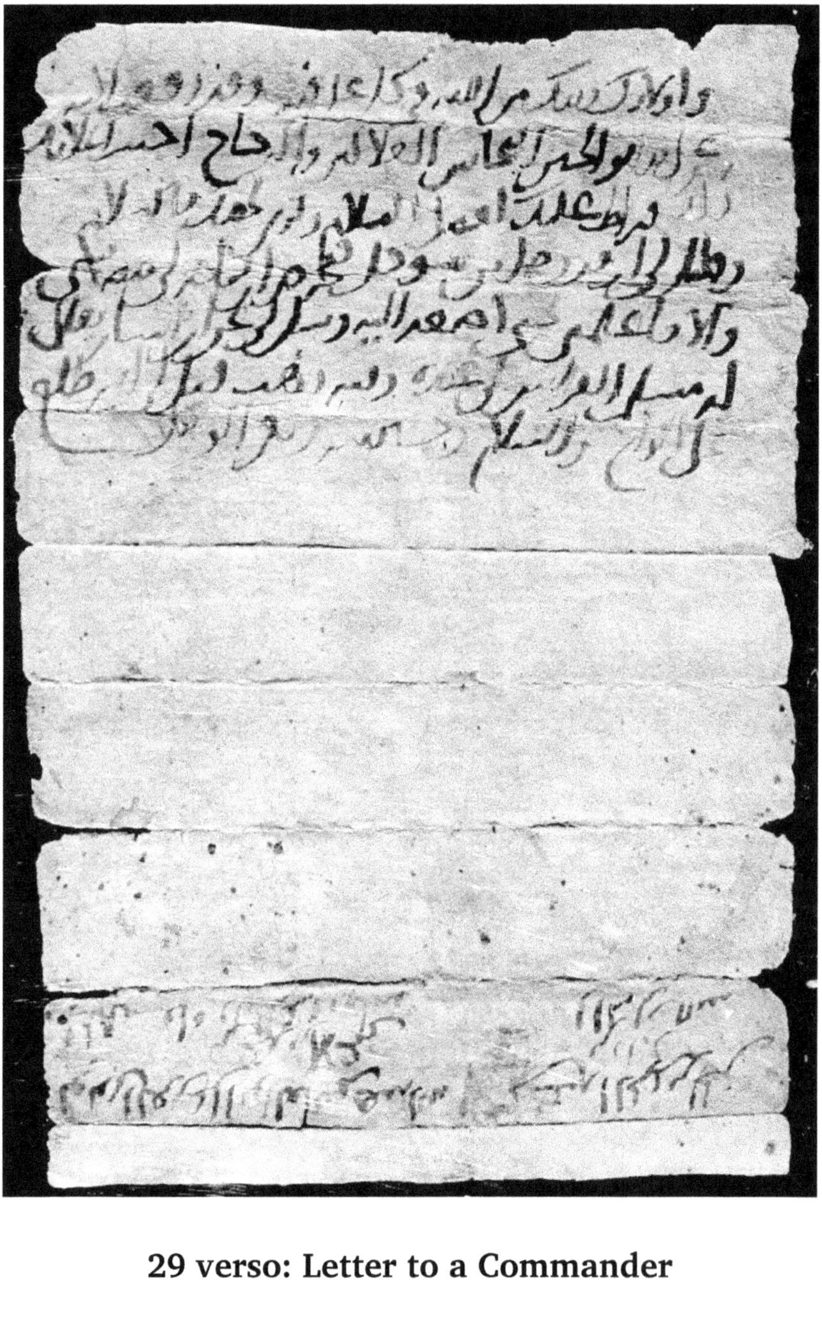

29 verso: Letter to a Commander

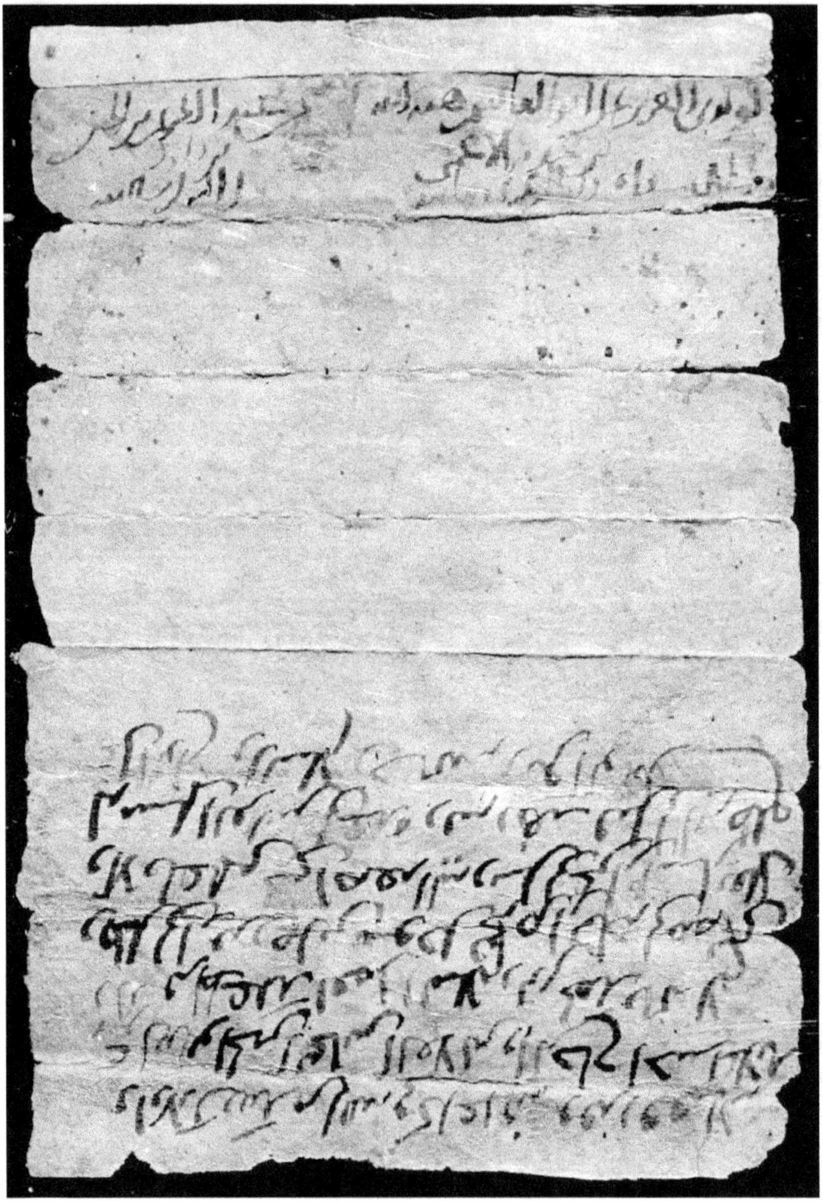

29 verso: Letter to a Commander

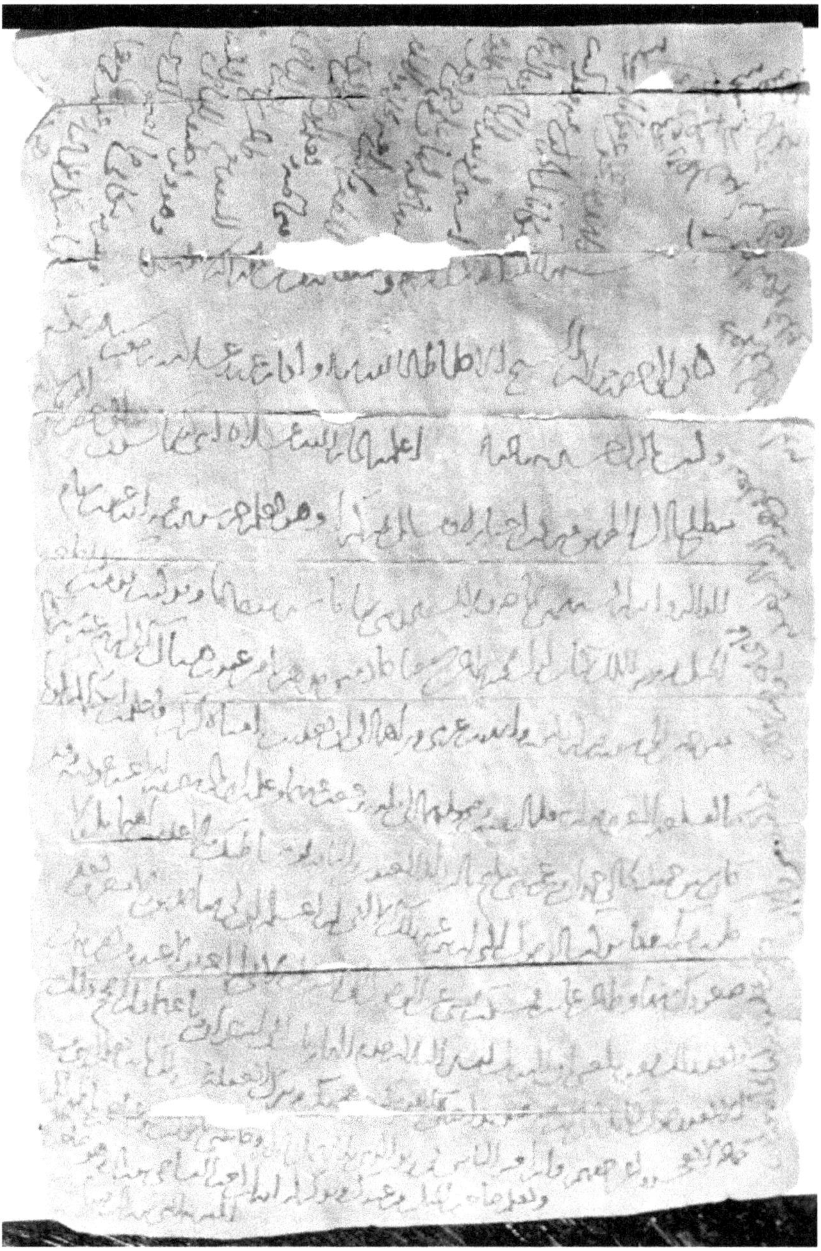

30 recto: Letter to a Dignitary

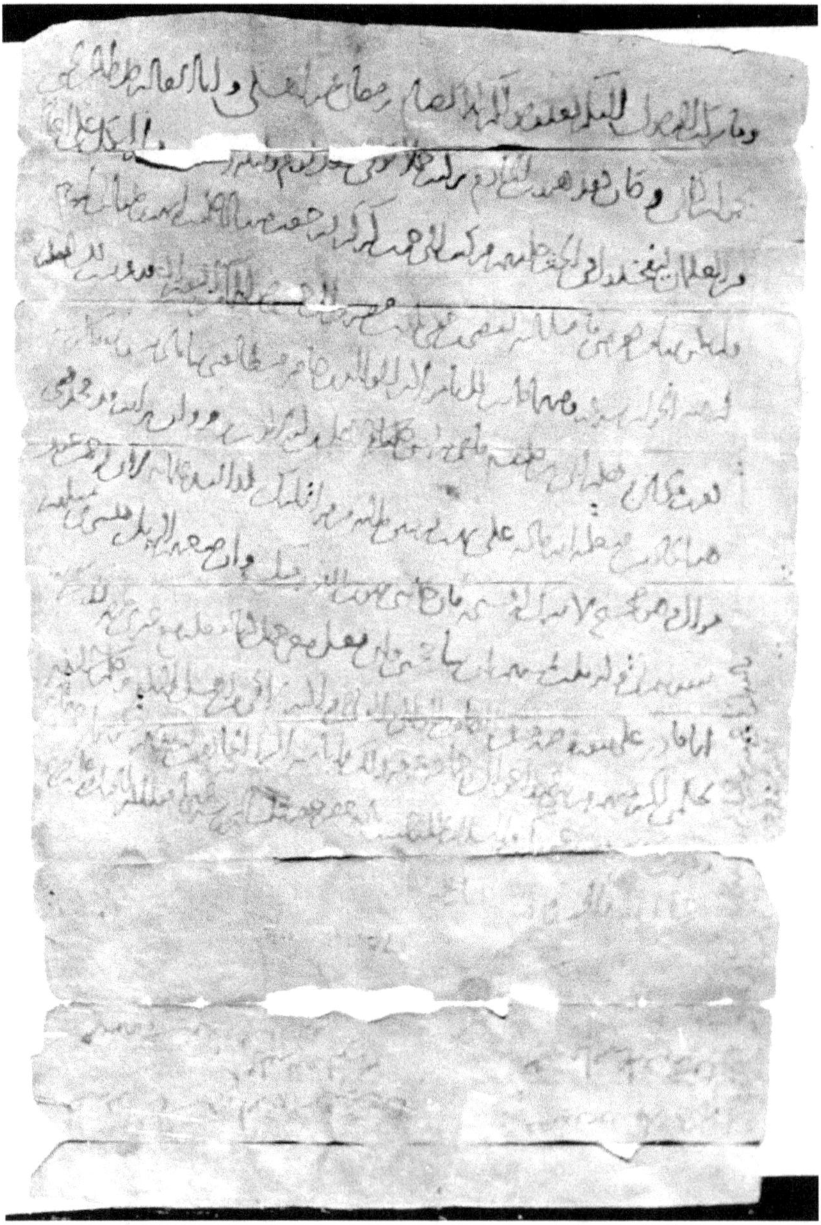

30 verso: Letter to a Dignitary

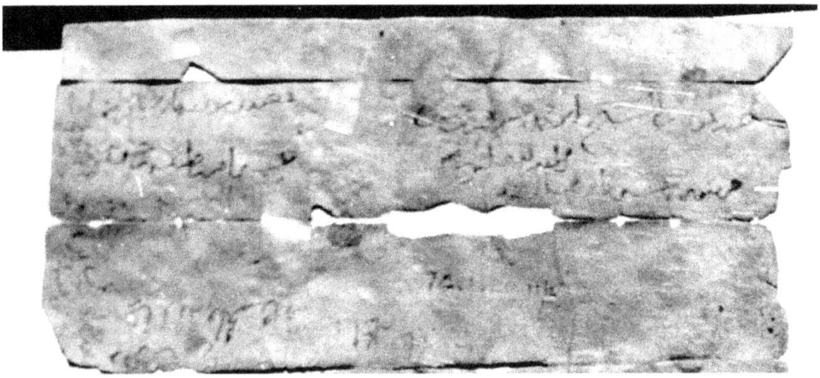

30 verso: Letter to a Dignitary

31 recto: Letter to a Dignitary

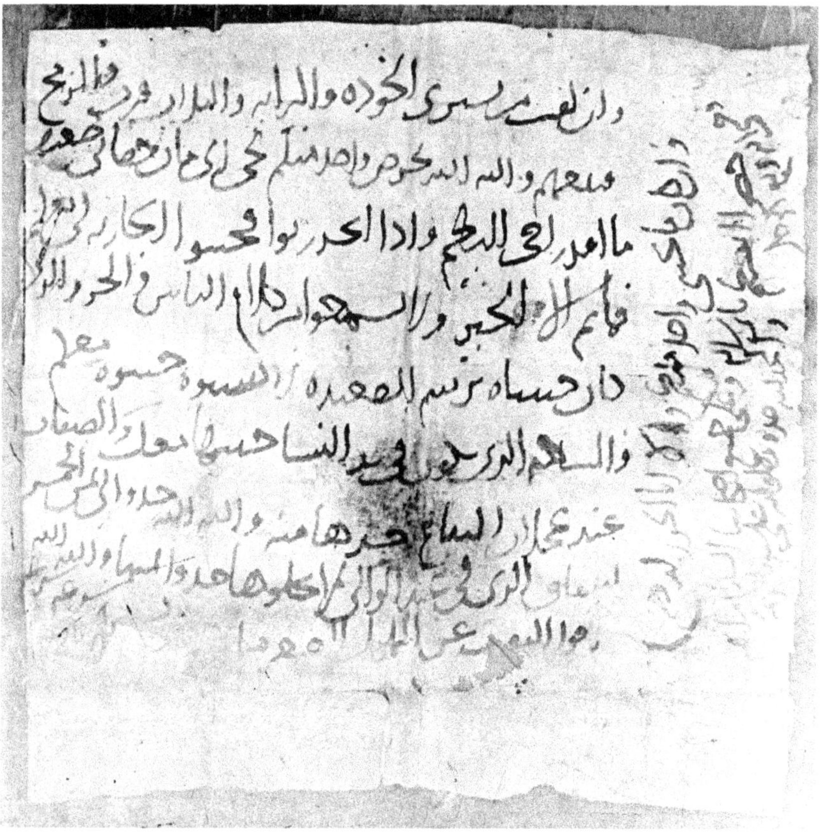

31 verso: Letter to a Dignitary

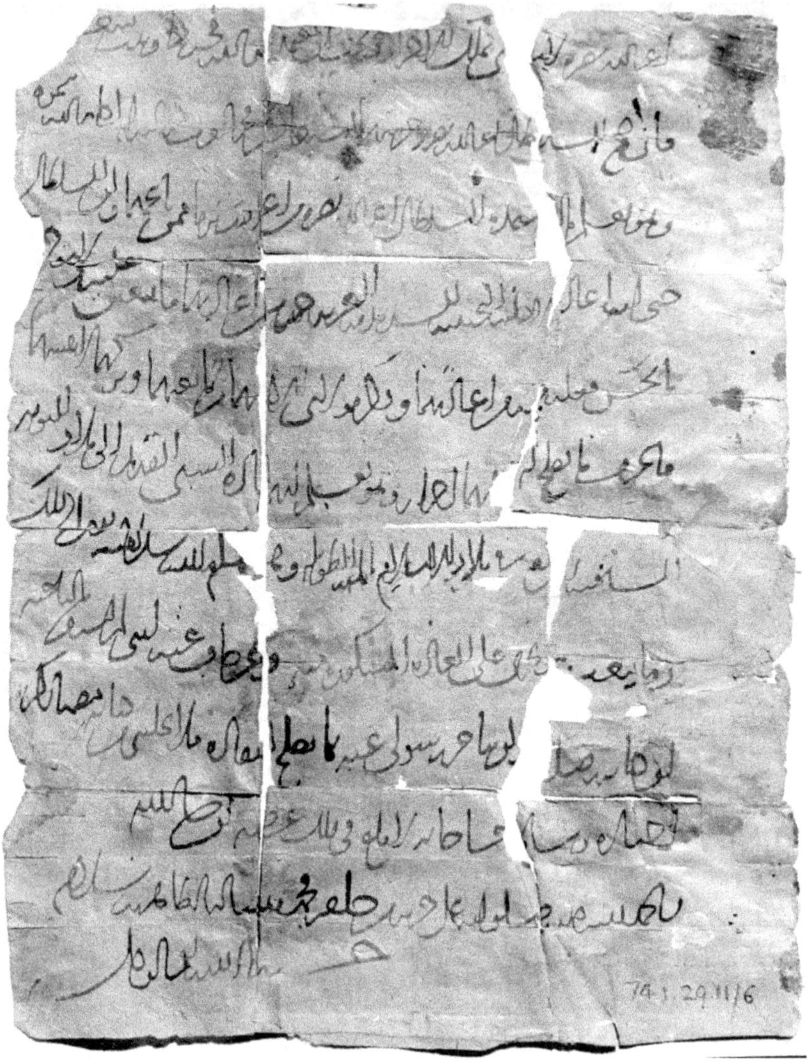

32: Letter to a Dignitary

33: Letter to a Dignitary

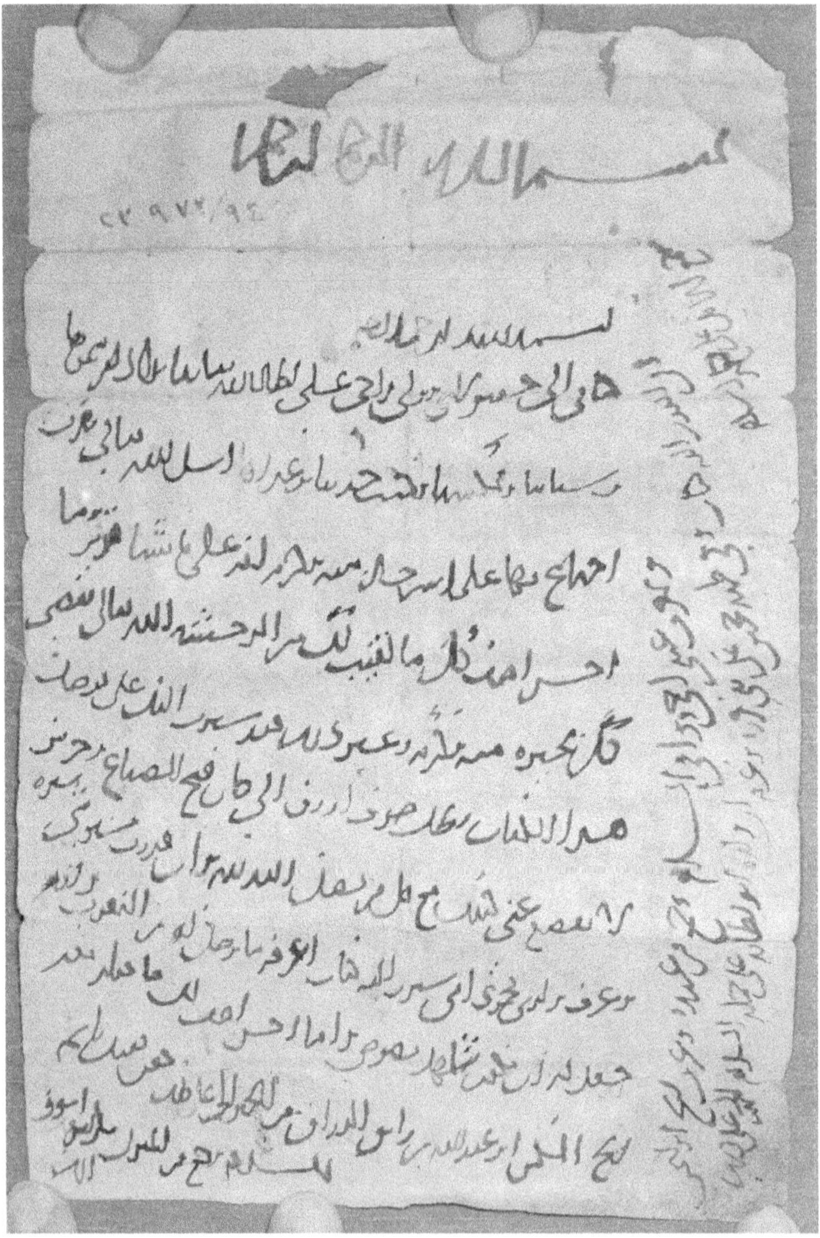

34 recto: Letter to a Dignitary

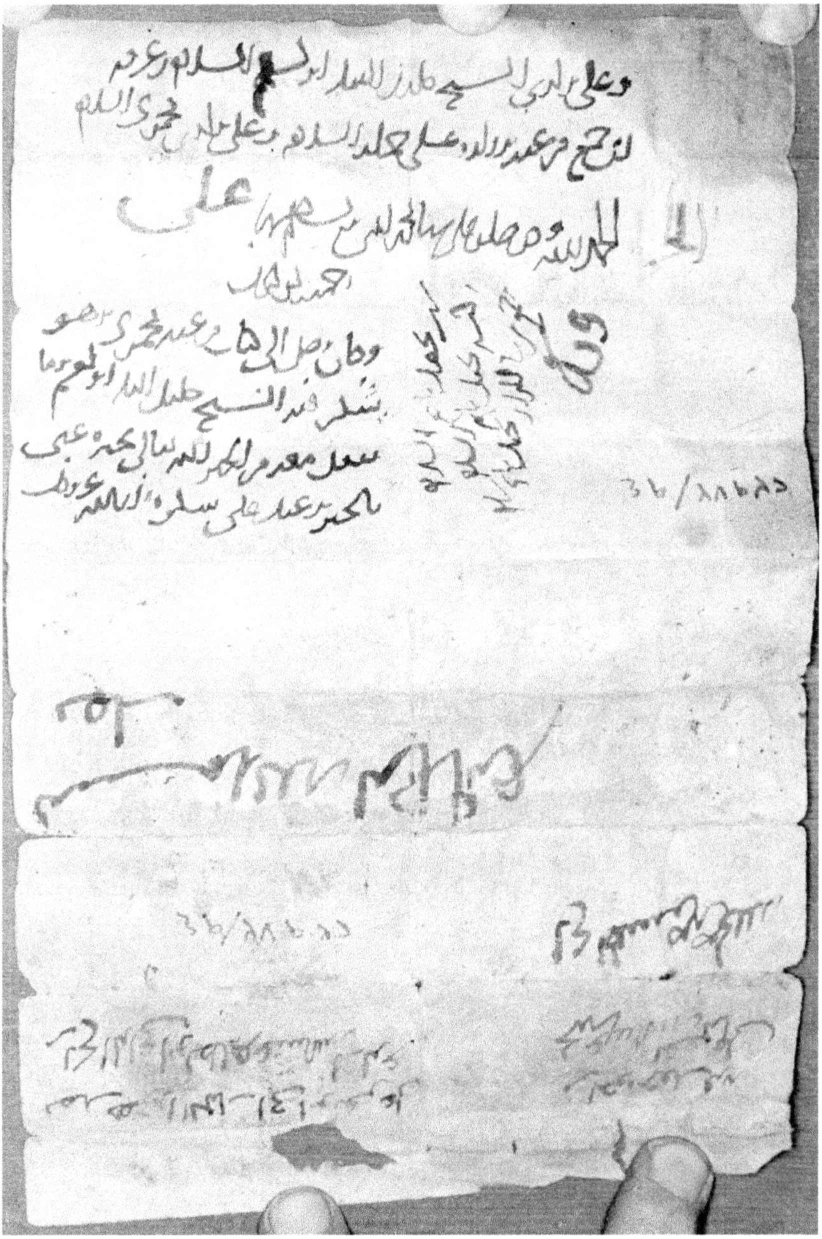

34 verso: Letter to a Dignitary

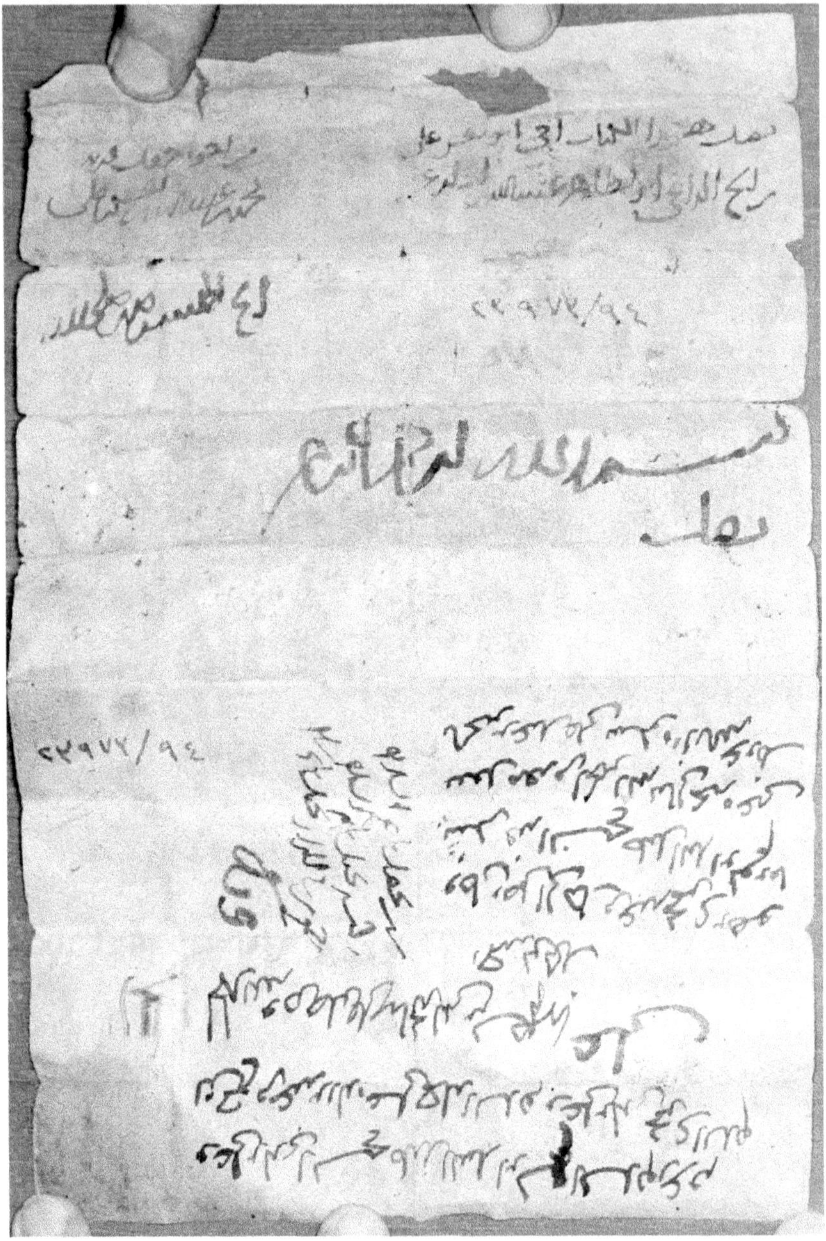

34 verso: Letter to a Dignitary

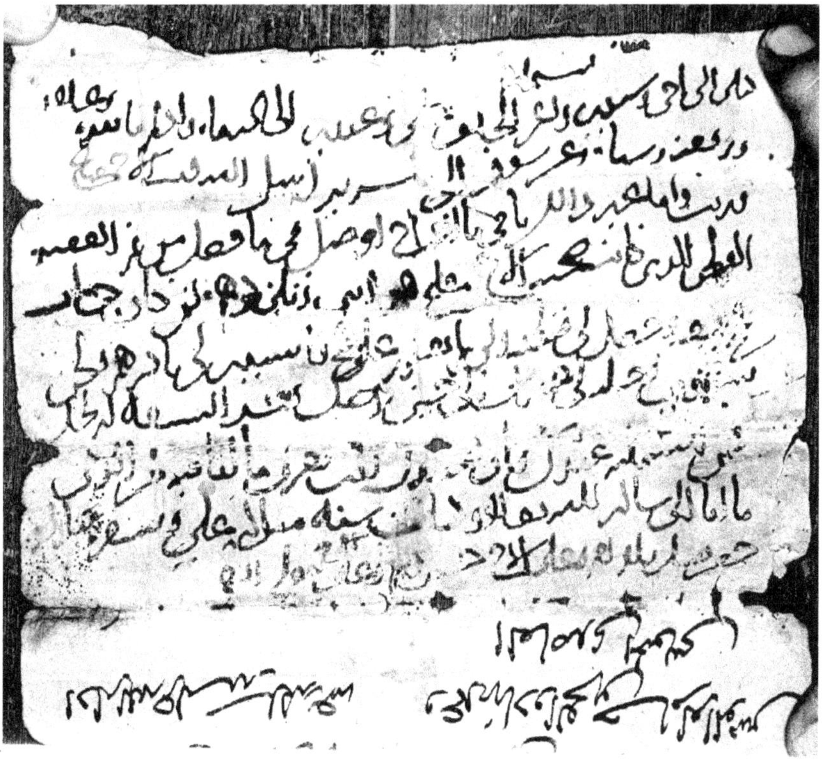

35 recto: Letter

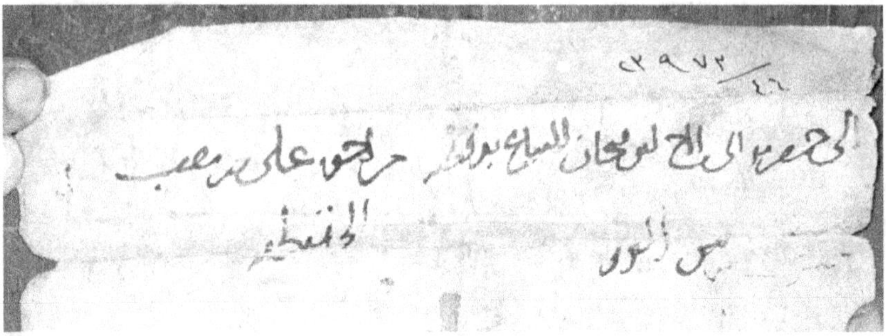

35 verso: Letter

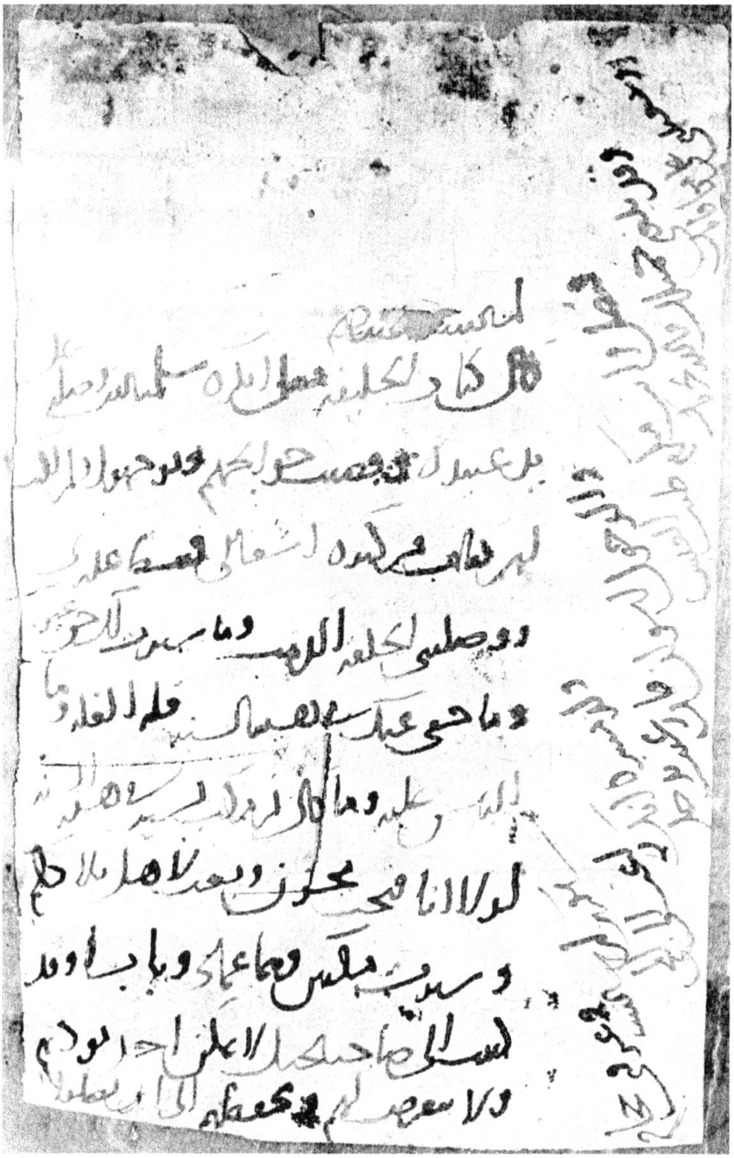

36 recto: Letter

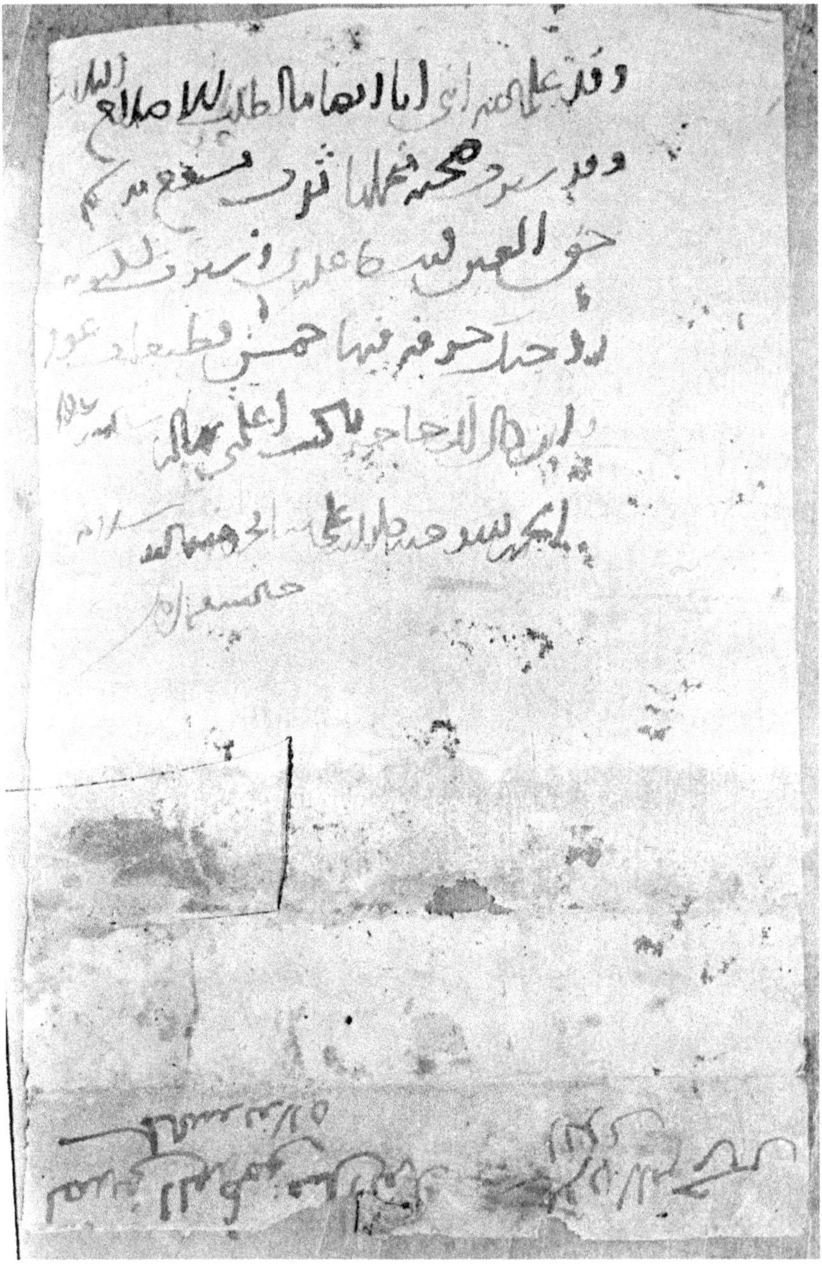

36 verso: Letter

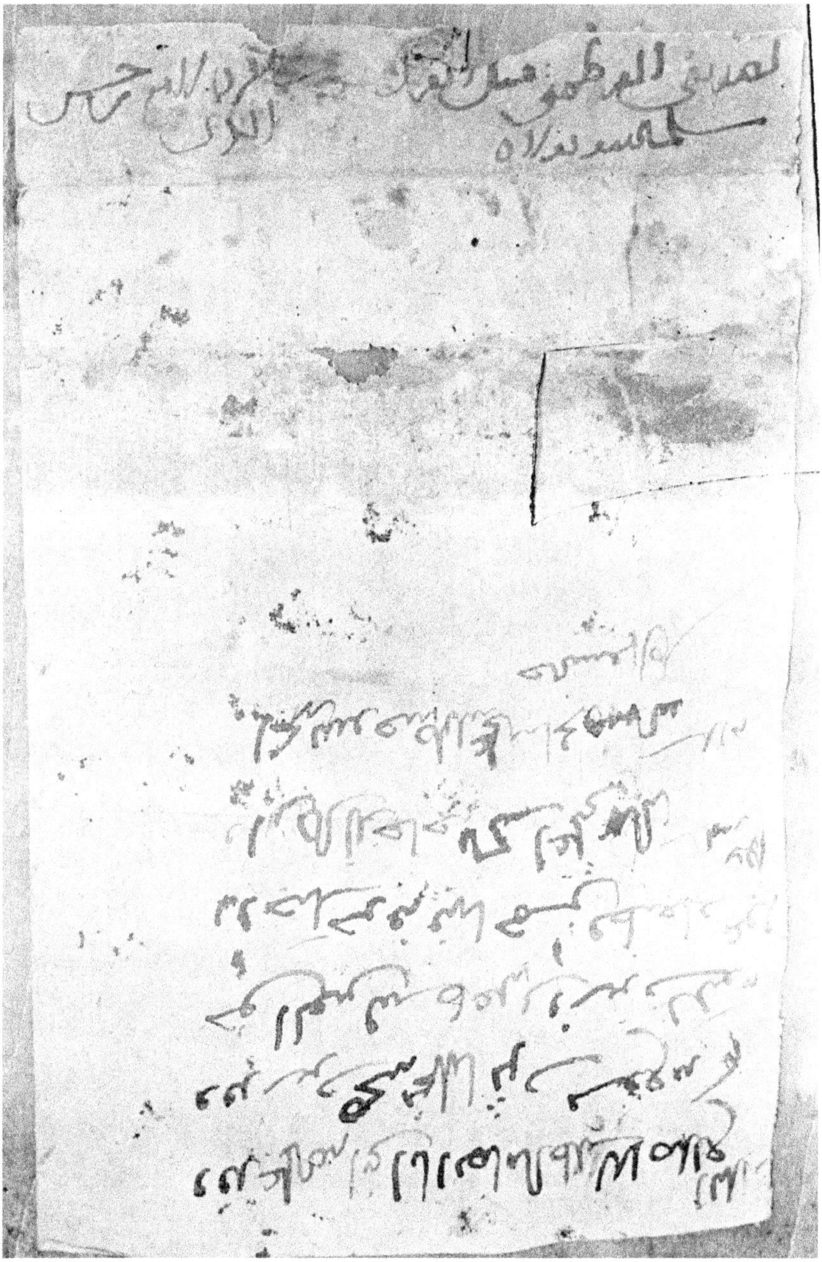

36 verso: Letter

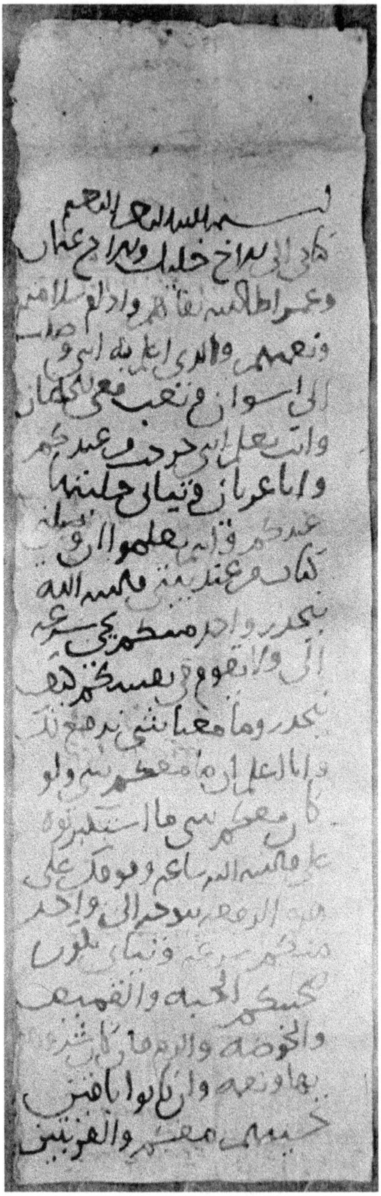

37 recto: Letter

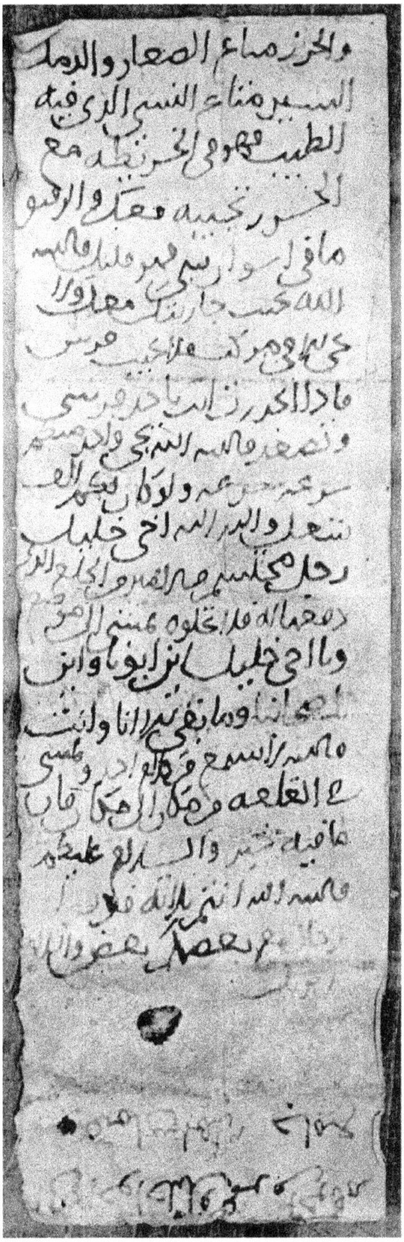

37 verso: Letter

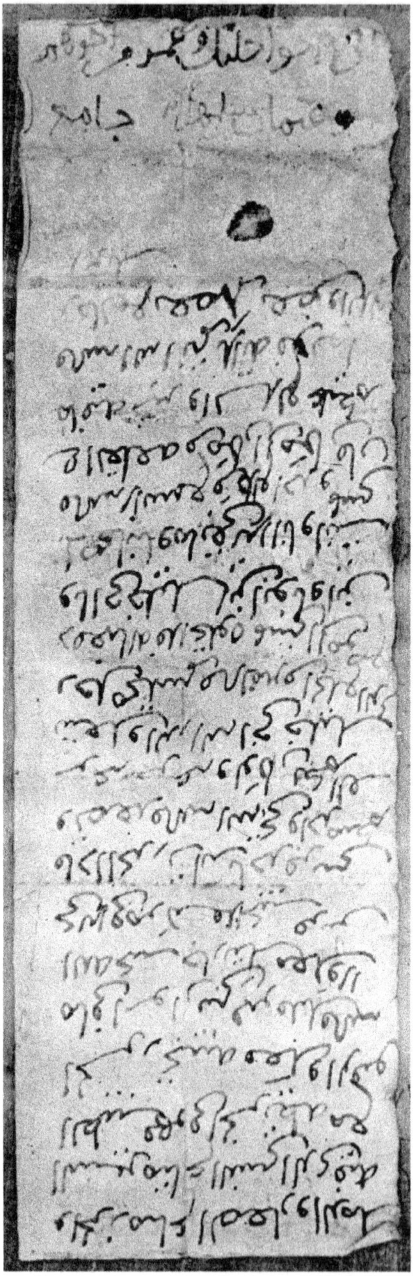

37 verso: Letter

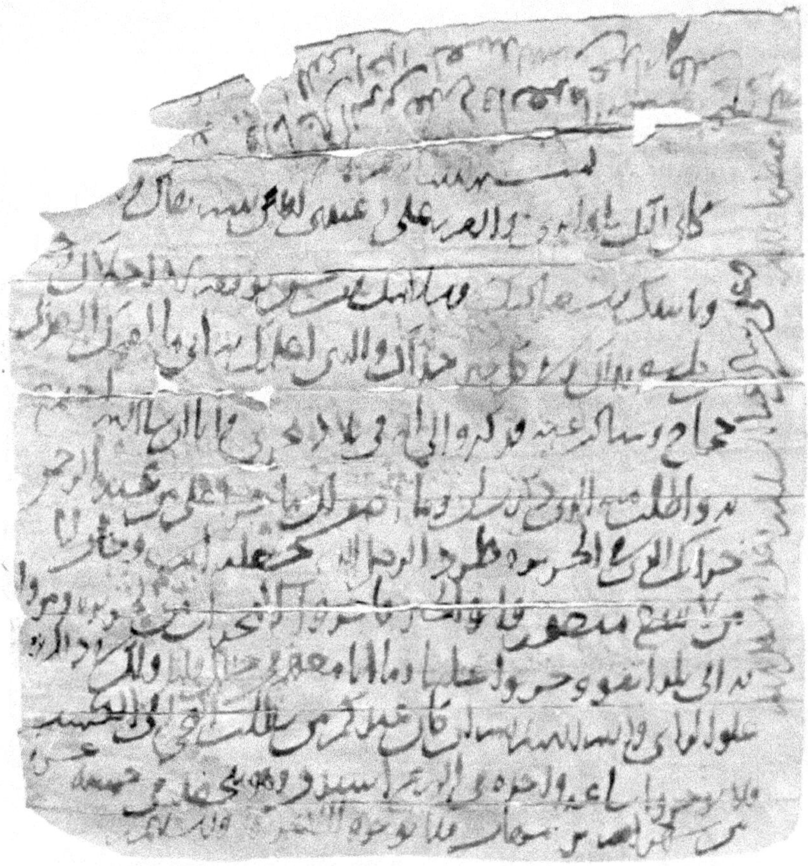

38 recto: Letter

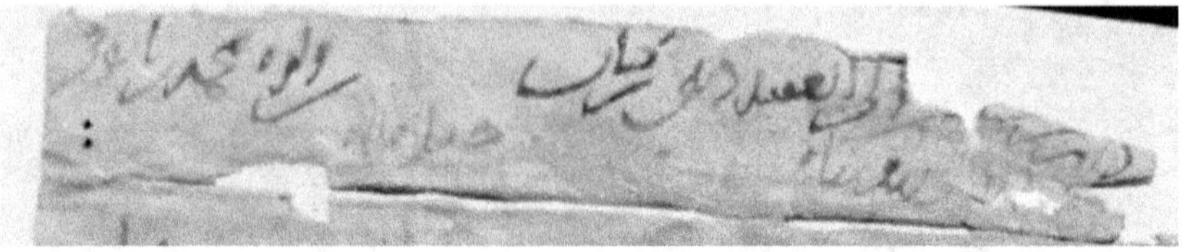

38 verso: Letter

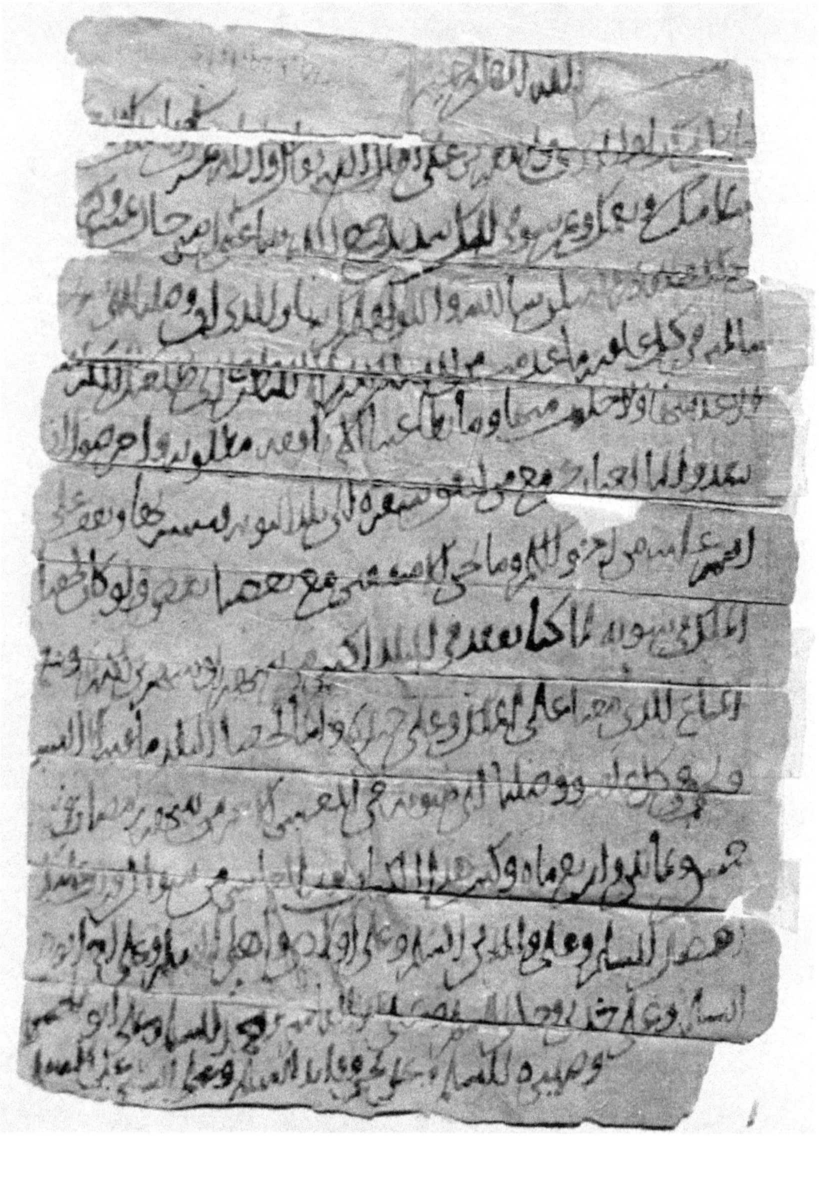

39 recto: Letter

39 verso: Letter

39 verso: Letter

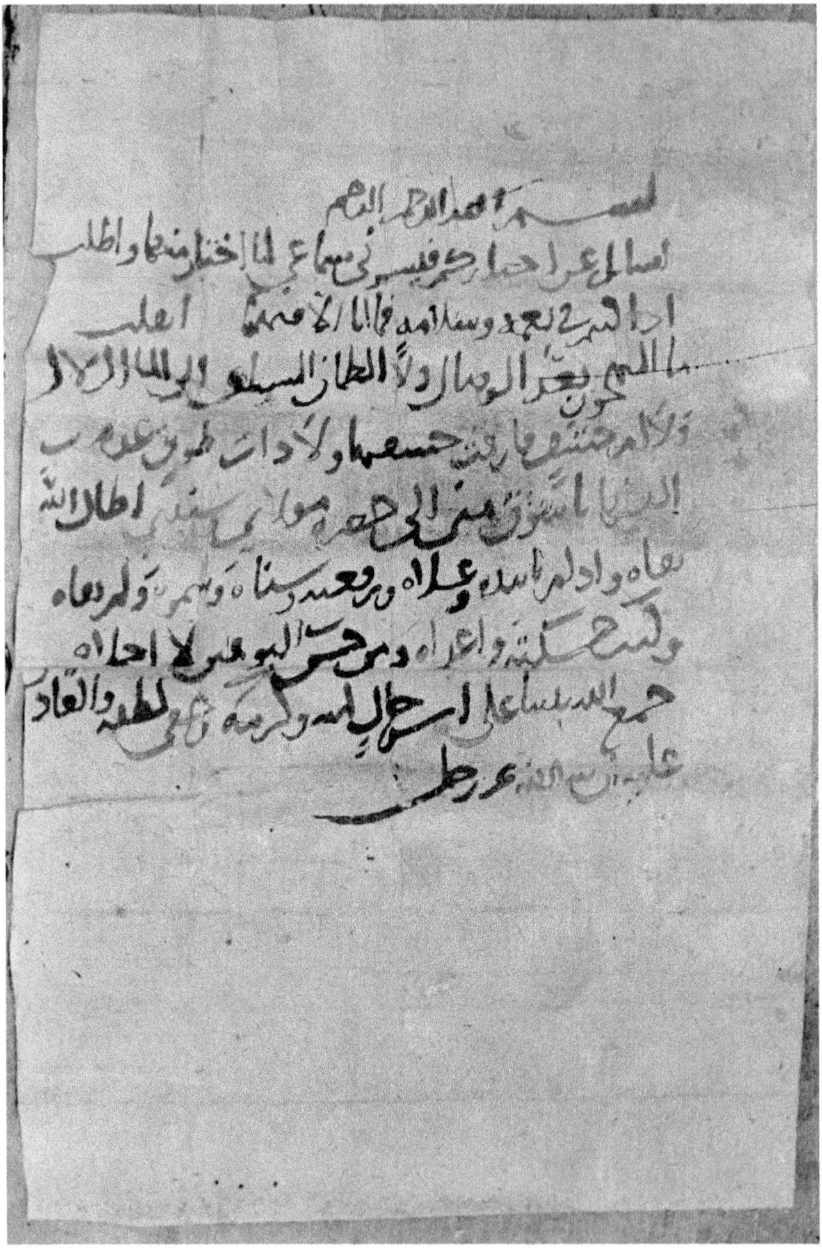

40: Letter

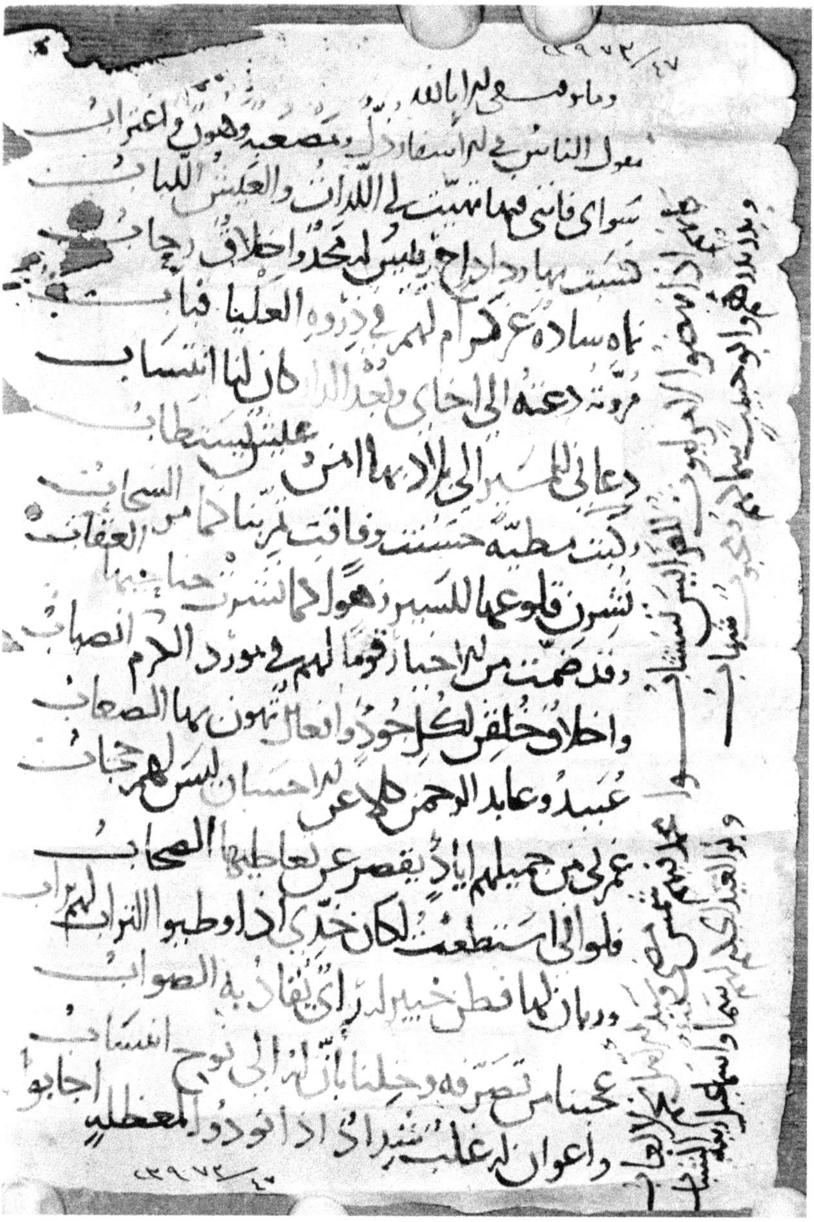

41: Poem of a Traveller

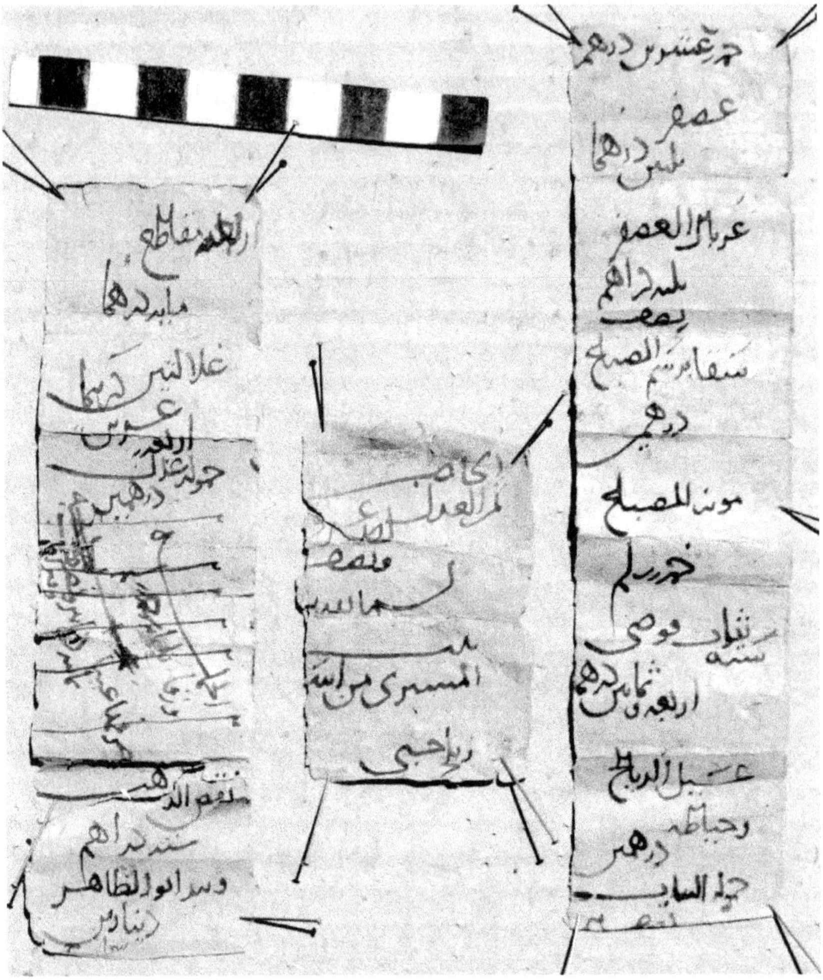

42 recto: Account

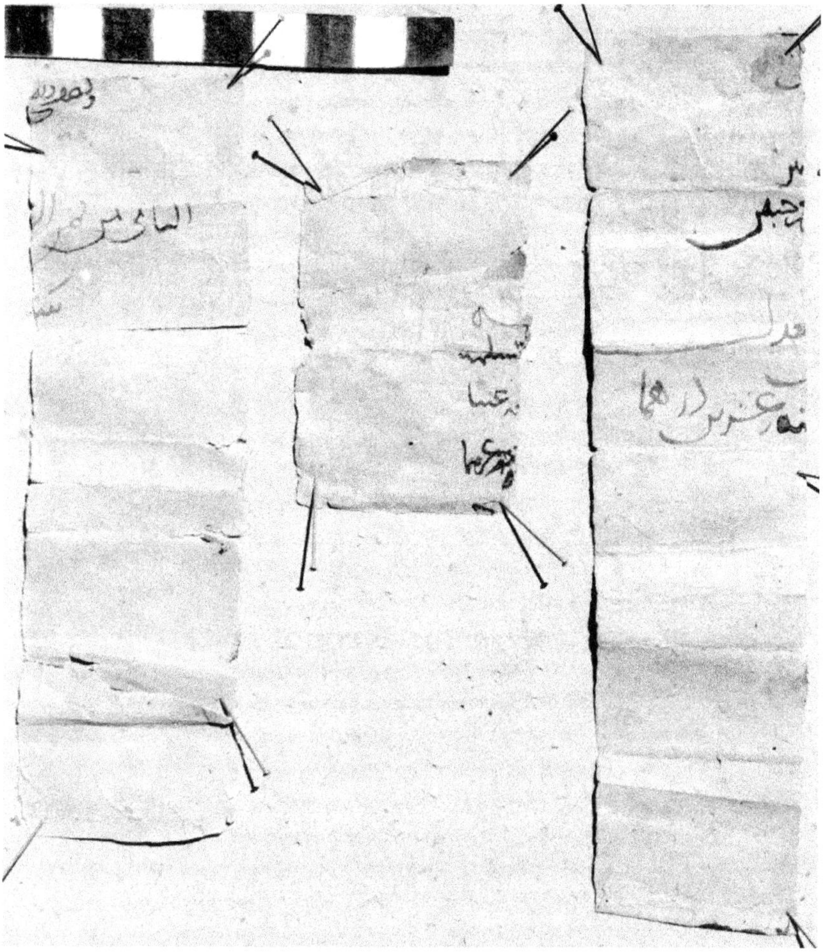

42 verso: Account

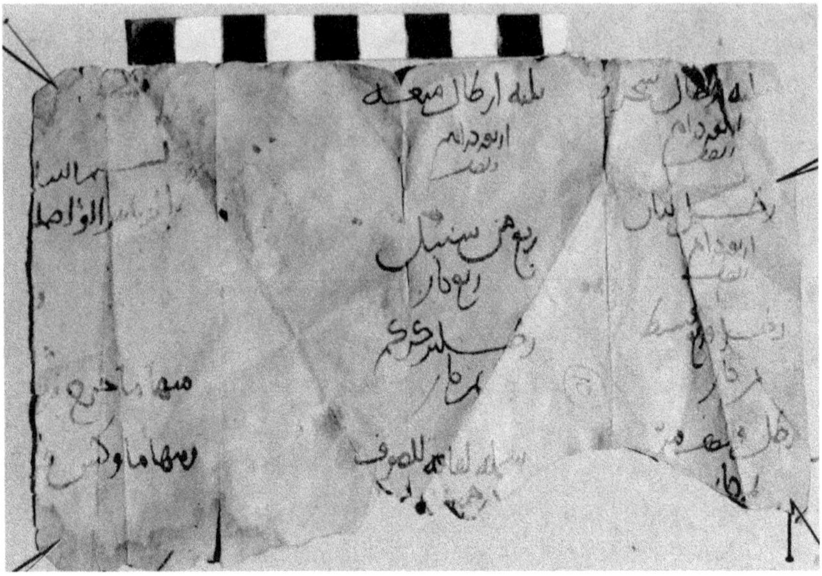

43 recto: Account

43 verso: Account

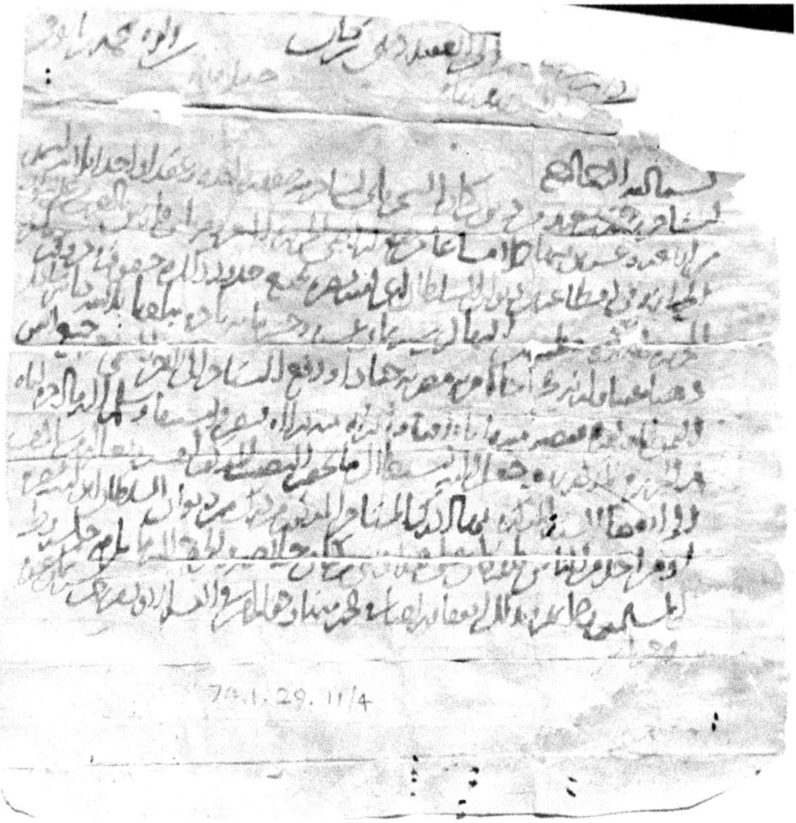

44: Lease of Land

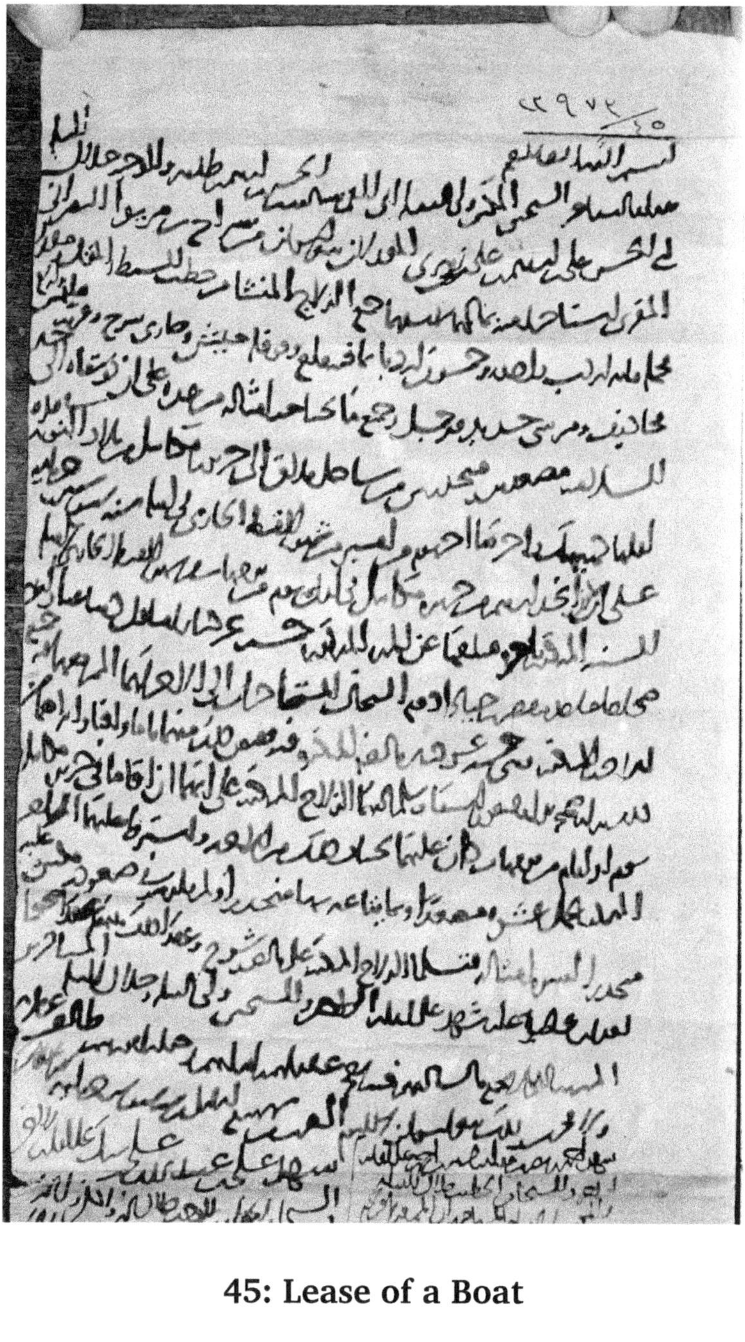

45: Lease of a Boat

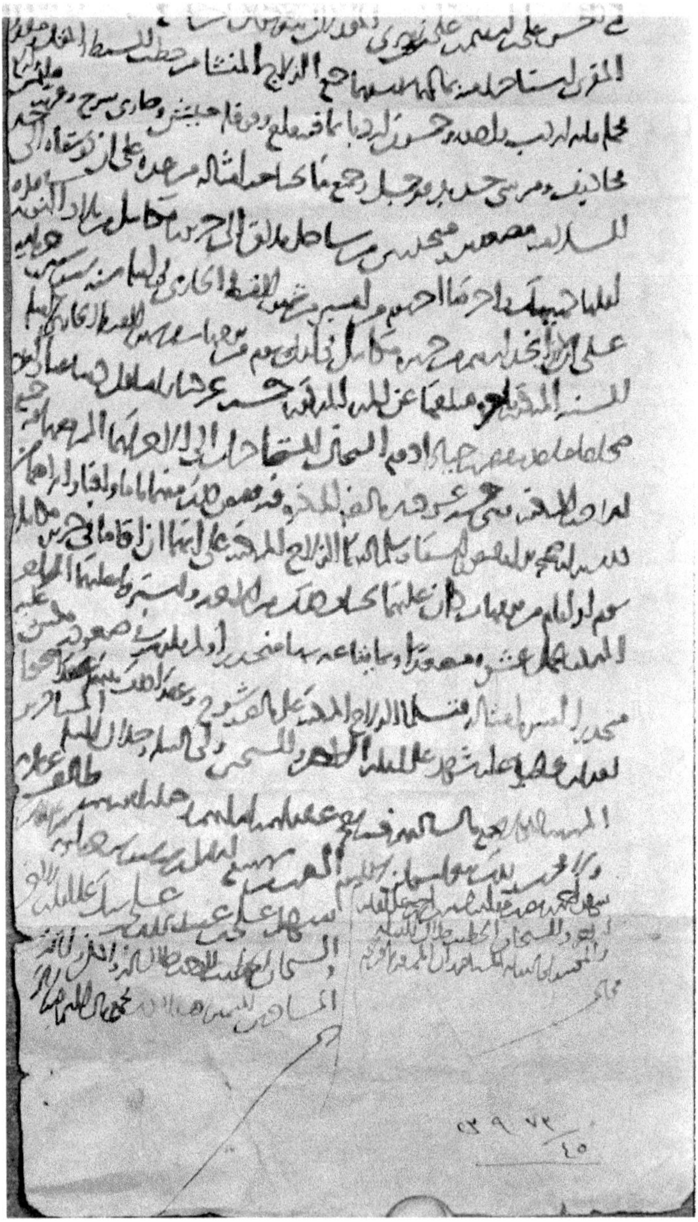

45: Lease of a Boat

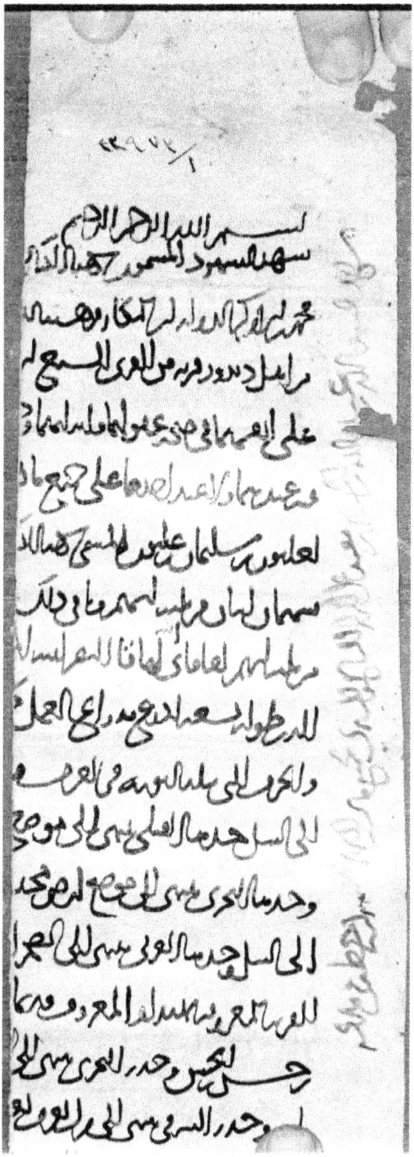

46 recto: Document of Testimony

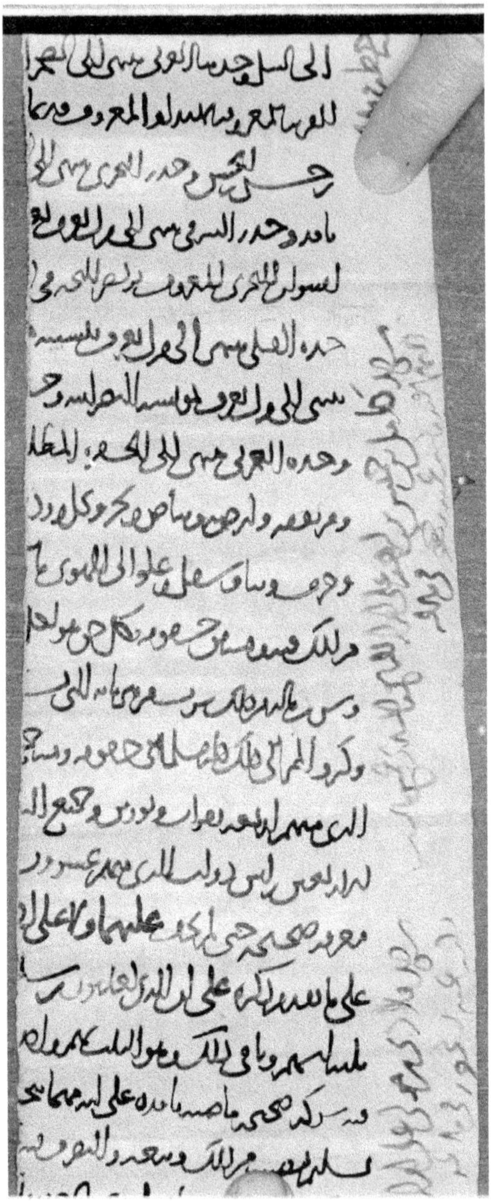

46 recto: Document of Testimony

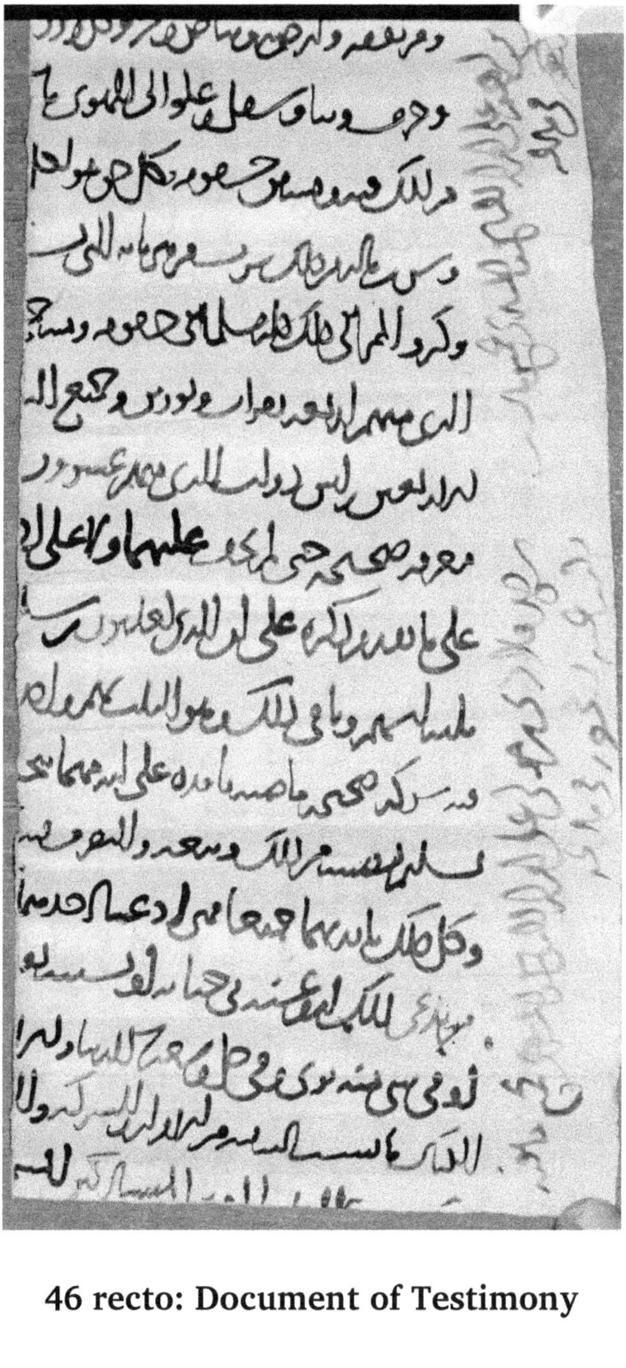

46 recto: Document of Testimony

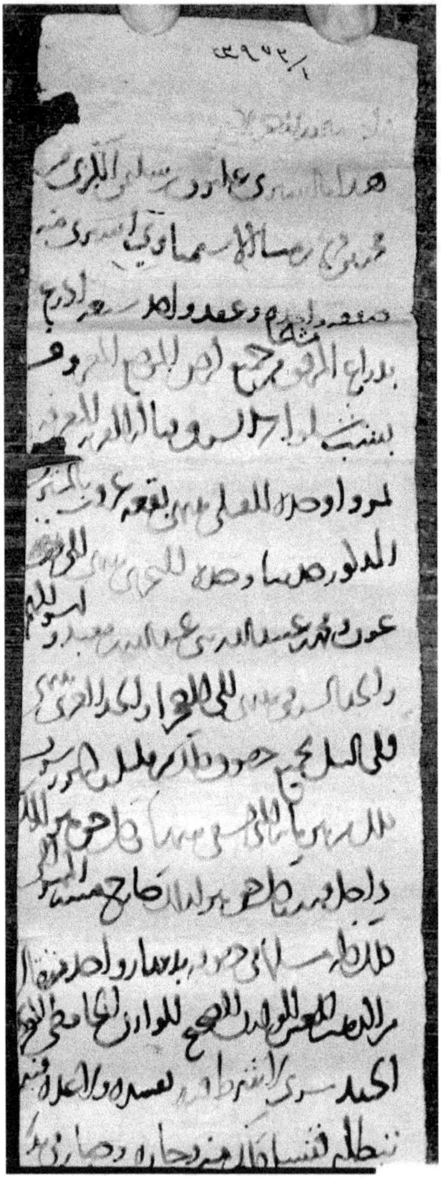

46 verso: Document of Sale

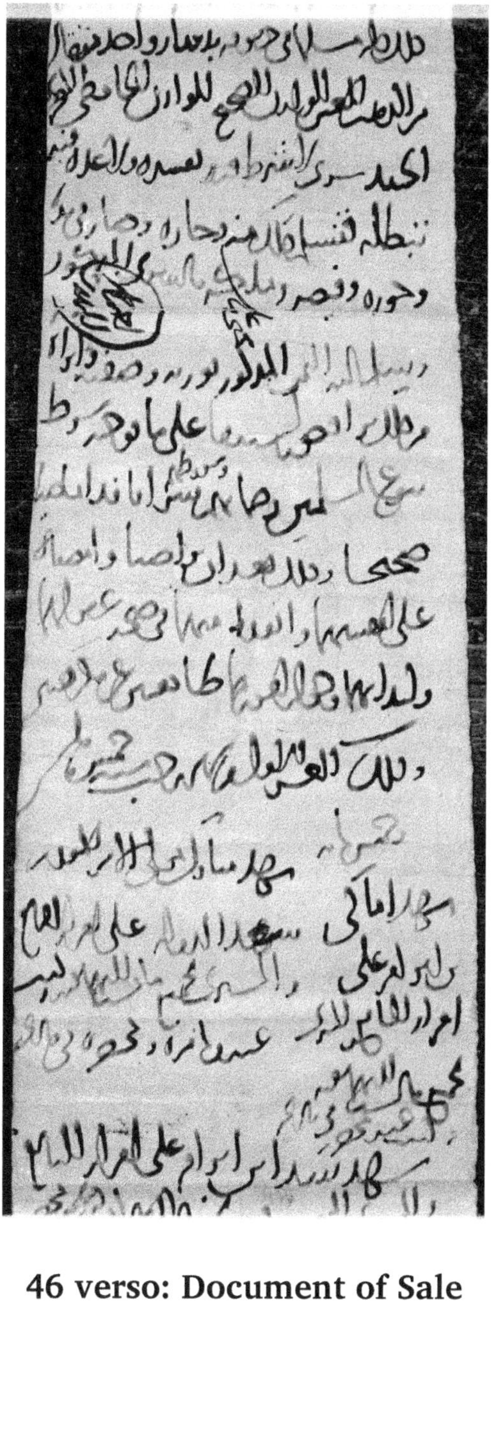

46 verso: Document of Sale

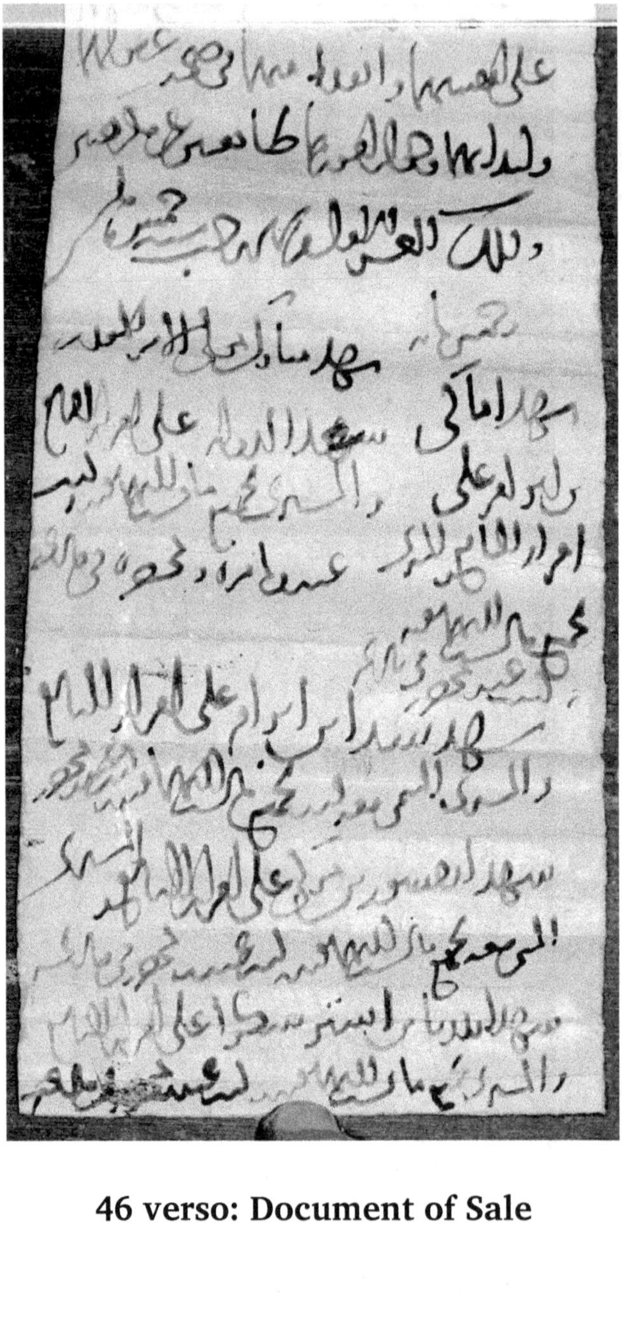

46 verso: Document of Sale

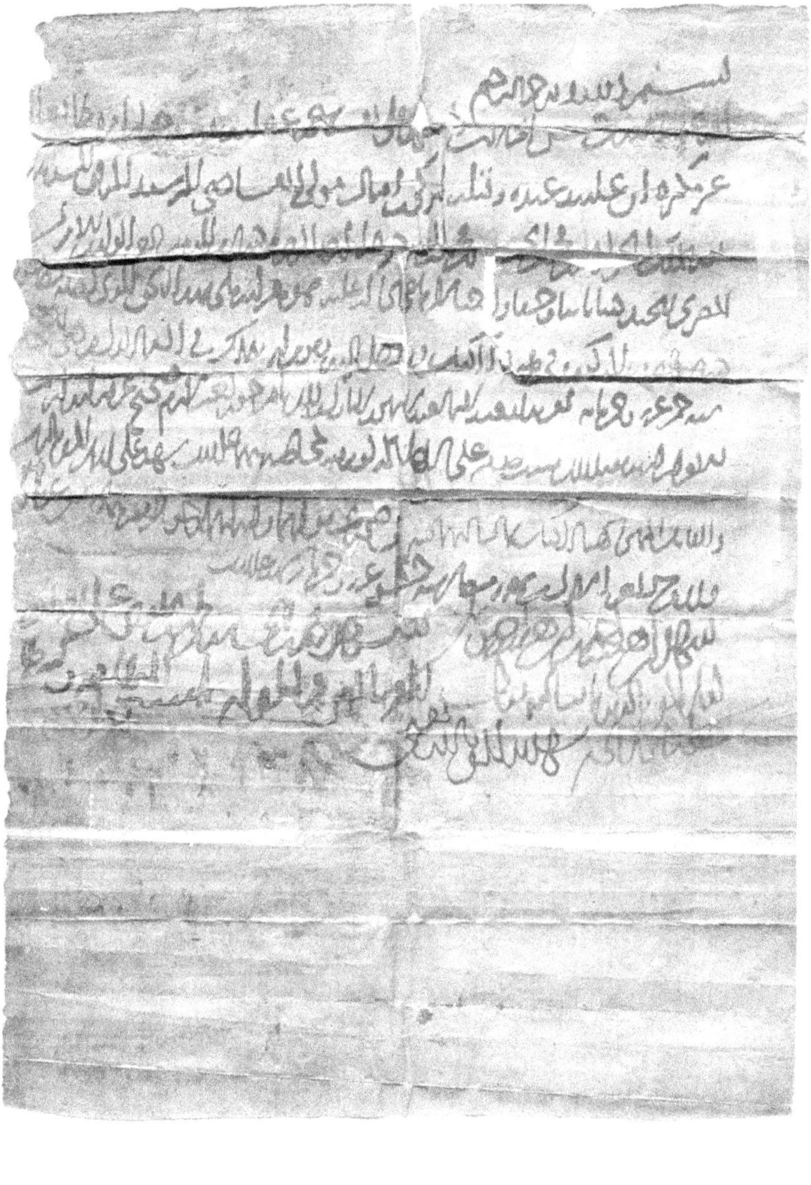

47 recto: Acknowledgement

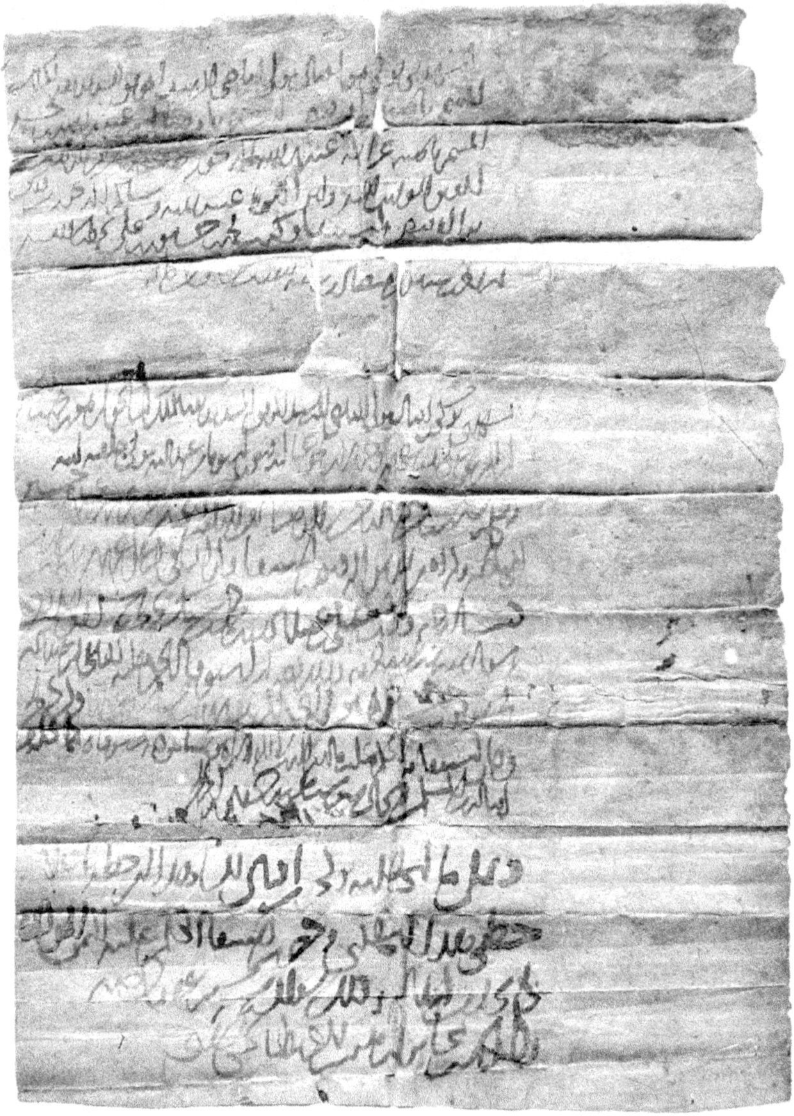

47 verso: Testimonies

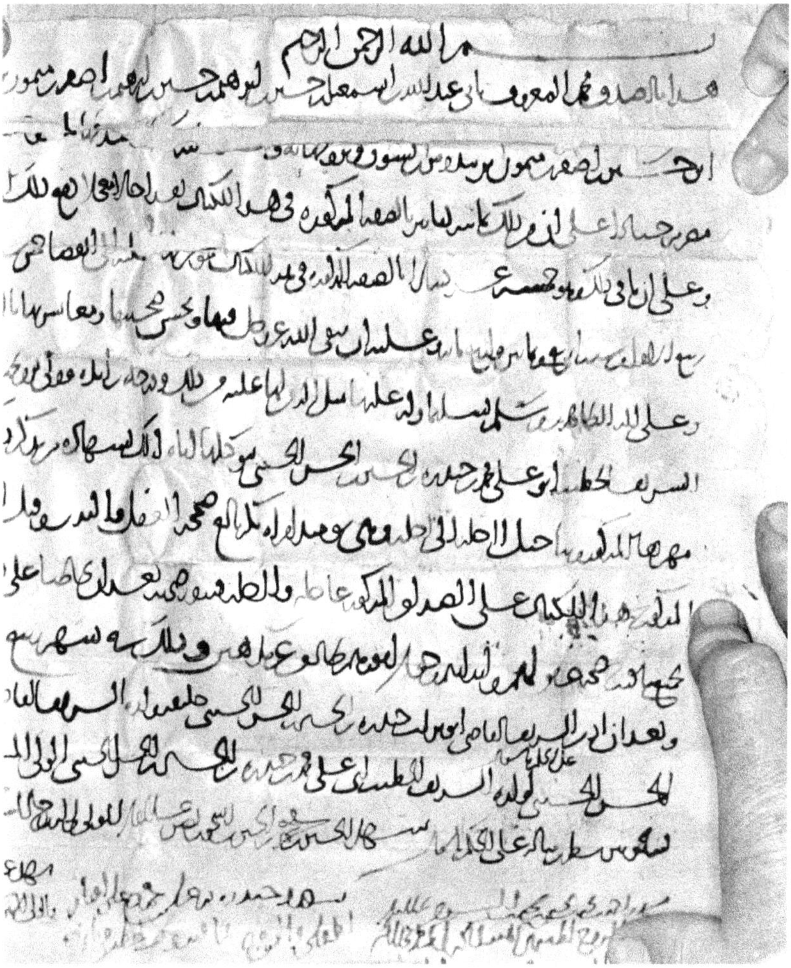
بسم الله الرحمن الرحيم

48 recto: Marriage Contract

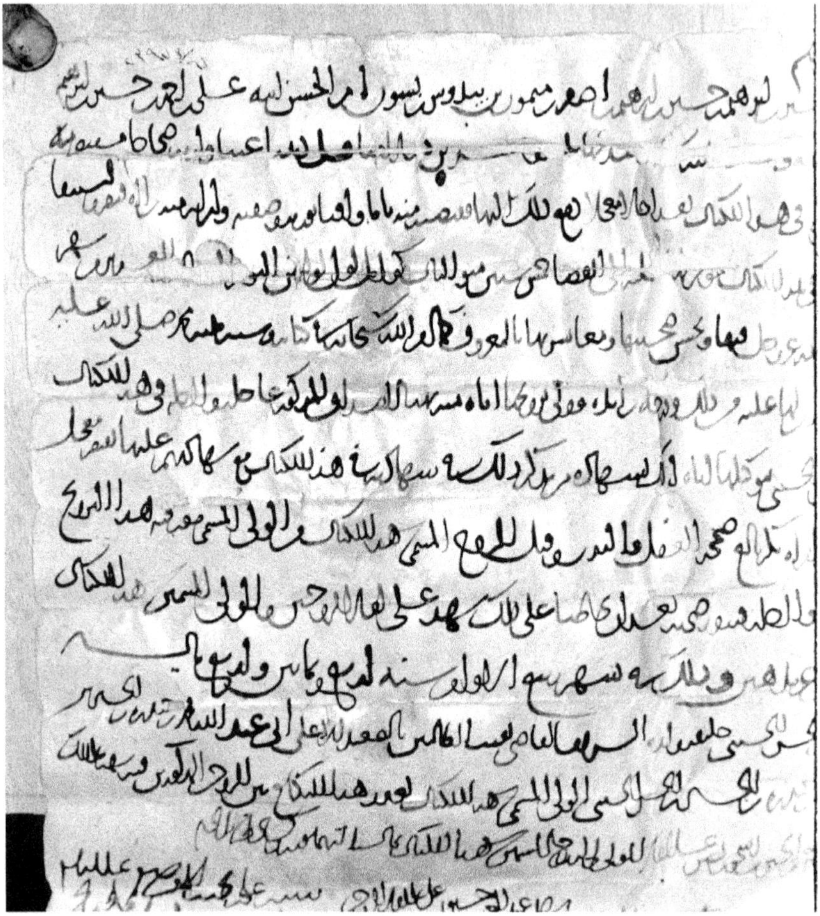

48 recto: Marriage Contract

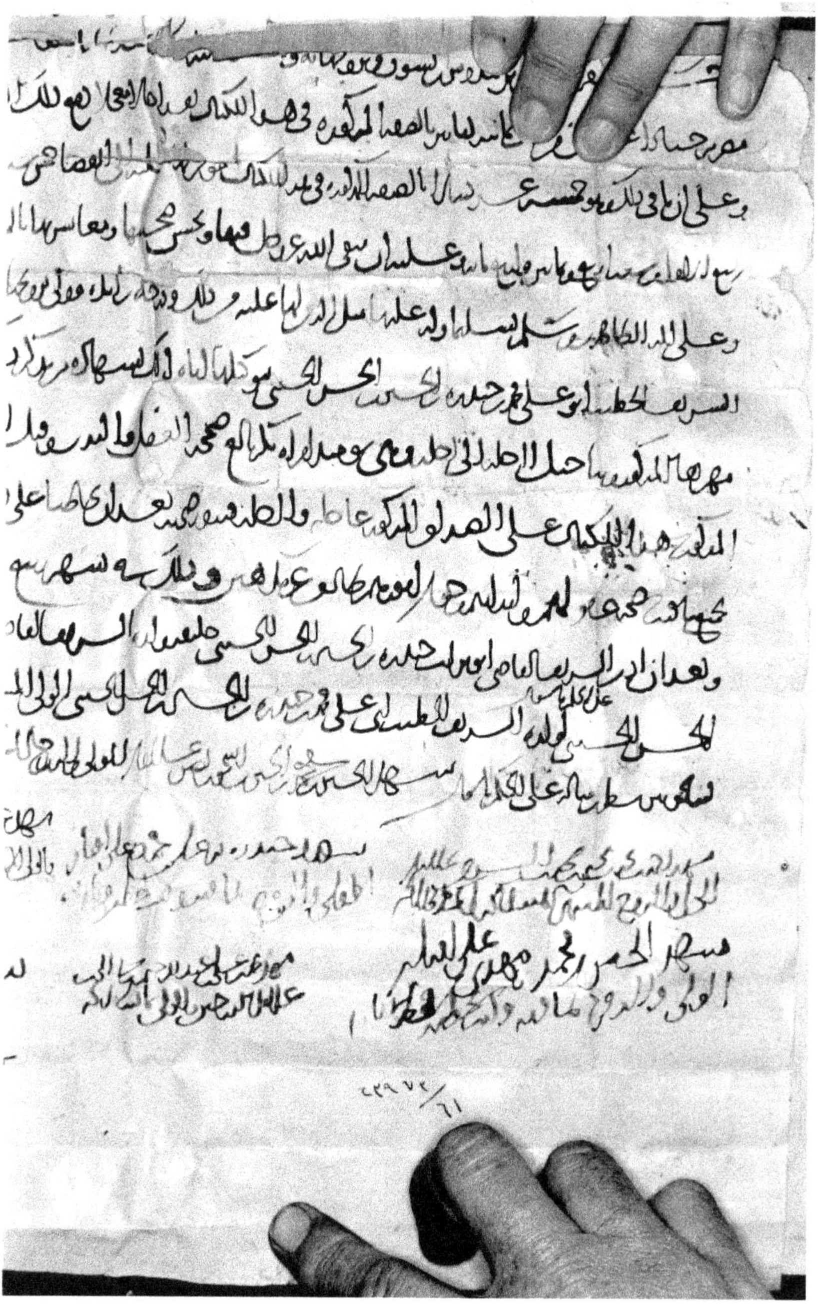

48 recto: Marriage Contract

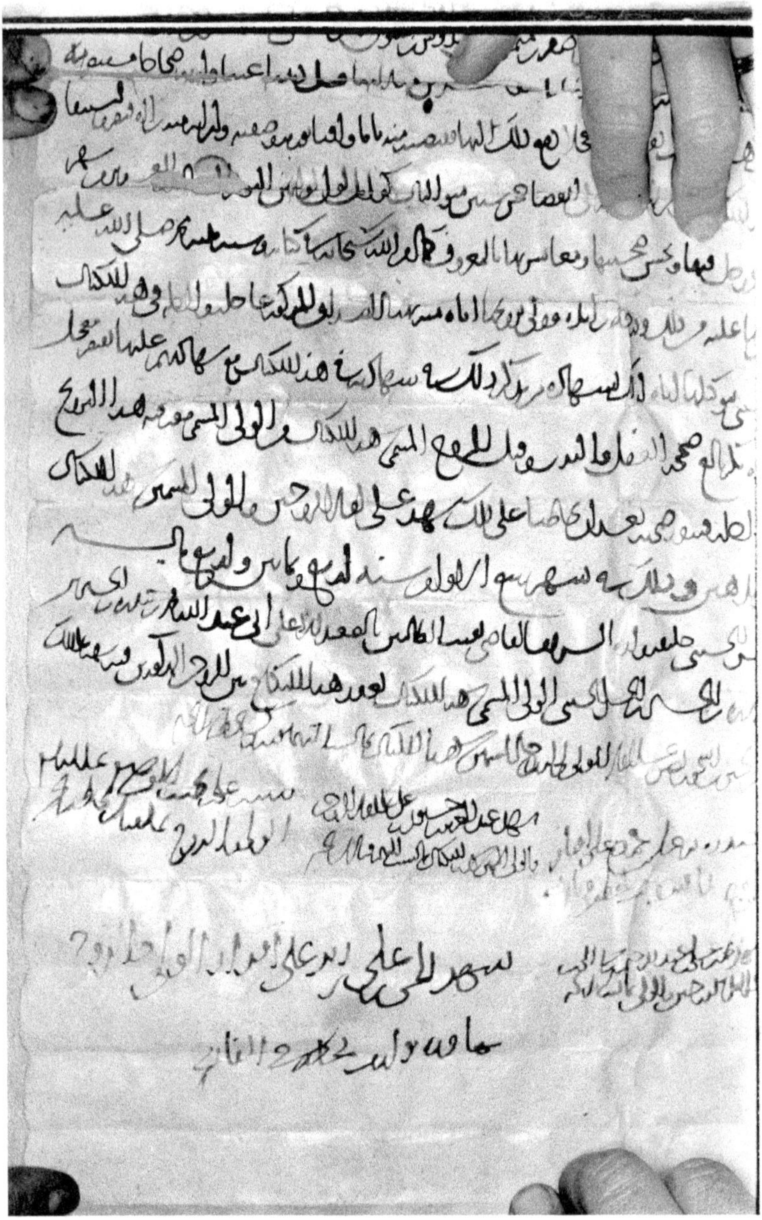

48 recto: Marriage Contract

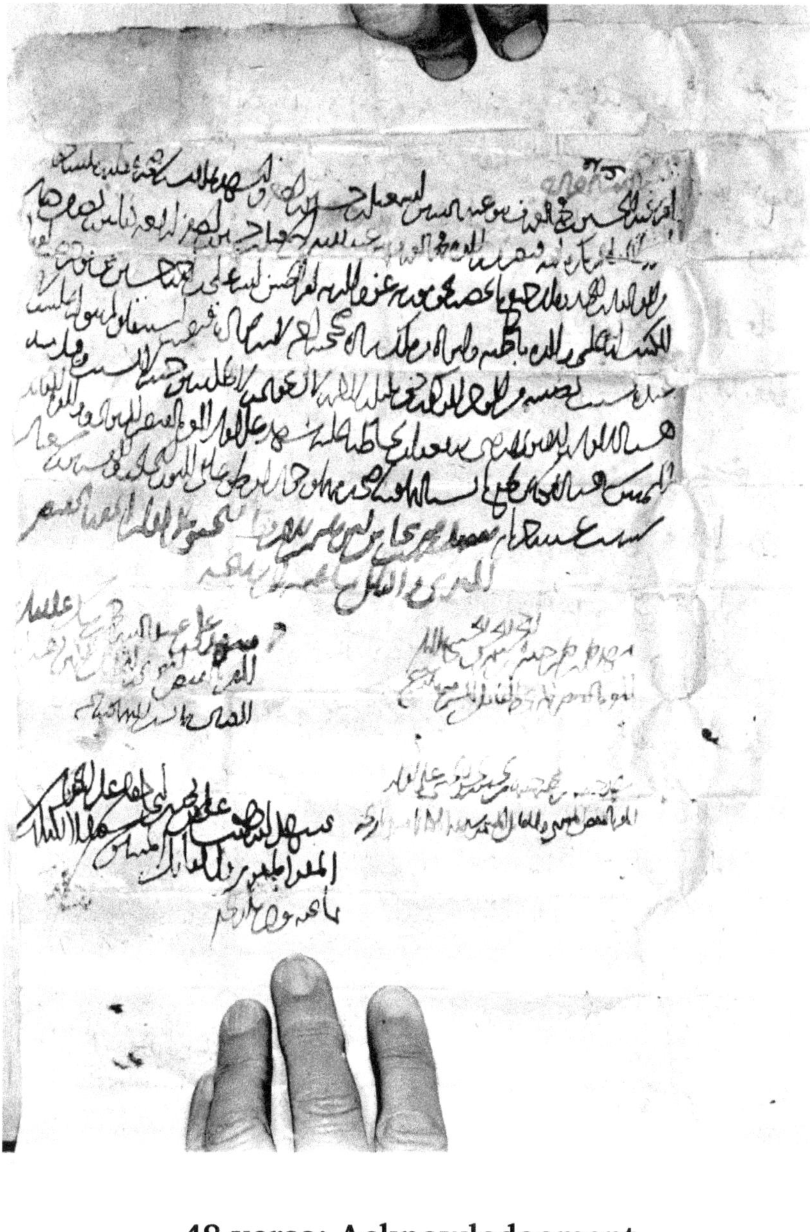

48 verso: Acknowledgement

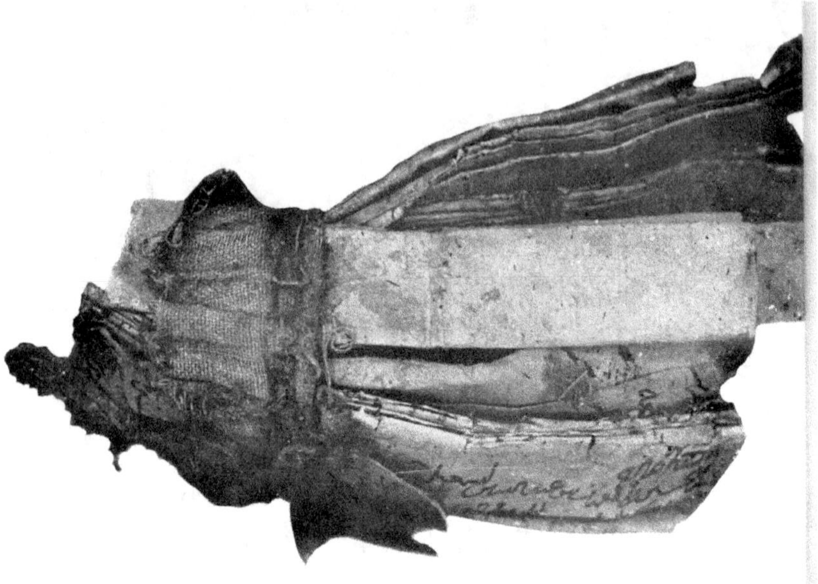

48 verso: Acknowledgement

Photograph from Plumley (1972)

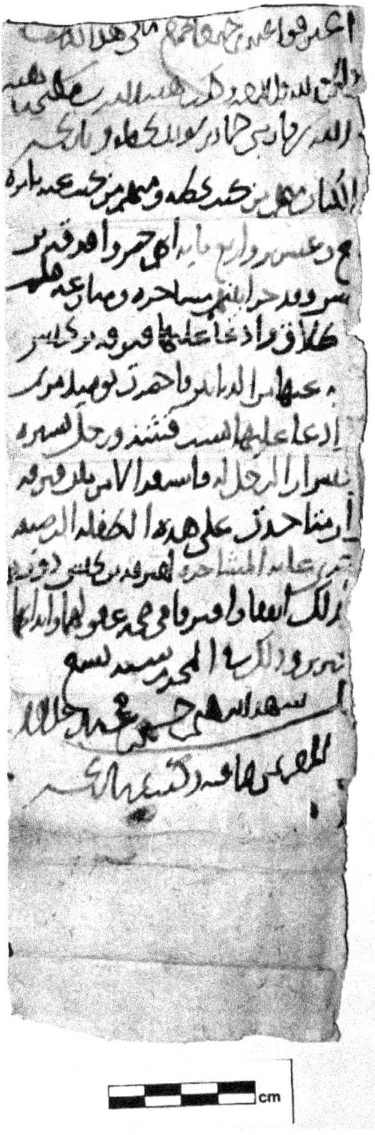

49 recto: Document concerning Division of Property after Divorce

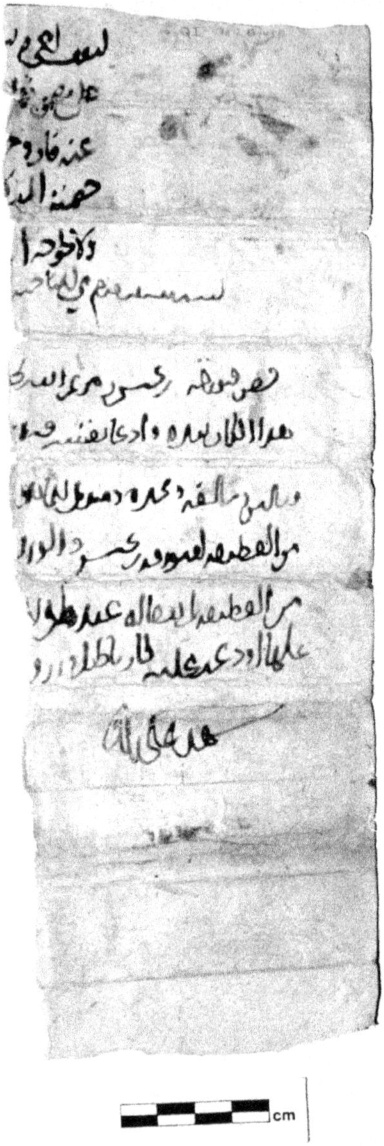

49 verso: Court Document relating to Divorce

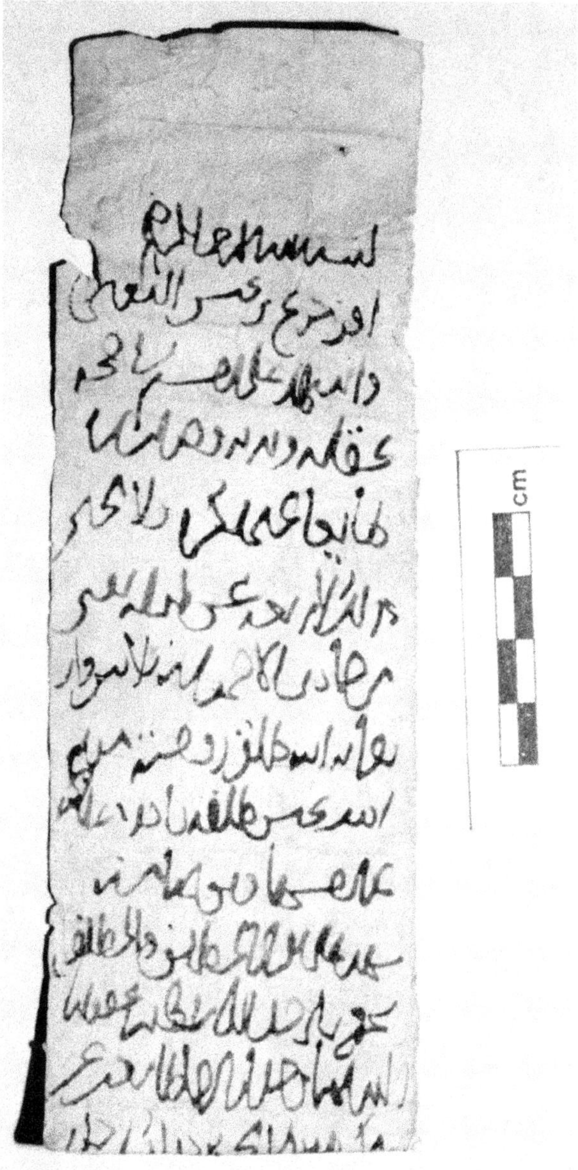

50: Acknowledgement relating to Divorce

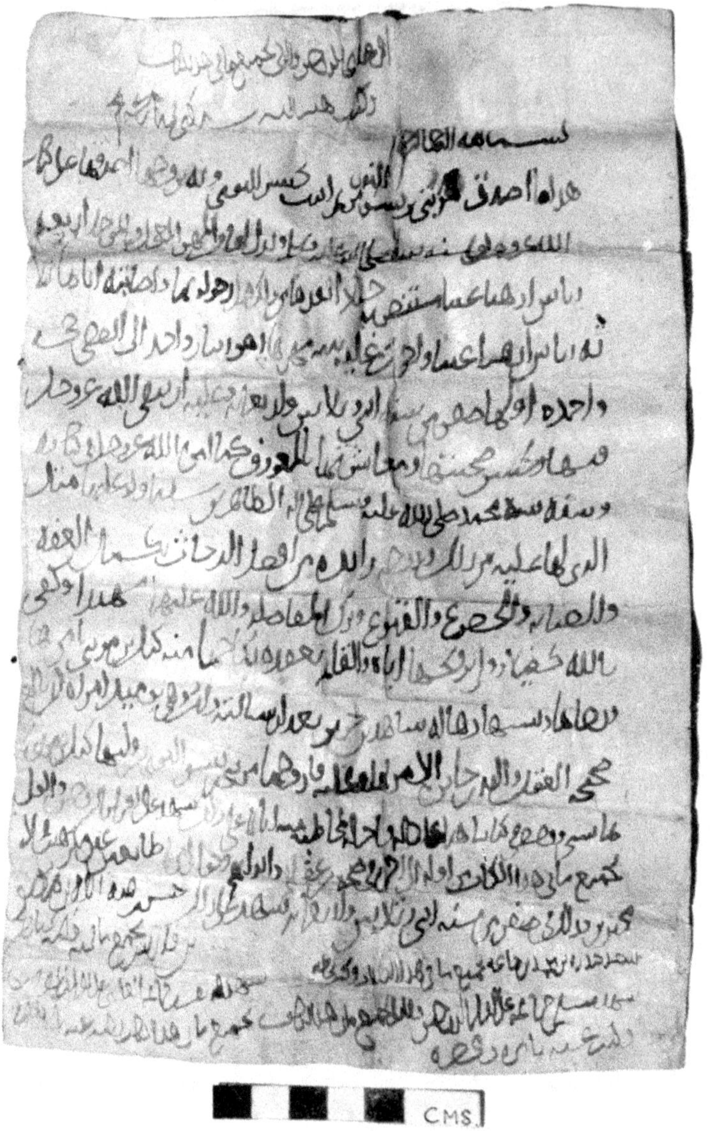

51 recto: Marriage Contract

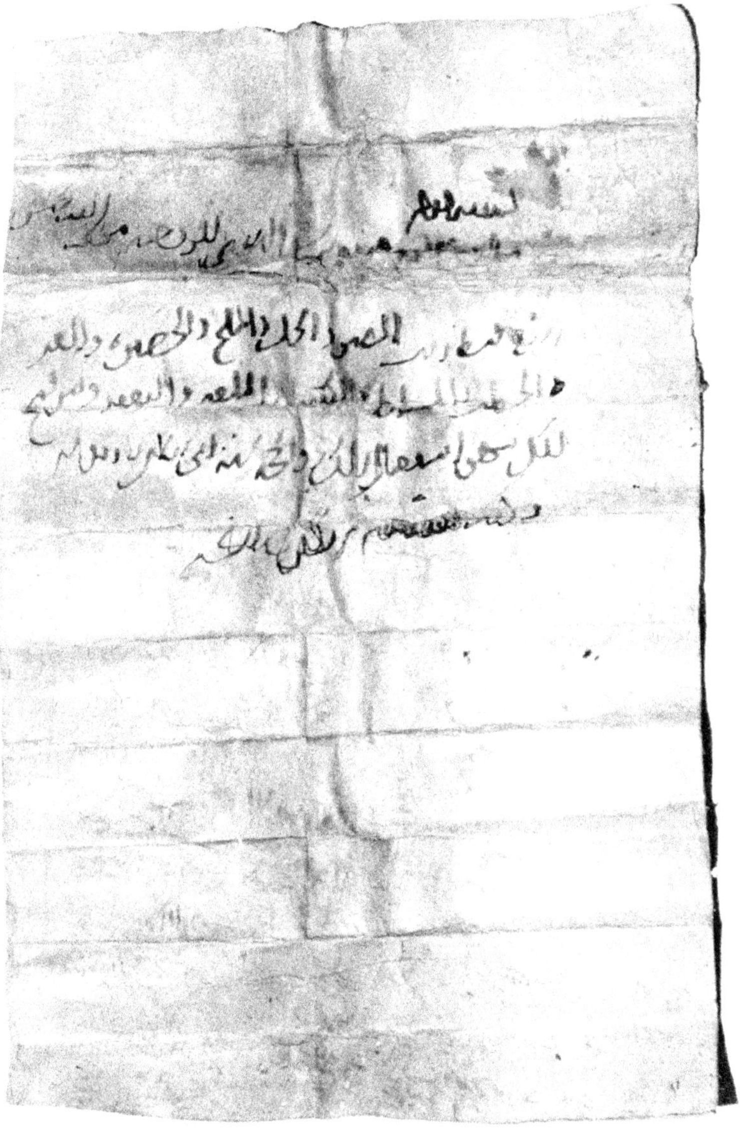

51 verso: Testimony

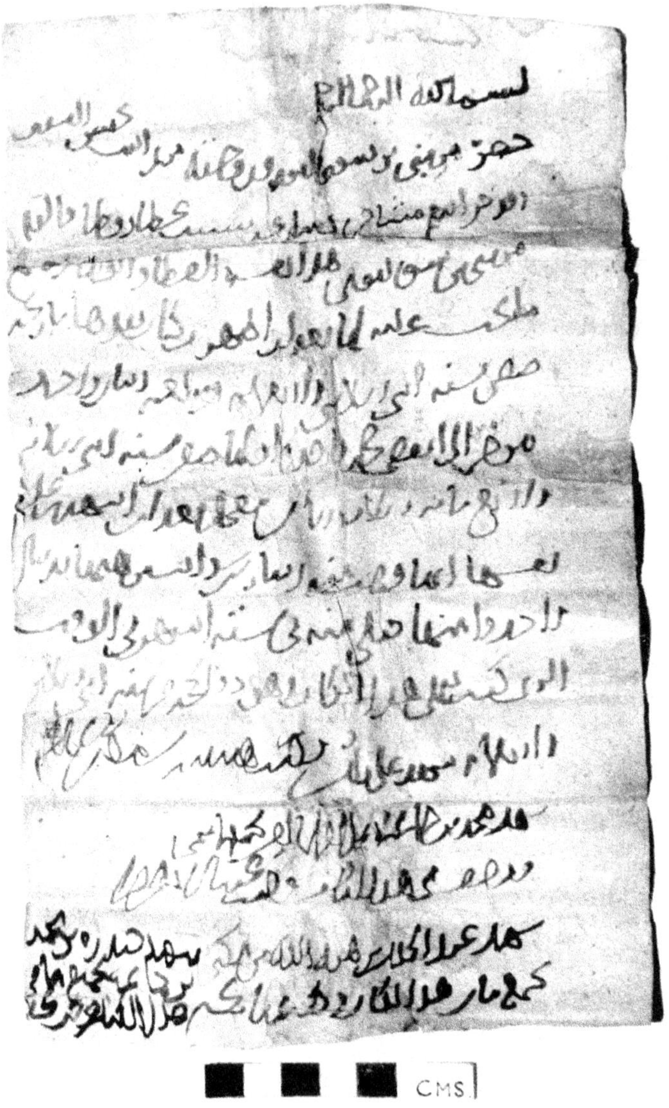

52: Court Record relating to Marriage

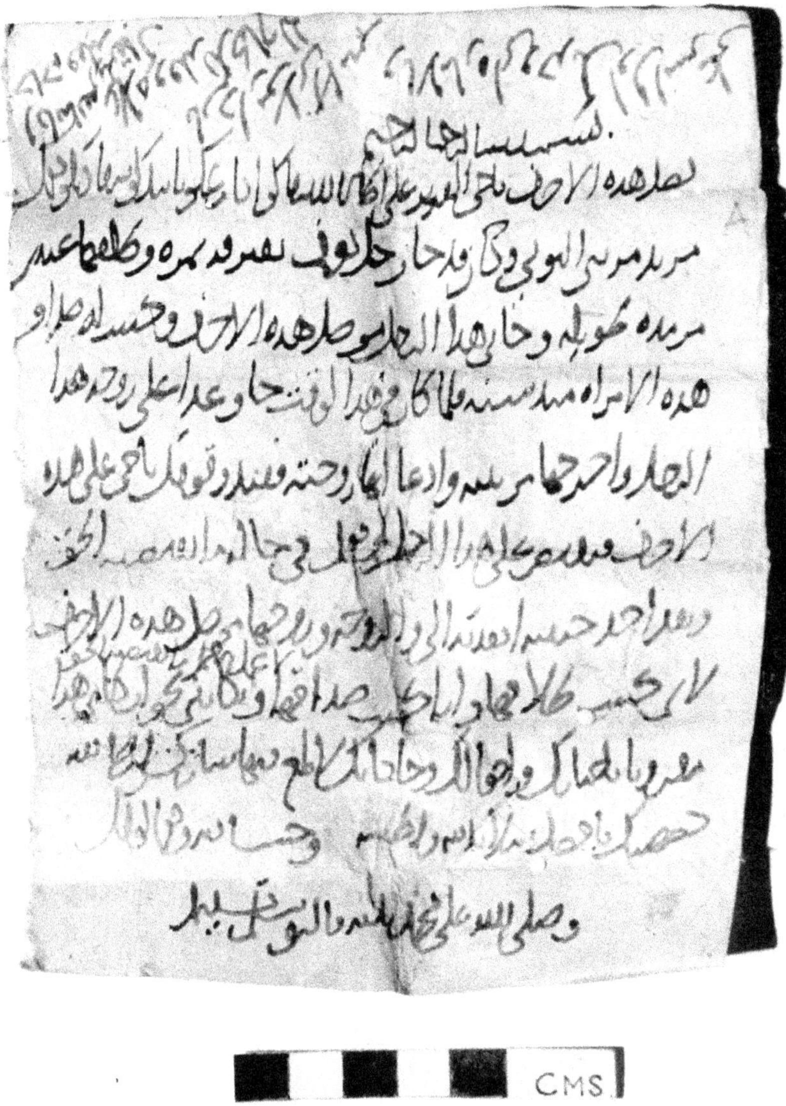
بسم الله الرحمن الرحيم

53 recto: Letter relating to a Marital Dispute

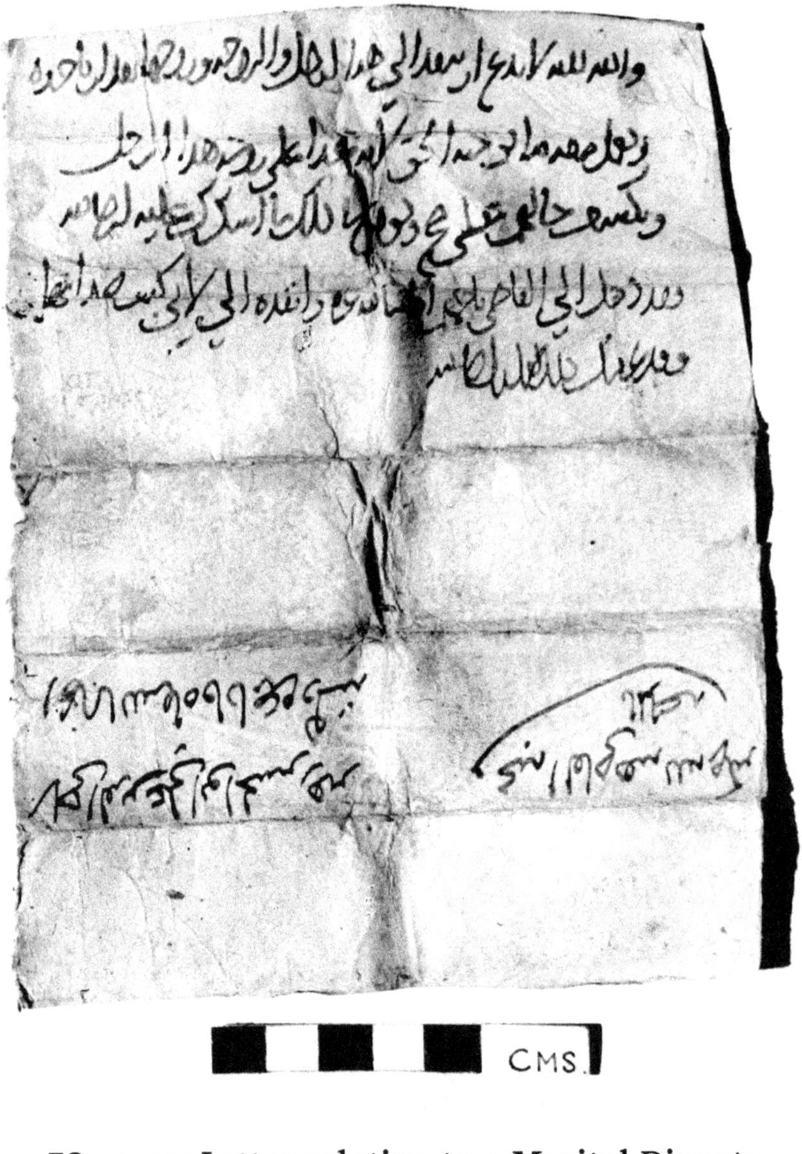

53 verso: Letter relating to a Marital Dispute

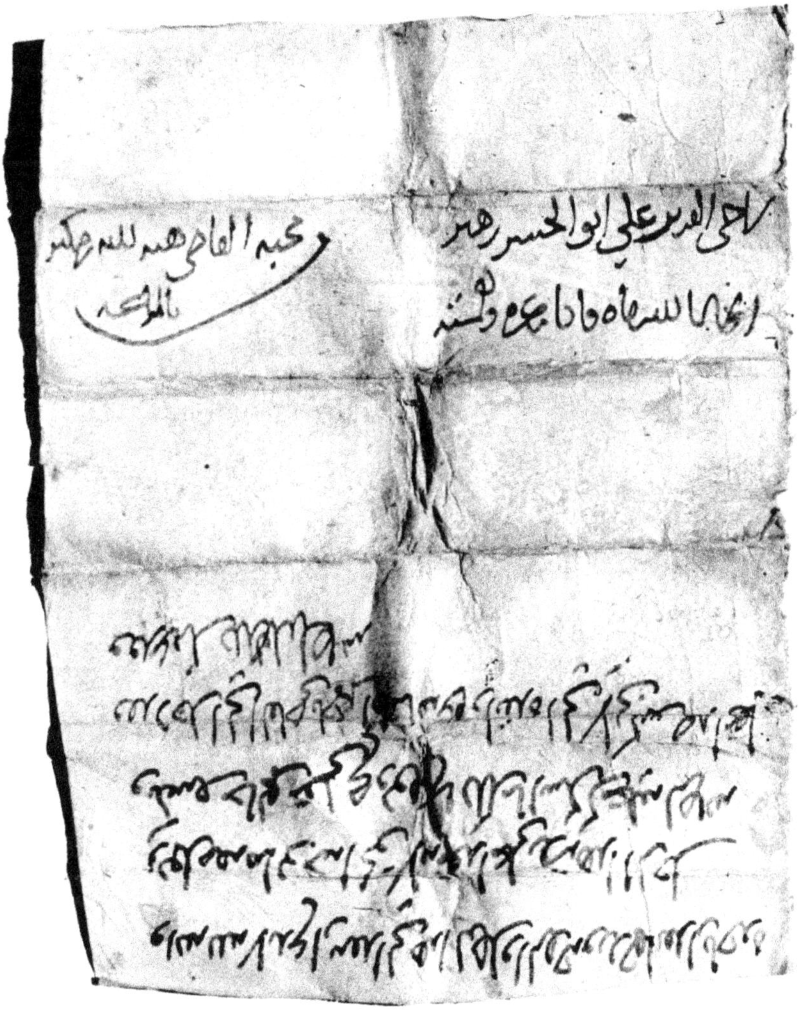

53 verso: Letter relating to a Marital Dispute

About the Team

Alessandra Tosi was the managing editor for this book and provided quality control.

Anne Burberry and Krisztina Szilagyi performed the copyediting of the book in Word. The fonts used in this volume are Charis SIL, Scheherazade New, SBL Greek, and Segoe UI Historic.

Cameron Craig created all of the editions — paperback, hardback, and PDF. Conversion was performed with open source software freely available on our GitHub page at https://github.com/OpenBookPublishers.

Jeevanjot Kaur Nagpal designed the cover of this book. The cover was produced in InDesign using Fontin and Calibri fonts.

Cambridge Semitic Languages and Cultures

General Editor Geoffrey Khan

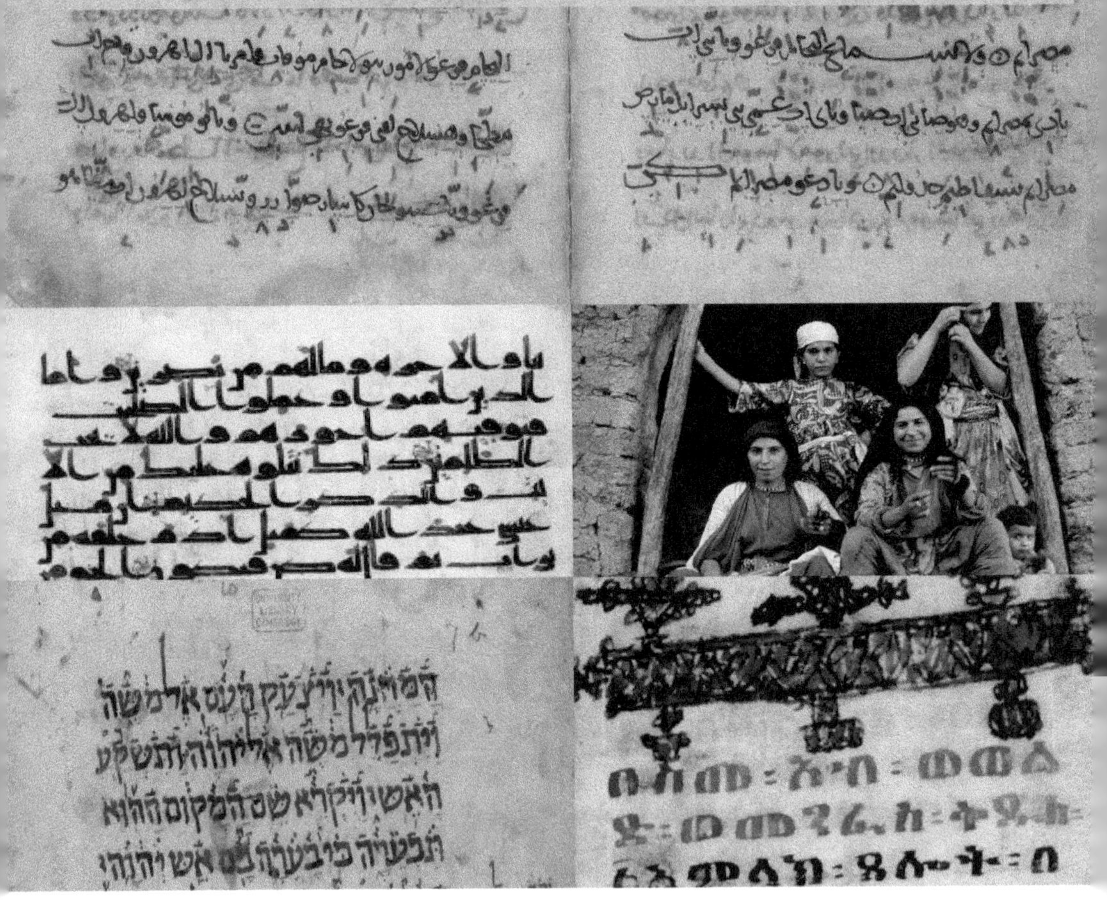

OPEN ACCESS

www.ingramcontent.com/pod-product-compliance
Lightning Source LLC
Chambersburg PA
CBHW050522300426
44113CB00012B/1916
* 9 7 8 1 8 0 5 1 1 2 3 0 3 *